PRAISE FOR

Updike

"A brilliant biography. . . . A delightfully rich book. . . . Highly readable. . . . The joys of *Updike* are based on discovering the autobiographical content of the tens of thousands of details that populate Updike's vast fictional universe."
—Orhan Pamuk, *New York Times Book Review*

"A hefty, thorough biography. . . . Begley does an impressive, conscientious job of marshaling evidence of Updike's many contradictions."
—Jonathan Dee, *Harper's*

"An honorable book. . . . Updike's exquisite words flowed, some felt, too freely and too amiably. . . . But it's one of the achievements of Begley's book that it so acutely demonstrates how it all, in fact, didn't come so easily. . . . Begley is a gifted literary critic."
—Dwight Garner, *New York Times*

"As a biographer, Adam Begley has a great many strengths—concision, eloquence, an eagle eye—and few of the usual shortcomings. He isn't puritanical, or reductive, or over-diligent. . . . If this biography succeeds in renewing general interest in Updike, then it will do so not by taking him down a peg or two but by showing that it is not a betrayal or even a disappointment but a bearable inevitability that the boy with the golden pen, the twinkly talking head, had been a human being after all."
—*Wall Street Journal*

"Adam Begley's *Updike* is a model of what a literary biography should be: rich with penetrating insights not only about the life but also about the work. It will enthrall longtime Updike fans and help create generations of new ones."
—Francine Prose

"Terrific. . . . Begley's book blends biography with a brilliant close read of Updike's work. . . . As insightful on the work as the life, it is a complicated and fascinating portrait of one of the great literary lives of the second half of the twentieth century."
—*Salon*

"'You have to give it magic,' John Updike explained of the stuff on the page, so much of it alchemically transmuted from his own experience; here was a man who could find pounding a mailbox into the ground to be an occasion for literature. Adam Begley has done him proud, offering up Updike the man and Updike the writer in an exuberant, stunningly choreographed pas de deux."

—Stacy Schiff

"A master storyteller comes to affably charming life in Begley's incisive biography. . . . Begley finds the truest reflection of the man in his work."

—*Vogue*

"Fabulous. . . . Updike fans will enjoy Begley's marvelous biography, which is as much about the man as the writer."

—*Entertainment Weekly*

"A beautifully written, richly detailed, and warmly sympathetic portrait of a great American writer."

—Joyce Carol Oates

"An insightful, compelling, discreet, and admirable biography. . . . In synthesizing a substantial amount of material through clear, intelligent prose, Begley does what I never thought possible: he writes a biography I wished were longer. He adeptly handles the arc of the larger life while sprinkling an array of engaging facts."

—*Christian Science Monitor*

"On the evidence of this judicious new biography, John Updike recorded in his fiction the most painful events in his life. . . . Begley demonstrates that Updike was more complicated than the twinkly public persona he created for himself."

—Robert Wilson, *The American Scholar*

"Begley is so much in command of his subject. . . . He has located the man behind the giant oeuvre."

—Sam Tanenhaus, *Prospect*

"Adam Begley tells the story of John Updike's life in art with brilliant tautness, as if he were writing a novel. He has rendered a portrait of the writer that shimmers with truth. This is literary biography at its highest level of excellence."

—Janet Malcolm

"An insightful and meticulously researched book. . . . A sustained, very fine work of literary criticism."

—*New Republic*

"A deeply researched biography. . . . Begley's reading of Updike's work is enlightening and devoid of academic jargon."

—*Miami Herald*

"A massive, engaging, and generally admiring work that enlightens, entertains, and gently probes the numerous cracks in Updike's character."

—*Cleveland Plain Dealer*

"Begley has done the gumshoe work of a thorough biographer. . . . The biography is full of those small, telling details that define the author's life. . . . Begley's biography sent me back to Updike's early works with renewed appreciation. He has set the standard for detailing the nature of Updike's private and public life."

—*Dallas Morning News*

"Adam Begley gives the writer the biography he deserves—a dexterous combination of literary analysis and life events. . . . The biography is graceful rather than ponderous, as much of a pleasure to read as Updike's prose."

—*Columbus Dispatch*

Updike

Updike

ADAM BEGLEY

HARPER  PERENNIAL

NEW YORK • LONDON • TORONTO • SYDNEY • NEW DELHI • AUCKLAND

 # 88314656

HARPER ● PERENNIAL

HarperCollins books may be purchased for educational, business, or sales promotional use. For information please e-mail the Special Markets Department at SPsales@harpercollins.com.

An extension of this copyright page appears on pages 535–36.

FIRST HARPER PERENNIAL EDITION PUBLISHED 2015.

Designed by Leah Carlson-Stanisic

The Library of Congresss has catalogued the hardcover edition as follows:

Begley, Adam.

Updike / Adam Begley.—First Edition.

pages cm

ISBN 978-0-06-189645-3 (hardcover)

1. Updike, John. 2. Authors, American—20th century—Biography. I. Title.

PS3571.P4Z556 2013

813'.54—dc23

[B]

2013039246

ISBN 978-0-06-189646-0 (pbk.)

15 16 17 18 19   OV/RRD   10 9 8 7 6 5 4 3 2 1

To Anne

Contents

Introduction

In addition to the relevant facts, winnowed from heaps of raw information, a biography ought to give a sense of what its subject was like to shake hands with or stand next to or drink coffee with. So here, before we burrow into the life and work, is a little vignette I hope will give a taste of John Updike, the flavor of the man as he appeared to me in the late fall of 1993, when I trailed behind him, playing Boswell for a day and a half. We were in Appleton, Wisconsin, at Lawrence University, where Updike's younger son had studied in the eighties. Updike had been invited to give the convocation address, dine at the home of the university president, and talk with students in a writing seminar. It was the sort of well-paid trip Updike made over and over again. He was on display as America's preeminent man of letters, showing off what he called his "public, marketable self"—a wonderfully controlled and pleasing performance that revealed, it seemed to me, a good deal about his private, hidden self.

He had barely sat down (we were at a buffet supper at the president's house, plates balanced on knees, guests in armchairs or perched on footstools) when a well-dressed woman sitting near him asked in a sweet midwestern voice, "Mr. Updike—did you write the wonderful story about the man who swims from pool to pool?"

"I wish I had," he answered at once, his voice honeyed like his interlocutor's; "that was John Cheever, 'The Swimmer.'" He grinned, and contained in that wolfish grin—his small mouth a sharp *V* in his long, narrow face—was a mixture of pure amusement, malice, and forbearance. "Perhaps now that John is dead I could lay claim to some of his stories." The assembled company exhaled with a long, relieved laugh. They were relaxing, surrendering to his charm.

Encouraged, the same woman spoke up again, asking if Mr. Updike, so famously prolific, was slowing down, thinking of retirement. Again, the response was instant: "Do you think I should? At sixty-one?" His tousled hair was nearly white, his eyebrows scruffy like an old man's. A network of fine wrinkles surrounded his eyes—but the eyes themselves were bright and lively ("he had a bona fide twinkle in his eye," said Jane Smiley, "maybe the only person I've ever known to really have such a thing"). He was tall and lanky but not remotely feeble or doddery. On the contrary, he exuded a vigorous self-confidence, an almost palpable centeredness. His voice, still sweet, had taken on a flirty, comically submissive edge, as if the advice of this midwestern Cheever fan could hasten his retirement and shape the end of an illustrious literary career. "I *have* been tidying up," he offered, along with another friendly, wickedly acute grin.

That moment of teasing social agility sparked my suspicion that the playfully mischievous, dazzlingly clever John Updike was a potentially dangerous individual, and that a gamut of conflicting emotions, not all of them kindly, were hidden behind the screen of his public persona. I think it was the hint of danger, subliminally communicated to the clutch of listeners in the president's blandly elegant living room, that made his performance in the role of celebrated author so appealing. Yes, he was a professional writer being professionally engaging, but he was also signaling—how? with that clichéd twinkle?—that his good behavior, his forbearance, had its limits.

At the time, I'd read only a few dozen Updike stories and a couple of the novels; when I finally read his memoirs, I found this apposite passage about an earlier trip to a midwestern university:

> I read and talked into the microphone and was gracious to
> the local rich, the English faculty and the college president,
> and the students with their clear skin and shining eyes and
> inviting innocence, like a blank surface one wishes to scrib-
> ble obscenities on.

Suspicion confirmed. Of course there was an undercurrent of aggression in all that expertly deployed charm, a razor edge to his ostensibly gentle wit. In one of the dazzling self-interviews with his alter ego Henry Bech, he lamented his own eagerness to please and ridiculed the whole notion that a writer should be "nice": "[A]s Norman Mailer pointed out decades ago, and Philip Roth not long afterwards, niceness is the enemy. Every soft stroke from society is like the *pfft* of an aerosol can as it eats up a few more atoms of our brain's delicate ozone, and furthers our personal cretinization." A nice, happy author? No, thanks. I found I liked him all the more.

It's possible, I suppose, that I was programmed to like him. My father and he were classmates in college, both of them majoring in English, and for a while after graduation, when my parents were living in Cambridge, Massachusetts, and Updike and his first wife had moved to Ipswich, less than an hour away, the two couples were friendly. Fifty years later, when Updike died unexpectedly (very few people knew that he was ill, let alone dying), my father sent me an e-mail version of an anecdote I'd heard before:

> One day for some reason John came to see us alone, in the early afternoon. We were in our living room, which was flooded by the afternoon sun. You were in your Easy Chair, a contraption in universal use then among advanced couples, which allowed the pre-toddler to recline rather as though he were in a barber's chair having his hair shampooed. One of John's less known talents was his skill as a juggler. He took three oranges from a bowl on the coffee table and began to juggle for you, and you began to laugh. Astonishing belly laughter.

According to this family legend, Updike was the first person to make me laugh. Part of me believed it, and believed it was a natural consequence of this early imprint that I found him congenial when I met him as an adult, the baby in the Easy Chair having grown up to be a literary journalist. Whenever we spoke (which wasn't often— all told perhaps a dozen phone calls and two extended face-to-face interviews), I was amazed and delighted by his gracious, professional manner, and by the sly undercutting of his public, marketable self. He wanted to let you know that he was perfectly aware of the falsity of the situation, and perfectly prepared to be amused by it, for the moment. He wanted to let you know that his real self was elsewhere.

This wasn't just a targeted trick, like juggling for a baby, deployed for the benefit of an admiring journalist; old friends and colleagues noticed it, too. "John could be funny and very friendly," said his Harvard friend Michael Arlen, "but you always felt that this was just a parallel universe we were occupying for the moment—the real universe was back at his desk." Roger Angell, Updike's *New Yorker* fiction editor for more than thirty years, observed how, near the end of each visit to the magazine's offices, he "somehow withdrew a little, growing more private and less visible even before he turned away." Angell called it the "fadeaway" and thought it had to do with being temporarily exiled from writing: "the spacious writing part of him was held to one side when not engaged, kept ready for its engrossing daily stint back home." He was there but not there—just as he was kind but subversive, and charming but dangerous.

Another confusion: Updike thought of himself, or *wanted* to think of himself, as "a pretty average person." So he said at age forty-nine. But since childhood he'd been assured that he was exceptional, brighter and more talented than the rest. And surely he was. A drum-roll of honors, prizes, and awards accompanies the very long list of his published books—sixty-odd in fifty-one years! The list and the accolades confirm that he was indeed extraordinary. His most obsessive fan, Nicholson Baker, whose *U and I* is easily the strangest homage he ever received, declared "unreservedly" that Updike was a genius (but rightly conceded that the word has no useful meaning). My ideas about this question are borrowed from Lionel Trilling, who wrote about George Orwell, "He was not a genius, and this is one of the remarkable things about him." Trilling thought Orwell stood for "the virtue of not being a genius, of fronting the world with nothing more than one's simple, direct, undeceived intelligence, and a respect for the powers one does have, and the work one undertakes to do." Updike once declared that his epitaph should be "Here lies a small-town boy who tried to make the most out of what he had, who made up with diligence what he might have lacked in brilliance."

Hard work, talent, "undeceived" intelligence—those three essential ingredients require a binding agent, which is ambition. The small-town boy aimed high, with posterity's judgment never absent from his thoughts. As a college student he dreamed of becoming a "universal artist," by which he meant someone both great and popular, lodged in the heart of the American people not just today but tomorrow. In the mid-sixties, he began to deposit his papers at the Houghton Library, where Harvard University stores its rare books and manuscripts, where scholars go to examine the literary remains of giants such as Ralph Waldo Emerson, Emily Dickinson, Henry James, and T. S. Eliot. For the next forty years Updike dutifully boxed up and delivered to the library first drafts and false starts and galley proofs—"the refuse of my profession"—as well as personal correspondence. Today the Updike archive, a vast paper trail, possibly the last of its kind, is irrefutable evidence of faith—his own and others'—in the enduring significance of his achievement.*

Predicting his eventual place in the pantheon of American literature is an amusing pastime, but no more useful than playing pin-the-tail with the genius label. In September 2013, the Library of America published two volumes of his collected stories; if that proves to be the first installment of a uniform edition of his work, one of Updike's fondest wishes will have come true. It's one of my fondest wishes that those books will mark the beginning of a surge in his posthumous reputation.

---

* Nine months after Updike's death, Harvard bought the archive from his estate for three million dollars; until then the university had merely been storing the material, hoping one day to own it.

> A man who has been the indisputable favorite of his mother keeps for life the feeling of a conqueror.
>
> —Sigmund Freud

I.

A Tour of Berks County

In the late spring of 1983, when John Updike's reputation as a writer had reached a pinnacle—having swept all three major literary awards for *Rabbit Is Rich* in 1982, he made his second appearance on the cover of *Time*, the headline on this occasion boasting, "Going Great at 50"—a freelance journalist named William Ecenbarger pitched an idea for a story to the editor of the *Philadelphia Inquirer Magazine*. The reporter wanted to write about the relationship between Updike's fiction and the geography of Berks County, Pennsylvania, what Updike called, with possessive emphasis, "*my* home turf." Ecenbarger planned to visit the city of Reading, where Updike was born; Shillington, the small town on the outskirts of Reading where he lived until he was thirteen; and Plowville, eleven miles into the countryside where he languished in frustrated rural isolation until he left for college. From these three places Updike drew the material that launched his career, the earliest novels (*The Poorhouse Fair*; *Rabbit, Run*; *The Centaur*; and *Of the Farm*) and dozens of short stories, some of them among his best. Plowville became Firetown; Reading, a middle-size industrial city in decline for all of Updike's adult life, became Alton (or Brewer in the Rabbit tetralogy); and beloved, small-town Shillington, sandwiched between the retreating countryside and the encroaching suburbs, was reborn as Olinger (with a long *O* and a hard *g*, as in "Oh, linger"). Together, they are the heart of Updike's America, its landscape and its history.

In short, Bill Ecenbarger had chosen a promising topic.

Given a green light by his editor, he dutifully sent an interview request to Alfred A. Knopf, Updike's publisher. No reply was forthcoming, but then, Ecenbarger hadn't expected one. (Thanks to a series of uncompromising pronouncements on the subject—"I really think being interviewed a great waste of time and energy, with results that generally leave you feeling embarrassed, or at least that you should clean your fingernails"—Updike had gained an unwarranted reputation for being media shy.) Unfazed, the journalist drove down to Shillington to have a poke around and do some research in the town's public library. No sooner had he begun quizzing the reference librarian about the famous local author than he felt an insistent tug at his sleeve. An elderly woman was at his elbow, peering at him through large tortoiseshell glasses.

"I know all about him," she said simply. "He's my son."

As any good reporter would, Ecenbarger took Linda Updike to lunch at a nearby restaurant. She, in turn, took him out to Plowville and showed him around the small sandstone farmhouse familiar to all devoted Updike readers. The key sights in the cramped interior were young John's narrow bedroom at the top of the stairs and, downstairs, long white shelves devoted to the books he'd written. "He told me when he left for Harvard," she said, "that he was going to fill those shelves. There's only room for one or two more." (By 1983, Updike had published twenty-three volumes; there were forty more yet to come in his lifetime.) She showed him the big, well-built barn made famous by "Pigeon Feathers." Ecenbarger remembers his guide as a soft-spoken, intelligent woman. A widow who had lived on her own for more than a decade, she was a little garrulous, manifestly proud of her son, and happy to claim some credit for having nurtured his talent.

Delighted by his stroke of luck, the journalist went home and began to write the article. Four days later, he received a phone call from Mrs. Updike. "Chonny will be here tomorrow," she said. "He's coming to put in my screens. He does it every year. Why don't you stop by?"

Needing no further encouragement, the next morning Ecenbarger presented himself at the farmhouse, where he was greeted by Mrs. Updike. She warned him that her son, still upstairs, was a bit grumpy. "He often gets that way when he visits," she confided.

Ecenbarger waited inside while Mrs. Updike went out to fill a bird feeder. He was examining the long bookcase crammed with the Updike oeuvre when the author himself appeared, wearing a navy wool watch cap, which he removed after poking his head out the kitchen door to test the morning temperature. "Let's go," he said. "I have a lot of other things to do today." Ecenbarger had the distinct impression that the celebrated author was doing his best not to vent his irritation at having an impromptu interview thrust upon him by his mother.

"I'll drive so you can take notes," Updike suggested as they left the house, "but I want to drive your car." Opening the door of Ecenbarger's Volkswagen, he added, "I've never driven a Rabbit before." That glint of humor set the tone for things to come: reluctant at first, Updike soon warmed up, teased by nostalgia into what became a marathon round of autobiographical tourism. All day long the two men drove around the county. In West Reading they passed the municipal hospital where Updike was born on March 18, 1932; in Shillington they parked in front of 117 Philadelphia Avenue, the white brick house where he grew up, an only child coddled by his parents and maternal grandparents; and finally they returned to Plowville, to the eighty-acre farm where he endured his lonely adolescence.

Bill Ecenbarger made the most of his scoop. He had every reason to be grateful to Updike and his mother: with their help (and a good deal of attentive reading) he produced an entertaining and informative piece of feature journalism. "Updike Is Home" appeared on June 12, 1983, illustrated with a photograph of a smiling Updike in front of the farmhouse, one hand in the pocket of his tan corduroys, the other cupped on the back of his neck. It's a coy, boyish pose, almost elfin; the fifty-one-year-old author looks like a sly kid.

His mother hovers in the background, a ghostly gray presence in the doorway of the house.

What Ecenbarger failed to realize—until several weeks after the publication of his article—was that the transaction had been mutually beneficial. The reporter filed one version of the story, and the fiction writer filed another: an Updike short story, "One More Interview," appeared in *The New Yorker* on July 4; it's about an unnamed actor who agrees, reluctantly, to drive around his hometown in the company of a journalist ("It would provide, you know . . . an angle"). Gradually the actor's resistance ("I can't stand interviews") melts away as the trickle of memories swells to a flood. Even as the reporter's interest wanes ("I think maybe I've seen enough. This is only for a sidebar, you know"), the actor finds he can't let go of this opportunity to revisit his small-town boyhood, to dream of his first love and his vanished, teenage self ("He wanted to cruise forever through this half of town").

Reading his *New Yorker*, Ecenbarger was astonished to find that he'd become muse to a great American writer. Updike had transcribed, verbatim, their exchanges, beginning with the helpful suggestion that the interviewee drive while the interviewer take notes, and extending to trivial back-and-forth unrelated to the matter at hand, such as the actor's surmise that the "wiry" reporter (whose "exceptionally tight mouth" Updike lifted, as it were, straight from Ecenbarger's face) had been a high school athlete:

> "Don't be modest. You played second base, didn't you?"
> "Center field, usually."
> "Same idea . . ."

The reporter's preferred position on the diamond was thus immortalized in Updike's fiction.

Other borrowed details: Just as Updike initially had trouble with the Rabbit's manual transmission, so the actor, driving the interviewer's car (not a Rabbit but rather "a Japanese model"), shifts "from first straight into fourth, with a fearful laboring of the engine." Ecenbarger told Updike that the article he was writing was more about the place than the author; the actor receives the same warning, phrased the same way. Describing the midcentury sartorial flair of the town's richer kids, the actor spells out for the interviewer the precise word he has in mind: "there was a word then, 'snazzy,' s-n-a-z-z-y"; Updike remarked on an unchanged aspect of Shillington and said he found it "cheery"—whereupon he helpfully spelled out the word, "c-h-e-e-r-y."

Updike chose to include in his tour the local lovers' lane— "where we used to neck," he explained to Ecenbarger. The actor steers the interviewer to the "necking place" and is amazed to find it still there. His thoughts turn to Ermajean Willis, the girl he'd "acquired" at age seventeen, and he drives the few blocks to her house.

> "My girlfriend used to live here," he confessed to his interviewer.
> "You had only one?"
> "Well, yes."

Parked in front of her house, the actor feels "swamped by love."

From the scant but sharply focused information divulged about Ermajean, it's obvious that she's one of many fictional incarnations of Nancy Wolf ("my only girlfriend"), a girl Updike wrote about as Nora in his 1989 memoir, *Self-Consciousness*.[*] We know she's the same girl because of a conspicuous architectural detail (a detail he mentions twice in *Self-Consciousness* as a feature typical of Shillington): the concrete balls decorating the retaining wall in front of both Ermajean's house and Nora's. Though he once insisted (unconvincingly) that the Shillington he used in his fiction was more a stage in his "pilgrim's progress" than an actual spot on the map, his instinct was always to borrow the signature detail from the bricks and mortar of the town.

What are we to make of this whole incident? Ecenbarger was at first mildly disturbed to find that in Updike's version, the actor doesn't enjoy playing tour guide. He slips from wary impatience and

---

[*] Updike changed her name to Nora in his memoir, presumably to protect her privacy. She died in 2009, just a few weeks after Updike.

annoyance into a bittersweet reverie that triggers a powerful romantic longing for a place and a time and a self forever gone. At the very
end of the story, the spell broken (in part because the interviewer is
plainly bored, blind to the "glory" of vivid private memories), the
actor reverts to a brusque, comic annoyance: "Keep your pencil out.
You son of a bitch, I'm going to tell you the names of every family
that used to live on this block." Ecenbarger had been under the impression that the courteous, even genial, Updike had quickly forgotten his irritation, that their nostalgic excursion had given the author
pleasure. (It very likely had: "I become exhilarated in Shillington,"
he once wrote, "as if my self is being given a bath in its own essence.")

Leaving aside the reporter's momentary distress, there was no
harm done. Updike took the incident, reshaped it slightly to accentuate the dramatic arc, and gave it the twist of the actor's final pet-
ulant outburst. Retaining intact the details that suited his purpose,
he adjusted others strategically—and so turned a day's drive into a
perfectly adequate *New Yorker* story, a slick comic vignette with a
moment or two of poignant depth. That was his job, Updike might
have said with a shrug, a profitable trick of alchemy.

Or digestion. In a story he wrote in 1960 about his maternal
grandmother (a story closely based on the facts of Katherine Hoyer's
life), he described with a startling simile the writer's creative process: "We walk through volumes of the unexpressed and like snails
leave behind a faint thread excreted out of ourselves." Twenty-five
years later, addressing an appreciative crowd in a packed theater in
downtown Albany, New York, Updike elaborated on his scatological
theory of the creative imagination: "Freud somewhere claims that a
child's first gifts, to its parents, are its feces, whose presentation (in
the appropriate receptacle) is roundly praised. And as in this primal
benefaction, the writer extrudes his daily product while sitting down,
on a healthy basis of regularity and avoidance of strain. The artist
who works in words and anecdotes, images and facts wants to share
with us nothing less than his digested life." The audience laughed, as
Updike surely hoped they would, but he was also making a serious
point. The joke depends on the scabrous suggestion that all writing,
including his own, is crap. We can dismiss that notion with a smile

and still see in it a speck of truth: the writer who feeds off his raw experience, walking through volumes of the unexpressed and then excreting or extruding fiction, is engaged in a magical transaction that produces wonders, a fabulous gift presented to the reader—but isn't there something ever so slightly repellent about this offering? Isn't there the hint of a foul odor? Fiction is a "dirty business," he once confessed; his art had "a shabby side."

A year or so after his encounter with Bill Ecenbarger, Updike wrote an autobiographical essay about yet another tour of his old neighborhood, a solo walk he took through streets he'd described in story after story—"a deliberate indulgence of a nostalgia long since made formal in many words." In "A Soft Spring Night in Shillington" (which ran in *The New Yorker* in late 1984 and eventually became the first chapter of *Self-Consciousness*), Updike voices his regret at plundering his memories of Shillington, "scraps" that have been "used more than once, used to the point of vanishing . . . in the self-serving corruptions of fiction."* His regret, his suspicion that in his writing he's betraying a place he loves ("a town that was also somewhat my body"), is balanced against the stubborn fact that he depends for his livelihood on the sale of his fiction—"scribbling for my life," he calls it. In his speech on creativity, he mentioned the "simultaneous sense of loss and recapture" he experienced when his memory seized upon a scene from his past he knew he could use in his fiction. This ambivalence stayed with him throughout his career,

---

* A trivial example, from "One More Interview," of a recycled "scrap": As the memories begin to flow, the actor suddenly recalls the exact pattern of the linoleum floor in his hometown barbershop, and how Jake, the barber, "could tap-dance or a least do a nimble shuffle-and-slide . . . performing with his broom for his audience of regulars." That detail (which pops quite naturally into the head of a thespian, a man who's spent his life on the stage) first surfaced in Updike's description of the Shillington barber in "The Dogwood Tree: A Boyhood," an autobiographical essay written twenty-three years earlier: "Nimble and bald, he used to execute little tap-dance figures on the linoleum floor of his shop." In "A Soft Spring Night in Shillington," Updike divulged the real name of this multitalented fellow and described the routine one more time: "Artie for a joke would do a shuffle-one, shuffle-two, tap-tap-tap on the hairy linoleum floor."

but he never gave up the habit of reusing the scraps that came his way; even the writing that isn't nakedly autobiographical is flecked with incidents and characters drawn from life with disconcerting accuracy—a host of Ecenbargers opportunistically fictionalized.

It's not too great a stretch to say that John Updike's entire career was an extended tour of his native turf, or that the later adventures in far-off places were made possible by the intensity of his preoccupation with his small-town beginnings. In one of his last poems, written just a month and a half before his death, when he already knew he was terminally ill, he thanks his childhood friends and high school classmates

> . . . for providing a
> sufficiency of human types: beauty,
> bully, hanger-on, natural,
> twin, and fatso—all a writer needs,
> all there in Shillington . . .

He began by writing down what had happened to him, at home, next door, and down the street, "the drab normalities of a Pennsylvania boyhood."* This became both his method and, for a time, his credo. His stated aim was to "realize . . . the shape, complexity, diffidence, and tremor of actuality." In the mid-seventies—in a lecture with a manifesto title, "Why Write?"—he declared, "We must write where we stand; wherever we do stand, there is life; and an imitation of the life we know, however narrow, is our only ground." But the accurate transcription of surface detail wasn't enough; in the service of his "relentless domestic realism," he dug deeper, mining the lode of family life, the lives of his friends and acquaintances, for buried nuggets of serviceable material. No one was spared this ritual excavation, not his parents, not his two wives, not his four children—as he conceded in *Self-Consciousness*, he exempted himself from "normal intra-familial courtesy." Or, more bluntly, "[T]he nearer and

---

* "Most of the best fiction is written out of early impressions," he once remarked, "taken in before the writer became conscious of himself as a writer."

dearer they are, the more mercilessly they are served up." In a heart-breaking interview for the 1982 public television documentary *What Makes Rabbit Run?* Updike's eldest son, David, acknowledged that his father "decided at an early age that his writing had to take precedence over his relations with real people." Later in the film Updike frankly concurs: "My duty as a writer is to make the best record I can of life as I understand it, and that duty takes precedence for me over all these other considerations." The writing took precedence even over his personal reputation: Updike's alter egos were at times convincingly hideous individuals. "I drank up women's tears and spat them out," he wrote in a late confessional poem, "as 10-point Janson, Roman and *ital.*"

In a *Paris Review* interview he gave twenty years before he published his memoirs, he made a pro forma attempt to deny that the autobiographical elements in his fiction were anything more than "teasing little connections." (It's worth noting that the interview was conducted in 1968, the year *Couples* was published; Updike would have been eager to discourage any investigations into the parallels between the adulterous high jinks in the novel and the state of his own marriage.) Although he couched his remarks in the unequivocal language of a legal deposition ("I disavow any essential connection between my life and whatever I write"), he never bothered to make it stick. He talked, in virtually the same breath, about the "submerged thread" of autobiography connecting his early books. (The thread, hardly submerged, was thick enough to wrap in a single package *The Centaur*, *Of the Farm*, and most of the stories in *The Same Door* and *Pigeon Feathers*.) And his disavowal was clearly forgotten by the time he made his speech on the creative imagination. "Creative excitement," he said on that occasion, "has invariably and only come to me when I felt I was transferring, with a lively accuracy, some piece of experienced reality to the printed page." The process put an insulating distance between his private self and his Updike-like characters: "I don't really feel it's me," he told an interviewer who asked if he felt he was exposing too much of himself in print. "The fact that it's happening on paper makes it seem very removed from me."

John Updike wrote about himself. Dozens of adverbs present themselves, all vying for the honor of capping that sentence so that it reveals the exact nature of his special brand of lightly fictionalized, peekaboo autobiography. John Updike wrote about himself copiously. That's indisputable and modestly neutral, but too vague. John Updike wrote about himself reflexively. (Why not push it further and say that he wrote about himself compulsively, or even—as some would claim—ad nauseam?) One could argue that he wrote about himself religiously, and there's a truth there: "Imitation is praise," he wrote. "Description expresses love." He also wrote about himself lucidly. That fits well, in part because *lucid* was one of his pet words, in part because it's friendly without necessarily implying approbation. Many of the adverbs that come to mind prejudge the issue, offering a ready-made verdict either aesthetic (he wrote about himself brilliantly, ingeniously) or moral (he wrote about himself honestly, bravely, with abiding curiosity). The verdict can of course go the other way: he wrote about himself indulgently, or ruthlessly, with callous disregard for his family and other, collateral victims. It's clearly safest to stick with the cautious neutrality of objective criticism. If you polled a seminar room stuffed with scholars and literary theorists you'd come away with a slippery exam question: John Updike wrote about himself ironically—discuss.

Of the many adverbs auditioning for the role, three seem particularly well-suited: John Updike wrote about himself *naturally*, then very quickly learned to write about himself *professionally*. On his best days, he wrote about himself *creatively*, and his fiction became part of his autobiographical legend. From an early age, prodded by ambition, he exploited with remarkable and enduring discipline his knack for imitating the life he knew. One of the wonders of his career is that he never lost interest in the material nearest to hand (just ask Bill Ecenbarger). Unlike the actor in "One More Interview," he was never jaded—never the weary sophisticate. (And he never tired of reliving his Pennsylvania boyhood: more than a third of the stories in *My Father's Tears*, published five months after his death, circle back to Shillington and Plowville and the family that nurtured him.) At the very end of his life, after five decades of prodigious literary production, when suddenly faced with the prospect of his own imminent death, he could still write about himself with what seemed, triumphantly, an artless ease.

> A wake-up call? It seems that death has found
> the portals it will enter by: my lungs,
> pathetic oblong ghosts, one paler than
> the other on the doctor's viewing screen.

The poignant intimacy of the valedictory poems published posthumously in *Endpoint*—the sense of a direct connection between the terminally ill poet and his sympathetic reader—is a heightened version of the effect Updike contrived to produce in his earlier autobiographical fiction: a self is exposed (the writing a kind of viewing screen), and from the moment we recognize and identify with this X-rayed character, the story begins to exert a powerful fascination. "We read fiction because it makes us feel less lonely about being a human being," he once remarked. The pen pals he provided for us were most often variations on the theme of John Hoyer Updike. Even critics who dismiss his work as snippets of experience padded out to make a story are implicitly acknowledging the compelling accuracy of the writing; with no knowledge of Updike's life, they assume they're reading fragments of autobiography. When we think we recognize his presence in the work, we're also recognizing its potent realism; as he pointed out, "only the imagery we have personally gathered and unconsciously internalized possesses the color, warmth, intimate contour, and weight of authenticity the discriminating fiction-reader demands." His alter egos seem real to us because they *are* real, or near enough. They seemed real, in any case, to the author.

Consider, for example, "Flight," a short story written at the beginning of 1959 that's every bit as densely autobiographical as "One More Interview," though in this case the Updike stand-in is Allen Dow, a seventeen-year-old high school student burdened with both Updike's family history and his "special destiny." Allen's mother tells him that he will transcend his small-town beginnings ("You're going to fly"), and this prophecy touches his "most secret self." His deep belief that he's somehow extraordinary coexists with a natural desire to be just like everyone else, and in the crosscurrent of those contradictory impulses a character is born with whom the reader forges a bond. Allen—who remembers being a "poorly dressed and funny-looking" teenager who "went around thinking of himself in the third person . . . 'Allen Dow smiled a thin sardonic smile' "—is like us, at once vulnerable and instinctively self-protective; his secret self is our secret self.

Although Allen is clothed in the particulars of the young John Updike's circumstances, circa 1949, a few strategic changes enhance the dramatic possibilities. Allen's maternal grandfather (in all other respects a portrait of Updike's maternal grandfather, John Franklin Hoyer) is dying, and his illness is making Allen's mother understandably miserable.* In her "desperate state," she launches a scarcely disguised assault on Allen's girlfriend, Molly; their teen romance, he tells us, "brought out an ignoble, hysterical, brutal aspect of my mother." Allen's "special destiny" is the main objection: he mustn't have a girlfriend who will hold him back. "The entire town seemed ensnarled in my mother's myth, that escape was my proper fate." Allen himself is ensnarled in the myth, and he, too, is cruel to Molly. This part Updike borrowed directly from his own experience. In *Self-Consciousness*, he explains that his relationship with his girlfriend Nora was fatally undermined by his mother's disapproval and the expectation that he would be moving on to better things: "I was never allowed to relax into her; the perfect girl for me would take me away from Shillington, not pull me down into it."

Here's how it was with Updike and Nora, a ruthless portrait of the author as a callow youth mistreating his girl:

---

* Though John Hoyer lived to be ninety and died only when Updike was a twenty-one-year-old senior in college, at Allen Dow's age, Updike was much distressed by his beloved grandfather's "heart-tearing" cough. In "Flight," the cough sounds "like a dry membrane tearing."

It was courtesy of Nora that I discovered breasts are not glazed bouffant orbs pushing up out of a prom dress but soft poignant inflections. . . . She was as fragrant and tactful and giving as one could wish; in the relative scale of our youth and virginity, she did for me all that a woman does for a man, and I regretted that my nagging specialness harried almost every date and shared hour with awareness of our imminent and necessary parting.

And here's how it is with Allen and Molly:

We never made love in the final, coital sense. My reason was a mixture of idealism and superstition; I felt that if I took her virginity she would be mine forever. I depended overmuch on a technicality; she gave herself to me anyway, and I had her anyway, and have her still, for the longer I travel in a direction I could not have taken with her, the more clearly she seems the one person who loved me without advantage.

In *Self-Consciousness*, Updike showcases the memory of a particular evening, after he'd suffered the humiliation of stuttering on the stage of the high school auditorium, when he hung around on the curb opposite Nora's house, "hoping she would accidentally look out the window or intuitively sense my presence, and come out to comfort me. And she did. Nora did come out, and we talked." In "Flight," Allen parks the family car opposite Molly's house on an evening when he's especially traumatized by his grandfather's illness, his mother's despair, and his own restlessness. Like Nora, Molly intuitively senses that he's outside her house and comes out to see him: "*She came.* When I have forgotten everything else—her powdery fragrance, her lucid cool skin, the way her lower lip was like a curved pillow of two cloths, the dusty red outer and wet pink inner—I'll still be grieved by this about Molly, that she came to me."

The memoirs give us the painful facts, a circumspect account delivered in a stiff, chilly tone barely softened by nostalgia; the short story, gentler but more devastating, draws us into a complex web of desire, guilt, and memory, the intensity of the emotion concentrated in that sexually suggestive close-up of Molly's lips. The story ends with a bitter quarrel between Allen and his mother, which results in a final betrayal of his girlfriend. In the memoirs, the betrayal is suggested rather than dramatized ("I did not let Nora's satiny skin and powdered warmth and soft forgiving voice prevent me from going on with my show"); the nostalgia is tinged with mild, passing regret. Updike, like his mother, believed in his own special destiny—his show must go on.

Allen Dow is haunted by remembrance and by the guilt that comes with escape—as was Updike, who once directed an interviewer's attention to the conclusion of "Flight," to the moment of the climactic quarrel, the moment, metaphorically speaking, when Allen leaves behind both his girlfriend and his mother. "This is the way it was, is," said Updike. "There has never been anything in my life quite as compressed, simultaneously as communicative to me of my own power and worth and of the irremediable grief in just living, in just going on."

This unusual glimpse of an author overawed by the conflated memory of an actual incident and his fictional rendering of that incident ("This is the way it was, is") invites the reader to erase the distinction between autobiography and fiction. Is Nora more real than Molly? Where should one draw the line between Allen's self-love and Updike's? Between Allen's cruelty and Updike's? Between Allen's remorse and Updike's? It's likely that the author himself couldn't have told us. His memories of his high school years would have been altered by the emotions stirred up in the excitement of writing "Flight" (and dozens of other autobiographical fictions) a decade after the events in question. He acknowledged this in the foreword to *Olinger Stories*: "Composition, in crystallizing memory, displaces it."* By the time he wrote "A Soft Spring Night in Shillington" in 1984 and told the story of his "only girlfriend," the difference between the living, breathing Nancy Wolf, the Nora of his memoirs,

---

* This same sentence is quoted on the back of the book, modified so as to make the case more emphatically: "Composition, in crystallizing memory, replaces it."

and the imagined Molly would have been blurred at best—and Allen Dow (who reappears as an alter ego in a later story) would have become part of Updike's mythic image of his teenage self.[*]

All of which adds to the authenticity of the fiction and therefore to its resonance. To the extent that we see ourselves in Updike/Allen, that our romance with our secret self also includes the suspicion that we're special (exempt from the common fate even as we seek to embrace common pleasures), we're complicit in the betrayal of Nora/Molly, dismayed to be her betrayer's partner in crime, aware of the load of remorse he will necessarily shoulder—and yet unable to condemn his adolescent urge to *get out*. To read the story sympathetically is to hear a melancholy echo of our own tenderest regrets.

The more Updike one reads, and the more one learns about his life, the more glaringly obvious it becomes that he was enthralled by the details of his own experience. Does it make him a lesser artist that he so often relied on self-portraits and transcriptions of actual events and circumstances? Perhaps it would if the portraits were documentary photorealism and the action unedited chronology: the prose equivalent of a live webcam. Though he announced his desire to "imitate reality with increasing closeness," he knew full well that there is no way of translating raw experience into words without altering it. And that was never his intention. He selected, he edited, sensing acutely the drift and propensity of seemingly unimportant actions, sharpening the blur of daily life so that meaning began to emerge; the altered, fictionalized story, now freighted with significance, displaced the less dramatically compelling reality. The particular brilliance with which he made his autobiographical material come alive on the page is part of the reward of reading him. In a curious way, the autobiographical elements deepen and complicate the reader's enjoyment: The informed reader learns to distinguish between the subtle magic of transcribed experience and the different, bolder magic of less securely tethered imaginative gestures.

---

[*] In the *Paris Review* interview, Updike remarked, "Once I've coined a [character's] name . . . I feel totally hidden behind that mask, and what I remember and what I imagine become indistinguishable."

PART OF WHAT allowed Updike the freedom to indulge his autobiographical impulse was his relationship with his mother, the elderly woman who tugged at Ecenbarger's sleeve in the Shillington public library, eager to talk about her son, the famous writer. To say that Linda Hoyer Updike encouraged her only child and nurtured his precocious talent is to understate and simplify an unusually close and complicated relationship. She helped him to become a writer (and he, when the time came, helped her); she offered him yards of advice and unstinting praise from the moment he set pen to paper. She was, as he put it, "an ideally permissive writer's mother," meaning that he was free to write exactly what he pleased, no matter how painful to his family. He explained that his parents shared an "un-middleclass appetite for the jubilant horrible truth," and that they were "never other than encouraging, even when old wounds were my topic." And a lucky thing, too, for he pinned his artistic courage on the notion that "only truth is useful. Only truth can be built upon."

His mother's respect for her son's unflinching honesty was noted by the biographer Ron Chernow, who went to see Linda Updike in Plowville in the early seventies when he was a young journalist eager to write something—anything—about John Updike. Chernow remembers asking her how it felt to pop up as a character in her son's fiction, specifically in *Of the Farm*.* According to Chernow, "She paused and said, 'When I came upon the characterization of myself as a large, coarse country woman I was very hurt.' She said she walked around for several days, brooding—and then she realized she *was* a large, coarse country woman." (Chernow hastened to add that although her personality wasn't at all coarse, the description accurately captured her look—the stocky build, the husky voice, the pleasantly plain face, the utterly unglamorous clothing.)

---

* When Bill Ecenbarger asked her the same question, she replied, "He portrayed me as he saw me, and I respect his vision." To Steve Neal, she gave a more ironic, media-savvy answer, saying that she was eager to become more like the character in *Of the Farm*: "I don't think I'm as witty, and I'm certainly not as tough, but I'm trying hard."

Although he habitually referred to her as a "would-be writer," Updike's mother was in fact, under her maiden name, Linda Grace Hoyer, a *published* writer—with what in any other family would seem an enviable track record. Between 1961 and 1983, *The New Yorker* published ten of her short stories.* In 1971, Houghton Mifflin published her novel, *Enchantment* (actually a series of linked stories, four of which had appeared in *The New Yorker*); and a few months after her death in late 1989, *The Predator*, a collection of stories, six of them from *The New Yorker*, was published by Ticknor and Fields.[†] Updike, once he'd gone to work at *The New Yorker*, was active in helping to get his mother's stories into the magazine; in fact, it's very likely that without his help she would never have succeeded. As she told Bill Ecenbarger, with clear-eyed modesty, "I had only a little gift, but it was the only one I got." She also told him, proudly, "Johnny knew it was possible to be a writer because he saw me trying."[‡]

Her published stories are all frankly autobiographical, and almost all set in a farmhouse identical to the one where she was born in Plowville in 1904, the only child of John and Katie Hoyer. Her first book, *Enchantment*, tells her life story in fifteen overlapping first-person installments: her own birth and childhood, her schooling, her marriage, the birth of her only child (who becomes a famous writer), and so on. It's the Updike-Hoyer household with a few minor alterations and embellishments and a great deal of spiritual reverb. In some of the earlier stories, when they were published in *The New Yorker*, the narrator's name is Linda; the stories were presented, in other words, as the author's memoirs. When she collected these stories in book form, Linda gave her alter ego the fanciful name of Belle Minuit, which matches her preoccupation with spells and omens, with various forms

---

* To put this number into perspective, *The New Yorker* published no fewer than 146 of her son's short stories—and just 13 by J. D. Salinger, another writer whose name was closely associated with the magazine.

† She lived to see the bound galleys of *The Predator* but not the finished book.

‡ He told an interviewer, "It probably wouldn't have occurred to me to be a writer if she hadn't been there doing it."

of "enchantment." Her second book is about an aging widow with the more plausible name of Ada Gibson; Ada lives alone in an isolated farmhouse in Pennsylvania, visited occasionally by her only son, a celebrated illustrator who draws covers for *The New Yorker*. You might expect that the various family portraits executed by mother and son would cause some confusion, but actually they tend to corroborate rather than contradict one another. The fictional elements are almost always easy to spot, and the emotional currents (especially between mother and son) ebb and flow in synchronized patterns.

Did John Updike learn the habit of writing autobiographically at his mother's knee? She certainly set an example. Her sister-in-law, Mary Updike, who had been Edmund Wilson's secretary at *The New Republic*, advised her as early as 1931 (a year before John's birth) to write "straight fiction" (as opposed to essays) and to use "material from your life on the farm." Linda took the advice; in fact, she didn't even bother to change Plowville's name. Both mother and son reproduced in intimate detail the family's domestic arrangements. Two years after her death, at a reading in Pennsylvania, Updike noted in a wry tone that "one of the disadvantages of two people writing out of the same household is that you tend to overlap material." He also revealed that his mother made a habit of showing him her stories. "I was really an editor before I was a writer," he said, milking the situation for laughs. "From quite young I was asked to read her things and comment on them, a sort of wearisome but awesome responsibility for a child of ten." He grew up, in other words, with the idea that it was perfectly natural to write stories about one's family and one's immediate neighborhood.

And yet most of his mother's energies did not go into writing autobiographical fiction. Her magnum opus ("frequently revised and never published," as her son repeatedly pointed out) was a historical novel about Ponce de Léon. "There was a novel," Updike recalled, "that slept in a ream box that had been emptied of blankness, and like a strange baby in the house, a difficult papery sibling, the manuscript was now and then roused out of its little rectangular crib and rewritten and freshly swaddled in hope." The comic hint of sibling rivalry in that fanciful description is echoed in his account (also oft-repeated) of the shock he experienced as a young child when his mother rebuked him, asking him to be quiet because she was busy writing: "I had not hitherto realized that I had . . . any competitors whatsoever." The novel, called *Dear Juan*,* was submitted to publishers again and again over the course of a quarter of a century and more. The image Updike frequently conjures to evoke the persistent futility of her efforts is of brown envelopes mailed off to New York—whence they were mailed straight back. Updike joined in this boomerang exercise at age eleven (though, in his case, he was sending off cartoons and drawings and, when he reached high school, light verse). Mother and son spent their time "plodding out to the mailbox to reap . . . rejection slips."†

Linda's rejection slips came with numbing regularity: she left behind multiple drafts of *Dear Juan*, two other unpublished novels, and dozens and dozens of unpublished short stories. Perhaps it's understandable, in view of that heap of spurned manuscripts, that Updike habitually referred to her as his "long-aspiring mother," that he relegated her, in a memorable and patently inaccurate phrase, to "the slave shack of the unpublished." If she was unpublished, then he had no need to address the quality of her fiction—which he almost never did in public. Here's a man who was never, it can safely be said, at a loss for words, but he had virtually nothing to say about the experience of reading his own mother's work—unless you count the last words of "My Mother at Her Desk," a late poem: "Mother typed birdsong." (The poem begins, "My mother knew non-publication's shame.") With that exception, he never used in his fiction the predicament of a hugely successful and prolific writer whose mother,

---

* The title is another blatant sign of Linda's preoccupation with her son: years later, when he had left for Harvard, she would sometimes begin her letters to him, "Dear Juan."

† For him, the relationship improved dramatically. In 1986, addressing the Forty-Eighth International PEN Congress in New York City, after decades of mailing off manuscripts and receiving money and critical acclaim in return, Updike spoke in praise of the U.S. Postal Service: "I never see a blue mailbox without a spark of warmth and wonder and gratitude that this intricate and extensive service is maintained for my benefit."

also a writer, struggles to get her stories into print. His silence on the subject may have something to do with his private reservations about her work, as well as his reluctance to draw attention to the boost he'd given her career (though as we know, he didn't usually shy away from exposing embarrassments, his own or others'). Most likely his silence demonstrates that in his mind, despite tangible evidence to the contrary, his mother simply wasn't a writer—she remained for him always an *aspiring* writer. Or, as he put it bluntly, brutally, in a poem composed after her death, "I took off from her failure." Another satisfying self-dramatization.

During her son's formative years, in any case, Linda easily generated more than enough aspiration for two. This was a woman who made lists of the university alma maters of anthologized short story writers (an exercise that eventually helped steer her son to Harvard College). Frank, forceful, exceptionally tenacious, and early on persuaded that her son would do great things, she infused John with confidence, determination, and a sense of security. She was his first audience, and gave him his first sense of himself as a performer. Like Allen Dow's mother, she convinced him he could fly. "I always did think he could fly without a machine," she told *Time* magazine, "but I don't know whether I was right in sharing that thought or not." He certainly got the message. "I was made to feel that I could do things," he told an interviewer. "If you get this feeling early and can hold it until you're 15, you tend never to lose it." By making "the great leap of imagination up, out of the rural Pennsylvania countryside . . . into the ethereal realm of art," his mother showed him how to set his sights somewhere beyond Shillington. Her own ambition, it should be noted, had no geographical dimension: she showed no inclination to leave Berks County. Though she seemed to her son to be "trying to reach beyond the street outside . . . toward a world we couldn't see," at the same time she seemed to be "hiding from the town, in our house and yard." Like Allen Dow, Updike had to cope with the complicated business of having a powerful, fiercely possessive mother who was simultaneously tightening her grip and pushing him up and out into the world—even as she herself was retreating from it.

The push-and-pull was aggravated by the unusually strong sense of place she passed on to her only child. Both mother and son believed that their identity was inextricably rooted in a specific location, but what's peculiar—in the dynamic of a parent and child who never spent more than a few days apart until he turned eighteen and left home for good—is that they were attached to different places: she to the farm in Plowville, he to his boyhood home in Shillington, the small town "synonymous" with his being.

It's no surprise, then, that in the Updike family mythology, the move in 1945 from Shillington to Plowville (which occurred on Halloween, as if for atmosphere's sake) is a momentous event. Told and retold in Linda Updike's *Enchantment*, her son's *The Centaur* and *Of the Farm*, and a good number of his short stories and autobiographical essays, the eleven-mile journey from one home to the next is the crisis to which Updike's childhood builds—and the ideal lens through which to examine the tangle of familial loyalties and tensions that shaped him and fed his early fiction.

The family saga begins, all accounts agree, with Linda Updike's own childhood, which, as she points out in *Enchantment*, set the pattern for her son's. Linda Grace Hoyer was an only child born into a household that consisted of two parents and two grandparents. The Hoyers' farm was for young Linda a paradise: "I began my life," says Belle Minuit, "with a sense of having visited the Garden of Eden." But where there's paradise, the threat of expulsion looms. In 1922, flush with tobacco money, John Hoyer sold the farm and moved with his wife into a white brick house in Shillington, at 117 Philadelphia Avenue. Hoyer, who'd done some teaching in his youth, never liked farming; now he planned to live off his stock market investments. The new house was on a half-acre corner plot; proudly middle-class, it was set back from the street and surrounded by an elaborate, neatly tended privet hedge.

The Hoyers moved into Shillington while their daughter was away at college—at Ursinus, in Collegeville, Pennsylvania, just outside Philadelphia. It was there that Linda Hoyer met Wesley Updike. They graduated in 1923 and were married two years later, after Linda had earned her master's degree in English at Cornell University.

In *Enchantment,* Belle presents her decision to wed one of her Ursinus classmates, George (the name both mother and son preferred for their fictional portraits of Wesley Updike), as the result of a "revelation" that left her with "no choice": In a scene disconcertingly reminiscent of the Annunciation, Belle hears a voice telling her she will bear a son, a special son who will be "truly representative of the clan" and fulfill her thwarted ambitions. She asks, "But what must I do to have this son?" The voice tells her, "Marry George." Just to make sure we get the picture, Belle repeats, "So . . . I had married George, because a son had been promised to me." Stranger than fiction is the fact that Linda repeated a watered-down version of this fable to a journalist: "I had this foresight," she said, explaining at once her marriage and her son's talent, "that if I married his father the results would be amazing."

Cemented by the birth of the promised child, the marriage lasted forty-seven years, ending only with Wesley's death—but no one would have called it a particularly happy union. According to her son, Linda always spoke of their long entanglement as something they were both powerless to change. Even the first year was tumultuous: The young couple settled briefly in Ohio, where Wesley worked as a field superintendent for a small oil and natural gas field—but Linda left abruptly, returning to her parents' house in Shillington. Wesley followed soon after. He worked as a hotel clerk in Reading for the next year until landing a job, in February 1927, as a lineman with AT&T.

The promised son, John Hoyer Updike, was born at a low point in the family's fortunes, the year in which Linda's father, still reeling from the stock market crash, saw the last of his investments shrink to nothing. In June, after five relatively happy years on the road as a cable splicer with the telephone company, Wesley lost his job. "Possibly the household that nurtured me was a distracted and needy one," Updike speculated; certainly it was a household "in severe Depression-shock." The only tangible reminders of their "pretensions to quality" were the white brick house itself and some of the furnishings, such as the upright piano in the parlor, the Tiffany lampshade over the dining room table, the good china.

The first year of Updike's life was—for the nation—one of unrelieved economic misery. The banking crisis was spreading panic, and a quarter of the workforce was unemployed. The Hoyers and Updikes suffered along with their fellow citizens. According to her son, Linda Updike had been "a belle of sorts, flashily dressed by her father in his palmy period"; now, in straitened circumstances, she decided to put her education to some use by teaching at the Shillington elementary school, an experiment that lasted less than a day. She found herself unable to control the students, and simply walked out of the classroom. Instead she went to work at a department store in Reading, selling drapery for a salary of fourteen dollars a week and leaving her baby boy in her mother's care. Her father and her husband both joined WPA work crews surfacing the roads in and around Shillington, "spreading oil and shovelling crushed stone." Her mother, in addition to looking after Johnny, sold asparagus and pansies from the garden and eggs from the chicken house at the bottom of the backyard. At Albright College in Reading, Wesley began taking education courses, which allowed him to start in the fall of 1934 as a mathematics teacher at Shillington High School, a job he kept until his retirement nearly thirty years later. Throughout the Depression, he worked summer construction jobs for extra cash. As his son put it, he was "running scared financially for much of his life."

To commemorate the first birthday of her baby boy, Linda insisted that the family plant a pink dogwood tree by the side of the house. The tree cost $5.25—a large sum in hard times—but it still bloomed eighty years later.

Little changed between 1932 and 1945. Linda quit her job in 1935, declaring that she would become a writer, and the baby grew into a boy and then an adolescent. If not quite the messiah Belle Minuit bargained for, he was at least a notably bright, good-natured child. Looking back on those thirteen years, Updike was struck by the "immutability" and "steadfastness" of his surroundings. The relative stasis, he wrote, was "an exceptional effect, purchased for me at unimaginable cost by the paralyzing calamity of the Depression and the heroic external effort of the Second World War." Shillington barely grew, barely changed. "I grew up in a town that was abnormally still." The essential feature of this "immutability," as far as young John was concerned, was the unaltered configuration of his family: mother, father, and maternal grandparents—no additions, no subtractions. Still channeling the unabashed egoism of early childhood, he declared that the five of them were "locked into a star that would have shattered like crystal at the admission of a sixth"— no room for a sibling, or "competitor," as he put it. In "Midpoint," his most ambitious and most explicitly autobiographical poem, he makes use of the same astral image:

> The fifth point of a star, I warmed
> to my onliness, threw tantrums,
> and, for my elders' benison, performed.

And here, too, he celebrated the absence of any "competitor":

> The brothers pressing to be born
> Were kept, despite their screams, offstage.

Alone in the spotlight, he accepted the applause of his adoring audience.

Half the household was elderly. His grandfather was nearly seventy when John was born, his grandmother perhaps a dozen years younger. John Hoyer is remembered in Updike's writing as a "lovely talker" who was "in his way a distinguished man," fond of quoting from the Bible in his wheezy voice and dispensing political opinions. (He was a staunch Democrat.) He had, according to his grandson, "that old-fashioned way of talking as a kind of performance." With the exception of his grandmother, everyone in the house was a talker, and the favorite topic was the family:

> I was raised among quite witty people who talked about themselves and each other all the time so that there was generated in the household a kind of running mythology which I've drawn upon. It was no invention of mine; I've been the witness who's tried to write a little of it down. All four adults

in that house where I grew up charged their very quiet lives with drama and suspense. They were Bible readers, especially my grandfather and my mother, and there was something of viewing their lives as an unfolding book, as a scroll that was being rolled out, and constantly examining it for significance . . . for God's fingerprints. Well, it just was somehow very exciting.

Early on, in other words, he learned the importance—the mythic importance—of daily doings.

Updike's grandmother, in memory, is silent or monosyllabic, a small, slight, dark woman with a sharp face, "always serving, serving others." Katie Hoyer contracted Parkinson's while the family was still living at 117 Philadelphia Avenue, and her husband's eyesight deteriorated, so that young John would have to read his newspaper to him, but otherwise the status quo remained undisturbed: the five of them close—perhaps, Updike later wondered, too close.

In "The Dogwood Tree: A Boyhood," he offers a glimpse of the family in action:

> My mother is pushing the mower, to which a canvas catch is attached. My grandmother is raking up the loose grass in thick heaps, small green haystacks impregnated with dew, and my grandfather stands off to one side, smoking a cigar, elegantly holding the elbow of his right arm in the palm of his left hand while the blue smoke twists from under his moustache and dissolves in the heavy evening air—that misted, too-rich Pennsylvania air. My father is off, doing some duty in town; he is a conscientious man, a schoolteacher and deacon, and also, somehow, a man of the streets.

Also absent from this picture is the cherished boy, "dear Chonny," sheltered by his family's solicitous care, blissfully unaware of financial pressures: "However pinched my guardians felt, they did not pinch me." He was protected, in fact, from any serious trauma; he "soaked up strength and love." Though he admitted in later life to torturing his toys (pleading guilty to abusing his teddy bear, Bruno, and mutilating a rubber Donald Duck), he was well-behaved, cautious—"squeamish," even—but cheerful and obliging, eager to play box hockey and roofball at the playground (his local heaven) in shorts and sneakers, a freckled boy well liked by the neighbors on Philadelphia Avenue and the teachers at the Shillington elementary school.

There were accidents and disappointments. At age five he was struck by a car on his way to Sunday school and spent a week in bed with a bandaged head. He liked girls in general (he "strained for glimpses of [their] underpants as they swung on the swings and skinned the cat on the jungle gym"), but all through elementary school, he loved one classmate in particular, a freckled girl with pig-tails and green eyes. This love went unrequited. He also suffered from hay fever, and a nervous tension that made his stomach ache at mealtimes and caused, at one point, his hair to begin falling out. At a tender age (ten or eleven), he was already spooked by the idea of death, his morbid brooding brought on by reading science fic-tion and contemplating a vast future so frighteningly evoked—he couldn't bear the thought of the "cosmic party" going on without him. Thanks to his superstitious grandmother, he developed a fear of ghosts. Those various complaints were mild, however, compared with his stutter, which embarrassed him acutely when he was still young. The speech impediment first tripped him up in high school; he never banished it entirely, but in later life it was more of a hes-itation—a barely noticeable catch in an otherwise fluent stream of words—than an outright stammer.* Worse still was the scourge of "red spots, ripening into silvery scabs" that erupted on his skin: psoriasis, inherited from his mother, first attacked when he was six (Linda wrote to relatives that it was the worst case she had seen outside of a book on skin diseases); it plagued him, with occasional surcease, for the rest of his life. Though not quite a sickly child, he was delicate, accustomed to having others worry about his health.

---

* "The paralysis of stuttering," he later theorized, "stems from the dead center of one's being, a deep doubt there."

The tranquillity of his childhood was troubled by Linda Updike's unpredictable moods—her "fits of anger," mostly aimed at her husband and her parents rather than her son. There was quarreling, "smoldering remarks," and the slamming of doors, an atmosphere of barely repressed rage:

> As I remember the Shillington house, I was usually down on the floor, drawing or reading, or even under the dining-room table trying to stay out of harm's way—to disassociate myself from the patterns of conflict, emanating from my mother, that filled the air above my head. Darts of anger rayed from her head like that crown of spikes on the Statue of Liberty; a red "V," during those war years, would appear, with eerie appositeness, in the middle of her forehead.

Her "stinging discipline," when John was late coming home, consisted of whipping his calves with a switch, "her face red with fury." But he also remembered the quiet of his mother's intense concentration when she was writing, and the companionable sound of her typewriter.

Her portable Remington features in a childhood memory of unalloyed delight: "I still carry intact within me my happiness when, elevated by the thickness of some books to the level of my mother's typewriter, I began to tap at the keyboard and saw the perfect letter-forms leap up on the paper rolled around the platen." He wrote his first story at the age of eight, typing it out on his mother's typewriter. The first sentence read, "The tribe of Bum-Bums looked very solemn as they sat around their cozy cave fire." He also wrote a long poem about an egg that was published in the grade school newspaper, *Little Shilling*. But despite this early flirtation with the writer's trade, his first love was cartoons—Mickey Mouse, to be precise. "Have I ever loved a human being," he asked himself, "as purely as I loved Mickey Mouse . . . ?" A passion for blank paper, for drawing, for tracing and comics, and for the movies merged eventually into a crystallized ambition: "What I really wanted to be when I grew up was an animator." He remembered the bliss of copying comics—

Mickey, Donald Duck, Barney Google—as he lay prone on the carpet. Starting in kindergarten, he was given drawing lessons by a neighbor, Clint Shilling. A photograph taken by his mother of nine-year-old John sitting on the steps of the side porch of the Shillington house ("one of my favorite places in the world") shows him dressed for church, intently studying a Big Little Book featuring Mickey Mouse. Contemplating this photo in his late sixties, he wondered whether Big Little Books ("chunky little volumes sold for ten cents, made of single panels from a comic strip opposite a short page of narrative text") eased his transition from wanting to be a cartoonist to wanting to be a writer.

The image that recurs again and again in his writing is of that young boy lying on the floor, busily drawing or tracing or coloring, or doing the same at the dining room table under the stained-glass lampshade, reproducing the comics and cartoon characters that he so loved, already certain that his efforts would meet with the unstinting approbation of his parents and grandparents. Here was the beginning of Updike the industrious artist. Even at the age of five, his mother told a journalist, "he worked." As he explained in his 1985 speech, the creative imagination "wants to please. It wants to please more or less as it has been pleased, by the art that touched it in its formative years." Part of the aim of those early artistic endeavors was surely to entertain—to placate—his mother. In a story called "A Sandstone Farmhouse," a sequel to *Of the Farm* written in 1990, less than a year after Linda Updike's death, there's an intriguing glimpse of a son coping with a mother patterned on Updike's own: "Even as a very small child he had been aware of a weight of anger his mother carried; he had quickly evolved—first word, first crawl—an adroitness at staying out of her way when she was heavy with it, and a wish to amuse her, to keep her light." As a grown man, remembering a visit with his mother to Plow Cemetery, he remarked, "Only in Pennsylvania, among my kin, am I pressed into such difficult dance-steps of evasion and placation." Those two words, *evasion* and *placation*, could be said to sum up Updike's nascent artistic impulse.

His childish worldview was innocently solipsistic: "My geography went like this: in the center of the world lay our neighborhood of Shillington. Around it there was greater Shillington, and around that, Berks County. . . . [N]ot all children could be born, like me, at the center of the nation. But that some children chose to be born in other countries and even continents seemed sad and fantastic. There was only one possible nation: mine." Though his street, Philadelphia Avenue, has been widened, and the chestnut trees that lined it have been chopped down, and though shopping malls have replaced the fields on the edge of town, his Shillington neighborhood remains largely unchanged. The town today is profoundly unremarkable— as it was then. As Updike wrote, "Cars traveling through see nothing here to make them stop; the town is neither young nor old, poor nor rich, backward nor forward." The ordinariness appealed to the boy, and it appealed also to the writer looking back on it, the writer who made it his business to "transcribe middleness with all its grits, bumps and anonymities."

For young John, the neighborhood was a magical realm oozing nurture and encouragement. In later life he traced his political orientation—especially his strong attachment to the idea of national solidarity—back to the stability and security of his environment during the war years. To leave Shillington even temporarily seemed to him a wanton waste. He disliked the Sunday country walks his parents took him on; they were too rural for his tastes: "I was a small-town child. Cracked pavements and packed dirt were my ground." Visits to country cousins (his mother's relatives), who were "hopelessly mired in farmerishness," confirmed his distaste; to him, "people who kept pigs, and owned mules, and grew corn, seemed unbearably sad."

The city proved more alluring. It was a twenty-minute trolley ride from Shillington to the heart of downtown Reading (still relatively vibrant in those early years), where he acquired a taste for urban atmosphere. Even before he reached adolescence, he was allowed to spend Saturday mornings in Reading, sampling "consumer culture, Forties style"; he bought comic books and art supplies and browsed the aisles of five-and-tens (McCrory's, Woolworth, Kresge's), making sure to save seven cents for the trolley home. Later, beginning with the summer after high school graduation, he worked as a copyboy at the *Reading Eagle*.

Other worlds beyond the town limits proved equally seductive. The Shillington movie theater, just two blocks from the house on Philadelphia Avenue, brought images of faraway places, in the newsreel and the travelogue that preceded the feature; and the feature itself might fizz with the glamour and escapist excitement of Hollywood. His parents began taking him to the movies when he was just three; starting at age six, he was allowed to go by himself, which he did almost fanatically—as many as three times a week—running all the way to the theater with a dime and a penny clutched in his hand.

At age twelve, he went to stay with his sophisticated aunt Mary (his father's older sister, who had worked at *The New Republic*). Mary made a big impression; as he remembered it, she had "a flapper's boyish figure and a dry tough way of talking—she made 'wisecracks'—and long flaxen hair wrapped in a big braid around her head." She had married her cousin, also called Updike, and was known in the family as MEUU, for Mary Ella Updike Updike. These other, more worldly Updikes lived in Greenwich, Connecticut, and seemed, to young John, to be rich—they lived, he thought, "the way people should live."

Mary took her nephew into Manhattan, to the Museum of Modern Art. Forty years later, recalling that "stirring, puzzling" first glimpse of the modernist aesthetic—Georges Braque and Jean Arp were the artists he remembered most clearly—he wrote, "I felt myself, in my aunt's shadow, moving through a kind of toy store, where the toys could not be bought or touched, only admired." His aunt boasted that she'd never seen a child so interested in a museum.

It was MEUU who gave the family a subscription to *The New Yorker*, for Christmas in 1944. Updike was bewitched; it was "the best of possible magazines." The cartoons delighted him, especially the draftsmanship of Alain (Daniel Brustlein), Robert Day, Garrett Price, George Price, and Peter Arno; he devoured James Thurber and E. B. White. Not yet thirteen, he was instantly desperate to become a contributor: "I loved that magazine so much I concentrated all my wishing into an effort to make myself small and inky and intense enough to be received into its pages." The urge persisted; as he told his first Knopf editor, "[P]eople assume I fell into the NYer right from Harvard's lap, but I had been trying for eight years." The magazine spoke to him, as it did to a large and rapidly increasing readership (the subscription base doubled between 1939 and 1949), of a glamorous urban world, graced with wit and sophistication, and a glittering, cultured lifestyle like that of the Greenwich Updikes—a way of living that could one day be his.

Although fervent, his desire to translate himself into the pages of the magazine did nothing to undermine his evident satisfaction with his lot in life—which he later claimed to have pondered with a precocious philosophical detachment: "The mystery that . . . puzzled me as a child was the incarnation of my ego—that omnivorous and somehow preëxistent 'I'—in a speck so specifically situated amid the billions of history. Why was I I?" And why was this speck so comfortably situated? Almost every word he wrote about his "beloved" hometown was a hymn of praise ("Time . . . spent anywhere in Shillington—was delicious") or a declaration of irrevocable citizenship ("My deepest sense of self has to do with Shillington"; "If there was a meaning to existence, I was closest to it here"; "Shillington was my *here*"). Like his mother, he looked back on his childhood haunts as a paradise:

> The Playground's dust was richer once than loam,
> And green, green as Eden, the slow path home.

Yet it's hard to know whether this love affair wasn't in part retroactive, the strength of the attachment a consequence of his exile—and an ongoing rebuke to his mother for insisting on dragging the family out to Plowville.* In "Shillington," an ode written on the occasion of the town's bicentennial, eight years after he'd left Berks County entirely, he pondered the play of recollection as the place itself changed over the years: "Returning, we find our snapshots inexact."

---

* In "The Black Room," a widowed mother who "finagled" her family's retreat to "an unimproved farmhouse" in the country complains to her grown son that his continuing devotion to their old house in town is a form of reproach: "I don't know why you always spite me by loving that house so."

The powerful final lines of the poem are packed with significance, especially in the light of the move from 117 Philadelphia Avenue to the sandstone farmhouse:

> We have one home, the first, and leave that one.
> The having and leaving go on together.

There was never any doubt about which was his first home, and subsequent departures from other places he lived (Plowville, New York City, Ipswich) always involved a reenactment of sorts, echoes, however faint, of that early exodus—"the crucial detachment of my life." In a story published in 1991, a year and a half after his mother's death, Updike captured with a memorable phrase the regret of a man who, fifty years earlier, had been detached from his hometown and "saw his entire life . . . as an errant encircling of this forgotten center." The having and leaving lasted half a century—lasted, in effect, a lifetime.

THE FAMILY LEFT Shillington on October 31, 1945. Updike's description of the actual moment of setting off—after the trick-or-treating and the departure of the moving van—is notably theatrical, and punctuated by bitter asides. His elderly grandparents were already out at the farm when John and his parents packed the last few items into the newly acquired secondhand Buick ("In Shillington we had never had a car, for we could walk everywhere") and drove away down the street: "Somewhat self-consciously and cruelly dramatizing my grief, for I was thirteen and beginning to be cunning, I twisted and watched the house recede through the rear window." If this is indeed how it happened, there can be no doubt that the cruelty of that self-dramatizing gesture was directed at his mother.

Almost as frequent as his hymns to Shillington are his complaints about the "dislocation to the country," which "unsettled" him and left him lonesome, bored—and, come summer, choked by hay fever. He had started junior high school the year before, and now, three months into his eighth-grade year, he was forced to commute to Shillington High School every weekday with his father. He resented being turned overnight into "a rural creature, clad in muddy shoes [and] a cloak of loneliness"; he resented being made to feel like "pretty much an outsider, in a family of outsiders." The resentment still gnawed at him decades later.

For Linda Updike to regain her childhood paradise, her son had to relinquish his. In a letter she sent him on the fifth anniversary of the move (October 31, 1950), she wrote, "If I had known then how much you hated to leave that house, I might not have had the courage to go." My guess is that she would in fact have found the courage—after all, she rode roughshod over the resistance of her eighty-two-year-old father, who had to endure a humiliating return to the farm he thought he'd put behind him a quarter of a century earlier. And she brushed aside the complaints of her husband (a "man of the streets" who liked to say that he wanted to be buried under a sidewalk); Wesley had to surrender to what he considered rural imprisonment. Only Linda's habitually silent mother voiced no objection to leaving Shillington. So why insist on imposing this relocation on the rest of the family? "I was returning to the Garden of Eden and taking my family with me. I thought I was doing them a great service," she told a television interviewer, echoing her fictional alter ego, Belle Minuit, and still looking defiant forty years after the fact.

Updike sometimes suggested that it was a financial decision. During the war, his mother went to work in a parachute factory ("where she wore her hair up in a bandana like Rosie the Riveter"), and with more money coming into the household, they could afford to buy back the Plowville farmhouse with its eighty-three acres (for which they paid a total of $4,743.12), and tell themselves that they were saving money by living in a smaller house in the country. But in fact Linda had resolved while still a young woman, before World War II—before the Depression, even—to recapture her birthplace and make it her home. Equally unconvincing is the claim advanced by Updike in the early 1970s that the move to Plowville was inspired by E. B. White's rustic adventures in Maine: "After reading White's essays in *Harper's* throughout World War II, my mother in

1945 bought a farm and moved her family to it." While it's true that Linda believed passionately, as her son put it, that "we should live as close to nature as we can," and it's also true that she claimed a mystic connection to those "eighty rundown acres of Pennsylvania loam," the notion that White's example was decisive seems far-fetched; it makes her sound frivolous, and trivializes the intensity of her determination.

Selfishness, plain and simple, surely played a role. But there was another important factor: she was bent on getting her son out of Shillington, on keeping him apart and different from the townsfolk. A thirteen-year-old in Plowville—how the name embarrassed him!—was quarantined from pernicious, lowering influences; he would be marooned on the farm for at least a couple of years, until he learned to drive. Even when he had his license, if he wanted to escape he would have to borrow the family car. In *Self-Consciousness* Updike wrote, "Shillington in my mother's vision was small-town—small minds, small concerns, small hopes. We were above all that." To an interviewer, Linda explained bluntly why she had done her best to break up John's attachment to his high school girlfriend: "She was of Shillington, this place I found so contemptible." Updike sometimes claimed to have inherited from somewhere an "authority-worshipping Germanness"; it certainly wasn't from Linda, who bristled at authority and stubbornly resisted conformity. In fact, she's the likely source of Updike's own intermittently inconvenient contrary streak.

As far as Linda was concerned, Plowville's virtues were amplified by its distance from town. Set in a lush, rolling landscape, the house, built in 1812, consisted of a combined kitchen, dining room, and living room downstairs, and two bedrooms and a sleeping alcove upstairs. It was barely big enough for four adults and a teenager.* For the first year or so there was no indoor plumbing, no central heating, no electricity, no telephone. "My reaction

---

* "The firmest house in my fiction, probably, is the little thick-walled sandstone farmhouse of *The Centaur* and *Of the Farm*. I had lived in that house, and can visualize every floorboard and bit of worn molding."

to this state of deprivation," Updike once said, "was to get sick. I was quite sick that year with colds and things, and huddled by this kerosene stove that was the only heat we had in the house." His mother may have thought that her family was somehow too good for Shillington—"above all that"—but in his eyes, the move to Plowville was a step down, a sign that they'd somehow lost the middle-class status proclaimed by the white brick house in town. It was a step down and a step back, too: while the rest of America was abandoning rural areas for town and cities, the Updikes were doing the reverse, rolling back the clock and implicitly rejecting the accepted model for socioeconomic progress.* And John couldn't even complain. If he expressed his preference for Shillington, he risked wounding or angering his mother: "My love for the town, once we had moved from it, had to be furtive."

For a perceptive child attuned to the dynamics of a close-knit family, one of the enduring lessons of the move to Plowville would have been the efficacy of his mother's resolve. Imposing her will on the rest of the family, Linda Updike overcame their objections because she knew exactly what she wanted and never wavered in her desire.† In *Enchantment*, Belle Minuit's father protests that the move back to the farm would be a mistake, "a retreat from life itself." He tells her, "I would rather die than go back to that place"; her response to this point-blank refusal is to ratchet up the melodrama: "We're moving back to that farm—if it kills us *all*." Whether or not Linda actually made any such drastic vows, the relocation was planned and executed entirely on her initiative. Looking back in his memoirs, Updike reckoned that from the time he was thirteen, his life, however fortunate, had "felt like not quite my idea." Moving out of his

---

* The father in "Pigeon Feathers" declares, "In this day and age only the misfits stay on the farm."

† According to her son, one of Linda's favorite sayings was, "Take what you want and pay the price for it." When she bought back the farm, part payment was adherence to the terms of an "inner bargain": she began going to church every Sunday morning—and kept it up for the next forty-five years. Downbeat by comparison, one of Wesley's favorite saying was "You don't get something for nothing."

hometown derailed him. "Shillington, its idle alleys and foursquare houses, had been my idea," he wrote; Plowville was emphatically his mother's idea. Unlike his mother, he never regained his lost paradise, though he did find a substitute in Ipswich. It's worth noting that this was the last time he allowed anyone else to dictate the terms of his existence. Any future exile would be self-imposed.

Whatever the precise mix of Linda's motivation, the relocation had immediate and enduring effects. In the short term, it meant that Updike had "extra amounts of solitude . . . to entertain," and he filled those hours with books, most of them borrowed from the Reading public library. P. G. Wodehouse was a particular favorite; he read through all fifty of the Wodehouse volumes on the library's shelves. He also devoured the works of a clutch of mystery writers (Agatha Christie, Erle Stanley Gardner, Ellery Queen, John Dickson Carr, Ngaio Marsh) and humorists (James Thurber, Robert Benchley, Stephen Leacock, S. J. Perelman). "A real reader," he explained, "reading to escape his own life thoroughly, tends to have runs on authors." The "peace and patience" of the Reading library, its comparatively vast spaces behind the imposing granite facade, offered a welcome contrast to the crowded farmhouse; he saw it as "a temple of books" that exuded an air of glamour—"A kind of heaven opened up for me there."* His mother, who had written her Cornell master's thesis on Sir Walter Scott's *The Bride of Lammermoor*, tried to get him to read Flaubert and a few other classics, but he persisted in reading mystery novels and humor. At age fourteen he borrowed *The Waste Land* and found, he later reported, "its opacity pleasingly crisp." The following year, on a visit to his aunt's house in Greenwich, he sampled a few pages of *Ulysses*—which instantly confirmed for him his preference for escapist reading.†

---

* In a late story, "My Father's Tears," the narrator remembers the Alton library, the fictional counterpart of the Reading library (both situated, with Updike's usual precision, on Franklin Street, two blocks from the train station), as "a place you felt safe inside"; it was a place, in other words, that combined the key elements of an Updike paradise: safety and escape.

† It wasn't until the very end of 1966 that he finally finished *Ulysses*.

Stranded on the farm, Updike devoured his library books, drew, copied cartoons, listened to the radio—and started to write. In February 1945, when he was a month shy of thirteen, his first article appeared in *Chatterbox*, the Shillington High School newspaper, to which he would eventually contribute 285 items (poems, stories, film reviews, essays, and drawings). In the summer after he turned sixteen, still wanting to please more or less as he had been pleased, he tried to write a mystery novel.

He was also sending out cartoon "roughs" to magazines such as *Collier's*, *The Saturday Evening Post*, and *The New Yorker*. Having heard that professionals used a rubber stamp to affix their name and return address, Updike acquired such an item (and remained faithful to this method for the rest of his life, always too frugal to switch to personalized stationery). He bought the 1935 anthology of *New Yorker* poetry so as to get a better fix on the kind of verse his favorite magazine preferred.* At age sixteen he had his first poem accepted—by a magazine called *Reflections*; a dozen or so followed during his years in Plowville. The publications were obscure, shoe-string titles (*The American Courier*, *Florida Magazine of Verse*), and the poems were almost all light verse—"a kind of cartooning with words," he called it. "Child's Question," a poem he published in *Chatterbox*, is representative of the precocious wit of the Updike juvenilia:

> O, is it true
> A word with a Q
> The usual U
> Does lack?
> I grunt and strain
> But, no, in vain
> My weary brain
> Iraq.

---

* One of the poems in the anthology, "Metropolitan Nightmare," by Stephen Vincent Benét, left a "deep dent" in him, he later confided to an editor.

Clever wordplay is the most conspicuous feature of his adolescent output, along with an insistent eagerness to please. He was fearless and energetic as well, qualities his mother worked hard to protect and promote.

He was, at around this time, learning to see with an artist's eye. This process is described in rather grandiose terms at the end of *The Centaur*, when teenage Peter, lying ill in bed on a bright, snowy morning, watches through an upstairs window as his father trudges off to work:

> I knew what this scene was—a patch of Pennsylvania in 1947—and yet I did not know, was in my softly fevered state mindlessly soaked in a rectangle of colored light. I burned to paint it, just like that, in its puzzle of glory; it came upon me that I must go to Nature disarmed of perspective and stretch myself like a large transparent canvas upon her in the hope that, my submission being perfect, the imprint of a beautiful and useful truth would be taken.

Whether or not he was stretching himself like a canvas, Updike was certainly noticing intensely, taking the imprint of his patch of Pennsylvania, gathering the material that would launch his career. His earliest writings confirm that his talent for careful observation—and a verbal facility that allowed him to express what he saw—came naturally to him, a built-in feature of his intelligence.

If his mother's aim was to encourage artistic endeavor, moving him out to Plowville was an inspired tactic. He later suggested that his creative talents "developed out of sheer boredom those two years before I got my driver's license."

It was after the move to Plowville that he stumbled into his first religious crisis, a sudden access of doubt, accompanied by—and largely caused by—a debilitating fear of death. (His description of a similar episode in his early thirties gives a visceral sense of his abject terror: "[I]t is as if one were suddenly flayed of the skin of habit and herd feeling that customarily enwraps and muffles our deep predicament." In Shillington, he had attended Sunday school at Grace Lutheran Church, and enjoyed a comfortable, untroubled faith. He accepted the blessing of a sometimes puzzling but generally benign deity. He was impressed by the idea that lusting after a woman in one's heart is as bad as actual adultery—which suggested that "a motion of the mind, of the soul, was an actual deed, as important as a physical act"; he registered the concept that God watches a sparrow's fall; and he took to heart the lesson of the parable of the talents: "Live your life. Live it as if there is a blessing on it. Dare to take chances, lest you leave your talent buried in the ground." After the move to Plowville, he attended Sunday school at Robeson Lutheran Evangelical Church and found himself beset by "painful theological doubts." He eased his fears with a tottery syllogism:

1. If God does not exist, the world is a horror-show.
2. The world is not a horror-show.
3. Therefore God exists.

Ignoring the weakness of the second premise (even in safe, sleepy Shillington some sign of the horror show must have been visible), he willed himself to believe. In his memoirs, he explains that his faith gave him his artistic courage: "Having accepted that old Shillington blessing, I have felt free to describe life as accurately as I could, with especial attention to human erosions and betrayals." In a sense, he's claiming divine sanction for his autobiographical impulse.

The trauma of his adolescent crisis of faith is brilliantly, indelibly captured in "Pigeon Feathers"—which also happens to provide a ruthlessly accurate map of the emotional terrain of Updike's extended family (minus the grandfather, who, for the purposes of this story, is already dead). Crowded into a primitive farmhouse are David Kern, a precocious thirteen-year-old, an only child; George, his restless father, a high school teacher prone to gloomy pronouncements, who "spent his free days performing, with a kind of panic, needless errands," anything to get away from the farm; Granmom, who hovers in the kitchen, "her hands waggling with Parkinson's disease"; and Elsie, David's mother, an angry, forceful, unhappy woman who's sometimes dreamy and distracted, sometimes nurturing and perceptive. Elsie has dragged the entire family from Olinger to Firetown, back to the house where she was born. The setup, to borrow a phrase from the story, is "grim but familiar."

The first line of the story insists on the damage done, on the emotional cost of leaving Olinger: "When they moved to Firetown, things were upset, displaced, rearranged." David's world is out of joint, and the physical disruption reflects an inner, metaphysical turmoil that exposes him to religious doubt and crippling terror at the thought of his own death. The rural isolation of the farm exacerbates his sense of dread; it forces him to face his crisis alone. The minister who teaches catechetical class in the basement of the Firetown church gives him only the sort of bland reassurance intolerable to someone in search of absolutes, and his mother and father aren't much help, either: "He had never regarded his parents as consolers of his troubles; from the beginning they had seemed to have more troubles than he. Their frailty had flattered him into an illusion of strength." David's religious doubts are eventually resolved to his own satisfaction (if not the reader's—the boy deduces from the beauty of nature evidence of a caring deity). As for his parents' "troubles" (the mother's anger, the father's "lively self-disgust"), the ugly bickering between them seems less a symptom of marital strain than a comforting routine; David notes that "they seemed to take their quarrels less seriously than he did." Nobody is content in the Firetown household (though the mother returns from her walk around the farm "flushed with fresh air and happiness"), but they'll bump along and get used to it.

Country life sharpened Updike's appetite for urban excursions: In the summer of 1946, he signed up for a bus trip to Philadelphia to see the Athletics host the Red Sox for a Sunday doubleheader—this was his first chance to see the great Ted Williams, who hit several home runs and earned himself a permanent place in Updike's pantheon of heroes. With Wesley he took the train to New York City (to see his father's brother, who was passing through, and in the hope of acquiring a book on Vermeer). Though the trip was a disappointment, faithfully documented in one of his earliest stories, "The

Lucid Eye in Silver Town," a seed was sown: "Towers of ambition rose, crystalline, within me."

The eleven miles between Plowville and Shillington meant that Updike's life, during the school year, was split in two: there was his mother's world on the farm, and his father's world, which revolved around Shillington High School. When he came to write what he called "the saga of my mother and father," Updike made a similar division, offering a portrait of Wesley and Shillington (or Olinger) in *The Centaur* and of Linda and Plowville (or Firetown) in *Of the Farm*. And just as Linda acknowledged her resemblance to the mother in *Of the Farm*, so Wesley saw himself in George Caldwell. In an interview, after disclosing that George was "assembled from certain vivid gestures and plights" characteristic of his father, Updike shared the following anecdote: "[O]nce, returning to Plowville after *The Centaur* came out, I was upbraided by a Sunday-school pupil of my father's for my outrageous portrait, and my father, with typical sanctity, interceded, saying, 'No, it's the truth. The kid got me right.'" Updike thought of *The Centaur* as his most autobiographical novel—especially because the motivating force behind it was the wish to "make a record" of his father.

Set over the course of three days in January 1947, the novel tells the story of George Caldwell; his fifteen-year-old son, Peter; and their strong but at times deeply uncomfortable relationship. Cassie, the wife and mother, makes only brief appearances, but she's a potent presence, even offstage. She engineered what Peter thinks of as his "martyrdom": the family's relocation to a "half-improved farmhouse," a "primitive place" he bitterly resents. "It had been my mother's idea," he reports. George empathizes with his son and, characteristically, shoulders part of the blame: "The poor kid. . . . We took him out of the town where he loved to be and stuck him in the sticks." It's the distance between the farmhouse in Firetown and the high school in Olinger where Peter is a student and George a general science teacher that provides the drama in the novel: first a broken-down car, then a snowstorm prevent father and son from returning home from school for two successive nights. Together in adversity, Peter and George reveal themselves to the reader.

The dual portrait of father and son is enriched and complicated by mythological parallels elaborated in alternate chapters. As James Joyce did in *A Portrait of the Artist as a Young Man* and *Ulysses*, Updike borrows from the Greeks to endow his characters with archetypal significance, reimagining Olinger High School as Mount Olympus (a glorification that also works, conversely, as ironic diminishment: the school's faculty is hardly godlike). Updike gives George the role of Chiron, the noble centaur (half human, half horse) who sacrifices himself for the sake of Prometheus (Peter) and suffers in his stead. (Prometheus, who had the audacity to steal fire from the gods and give it to mankind, was chained to a rock in punishment and left there to languish. Think of the rock as the farmhouse in Firetown, and the analogy becomes clearer. There is, mercifully, no liver-eating eagle in the picture.) The nonmythic reality is that George endures a daily martyrdom to support his family, suffering so that Peter won't have to—so that he can, eventually, escape from captivity. George's travails are compounded by hypochondria; he's convinced himself that he's dying of cancer.

As Updike pointed out when he accepted the 1963 National Book Award for *The Centaur*, both the book and the hero are centaurs, divided entities. The novel is a daring mix of remembrance and myth, of visually precise detail and fantastic allegory; George combines a drudging, plow-horse devotion to duty with a subversive, almost anarchic streak that tempts him—nearly, but not quite—to kick over the traces. In his acceptance speech, Updike made an eloquent case for accuracy as the writer's necessary virtue—and indeed, one of the most impressive features of the novel is the vivid realism of the chapters narrated by Peter, who observes himself and his father with brutal clarity. But even when the narrative is cloaked in myth, even when he appears in the guise of Chiron, George Caldwell is a dead ringer for Wesley Updike (about whom, his son later explained, there was "an ambivalence that seemed to make him very centaur-like").

Born in Trenton, New Jersey, in 1900, Wesley Russell Updike grew up precariously in a once-prosperous family, youngest child of a clergyman, Hartley, who failed in the ministry, failed in business, and died an invalid.* Not surprisingly, Wesley was "caught in some awful undercurrent of discouragement," and though he grew to be a tall, slim young man with a modest athletic talent—his nose was repeatedly broken playing football, as a linesman, in high school and college—he seems to have had little talent for happiness. He compensated for his gloomy disposition with gallows humor, fits of antic eccentricity, and what his son called an "inveterate, infuriating, ever-hopeful gregariousness." Like many of Updike's fictional fathers, he was a man of contradictions, "stoic yet quixotic, despairing yet protective." A faithful deacon in the Lutheran church who taught Sunday school after teaching all week in the high school, he remained an outsider in Shillington, never quite "clued in," never invited to join the local Lions Club or the Masonic Lodge. Updike recalled the "somehow *wounded* air he had"—but also his upright posture and striding gait. Restless and sociable, uneasy and aggrieved, forever running inscrutable errands, Wesley prowled the pavement, eager to participate and certain that he would be left out. "Life," Updike concluded, "had given my father a beating."

He was, nonetheless, an enduring role model. A decade after Wesley's death, Updike acknowledged that his anxious, care-ridden father "really did communicate to me all I know about how to be a man"—and managed, remarkably, to impart "a sense of joy." Wesley's paltry salary ($1,740 a year in 1947, when his son was a sophomore in high school; $6,400 by the time he retired in 1962) did nothing to assuage his abiding fear of the poorhouse; he was the family's sole means of support. The gallows humor must have helped—Wesley was famous around town for his grim clowning, a repertory of gags that included lying down in the classroom and shouting, "Go ahead. Walk all over me. That's what you want to do." Or pulling out the cap gun he kept in his desk and shooting himself in the head. Or giving a Nazi salute when classroom discipline broke down. Some of this foolery made his son cringe. But Updike also remembered feeling a surge of pride at seeing his father perform in school assembly,

---

* Updike wrote: "[T]he stain of unsuccess ate away at my grandfather's life as if in some tale by Hawthorne."

where he could make the entire auditorium roar with laughter. John was in his father's math class for all three years of junior high school; for eighth grade, his father was also his homeroom teacher. The enforced proximity revealed to the teenager "the agony of the working teacher"—the struggle to maintain discipline, the wearying routine, day after day—and put him, curiously, in the position of becoming his parent's champion and protector. In *Self-Consciousness*, he writes about avenging with his own success the "slights and abasements" visited upon his father.

The Centaur is a token of that success, and one of its wonders is the delicate balance Updike achieves in portraying George's character. A tragic figure and a figure of fun, at once deeply irritating and convincingly lovable, he is, as Updike liked to say, a *good* man. And a maddening one. Peter Caldwell feels about him pretty much the way Allen Dow (in "His Mother Inside Him") feels about *his* father: a mix of "admiration, exasperation, and pity." Worried about his father's health (the cancer George believes is incubating in his bowels), about the precarious family finances (George secretly borrows from the school's athletic funds, as did Wesley Updike), about his problems with discipline in the classroom ("the kids goaded him to the point of frenzy"), Peter makes a vow to "protect" him.

Though his love for his father just about trumps his exasperation, and though the two of them are allied in their distaste for the farm ("I hate nature," says George. "It reminds me of death"), the stronger bond by far is between mother and son. She exerts a "magnetic pull" over him, and together they make for themselves a "little intricate world" from which George ("that sad silly man") is excluded—the "romance" of mother and son is far more compelling than that of husband and wife. But here, too, there's a breach. When Peter wanders in the city of Alton, alone and unencumbered, excited by what seem to him cosmopolitan delights, and feeling released from his everyday world and its galling inconsequence, he realizes that relishing urban freedom is a kind of betrayal:

> I thought guiltily of my mother, helpless at her distance to control or protect me, my mother with her farm . . . her dis-

satisfaction, her exhausting alternations of recklessness and prudence, wit and obtuseness, transparence and opacity, my mother with her wide tense face and strange innocent scent of earth and cereal. . . . [O]f her own will she had placed ten miles between us; and this rejection on her part made me vengeful, proud, and indifferent: an inner Arab.

More than a sign of solidarity with his father, Peter's preference for Alton (and Olinger) is bound up with a defiant impulse—a rebellion against his mother.

She's the same woman in *The Centaur*, in "Pigeon Feathers," and in "Flight"—all three present an unmistakable likeness of Linda Updike. It's always the mother's decision to haul her family out of Olinger to the farmhouse in Firetown that underpins the action, whether it's trying to return home (*The Centaur*), trying to leave home ("Flight"), or solving a crisis triggered by the "upset" of having moved home ("Pigeon Feathers"). Her act of will becomes, in a sense, his inspiration. Updike acknowledged as much, obliquely, in "Cemeteries," an essay he wrote in 1969 and published in the *Transatlantic Review*. He recalls a visit to the family burial plot in Plowville with his mother, who wanted him to agree to be buried there, next to his parents. He avoided saying yes, but felt the urge to disguise the "evasion" with some banter and buffoonery. He asks himself, "Why is it that nothing that happens to me is as real as these dramas that my mother arranges around herself . . . ?" For the first decade of his writing life, it was the very real fact of Linda's great drama (her Plowville paradise regained) that fed his fiction.

Updike poured into *The Centaur* not just his feelings about his parents but also all the intimate experience he had of small-town high school, both as a student and as the son of a teacher. The janitor with his broom, the other teachers with their quirky self-importance, the lecherous supervising principal, the basketball games, the swim meets—all are intently observed and transferred onto the page with energy and wit. Peter's schoolmates, both en masse and in particular, are portrayed with unsentimental rigor. They're mostly dull and ordinary kids, but as a group they're somehow thrilling—collectively capable of a "gaudy and momentous" gesture. Part of Peter knows that he's a cut above, college-bound, destined to achieve a worldly success beyond the grasp of his Olinger cohort, but he's still desperate to hold his place in his chosen clique. He's divided between his high aspirations (he wants to be a painter; he venerates Vermeer) and the wish to emulate his shiftless idol, Johnny Dedman, who "performed exquisitely all the meaningless deeds of coördination, jitterbugging and playing pinball and tossing salted peanuts into his mouth." Peter's relationship with his girlfriend, Penny, is typical.* He describes her as "small and not unusual," thinks of her as his "poor little dumb girl," and speculates that it's a "delicate irresolution of feature" that makes her, just possibly, "worthy" of him. And yet, despite the disdain he fails occasionally to conceal—he is, after all, an "atrocious ego"—he loves her as best he can. We're told, toward the end of the novel, that Peter sees "other people as an arena for self-assertion," a harsh judgment but not entirely unfair.

Updike's assessment of his own "obnoxious" teenage self is no more flattering. In his memoirs, he paints a picture of a kid whose "frantic ambition and insecurity" turned him into a pest: "skinny, scabby, giggly, gabby, frantic to be noticed, tormented enough to be a tormentor, relentlessly pushing his cartoons and posters and noisy jokes and pseudo-sophisticated poems upon the helpless high school." There's a stiff measure of retrospective false modesty in that litany, his failings exaggerated for comic effect, but there's no doubt that the young Updike craved attention and acceptance. Parking meters made their first appearance in Shillington in the late 1940s, and Updike could never resist leapfrogging over them, his exuberance and exhibitionism working hand and hand.

---

* Implausibly, Updike has made Peter and Penny a full two years younger than he and Nancy were: Penny is supposed to be in the ninth grade, a fourteen-year-old; Peter in the grade above. Following the precedent set in "Flight," the boy gives little; the girl will nevertheless "sacrifice" for him.

"Himself a jangle of wit and nerves"—that terse description, from an unpublished draft of a story written in 1960, is a faithful snapshot. He worked extensively on the class yearbook and was an associate editor of *Chatterbox*, co-valedictorian, and popular enough (and pushy enough) to be elected class president, though he later came to think of his election as a mistake; in his memoirs he wrote, "I did not, at heart, feel I deserved to be class president."

He seems, in any case, to have preferred his daredevil self: "In Shillington, to win attention and approval from my classmates, I would get out on the running board of my family's heavy old black Buick and steer the car downhill through the open window, while my thrilled passengers squealed within." School friends remembered "some pretty hairy rides" in that car, including lunchtime games of chicken. This was the rebel who "smoked and posed and daydreamed," soaking up "high-school sexiness" in a booth at the back of Stephen's Luncheonette on Lancaster Avenue. That's where he learned the art of sophisticated smoking—"how to inhale, to double-inhale, to French inhale, and (just barely) to blow smoke rings." One friend described him as "the original flower child," with uncombed hair and unbuttoned shirt, a Kool dangling from his lips, hunched over the pinball machine. Everyone agrees that "Uppie" was a sloppy dresser, habitually unkempt, and that he seemed to subsist on cigarettes, cookies, and baloney. At Stephen's, where half the school would hang out after the last class let out at twenty past three, John gobbled salt-encrusted hamburgers washed down with coffee. He would linger after the other kids dispersed, waiting for his father so they could drive together back to Plowville. Again and again in his writing he revisited that luncheonette, a place thick with "cigarette smoke and adolescent intrigue," Frankie Laine or Doris Day on the jukebox competing with the pinball's "rockety-*ding*." In *The Centaur*, this teenage paradise is Minor's Luncheonette, and it's more important to Peter than school—he thinks of it, in fact, as the center of his life apart from his mother.

Updike's collection of high school pals—they called themselves Our Gang—congregated at Stephen's or at the house of a classmate named Joan Venne. As he saw it, he was a sort of marginal character who had forced himself into the "jet set of Shillington High." He wooed them with slapstick: "I developed the technique of deliberately falling, as a way of somehow exorcising evil spirits and winning approval and defying death. . . . I spent a lot of time in high school throwing myself over stair railings." That may have gotten their attention, but what held it was his wit. He made them laugh, amusing them just as he had amused his mother. The Shillington gang was in some ways more important to him than any other. His high school friends stayed with him all his life in that he continued to see them at class reunions every five years. (By contrast, after he left Ipswich in 1974, he dropped his friends there entirely.) Inserting himself into a gang, or gathering one around him, became his preferred mode of social engagement. He had individual friends, to be sure, but he also needed a crowd, a group in which he could both stand out and blend in, draw attention to himself and disappear from view. Shillington and Ipswich, the places where his gang was most cohesive (and most adoring), were the places where he was happiest.

Shillington (Olinger)—the world of *The Centaur*—was the world Linda Updike hoped her son would transcend. A part of him wanted nothing better than to kill time in the "clamorous and hormone-laden haze" of Stephen's; his mother could think of nothing worse. In *Of the Farm*, Joey Robinson's mother explains why she was so desperate to get the teenage Joey out of Olinger: she couldn't bear the thought of him becoming "an Olinger know-nothing. . . . I didn't want my only child to be an Olingerite; I wanted him to be a *man*." She complains that the residents of Olinger "with absolute seriousness consider it the center of the universe"—a clear echo of Updike's boyhood sense of geography.

Joey was no more likely to become a self-satisfied Olingerite than Updike was. In all these fictions, the mother predicts that her only son will fly, and so he does, though there's a certain ambiguity about what exactly he's escaping. When Updike drew a critic's attention to the "central image of flight or escape" in his early work, he underscored the sense of loss and guilt that dogs the escapee: "[I]n time as well as space we leave people as if by volition and thereby incur guilt and thereby owe them, the dead, the forsaken, at least the homage of rendering them." The ambitious young man, pushed by his mother to get out, succeeds brilliantly—and is consumed by remorse, because his success reveals to him that he was fleeing not just the trap of small-minded small-town life but also a willful, dangerously brilliant, unhappy mother and a martyred, ineffectual father. He was leaving behind difficult, unsuccessful parents who stewed in a "hothouse world / Of complicating, inward-feeding jokes," parents who labored, as he put it in his memoirs, "under some terrible pressure of American disappointment." To the *Paris Review* he explained:

> The trauma or message that I acquired in Olinger had to do with suppressed pain, with the amount of sacrifice I suppose that middle-class life demands, and by that I guess I mean civilized life. The father . . . is sacrificing freedom of motion, and the mother is sacrificing in a way—oh, sexual richness, I guess; they're all stuck.

That vague, enigmatic allusion to his mother's sacrifice may be related to one of the more perplexing lines of dialogue in *The Centaur*, in which Cassie, the wife and mother, standing in the kitchen with George and Peter, declares out of the blue, "If there's anything *I* hate . . . it's a man who hates sex." Further clues to this mystery can be found in a *Vanity Fair* profile in which Updike mused in studiously general terms on mother-son relations: "I suppose there probably are a fair number of mothers who never find completely satisfactory outlets for their sexual energy and inflict a certain amount of it on their male children. Without there being anything hands-on or indecent." His mother's frustrations were reason enough for him to plot his escape—and a perpetually fresh source of guilt.

Despite all the time wasted playing pinball in Stephen's, his high school grades were impeccable, nothing but As from seventh to twelfth grade. Linda and Wesley had driven him up to see Harvard in the summer of 1949, and John never forgot his first glimpse of the college's linked quadrangles with their arching elms ("The old place was alive"). When he received scholarship offers from both Harvard and Cornell, the choice seemed clear.* He spent the summer of 1950 working as a copyboy and Teletype operator at the *Reading Eagle*, and in September traded Plowville for Harvard Yard.

How long had he been dreaming of escape? Since the move out to the farm? Or was it earlier still? In "The Dogwood Tree," he claims that even as a boy, he saw art—whether drawing or writing—as "a method of riding a thin pencil line out of Shillington, out of time altogether, into an infinity of unseen and even unborn hearts." Was that nascent artistic ambition a sign of his "gnawing panic to excel," or the first stirrings of an impulse to flee? A combination of both. "What did I wish to transcend?" he asks in his memoirs, "My beloved Shillington—can it be?" The answer, though muffled by the convoluted syntax of ambivalence, was yes:

> Some falsity of impersonation, some burden of disguise or deceit forms part of myself, an untrustworthy part that can collapse at awkward or anxious moments into a stutter. The burden was present even in Shillington, perhaps as my strong desire, even as I strove to blend in and recognized each day spent there as a kind of Paradise, eventually to get out.

That "strong desire" (in "Leaving Church Early" he calls it, "How to Get Out of Here: my dastardly plot") figures as an element of Updike's "avenging mission"—the idea being that he would make a name for himself elsewhere to "show" Shillington, to avenge his father: "Leaving Pennsylvania, where my father had been pinned by necessity, was . . . a spurning on his behalf." The entire complex transaction, the effort put in by all parties to get from A to B—from cherished only child to triumphant but tarnished refugee—became the stuff of Updike's novels and short stories.

---

* Curiously, Princeton, to which he had also applied, turned him down. It's often stated that he went to Harvard on a full scholarship; in fact, the annual Harvard College tuition in 1950 was six hundred dollars, and he was offered only four hundred dollars in financial aid for freshman year. His aid package increased over the years, and by the time he graduated, tuition was fully covered.

A late story, "My Father's Tears," begins with a farewell scene: parents dropping off their only child, Jim, at the railway station in Alton. It's the end of spring break, and he's returning to Harvard; they're going back home to the little sandstone farmhouse where the family, a pair of grandparents in tow, have moved at the mother's instigation. It's the familiar grim setup, with the usual tensions:

> The house of my childhood, in the town of Olinger, a mere trolley-car ride from Alton, had been a long narrow brick one, with a long back yard, so there were places to escape to when my mother was, in my father's bemused phrase, "throwing an atmosphere." But in the new house we could all hear one another turn over in bed at night, and even the out-of-doors, buzzing with insects and seething with weeds, offered no escape from my mother's psychological heat. I had grown up with her aggrieved moods, turned on usually by adult conflicts out of my sight and hearing. She could maintain one for days until, coming home from school or a friend's house, I would find it miraculously lifted. Her temper was part of my growing up, like Pennsylvania mugginess.

Jim wants to escape, in this passage, from his mother and her psychological heat, but in the story as a whole, the issue is his escape from Pennsylvania. On the platform of the station, he shakes his father's hand and sees that tears glitter in his eyes: "I was going somewhere, and he was seeing me go."

The train approaches, and Jim boards: "My parents looked smaller, foreshortened. We waved sheepishly through the smirched glass." That's it; he's gone. "I opened my book—*The Complete Poetical Works of John Milton*—before Alton's gritty outskirts had fallen away." From a literary point of view, it looks as though remorse is setting in quickly; surely it's *Paradise Lost* he's studying. Not at all: the next paragraph finds us already in Boston, where a waiting girlfriend embraces him on the platform, and we learn the name of the poem he'd been reading as the train hurtled northward: *Paradise Regained.*

But there's a final twist to the tale, yet another layer of ambivalence. We learn late in the story that Jim, who has lived his entire adult life in Massachusetts, goes back every five years (as Updike himself did) to his high school class reunion—the most recent was his fifty-fifth. "I have never really left Pennsylvania," he tells us; "that . . . is where the self I value is stored, however infrequently I check on its condition."

> What is the past, after all, but a vast sheet of darkness in which a few moments, pricked apparently at random, shine?
>
> —"The Astronomer" (1961)

II.

The Harvard Years

"I have never really left Pennsylvania"—Updike may have harbored a similar sentiment in some nostalgic corner of his heart, and Berks County always remained his richest source of inspiration, but of course he did move away. He got out; he escaped; and as his mother predicted, he flew. When I interviewed him at the Ritz Carlton hotel in Boston in the fall of 2003, just before *The Early Stories* was published to loud acclaim, he was a grand, celebrated author, seventy-one years old and the perfect picture of a New England gent—spry, white-haired, smartly tailored in his herringbone tweed, tan corduroy trousers, and polished brown loafers. In the half-century since he'd waved good-bye to Plowville, all visible traces of his Pennsylvania boyhood had been erased. Effortlessly articulate (except for a very occasional stammer, which he suppressed, visibly but successfully), he was smoothly cosmopolitan, friendly, and humorous. Because this was a press interview, he was also sensibly guarded; he'd long since mastered every facet of his role as a professional man of letters, including the neat trick of beguiling the interviewer while keeping him at arm's length. We sat and talked for over two hours in the hushed Ritz bar, at a table pressed up against a huge picture window looking out over Boston Public Garden. (This had been his preferred venue for interviews, he said, ever since his second wife had banned journalists from their home on the North Shore.) "In a way I went abroad when I left Pennsylvania," he told me. "I feel free in New England, free of being my father's son and my grandfather's grandson." This was a standard Updike line, repeated with variations to a succession of journalists over the decades; by 2003 his father had been dead for thirty years and his grandfather for half a century, so it was no great surprise that Updike felt emancipated from their influence. I wish I had asked him about the more powerful character in his family; fourteen years had passed since his mother's death—was he free of being her son?

He certainly wasn't when he quit Pennsylvania as an eighteen-year-old and found himself "abroad" in Cambridge, Massachusetts. John and his mother drove up alone; classes at Shillington High were already in session, so Wesley stayed home. They left Plowville on September 20, 1950, stopping for the night in Greenwich at Aunt Mary's. The next day, they arrived at Hollis Hall, a large, redbrick dormitory on the west side of Harvard's Old Yard, which in those days was graced with tall, spreading elms.

Linda wrote to her son from her hotel room opposite the Cambridge Common just hours after they parted, the first volley in an extraordinary correspondence that continued until the week of her death, nearly four decades later. During his freshman year, she wrote virtually every day—in other words, she appeared in his mailbox in the morning, a palpable, reassuring presence thanks to her remarkable skill as a letter writer. Nearly all these missives were typed out on her Remington, single-spaced and generally a page long; they came stuffed with fresh news of the farm, a detailed emotional weather report, and heaps of encouraging maternal advice on topics ranging from the medical to the literary. John wrote back often, about every three days to begin with, then once a week. Proud of her letters, he preserved them all, and even suggested that after graduation they sit down together and edit them, cutting out the purely personal, so that they would be "ready for posterity." In every letter, she conveyed the sense that the two of them were in cahoots, partners in a project with the twin aim of sending art out into the world and sending John out into the world. The very first one, on Commodore Hotel stationery, ends with a typically probing query: "Goodnight—Is it Mamma? Linda? What am I to a Harvard man?" Teasing, flirtatious, demanding, her question betrays both pride in her son and well-founded apprehension about her role in his new life.

She knew what John would soon come to understand: that four years at Harvard would transform him in irreversible ways. By the time he left Cambridge with his bachelor's degree in June 1954, Updike had achieved success of a kind the excitable, insecure kid who savored idle hours in Stephen's Luncheonette could only have dreamed of. The Harvard graduate was a married man flush with prizes and academic honors, courted by publishers and only weeks from fulfilling his cherished ambition of appearing in *The New Yorker*. A few months after graduation, he and his bride sailed for Europe—off to Oxford on a fellowship. He was well and truly launched. "Harvard took me," he later reflected, "a raw youth out of Pennsylvania . . . and made me to some modest degree an educated man"; he added that there was a cost: "I lost something very essentially me." In "Apologies to Harvard," he pictures the college's role in this transformative process in "gourmet terms":

> To take me in, raw as I was, and chew
> And chew and chew for one quadrennium,
> And spit me out, by God, a gentleman.

He adds that he felt "little gratitude" for all that well-intentioned Ivy League mastication. In fact, he felt an urge to trash his alma mater, to tell people that he was "in some obscure way ashamed of the Harvard years," that he had been "obscurely hoodwinked" and "pacified" by the college. He once said, reaching for another bold metaphor, "I felt toward those years, while they were happening, the resentment a caterpillar must feel while his somatic cells are shifting all around to make him a butterfly." Though it was exactly what he wanted, what he worked so hard for, his time at the most famous of elite American universities sealed his betrayal of Shillington. Having emerged from the cocoon a Harvard man, he would be in some sense forever alienated from Shillington—though not, of course, in his memory and in his writing, where his hometown remained lovingly enshrined. The metamorphosis necessarily added to the store of guilt associated with *getting out*: "We have one home, the first, and leave that one. / The having and leaving go on together."

Although he had the habit, which persisted well into middle age, of thinking of himself as a hick or a hillbilly, Updike was never, not even as a teenager, as raw as he implied. It's true that until the age of eighteen he spent no more than a half-dozen nights outside Berks County, but both his parents had been to college; his mother possessed an advanced degree from an Ivy League university; his high school education was certainly adequate; and his home, though for the last five years a primitive, isolated farmhouse, was nonetheless a lively place where intellectual and artistic achievements were prized. Working as a copyboy at the *Reading Eagle*, he consorted with reporters and editors in a "palace of print" and honed his typing skills. In short, he could hardly be counted among the most disadvantaged and backward of freshmen. Yet "the shock of Harvard," as he later called it, was jarring all the same. Updike, who would become the poet laureate of American middleness, had left behind his familiar, homespun America and landed, with a bump, in an exclusive zone of rare privilege, a place far removed from the comfort of the mainstream.

His first year was marked by homesickness, hemorrhoids, and an understandable case of performance anxiety. The straight-A student from the small-town high school worried about his grades, especially in Latin (a full year of Lucretius and Virgil)* and math, which he briefly considered choosing as his major; the prolific contributor to *Chatterbox* worried about getting elected to the *Lampoon*, Harvard's legendary undergraduate humor magazine. At night he was troubled by bouts of insomnia; during the day, his "freshman melancholy" took over. He suffered a succession of colds, eye infections, and

---

* Updike's high school Latin wasn't good enough to exempt him from the English department honors requirement—hence his arduous year of Latin 1.

stomach complaints, some of which required visits to the university health service. He also went to the infirmary for chest pains, though X-rays showed nothing sinister; it eventually occurred to him that smoking thirty or forty cigarettes a day might have contributed to the problem. His mother was concerned about his health (and he was, too—his hypochondria was operating at full force), but most of these ailments were nothing more than the jitters of a sensitive boy from the provinces plunked down in the midst of an accomplished peer group from all over the country, many of them expensively educated at private schools, some slick with big-city smarts, some eccentric in ways unknown to Shillington. He confessed to his mother that he was frightened by the intelligence of his classmates and the variety of talent they displayed. When his fear and unhappiness passed, when he realized toward the end of freshman year that he would prosper at the college, his psychosomatic illnesses largely vanished—leaving him just the psoriasis and the stammer to contend with.

The student body at Harvard, though more diverse than it had been in the 1920s, say, when it was overwhelmingly WASP, was still notably preppy at midcentury, with the well-groomed private school boys topping the social hierarchy and setting the tone. In the immediate aftermath of the war, veterans on the GI Bill, worldly-wise and full of purpose, made the college particularly vibrant, but most of them had graduated by 1950. The prewar status quo (elitism, somewhat diluted by a vigorous assertion of the meritocratic ideal) reimposed itself with impressive rapidity, though as a hangover from the war years and the Depression, some of the undergraduates may have worked a little harder, with an eye on a safe corporate career. One thing, certainly, had changed for good: coeducation in the classroom. Beginning in 1943, Radcliffe women were allowed to enroll in nearly all Harvard courses, though they continued to live on a separate campus, and their visits to Harvard dorms were regulated by strict parietal rules (not always strictly enforced).

Hollis, where the rooms were relatively cheap, was unusually free of preppies; almost all the students in the dorm came from public schools, and many were on scholarship. Updike shared Room

11, on the third floor, overlooking the Yard, with a kindred spirit, a powerfully intelligent young man named Robert Christopher ("Kit") Lasch, who went on to become an eminent historian and cultural critic. (His most famous book, *The Culture of Narcissism*, was a national bestseller in 1979.) Lasch, who died in 1994, grew up in Omaha, Nebraska, then Chicago, and came from a family even more conspicuously articulate than Updike's. His father, who'd been a Rhodes Scholar, was a newspaperman who would go on to win a Pulitzer Prize for his editorial writing; his mother, equipped with a doctorate in philosophy from Bryn Mawr, eventually taught logic at the university level. The roommates became friends, though Kit was both volatile and solemn: "prickly," as Updike put it. The pressure to get along with an assigned roommate surely helped John to accept Kit as a companion rather than a rival, but he couldn't help thinking that putting two would-be writers in the same small room was like "rubbing two tomcats together." As it happened, the friendship helped him get through what he later called the "compression bends" of freshman year. Both boys were exceptionally hardworking, ambitious, and academically successful; both wrote all the way through college. One of Kit's short stories was published in his senior year in *The Harvard Advocate*, the venerable undergraduate literary magazine. He also wrote poetry, and even a novel, which remained unpublished. John told his mother about his roommate's literary aspirations, and when Kit visited Plowville over spring break in freshman year, Linda asked both boys to read the latest draft of her much-revised historical novel, *Dear Juan*, which they did. Kit, when he got back to Cambridge, sent her a kind but stiff letter of appreciation.

Lasch's letters home to his parents, almost comically self-serious documents, offer many sharp glimpses of his "roomie." On September 26, only five days after they'd first met, Lasch summed up his impression of his new friend:

> My roommate has stood the test of time better than any of the other people in the hall. He is a very intelligent kid; his i.q. is round 150 or something like that. He writes poetry,

stories, and draws cartoons and sends all of these to various magazines. He has even had a few things accepted. He is more industrious than I, but I think his stuff lacks perception and doesn't go very deep. He is primarily a humorist. As he himself admits, he is probably a hack. At least, he has more of the hack in him than the profound artist. He is very funny, and is the first person I've met who seems to appreciate my own humor.

One can imagine the dorm room chatter that furnished Lasch with the material for these peremptory judgments—Updike, eager to impress, letting slip his IQ (which is comfortably in the genius range), and mentioning the poems he'd sold to obscure magazines; and then, worried that he'd been boastful (after discovering the fact that Kit's own submissions, to *The Saturday Evening Post*, *The Atlantic Monthly*, *Harper's Magazine*, and *The New Yorker*, had all been rejected), making a self-deprecatory quip about being just a hack. Luckily, the exchange of manuscripts that led to Lasch's private reservations about his roomie's capacity for profundity didn't give rise to any immediately destructive jealousy on either side. Competition eventually eroded their friendship, with most of the blame on Kit's side, but for that first year, they were a well-matched pair. In a poem written after Lasch's death, Updike remembered the "unexpressible friction" between them—and also a kind of love.

In March they agreed to stick together sophomore year, and having applied to Lowell House along with another boy from Hollis, Reginald Hannaford, they were rewarded with exactly the suite of rooms they wanted, on the top floor, E-51.

Because they worked so hard, Updike and Lasch managed only a meager social life as freshmen. They went to the movies at the UT, in Harvard Square, a vast, plush movie theater that presented a nightly double bill; or they took the T to Boston's Back Bay to the Exeter Street Theatre, a converted Spiritualist church built in Romanesque Revival style. (That first year they saw, among others, *King Solomon's Mines*, *Kind Hearts and Coronets*, and *All About Eve*; after his first-semester Latin exam, Updike took in an afternoon double feature: Joseph Cotten in *Walk Softly, Stranger*, and James Stewart in *The Jackpot*.) Sometimes he dropped by at Cronin's, a scruffy student haunt with comfortable booths. On Saturdays, if there was a home football game, they would trudge across the river to the stadium at Soldiers Field to witness the almost inevitable defeat. John played some poker in the dorm, and on Sunday mornings slept late and treated himself to a cinnamon doughnut and a cup of coffee at Daley's Pharmacy (a "haven from Latin and Calculus")—and that's about it. Whereas Lasch made several visits to the women's college at Wellesley, he reported to his parents that his roommate didn't go on a single date during the fall semester.

Updike was at least somewhat constrained by the offstage presence of Nancy Wolf ("Nora" in Updike's memoirs, the "so-called girlfriend," as Lasch dubbed her), who was back in Shillington, a senior at the high school. In the run-up to Christmas vacation, following an argument with his mother (sparked when she discovered that he'd put in a telephone call to Nancy but not to his parents), Updike vowed not to see Nancy while he was home. His resolve failed him: on January 11, Lasch wrote to his parents that Updike had "spent a good deal of time with his high-school flame, the infamous Nancy, who seems to have made her move and got her talons even more firmly fastened in him." Agreeing with Linda (and, so it seemed to Updike, with nearly everyone in Shillington) that this long-distance affair was a poor idea, Lasch expressed regret that the inevitable end of the romance had been delayed: "It is too bad; he just seemed to be getting loose." But even if he'd succeeded in shaking free from Nancy, Updike's work habits and his various ailments would probably have kept other girls out of the picture.

He wrote relatively little about his college years ("Harvard has enough panegyrists without me"), but "The Christian Roommates," written in 1963, is set in a Harvard dorm exactly like Hollis. Interestingly—unusually—he put himself and his roommate off to one side, as foils to the central characters, Orson Ziegler and Henry ("Hub") Palamountain, a comically mismatched duo whose fraught relations are the story's main concern. Straight-arrow Orson professes to hate Hub (who's as bizarre as Orson is normal), but Updike hints broadly that what he feels is something closer to love; the roomies' "marriage," though more fractious, is as teasingly homoerotic as Ishmael and Queequeg's cozy first night at the Spouter-Inn.

Updike calls his alter ego Kern (as he does in several other stories, including "Pigeon Feathers"); Lasch's stand-in is called Dawson. The caustic description of the pair—both of them ace students and aspiring writers—is a faithful likeness of the Harvard freshmen who lived in Room 11. "Dawson had a sulky, slouching bearing, a certain puppyish eagerness, and a terrible temper. He was a disciple of Sherwood Anderson and Ernest Hemingway and himself wrote in a stern, plain style.* He had been raised as an atheist." Kern, a churchgoer who "smoked and talked incessantly," is sketched with economy and ruthless detachment: he's a Pennsylvania farm boy "bent on urban sophistication,† riddled with nervous ailments ranging from conjunctivitis to hemorrhoids"; Orson, the story's protagonist, likes Kern but also detects in him something "subtly vicious." The dynamic between Kern and his roommate Dawson is delicate, even though they're pals. Kern feels he has to placate the sulky Dawson, to tiptoe around his temper; between them they deploy "a battery of running jokes." (Thanks to his mother, Updike was adept at coping with the hazards of sharing close quarters with someone short-tempered and unpredictable.)

"The Christian Roommates" offers a sobering look at how challenging Harvard could be, socially as well as academically, for the incoming freshmen. In the dorm are two "Negroes" ("Carter was from Detroit and very black, very clipped in speech, very well dressed. . . . Young was a lean, malt-colored boy from North Carolina, here on a national scholarship, out of his depth, homesick and cold"); neither

---

* The prose style Updike attributes to Dawson is a wickedly accurate description of the gruff, humorless writing in Lasch's letters home.

† In the *New Yorker* version, Kern is "*driven by* an unnatural sophistication." When Updike revised the story, nearly forty years after he'd written it (and fifty-odd years after the events described), he chose to emphasize Kern's aspirations rather than his accomplishments.

of them graduates. Another casualty, Petersen, an "amiable Swede" from Minnesota, also drops out, whereas his roommate, Fitch, "a child prodigy from Maine," hangs on—after suffering through a full-blown nervous breakdown at the end of his first year. More resilient are the two Jews, Silverstein and Koshland, both from New York, tough and savvy kids who "treated Cambridge as if it were another borough." Taking his cue from the relatively preppy-free Hollis, Updike deliberately populates the dorm with public school graduates; he's not interested in the many freshmen who had the advantage of being "launched by little Harvards like Andover and Groton"—though he insists, melodramatically, that even the preppies will eventually have their difficulties: "the institution demands of each man, before it releases him, a wrenching sacrifice of ballast." That sacrifice comes soonest for those students who have neither an East Coast pedigree nor the prep-school background that is usually part of the package.

Orson Ziegler, a doctor's son from South Dakota, is a case in point. Though he arrives on registration day confident and decisive about his future (he, too, will be a doctor), the shock of Harvard nearly derails him. Part of his problem is the irritation of living with the exasperatingly smug and militantly eccentric Hub (who tears up notices from the draft board without opening them and scatters them out the window), but he's also overwhelmed by his studies: "Orson perceived how little he knew, how stupid he was, how unnatural all learning is, and how futile." The fact that he earns three As and a B in his first semester is neither a consolation nor a cushion against the strain of the second semester, when his anguish takes on a frightening aspect: "As spring slowly broke, he lost the ability to sleep. Figures and facts churned sluggishly in an insomniac mire. His courses became four parallel puzzles. . . . Sleepless, stuffed with information he could neither forget nor manipulate, he became prey to obsessive delusions." Balanced on a "high wire of sanity," and nearly tipped into the abyss by his hysterical reaction to Hub's loopy antics, Orson finishes his exams and escapes home. The last three paragraphs of the story take a synoptic view of the roommates' respective fates. Hub becomes an Episcopalian priest and eventually a missionary in South Africa;* Orson fulfills his ambition and leads an "honorable" life as a physician in his hometown in South Dakota. "In one particular only—a kind of scar he carries without pain and without any clear memory of the amputation—does the man he is differ from the man he assumed he would become. He never prays." This ominously announced apostasy is the "sacrifice" Harvard has demanded of him. As the portentousness of those last lines suggests, "The Christian Roommates" is not one of Updike's best stories.

Updike's achievements at Harvard were more spectacular than Orson's, and he emerged with his faith effectively intact. And yet it would be a mistake to think that his academic success came easily. He worked for it with the driving energy and keen concentration that he would later bring to his writing. At the same time, he had to develop a self-protective disregard for the demands and strictures of the social hierarchy, a "feigned haughtiness," as one classmate described it. Almost everyone who knew Updike at the time stresses that he was *different*—a little odd, and certainly not a mainstream Harvard type. He looked different and he dressed differently. Knowing this—as any self-conscious young man necessarily would—can't have been comfortable. But adversity has its rewards. Just as the boredom and isolation of Plowville pushed him to develop his creative talent, so the social pressure at Harvard hardened him and reinforced his desire to put his talent to use.

AFTER THE EXCITEMENT of shopping for his courses (in addition to Latin, math, and freshman English, he chose Social Science 1, a history course grandly entitled Introduction to the Development of Western Civilization), there was the equally serious business of the *Lampoon* tryouts. Updike was keenly aware of the magazine and its

---

* Hub is closely modeled on the late Edward A. French, a notoriously eccentric character in the Harvard class of '54, an ardent pacifist and vegetarian who became a minister, then a missionary in Africa. By coincidence, French later spent twenty-nine years (from 1967 to 1996) as the rector of Ascension Memorial Church in Ipswich, Massachusetts, the town in which Updike lived for seventeen years.

illustrious alumni (including Robert Sherwood, William Randolph Hearst, and Robert Benchley, one of his idols); the opportunity to join its editorial staff had been an important factor in his choice of Harvard over Cornell. The summer after high school, while he was rubbing elbows with the journalists at the *Reading Eagle*, he'd seen an article about the *Lampoon* in a magazine called *Flair*, complete with a photograph of the undergraduate editors and samples of their cartoons and verses. He was still dreaming of becoming a cartoonist, and he knew that the *Lampoon*, if he could make the cut, would be an auspicious beginning. Needless to say, his mother was cheering him on.

But the Lampoon is not just a magazine; it's also an exclusive undergraduate club housed in a curious flatiron building that sits parallel to Mount Auburn Street, crouched like a friendly, slightly goofy sphinx with a jolly face staring out of a tower topped by a copper ibis. The interior, equally eccentric and ostentatious, well worn, comfy, dimly lit, is unmistakably that of a clubhouse. Though he claimed to have been blissfully ignorant as a fresh-man of the social dimension of the organization he was so eager to join, Updike did write to his mother, after his first visit, about the "soft-spoken aristocrats" he met there. Twenty years later, in an introduction to a *Lampoon* anthology, he described the place as "an outcropping . . . of that awful seismic force . . . Wasp Power." His jocular tone partly obscures the seriousness of his point: "The Lampoon is a club and, as do all clubs, feeds off the delicious im-mensity of the excluded." The Castle, as the Lampoon building is known, was an elitist stronghold well defended by a cohort of young Boston Brahmins, in the midst of an unabashedly elitist university. And yet Updike prospered there, proving that he could be at once clubbable—this was only the first of several exclusive in-stitutions he would join over the course of a lifetime—and blessedly immune to ambient snobbery. He held his own among the Boston blue bloods and the New York sophisticates. If the well-to-do so-cial members of the Lampoon bothered him, he gave little sign at the time; and he didn't become a snob himself. He could enjoy the pranks and the alcohol-fueled fun without inquiring into the pedigrees of his fellow revelers or indeed what he called the "social engineering" that went into all the merrymaking. With hindsight, he judged that the Lampoon was "saved from mere sociable fatuity by being also *The Lampoon*, a magazine." (By the same token, one could say that Updike himself was saved from snobbery by his devotion to work—he was too busy, too driven, to give himself airs.) And as it happened, the magazine was ideally suited to Updike's tastes, talents, and prodigious energy: when it started in 1876, it had been modeled on *Punch*, the British humor magazine, but it had recently begun to ape *The New Yorker*, the object of Updike's ambition from the age of twelve.

The competition to become a Lampoon member began near the start of each semester, and the candidates were elected (or not) several months later. The successful candidates were then subjected to "Fools' Week," a prank-filled initiation. Always in a hurry to get ahead, Updike decided against waiting until spring, so on the appointed evening at the end of September, only a week or so after he'd arrived in Cambridge, he turned up at the Castle to try his luck. One of the upperclassmen on hand to inspect the new crop of prospective fools was Michael Arlen, son and namesake of the author of *The Green Hat*. Arlen père had been a literary celebrity in London in the 1920s, and his son grew up in the south of France, went to boarding school in England, and then came to America just before the war. Two years ahead of Updike, young Michael Arlen was possessed of all the panache the kid from Pennsylvania was so eager to acquire. Arlen's account of that evening gives an indication of the distance Updike still had to travel:

> It was a rainy night—improbable to remember across those many years, but there's the objective correlative: so many of the freshmen, including John, were wearing galoshes. (Upperclassmen were far too cool, too in league with the devil, to do that.) There was John—a little taller than most, a shock of hair, prominent nose. He had a book bag in which he was carrying *framed* cartoons from the Shillington high-school newspaper.

Though he may have been aware that his clothes were wrong—*wonky* is the term Updike preferred—he was still too green to know that framing one's own cartoons was a blatant faux pas.

A surprising number of Updike's classmates vividly remember his freshman year clothes and distinctly nonpreppy appearance. He wore a green corduroy jacket and wide, knitted ties, and his hair looked like he'd just dragged himself out of bed; with his long limbs, thin face, and angular features, he resembled his own cartoons of a court jester. Later, once he'd settled in (and began to jettison the clothes his mother had bought him in Reading), he dressed in the English major's de facto uniform—a gray coat and narrow necktie—but he was never, as an undergraduate, slick or polished. He bounced up and down—vaulting over parking meters as he'd done in Shillington—so excited was he by the Cambridge scene. He sometimes whinnied when he laughed, and cackled in an endearing way at his own corny jokes; his smile, a deep *V,* was crooked; and he stammered, of course—not for show, as some effete Poonsters did, but because at times he genuinely couldn't get the words out.

If not for his evident talent and enthusiasm, the Lampoon's contingent of tweedy, soft-spoken aristocrats would have blackballed him. Luckily, it was immediately apparent to a few of the more perceptive members that he would be an asset to the magazine, and on that basis he was elected. Arlen remembers that "John seemed a cut above even the talented people there. Everyone thought he was unusually gifted." There was no mistaking his eagerness; once he'd joined,* he became an avid participant in the brainstorming "gag sessions," and a relentlessly prolific contributor to the magazine—in some of the issues, over half of the artwork (signed "JHU," for John Hoyer Updike) was his. "An undergraduate magazine," he later explained, "creates a wonderfully ongoing vacuum for those who want

---

* More than half a century later, Updike told a fellow Lampoon alumnus that the initiation fee of one hundred dollars (substantially more than he could afford) was waived in his case. Other alumni, interviewed about Updike's election to the Lampoon, said it seemed likely that the fee was indeed waived—despite the "snobbish opposition" of the "social" members.

to fill it." Although Updike was elected as a cartoonist ("he was much fonder of his cartoons than anyone else," according to Arlen), what his fellow Poonsters came to prize most was his light verse. "It was a disappearing craft, like harpsichord tuning," said Arlen, "but John was writing, even in freshman year, almost *New Yorker*–level light verse. He could turn it out effortlessly, and we were always short of material."

According to one Lampoon colleague, the magazine's chronic shortage of material could be blamed on the feckless high spirits of the majority of the Poonsters:

> The main problem with the gag sessions was that most of the members . . . didn't really give much of a damn about the quality of the material that went into the magazine. But then it was a very old tradition of the *Lampoon* that a serenely blasé attitude toward the subscribers, as well as to the public at large, was the only possibly correct attitude. . . . What [most members] honestly wanted to do when they came to the building, to put it very simply, was just horse around and have a good time. As a result of this, the gag sessions in the Sanctum, during which we were all supposed to submit our ideas for the approval of the board, always deteriorated very quickly into scenes of hilarity out of which, more often than not, nothing whatsoever that could actually be used in the magazine emerged.

With his "romantic weakness for gags"—inherited from his father, along with his talent for pratfalls—Updike was a willing participant in the Lampoon's elaborately orchestrated "social frivolity." During his Fools' Week in February 1951, he starred in a stunt he remembered with what seems today somewhat misplaced pride; he called it his "one successful impersonation." Disguised as a blind cripple selling pencils, he stationed himself in front of Widener Library; a couple of his fellow fools, dressed as priests, bought some pencils and then began to argue with him, claiming to have been short-changed. The quarrel drew a crowd—whereupon the two "priests" pulled large codfish from under their cassocks and pelted him, in his blind cripple disguise, with the day's catch.

He was happy to play the clown, but not necessarily at ease. Months after his election and the high jinks of Fools' Week—and despite a rapid start as a contributor to the magazine—he remained anxious about his status. Charles Bracelen Flood, a senior who was ibis (vice president) of the Lampoon during Updike's freshman year, and who'd recently been given a contract by Houghton Mifflin to publish a novel he was writing in Archibald MacLeish's creative writing seminar, remembered his surprise at having to bolster Updike's confidence with a verbal pat on the back:

> At the end of one of the last-of-the-spring-term informal dinners, John asked if he could speak to me. The two of us stood by ourselves just inside the Lampoon's side door on Bow Street, and he began to talk. I think he wanted reassurance that he fitted in, and I was able to provide that. I assured him that everyone liked him, and I think I added that we all thought that he had a lot of ability. He nodded and seemed satisfied with our brief conversation, and we parted.

Updike's steady march up the masthead could only have been encouraging. He was elected narthex at the end of freshman year; ibis the next year; and finally, at the end of junior year, president.* According to Ted Gleason, who was in the class behind Updike, "John did everything, absolutely everything for the *Lampoon*: wrote, drew, ran the entire effort. . . . The *Lampoon* was Updike." When Gleason joined in the spring of 1952, Updike happened to be "curator" of Fools' Week, which meant he was responsible for devising the stunts Gleason and the rest of the fools would be required to perform. One fool had to measure Harvard Square with a codfish at eleven o'clock on a Monday morning. (Cod seem to figure prominently in the repertory of Lampoon pranks.) Gleason and two others were told to go to the Boston Garden, where Barnum and

---

* The title narthex is bestowed on a promising young Poonster.

Bailey's circus was performing, acquire twenty pounds of elephant dung, and ride back to Harvard Square on the T with the dung wrapped in a baby's blanket, cradling this odorous infant in their arms and feeding it from a bottle. The entire group was made to hire a horse and wagon and drive down Massachusetts Avenue (dressed in ridiculous fool costumes), dispensing grapefruit juice and vodka from a trash barrel. And, most ambitiously, Updike dreamed up an absurdist spectacle (not unlike the drama of the blind cripple and the priests) that drew a large and appreciative lunchtime crowd to a street adjacent to the Yard: a fool disguised as an old man driving an ancient jalopy was hit from behind by a car packed with fellow fools; the old man jumped out and swore at the others in Italian, whereupon they poured from their car carrying sledgehammers and crowbars and proceeded to utterly demolish the jalopy—then drove off lickety-split, leaving the ruined vehicle in the road.

In addition to the pranks and the motley parades, there were parties held in the Castle, in the upstairs room known as the Great Hall, dances complete with Radcliffe girls and even, on one occasion, the music of a three-piece combo. Among the more impressive Lampoon members was the multitalented Fred Gwynne, later famous on television as Herman Munster, patriarch of the Munster household, who was a class ahead of Updike. Doug Bunce, a curious character, also multitalented and often in trouble with the university, actually took up residence in the Castle. An outsider, like Updike, Bunce burrowed deep into the Lampoon and became a de facto insider.* Even more remarkable was Updike's classmate Prince Sadruddin Aga Khan, son of the hereditary imam of the Shia Ismaili Muslims, who roomed sophomore year in Eliot House with Paul Matisse and Stephen Joyce. According to Harvard legend, this constellation of roommates prompted the master of Eliot to brag, "Where else would you find, in one room, the grandson of Matisse, the grandson of Joyce, and the great-great-great-great-grandson of

---

* After Bunce left Harvard, he changed his name to Douglas Fairbairn. He told the story of his Harvard years in his autobiography, *Down and Out in Cambridge.*

God?" Updike made use of Sadri Kahn's fabulously exotic background in a flimsy short story set at Harvard, "God Speaks," about Gish Imra of Nuristan, a fabulously wealthy undergraduate princeling, putatively divine, who drives around Cambridge in a red MG. Gish plays tennis with the narrator (who learned his tennis on "pitted public courts in Pennsylvania"), and they strike up a brief, casual friendship. Updike took these flashes of eccentric Lampoon glamour in stride, knowing that he himself was in a sense exotic; he learned to bask in the pleasure of club solidarity, and even acquired a brace of nicknames (Upchurch and Upsurge), a reassuring sign of acceptance.

Over the course of his four years, he supplied the magazine with seven cover illustrations, more than a hundred cartoons and drawings, sixty poems, and twenty-five prose pieces—a prodigious output from someone as serious as Updike was about his studies. His mature judgment on this body of work was not entirely flattering and curiously skewed: "[T]he drawings now give me pleasure to contemplate," he wrote in 1984, "the prose pieces pain, and the poems a guarded sensation in between." He was in fact a moderately skilled cartoonist with some funny ideas and what looks like the beginning of a personal style, but it would be hard to argue for genius in the artwork he did for the *Lampoon*. He liked Chinese jokes: a birthday party where a table of little Chinese kids are singing "Happy Birthday, Tu Yu" to their little friend; or coolies, unimpressed by a union agitator, saying, "Why *shouldn't* we work for coolie wages?" He also liked to draw jesters; one of his most charming is a jester in a simmering cauldron (being cooked by absent cannibals, one supposes) who obligingly reaches over his head with a salt shaker to adjust the seasoning. It's possible that the pleasure he derived in later life from looking at his own drawings was mostly a matter of remembering "the happiness of creation, the rapture of creating something out of nothing."

But even as he was churning out cartoons to fill the next issue, Updike recognized that other artists on the Lampoon (especially Doug Bunce and Fred Gwynne) were more skilled and sophisticated than he was—"the budding cartoonist in me, exposed to what I thought were superior talents, suffered a blight." It was, in effect, the first time he encountered serious competition in a creative endeavor.

Updike's written work is another matter: it shows a rare talent emerging. Of the light verse he published in the magazine, he liked four poems well enough to include them in his first collection.* "Mountain Impasse," written in the spring of his junior year and inspired by a quotation lifted from *Life* magazine (in which Stravinsky imperiously declared, "I despise mountains, they don't tell me anything"), is wonderfully witty, cleverly constructed, and flawlessly polished, as the first stanza promises:

> Stravinsky looks upon the mountain,
> The mountain looks on him;
> They look (the mountain and Stravinsky)
> And both their views are dim.

That summer, he wrote his brief lyric meditation on what he later called "the mythogenetic truth of telephone wires and poles"; it ends with a flash of enchanting poetic imagination, the dip of the wires reconceived as "the flight of a marvelous crow / No one saw: / Each pole, a caw." That surreal vision—a long leap ahead of even the most skilled undergraduate humor—depends on a gift more precious than verbal ingenuity.

Easily the most ambitious and accomplished of his *Lampoon* stories is "The Peruvian in the Heart of Lake Winnipesaukee," a broadly comical meditation on identity and self-knowledge. Conventional in structure (a straight first-person narrative), it's nonetheless fresh and original—there can't be many other stories about a barefoot South American's journey of self-discovery at a New Hampshire summer camp, especially not ones that feature body paint, operatic arias, and a stolen canoe. It was included in the issue published in September 1953, for which Updike drew the cover (a chicken with a pince-nez and a Harvard sweatshirt confronted by an egg labeled "Class of

---

* "Poetess," "The Population of Argentina," "Why the Telephone Wires Dip and the Poles Are Cracked and Crooked," and "Mountain Impasse."

'57" and bearing the instruction "HATCH ME"). The same issue contains numerous line drawings signed JHU and a sample, too, of his light verse: a poem called "The Hypocrite," about a dandy who wears dirty socks. He was truly a one-man band.

When asked to reflect in later life on his Harvard experience, he often responded with nostalgic riffs about the Lampoon Castle—he'd dredge up memories of gag sessions in the Sanctum, or "the smell of wet old magazines that arose from the cellar," or the chaotic camaraderie of the Thursday evening dinners served in the Great Hall. He also remembered the lonely bliss of doing cartoon work for the magazine in his narrow, attic-like room on the fifth floor of Lowell House. In an autobiographical essay, he offered a vivid snapshot of himself bent over his Bristol board, "my lower lip sagging in the intensity of my concentration, a cigarette smoking in an ashtray near my eyes. . . . The nervous glee of drawing is such that I sometimes laugh aloud, alone." He labored tirelessly because he greatly enjoyed the mechanics of what he was doing, both the drawing and the writing; because he loved seeing his work in print; and because his involvement gave him a secure identity around the Yard. But even before he arrived at Harvard, he knew that the Lampoon was an effective stepping-stone, that it would get him noticed in the wider world—which it did.

It was through the Lampoon old boy network that Updike made his first promising connection with the New York publishing world. Edward Streeter, a Lampoon alumnus who graduated in the class of 1914, was a banker who wrote popular novels in his spare time, among them *Father of the Bride* and *Mr. Hobbs' Vacation*, both of which were made into successful Hollywood movies. Impressed with Updike's work in the *Lampoon*, Streeter tipped off his good friend Cass Canfield, who was chairman of Harper and Brothers. In April of his senior year, Updike received a letter from Canfield—care of the Lampoon—asking to see some of the young man's writing (including the piece "about the Peruvian"), and suggesting that he would welcome the submission of a novel about undergraduate life. Updike replied with a long letter explaining that a novel of undergraduate life was "not my meat" ("Somehow, the people I knew in high school still seem much larger and worthier than my friends at college"); he offered instead a description of two different novels he had in mind, one a satire, the other a tragedy. The satire was to be about a woman named Supermama who is perfect in every way—beautiful, brilliant, superbly capable—and therefore insufferable in the eyes of the opposite sex. (It's not hard to see Linda looming in the background of that one.) The tragedy was to be about a man who's determined to be pure and virtuous—and therefore sows havoc around him. Updike admitted that perhaps both of these conceptions were "thin." Canfield made vague, encouraging noises about Updike's rather unlikely projects, and sagely suggested that he "choose the one which upon reflection shapes up as the best narrative." The publisher stayed in touch, faithfully reminding Updike of his interest. Persistence pays: Updike eventually promised that Canfield would get first look at anything he wrote for "book publication." He kept that promise, with the result that in March 1958, his first book, a collection of poems called *The Carpentered Hen and Other Tame Creatures*, was published by Harper and Brothers.

His undergraduate writing also attracted the attention of a powerful *New Yorker* editor, Katharine White. Although she made no effort to contact him, she kept an eye out for his submissions. As she wrote in the letter that contained his first-ever *New Yorker* paycheck (fifty-five dollars for "Duet, with Muffled Brake Drums"), the quality of Updike's light verse in the *Lampoon* had given her hope that one day he might become a contributor.

It's no wonder, then, that once he was a comfortably established man of letters, Updike looked back at the Castle with warm feelings of unclouded affection. His strenuous undergraduate efforts not only smoothed his path to *The New Yorker* but also led to the publication of his first book: Lampy had in effect launched his professional career. But in 1956, when his student days were fresh in his memory, his feelings were mixed at best.* Less than two years out of

---

* At the very end of his life he declined to participate in an oral history of the Lampoon. He didn't want to give any more interviews, he said, "about foolery that has pretty much faded from my memory."

Harvard, not long after he'd started to work at *The New Yorker*, he wrote a story with a Salingeresque title—"Who Made Yellow Roses Yellow?"—that casts a less flattering light on the Lampoon. The brief reunion of two college friends gives Updike a chance to explore the snobbery and resentment bubbling away beneath the show of camaraderie at the *Quaff*, a clubby campus humor magazine, an obvious stand-in for the *Lampoon*.

Hoping to find a job in advertising, twenty-five-year-old Fred Platt arranges a lunch with his pal Clayton Thomas Clayton, who's been scooting up the corporate ladder via the publicity department of a giant chemical company. Fred, who is from a rich and distinguished New York family, had helped Clayton get onto the *Quaff* ("Sans *Quaff*," Fred thinks, "where would Clayton be?"). Now, with a genial sense of entitlement, Fred feels he ought to be offered employment, especially since getting Clayton elected to the magazine had been an awkward task. A scholarship student from a provincial public high school, Clayton had turned up as a freshman at the *Quaff* Candidates' Night with an armful of framed cartoons (exactly as Updike had). The tweedy set dismissed him as "wonky" and "right out of the funny papers"; they thought it "pathetic" that his drawings were framed; they sneered at his "cocoa-colored slacks and sport shirts." But Fred, recognizing that the nervous kid with the ridiculous name had talent ("The point was he could draw"), sensing that he could be helpful to the magazine, and wishing also to be kind, insisted that Clayton Thomas Clayton be elected. And it seemed at first a fine thing: "His *Quaff* career had been all success, all adaptation and good sense, so that in his senior year Clayton was president, and everybody said he alone was keeping silly old *Quaff* alive." (Thus far, Clayton is Updike's double, step for step.) Later, with the benefit of hindsight, Fred saw that instead of keeping the *Quaff* alive, Clayton had caused "the club, with its delicate ethic of frivolity," to wither: "The right sort had stopped showing up."

By the "right sort," Fred means people like him—elegant, privileged sophisticates. Clayton, by contrast, is all vulgar business. He says things like "People are always slamming advertising, but I've found it's a pretty damn essential thing in our economy." We're told that Clayton loves work; Fred thinks it's all Clayton knows how to do: "His type saw competition as the spine of the universe." Here, too, Clayton resembles Updike: in the words of his Lampoon friend Michael Arlen, "John was always a striver. He took pleasure and satisfaction from being a striver. He could outwork anyone." But Updike and Clayton differ in that Clayton, who has neither charm nor wit, is still (three years out of college) stubbornly gauche; and he still seethes with resentment against the "tin gods" who snubbed him at college.

Who did Updike think was the "right sort"? Did he favor feckless Fred, the upper-class dilettante, or industrious Clayton, the middle-class go-getter? On the whole, Clayton comes off worse, but only because Updike plays on the reader's own snobbery by making Fred charming and Clayton crass. Though Fred gets the last word, his triumph is hollow. Frustrated in his quest for a job, having decided that Clayton is "helplessly offensive," Fred mocks him when they're saying good-bye—gratuitous cruelty that leaves a sour taste. Updike's evenhanded treatment of the whole encounter suggests that by 1956 he had achieved a detached and mature understanding of the Lampoon social dynamic. But that doesn't mean he had found it easy to be a Clayton-like character in the midst of the tin god contingent. In his sophomore year a campus rumor circulated about a drunken dinner at the Castle punctuated by an outburst from a bleary Updike who climbed onto the table to denounce his fellow Poonsters as goddamn shitty snobs. Years later he described himself as an angry young man during his college career, but if so, there's no indication that he acted on his anger; more likely, he looked back and thought he *ought* to have been angry.

INNOCENTLY OBLIVIOUS TO these pressures and resentments, Updike's parents were thrilled by his success at the Lampoon—"one of the most exclusive of all exclusive societies," as Linda called it. She added, in oracle mode: "Once in a while, perusing the dictionary, I meet Icarus and remember that certain very real and special dangers are prepared for all men who leave the muddy routine that seems to be the usual lot of God's creatures. And yet a moment free in the air is probably worth a lifetime in the mud." Whenever a new issue of the magazine was in the offing, her letters were full of proud anticipation. And soon enough his parents had other reasons to be pleased. Though his grades weren't at first uniformly excellent (Latin dragged down his freshman year average), and though he claimed to have "peaked" as a scholar in his junior year, his academic record was remarkable enough for him to qualify as one of Phi Beta Kappa's "Junior Eight," which meant that he was among the top ten scholars in a class of more than a thousand. He eventually graduated summa cum laude—a fitting tribute to his intelligence and diligence.

Because most of his courses were in literature, the bulk of his work consisted of reading. It was during these four years—a period when the Harvard English department was particularly strong—that he laid the groundwork for what became, in time, a monumental erudition. In his memoirs, he recalled a moment of special happiness on the day he attended the introductory meeting of Hyder Rollins's course in late Romantic poetry:

> As I settled into the first lecture, in my one-armed chair, my heart was beating like that of a boy with a pocket of heavy nickels as he walks through the door . . . of a candy shop. It would be bliss . . . I thought, to go on forever like this, filling in one's ignorance of English literature slot by slot, poet by poet, under the guidance of tenured wizards, in classrooms dating from the colonial era, while the down-drooping golden-leaved elm branches shivered in the sunlight outside in the Yard.

Chief among the tenured wizards was Harry Levin, whose lectures on Shakespeare, "delivered with a slightly tremulous elegance" to a capacity crowd in Emerson Hall, stressed the idea of "dominant metaphor." To Updike, Levin's resolutely textual approach, orthodox New Criticism with the emphasis on explication, was a revelation: "That a literary work could have a double life, in its imagery as well as its plot and characters, had not occurred to me." It's a lesson he never forgot, and one he put to use even in his earliest fiction, where patterns of imagery and metaphor complement and complicate the narrative. Even if the subject and tone of his first stories ("Friends from Philadelphia," say, or "Ace in the Hole," which he wrote in the fall of his senior year) are decidedly nonliterary, they were designed to repay with interest the kind of close textual analysis favored by Levin.

Though he concentrated on the poetry of the English Renaissance, Updike also took courses on Anglo-Saxon poetry, on the metaphysical poets, on Spenser and Milton, on Samuel Johnson and his times (a celebrated course taught by Walter Jackson Bate), on Tolstoy and Dostoevsky, and on George Bernard Shaw. He enrolled in a series of writing courses. In sophomore year he was taught by a "staid, tweedy" poet and Chaucer scholar named Theodore Morrison, who favored modern masters, read aloud from Hemingway, and allowed Updike to submit chapters of a novel. The next year, there was Kenneth Kempton ("the least tweedy of writing instructors"), who read aloud to his class the J. D. Salinger stories then appearing in *The New Yorker*, another revelation for Updike. Listening with rapt attention, he discovered fresh possibilities for the short story, among them the idea that religious concerns could be smuggled into an urban setting populated by young people not unlike him. "It's in Salinger," he later acknowledged, "that I first heard . . . the tone that spoke to my condition." He was especially wowed by "Just Before the War with the Eskimos," which taught him that a "good story could be ambiguous, the better to contain the ambiguity of the world"—a notion he put to work in a number of early stories (including "Who Made Yellow Roses Yellow?"). In his senior year, his writing course was taught by Albert Guérard ("the very model of a cigarette-addicted Gallic intellectual"), who turned Updike away when he first applied as a sophomore but now recognized his talent—and even urged him to send a story to *The New Yorker*. (Though it was rejected at the time, a year later Updike submitted a lightly revised version, which was accepted.)

Little by little he was rethinking his ambitions, largely because he now recognized that he was a better writer than a cartoonist. The novel he was writing in installments for Morrison's class, three thousand words every two weeks, was called *Willow*; it was set in a small town not unlike Shillington.* In a letter to his parents, Kit grumbled about John's easy schedule—"None of his courses seem to demand any work. And all he does is write his novel." The next letter provided detail, delivered in Lasch's typically wry tone: "Updike keeps plowing ahead on his novel. He has written about ninety pages. Some of it is very good. The book . . . is about high school. He is well qualified to write that book." Updike disagreed with that last judgment. Although Morrison was kind and encouraging (as well as shrewd), his encouragement wasn't enough to prevent Updike from abandoning *Willow*. Years later he described it as "a kind of younger *Couples*" (a gang of teenagers' tangled love affairs) and "terribly amateurish."

By the time he graduated, he later estimated, he was "eighty-five percent bent upon becoming a writer." His Smith Corona had displaced Bristol board. Perhaps he would have been a hundred percent committed to the writing life had he earned a spot in the most prestigious Harvard creative writing course, Archibald MacLeish's English S, a yearlong seminar limited to twelve students. Updike twice applied and was twice rejected, a rare setback in an otherwise monotonously triumphant career.†

In small part because he hadn't entirely given up the idea of making his living as a cartoonist, he enrolled in the spring of his sophomore year in a drawing class taught by Hyman Bloom, an Abstract Expressionist painter whose reputation was just reaching its peak. Updike later remarked that Bloom's ultralight pedagogical

---

* He gave the name Willow to the hero's hometown in *Villages* (2004), his last and most nakedly nostalgic account of a Shillington boyhood.

† Edward Hoagland, who was accepted into MacLeish's seminar in the fall of 1953, notes that Updike's rejection had long-term consequences. A Boston publishing house, Houghton Mifflin, traditionally snapped up the first books of promising young Harvard writers—but according to Hoagland, "the trouble was that Harvard's writing teachers had not recognized Updike's talent . . . and so the wider Harvard-Boston establishment . . . missed him too." Boston's loss was New York's gain.

touch ("his utterances were few, he muttered when he emitted them, and he moved about the classroom on shoes notable for the thickness and the silence of their soles") taught him that "art was a job you did on your own." Actually, Updike's other, rather more pressing reason for enrolling in Bloom's Advanced Composition was precisely to avoid being on his own: he was pursuing Mary Pennington, a Radcliffe fine arts major he'd met the previous semester—pursuing her successfully, as it turned out. John and Mary were married a year later, and for the next two decades, art was a job he did in the thick of the large and lively family they started together.

They met in Frederick B. Deknatel's course on medieval sculpture in the fall of 1951, and got to know each other smoking cigarettes after class on the steps of the Fogg Museum, where the art history classes were held, and then over coffee. They collaborated on a term paper, and when Mary failed to appear for the final exam, Updike heard to his dismay that she was in the hospital. He rushed to Mass General, where he discovered that she was suffering from a platelet deficiency and would be released in a week; in the meantime, he visited her every afternoon. Lasch found this behavior worrying and told his parents that Updike was "losing sight of his initial purpose in being here"—but when Kit finally met the "lady love," he conceded that she was "a charming girl." John didn't mention his new girlfriend to his mother until mid-December, and when he did, Linda was uncharacteristically silent on the subject. At the beginning of February she passed a tight-lipped judgment: "She sounds alright to me"; he escorted Mary to the Lowell House Dance at the end of that month, and a week later felt free to tell Linda how happy Mary made him. In April, hoping to slow things down, his mother expressed tentative misgivings, but John fought back, and in May he invited his girl home to Plowville for a June visit, after exams. By November there was open talk of marriage; and in early January 1953, Mary's parents gave a small party to celebrate the engagement. The marriage took place five months later, in Cambridge.

That Linda didn't disapprove, that she made no concerted effort to hinder or delay the progress of the courtship, was an unexpected blessing. John's romance with Nancy Wolf had suffered as a result of his mother's unwavering opposition. In December of his freshman year, he'd received a letter containing a maternal broadside against Nancy, triggered by Wesley's report on the girl's behavior at Shillington High School, where she flaunted tokens of her attachment to the successful Harvard man. "I am no longer amused by her flutterings," Linda wrote. "I think I know now how much of her energy she uses up in being attractive and how easily her charm will break under pressure. Daddy adds the last straw by saying that 'she's got him.' Be that as it may, don't ever forget that she ain't got me and I can sputter just as long as she can flutter." Against the odds, Nancy was still part of the picture when John came home for Christmas vacation. But in February, with his second semester of college under way, Linda's sputterings finally achieved the desired effect: John broke it off. Until Mary Pennington materialized in the fall of sophomore year, he led a monkish existence of hard work and conspicuous celibacy. And then suddenly he was eager to marry. The prospect of sealing his escape from Linda surely spurred him on.

When Kit visited Plowville during spring break of sophomore year, he found "an air of slight unrest in the house," which he attributed to the poor health of John's grandparents—and to John's budding romance with Mary. "I cannot say how much this has upset the balance," Kit wrote to his parents, "but I had foreseen that, if nothing else, Updike's interest in home would be greatly diminished by it."

In an early, unpublished version of "Homage to Paul Klee; or a Game of Botticelli,"* another short story Updike set at Harvard, the protagonist, a wide-eyed innocent named Isaac, observes the coeds from "the neighboring young ladies' college" as they traverse the diagonal paths of the Yard, and comes to a decision: "Isaac wanted one, he was desperate to have one. . . . But who was he? An ignoramus; an inlander. Nevertheless, he would get one." By the end of his freshman year, Isaac (like Updike) begins to feel at home on

---

* Updike chose not to include "Homage to Paul Klee" in *The Early Stories*; it was only ever published in an obscure Unitarian journal called *The Liberal Context*.

campus; seeing himself objectively, "he ticked off his baggy-elbowed tweed coat, his unpressed suntans, his button-down shirt, his striped tie, his groping-for-exactitude self-deprecatory stammer, his nicotine-scalded fingers; and realized he belonged here." Next term, emboldened and relaxed by his sense of belonging, he meets Martha in a medieval art course and woos her—grabbing her attention and making her laugh with a succession of pratfalls. (Updike told *Time* magazine that he pulled similar stunts with Mary: "I courted her essentially by falling down the stairs of the Fogg Museum several times." According to Mary, the pratfalls were staged on the Widener steps—a better venue for a breakneck wife-wooing.)

Never quite as coolly calculating as Isaac, Updike at the time was in the grip of young love, and probably not aware of seeking out any particular type of woman. And yet in Mary Pennington he found someone instantly recognizable as a Radcliffe girl, someone who fitted in effortlessly with the college scene—unlike Updike, who saw himself as an outsider, a loner who had to exert himself to blend in. In the much shorter, published version of "Homage to Paul Klee," the protagonist's name has been changed to Sam, his avowed determination to acquire a Radcliffe girlfriend is left out, and so are the details of their first meeting. But we do learn that the girlfriend (whose name is still Martha) "had lived all her life in Cambridge," and that thanks to her "broad and luminous culture," she plays a mean game of Botticelli. A similar character appears in "Museums and Women," a story Updike wrote in 1962; unnamed, she's identified by the narrator, William Young, as "the girl who was to become my wife." She's smoking a cigarette, standing out in the cold on the steps of the campus museum in "threadbare sneakers from which her little toes stuck out" (a detail lifted from reality that also appears, nearly verbatim, in the early draft of "Homage to Paul Klee"). William recognizes her from the medieval art class he's taking and stops to talk with her. He courts her, attracted at least in part by her air of "careless authority":

> She was a fine-arts major, and there was a sense in which she contained the museum, had mastered all the priceless

and timeless things that would become, in my possessing her, mine as well. She had first appeared to me as someone guarding the gates.

Similarly, in the draft version of "Homage to Paul Klee," Isaac contemplates Martha's size (like Mary Pennington, she's taller than average) and reflects that "in possessing her . . . he seemed to be possessing a whole world." In a moment of epiphany, he sees her as a member of a social class "that has had the time and fortune to grow grace and knowledge and courtesy in its blood." This passage is capped with a romantic vision of upward mobility couched in prose purple enough to make F. Scott Fitzgerald blush:

> The territory he had battled for as an invader was in her inherent; so his sense of her size measured a conquest immeasurably vast and sweet, and lifted him into a happiness boundlessly proud.

These fictional accounts of his courtship suggest that Updike, looking back after a decade or so of marriage, became conscious of his own social climbing; he recognized an underlying motive in his attraction to Mary: She was someone "guarding the gates"—someone who could usher him into an agreeably refined future.

At the time, Updike expressed no social ambition whatsoever. He was perfectly content to be the country boy on the staff of the *Lampoon*. But as for artistic and intellectual ambition—it would be hard to overstate the scope of his dreams. While he was at work on *Willow*, he wrote to his mother about what was missing from the American literary scene. "We need a writer who desires both to be great and to be popular," he told her, "an author who can see America as clearly as Sinclair Lewis, but, unlike Lewis, is willing to take it to his bosom." A great writer who loved America, he thought, could "produce an epic out of the Protestant ethic." Though not quite ready to throw his hat in the ring—Rabbit was still a decade distant—Updike was already sizing up the job. In junior year, a few months before his marriage, he wrote, "I feel I am on the lip of a great jump forward, and this jump might carry me into the charmed circle." The charmed circle he had in mind was *The New Yorker*, not the Social Register.

In the long summer months after Mary's visit to Plowville, when John was again working at the *Reading Eagle* and Mary was wait-ressing in Cambridge, he sent her letters about his writing and the struggle to get into print and the bitter disappointment of rejection slips. He was certain that he was going to fly, as his mother promised he would. Mary believed it.

She was two years older than John, and had grown up in Cam-bridge with a younger sister in a highly cultured, politically progres-sive household. Her father, Leslie Talbot Pennington, an intellectual with a scholarly bent, was a Quaker who converted to Unitarian-ism, went to the Harvard Divinity School, and became minister of the Unitarian Church in Harvard Square, where his daughter was later married. Her mother, Elizabeth Entwistle Daniels, had been to Radcliffe (class of 1923), and taught Latin at Buckingham, a private day school in Cambridge. In 1944, Leslie Pennington was appointed minister of the First Unitarian Church in Chicago, and Mary moved to the Midwest with her parents. She stayed for only a few years before returning to Cambridge to live with family friends and spend her last year of high school at Buckingham before enroll-ing at Radcliffe in 1948.

Mary was a very attractive undergraduate, a smart, good-looking, and capable young woman with a broad, engaging smile and a dash of bohemian style—sandals, ballet slippers, peasant blouses, dark hair worn long or cut dramatically short, no makeup, no lipstick. Her bicycle is mentioned nearly as often as her smile: she's wheeling it across the Yard, or pushing it purposefully down Massachusetts Avenue, with John trailing a step or two behind. One of John's Harvard friends told me about meeting him for the first time—but John barely figures in the story: "I saw this girl in the li-brary who was just stunning. There was this skinny guy across from her but I didn't pay him any attention."

Beginning in the second half of her last year at Radcliffe, Mary lived with a roommate (a friend from Chicago called Ann Rosenblum) in a small penthouse apartment perched atop a redbrick Victorian building on Sparks Street; Ann papered the bathroom walls with *New Yorker* covers. After graduating, during John's junior year, Mary found a job as an unpaid apprentice teacher at the Shady Hill School, first with the fifth grade, then in the studio, teaching ceramics and painting. Evenings and weekends, she was often spotted in Updike's Lowell House room. One of his Lampoon colleagues recalls being surprised to find her "in residence," and wondering what John "did with the inevitable roommate."

Actually, there were several junior year roommates. Kit and John were still up on the fifth floor, but they'd moved across the hall, to E-52, a four-man suite. Choosing from the pool of Lowell "floaters" (residents in search of roommates), they added a senior named Charles Neuhauser. Meanwhile, Reginald Hannaford had withdrawn from college in order to receive psychiatric care,* and he recommended that they take in his place a sophomore named David Archibald.

Still remarkably concentrated on his work, Lasch was on his way to compiling a first-rate academic record capped by a summa in history and the 1954 Bowdoin Prize for best senior essay. He was also taking writing courses, churning out short stories, and announcing every so often to his parents that he was at work on a novel. At the very beginning of junior year, he and Updike collaborated on a short play for the Congregational youth group (of which Hannaford and Archibald were members). After John and Kit polished off the play in an afternoon, Lasch told his parents, "If only he would write a musical with me. We would be a great combination, with his brilliance and my capacity for drudgery."

John was still confiding in Kit during his last semester at Lowell House. He let his roommate know when he was briefly seized with cold feet about marriage ("The financial aspect is beginning to weigh on him," Kit reported to his parents). And yet their friendship

---

* Hannaford was the model for Fitch in "The Christian Roommates"—but in the story, Updike rearranged the chronology, sending him away with a nervous breakdown at the end of freshman rather than sophomore year.

was clearly strained in those final years at Harvard, partly because of Lasch's moodiness and his fits of belligerence, and partly because of their academic rivalry—the competition, so fruitful freshman year, began to grate as the stakes grew higher. A false rumor circulated on campus that Kit had lost his temper with John one day during junior year and that the quarrel had come to blows. It's certainly true that Kit failed utterly to suppress the note of bitter envy when he described to his parents John's latest triumph:

> Updike was elected to the Phi Beta Kappa society, one of only eight juniors so honored. I of course was passed over. I don't really mind it except for the implied superiority of Updike over me. If he really is a better student than I am, then I fear for myself. His seems a pedantic and lazy mind, and one limited to a small area of knowledge. But he does get better grades.

It's hard to act the part of a genial roommate when you're prey to that kind of resentment. Lasch was envious, and his envy obviously clouded his judgment: Updike may have been lazy the way many young men at college are lazy—unhelpful in matters of housekeeping, say—but he never exhibited any sign of having a lazy or pedantic mind. Lasch knew it, too; this outburst came only six months after his spontaneous acknowledgment of his roommate's brilliance. Mary—John's fiancée as of January 1953—realized there was a kind of battle between the two of them, the nature of which she never fully understood; it's possible that she herself contributed to the tension. Thanks to Mary, Updike was moving on. He was less interested in home life, as Kit observed—and he was less interested in dorm life, too.

Charles Neuhauser, one of the two new junior year roommates, was a poet, high-strung and uncompromising. He and another friend of Updike's, David Chandler, both of whom were on the editorial board of the *Advocate*, privately printed a slim volume of their poems, *An Antique Drum*, recouping the cost by selling copies to friends. Updike bought one, and probably still had it on hand in

1969 when he wrote a story, "One of My Generation,"* a satiric portrait of a relentlessly literary roommate who writes tortured poems full of exotic, overheated imagery (lifted, unkindly, from *An Antique Drum*). The story is weak and sour, but it opens a window, somewhat distorted by caricature, on the book chat of Harvard English majors circa 1954. Ed Popper, the poetically inclined, somewhat unhinged roommate modeled on Neuhauser, insists on ranking, like some minor-league T. S. Eliot, the English poets. The narrator, a nameless, featureless version of Updike, is impressed by Popper's fixation on Robert Lowell, by his "passionate discrimination" in making literary judgments ("Literature had ceased to be his study and become his essence, an atmosphere he merely breathed"), and by the minuscule knot in his necktie ("the tiniest, driest, most intense necktie knot I had ever seen"). Both roommates are committed to the kind of close textual analysis favored by Harry Levin:

> To train one's mind to climb, like a vine on a sunny wall, across the surface of a poem by George Herbert, seeking the handhold crannies of pun, ambiguity, and buried allusion; to bring forth from the surface sense of the poem an altogether other, hidden poem of consistent metaphor and, as it were, verbal subversion; to feel, in Eliot's phrase, a thought like an emotion; to *explicate*—this was life lived on the nerve ends.

Despite his devotion to poetry and his neurotic tendencies, Popper (like Neuhauser) ends up working for the CIA—which is the punch line, so to speak, of the story. The narrator weighs his generation against the "riot-minded" youth of the late sixties, with their "drug-begentled eyes" and their contempt for the "power structure"; the Pentagon protests of the flower children, he points out, are aimed at old English majors, poetry lovers adept at exegesis—in other words, people just like Ed Popper.

---

* Like "Homage to Paul Klee," "One of My Generation" was left out of *The Early Stories*.

"One of My Generation" gives an indication of how far Updike traveled from Shillington High to Harvard College. He arrived in Cambridge a "cultural bumpkin," having read very little but mystery novels, science fiction, humor writing, some Hemingway, some Thornton Wilder, and random volumes picked up on a whim. At age fourteen, having borrowed from the Reading public library Edmund Wilson's newly published *Memoirs of Hecate County*, he was given his "first and . . . most vivid glimpse of sex through the window of fiction." For high school English he read *Macbeth* and *The Merchant of Venice*, but not *Hamlet* or *King Lear* or *Antony and Cleopatra*. Now, just a few years later, the names of seventeenth- and eighteenth-century English poets—Cowley, Traherne, Cowper—tripped off his tongue. Midnight found him in his dormered room in Lowell House, a cigarette in one hand, Spenser's *The Faerie Queene* in the other, alive to the glamour of becoming a connoisseur of the classics. Having discovered Swift and Pope, he discovered in himself "a yen to read great literature." He had been rocketed into a literary universe; he remembered how he and his fellow English majors "worshipped, and gossiped about, Eliot and Pound and those other textual Titans." Instead of playing pinball after class, he was attending poetry readings: Carl Sandburg, E. E. Cummings, Dylan Thomas, Wallace Stevens (a native of Reading and therefore the object of Updike's close scrutiny). Eliot, whose towering reputation seemed "like an encompassing gray cloud, the very atmosphere of literature," also read on campus, but Updike stood so long in line waiting to get into Sanders Theatre that he fell asleep during the reading.

Sometimes the Harvard scene got to be too much for him. In junior year, writing to a high school classmate just before Christmas break, he was desperate to hear of any plans for a New Year's Eve party in Shillington: "The only thing that has sustained me in this orgy of erudition is the vision of a beautifully non-intellectual brawl during the holidays." The party materialized, a sloppy ad hoc affair attended by his whole gang of friends; five years later Updike captured it with exquisite precision in one of his finest stories, "The Happiest I've Been."

His grumbling about an "orgy of erudition" was mostly a pose for his pals back home. He really did worship the textual titans; this was a time in American life, as he later remarked, when literature "was revered as it would not be again." After almost half a century he still remembered going to hear Robert Frost at Sanders Theatre, an event attended by "the flower of the English faculty," including the distinguished poet and professor Archibald MacLeish—the man who twice declined to admit Updike to his writing seminar. Though Updike warned that his memory of the evening was fallible, the details he provided when he wrote about it are sharply etched, and the scene is compelling, a vivid snapshot of a literary and political moment. MacLeish had recently written a radio play called *The Trojan Horse*, the burden of which was an anti-McCarthyite message: the United States should bar the gates to the Trojan horse of totalitarian tactics of the sort practiced by the junior senator from Wisconsin. Frost evidently disagreed, and after he'd finished reading his poems, he indulged, as he often did, in some extemporaneous commentary; he took as his text MacLeish's liberal notion that all manifestations of totalitarianism are anathema.

"You know," he told his old friend and admirer in the astonished hearing of us worshipfully assembled undergraduates, "if you're going to beat a fella, you got to get to be like him." He may have said "sort of like him" or some such qualification, and I believe he continued a while on this theme, long enough for his anti-anti-McCarthyite drift to register. It was Frost in action, cruelly playful, a cat reaching out from the stage to tease its mouse, an eminent mouse who had been faithful in the hospitality, cordiality, and homage he had granted, over the years, to the greater poet. . . . As I remember it, Frost didn't raise his voice, and spoke as if helpfully, to an obtuse student. MacLeish smiled, slightly, through the assault; he knew his man, and perhaps had heard it all before. But we of the young audience had not, and this flash of bullying rather soured, for me, the charm of hearing [Frost's poems] in the voice of their maker.

Was it a form of delayed revenge to replay the scene of this "assault" on MacLeish? Though Updike claims to have been put off by Frost's "bullying," it doesn't appear to have dimmed his admiration for the "greater poet"; he goes on, in fact, to praise Frost for breaking loose from "consensual politics." It's possible that when he wrote those lines, Updike was thinking back on his own experience as a reluctant supporter of the Vietnam War beset by *bien-pensant* antiwar critics.

In his undergraduate years, Updike's politics were nothing if not consensual, as he indicated with this humorous checklist of his unimpeachably liberal responses to the era's various "excitements": "Joe McCarthy (against), Adlai Stevenson (for), the Checkers speech (against), the Korean War (for, as long as somebody else was fighting it)." He retained a "vivid civic memory" of signing up, along with his assembled classmates, for a student deferment. He no more questioned the justice of this temporary exemption from the draft than he did the overwhelmingly masculine tone of his university ("Not one class I took," he noticed years later, "was taught by a woman"). Like many of his classmates (but unlike Kit Lasch, who canvassed for Stevenson), he paid very little attention to the political issues of the day. In "Apologies to Harvard," he wrote, "We took the world as given." As far as he was concerned, the salient—and, in retrospect, scandalous—characteristic of his college cohort was a kind of unthinkingly conventional, atomized, unaware selfishness: "*We did not know we were a generation.*"

After junior year, in any case, he was half of a newlywed couple; he had many things on his mind other than politics. The wedding in late June, at the Crothers Chapel of the First Unitarian Church in Harvard Square, attended by both sets of parents, came off nearly without a hitch—except that the dazed groom somehow forgot to kiss the bride. For the honeymoon, they borrowed a house from one of Leslie Pennington's parishioners, a small cottage behind an apple orchard in Ipswich, Massachusetts; they stayed for a long weekend, playing croquet and bicycling in to town and out to the beach, where Mary, in a bright blue bathing suit, convinced her husband to brave the chill June waters. The sun burned his nose and planted an idea—life by the beach might keep his psoriasis in check. For ten weeks that summer they worked at a YMCA family camp in New Hampshire, on Sandy Island, in the middle of Lake Winnipesaukee (where he gathered the material for "The Peruvian in the Heart of Lake Winnipesaukee"). John was the camp registrar, and ran the office, while his bride minded the store; they were paid $150 each, plus room and board. They bunked in a small, secluded cabin. He did some writing and even sent off a couple of poems to *The New Yorker*. Both were rejected, but gently, and he was encouraged to send in more light verse. In late August, Mary's parents drove them down to Plowville; they arrived in the late afternoon to find that Linda's ninety-year-old father, John Franklin Hoyer, had died a short while earlier. The happy homecoming turned into an impromptu wake, a coincidence that inspired stories by both John and Linda.

For John's senior year, the young couple rented the cheapest apartment they could find. For thirty-five dollars a month, they got a fairly big room that served as kitchen, dining room, living room, and music room—it contained both an upright piano and the table where they ate. There was a tiny bedroom and a tiny bathroom. At least it was a nice neighborhood, a pleasant ten-minute walk from the Yard. They had a cat, Ezra (after Ezra Pound), who came in and out of the window—inspiration for a short story, "Spring Comes to Cambridge," which Updike submitted to *The New Yorker*. It was rejected on the grounds that the quota of cat stories had already been filled. (This was not the end of Ezra's literary career. He was taken to Plowville when John graduated, and years later Linda wrote a story about him, "The Predator," which *The New Yorker* did accept.) In the cover letter Updike sent in with "Spring Comes to Cambridge," he asked if he could come to New York to discuss the possibility of finding work at the magazine. The rejection, from William Maxwell, came with a discouraging reply: "About the job—there doesn't seem anything at this time that would be right for you, and I wouldn't think it sensible for you to make a special trip down to talk about it." A polite, unequivocal no.

UPDIKE WAS TOO busy to brood. He was intent on achieving highest honors, and at the same time laying the groundwork for his future career by churning out a steady stream of drawings, light verse, and humorous prose for the *Lampoon*, and short stories for his writing classes. There were hurdles to clear, some trivial, some momentous. Harvard required that he pass a swimming test before graduating, which meant overcoming a history of hydrophobia ("I managed a froggy backstroke the length of the pool"). His oral examination by the English department went poorly; one of the examiners quoted Horace in Latin, and the examinee wobbled—"a babbling display of ignorance," he judged it. Although he complained that his senior thesis on Renaissance poet Robert Herrick was dull, it won the second Bowdoin Prize for best undergraduate essay in English. (Second prize was worth $300 that year; first prize, worth $500, was snagged by Kit Lasch for an essay on the rise of American imperialism in the late nineteenth century.) Updike also won the Dana Reed Prize ($100) for distinguished writing in an undergraduate publication, for a parody of Milton in the *Lampoon*, and a Knox Fellowship. Worth $2,400, the Knox was for study abroad, and it determined his immediate fate: he applied to the Ruskin School of Drawing and Fine Art in Oxford, England, and was accepted for the following academic year.

Asked by a classmate why he chose the Ruskin, he replied, "Because it's always been my ambition to be the next Walt Disney, but to do that I need to perfect my drawing." This wasn't a flip remark. Disney's *Peter Pan*, which came out halfway through Updike's junior year, went on to become the highest-grossing movie of the year. When Updike saw it a week after it opened, he was amazed by the variety of people seated around him in the theater, all evidently enjoying themselves. He was reminded of the hugely important cultural role of the animator—a "universal artist," and the object of Updike's envy. Harvard had steered him away from his dream of becoming a cartoonist, but his elitist education hadn't dimmed his enthusiasm for a medium with mass appeal. In a relaxed moment a month before graduation, he told his mother that he really shouldn't worry so much about achieving highest honors: "If I were reasonable, I wouldn't care at all, since the exact color of my degree will have little bearing on my ability to write and draw and sing my way into the heart of the American people." He wanted to entertain, and he wanted to be loved—if possible, universally.

Meanwhile, his reputation as a brilliant English student and the engine behind the *Lampoon* was spreading rapidly. Peter Judd, who was then president of the Signet, a venerable literary society with a handsome clubhouse on the corner of Dunster Street and Mount Auburn, took the unusual step of inviting Updike to join in his senior year—bypassing the usual selection process (most members are elected sophomore or junior year) and waiving the membership dues. "I seem to remember John accepting in a somewhat embarrassed way," said Judd. "I can't remember him in the clubhouse." He joined, but stayed away—until several years later when he was living in nearby Ipswich.

Judd, who roomed in Lowell House, had vivid memories of Updike:

> That long face with the nose accentuated in profile caught
> the attention. No one else in the dining hall looked like this
> rangy fellow who had none of the panache that many Har-
> vard boys assumed in those days, who dressed simply and
> didn't seem to mix.

Lowell was known in the mid-fifties as the intellectuals' house; the dining room discussions were raucous, opinionated, and sometimes pretentious. There was much dropping of literary names, especially of twentieth-century modernists. Updike did not participate. "He never liked intellectuals," said one college classmate; he avoided anyone who could outthink him, anyone who might represent competition. He also avoided the *Advocate* crowd and the writing class enthusiasts: "I was kind of a loner there too in a way," he told *Time* magazine in 1968. "I never was really with any literary group, and I felt that I was slightly an oddball." He and Mary often ate by themselves in the Lowell dining room, or with a roommate or two—the couple were a fixture there on Friday and Saturday nights. He was considered cool by some, aloof.

There are notably few references to Updike in Lasch's letters home during senior year. Late in the fall he makes a cameo appearance, helping out when Kit and his girlfriend need a place to sleep somewhere near New Haven on the night before the Yale game: John suggested they stay in Greenwich with his aunt Mary, recently widowed and happy to have some company. Otherwise, it's as though John had dropped out of college. It's tempting to read into Lasch's silence a brooding jealousy; there's no mention in his letters of any of the writing John was publishing in the *Lampoon*, no mention of his summa, no mention even of his second place in the Bowdoin competition. But the more likely explanation for the cooling of their friendship is that Updike was living off campus with his wife, studying hard and writing when he wasn't studying, and therefore somewhat disconnected from undergraduate life. No longer roommates, he and Kit rarely saw each other. Their correspondence after college, though perfectly friendly, was infrequent—they exchanged fewer than two dozen letters over the course of four decades—and, after seeing each other a few times in New York in the mid-fifties, met up only once or twice more before Lasch's death in 1994. A friendship that was for a brief while as close as any Updike ever had simply petered out.

Updike's "dull" thesis on Herrick has a forbidding title: "Non-Horatian Elements in Herrick's Echoes of Horace." Though it suffers in places from a plodding tone, it's a nearly flawless academic exercise, dutifully demonstrating the author's mastery of his subject as well as his ability to marshal evidence and draw plausible critical conclusions. His confidence is striking (he spars with T. S. Eliot in his introduction), as is his willingness to deploy ostentatiously unscholarly metaphors ("Horatian echoes . . . are sprinkled throughout the poem like flavoring in a smooth broth, quite unlike the rough stew of 'A Country Life,' where chunks of Horace float in an alien gravy"). More important, he seems to have found in Herrick's poetry a congenial model for his own writing. Consider this appreciation of Herrick's humility, which stems, according to Updike, from a "Christian awareness of the smallness of earthly things":

His poems are short, his subjects are trivial, his effects are delicate. Yet at the same time he is willing to describe tiny phenomena with the full attention and sympathy due to a "major" theme.

That could serve as an accurate description of Updike's early fiction. At least one scholar has suggested that the conclusion of the thesis "sounds a programmatic note for Updike's later career." Humility is again the essential feature:

> Compared with Catullus and Donne, Horace and Herrick do not feel deeply. Compared with Vergil and Milton, they possess little dramatic power. But by writing with care and by writing about things, however trivial or fanciful, which excited their imaginations, Horace and Herrick have created some of the world's most graceful poetry.

It would be absurd to claim that Horace and Herrick had a determining influence on Updike's early writing (his principal debt at this point, as he later admitted, was to Hemingway), but he does pay similarly sympathetic attention to "tiny phenomena," and he achieves similarly graceful effects. Carefully crafted, with a fine attention to the texture of provincial lives (circumscribed lives that nonetheless excited his imagination), his undergraduate stories are modest in ambition and somewhat cautious; though he evidently wasn't yet ready to take emotional or intellectual risks, he could handle with enviable dexterity (and Herrick-like humility) "the smallness of earthly things."

In the fall of senior year, he submitted to Albert Guérard's English Jb a short story called "Flick," about a young man who's just lost his job on a used-car lot. Flick is the nickname of the protagonist, Fred Anderson, a less savvy, more anxious version of Harry Angstrom. Like Rabbit, Flick is a high school hero whose skill with a basketball has not translated into post–high school success. He's married to a classmate, Evey, and they have a baby girl—but Evey has to work full-time, and their third-floor apartment is small and shabby. In other words, losing his job is a serious matter, and Flick dreads breaking the news to his smart-mouthed wife ("She'll pop her lid").

The echoes of Hemingway, as in this terse evocation of Flick's anxiety, are a reminder of how pervasive Papa's influence was at mid-century:

> His stomach was a little tight. It had been like that when he walked to the gymnasium alone in the dark and could see the people from town, kids and their parents, crowding the doors. But the locker room would be bright and hot, and the other guys would be there, laughing and towel-slapping, so the feeling went away. Now there were whole days when it didn't go away.

Elsewhere, what catches the eye—what caught Guérard's eye (he praised Updike's authentic portrait of "ordinary, 'everyday' damnation")—is the telling use of minute, convincing detail. Relying strictly on dialogue, gesture, and bursts of clear-eyed description, Updike shows us (without telling us) that things won't get any better for Flick and Evey, though Flick still tries to summon some of the old high school magic to block out the grim reality of their predicament. Here is Flick, fresh from being fired, driving home, listening to the radio:

> [H]e picked a cigaret from the pack on the sunshield, hung it from his lower lip, snapped a match across the rusty place on the dash, held it to the cigaret, dragged, and blew out the match, all in time to the music. He rolled down the window and flicked the match so it spun end over end right into the gutter. "Two points," he said and laughed for a syllable. He cocked the cigaret toward the roof and sucked the smoke way in, letting it bounce out of his nostrils a puff at a time. He was beginning to feel like himself, Flick Anderson, for the first time that day.

This is fast-paced, entertaining prose based on keen observation of lived life—already an achievement for a twenty-one-year-old still in college. What makes it especially good is the rich detail: the rust on the dashboard; the hint of foreshadowing in the match's trajectory; the unforced allusion to basketball, source of Flick's brittle self-esteem; the way he tries to calm his nerves with rote physical gestures. It adds up to a convincing psychological and sociological snapshot of a young, distressed, working-class American circa 1953. From his father, Updike had heard many stories about how the students at Shillington High School, especially the star athletes, fared after graduation. "Flick" captures the type exactly, by showing us a quirky, undeniably real individual. Impressed, Guérard suggested to Updike that he submit the story to *The New Yorker*.

"Flick" was rejected, but a year later (after several poems and another story had been accepted) he resubmitted it as "Ace in the Hole." Though the nickname of the protagonist (now Ace) had changed along with the title (now a clever play on words), the story published in the April 9, 1955, issue of *The New Yorker* is otherwise almost exactly the same story Updike handed in for his Harvard writing class.

Richly evocative of a particular time and place, the original version takes its sociology for granted; it focuses narrowly, without making any explicit judgment whatsoever, on an hour or so of Ace's unhappy afternoon. When Updike revised the story nearly fifty years later for *The Early Stories*, however, he superimposed a layer of ethnic and religious tension: Evey is now a Roman Catholic, and defensive about it; Ace allows himself to call an Italian-looking kid who taunts him a "miserable wop"; Ace's boss has a new name (Goldman instead of Friedman); and Ace, offering his opinion of his boss, who's just fired him, reveals what looks like an anti-Semitic streak: "He just wanted too much for his money," he says. "That kind does." These changes are significant, if only because they underscore the clean simplicity of the earlier version, which is like a peephole on a world utterly different from the Harvard milieu in which it was written. The lively accuracy of the scene he paints is its own reward; it pleases, much in the way Herrick pleases, because it treats—to borrow Updike's undergraduate assessment of the poet—"tiny phenomena with the full attention and sympathy due to a 'major' theme." Or to put it another way, he fulfilled, age twenty-one, his writerly duty as he still saw it half a century later: "to give the mundane its beautiful due."

The same can be said for "Friends from Philadelphia," a story he wrote immediately after graduation, at the Penningtons' summer place, in South Duxbury, Vermont, near Montpelier. He and Mary took the train north, and a neighbor picked them up and drove them out to the farmhouse, a rustic spot three miles off the main road, up the side of a mountain. Leslie Pennington had bought the property for two hundred dollars during the Depression, and the family used it only during the summer months. John and Mary had volunteered to open it up and get it ready for her parents' arrival. John didn't really like the house—it was too much like Plowville, and even more isolated—but once they'd done their chores, there was certainly plenty of time to write.

He typed out "Friends from Philadelphia" on his father-in-law's typewriter and sent it off to *The New Yorker*. By the time he received a letter from William Maxwell (dated August 5) announcing that the magazine was "delighted" with the story, and inviting him to the city to discuss over lunch his future as a *New Yorker* writer, Updike and his wife had migrated south to Plowville, trading one set of parents for the other. He never forgot the moment when he retrieved the envelope from the mailbox at the end of the drive, the same mailbox that had yielded so many rejection slips, both his and his mother's: "I felt, standing and reading the good news in the midsummer pink dusk of the stony road beside a field of waving weeds, born as a professional writer." To extend the metaphor, though the gestation period that led to this gratifying birth had been quite long (he'd fallen in love with the magazine a full decade earlier), the actual labor was brief and painless: he passed from unpublished college student to valued contributor in less than two months—"the ecstatic breakthrough of my literary life," he later called it.

His very first *New Yorker* short story (following the acceptance of two poems "Duet, with Muffled Brake Drums" and "Ex-

Basketball Player"), "Friends from Philadelphia" also marks the first appearance of John Nordholm, Updike's original Olinger alter ego, one of a succession of fictional teenage boys blessed and burdened with the author's character traits and family situation. Like "Ace in the Hole," the story appears at first to be a modest affair. There are only four characters, and the action, which amounts to a trivial errand, is complete in little more than half an hour: fifteen-year-old John Nordholm, trying to buy a bottle of wine at his mother's behest for the eponymous friends from Philadelphia, enlists the help of the Lutz family—Thelma Lutz, his classmate, and her parents. Again, the heart of the story is the revelation of character through dialogue, detail, and gesture. John is too young—too young to buy wine and too young for Thelma (just barely). The first line of the story ("In the moment before the door was opened to him, he glimpsed her thigh below the half-drawn shade") suggests that John is on the brink of new experiences; the door will be opened, the shade will be raised, and the mystery obscurely typified by that glimpse of thigh will be laid bare. But not yet. "Friends from Philadelphia" is cheerful and sly; it winks broadly at sexuality ("When she looks like that, John thought, I could bite her lip until it bleeds") without allowing the clamor of adolescent urges to take center stage. John and Thelma play somewhat larger roles than Thelma's mother and father, but each of the four characters is complex enough to excite the reader's curiosity. As a result, the story never feels slight—a faint air of mystery gives it depth and poignancy, and balances the gentle comedy.

In the introduction to *Olinger Stories*, Updike felt obliged to respond to the charge that the story has no point: "The point, to me, is plain, and is the point, more or less, of all these Olinger stories. *We are rewarded unexpectedly.*" The reward, in this case, takes the form of a twist at the very end of the story: the bottle of wine Thelma's father buys (and pays for), a Château Mouton Rothschild 1937, is much finer than anything John or his parents would have thought to ask for, an act of random generosity that lifts the ending like an exclamation point.

Updike gave competing versions of the genesis of the story (which not only launched his professional career but remained, despite his prodigious output, his mother's favorite). At one point he claimed he was reacting against the sardonic tone of a John Cheever story, "O Youth and Beauty!" (which was published in *The New Yorker* a full year earlier, in the summer of 1953): "Cheever's story involved drunkenness and a sudden death by pistol shot, and to my innocent palate it tasted as rasping and sour as a belt of straight bourbon. I thought to myself, 'There must be more to American life than this,' and wrote an upbeat little story, with an epiphanic benefaction at the end, to prove it." It's true that in his senior year Updike had taken against Cheever, calling him "one of my greatest enemies" and deploring his cocky writing and his anger at his miserable characters. But in the introduction to *The Early Stories* (written nearly half a century after the fact), he gave credit to J. D. Salinger. Leaving Cheever out of it entirely, Updike confided that the unexpectedly excellent bottle of wine (the "epiphanic benefaction") "owes something" to the dead Easter chick in the bottom of the wastebasket at the end of "Just Before the War with the Eskimos." Neither account is wholly persuasive. More important than either Cheever or Salinger was the inspiration Updike drew from setting the story in Shillington—or Olinger, as he decided to call it several years later.

Though he never gives the name of the place where Thelma lives, he was picturing his hometown, inhabiting the location with a ferocious intensity, creating Olinger with the force of his Shillington memories. In a letter to his editor, he specified that the Lutzes' house is at 17 Spruce Street and the liquor store at the corner of Lancaster Avenue and Sterley Street. He had in mind both an exact address and real people. The characters were immediately recognizable to any Shillington reader as John himself and the family of his classmate Joan Venne.

Looking back ten years later, he had the impression that "Friends from Philadelphia" was written by someone to whom "everything outside Olinger—Harvard, marriage, Vermont—seemed relatively unreal." He entered completely into the world of his story, the recollected world of a tall, awkward, eager small-town teenager named John; in the grip of this creative fervor, he lost sight of his current surroundings—his wife, her parents' lonely farmhouse, the chill of the early summer evenings—and saw only the Shillington of his boyhood.

He paid his hometown another virtual visit in a poem written in midsummer called "Ex-Basketball Player," which *The New Yorker* accepted three days before "Friends from Philadelphia." Updike's most popular poem, widely anthologized and often taught in school, it's a portrait of Flick Webb, a sadder, more remote sibling of Ace Anderson (whose name was Flick in the first draft of the story). Here, too, the geography is exact, and cleverly blended into the narrative, the mise-en-scène being an abortive sprint up the court:

> Pearl Avenue runs past the high-school lot,
> Bends with the trolley tracks, and stops, cut off
> Before it has a chance to go two blocks,
> At Colonel McComsky Plaza. Berth's Garage
> Is on the corner facing west, and there,
> Most days, you'll find Flick Webb, who helps Berth out.

The garage itself, with its anthropomorphic gas pumps, is pure Olinger, and so is the luncheonette where Flick spends his time when he's not working, the details lovingly observed and ingeniously shaped to fit the requirements of a lyric poem.

Even as he was meditating on postgraduation failure, Updike was achieving exactly the opposite. "I had given myself five years to become a 'writer,' and my becoming one immediately has left me with an uneasy, apologetic sense of having blundered through the wrong door." The proximate result of his rapid launch was twofold: a redoubling of his ambition (he peppered *The New Yorker* with submissions in the weeks after his breakthrough) and, perversely, a simmering, low-key grudge against his alma mater.

In "The Christian Roommates," Updike wrote that Harvard "demands of each man, before it releases him, a wrenching sacrifice of ballast." To judge from other equivocal remarks about a college career that changed his life in many ways, he obviously felt that he himself had made some such sacrifice. What kind of ballast had he felt obliged to jettison? And was the loss truly wrenching? Harvard made him an outsider in Shillington—a blow, to be sure, though the distance this estrangement opened up allowed him to use the town for his fiction. Harvard took away Shillington, but it gave him Olinger—or, at the very least, sharpened the tools he would need for the excavation of his home turf. And yet instead of feeling grateful to the institution, he felt grateful to the town. It was Shillington he thanked in the poems collected in *Endpoint*, when he knew he was dying (" . . . Perhaps / we meet our heaven at the start and not / at the end of life"). For having finished off the project begun by his mother when she insisted on moving him out of Shillington to the Plowville farmhouse, the college received no thanks at all. If anything, he associated it with his betrayal of the town he'd loved as a child and still cherished in memory.

"Four years was enough Harvard. I still had a lot to learn, but had been given the liberating notion that now I could teach myself." His formal education was at an end; his education as a writer was under way. He was, for now, an arrow aimed at the bull's-eye of *The New Yorker*.

The day before he sailed for England to take up his place at Oxford's Ruskin School, he stopped by the magazine's offices at the invitation of William Maxwell, the editor who'd sent the momentous letter accepting "Friends from Philadelphia." The *New Yorker* waiting room was blandly anonymous, and the linoleum corridors a drab maze, but the young college graduate was nonetheless dazzled by the visit. Maxwell showed off his sunny office, then ferried him a short distance along Forty-Third Street for lunch at his club, the Century Association, a venerable establishment housed in an elegant and imposing Beaux Arts building designed by McKim, Mead and White. Updike himself would become a member of the Century in 1972—the membership is composed of "authors, artists, and amateurs of letters and the fine arts"—but on the day of that first lunch, September 3, 1954, he was being vetted by an even more exclusive organization.

That afternoon, Maxwell sent a memo to his colleague Katharine White; it offers a shrewd portrait of the twenty-two-year-old writer:

Just a note to tell you that Updike turned up and I took him to lunch. Had you met him? Very modest, shy, intelligent humorous youngster, slightly gawky in his manner and already beginning, being an artist, to turn it into a kind of style, by way of self-defense.

In later years, Maxwell emphasized the idea that Updike was putting on an act. "The first time I took him to lunch," he told a journalist in 1972, "John was amusing and charming—and pretended to an awkwardness he clearly didn't feel. I knew that he couldn't be that talented and perceptive and still be a country boy." Maxwell wasn't alone in identifying Updike's manner as a kind of self-defense. Others noted that he paraded his mix of teasing humor and gawkiness (the uneasy, apologetic, blundered-through-the-wrong-door routine) in order to keep the world at arm's length. One old friend called it his "passive-aggressive aw-shucks pose." Another friend who met Updike in the early days at *The New Yorker* disagreed with Maxwell's suggestion that the "youngster" was "very modest." This friend believed that "despite the veneer of shyness, John was confident in his way of being." In any case, Maxwell liked the youngster very much; with the blessing of William Shawn, the magazine's editor, he offered Updike a job, telling him that when he got back from his year in England there would be a place waiting at *The New Yorker*, a message repeated by Katharine White nine months later when she and her husband visited Oxford. The door was now open to the most successful and prestigious magazine of the day—"the object," as Updike put it, "of my fantasies and aspirations since I was thirteen."

It's worth pausing here to marvel at the unrelieved smoothness of his professional path. Is there an American writer who so quickly and painlessly established himself with a magazine that could provide a lucrative, conspicuous, and highly respected venue for his work? F. Scott Fitzgerald made a great deal of money in his twenties writing for *The Saturday Evening Post*, but he later came to see the association as a blot on his literary reputation—and nobody would argue that the manic Fitzgerald had a smooth ride. Among the other twentieth-century American writers who made a splash before their thirtieth birthday (the list includes Upton Sinclair, Ernest Hemingway, John O'Hara, William Saroyan, Norman Mailer, Flannery O'Connor, William Styron, Gore Vidal, Harold Brodkey, Philip Roth, and Thomas Pynchon), none piled up accomplishments in as orderly a fashion as Updike, or with as little fuss. If he was, as he later claimed, angry, he tamped it down. He wasn't despairing or thwarted or resentful; he wasn't alienated or conflicted or drunk; he quarreled with no one. In short, he cultivated none of the professional deformations that habitually plague American writers. Even his neuroses were tame. Except for his psoriasis, his stutter, and his intermittent religious doubts, he faced no obstacle that hard work and natural talent couldn't overcome.

This frictionless success has sometimes been held against him. His vast oeuvre materialized with suspiciously little visible effort. Where there's no struggle, can there be real art? The Romantic notion of the tortured poet has left us with a mild prejudice against the idea of art produced in a calm, rational, workmanlike manner (as he put it, "on a healthy basis of regularity and avoidance of strain"), but that's precisely how Updike got his start. When he arrived at *The New Yorker*, he hadn't yet written anything resembling a masterpiece (he sensibly aimed at the achievable goal of turning out stories and poems his favorite magazine would be likely to buy), but he was building for himself, plank by plank, a stable platform on which to perform more daring feats.

If ever a writer, a magazine and a time were made for each other, the writer was John Updike, the magazine was the *New Yorker* and the time was the 1950s.
　　—Ben Yagoda, *About Town: The* New Yorker *and the World It Made*

III.

The Talk of the Town

The arrow took a detour en route to the target. John and Mary, who was by now two months pregnant, sailed from New York on September 4, 1954, aboard the RMS *Caronia*. Waving good-bye from the pier were both sets of parents, two aunts, a great-aunt, and friends from Cambridge. Although Mary was very seasick, they both found the crossing quite wonderful; luxurious, even for passengers who weren't traveling first class; and exciting: neither of them had been to Europe before, and this was the first great adventure of their married life. They arrived in Southampton after ten days at sea, made their way by train to Oxford, and set about finding a place to live.

Their address for the next ten months was a basement flat at 213 Iffley Road, a half-hour walk from the Ruskin School of Drawing and Fine Art (housed, in those years, in a wing of the university's Ashmolean Museum). Their comfortably furnished sitting room was three steps down from the street; looking out the bay window, they could watch the legs of passersby. A long corridor led to a bedroom heated by a metered gas fire, a bathroom with a tub and a sink, and a kitchen with a cold stone floor. Outside the kitchen door, in the small backyard, was the outhouse, a feature of midcentury English plumbing that brought back memories of Plowville.

Though dank and gray, pinched by British postwar austerity and their own modest means, and made gloomier by bouts of homesickness, the young couple's Oxford interlude was nonetheless an idyll of sorts. John had nearly a month to get settled before his art classes began. Mary registered with the maternity ward of Oxford's Radcliffe Hospital, which told them to expect the baby on or about March 20, 1955. The National Health Service wanted all mothers to give birth at home if they possibly could, and declared that that was what Mary should do, but she tearfully insisted that she could *not*—that she had no relatives in the country and needed the reassurance of a hospital staff. She got her way, but was soon attending compulsory natural childbirth classes.

When the Ruskin opened its doors in October, Updike was put to work drawing from plaster-cast copies of antique statues tucked away in far-flung corridors of the Ashmolean; he also painted still lifes of fruit and crockery. By mid-November he'd been "promoted" to the life drawing class; he complained, comically, that the model kept staring at him and sneering ("Nothing like a sneering nude to set a man's pencil trembling"). In the winter term, calculating that she had several months before the baby was born, Mary enrolled as a part-time student and joined one of John's still-life classes. As far as his future was concerned, the Ruskin was a dead end: by the time he left England, his dream of becoming the next Walt Disney had been definitively abandoned, largely because his writing career was flourishing. And yet his association with the school remained a source of bemused pride; in the vast majority of his books, even those published more than a half century after he'd put his paintbrushes away for good, he continued to cite on the jacket flap, in the caption beneath the photo of the gradually graying author, that year in Oxford (and occasionally the Knox Fellowship that funded it). Studying at the Ruskin did improve his draftsmanship, but even he could now clearly see where his talent lay. (A talent demonstrated in the exact and evocative prose he summoned to describe the school's grand museum home: "the sooty, leonine sprawl of the

Ashmolean.") He said that his year of professional training in the visual arts sharpened his writing: "I've never done anything harder than try to paint things the way they are. The amount of concentration it takes to mix a color and put it in the right spot was really a very good lesson for me as far as accuracy in all things artistic." Another, more concretely profitable benefit was a short story, "Still Life," written in 1958 and promptly sold to *The New Yorker*, about a young American studying at the Constable, a British art school housed in a "vast university museum."

At Christmas they went to Paris for a week. Directly across the Seine from Notre Dame they found a large but shabby room with a flaking ceiling and a bidet (which John thought "blandly obscene") next to the bed; the floor-to-ceiling windows looked out on the cathedral. Despite the cold, they wandered on foot through the city, climbing to the top of Notre Dame, though Mary was by now six months pregnant. Like good art students, they explored the Louvre. They spoke so little French, as John remembered it, that in restaurants they could order only "omelette aux champignons":

> Mary, in need of a bathroom, asked, as Radcliffe French 101 had told her to . . . for the salle de bain.* "Salle de bain!? Ut, ut, alors"—all the waitresses, cooks, etc. rushed forward to examine this charming (and by now fiercely blushing) young American lady to discover why, at eleven o'clock in the morning, she needed, in a restaurant, such abrupt ablution. It was, of course, a toilette she needed. Ah, toilette, toilette—and everything came right at last.

Paris is largely absent from Updike's fiction, but that particular scene came back to him, years later, with "almost unbearable affection."

In the week before their trip to Paris, he'd written "March: A Birthday Poem," which *The New Yorker* bought in January and pub-

---

* Actually, Mary never studied French at Radcliffe; she was relying on the classes she took in high school.

lished in mid-February. A celebration of the month in which his first child would be born, it's the best verse Updike wrote in Oxford, playful but essentially serious, keenly observed, wide-ranging, and imbued with a kind of folk wisdom, as though the young poet were eager to claim a degree of maturity before becoming a parent:

> The color of March is the one that lies
> On the shadow side of young tree trunks.

Despite the long, bouncy bus rides the couple took through the countryside hoping the jolts would bring on labor, the baby was late. As the last days of March trickled away, Updike saw the joke coming—sure enough, Elizabeth Pennington Updike was born on April Fools' Day. Updike's only consolation was that at the early morning hour when Elizabeth came into the world, it was still March in the United States—just barely.

John's parents had to content themselves with drawings of Elizabeth sent in the mail, accompanied by a burst of rapturous emotion; later there were photos, and humorous, baffled descriptions of the neonate's endearing habits. Mary's parents, however, had an early chance to see their granddaughter in the flesh. The Penningtons arrived in England shortly after Easter, for a three-month exchange: Leslie was to serve as minister at the Unitarian Church of Liverpool, while his English counterpart took up duties in Chicago. The Penningtons and the young Updikes, baby Elizabeth included, spent a week together in the Lake District, walking and admiring the scenery.

It was on this otherwise happy excursion—the weather was excellent—that John and Leslie had their first long religious discussion, which was fraught, according to Mary: "I think John really disapproved of Unitarian theology, and was trying to hold on to his own faith. They were quite quarrelsome and I was shocked. He was insulting my father, who took it pretty calmly." Updike confessed in *Self-Consciousness* that he and his "gentle" father-in-law had "tense" arguments in which John "insisted that the object of faith must have some concrete attributes"—that is, that God must be actual, Christ divine, and the human soul immortal. He was, essentially, attacking Unitarianism—and hence Leslie's ministry. The mild Unitarian outlook, exemplified by Leslie's notion that the "human need for transcendence should be met with minimal embarrassments to reason," was an insidious threat to the tenets of John's sometimes wobbly faith: the Lutheran doctrine of sacramental union, for instance, is meaningless if one isn't prepared to believe in the "concrete attributes" of the Eucharist. That kind of belief, which John grew up with, puts reason under pressure. Though the dispute was awkward for Mary, her father, however gentle, was resolute in his beliefs; he stood his ground (as John's own father would probably not have done), and John, unused to contending with a strong male figure, refused to drop it, even for Mary's sake. In fact, Mary's presence probably made John more stubbornly argumentative.

He went to church a few times during the year in England, but not regularly. He told his mother he was trying hard to be a Christian. To ward off doubt, he turned to theology: G. K. Chesterton, the French philosopher Jacques Maritain, C. S. Lewis. He remembered with particular fondness a pamphlet by Ian T. Ramsey, an Oxford don who later became bishop of Durham, called "Miracles: An Exercise in Logical Map-Work." Although clearly uneasy about his faith, John did not share his worries with Mary.

In letters to Harvard classmates he complained of the damp and the cold ("The English climate doesn't seem suited to anything but trying to build fires and going to sleep") and the natives ("Englishmen are astoundingly ignorant about the U.S. . . . and proud of it. A bad lot. Easy to see why the 19th century, author of all our woes, was so mismanaged—the British were in charge"). He asked for baseball news and despaired of ever understanding cricket. The infrequent gripes are either lighthearted or tongue-in-cheek. He might as easily have complained of his homesickness or the disorientation of being a stranger in a strange land. The aim of the letters was at least in part to solicit replies. Linda helped in that regard, showering the young couple with the news from Plowville, along with her bracing brand of encouragement. Coming from across the Atlantic, these maternal missives were suddenly very welcome.*

On the whole, isolation and foreignness seemed to work in Updike's favor: he kept up the furious rate of production he'd achieved the previous summer. "He typed automatically, whenever he could," according to Mary, often at a little table by the bay window. *The New Yorker* bought three new stories, "Tomorrow and Tomorrow and So Forth," "Dentistry and Doubt," and "The Kid's Whistling," along with a dozen poems, so that by April he'd triggered a "quantity bonus" in his agreement with the magazine; for the rest of the year his work commanded a higher rate. He was already, in other words, a frequent contributor.

Relations with the magazine were formalized even before the Updikes had settled in at Iffley Road. A letter from Katharine White dated September 15, 1954, and addressed to "John H. Updike, General Delivery, Oxford," proposed that he sign a "first-reading agreement," a scheme devised for the "most valued and most constant contributors." Up to this point, he had had only one story accepted, along with some light verse. White acknowledged that it was "rather unusual" for the magazine to make this kind of offer to a contributor "of such short standing," but she and Maxwell and Shawn took into consideration the volume of his submissions (including the stories and poems that had been rejected), and their overall quality and suitability, and decided that this clever, hard-working young man showed exceptional promise. In return for a first look at his "verse, fiction, humor, reminiscence, casuals, etc.," *The New Yorker* agreed to pay him 25 percent "extra" for any work it did buy, plus a quarterly "cost of living adjustment" (known in-house as a COLA), which usually amounted to a bonus of about another 25 percent. To further sweeten the deal, White included a check for one hundred dollars—"a symbol of our good faith," she said, "to bind the bargain."

---

* "While he had been abroad, his mother's letters—graceful, witty, informative, cheerful—had been his main link with home" (from "Home," a story Updike wrote in March 1960).

It sounded like a generous deal—Updike signed without hesitation—and he made a considerable amount of money from his *New Yorker* fiction right from the start. But White's phrase—"bind the bargain"—is a reminder that the purpose of the deal was in fact to bind the young writer to the magazine. The truth of the matter is that *The New Yorker* paid what it liked (above a certain minimum). "We price every manuscript separately according to what we think its value is to us," White frankly acknowledged, "and this pricing may, I suppose, often seem whimsical to a contributor. It is." Some of Updike's contemporaries (notably John Cheever) were consistently underpaid by the magazine—but this shabby treatment seemed curiously arbitrary, or as White put it, whimsical. Updike himself was never underpaid; on the contrary, he reaped immediate benefit from the first-reading agreement: for "Friends from Philadelphia," the story he sold before signing the agreement, he was paid $490; for his next, "Ace in the Hole," he was paid $612.50; and for his third, "Tomorrow and Tomorrow and So Forth," $826. For Updike, at the time, these were staggeringly large sums. His father's yearly salary was $1,200; the idea that he could earn more than his father with just a few stories made a lasting impression.[*]

Of course, there were also many, many rejections; over the course of the year, *The New Yorker* turned down roughly half the work he submitted. He weathered each verdict without protest. ("In many ways," he bravely claimed, "a rejection is more bracing than an acceptance.") Early on, he tried submitting rejected poems to other magazines, *Punch*, say, or *The Atlantic Monthly*, but he met with scant success, and soon enough he was writing with only *The New Yorker* in mind. The magazine with the first-reading agreement was thus the only one doing any reading at all; in the early years, a story or poem that was turned down was almost always abandoned rather than revised.

---

[*] Updike's Form 1099 shows that *The New Yorker* paid him a total of $1,003 in 1954. Considering that he had graduated from college only in June, and that from October he was enrolled at the Ruskin, it was a handsomely remunerative first year as a writer.

He was exceedingly polite in his long-distance dealings with the editors, saying thank you again and again, making it clear that he venerated *The New Yorker* and was grateful even to be in glancing contact with it. To both White, who edited the majority of the work he sent from England, and Maxwell, who took charge when she was away from the office, he expressed his confidence in the magazine's judgment and admiration for its legendary attention to detail. Very quickly he added a flirty personal edge to his correspondence. His letters were professional, in that he was negotiating from across the Atlantic the business of getting his words into print in the best possible shape—but he also wanted to make friends. And he did.

His first conquest was Katharine White. A formidable woman who went to work at *The New Yorker* in 1925, just six months after Harold Ross founded it, she was almost single-handedly responsible for the magazine's emergence as a prestigious venue for serious fiction. Over the course of her career, she edited John O'Hara, Vladimir Nabokov, Jean Stafford, and Mary McCarthy, to name just a few. In her obituary, William Shawn wrote, "More than any other editor except Harold Ross himself, Katharine White gave *The New Yorker* its shape, and set it on its course." Born Katharine Sergeant to a Brahmin family in Boston, she arrived at the magazine as Katharine Angell (her first husband was Ernest Angell, a lawyer with whom she had a son, Roger, who eventually became Updike's editor—an unusual dynastic succession); in 1929 she married a younger *New Yorker* colleague, E. B. ("Andy") White. By the time she began editing Updike, she was in her early sixties, and treated him, as she did her other authors, with a firm maternal hand, mixing encouragement with the occasional reproof. She also made evident her affection for him. Ten years after her death in 1977, he wrote about the warmth she conveyed, her "aristocratic sureness of taste," her "instinctive courage and integrity," her "ethical ardor"; he also stressed that her "good humor and resilience were as conspicuous as her dignity and (when provoked) her hauteur." All these qualities (and also a meticulous, sometimes comical attention to minutiae) are on display in the letters that arrived almost daily at the Updikes' basement flat. They provided what Updike (like any writer just starting out) needed most: critical approbation from someone who radiated commanding authority.

White was motherly, but not like his mother. Though they were both forceful, tenacious, intelligent women with strong opinions, their styles were utterly different: Linda Updike had none of Katharine White's polish and none of her "hauteur"; she was more impulsive, irascible, and unconventional than the *New Yorker* editor. Twenty-three years of coping with his mother had nonetheless been excellent training for Updike's first important relationship of his professional career. In particular, his correspondence with his mother during the Harvard years prepared him for the challenge of coping at a distance with another demanding character who was observing him intently and doing her best to further his career.

By taking scrupulous care with his work, by engaging sympathetically with every aspect of his writing, from subject matter to punctuation, White encouraged Updike's equally scrupulous commitment. They bonded over dashes, colons, and commas—most amazingly in an exchange of letters in the last two months of 1954 concerning two poems, "The Sunflower" and "The Clan." She wanted to make his punctuation consistent; he wanted to make his light verse flow in a manner pleasing to the ear and the eye. When he suggested changes to the proof of "Sunflower"—literally begging for a colon rather than a dash at the end of a particular line ("A colon is compact, firm, and balanced: a dash is sprawling, wishy-washy, and gawky. The colon suggests the Bible: the dash letters and memoirs of fashionable ladies")—she replied with a three-page "treatise on punctuation" and a transcription of the relevant paragraph from H. W. Fowler's *Dictionary of Modern English Usage* (the standard reference at *The New Yorker*, thanks to Harold Ross, who always kept a copy handy). She urged him to "try to feel more kindly toward the dash"—and closed with characteristic graciousness: "I want to add that I am delighted to find anyone who cares as much as this about punctuation and who is as careful as you are about your verse. . . . And I thank you for a very interesting and amusing letter."

The back-and-forth between these two sticklers grew more and more affectionate; in March, she suggested that soon she would have to "break down" and begin her letters "Dear John." In the same missive, she announced that she and her husband were planning a trip to England in the first weeks of June, and proposed that they visit the Updikes in Oxford. As the plans for this visit took shape, he continued to address her as "Mrs. White" (he never graduated to "Dear Katharine"), but he now launched freely into personal matters, with a charming description, for example, of the infant Elizabeth; he sent bulletins, as the baby grew, giving her precise weight.

An intelligent, fastidious, clear-sighted editor, White did Updike far more good than harm—but her advice wasn't always for the best. She steered him away from writing about his Pennsylvania background, and discouraged him from indulging in wistful reminiscence, which turned out to be one of his most fruitful fictional modes. In February, rejecting a story called "Have a Good Life," about a young man from a small town very much like Shillington who plays a game of pickup basketball on his last day at home before going off to get married, White suggested that he should avoid stories in which "a young man looks back nostalgically at his basketball-playing days."* She noted that they had two similar items by him awaiting publication ("Ace in the Hole" and "Ex-Basketball Player"), and warned of a glut of characters looking back regretfully: "[W]e get so many that we have to be extra severe in our judgment of all stories on this theme." Eager as always to please, Updike apologized, admitting that he hadn't noticed how often he was writing about nostalgia, and as a result of her intervention, there were no more stories about his youth for the next two years. Not until she'd retired and he'd left New York for Ipswich did he produce "The Alligators" and "The Happiest I've Been," two Olinger stories dripping with nostalgia (the latter featuring John Nordholm, the boy from "Friends from Philadelphia")—a breakthrough that allowed him to write some of his finest fiction. It's a dirty trick of literary fate that White's description of the kind of story Updike should avoid—a young man who

---

* "Have a Good Life" is set in Willow, as was the eponymous novel Updike began in his sophomore year at Harvard and abandoned about two thirds of the way through.

looks back nostalgically at his basketball-playing days—is precisely the starting point for *Rabbit, Run*, his first major success.

Very few of White's judgments were off the mark. She encouraged him, for instance, to write about "the domestic scene and the subtleties and affectionate and agonizing complexities of husband-wife-children relationships." Her taste was for short stories about relatively refined characters—better educated and more privileged than would ordinarily be found in Shillington. Confronted with Berks County material, she expressed the hope that he would choose "an entirely different locale"—England, for instance. She suggested he try writing about "a young married American who is doing graduate work at Oxford." Updike obliged with a story that's essentially made to order.

"Dentistry and Doubt," which he sold to *The New Yorker* in April (shortly before his theological altercation with his father-in-law), is a slice of Updike's English life, about a young American clergyman's visit to an Oxford dentist's office. The clergyman, Burton, is writing his master's thesis on Richard Hooker, an early Anglican theologian. As he endures the dentist's ministrations ("Now, this may hurt a little") and the stilted small talk specifically tailored for an American patient ("What part are you from?"), Burton's mind drifts to the religious doubts he was experiencing earlier that morning, a brief tussle with faith that gives the story some heft. But the best thing about "Dentistry and Doubt" is the intensely observed detail, Burton's catalogue of sights and sensations, all made more vivid because they're unfamiliar, this being his first visit to a foreign dentist.

Katharine White gratefully expressed her approval: "We think it is the best written prose you have done yet." And indeed, Updike's prose is subtly different in this story—bolder and richer—a sign perhaps that his training at the Ruskin was already having an effect. But the Ruskin must share any credit with Henry Green, whose novels Updike discovered soon after he arrived in England.[*] Green's influ-

---

[*] A few months later, Updike read his first Nabokov, "Pnin's Day," in the April 23, 1955, issue of *The New Yorker*.

ence helps to account for a new softness in Updike's writing—a lingering, tender touch—and a new daring. The syntax is looser, more flowing, and the metaphors more striking. Updike gives us Burton's view from the dentist's chair with minute precision, and an audacious simile: "The dentist's eyes were not actually gray; screwed up, they seemed more brown, and then, as they flicked toward the tool tray, rather green, like pebbles on the bed of a fast-running creek." When the drilling is done, Burton becomes aware of the dentist's array of tools "as things in which an unlimited excitement inhered." Updike lists various items—tweezers, picks, drill burrs, tiny cotton balls—and tells us that they traveled to Burton's senses "burdened with delight and power." Here, as in the many lively descriptions of the birds at the feeding station outside the dentist's window, one can see the early traces of Green's enduring influence.*

The first sentence of Updike's introduction to a Penguin Classics edition of three Henry Green novels, *Living, Party Going,* and *Loving,* begins, teasingly, "If I say that Henry Green taught me how to write . . . ," and then sidesteps the issue by asserting that writing isn't learned. Part of what appealed to Updike was that he and Green (another unusually precocious talent) shared certain writerly traits, including a fascination with seemingly unimportant quotidian detail. There was admiration, and also the shock of recognition. "He is a saint of the mundane," Updike wrote, "embracing it with all his being." Updike praised the "intensity of witnessing" in Green's "limpid realism." Green's accomplishment reassured Updike that his own inclination was leading him along the right path. Green unlocked in him a lyrical impulse, and spurred him to make his prose style an active, expressive element in his fiction. Also important were Green's "formal ambitiousness" and his "allegiance to the modernistic tradition." Along with Proust, whom Updike began to read the next year, when he was living in New York, Green served as a kind of literary

---

* Updike had perhaps already noticed, when he wrote "Dentistry and Doubt," that Green was particularly interested in birds: "[T]hey play flitting, cooing chorus to book after book," he wrote in a review of Green's first novel, *Blindness,* when it was reissued in 1978.

goad: "Both quite bowled me over," Updike remembered, "showing me what words could do, in bringing reality up tight against the skin of the paper." He gave the two authors credit for a "considerable expansion" of his literary ambitions. Although "Dentistry and Doubt" isn't actually all that much more ambitious than "Ace in the Hole" (and it would be hard to claim that it's a better story), Green had left his mark. Updike added him to the pantheon of modern "textual Titans" he'd worshipped at Harvard—the difference being that now, less than a year out of college, he began to hope that he, too, might one day be hailed as a titan.

Not all his encounters with eminent literary figures took place between the covers of a book. At a tea party in Oxford, Updike met his first celebrated author, the Irish novelist (and *New Yorker* contributor) Joyce Cary, and found him to be "full of a tender excitement, the excitement of those certain they are loved." Updike's Lowell House classmate Peter Judd, who was studying at Magdalene College, drove him to London in his Hillman Minx convertible to meet James Thurber. The occasion had been arranged by a Radcliffe friend, Nora Sayre, whose father, Joel Sayre, was a longtime *New Yorker* contributor. Her idea was that the magazine's future should come face-to-face with its past. (Though Thurber was still contributing stories and cartoons to the magazine in the 1950s, he was no longer as prolific as he'd been in previous decades.) Sayre knew, moreover, that Updike adored both Thurber's drawings and his writing. And yet the meeting was a flop. A tall, big-boned man with an unruly thatch of white hair, Thurber was by this time completely blind. After being led into the room by his wife, he launched into a monologue that lasted all afternoon. The assembled youngsters listened with rapt attention—except for Updike, who was dismayed to discover that he was bored by the rote recitation of anecdotes he'd read with delight as a child. He later claimed to have made some fawning attempts at conversation with the great man, but, according to Judd, Updike "rose to no bait, asked no questions." He was "diffident"—"clearly not willing either to present himself as a rising star or to sit at the feet of the master." The experience had the unfortunate consequence of diminishing his pleasure in Thurber's work.

Despite the disappointment of the encounter with Thurber, Updike was eager to greet his *New Yorker* editor Katharine White and her husband, E. B. White, another childhood hero and a great favorite of his mother, who adored White's essays about his Maine farmhouse. The Whites, who were stopping in Oxford on the way to the Cotswolds, pulled up outside the basement flat on Iffley Road in a black limousine driven by a liveried chauffeur, a fact the instinctively decent and unassuming Andy White remembered with considerable embarrassment. Whereas Thurber was oblivious, absorbed in his own performance, White was scrupulously attentive to those around him; when he spoke, what he said was designed to put his listeners at ease. His wife, who surprised the Updikes by being plump and short, as opposed to tall and regal, also thrilled them by reiterating over lunch William Maxwell's promise: a job at *The New Yorker* would be waiting for John when he returned from Europe.

The Updikes left England in early July, first traveling by train to Liverpool to stay with Mary's parents, then sailing from there aboard the MV *Britannic*. They were greeted at the docks in Manhattan by John's parents and Mary's aunt and great-aunt, then taken by Wesley and Linda back to the farm in Plowville, a car ride revisited in "Home," a story Updike wrote five years later. He lifted one incident from the journey—the young wife accidentally tipping a live ash from her cigarette onto the naked tummy of her baby girl—straight from life. The story also features vivid thumbnail portraits of Updike's parents, similar to ones he'd already produced in "Flight" and "Pigeon Feathers," miniatures that would be expanded in *The Centaur* and *Of the Farm*.

He had written from Oxford to arrange a job interview with William Shawn. After a few days at home in Plowville, he set off for Manhattan in his brand-new car (the family's first; his father could afford only used cars), a 1955 four-door Ford coupe, waterfall blue. Paid for with his *New Yorker* earnings, the Ford had been the subject of earnest transatlantic negotiations; John gave his father detailed instructions about the precise model and color he wanted, and stressed the importance of a radio.* His mother accompanied him to New York, and though the car performed flawlessly, the trip ended in failure: they never made it to the city. There are two accounts of this odd little episode, one from a memoir of Shawn that Updike composed in 2000, the other from a story Linda wrote in the sixties called "The Mantle and Other Blessed Goods." Updike remembered driving to the interview "with my mother along for the ride." He became "hopelessly lost in a traffic jam under the Pulaski Skyway in New Jersey; it was my humiliating task to find a phone booth and call [Shawn] to say, while trucks roared overhead, that I would be hopelessly late." Shawn politely offered to wait, but Updike insisted on turning back and rescheduling the appointment for the next day. Linda's version makes use of the same facts but ends with the narrator's italicized conviction that the next day her son would be driving to the city on his own: "[He] would make *this* trip alone." The emphasis practically begs the reader to ask why the mother had ever even thought of tagging along with her adult son to "meet the man who was going to be [his] first employer." In Linda's story, as in real life, the answer is that she thought of herself as enmeshed with his career. *The New Yorker*, for Linda as for Updike, was Mecca; she wanted to take part in the pilgrimage. And her son clearly had difficulty opposing her wishes. He could only thwart her accidentally, by getting hopelessly lost in a traffic jam.

No harm done: the next day, he got back into the Ford and made the journey without incident, all by himself. Shawn offered him the promised job.

Finding a place to live in the city meant more trips to town in the new car, and there was also an unavoidable visit to a Manhattan draft board. Because of the poor condition of his skin, which had been starved of sunlight in England, he was exempted from military service; on his form the examining doctor wrote, "4-F: Psoriasis." John felt relieved, though somewhat guilty, and Mary was delighted. Linda, according to John, "seemed saddened, as if she had laid an

---

* The car radio figures prominently in *Rabbit, Run*.

egg which, when candled by the government, had been pronounced rotten."

John, Mary, and four-month-old Elizabeth moved into a small apartment at 126 Riverside Drive, near Eighty-Fifth Street on the Upper West Side. Despite the crumbling ceiling, the odd triangular kitchen, and the carpet, to which Mary took an instant dislike, Updike thought the place was fine and admired the view across the Hudson River to New Jersey. The apartment was on the fifth floor, reached by a tiny, creaky elevator. Outside the front door of the building were steep, rounded steps down to the sidewalk, difficult to negotiate with the baby carriage, and beyond the sidewalk was the speeding traffic on Riverside Drive. Just to get out of their apartment, in other words, they had to negotiate a series of specifically urban challenges.

John began work as a reporter for The Talk of the Town on Monday, August 15, 1955. He was installed on the eighteenth floor, in a spartan cubicle equipped with a typewriter, a metal desk, a telephone, and a supply of freshly sharpened pencils. "It was all pretty monastic," according to Anthony Bailey, an Englishman a few months younger than Updike who started work as a Talk reporter in early 1956 and became his lifelong friend. "I found myself in an office right next door to him," said Bailey. "Ten o'clock was opening time, and I generally got there around ten-thirty. John would already be at his desk. You could hear his typewriter going—going from dawn to dusk, it seemed to me. It was very intimidating; his work rate was astonishing." (Actually, dawn was out of the question: always a late sleeper, Updike rarely reached the office before nine-thirty.) As astonishing as his work rate were the ease and rapidity with which he settled into his new environment. He was unhappy for a couple of weeks, mostly because he couldn't see how he would make time for his own writing, but by mid-September his misgivings had vanished. The job suited him perfectly. There was no period of adjustment, no apprenticeship; he appeared on the scene fully formed. Said Brendan Gill, who'd been at the magazine for two decades when Updike arrived, "He struck *The New Yorker* like an absolute bombshell." As Bailey put it, "John was the star." During the nineteen months he worked at the office, the magazine published more than three dozen of his Talk pieces (many of them classics of the genre), a half-dozen of his short stories, another half-dozen parodies, and a steady stream of light verse. The time he spent in the building working alongside the staff writers and getting to know the editors helped cement what would become the longest and most important professional association of his career.

"If ever a writer, a magazine and a time were made for each other, the writer was John Updike, the magazine was the *New Yorker* and the time was the 1950s." Ben Yagoda made that sweeping claim in *About Town: The* New Yorker *and the World It Made*, and it would be hard to refute.* The American economy was ascendant, the magazine was ascendant, Updike was ascendant—and the confluence of these trends flattered all parties. Writing to Maxwell four decades later, Updike confessed that "ever since you accepted in one summer 'Duet, with Muffled Brake Drums' and 'Friends from Philadelphia,' I have been in a writerly bliss nothing could shake." Maxwell, as early as 1958, assured Updike, "It is a slightly different magazine because you are now published in it." (That may sound like faint praise, but *The New Yorker* has always been notoriously resistant to change; Updike had caused the mountain to move.) From the beginning, and sometimes to his chagrin, critics identified Updike as a typical *New Yorker* writer, as though he had been concocted in-house, the product of a singularly fruitful editorial meeting. Everything was going right for the magazine (from 1950 to 1964, circulation grew by 40 percent, ad pages by 70 percent, and prestige and influence by an unquantifiable yet unmistakable degree)—surely the sudden appearance of the wunderkind Updike was simply part of that fabulous chain of success.

To leaf through *The New Yorker* at midcentury was to celebrate a nation and a city triumphant. In that postwar moment, New York became the center of the world—"continuously insolent and alive,"

---

* Updike praised Yagoda's book as an "excellent, equable, thorough history of the magazine."

in Cyril Connolly's memorable phrase, the mighty beating heart of the most powerful country on the globe.* "The city," E. B. White rhapsodized in 1948, "is like poetry. . . . The island of Manhattan is without any doubt the greatest human concentrate on earth, the poem whose magic is comprehensible to millions of permanent residents but whose full meaning will always remain elusive." *The New Yorker* was both a gloss on that poem and a mirror reflecting its magic. Although it attracted a growing number of suburban and rural readers, not all of whom shared in the rising postwar prosperity, the message broadcast in its pages, in the advertisements as well as the short stories, casuals, columns, reported pieces, and reviews, was cosmopolitan, affluent, upwardly mobile. When Updike called to mind the typical *New Yorker* reader of the time, the words he used were "pampered and urban"—certainly the condition to which many aspired.

And yet these upwardly mobile middle-class readers were sensitive enough to have qualms about avid economic and social aspirations. The ads in the magazine—the vast majority of them hawking luxury goods—mostly pandered to naked snobbery and greed. Sometimes they challenged the consumer to be more "modern," or winked at the bad taste of others; occasionally they offered forthright instruction in the art of living. The content of the magazine inclined in somewhat different directions. The cartoons often gently mocked the conspicuous consumption of the rich, and sometimes even cast an eye over the precincts of the poor. In the writing, lowlifes came in for much scrutiny, notably in profiles by A. J. Liebling and Joseph Mitchell. The magazine had a well-developed social conscience, and played, at times, the role of crusader, exposing national and international wrongs—this was the magazine that devoted the entire editorial space of a sixty-eight-page issue, just a year after the United States dropped two atomic bombs on Japan, to John Hersey's

---

* Updike wrote a Talk of the Town piece about loafing in Bryant Park, near the intersection of Fifth Avenue and Forty-Second Street; he called it "the bull's-eye of our city": "As surely as if we were in the Forum of 169, on the Ile de la Cité in 1260, or in Piccadilly Circus in 1860, we sat now, in 1960, in the center of Western civilization."

"Hiroshima." Seduced by ads for jewelry and perfume, liquor and furs, but braced by the probity of the editorial content, *New Yorker* readers could allow themselves to feel slightly superior to the grasping multitudes. They were consumers, too—but they consumed tastefully, conscientiously. They belonged, or wanted to belong, to an elite club, a meritocratic aristocracy, and liked to think of the magazine as an island of civilization, a virtual community of the *bien-pensant*. (All clubs, as Updike remarked of the Lampoon, feed off "the delicious immensity of the excluded.") A 1946 *New Yorker* marketing pamphlet boasted that its readers were "at least all of the following: Intelligent, well-educated, discriminating, well-informed, unprejudiced, public-spirited, metropolitan-minded, broad-visioned and quietly liberal." Who wouldn't want to join such an enlightened crew?

It's important to remember that when he fell in love with it, *The New Yorker*, though ascendant, was hardly the only game in town, as it would be just a few decades later. An aspiring writer might more plausibly have set his or her eyes on *Life* or *The Saturday Evening Post* or *Collier's* or *Cosmopolitan*—all of which could claim a much wider circulation, and paid much higher fees to freelancers. By comparison, *The New Yorker* was still a small magazine. But it spoke to Updike in irresistible, seductive tones. As a thirteen-year-old, he had been ready to reshape himself radically so that he could literally merge with it: "I loved that magazine so much I concentrated all my wishing into an effort to make myself small and inky and intense enough to be received into its pages." Reporting for work at age twenty-three, he was still desperately eager to be received into its pages—but less willing to transform himself and his writing to achieve that end. In the marketing department's crowing checklist of *New Yorker* qualities, there was at least one that didn't exactly suit the young man from Berks County: "metropolitan-minded."

Otherwise, yes: Updike and *The New Yorker* in the fifties—it was indeed a perfect fit. Yagoda wisely refrained from stretching his claim to include New York City itself. Despite his adolescent fantasies of escaping Plowville for the glittering metropolis, epicenter of sophistication, Updike and the City of New York were not, in fact, made for each other. When he arrived in town, the possibility of becoming a New York writer was still open to him. In theory, he could have chosen urban life as his great subject and embraced the bustling literary scene as a natural habitat (the way, for example, Norman Mailer and Harold Brodkey did at about the same time). Instead, less than two years after he arrived, Updike retreated to Ipswich, Massachusetts, and he made New England his home for the rest of his life. His urban stint did play an important part in shaping both his writing and his idea of himself, but mostly in a negative sense. Turning his back on the splendors of midcentury Manhattan, he elected to leave. He would not be a New York writer, and New York would not be his subject.

The decision came after a brief but thorough immersion. The Talk of the Town was in those days more geographically focused than it is today; its purview was mostly Manhattan, with only rare excursions beyond the outer boroughs. As a Talk writer, Updike had to walk a local beat, to know the cityscape inside out—sometimes literally, as in the delightful piece published in early 1956 in which he reports on an ingenious feat of urban navigation: how to make one's way from the Empire State Building to Rockefeller Center without ever setting foot on either Fifth or Sixth Avenue. (The trick is to pass through and under city blocks, thanks to vast department stores, arcades, and conveniently located subway stations.) His work peeled open the city for him, and provided material for the short stories he wrote during and immediately after his stay. His press pass access—the reporter's license to poke around, to eavesdrop, to stare openly—earned him a fund of expertise, urban know-how he would draw on for the rest of his life; it gave him the courage to create in the mid-sixties an alter ego, Henry Bech, who is a New Yorker through and through. His Talk job, in other words, allowed him to claim the city as his own, even after he'd left, even though a fundamental part of him had resisted it all along.

His first assignment was to investigate Magi-Green, "a lawn invigorator that dyes grass green." It was a somewhat unusual assignment in that it entailed a visit to the out-of-town headquarters of the Lockery Company, makers of Magi-Green, which was located in Southampton, New York, near the end of Long Island. Updike, on a whim, decided to drive—and to take his little family along. In an account of this adventure, written decades later, he emphasized his "country innocence"—he had no idea how *long* Long Island was, how heavy the traffic would be, or that having the Ford in New York was a mistake to begin with. By the time they reached their destination, Mary and Elizabeth were "so wilted as to need a rejuvenating spray themselves." But Updike got the job done nonetheless, and the resulting journalistic trifle is mildly amusing and fairly typical of The Talk of the Town, save for the exurban expedition and a subject matter (lawn care) so quintessentially suburban. The reporter ("we," by hallowed *New Yorker* convention)* gathers a comically copious amount of information about the product, allows its makers to display a comical commercial enthusiasm, and adds to the comedy by appearing (almost) to share that enthusiasm. It's a gentle kind of wit that Updike mastered on the spot. Within a few days, William Shawn telephoned him at the Riverside Drive apartment and offered him a promotion: henceforth Updike would be a Talk *writer* rather than a Talk reporter, which meant that his pieces would bypass the magazine's rewrite men—and that he'd earn two hundred dollars per piece.†

The Talk of the Town was essentially ephemera, one of the least consequential sections of the magazine; most of the items were designed to amuse, and the amusement was generally fleeting. Updike remembered three types of Talk story: "interviews, 'fact' pieces, and

---

* In the foreword to *Assorted Prose*, Updike writes, "Who, after all, could that indefatigably fascinated, perpetually peripatetic 'we' be but a collection of dazzled farm-boys?"

† There are few topics murkier than *The New Yorker*'s arrangements for paying its staff writers. Each had a different deal. It seems that during his time with The Talk of the Town, Updike was given a $100 weekly "drawing account"— essentially an advance against his actual earnings. By writing two Talk pieces a month, he could "offset" the sum deposited into his account. The idea behind this arcane system was to make life more secure for freelancers who had a mortgage or school tuition to pay; of course it had the corollary effect of tying the writers to the magazine.

'visits.'" His Magi-Green piece was a visit piece (fortified with facts trumpeted by the Lockery Company), and visits became his specialty. He preferred them because they required "no research and little personal encounter." He developed the knack of planting himself in a particular place—Central Park, the cocktail lounge of the Biltmore Hotel—and simply looking and listening, making himself utterly receptive to sensory impression, noticing everything. Having soaked up the ambience, he put his writing skills to work: "An hour of silent spying" was followed, as he put it, by "two hours of fanciful typing." (The average Talk piece was seven hundred to eight hundred words.) He made the job of translating his perceptions into "*New Yorker*-ese" look effortless. "His success rate was a hundred percent as far as one could make out," said Tony Bailey. It was true; every single item Updike wrote for The Talk of the Town the magazine printed. According to Brendan Gill, who was one of the Talk rewrite men, "It was perfectly obvious that he was writing better Talk stories than anyone who had ever written them."

Which is partly why he stopped. It was both too easy for him and a waste of his talent. Although writing them was clearly good training for someone working in a realist tradition, and although he often achieved in them a slender poetic perfection, too many of his Talk pieces merely displayed "a kind of contemptuous harried virtuosity in a narrow vein indeed"—a withering phrase he used to describe a visit piece he wrote in January 1957. Feeling unwell, he toured the National Motor Boat Show at the New York Coliseum, and found that the boats resembled cars, bullets, birds, and flying saucers. "It may have been the absence of water, or the fact that we were running a fever, but nearly everything we saw at the Coliseum looked like something else." Expertly clever and engaging, the piece playfully examines the ramifications of a sardonically posited marketing principle: "No doubt it is a law of an expanding economy that once a thing looks like its natural self, its appearance must be perverted, or people will be satisfied with the model they already have." Updike doesn't allow his cynicism about the designers' commercial motivation to spoil the fun; he gives us a gee-whiz guided tour of the pleasure craft and their "perverted" appearance. The prose is breezy and sharp and tremendously self-assured. Updike once defined "*New Yorker*-ese" as "big-town folksy," which is accurate enough, though it doesn't account for his astonishing fluency, his ability to switch on a current of cheerful intelligence that sparked and fizzed without seeming precious. It was exactly what the magazine wanted—but it wasn't enough to satisfy a young man's ambition. "It seemed unlikely that I would ever get better at Talk than I was at twenty-four," Updike explained. "A man who would be an artist is obliged to keep working where he might improve." Also, Talk pieces in those days were unsigned—they did nothing to secure him a place in the public eye.

His artistic aspirations were pinned on the work he was doing outside office hours. The bouts of furious morning typing in the spartan eighteenth-floor cubicle eventually resulted in a six-hundred-page manuscript—an autobiographical novel, never published, called *Home*—and a run of eight short stories: "Toward Evening," "Snowing in Greenwich Village," "Who Made Yellow Roses Yellow?" "Sunday Teasing," "His Finest Hour," "A Trillion Feet of Gas," "A Gift from the City," and "Incest." These stories, written between November 1955 and April 1957, are a remarkably homogeneous New York City series: all are set in Manhattan; all but one feature a married couple modeled more or less exactly on Mary and John; and all are about young people adjusting to urban life and expressing, directly or indirectly, their aspirations and anxieties. Broadly speaking, the stories explore the treacherous allure of big-city sophistication, its potentially corrupting influence—weighed against the danger of clinging to country innocence, to a provincial youth's naïveté.

This, for as long as he was living in the city, was a constant preoccupation. Despite his brilliant career at Harvard, his year in Europe, and his instant, seemingly effortless mastery of the "big-town folksy" *New Yorker* idiom, the young Talk writer was still uncomfortable about becoming cosmopolitan. He still thought of himself as a dazzled farm boy, an "inlander" (hence an outsider), a hick with an "innocent longing for sophistication," a rube lured by the promise of "urban romance." And yet to shed that identity and embrace New York unreservedly was to betray, again, his beloved

Shillington; to adopt a seamless urbanity was to deny, in a sense, his parents, both of whom embodied a kind of antiurbanity; to become a city slicker was to turn his back on the awkward, scabby kid who'd been the object of his family's adoring attention. At this age, his ambition still wasn't social; it was professional. He craved success, yet was wary of its trappings.

The first of his New York stories, "Toward Evening," makes significant use of the glorious view from the Riverside Drive apartment. It begins by tracing with documentary accuracy the bus journey up Broadway from his midtown office of a young man named Rafe; it continues at home, an intimate domestic scene with Rafe, his wife, and their baby daughter (like the Updikes, this little family lives on Eighty-Fifth Street, overlooking the river); and it ends, after dinner, with Rafe gazing out the window across the expanse of the Hudson, smoking a cigarette and meditating, elaborately, on the origins of the neon Spry sign flashing red and white below the dark Palisades. His postprandial musings are exaggeratedly worldly-wise, a mini Talk piece that exposes, with a mild cynical edge, how the wheels turn in a modern corporate setting. (Spry was a national brand of vegetable shortening manufactured by Lever Brothers.) The reverie comes to a close with this Kiplingesque coda: "Thus the Spry sign (thus the river, thus the trees, thus babies and sleep) came to be." Balanced against Rafe's knowing, up-to-the-minute New York riff is the timeless mystery of creation. Stepping back—out of Rafe's point of view—Updike ends the story with a reminder of cosmic inscrutability:

> The black of the river was as wide as that of the sky. Reflections sunk in it existed dimly, minutely wrinkled, below the surface. The Spry sign occupied the night with no company beyond the also uncreated but illegible stars.

The "uncreated but illegible stars" and the vast, unknowable, godless universe they suggest mark the limit of Rafe's understanding—and ours. This acknowledgment of human ignorance—a kind of anti-epiphany—conjures, in turn, the possibility of divine knowledge;

anyone with a religious disposition (Updike, say) is bound to read in the "illegible" stars the possibility of a divine plan.

Rafe is exactly Updike's age, and what we learn of his family history matches Updike's. Educated, cultured, clever, and observant, he's also lustful, somewhat spoiled, a touch self-satisfied. In the version published in *The New Yorker*, we're told a little about his job in a midtown office: "The strange thing about the place where he worked was not that the work didn't matter but that everyone engaged at it knew it."* It's not much of a stretch to think of Rafe as a writer for The Talk of the Town engaged in producing charming ephemera. As his bus lumbers up Broadway, he amuses himself by playing a game with the numbers on the east side of the avenue: "1832, 1836, 1846, 1850 (Wordsworth dies), 1880 (great Nihilist trial in St. Petersburg), 1900 (Rafe's father born in Trenton), 1902 (Braque leaves Le Havre to study painting in Paris), 1914 (Joyce begins *Ulysses*, war begins in Europe)." It's another mini-Talk piece, an idea Updike might have hatched for his day job and then decided to use in his fiction instead.†

On the bus, when he's not playing clever games, Rafe eyes the female passengers. First he admires a "beautiful girl" who's reading the second volume of Proust, *À l'ombre des jeunes filles en fleurs*;‡ then he becomes conscious of a "young Negress" who briefly excites his sexual desire. Rafe's interest in these women is bracketed by reminders of religious stricture: he got on the bus at St. Patrick's Cathedral

---

* In the version published in *The Same Door* and then collected in *The Early Stories*, Updike radically trimmed the opening paragraph of "Toward Evening," eliminating almost all mention of Rafe's job; we eventually learn, in passing, that he works in an office—the rest is left to the imagination.

† Six months later another bus, this one with a sign reading "Capacity 26 Passengers," inspired a charming bit of light verse, "Capacity," in which every passenger is catalogued from *A* to *Z*—"affable" to "zebuesque"—except *U*, presumably the poet himself.

‡ Updike later noted, "I began to read Proust in the first months I lived in Manhattan, on Riverside Drive. I was twenty-three, newly a father, newly employed."

(in those days, buses on Fifth Avenue ran north as well as south); and he thinks to himself, just as he's about to get off, "Dress women in sea and sand or pencil lines, they were chapters on the same subject, no more unlike than St. Paul and Paul Tillich." Theology and adultery are twinned subjects in both Updike's work and his life. In the context of this story, we see a young man whose wandering eye makes him feel reflexively guilty—he is, after all, on the way home to his wife and baby.

The scene inside Rafe's apartment is, as usual, conspicuously autobiographical. The baby is called Liz, like John's daughter, and she's not interested in the mobile her father has brought home for her—though Updike himself was moved to write a poem about the item ("Mobile of Birds") a couple of years later. The wife (Alice in *The Same Door*, unnamed in *The Early Stories*) is bored at home, no surprise given her "confined existence." Though she's briefly irritated by Rafe's dreamy, absentminded habit of ignoring her questions about his work, she's a conscientious housewife who cooks her husband's favorite food, prepared with his allergies in mind and served on "the eccentric tilting plates in which, newly married, they had sailed the clean seas of sophistication."* (Even this tiny detail is drawn from life: the Updikes owned a pair of brown, tilting plates they'd bought in a Cambridge hardware store for their first apartment.)

Rafe is well launched on the clean seas of sophistication. His daydream about the Spry sign is an obvious indication that he thinks of himself as suavely in the know. He effortlessly imagines, in precise detail, how the sign came to be, a chain of human events that stretches from an executive's whim as he drives his secretary home to Riverdale to the exact moment (3:30 on a windy Tuesday afternoon in November) when eighteen men finally finish the job of fixing the neon beacon in place. But Updike undercuts Rafe in the last sentence of the story with his reference to the "also uncreated but illegible stars"—which tips off the careful reader to the fact that Rafe's urbanity is tinged with vanity and hubris. Brilliantly fash-

---

* The phrase about sailing the "clean seas of sophistication" is a late addition; it underscores the idea that the couple's urban polish is freshly acquired.

ioned out of mundane autobiographical material, the story is a sociologically precise slice of a bright young New Yorker's very ordinary day. But it can also be read as a kind of cautionary tale: the savvy Talk of the Town writer reminding himself not to lose his humility (or succumb to temptation) as he makes his way in the brave new world of the big city.*

Kit Lasch, who was now a graduate student in history at Columbia, came to dinner a few times at the Updikes', and fired off his impressions to various correspondents. On his second visit, he was invited to dinner with an "eligible young lady." According to Lasch, John and Mary "stood by with the air of elderly chaperones. When it was time for the young folks to go, Updike, in a very grandfatherly way, proposed to walk us to the subway, but at the door he evidently thought better of it, relented, and allowed us to walk the two blocks unescorted. It was quite an adventure." He takes up the same theme in his next letter, complaining that the Updikes "have become very ceremonial"—the implication being that John's success has gone to his head. Lasch saw signs of pomposity in every gesture: "They invite you to dinner weeks in advance, and if you had a hat in hand they would relieve you of it at the door, and make a big point of doing so." It seems obvious that Lasch was still struggling with his envy, and that the friendship was in serious disrepair. But he was nonetheless quite right about Updike's preoccupation with how to greet guests and how to say good-bye to them. Hospitality was very important to him; he felt the need to master its rituals and ceremonies. Part of him wanted to appear elegantly nonchalant, and yet he was still at this point something of a novice.

---

* It's possible that Updike, gazing on the Spry sign and imagining the workings of the corporation responsible for erecting it, may have found his thoughts turning to *The New Yorker* and how the magazine itself came to be. As he knew, it was bankrolled in the early years by Raoul Fleischmann, an heir to the General Baking Company whose family had made a fortune with Fleischmann's Yeast, a baking ingredient, like Spry, and just as heavily advertised. Updike grew up thinking of *The New Yorker* as a bright, shiny cultural artifact; it was a beacon of sophistication for a wide-eyed country boy. Now he knew it from the inside, as company with a product for sale, launched as a business venture and profitably managed by employees of Raoul Fleischmann.

By the time "Toward Evening" was published in *The New Yorker*, the Updikes were no longer living on the Upper West Side. Early in 1956, the family moved downtown to 153 West Thirteenth Street, to a slightly larger, floor-through apartment with two fireplaces and a tiny kitchen. Because the living room, dining room, and kitchen were at the front of the apartment, there were three windows looking out over West Thirteenth Street. In the back were a big bedroom and bathroom. This pleasant spot was the setting for "Snowing in Greenwich Village," the first of eighteen stories that track the marital dramas of Richard and Joan Maple. Seen in the light of the Maples' long domestic saga, this story, set on the day after they've moved into a new apartment in the Village, seems a harbinger of things to come: Richard's "close" call with the Maples' friend (now neighbor) Rebecca Cune marks the inception of a damaging adulterous impulse; the various affairs that will undermine the marriage are foreshadowed in the tense moments of the story's ending (the kiss that Rebecca perhaps invites but that Richard refrains from bestowing), and in the exquisite final sentence, mixing relief, regret, desire, and release: "Oh but they were close."

The few minutes Richard and Rebecca spend alone together—he walks her home at Joan's urging after their evening drink, then accepts an invitation to come up and see where she lives—tilt the story so that it seems to be mostly about the possibility of an extramarital dalliance. But the first two thirds are only very subtly infused with sexual tension, if at all. The overt concern is with the modern manners of a young couple entertaining a more polished and experienced friend. We're told in the very first paragraph about Richard's difficulties with "hostly duties" such as the taking of coats from newly arrived guests; the emphasis is on his youth and inexperience. This particular guest, Rebecca, has evidently been living in the city longer than the Maples; she tells them about her previous apartments, spinning yarns in a distinctive patter, thrilling her hosts with her somewhat louche adventures. "Rebecca's gift, Richard realized, was not that of having odd things happen to her but that of representing, through the implicit contrast with her own sane calm, all things touching her as odd." Rebecca is possessed of what William Maxwell detected in Updike during their first lunch together: a style.

The Maples are not so far advanced; "they did not regard themselves . . . as raconteurs." (And yet that's what Updike had necessarily become, in his professional life, a good Talk piece being essentially a cleverly elaborated anecdote.) The couple's new apartment is larger than anywhere they've lived in the two years since they were married; at last they have room to unpack their wedding presents. They have, for the first time, a mantel. They offer Rebecca expensive sherry, and cashews served in one of the newly unpacked wedding presents, a silver porringer (a detail plucked straight from the Updikes' cupboard, though in fact it was a baby present, not a wedding present). This is a young couple with aspirations, both material and cultural—though the Maples have retained, thus far, their country innocence. They exclaim in wonder at the mounted policemen who gallop noisily down Thirteenth Street; and when they see that it's snowing, they exclaim again—or at least Joan does. Richard, who works in advertising, is already a little farther along the path of studied cool. Like Rebecca, he poses, parading attitudes for effect. But he's not particularly good at it. Young-looking and faintly awkward (he stutters at the crucial moment), he's charmingly inept—working, like Updike, on a stylized aw-shucks act.

Richard (like Rafe in "Toward Evening") has a wandering eye; he's aware that by accepting an invitation to tour Rebecca's apartment, he's "trespassing beyond the public gardens of courtesy." Following her up the stairs, he feels guilty, but his guilt-inflected self-consciousness is a sign of virtue, of innocence threatened by corruption. He has yet to achieve the sophistication of a man capable of casual adultery.

Updike was as innocent as Richard, as the fallout from the story made clear. Rebecca was very obviously modeled on a friend of the Updikes, and though she accepted the story with polite good grace, saying only how "spooky" it was to be reading a *New Yorker* and find oneself in it, her on-again, off-again boyfriend berated Updike for his callous and thoughtless behavior. The boyfriend's harangue was ferocious enough to sink both Mary and John into a weekend-long funk. Feeling guilty and ashamed, Updike reconsidered two pet theories. The first was "that a writer of short stories has no duty other than writing good short stories"; the second, that "nothing in fiction rings quite as true as truth, slightly arranged." He knew that the second theory was still valid, but now realized how harmful it could be. His remorse, though genuine, lasted no time at all; "the truth, slightly arranged" remained the foundation of his fiction.

In his next story—"Who Made Yellow Roses Yellow?"— Updike was even more explicit about pitting an urban sophisticate (an upper-class New York dilettante) against a gauche provincial, a middle-class go-getter who's succeeding in advertising but who remains socially clueless ("hopelessly offensive") in the eyes of his snobbish friend. Sophistication takes a knock in "Who Made Yellow Roses Yellow?"—as it does in "Sunday Teasing," in which a vain young husband who has bullied his wife with a display of cleverness experiences a moment of sharp regret. The title of "Sunday Teasing" announces a religious theme. The husband, Arthur, has decided to dispense with Sabbath sermons: instead of going to church, he will spend his Sunday morning in the apartment reading St. Paul and Unamuno.* His do-it-yourself religious observance smacks of pride. Later, when a friend comes to lunch, Arthur shows off in front of his wife, Macy, and their guest; he behaves obnoxiously, goading Macy and causing her pain. Though proud of his intellect ("the sacred groves of his mind"), he's out of tune with his wife's emotions, and is therefore baffled when, in the evening, after their guest has gone, she begins to weep. Contrite, he does penance by washing the dishes. In a sinuous final sentence, complete with italicized epiphany, awareness comes crashing in on him: "As he stood at the sink, his hands in water which, where the suds thinned and broke, showed a silvery gray, the Sunday's events repeated themselves in his mind, bending like nacreous flakes around

---

* During the early months of his stay in New York, Updike was himself engaged in anxious theological investigations. This was when he first read Kierkegaard: an Anchor edition of *Fear and Trembling* and *The Sickness unto Death* bound together.

a central infrangible irritant, becoming the perfect and luminous thought: *You don't know anything.*"

Like "Toward Evening" and "Snowing in Greenwich Village," "Sunday Teasing" reads like a public confession, and a warning Updike is sounding for his own benefit. Precisely autobiographical in setting and detail, these stories show a young writer maturing on the page, working out what sort of person he would like to become, and worried, too, that the sophistication he'd innocently dreamed of was corrupting his most intimate self.

One of the weaker New York stories, "A Trillion Feet of Gas" has the virtue of broadening Updike's sociopolitical range. The cast of characters includes a Texas billionaire, an Upper East Side grandee, and a disapproving British intellectual, as well as lightly disguised versions of John and Mary—Luke and Liz Forrest, a young newsmagazine writer and his pregnant wife whose "bohemian" taste in interior decorating "ran to bamboo and Klee."* The expanded canvas allows Updike to make topical references to the presidential elections of 1956 (the Texan is a reluctant supporter of Eisenhower, or "Aahk," as he calls him); this is the first time Updike introduced overtly political concerns into his fiction. He blends these with a version of Henry James's "international theme": Donald (the Forrests' English houseguest) is visiting the United States "in the show-me mood of a cultural delegation." The Texan, meanwhile, is an emblematic figure; to meet him, Luke tells Donald, is to gaze "into the heart of a great nation."

The story takes place in the duplex apartment of rich New Yorkers at a "high-toned address off Park Avenue." The Forrests have been invited to dinner, and they've brought Donald along with them. At table, Luke takes it upon himself to amuse the assembled company, mostly by making fun of Donald (the Forrests liked him better when they met him on his home turf in Oxford). As a gag, part of an elaborate dig at the Brits, Luke mimes the familiar scene

---

* Mary Updike, who liked Klee (but preferred Cézanne), was pregnant with their second child when her husband was writing "A Trillion Feet of Gas"; David Updike was born eight weeks later.

from the movies of an idol teetering: "[H]e wobbled rigidly in his chair and then with horrible slow menace fell forward, breaking off the act just as his nose touched the rim of his water glass."

Luke's "act" is teasingly similar to Updike's pratfalls on the steps of the Fogg when he was wooing Mary, and also to a stunt he pulled in an elevator at work in the presence of his friend Tony Bailey. The *New Yorker* elevators were fraught territory, according to Bailey, partly because the claustrophobic William Shawn was famously terrified of them, and partly because at busy times of the day they were crammed with grimly silent office workers—"there was this really intense nonspeaking atmosphere," said Bailey.

> I got in with John one day on the eighteenth floor—we were going for lunch or something—and John pretended to faint. It was absolute pretense. It was purely an act—to take the highly charged atmosphere out of the elevator and focus it entirely on himself. It was a gag, but he couldn't help it somehow. It was almost as if he *was* fainting, but he wasn't— he was smiling throughout, and he went right down to the floor, and everybody was horrified. It was John's hypersensitivity to everything, which he turned into some kind of trick. He was feeling the pressure generated by nobody talking, everybody getting in there together and not wanting to be in there together. But only John would have turned this into some kind of comic demonstration.

Updike's fondness for gags and practical jokes, which budded in high school and blossomed at the Lampoon, was still in flower when he reached *The New Yorker*. Even though he was now the young patriarch of a small but growing family, and made his living by entertaining readers in the pages of a fashionable glossy magazine, he still liked the idea that with a well-timed performance he could rivet the attention of an audience; like Luke, he found it "comforting to know that he could still make people laugh."

And Luke, like Updike, is very aware of the effect of his clowning. He's conscious of the tension between the Texan—his trillion feet of natural gas are a blatant symbol of America's brash power—and Donald, the delegate from the Old World whose "maddening quiescence" so irritates the Forrests. Luke's high jinks and his teasing diffuse the tension by bringing it out into the open; in the final sentence of the story, he aims a mocking remark squarely at his British friend: "'You're afraid,' he said loudly, 'of our hideous vigor.'" The simple dichotomy of muscular American innocence and sneering European decadence is complicated by Luke's ironic awareness of his own role in this overdetermined transatlantic drama; he hams up his part deliberately—winking broadly, as it were, to let us in on the game.

When Updike was first married, he cast himself as the raw provincial, the inlander; his bride, with her New England background, was by default the more cultured and refined of the couple. She was at home in Cambridge; he was not. In the New York stories, written several years later, the roles are reversed: the wife is naive and unworldly in comparison with the husband. In "His Finest Hour" and "A Gift from the City," the two weakest and least autobiographical of the series, the wife is kind, sensitive, attractive, and ever so slightly dim. Rosalind, in "His Finest Hour," is "optimistic and unselfconscious. Her gaps in judgment were startling." In both stories, the wife's naïveté, her relative lack of street smarts, is a catalyst in the narrative. In New York, where both he and Mary were outsiders, Updike no longer saw his wife as someone who would lead him to a loftier place. "He was participating in the life of the city," Mary remembered, "and I was home with children. On special occasions I could go to a museum or go shopping at Lord and Taylor or Bonwit Teller."

One characteristic all the New York stories have in common is that they're peopled with likely *New Yorker* readers. The young couple in "Incest," for example—yet another version of John and Mary, this time called Lee and Jane—are college educated, living in a small, pleasant New York apartment furnished with bamboo chairs, a modernist sofa, a makeshift bed, bookshelves filled with books. They're familiar with Proust and Freud and the pediatric pronouncements of Dr. Benjamin Spock. Manifestly bright and proud of his intellectual attainments, Lee is also enough of a baseball fan to feel "spiritually dependent on Ted Williams." Jane sips vermouth after dinner, listen-

ing to Bach on the record player while she reads *The New Republic*—
if the story hadn't been intended for publication in *The New Yorker*,
surely she would have been reading that magazine instead.

The settled domestic scene in "Incest" is troubled by Lee's libid-
inal restlessness, which is implied rather than explicitly stated. At
the beginning of the story he tells Jane about one erotically charged
dream, and at the end he dreams another, even more sexually suggestive, about his daughter, a toddler with the same name as her
mother. This was the golden age of Freud in America, and Updike
would have expected his *New Yorker* readers to be at least vaguely
familiar with popularized versions of the arguments proposed in *The
Interpretation of Dreams* and *Three Essays on the Theory of Sexuality*.
"Incest" is a Freudian playground crowded with symbols that hint at
latent currents of psychic energy, sinister complexes percolating in
the subconscious minds of the parents as well as the child. Lee's erotic
dreams (which were, Updike told Maxwell, "substantially" his own),
his ambivalent thoughts about his wife's appearance (though they've
been married only three years, her face "showed age"), his frustrated
attempts at flirting with her—it all adds up to an unsettling picture
of a young marriage under pressure. As in "Toward Evening" and
"Snowing in Greenwich Village," we're presented with a husband exposed to temptation, either his virtue or his integrity at risk.

Writing about provincials in the big city, young folk testing out
degrees of urban sophistication and flirting with corrupting influences, Updike was part of a feedback loop: borrowing from the stuff
of his own life, he was showing subscribers images of themselves,
city-dwellers and aspiring city-dwellers working to achieve an easy
urbanity, a modern, cultured, upscale way of living—and not entirely comfortable with the results. The self-portraits in these stories
reveal a young man at once craving and resisting assimilation to a
powerfully attractive, occasionally frightening milieu. That milieu
was the city, of course—and it was also, more urgently, *The New
Yorker* as a place of employment, as a venue for his work, and as a
badge of writerly identity. The question of whether he would be a
New York writer was swamped by the question of whether he would
be a *New Yorker* writer.

Curiously enough, in light of his close and enduring identification with the magazine, the answer was not an unqualified yes. He
needed *The New Yorker*, if only because he needed to make a living;
and despite his new familiarity with its inner workings, he revered
it—and continued to do so. Even after the tenacious William Shawn
was pushed aside in 1987 and replaced by Robert Gottlieb, even
after the shock of Tina Brown's tenure (1992–1998) and the advent
of David Remnick, Updike continued to think of it as "not only the
best general magazine in America, but perhaps the best that America
has ever produced." Being a valued contributor; working alongside
his fellow staff writers, some of them legendary; forming an integral
part of a corporate entity, the most excellent of its kind—all this certainly appealed to him, but not with the same force as his personal
aspirations. Always in some corner of his mind he was the cherished
only child, and he would eventually have to insist on being a one-
man show; his aim was to achieve individual rather than collective
excellence. Although *The New Yorker* would never have discouraged
that ambition, his presence in the office, once he proved himself
to be versatile, eager to please, and infallibly competent, was a sore
temptation: how could editors, faced with the pressing weekly task
of finding material to fill the pages, resist the urge to make use of
him, to co-opt him? Even before he was installed at his metal desk
on the eighteenth floor, Katharine White regularly asked him for
humor and light verse: she wanted him to be funny, timely, and
above all prolific.*

In England, he had found topical subjects hard to come by. The
American newsmagazines he used to rely on for inspiration when he
churned out copy for the *Lampoon* were out of date by the time they
reached Oxford, and he felt uncertain and out of touch. But once
settled in Manhattan, he began to contribute casuals (the magazine's
catchall term for humorous prose): a parody of *Life* magazine; of

---

* The magazine was considerably fatter in the late fifties. For example, the issue in which "Sunday Teasing" appeared (October 13, 1956) ran to 204 pages.
During the fall season, the magazine often hit the upper limit set by Shawn:
248 pages.

Kerouac's *On the Road* ("On the Sidewalk"); of a T. S. Eliot lecture; of Harry Truman's memoirs. In the issue of January 26, 1957, is a piece entitled "Notes," which was never included in any of Updike's omnium-gatherums, possibly because it's hard to classify: "Notes" isn't a parody, exactly, and it's certainly not a book review. Prompted by newly published volumes of verse by John Berryman and Marianne Moore, both footnoted, it gently mocks the "self-exegesis" of the poets' *Waste Land*–like explanatory footnotes, an *apparatus criticus* alternately pretentious and condescending. In making fun of densely allusive highbrow poetry and the enthusiasts who champion it, Updike was making fun of himself and his passion for textual titans.* Despite his burgeoning artistic ambitions and his educated taste for high culture, he was still leery of exhibiting the telltale signs of literary sophistication. Aware of his own ambivalence, he made the clash of high and low culture a feature of both his casuals and his poetry.

The poems he was publishing in *The New Yorker* were mostly delicious froth, ingenious, well-crafted silliness. He'd been writing light verse—he defined it as verse that takes its spark from "the man-made world of information," from "language and stylized signifiers"—for more than a decade, beginning with his many contributions to *Chatterbox* and the *Lampoon*, but at Harvard and Oxford he'd also written poems in a more serious vein, poems derived, as he put it, "from the real (the given, the substantial) world." The serious poetry stopped while he was in New York. About half of the fifty-five poems in his first book, the slim, cheerful volume called *The Carpentered Hen*, were written while he was living in the city; all but one of those he classed as light verse†—which was what the

---

* Decades later, he provided generous notes for his *Collected Poems, 1953– 1993*, most of them autobiographical (and therefore a kind of self-exegesis), but neither condescending nor pretentious.

† The exception is "Tao in the Yankee Stadium Bleachers," which he wrote having taken Arthur Waley's *Three Ways of Thought in Ancient China* to the ballpark and peeked at it between innings. Perhaps not light verse, but not exactly heavy, either.

magazine wanted at the time, though Howard Moss, the poetry editor, never said so explicitly. In the 1950s it was still a relatively common, marketable genre that enjoined a certain amount of prestige. Harper and Brothers, which published *The Carpentered Hen*, also published the work of a number of other *New Yorker* writers, including E. B. White and James Thurber; the house was willing to print a young writer's collection of verse, but the idea was that more substantial work would be coming along soon.

A couple of months after he started at the magazine, he produced a poem making fun of a flag-waving, chest-beating editorial in *Life*, "Wanted: An American Novel." The gist of the editorial was that our anguished "hothouse literature" must perk up; instead of agony and gloom, the editorialist asserted, what was needed was more vigorous and manly writing reflecting the power and prosperity of our great nation. *Life* was calling for "a yea-saying to the goodness and joy of life." Updike responded with "An Ode":

> I'm going to write a novel, hey,
> I'll write it as per *Life*:
> I'm going to say, "What a splendid day!"
> And "How I love my wife!"

The poem, classically divided into strophe and antistrophe (mock pretension that adds an amusing absurdist touch), concludes with a pun silly enough to deflate an army of jingoistic editorialists:

> For *Life* is joy and *Time* is gay
> And *Fortune* smiles on those
> Good books that say, at some length, "Yea,"
> And thereby spite the Noes.

The gagster in him could hardly resist the opportunity to indulge in this kind of bright playfulness. Certainly he was going to write a novel (though hardly "as per *Life*")—in the meantime, his employer encouraged his penchant for "cartooning with words," and rewarded him for doing so.

Writing for The Talk of the Town, a plum post by any reckoning, and at the same time having his short stories, casuals, and light verse published in the magazine—this was more or less exactly the adult future he'd dreamed of since adolescence, his "sole ambition" ecstatically fulfilled. William Maxwell warned him in a letter just before he reported for duty, "If there is anything to be said against working for *The New Yorker*, it is that it makes the thought of working anywhere else too appalling." Sure enough, this was Updike's first and last regular employment—and his only firsthand exposure to the culture of a busy corporate office. His fellow workers, though, were mostly as intent as he on the lonely business of reading and writing, so it was not a particularly sociable environment. The exception was Brendan Gill, a lifelong staffer, "the only gregarious man on the premises," who regularly scooped up young Updike and led him off with several colleagues—Tony Bailey and Joe Mitchell, say—to the Blue Ribbon, where the waiters were clad in white aprons and the knackwurst was famously succulent, for a bantering midday meal.

The offices at 25 West Forty-Third Street were shabby, and cluttered with stacks of old phone books. The ambience was more like a newspaper than a glossy magazine; "everything," Updike remembered, "was slightly dusty and funky." The grimly functional décor and the pervasive hush suited his relentless work ethic, his ability to shut out for hour after hour everything but the task at hand. The newspaper feel was a hangover from the days of Harold Ross (himself an unreconstructed newspaperman), who died in 1951; the hush had more to do with his successor, the notoriously soft-spoken William Shawn. When Updike claimed his desk on the eighteenth floor, four years after Ross's death, Shawn was very much in charge—indeed, he was essentially the sole arbiter of what went into the magazine, a consolidation of editorial power unknown in Ross's day. It was Shawn who "handled" Updike's Talk pieces, and the two quickly established an amicable if distant rapport—distant mostly because Shawn was shy and Updike was in awe.

Nowadays Shawn is nearly as famous for his oddities as for his editorial prowess. The catalogue of his phobias and behavioral tics, the intrigue (especially his decades-long office romance with Lillian

Ross, which was meant to be a deep, deep secret and became, with the passage of time, merely the obvious but unmentionable status quo), the passive-aggressive manipulation of colleagues and contributors, the velvet tenacity of his grip on power (Maxwell once observed that in Shawn were combined the best features of Napoleon and St. Francis of Assisi)—it's all almost enough to make us forget the astonishing success with which he steered the magazine.

After Shawn died in 1992, Updike wrote a tribute for the pages of *The New Yorker*, a curiously equivocal document that ends with the disturbing image of Shawn "pinkly crouched behind his proof-piled desk." From the very first sentence, in which he remarks on Shawn's "unfailing courtesy and rather determined conversational blandness," Updike's praise is undercut by less flattering observations. All told, the image conveyed is of a quiet, shy, morbidly polite, deceptively passive character with a peculiar and powerful intelligence, a magician who weekly managed heroic editorial feats "without moving a muscle." An admiring portrait, perhaps, but not an affectionate one. Eight years later, after the publication of a spate of books about Shawn's tenure at the magazine, Updike restated his views, adding richer praise and darker hints of censure:

> His sense of honor, his sometimes venturesome taste, his wish to make every issue a thing of beauty permeated the magazine; if he did . . . stay at the helm too long, and did employ deception in his personal and editorial life, he remains, for me, a model of acumen and kindness, with something truly otherworldly in his dedication to exalted, disinterested standards within the easily sullied, and increasingly crass, world of the printed word.

Updike's private feelings about Shawn were more sharply ambivalent, but in his public utterances he remained loyally deferential to the man who had done so much to determine his literary fate.

That public loyalty was richly earned. Shawn recognized right away the value Updike's work, and foresaw that this particular "dazzled farm-boy" would quickly become a key contributor.

When in the summer of 1961 Updike volunteered to begin writing book reviews, Shawn agreed immediately; later that same year, Shawn approached him about becoming the magazine's television critic. Updike sensibly declined on the grounds that, in Ipswich, he couldn't watch any of the local channels available in the metropolitan area; he admitted, however, that he was tempted by the security of a critic's regular salary. Though Shawn occasionally made known (through White or Maxwell) his appreciation of Updike's fiction, he was more likely to praise the nonfiction. For example, along with the check sent to Updike for his celebrated Our Far-Flung Correspondents piece about Ted Williams's last at-bat, "Hub Fans Bid Kid Adieu," was a note from Shawn expressing, in so many words, his "gratitude and admiration." There's no record of his opinion of Updike's verse, but we can deduce that he approved from the sheer number of poems accepted by the magazine over the years. In 1965, when Updike published his first collection of essays, *Assorted Prose*, he dedicated it to William Shawn, an appropriate choice for at least two reasons: a nod from Shawn had allowed about three quarters of the material in the collection to run in his magazine; and it was Shawn (even more, perhaps, than Katharine White) who saw in Updike an all-purpose writer of "assorted prose"—who recognized, in short, a budding man of letters.

However well disposed, Shawn was an enigmatic benefactor, an "ineffable eminence," a secretive wizard whose verdict ("the message was commonly expressed, 'Shawn says yes' or 'Shawn says no'") was inscrutable and beyond appeal. The maternal Katharine White, who guided Updike with gentle patrician firmness to a settled place in the stable of *New Yorker* writers, and who set a rigorous precedent for all his subsequent editorial dealings, was a friendly, admired mentor. William Maxwell, who began his career as White's assistant, played an entirely different role from those two Olympian figures. Maxwell was involved in a more intimate way both with Updike's writing and in his personal life, and became a close, trusted friend; the friendship, abiding and sincere, was a product of a long, unusually fruitful, and nearly frictionless professional collaboration.

When White retired to her husband's farmhouse in Maine, which she did in stutter steps beginning in 1955, Maxwell took charge of editing Updike's stories, a duty he embraced like a labor of love and relinquished only when he in turn retired. Because Maxwell (born in 1908) was old enough to be Updike's father, you might have expected his relationship with the younger man to be paternal or avuncular; and because Maxwell was himself an accomplished novelist (acclaimed by critics and revered by his fans, but never reaching as broad an audience as he would have liked), one might have expected him to present himself as a mentor. In fact, he had a talent for nimbly avoiding the appearance of exerting authority of any kind (which is not to say that he was passive-aggressive like Shawn); his idea of editing was to hover like a good angel over Updike's shoulder, giving him the occasional nudge. *Caretaker* is the word Updike used to describe him: "He was, in effect, the caretaker of my livelihood"; as usual, it's exactly the right word. Updike sensed the older man's "intensity of care and even affection" for the stories they worked on together, and this solicitude made him feel "cherished." Maxwell was forty-six when they met (twice Updike's age), and the younger man admired his gentle, serious demeanor, his air of mild urbanity, his soft-spoken reverence for writing. Updike later remarked that on first impression he "conveyed a murmurous, restrained nervous energy and an infallible grace"—Fred Astaire came to mind.

Their friendship—as opposed to their friendly professional dealings—didn't fully blossom until after Updike moved to Ipswich. In fact, he didn't even meet Maxwell's wife and daughters until September 1957, when he stopped by their apartment during a brief stay in the city. A month later, just before Thanksgiving, the Updikes visited the Maxwells at their country house in Yorktown Heights, New York—the first time the two families came together. The visit went well; it was the highlight, Updike claimed, of his family's Thanksgiving vacation, which included a stop in Greenwich at his aunt Mary's house and a longer stay in Plowville. From that point on, Updike's correspondence with Maxwell is warmer, more relaxed and rambling, peppered with jokes, family news, and curious trivia. His editor brought out the best not just in his stories but also in *him*: the letters are affectionate and generous, serious when the topic calls for it, but otherwise lightly playful; they seem genuine, unforced, and unmediated—with Maxwell he clearly no longer felt the need, as he had when they first met, to adopt a pose or strike an attitude. He surely sensed that the older man admired him sincerely and expected great things of him. In fact, when he recommended Updike for a Guggenheim in the fall of 1958, Maxwell told the fellowship committee, "If he doesn't get the Nobel Prize, it will be the Swedes' fault, not his."

In his own fiction, Maxwell returned again and again to his boyhood haunts in Lincoln, Illinois. It's no surprise, therefore, that unlike Katharine White, he was receptive to Updike's penchant for nostalgia. Not long after the cheery Thanksgiving visit, during a tête-à-tête lunch at the Century, he encouraged Updike to revisit Shillington in the pages of *The New Yorker*. Updike had been telling him about his school days, remembering an unrequited crush on a sixth-grade girl—whereupon Maxwell said, "That's a short story." Updike went home to Ipswich and, in the first week of the new year, wrote it down more or less the way he'd spoken it; the result, "The Alligators" (the first story in which the name Olinger is given to the hero's hometown), was published in the magazine several weeks later. Maxwell thought the finished product read like one long poem—praise that thrilled Updike and made him itch to write more about his Berks County childhood. That kind of helpful intervention occurred with surprising regularity over the next two decades.

There are of course difficulties involved in having a friend for an editor. "The relationship," as Updike acknowledged, "is to some extent adversarial." He admitted to having been vexed by the rejection of certain stories; and when he complained about the "meddlesome perfectionism" of *New Yorker* editors, Maxwell, though unnamed, was one of the guilty parties. Updike knew that Maxwell enjoyed "a good verbal tussle" when he edited a piece, but Updike did, too, so there was never any rupture, nor even lingering annoyance. He recognized that Maxwell, as Mary reminded him, was "part of a machine for getting out a certain kind of magazine"; behind his editorial decisions loomed the omnipotent Shawn and the increasingly ponderous *New Yorker* tradition. Also, Maxwell was preternaturally tactful, and Updike, thanks to his mother, adept at avoiding confrontation. There was never a chance that Maxwell, by nature cautious, would push the young Updike in a daring or different direction. If he ever put a foot wrong, if he ever hampered his writer or sold him on poor advice, there's no record of it. At the end of their twenty-year collaboration, Maxwell wrote, "Could there have been an easier or happier association I ask myself, who perhaps shouldn't be the one to do it. But when I look back at the long line of stories that passed between us, I can only smile with pleasure." For his part, when he stumbled on a trove of old *New Yorker* letters full of his editor's attentive, affectionate, encouraging advice, Updike waxed ecstatic, remembering with sentimental fondness the delicate ministrations of his "caretaker."

However easy and mutually beneficial his relations with the magazine, he knew that he should be expanding his professional horizons—in other words, that he should start publishing books. Like many of *The New Yorker*'s star contributors, including E. B. White and James Thurber, he turned to Harper and Brothers, a venerable publishing house established in the early nineteenth century. Updike's choice was made easy by the fact that he'd already promised the head of the house, Cass Canfield, a first look at anything he wrote for "book publication." Early in 1957, in response to Canfield's yearly reminder, Updike indicated that he had very nearly finished work on a novel, and was also eager to publish a collection of light verse and a collection of stories.

By then, however, he'd already made the decision to quit *The New Yorker* and leave Manhattan.

THE UPDIKES' SECOND child, David, was born on January 19, 1957. It was immediately apparent, when mother and baby came home from the hospital, that they would have to move out of the apartment on West Thirteenth Street; a family of four needed more space. They planned to look for a new place near a park, with an elevator, if possible. One week after the baby was born, on Mary's twenty-seventh birthday, as it happened, the Updikes were invited to a party at Brendan Gill's house in Bronxville. Mary couldn't go because she was nursing her newborn, but John decided that he would go anyway. Though she was unhappy about being left behind on her birthday, Mary kept her feelings to herself—her mother was staying with them, helping out with Elizabeth, now a toddler of nearly two, and she didn't want her disappointment to show. John set off in his Ford coupe, taking with him Tony Bailey and Faith McNulty, another Talk reporter. He returned several hours later with his mind made up: he told Mary that night that they should leave New York entirely. It was obvious that something had upset him, but he wouldn't say what it was, except that he had the feeling, an overwhelming feeling, that he had to get out of the city—or else he would become like everybody at the Gills' party, the writers and hangers-on all competing with one another.

Half a century later, after seeing McNulty's obituary in the newspaper, Updike wrote to Bailey saying that the obit had summoned up a "dreamlike" recollection of the party—"the great and the near-great looking tired and tiddly"—and of the drive back from Bronxville: Bailey and McNulty quarreling about something, a distracted Updike ending up on the wrong side of the East River, and Bailey pointing out the view of the Manhattan skyline "shimmering across the water." Looking back on that evening and his impulsive decision to leave New York, he wrote, "A major turning point in my life, I see now."

The Gill residence in Bronxville, described by its owner as "a large, semi-ruinous mock-Tudor mansion," was an imposing pile. The guests would have included a sizable *New Yorker* cohort—the art editor, James Geraghty; cartoonists Charles Addams and Peter Arno; and writers Wolcott Gibbs, A. J. Liebling, Geoffrey Hellman, St. Clair McKelway, Philip Hamburger, E. J. Kahn Jr., Niccolò Tucci, and Robert Coates, among others. Despite the size of Gill's house, the noise of the booze-fueled chatter and the prodigious volume of cigarette smoke may have produced a claustrophobic effect—too many old tweed jackets and gray flannels, too much understated wit. Updike's brief description of the festivities—"the great and the near-great looking tired and tiddly"—is of course based on a fifty-year-old memory, as is his account of the drive home with quarrelling colleagues and the picture-postcard view of the skyline. But even taking into account the vagaries of memory and the seventy-three-year-old's lifelong habit of massaging his past into pleasing dramatic shapes, it seems safe to say that at that particular moment in early 1957, any large gathering of *New Yorker* staff—sober or not, illustrious or less so—was bound to stir up his competitive instinct. And if they were indeed looking "tired and tiddly," that dispiriting aspect would have reminded him, like a nagging sore, of his own unfulfilled ambitions.

The excitement and glamour of living in New York had always, for Updike, come bundled with less agreeable sensations. He felt "crowded, physically and spiritually" by the city's "ghastly plenitude, its inexhaustible and endlessly repeated urban muchness." He groused about a literary scene "overrun with agents and wisenheimers" all too willing to give a twenty-four-year-old helpful hints about how he should live his life. This barrage of advice, some of it from fellow writers (the competition), some of it from editors and publishers, compounded his discomfort. According to Michael Arlen, his Lampoon friend who was at the time working at *Life* magazine and would later join *The New Yorker*, this kind of complaint was a regular lunchtime refrain as early as 1955. Updike, Arlen said, worried that "whatever you might do or achieve in New York, you could never feel important because there was always greater or at least noisier stuff going on all around you." Arlen was under the impression that Updike had been plotting an exit for some time, that his ambition required him to be a big fish in a little pond. In his letters home, Updike first mentions, in May 1956, his desire to escape both *The New Yorker* and the city: "Not quite right for me, as the rejection slips say." The Bronxville party, in other words, should be thought of as accelerating a process already under way.

The genial host offered a prime example of the kind of career Updike had no intention of pursuing. At age forty-two, Gill had been at *The New Yorker* for twenty-one years—half his life. Charming, talented, ebullient, relentlessly energetic—it's hard to imagine him looking tired, however tiddly—he was also a graceful, engaging writer admired for his commitment to the magazine. But divide the room into the great and the near-great and he would without a doubt fall into the latter category. As Updike observed in a memorial tribute, Gill "came to *The New Yorker* young, as a writer of short stories, and stayed as a jack of all trades"; he failed to "take his own artistic gifts quite seriously enough." Updike wasn't going to make that same mistake. He wanted to be an artist, not an "elegant hack," as he put it in a letter to his mother, who would have agreed wholeheartedly. After a year and a half at the magazine, his immediate professional ambitions had been met. New and lofty cultural ambitions had meanwhile sprung up in the breast of the young man who had once hoped to be the next Walt Disney—and to those ambitions, the magazine itself was an obstacle.

The guest of honor at the Gills' was Victor Gollancz, a British publisher with nearly two dozen *New Yorker* writers in his stable, who was visiting on his yearly American tour. Gill had written to Gollancz a few months earlier to tell him about Updike, calling him "easily the finest writing talent that has shown up on this magazine in the twenty years that I've been here." Gollancz was understandably eager to meet this young phenomenon. In the thick of the crowded party, they had a lively chat about Updike's work-in-progress, *Home*, which Gollancz offered to buy sight unseen; about book printing, always a topic dear to Updike's heart; and about the philosopher A. J. Ayer—because Gollancz thought Updike resembled Ayer: each had a thin face and a long nose. Updike, for his part, found in Gollancz (also a striking individual, bald, bespectacled, and mustachioed, with dramatically dark, bushy eyebrows) exactly his idea of what a publisher should be: "gallant, wise, and willing to lose money on a book." This encounter was the beginning of a complicated relationship built on mutual admiration that nonetheless ended badly—and it was also a reminder that writing Talk pieces and casuals for *The New Yorker*, filling his quota so as to achieve his "quantity bonus," was not going to be Updike's lifework. It was time to publish a book.

A nostalgic thumbnail self-portrait he contributed to *Horizon* magazine offers a glimpse of the earliest stirrings of his new ambitions. It was the autumn of 1955, when he was freshly arrived in New York and already making a splash at the magazine. Everything was falling into place for the young author, and it was in this "atmosphere . . . of dreams come true" that he succumbed to the influence of yet another textual titan.

> While our baby cooed in her white, screened crib, and the evening traffic swished north on the West Side Highway, and Manhattan at my back cooled like a stone, and my young wife fussed softly in our triangular kitchen at one of the meals that, by the undeservable grace of marriage, regularly appeared, I would read.

He was reading the first volume of Proust, and his very Proustian remembrance of that "paradisiacal" moment continues with a description of the powerful effect *Swann's Way* had on him:

> It was a revelation to me that words could entwine and curl so, yet keep a live crispness and the breath of utterance. I was dazzled by the witty similes . . . that wove art and nature into a single luminous fabric. This was not "better" writing, it was writing with a whole new nervous system.

Proust—together with Henry Green—upped the ante; as Updike put it, "Those two woke me up." They encouraged his belief that the dream of high artistic achievement could also come true— just at the moment when his new employer expected from him something decidedly more ordinary. In those first busy months in New York, he fretted that his career as a freelancer might be over, that he would never be able to write serious fiction in the evening after writing Talk pieces during the day. His solution to that problem— writing for himself in the office before the workday began, a stolen morning hour alone in his bare eighteenth-floor cubicle—didn't solve the larger problem. Caught up in the excitement of his success at *The New Yorker*, he ignored the stark choice his aspirations would eventually force on him: stay at the magazine and risk becoming an elegant hack, or gamble on a freelancer's precarious life and commit to the dream awakened in him by Proust and Green.

In some later accounts of his "defection" from *The New Yorker*, the pressure of having a toddler and an infant at home weighs as heavily as concern for his career—"the city itself," he wrote, "was no place to raise a family or hatch novels." But it was the unhatched novels rather than the children that tipped the scales. Although he'd written a sequence of stories set in the city, he felt that New York was not his fictional turf—it was "too trafficked, too well cherished by others." He had the impression, moreover, that in Manhattan he was exposing himself to only a thin slice of the American scene. He later complained that "immense as the city is, your path in it tends to be very narrow. I only knew people I went to college with and other writers." And the metropolitan magic was wearing thin; he called it "a vast conspiracy of bother." He wrote, "When New York ceased to support my fantasies, I quit the job and the city."

His path in the city was narrow also because at this stage he wasn't an especially adventurous young man. The self-declared prophet of "middleness" was squeamish about the extremes lying in wait up and down Manhattan from Harlem to the Lower East Side to Park Avenue. Blacks, Jews, aristocratic WASPs—all these were foreign to him. In a fundamental sense, he didn't feel safe in New York. And thanks to his inherited "Depression mentality," he balked at the cost of city living. If the magic was wearing thin, one suspects that it was partly because he'd closed his eyes to it.

Pushed out by the crowds, and by his anxieties, and pulled along by a secret faith in his own grand literary destiny, he announced to Shawn that he would leave town and become a freelance writer. He cited his growing family as his excuse. Shawn ("sweet as a mint paddy") promptly volunteered to find him a larger, more suitable apartment, but that generous gesture addressed only the most superficial aspect of the problem. And so, at the end of March, a week after his twenty-fifth birthday, John and Mary and their two children decamped to Ipswich. "The crucial flight of my life," he called it, perhaps forgetting that he'd already described his exile from Shillington at age thirteen as "the crucial detachment of my life"—one difference being that when he looked back on the flight from Manhattan, it was almost wholly without regret. In 1968 he told *Time* magazine that New York City was "always still where I live in my heart, somehow," and in a documentary filmed in the early eighties, he claimed, riding in a yellow taxi from LaGuardia to Manhattan, to still feel like a citizen of New York: "My money comes out of here, and my manuscripts go towards here, and in a funny way when I come down I feel like I'm going home"—but I suspect he said these things only to please the interviewer. To *Time*, he owned up to a "sneaking fondness for elegance, for people whose apartments are full of money and the martini comes all dewy and chilled." And then he launched into this remarkable riff:

> There's a certain moment of jubilant mortality that you get on a Manhattan street—you know, all these people in the sunshine, all these nifty girls with their knees showing, these cops, these dope addicts, everybody swinging along, and they're never going to be in the same pattern again and tomorrow a few of them will be dead and eventually we'll all be dead. But there's a wonderful gay defiance that you feel in New York in the daytime.

A fabulous tribute, but it smacks of performance rather than sincerity. Another, more compact expression of his feelings—"being in New York takes so much energy as to leave none for any other kind of being"—takes into account his most pressing priority, which was to secure for himself time and space to write.

He left New York without ever detaching himself from *The New Yorker*. As he was about to discover, geographical distance alone would do little or nothing to separate him from the magazine in the eyes of various prominent critics. On his last Sunday in town, a review appeared in *The New York Times* of John Cheever's *The Wapshot Chronicle*. The reviewer referred in the very first sentence, as though it were common knowledge, to the "many critical strictures" aimed at "the *New Yorker* school of fiction." He then expressed his hope that Cheever would "break loose" from the group, and applauded the point at which the novel finally "breaks through the proper confines of 'sensibility' in the typical *New Yorker* story." For Updike, who was by this time appearing in the magazine as often as any other short story writer (more frequently, in fact, than Cheever) and whose fiction relied less on incident than sensibility (fine perception, gestural nuance, delicately modulated tone), this amounted to a direct attack.

An attack, in this case, launched by Maxwell Geismar, a respected literary historian and critic who taught for many years at Sarah Lawrence College. A year later, Updike read another Geismar essay, this time in the *Saturday Review*, which associated the *New Yorker* school with the "very shallow sophistication" of F. Scott Fitzgerald's early work. Geismar opined that "Fitzgerald was the J. D. Salinger of the Twenties . . . and a natural *New Yorker* writer." The links here between Fitzgerald, Salinger, the *New Yorker* school, and very shallow sophistication are rather tenuous, but the essay nevertheless threw Updike into a funk. He was so distraught that William Maxwell felt obliged to send his "depressed" author a two-page, single-spaced letter dismissing Geismar as an "incompetent" and "undiscerning" critic. Maxwell's defense of Updike's fiction is more than a consoling epistolary pat on the shoulder; it's a witty and perceptive analysis of what the young writer was up to. It begins with a reminder that Maxwell's editorial touch was generally light (and hence that Updike was not a creature of the magazine), and ends with an ad hominem jab at the enemy:

> I don't find your work shallow, I don't see any danger of its becoming that way, and if it does become that way, I will (in my heart) hold you, not myself responsible. There is a sentence of Turgenev's that [Edmund] Wilson quotes in his introduction to Turgenev's literary memoirs that is very much to the point: ". . . Believe me, no man of real talent ever serves aims other than his own, and he finds satisfaction in himself alone: the life that surrounds him provides him

with the contents of his works; he is its <u>concentrated</u> <u>reflec-</u>
<u>tion</u>. . . ." That's what you are right now, old boy, and that's
what I hope you will continue to be, and it's not shallow for
the simple reason that life itself is not shallow. Nobody's life
is, not even Maxwell Geismar's.

The argument is essentially that Updike is his own man and his
fiction reflects his personal circumstance and is therefore also his
own.* When it comes to the related questions—whether Updike's
fiction can be justly described as shallow or sophisticated, or both,
and whether it's fair to lump it with a so-called *New Yorker* school—
Maxwell pivots deftly, evasively, and points out that Harold Ross,
who stamped the magazine with his personality, was hardly a sophisticated character. Finally he asks, "Are you or aren't you, in <u>your</u> heart,
pleased and happy to see a story of yours in *The New Yorker*?" The
answer could only be yes—but that didn't stop Updike from squirm-
ing with discomfort whenever he saw criticism leveled at the fiction
in the magazine. At this point his reputation as a writer rested solely
on his stories, all of which had appeared in *The New Yorker*. He felt
personally singed by any blast aimed at the magazine and its school.

Was there such a thing, at midcentury, as a typical *New Yorker*
story? Did a *New Yorker* school of fiction exist? Certainly the magazine favored quiet, lucid, and subtle over brash, baffling, and daring.
A polite, genteel tone held sway: nothing radical, nothing transgres-
sive, nothing in bad taste. In his *Paris Review* interview, Maxwell
bobbed and weaved his way to a few general remarks about the fiction in the magazine:

> Irwin Shaw when he was a young man said once that in the
> typical *New Yorker* story everything occurs at one place in
> one time, and all the dialogue is beside the point. It was not,

---

* This line of thought evidently struck a chord. In his mid-seventies manifesto
("Why Write?"), he declared, "We must write where we stand; wherever we
do stand, there is life; and an imitation of the life we know, however narrow,
is our only ground."

at the time, a wholly inaccurate description. . . . Something that *is* characteristic of the writers who appear in *The New Yorker* is that the sentence is the unit by which the story advances, not the paragraph, and the individual sentence therefore carries a great deal of weight and tends to be carefully constructed, with no loose ends. And style becomes very important.

There was just enough truth in the various generalizations to make the idea of a *New Yorker* school a credible target for critical dissent. It's true, for example, that until Donald Barthelme crashed the party in 1963, innovation and experimentation usually had to be smuggled into the pages of the magazine. Updike himself complained of a certain "prudery" and an "anachronistic nice-nellyism." Critics such as Geismar—a champion of naturalism who wanted to see harsh truths aired, who wanted readers to be shocked out of their complacency—were bound to be impatient with the standard *New Yorker* fare.

Actually, many of the writers who appeared in the magazine (Nabokov, for one), and even some who were dubbed "*New Yorker* school," such as Cheever and Salinger, *were* subversive, but in the quiet, lucid, subtle way that suited the editors. If Updike had considered the matter calmly and rationally, he would have ignored the passing gibes, or told himself that they were, as Maxwell insisted, examples of incompetent criticism; instead he fretted and stewed, concerned that his relationship with the magazine would distort perception of his work and prejudice critics against the novel he would shortly be publishing.

Soon his sensitivity extended to any disparaging remark about *New Yorker* contributors. In June 1960 he read a short article in *Time* magazine reporting on the dim view taken by Alfred Kazin, a distinguished literary critic, of recent Broadway theater. Dismissing what he called "Westport comedy," Kazin ridiculed the kind of character featured in those dramas: well-heeled Freud-spouting intellectuals, exurban and adulterous, among them "the artist for *The New Yorker*, that safe citizen of our times" who works "in a slightly Bohemian reconverted barn." It was clearly a throwaway line—Kazin was himself an intellectual and a sometime contributor to the magazine—but Updike took umbrage and dashed off a long, sour note to Kazin accusing him of spouting "smug humbug."* It's an ill-judged, unintentionally revealing document:

> I notice in *Time* a reference to "the artist for *The New Yorker*, that safe citizen of our times." I don't know why this kind of thing, so regularly emitted by Leslie Fiedler, Maxwell Geismar, etc. invariably causes me pain, nor why I am driven to the indiscretion of writing to you. Perhaps because I expect better of you, since your criticism is so good when it is directed at real subjects. I submit that the *NYer* is not a real object of criticism; that remarks should be directed toward individual contributors. Unlike contributors to *Time*, the magazine's contributors do sign their names and therefore should not be saddled with the sins, real and imagined, of other contributors.

Updike's argument about the magazine not being "a real object of criticism" is far less compelling than the bizarre spectacle of an author trying his best to shield himself from a blow directed at someone else entirely. The fact that the blow is glancing and possibly even inadvertent makes no difference—he can't stop himself:

> I honestly believe that . . . no attempt is made to get a *New Yorker* kind of story; that, in the minds of the editors, no such kind exists. And that I have never seen in print any kind of case made out for the corporate identity of *New Yorker* fiction; and that the clearest notions of such a corporate identity exist in the minds of those who read the magazine least.

---

* The letter is handwritten (somewhat unusually for Updike) on all four sides of a folded sheet of notepaper; the cramped writing space suggests that perhaps Updike was uncertain about the message he was sending. If he'd typed out his rant on a full-size sheet, perhaps he would have thought better of mailing it.

It's possible that he convinced himself of the honesty of these beliefs, but it seems more likely that he was in the grip of a desire that
distorted his judgment: He was desperate to imagine that his stories
could be read in *The New Yorker* and yet stand apart. He wanted to
benefit from the magazine's corporate identity and yet be seen as a
solo act; he wanted *New Yorker* cachet to rub off on him without
being tagged with a label.

Part of his aversion to the idea of a *New Yorker* school was a reflexive denial of a truth he elsewhere happily acknowledged: that he
was indebted to fiction he'd first read in the magazine, including stories by Cheever and Salinger. Though he admired both writers and
was influenced by both, any remark from a critic that lumped him
with them made him prickly and defensive, symptoms of what Harold Bloom would call the anxiety of influence.* When he was more
securely established, Updike mastered a more decorous response
to remarks about typical *New Yorker* stories, but in the late 1950s,
while he was still finding his voice, it was a topic almost guaranteed
to trigger a show of petulance.

When he left New York, fleeing the crowds and also the corrupting influence of a certain kind of big-city sophistication, he
was—in a halfhearted, conflicted way—trying to escape from *The
New Yorker* as well. Needless to say, he failed utterly.

---

* Updike was dismissive of what he called "Harold Bloom's torturous dramatization of literary history as a running battle between creative spirits and their
oppressive predecessors."

> [M]y conception of an artist . . . was someone who lived in a town
> like Shillington, and who, equipped with pencils and paper, practiced
> his solitary trade as methodically as a dentist practiced his. And
> indeed, that is how it is at present with me.
>
> —"The Dogwood Tree: A Boyhood" (1962)

IV.

Welcome to Tarbox

Ipswich was Shillington redux, paradise regained, a home to rival his first home, a place where he could plunge in fearlessly, without reservation, no longer needing to pose as an outsider. This is where he reached his prime: "If Shillington gave me life," he wrote in *Self-Consciousness*, "Ipswich was where I took possession of it." A small Colonial town two miles from the seashore and about thirty miles north of Boston, it was the scene of some of his sweetest triumphs: his first eight published novels were written in Ipswich, along with a majority of his best short stories and his most ambitious poetry. He arrived a promising young magazine writer without a single book to his credit and departed, seventeen years later, a consummately professional author—a bestselling, prizewinning novelist with a burgeoning reputation as a leading man of letters. By 1974, the year he left, he was not only a critically acclaimed, paid-up member of the literary establishment, but also rich (thanks to steady *New Yorker* earnings and a swelling stream of book royalties) and famous (thanks to the notoriety of *Couples*). His younger son and daughter

were born in Ipswich, and all four of his children thrived there—
"Children are what welds a family to a town," he once noted. But
it was also in Ipswich that the family imploded, his marriage to
Mary wrecked by a daisy chain of adulterous affairs. The peaks and
troughs of Updike's Ipswich life were extreme, and the turbulence
shook up his poetry and prose, real-life drama reenacted on the page.

Why Ipswich? They both knew it—Mary from childhood, John
from their honeymoon weekend—and they both liked it. John remembered "something comfortingly raggle-taggle" about the center
of town. "It felt," he wrote, "like a town with space, where you could
make your own space." They thought briefly of returning to Cambridge after New York; they knew they could be happy there, but
ruled it out after deciding that it would be too much like going back
to college. Updike once claimed that he'd moved to New England
to be closer to his Red Sox hero, Ted Williams. More plausibly, he
maintained that he chose Ipswich for its coastline, the famously
beautiful, unspoiled Crane Beach, where he hoped on sunny days
to bake away his psoriasis. That practical consideration, however,
counted for less than the tug of nostalgia. Ipswich and Shillington
are different in many respects; the Colonial history of Ipswich, its
unusually large number of pre-1725 houses, and its proximity to
the shore give it a distinctive flavor, whereas Shillington was always
blandly typical—ordinariness part of its enduring appeal. Shillington was already a suburb when Updike was a child, the few miles
to Reading shortened by a trolley line. Ipswich in 1957 was safely
distant from Boston's urban sprawl, though connected by commuter
rail. The drive to the city was about an hour's journey, part of it
through cultivated farmland. All the same, both Ipswich and Shillington were unmistakably small-town, and that was the key element as far as he was concerned. "A small-town boy," he wrote, "I
had craved small-town space." He was looking for a little pond with
room enough for a big fish. He also needed, after New York, to re-
establish his connection with "the whole mass of middling, hidden,
troubled America."

Ipswich changed and grew during his time there, but its essential character remained the same. It was a town of fewer than seven

thousand in 1957, and more than eleven thousand when he left. Part of what John and Mary liked about it was the crazy-quilt ethnic makeup of the population, with large Greek, Polish, French Canadian, and Irish contingents mixing with the old Yankees, all contributing to what Updike called "mini-city perkiness." Despite the natural beauty of the coastal setting and the rich history—Ipswich bills itself as "The Birthplace of American Independence," a claim based on a 1687 tax protest—the town's style is markedly casual. Updike thought of it as "a maverick kind of place." Many streets are dotted with seventeenth- and early eighteenth-century houses, but there was no historical district when he arrived, nothing precious or preening about it; as he remarked, "Ipswich is traditionally careless of itself."

Decision made, destination chosen, he quickly put the plan into action. He took an early morning train to Boston, and from there Mary's former roommate, Ann Karnovsky (née Rosenblum), drove him out to Ipswich to look for a place to rent. The idea was to take a twelve-month lease and consider it a trial period. They looked at an apartment for $200 a month, and the real estate agent also showed them some properties for sale. The house John and Ann settled on was a small wood-frame cottage called Little Violet. (It was painted lavender.) Because the agent didn't have a key, they saw it only from the outside, peeking in through the windows at the downstairs rooms. There was a barn, a carport for the Ford, and two acres of land. The house was a couple of miles south of the town center on Essex Road, with no immediate neighbors. The view out the back, over a meadow fringed by woods, gave the property an idyllic country feel. The rent was $150 a month.

With John suffering from a slight case of mumps, the family moved into Little Violet at the end of March, camping out in the semifurnished house until the first week of April, when movers brought the furniture from the apartment on West Thirteenth Street. There were only two bedrooms, both upstairs, but there were two bathrooms, and a marble-floored room at the back that became John's study. From his desk he could look out over the meadow—"a writer's paradise," he told his mother. To his *New Yorker* colleagues he said that the whole family loved the house, even ten-week-old David. Perhaps it was the fresh air, or the excitement of a new house, but Elizabeth, just two, took to waking at dawn, an exhausting routine for her parents.

One of John's first projects at Little Violet was to erect a mailbox at the end of the driveway on Essex Road (and thereby establish a Rural Free Delivery address); he then wrote a poem about it. In Plowville, the mailbox had been the place where he and his mother would "reap" rejection slips; "Planting a Mailbox," with its cheerful mock-horticultural instructions ("Don't harrow, weed, or water; just apply / A little gravel. Sun and motor fumes / Perform the miracle; in late July, / There a post office blooms"), suggests that he was hoping for better results in his new home, a bountiful crop of mail. As if conjured by this two-part ritual, the postman delivered good news less than a fortnight after their arrival, news that could be seen as a validation of the move to Ipswich. Updike had wanted to break out of *The New Yorker* and establish an independent career as a freelancer, and here was Cass Canfield writing to announce that Harper and Brothers was prepared to publish a collection of his light verse. In the same letter, Canfield inquired pointedly after the progress of the novel: "We are all looking forward greatly to seeing the manuscript," he wrote, a reminder that publishing a budding author's light verse, however entertaining, was not Harper's main objective. Updike needed no encouragement on that score: he wanted to be a freelance writer, but more specifically he wanted to be a novelist.

In early May, Updike met in Boston with his Harper editor, Elizabeth Lawrence, who traveled up from New York to discuss the terms of the contract for the volume of poetry, which he planned to call *Biscuits for Cerberus*. This first encounter went smoothly; Updike charmed his editor, who followed up with a long, swooning letter: "Didn't we have a pleasant meeting last Monday? I came away feeling well rewarded. It was really great fun." She also gave her initial reaction to the six-hundred-page manuscript, typed out on yellow *New Yorker* scratch paper, of the novel *Home*, which Updike had handed over in Boston. Having read only the first half, she gave a guarded response, but on the whole her impression was positive:

"It gathers power as it goes. There are lovely things in it. And, best, it is written with the muscles and perceptions of a novelist." She made it clear that she wouldn't be offering any further opinion until the manuscript had been read by Canfield and Simon Michael Bessie, another high-ranking Harper editor. In the meantime, she appended a list of sixteen poems that she and "several readers" judged "not up to the best of the collection." The list includes "Ex-Basketball Player" (now his most frequently anthologized poem), "Shipbored," "Youth's Progress," and "Lament for Cocoa"; many of the flagged poems are delightful, and most had already appeared in the pages of *The New Yorker*. In the end Updike dropped only three of the sixteen.

Boyishly thrilled to be publishing his first book and keen to establish good relations with Harper, he turned a blind eye to unmistakable signs of mixed feelings on the part of Lawrence, Canfield, et al. When in mid-June *Home* was formally rejected, Updike made not a peep of protest. The rejection letter, nominally from Canfield but citing the opinion of his colleagues, praises Updike's writing and the "acuteness" of his observation; it reaffirms the publisher's confidence in him "as a writer and as a novelist." The verdict, however, was unanimous: "[N]one of us feels that the book would attract a substantial audience, primarily because in its present form the action does not compel the reader's attention." The advice was that he should "put the manuscript aside for awhile," advice that clearly made an impression: he put it aside permanently. Writing to William Maxwell in the late seventies, Updike implied that he and Lawrence had together agreed on this course of action; in a 1969 interview, however, he made it sound as though shelving the manuscript of *Home* had been his own idea: "It had been a good exercise to write it, but it really felt like a very heavy bundle of yellow paper, and I realized this was not going to be my first novel—it had too many traits of a first novel."*

---

* A decade earlier, in 1959, he told an interviewer that after he finished *Home*, he made the decision not to rewrite it, but rather to "chalk it up to practice." There was no mention of a publisher rejecting it.

Home is largely composed of the kind of nostalgic Berks County material that Katharine White had advised him against submitting to *The New Yorker*. It's the Olinger chronicles presented as a continuous narrative stretching from his mother's teenage years to his own, retracing the familiar Hoyer/Updike saga—the same constellation of only child, unhappy parents, elderly grandparents, the same to-and-fro between a small Pennsylvania town and an isolated farmhouse. Canfield referred to it as "the family novel." It contains characters and situations Updike later recycled in various stories, notably "Flight" and "Pigeon Feathers," and two novels, *The Centaur* and *Of the Farm*. It was his story, his material—and also his mother's: Linda would retell her part (roughly the first half of *Home*) in her two books. With hindsight, it's easy to say that by following Harper's advice and suppressing this autobiographical bil-dungsroman, Updike did himself a big favor. The decision allowed him to make more considered and economical use of the material; as he later admitted, "every incident with any pith turned up later somewhere else."

He put the manuscript in a drawer and went straight to work on a new novel, which was only glancingly autobiographical—which had, in fact, none of the traits of a first novel ("wretched genre," he exclaimed in an early interview, still bitter about his struggle with *Home*). Set two decades into a not-quite-Orwellian future, *The Poor-house Fair* imagines life inside the Diamond County Home for the Aged, where John F. Hook, a ninety-four-year-old former teacher with strong religious views (a character closely modeled on John F. Hoyer, Updike's maternal grandfather), opposes the secular and pro-gressive views of Stephen Connor, the "prefect" in charge. Updike had mentioned to Lawrence when they met in Boston that he was already at work on another novel, and it became a kind of fig leaf to cover the embarrassment of *Home*'s sad fate: Harper now pinned its hopes on the new manuscript.

Having finished off two final New York stories in early April—"A Gift from the City" and "Incest"—he wrote "Walter Briggs," his first story set in Ipswich. It has a comically tortured publishing history: it suffered through repeated title changes, and didn't run until nearly two years after it was submitted. The wrangles over "Walter Briggs" were lighthearted (in part because the stakes weren't especially high), but it's clear from the exchanges with Maxwell and White that Updike was learning to hold his ground in editorial disputes. He sent the story off in late June under the title "Walter Palm," telling Maxwell that Mary found it insubstantial and that it should perhaps be published under a pseudonym. When it became clear that *The New Yorker* was in fact going to accept it, an alarmed Updike explained that Walter Palm was an actual person's name and that the story was therefore libelous. Updike had once again lifted a character wholesale from life and pinned him to the page—in this case a retired man the Updikes had encountered at the YMCA family camp on Sandy Island the summer they were married. The character is peripheral to the story; the only important things about him are his name and the fact that the young husband and wife at the heart of the story both remember him as a background figure, a passing acquaintance in the first, romantically charged months of their marriage.

Walter Palm was a retiree who spent the entire summer at the camp playing cards and shuffleboard and fishing in Lake Winnipesaukee. He's described in the story as a fat man with a sly smile, lazy and complacent; although there's nothing more offensive than that, it's hardly surprising that Updike would want to change the name. And yet the name is integral to the story, part of an improvised memory game the young couple play on their way back home from Boston in their car: Clare tests her husband, Jack, on his knowledge of the names of the staff and residents of the camp. When she asks for the name of the fat man with the floppy fisherman's hat, Jack can come up with only the first name, Walter. Later, lying in bed after Clare has fallen asleep, replaying scenes from their honeymoon idyll, the rustic, candlelit cabin at the summer camp, redolent of romance, Jack suddenly remembers—the surname pops into his head. He whispers it to his wife, knowing he won't wake her, a bittersweet moment that reveals both the fissures in their marriage and his helpless nostalgia for those early days.

And what name, exactly, does Jack whisper? "Walter Palm" in the unpublished first draft; "Vergil Moss" in the version printed in

The New Yorker; and "Walter Briggs" in the version printed in *Pigeon Feathers*, Updike's second collection of stories. Along the way, Updike floated a handful of alternatives, including Edgar Sell, Edgar Moss, Edgar Neebe, Walter Bey, and, enjoying the joke, William Shawn.*

In all its various incarnations, "Walter Briggs" borrows freely and with unguarded precision from Updike's own experience. Clare and Jack have been married five years and have two children, a girl of two and an infant boy. Clare resembles Mary down to the cadence of her speech and her habit of going around barefoot. Jack, meanwhile, driven by competitive urges and prone to mildly malicious teasing, is glib and funny, hypersensitive and obscurely dissatisfied; he yearns for intimacy but is in fact himself somewhat withdrawn and self-absorbed. He worries that the excitement has faded from his marriage, and he reflexively blames his wife. He is more fully characterized than she is: whereas the reader is privy to some of his thoughts, none of hers are revealed. The couple closely resemble Jane and Lee from "Incest," and also Joan and Richard Maple from "Snowing in Greenwich Village"—in all three stories, Updike mines a domestic vein, exploring, as Katharine White urged him to, "the subtleties and affectionate and agonizing complexities" of how husband and wife get along.

Though he pilfered details from life to dramatize the young couples' marital relations—looks and gestures and quips that speak of stresses and strains—it would be wrong to assume that the stories accurately reflect the state of his own marriage at the time. The stories highlight difficulties, submerged or half-submerged family tensions that animate ordinary domestic scenes. Like many of her fictional avatars, Mary had learned to maintain "a self-preserving detachment." He clamored for attention; she occasionally withheld it. Acutely sensitive from childhood to the shifting moods

---

* The joke continued: the surname he finally picked was again that of a real person, his Harvard friend Austin Briggs. Bizarrely, in a 1968 Penguin edition of *The Same Door*, published in the United Kingdom, Updike inserted the original version of "Walter Palm"—its only unbowdlerized appearance.

of those around him (and to his own state of mind), John registered every twitch of annoyance, heard the echo of every private disappointment—but that's not what filled his day, or Mary's. The mood at Little Violet was cheerful; family life was busy, sometimes noisy and chaotic, as in any household where there are two children under three. Despite the burden of parenting, the relationship between John and Mary was warm and collaborative. She read his stories, poems, and casuals as soon as he had finished them, and again when editorial suggestions had been made, and sometimes even when they returned as author's proofs. She was forthright in her opinions, and her husband regularly quoted her in his letters to Maxwell. When he was working on "A Gift from the City," for example, Mary was disturbed that the "young Negro" who's the catalyst for the action of the story is never given a name but repeatedly referred to as "the Negro." John wrote to Maxwell a short letter in which Mary's judgment is cited on three separate issues including the problem of "the Negro"; Maxwell, when he received this missive, circled Mary's name and scribbled at the top, "one wife, one editor is all a man should have." In fact, she never edited her husband's work, strictly speaking, and her comments carried no special weight with *The New Yorker*—"the Negro" remained nameless after all—but it's clear that Updike relied on her as a first reader and respected her views. He called her a "pricelessly sensitive reader" and acknowledged that she advanced her shrewd opinions with gentle tact. When he mentioned Mary in his letters to Maxwell and White, there was no doubting his affection or the strength of their bond.

For his part, John was a conscientious father, a help to his wife and loving with the children. "He was good with the first baby," according to Mary, "and then he got better and better. He was willing to give baths and feed babies and bring me a baby to nurse in the middle of the night, to burp them. But he didn't wash diapers, which I had to do by hand until I could find a Laundromat or a diaper service." Although he was of some help with domestic chores, most of the housework and child care fell to Mary, if only because in Ipswich he soon established a regular routine that ate up most of the daylight hours. From breakfast until late lunch, he wrote. In that summer of 1957, when he was working on *The Poorhouse Fair*, he made up his mind to produce a minimum of three pages every morning (and many mornings, he did better). In the afternoon, he attended to other business—resolving editorial issues on stories and poems that had been bought by *The New Yorker*; checking and correcting galleys and proofs; and reading, for himself and also for the magazine, which was perpetually clamoring for casuals and light verse. His reading time often extended into the evening; his family reports that he always had a book in his hand. (The only place he didn't read was in bed.) His schedule remained essentially the same for the next fifty years. He never seems to have had any difficulty in getting himself to start work, or to sit still and concentrate for the number of hours necessary to meet his three-page quota. It sounds like a contradiction in terms, but he was effortlessly industrious.

Some of his afternoon reading was a way of courting inspiration for humorous writing. He'd flip through magazines and newspapers on the lookout for an item worth spoofing, some germ that might grow into a full-blown satire.* To Katharine White, who wrote in midsummer asking for casuals, he replied, "I came up here to get into a novel-writing groove. And have succeeded to the extent that I haven't an idea in my head." In September, when he'd nearly finished revising the draft of *The Poorhouse Fair*, she repeated her request, begging for "something funny and reasonably short"; he came up with "And Whose Little Generation Are You? Or, Astrology Refined," a quirky riff on the folly of classifying people according to their generation (as in the "Lost Generation" and the "Silent Generation"). The idea came to him when he picked up an article by literary critic Leslie Fiedler in the May issue of *The New Leader*, a bloated essay ripe for parody, full of dubious, would-be-clever classifications.

---

* The Updikes subscribed to a variety of mainstream publications, including *Life*, *National Geographic*, *The Atlantic*, *The New Republic*, *Saturday Review*, and also some smaller, left-wing journals: *Commonweal*, *Commentary* (which lurched to the right in the seventies), and *The Catholic Worker*. John, Mary explained, wanted to understand liberal positions.

The specific irritant was a self-serving assertion about Updike's age group: "The young, who should be fatuously but profitably attacking us, instead discreetly expand, analyze, and dissect us. How dull they are!" Updike actually quotes this pompous expostulation at the end of his casual, adding a clever kicker: "Anyone found discreetly expanding Leslie Fiedler may be assumed to be Silent." Most of the casual is taken up with "The Roll of Generations," Updike's tongue-in-cheek description of the cohort born each year from 1925 to 1934 (the Silent Generation). For the year of his own birth, he veers surreally into field guide jargon:

> b. 1932 The Cooler Generation. Much smaller and decidedly thinner than a song sparrow. Mostly blue-gray above, white beneath; white eye-ring, white-sided black tail. Voice: sharp *speeng*; high wiry *chee zee zee*. Prefers woodlands. Breeds north to southern parts of New Jersey, Michigan, Iowa. Winters along coast north to South Carolina.

Although amusingly absurd, this is hackwork, what he hoped to avoid by leaving New York—he would have called it an "afternoon labor." The morning writing slot was reserved for higher purposes.

Many afternoons were filled, starting in the late summer of that first year, with long-distance fiddling with the contents, design, and title of his book of poems, which Harper had scheduled for publication in March 1958. The name of the book changed even more frequently than that of "Walter Briggs"; after *Biscuits for Cerberus* came *Celery Hearts, Gingerly, Enough Poems, Noble Numbers, Round Numbers, Verse, Wellmeant Verse, Whatnot, Hoping for a Hoopoe* (which became the title of the English edition), and *The Carpentered Hen and Other Tame Creatures*, the title Harper finally agreed to at the beginning of October. Finding the perfect title was a team effort, husband and wife (and mother) mulling over the possibilities. Each time he came up with a new idea, he tried it out on Mary; if it won her stamp of approval, he put it forward to Harper with a surge of confidence. Other matters he wrestled with on his own. He was as deeply involved in the making of this first book as he was in the making of the scores that followed. From the beginning, he was passionate about the physical object, the item you held in your hand—the feel of it, the look of it, even the smell of it. Early on he insisted to Lawrence that he had to have the last word on any editorial changes, however small; in the months that followed he sent off long, precise letters concerning typography and layout, the weight and color of the paper, the jacket illustration, and the design of the title page. No detail was too tiny for him to consider, and his focused attention summoned a corresponding attentiveness at Harper. When the book finally appeared he was delighted. Relieved not to find a single typo, he exclaimed, "The poetry book is a <u>lovely</u> job"—though he noted changes he would like to make to the layout of a couple of poems if ever there was a second printing. He told Lawrence how pleased he was that on the shelf the spine of the book was just as tall as the last section of Pound's *Cantos*.

In later life he remembered Elizabeth Lawrence, indistinctly, as lanky and prissy, professionally capable but rather humorless. He liked her crisp voice over the telephone. When he wrote to her, his tone was businesslike but not unfriendly, occasionally sarcastic and jokey, but not flirtatious (as he was now and then in his letters to Katharine White); they certainly never settled into the kind of free-wheeling good fellowship he enjoyed with Maxwell. When Updike waxed ironic, Lawrence was sometimes puzzled ("Is the young man joking?" she scrawled at the top of one of his letters; "I can't decide"). She liked him, and wanted to hold on to him as a Harper author, but despite her good intentions and a flurry of behind-the-scenes maneuvering, she was too cautious and insufficiently deft to secure his loyalty.

The endgame played out as a two-month, slow-motion crack-up that would have shaken the confidence of a less sturdy writer. Shortly after he delivered the manuscript of *The Poorhouse Fair* in mid-December, he heard positive noises from Harper—Lawrence professed to be interested and admiring. Then, in a letter she sent off on the last day of 1957, she reversed field, telling him that she was "troubled about the impact of the story as a whole"; the second half, and in particular the ending, seemed weak to her, but as with *Home*, she was withholding final judgment until she could provide "a round-up of opinions" from other readers.

In addition to those other readers, Harper sought advice and assistance from Victor Gollancz, who had already bought the U.K. rights to *The Carpentered Hen*. Canfield was hoping that his British counterpart would offer to publish *The Poorhouse Fair*—subject to certain stipulated changes. The idea was to present a unified front; as Canfield put it in a letter, if Harper and Brothers and Victor Gollancz Ltd. took a "joint approach," asking for roughly the same revisions, Updike would be more likely to comply. The plan collapsed, partly because Gollancz liked the book more than Canfield and Lawrence (on the evidence of the novel, the Englishman thought the budding author "too good to lose") and partly because, as Lawrence recognized early on, Updike had a precocious sense of the sanctity of his own artistic aims: he was never inclined to compromise on what he considered essential matters, even when faced with concerted pressure. She declared that it would be "a mistake to publish [the novel] as it stands" and recommended that he cut it by a third and turn it into a "novelette," a term that surely rankled. His response was to ask, politely, with expressions of regret, for a more precise accounting of the book's defects—and to request the return of the manuscript. "I think we knew already," Lawrence wrote to Canfield in a scribbled note at the top of Updike's letter, "that this is a young man you take or leave, as is." She nonetheless elaborated on her concerns, in a two-page letter that for Updike closed out the possibility that he would ever come to terms with Harper. She argued that the central thematic conflict (identified by Updike as "humanism vs. supernaturalism") is "not carried to a satisfactory or satisfying conclusion." (What she refrained from telling him was that she believed the novel's fate in the marketplace "could be dismal."*) Updike responded to her letter by saying he had always intended to

---

* Gollancz took a similarly dim view of the novel's commercial prospects: he wrote to Mike Bessie, "I doubt whether we shall sell more than about 1500 copies of this particular book." He published it all the same.

leave the thematic conflict unresolved; "You went to the heart of its unacceptability to Harper," he wrote, "which is also the heart of the book." In subsequent letters, Lawrence tried to reassure Updike that "the doors at Harper's are wide open," not just to him but to the novel; he remained convinced, however, that they were shut tight. He complained to Maxwell about the difficulty of convincing Harper that it had in fact turned the novel down.

Indeed unwilling to let go, Canfield wrote to Katharine White to ask whether she thought Updike might be cajoled into making revisions. She replied with a long, exceptionally frank letter that failed to answer the question—she was in Maine; she no longer "handled" Updike, was less frequently in touch with him, and therefore couldn't know how he was likely to react—but she did deliver an opinion on the state of his career. She was not surprised that Canfield didn't like the novel—"I always felt that he was starting to write one too soon." She continued in the same vein:

> It is still a moot question whether fiction is his best vein, though please never say this to him. He is, perhaps, too versatile for his own good and my personal feeling is that he is at his best when writing satire and humor and perhaps even essays. But I doubt that he thinks so at the moment, and every so often he writes a really brilliant short story that is novelistic in treatment, so I could well be wrong.

She lamented the trend of publishers pushing their authors to produce novels rather than books of short stories or humor or satire— "so in the minds of young writers like John . . . the novel is *it*—is 'a must.'" Having vented her general frustration, she returned to the case of the young writer in question:

> Well, I'm keeping my fingers crossed for John. Anything could happen to him—good or bad. We all worry about him, and he is so very self-doubting, though putting up a front of being just the opposite, that he is probably sunk by Harper's decision on his novel.

White's worry is a reminder of how precarious his situation was, and of how difficult it was to interpret behavior that veered from youthful bravado (John in amiable jester mode) to uneasy, awkward, and apologetic (John's aw-shucks pose, which could easily be mistaken for a lack of confidence). Two novels in a row had been turned down—or at least that's the way *he* saw it. Although he had a book of light verse on the way, and an enviably smooth working relationship with *The New Yorker*, his only source of income was his writing (he estimated in late 1958 that he was making ten thousand dollars a year), and he had a wife and two tiny children to support. White believed he was self-doubting, but there's actually no sign that he was "sunk" by the rejection; it did no apparent damage to his self-esteem. On the contrary, only four days after hearing the bad news from Harper, he felt self-assured enough to buy his first house.

The lease on Little Violet was due to run out at the end of March, and the Updikes, thoroughly settled after just ten months in Ipswich, took the plunge. They bought a classic saltbox, a large seventeenth-century house complete with a massive central chimney and a plaque beside the front door with the name and date: the Polly Dole House, 1686. Squeezed onto a small plot on the corner of East and County Streets, it was just a few blocks from the center of the town. The upstairs was a warren of small rooms, more than a family of four would normally need, but John wasn't in the mood for caution or restraint. The big downstairs living room, with its foot-wide floorboards and walk-in Colonial fireplace, perfectly expressed his expansive sense of well-being. Just when Katharine White expected him to be rattled, he made a grand gesture of faith in his future prospects, taking out a mortgage to finance the $18,500 purchase. "I am now deeply in debt and quite panicked," he told Maxwell, comically exaggerating his anxiety with a description of the house as a fourteen-room tumbledown pile teetering on a corner plot shared with the neighborhood dump. One reason for his high spirits was a lift given him by *The New Yorker*: Maxwell had just accepted "The Alligators" (the story in which Olinger was given its name), and Updike felt, as he told his editor, a tremendous sense of excitement; he declared himself "ready to disgorge the whole mass of Pennsylvania." That is what he then did over the next half-dozen years, spinning out a dazzling sequence of stories—including "The Happiest I've Been" (written just three weeks after "The Alligators"), "Flight," "Pigeon Feathers," and a run of others, all collected in *Olinger Stories* (1964)—as well as *Rabbit, Run*; *The Centaur*; and *Of the Farm*. Tapping into the rich vein of Berks County material, buying real estate in Ipswich, and weathering the rejection of *The Poorhouse Fair*—all in the space of a few days in late January 1958—Updike (still shy of his twenty-sixth birthday) was indeed at a juncture where, as White put it, anything could happen to him. But he knew what he'd accomplished so far, and he knew what he still had inside him ("I was full of a Pennsylvania thing I wanted to say"), so he pushed ahead, trusting in his talent.*

His optimism and his faith in his writing were rewarded almost instantly. Tony Bailey, his *New Yorker* pal, visiting Ipswich at the end of February with his new bride, listened sympathetically to the story of Harper's obtuse hesitation and suggested that Updike send a carbon copy of the manuscript of *The Poorhouse Fair* to Stewart ("Sandy") Richardson, an editor at Alfred A. Knopf. Updike took Bailey's advice. Less than two weeks later, a "wildly enthusiastic" Richardson bought the novel, accepting it without reservation. By the end of March, Updike was under contract with Knopf; he would stay with the publisher for the rest of his life.

For an author with literary ambitions and a passion for attractive, well-made books, Alfred A. Knopf was the ideal place to be. By the time Updike appeared, it had been for several decades the premier literary publisher in America, well known for beautiful bindings and brilliantly designed dust jackets. Run by its eponymous founder and his wife, Blanche, a flamboyant, globetrotting couple who were in their mid-sixties (and often at each other's throats) when Updike signed his first contract, the company specialized in

---

* No sooner had negative word arrived from Harper than he set to work on yet another new novel, *Go Away*, which he abandoned a year later, having accumulated some 250 pages of typescript. To his mother he described it as "a long account of the good old days in Shillington."

novels and poetry; D. H. Lawrence, Willa Cather, H. L Mencken, Robert Graves, Wallace Stevens, Langston Hughes, and John Hersey were among the American and English stars on the list. The house also published in translation a great many distinguished authors, including Thomas Mann, Knut Hamsun, Jorge Amado, André Gide, Albert Camus, Jean-Paul Sartre, Yukio Mishima, and Yasunari Kawabata. Far and away its greatest commercial success was the publication in 1923 of a slender book of prose poems by a Lebanese-born writer, Khalil Gibran; *The Prophet* went on to become one of the bestselling books of all time, and a constant stream of revenue for the publisher.

Even before he'd signed his Knopf contract, Updike sent Sandy Richardson a long letter about the dust jacket (with sketches enclosed) and the design of the "inner aspect of the book," down to the tiniest detail of typography. He was jumping right in, as he had with Elizabeth Lawrence, eager to master the ins and outs of the printing process and hoping to influence every aspect of production. Richardson greeted his three-page missive with alarm and amusement, calling it "fine and helpful"—then asking, "Do I sense here a universal man?" They established from the beginning a bantering rapport, trading witticisms with competitive fervor, and might have become fast friends had Richardson not been fired in mid-November 1958, just weeks before the publication of *The Poorhouse Fair*.

In the normal course of events, Updike might have had fairly limited contact with Alfred Knopf himself, but because of Richardson's sudden dismissal, and because Updike never had an agent and was always obsessively attentive to design and production—an obsession Knopf shared—for several years publisher and author exchanged letters on a weekly, sometimes daily basis. The tone of Updike's letters was amiable, even friendly, but not playful, and not affectionate or conspiratorial as it was with Maxwell. A brilliant publisher with a genuine enthusiasm for literature, Knopf was a vibrant character: portly, with Burnside whiskers, and proud of his sartorial flair—he favored brightly colored shirts and vivid neckties. Updike described him as a cross between a Viennese emperor and a Barbary pirate. In the office, he was prone to bullying; he permitted himself to harangue his employees, to batter them with barbed memos, and to fire them summarily, as in the case of poor Richardson. The friction with his wife was the stuff of company legend. To Updike he was unfailingly polite and occasionally avuncular; he was thorough, businesslike, and decisive, which suited Updike just fine—he didn't want to be any friendlier with the Knopfs than professional courtesy required. In the beginning, anyway, he was content to have found another publisher so quickly and easily. In early November 1958, when he finally held in his hands a finished copy of his first novel, he was dizzy with delight.

"I wrote *The Poorhouse Fair* as an anti-novel," he once told an interviewer, underscoring an affinity with what came to be called the "nouveau roman." Elsewhere he claimed that he wrote it as "a deliberate anti–*Nineteen Eighty-Four.*" While it's true that *The Poorhouse Fair* has an unconventional form (a "queer shape," he called it), not entirely unlike that of certain avant-garde French novels of the 1950s, and that it presents a future nowhere near as scary as the one Orwell imagined, Updike's novel is perhaps better described as an anti–*first* novel. The great majority of first novels dote on the author's younger days, offering a backward glance masquerading more or less successfully as fiction; but Updike's first novel looks forward twenty years, peering uncertainly at a mildly dystopian tomorrow, and the characters (none of whom even remotely resembles the author) are mostly geriatric. More than half a century after its publication, *The Poorhouse Fair* remains, at first glance, a very odd debut—why was this very young man writing about the very old? And why was he fooling around with prognostications?

Trying to explain himself with the awkward self-consciousness of an author obliged to defend his work, he told Elizabeth Lawrence that the novel was about the future—"what will become of us, having lost our faith?" It begins and ends with more questions ("What's this?" and "What was it?"). As the story wends its way to a nonconclusion, after the anticlimactic stoning of the prefect Connor, the narrative is overwhelmed by a babble of disembodied voices, some familiar but none explicitly identified. Questions go unanswered; strands of other stories intrude, and those stories, too, are left hanging—as Updike conceded, his novel is radically indeterminate, a celebration of life's inconclusiveness. One could argue that there's a kind of modesty in presenting to the world a first novel that simply shrugs and stops, unwilling to propose any solution to the thematic conflict or a satisfying sense of closure to the plot. On the other hand, it's hard to be humble about a tour de force. To pull off this open-ended novel, he needed a healthy measure of artistic hubris, confidence in the naked power of his writing.

His courage came from two very different sources: Henry Green's example (acknowledged handsomely, albeit belatedly, in an introduction to a 1977 edition of Green's *Concluding*); and the power of Updike's own boyhood memories. He traced the inspiration for the novel to a visit made to his parents in March 1957, just days before the move to Ipswich. He had seen that the County Home that used to stand at the end of his street in Shillington, an immense poorhouse set in acres of grounds, a looming feature of his early years, was being razed. ("Out of the hole where it had been came the desire to write a futuristic novel in commemoration of the fairs that I had attended [there] as a child.") He also wanted to commemorate his maternal grandfather, John Franklin Hoyer, who had died in September 1953, shortly after John and Mary were married. Because his grandfather (and grandmother) featured vividly in his earliest memories, Updike "had no fear," as he told an interviewer, "of writing about old people."

John Hoyer—"in his way a distinguished man"—was a looming presence in a household where young John was the only child. Although there was tension between Linda and her father (tension often dramatized in her fiction, and which in real life caused her temper to flare), between the old man and his grandson, who was named after him, there was a strong bond of affection. "He loved me, and I loved him," Updike remembered a half century later. "His creaking high-buttoned shoes, the eloquence of his slightly wheezy voice, the stoic set of his mouth beneath his grizzled mustache, the afterscent of his cigars were present to me, day after day, throughout my growing up." John F. Hook, one of the two central characters in *The Poorhouse Fair*, is an "oblique monument" to John F. Hoyer, an affectionate, clear-eyed portrait that speaks with the voice of the original. When at the end of the novel, a tired Hook says, "The time is ap-proaching when us old fellas should be climbing the wooden hill," Updike is not only mimicking the characteristic cadence of his grandfather's speech (the hint of performance, and the exaggerated separation of syllables in "ap-proaching") but also borrowing one of his pet expressions (calling a flight of stairs "the wooden hill"). Hook and the other inmates of the poorhouse are entirely convincing—in itself a remarkable accomplishment—but what's even more remarkable is the sympathy with which they're drawn; Updike evidently transferred to these old people his openhearted reverence for his grandfather.

The inventory of items Updike borrowed from Henry Green's *Concluding* (1948) is ample and accurate:

> [A]n old estate housing a vague State-run institution (a girls' school, in Green's case), a not-too-distant time-to-come (fifty-five years hence, *Concluding*'s jacket flap stated in 1948), an elderly monosyllabic hero (Mr. Rock), a multileveled action drifting through one day's time, a holiday (Green's fête, Founder's Day, even falls like the poorhouse fair, on a Wednesday), heraldic animals, much meteorological detail, and a willful impressionist style.

Of course an impressionist style can't be imitated without the talent to do so, and in general the borrowing doesn't diminish Updike's achievement, which was to combine two traits he admired in Green: an "offhand-and-backwards-feeling verbal and psychological accuracy" and "absolute empathy." The result was exquisite writing and a wonderfully sensitive portrait of characters who might have remained foreign and remote.

As Whitney Balliett noted in *The New Yorker*'s review of *The Poorhouse Fair*, it's a "classic, if not flawless" example of a poetic novel.* The events at the Diamond County Home for the Aged were meant to take place some two decades in the future, but even when the novel was published, its setting seemed more dreamlike (surreal and unsettling) than futuristic; Balliett thought it less a novel than a "poetic vision." Though extravagant in his praise of the young author's prose (a "poet's care and sensitivity lie lightly on every word, on each hand-turned sentence, in each surprising and exact metaphor and simile"), Balliett complained about a lack of "emotional content" and worried that the reader might come away from the book "untouched." He added a parenthetical comment that rings especially true from the distance of more than half a century: "curiously, one never thinks of *liking* or *disliking* it." The skill on display makes it an easy novel to admire, even if a perceptible degree of emotional restraint does muffle its impact. It's not a book that appeals to the heart, but it would be unfair to call it heartless; the fully realized humanity of the characters, especially the elderly poorhouse inmates, is proof of the author's compassion, a capacity for fellow feeling somehow missing from the narrative itself.

Balliett's verdict—"Mr. Updike is a writer's writer"—must have pleased a young man who had set up as his idols Green, Proust, Kafka, and Joyce, and perhaps *The Poorhouse Fair* is best read today as a statement of writerly intent and a demonstration of precocious talent, as though the young author were presenting his credentials as an aspiring textual titan. There are passages where the writing seems a pure expression of joy, of intense pleasure taken in the act of composition. When, for example, an elderly inmate passing through the poorhouse infirmary frets about hospitalization and surgery, the subject is grim, the prose incongruously ecstatic:

> Even more than black death he dreaded the gaudy gate: the mask of sweet red rubber, the violet overhead lights, the rattling ride through washed corridors, the steaming, breath-

---

* Such was the magazine's lofty sense of its own integrity that it never hesitated, at midcentury, to review books by its own regular contributors—without deigning to note the affiliation or acknowledge the apparent conflict of interest.

ing, percolating apparatus, basins of pink sterilizer, the firm straps binding every limb, the sacred pure garb of the surgeons, their eyes alone showing, the cute knives and angled scissors, the beat of your own heart pounding through the burnished machinery, the green color of the surgeon's enormous compassionate eyes, framed, his quick breath sucking and billowing the gauze of his mask as he carved.

In an essay about fictional houses, Updike recalled "the thrill of power with which, in my first novel, *The Poorhouse Fair*, I set characters roaming the corridors of an immense imaginary mansion"— that is, the corridors of the poorhouse. The power to imagine, to invent, to play, gave him a kick more powerful than the craftsman's quiet satisfaction in a job well done. Echoes of that thrill are clearly audible in the sentences just quoted; one can readily imagine his excitement, imagine him sitting alone at his desk in the back room of Little Violet, his head teeming with bright descriptive phrases and freshly minted characters. He was happy, even jubilant—and this explains, in part, how he came to be so prolific an author: he wanted to recapture that feeling, to enjoy again and again the rush of euphoria.

This particular novel also served deeper needs. The struggle between Hook, armed with unshakeable religious convictions, and the radically secular prefect, Connor—a well-intentioned humanist who's not just areligious but also someone who's "lost all sense of omen"—is an imaginative projection of his own ongoing spiritual crisis. The clash of these characters is unresolved because the author's internal conflict was, too. Fear of death is endemic in the poorhouse, if only because the aged inmates are inescapably conscious of the grave—but again, their anxiety reflects Updike's own. He was anxious about the future as well ("What will become of us . . . ?"), perfectly understandably in the circumstances: he'd recently quit his job and moved with his young wife to a new town, infant and toddler in tow; the book he'd worked on for more than a year, *Home*, his novel about the past—his own and his family's—had been spurned; he had no fixed salary to depend on. Only recently settled in Ipswich, and not yet entirely settled professionally, he wrote about what happens next in a book whose title alludes to one possible outcome: the poverty attendant on failure. As he candidly acknowledged, he inherited a Depression mentality: "My father was always afraid he'd have to go to the poorhouse any minute . . . and I guess I work hard because I have the same fear." Unfounded and outdated, that worry was still intermittently potent.

It could be that he was also writing about his recurring urge to escape. In the early 1990s he gave the keynote speech at a Chicago Humanities Festival on the large topic of freedom and equality; in it he mentioned the major action of *The Poorhouse Fair*: "My first novel . . . showed the rebellion of the inmates of a charitable institution against their nobly intentioned, even saintly administrator; with an ineffectual hail of rocks, they voted against his benevolent order. . . . Is not such a rebellion against a benevolent but confining order a deeply human protest?" It's perhaps too far-fetched to think of the poorhouse as in some way analogous to the benevolent but confining order of *The New Yorker*, with Connor a transfigured version of the "saintly" Mr. Shawn. But Updike did begin *The Poorhouse Fair* in the immediate aftermath of his "defection" from the magazine; and a year later, when Knopf accepted the novel (on virtually the same day that Harper published *The Carpentered Hen*), Updike's liberation was complete. He told Richardson that he wanted the book "disentangled" from the Forty-Third Street nexus: "I love the magazine like a parent, but I wrote the book as a distinct activity." *The New Yorker* would remain a steady source of "whale-sized checks," but now, with a novel sold and a book of verse already printed and on its way to bookstores, he could claim the status of a bona fide freelance author. His flight from New York was precisely the escape he'd hoped for: he was now a solo act.

A solo act with a new, adoring audience. By the time the family moved into the new house at 26 East Street, just a few days after John's twenty-sixth birthday, he and Mary were already part of a clearly defined social set, a group of Ipswich residents who had coalesced the previous autumn, when "Sunday sports"—a vigorous afternoon game of touch football (or basketball, or volleyball) followed by drinks—suddenly became a weekend ritual, sacrosanct in the Updike household.

"My wife and I found ourselves in a kind of 'swim' of equally young married couples," he reported in *Self-Consciousness*. "There was a surge of belonging." The first stirrings of their social life actually came thanks to music, not sport: soon after they moved into Little Violet, the Updikes received a phone call from a couple who were planning to form a recorder group. Three couples were involved at first; they met to play chamber music on alternate Wednesdays. Mary played the alto recorder, John the tenor. By the end of May, John could report to Bill Maxwell that Mary played very well; in June, on a trip to New York, he bought himself a new instrument. Despite his devotion to the jukebox tunes of his youth, he had never thought of himself as particularly musical. (When he was a boy, his Shillington piano lessons came to nothing.) Now, however, he diligently set about learning to read music.

With the warmer weather, the young families of Ipswich began to spend sunny days at Crane Beach, and the Updikes' circle of friends expanded—the children mingling, then the mothers, then the fathers. The fathers began playing touch football together, and within a year or so the contours of the group—roughly a dozen couples, with half that number as the nucleus—were more or less fixed. The "surge of belonging" included cultural and community activities. In addition to the Sunday sports and the recorder group, there was a foreign policy discussion group, a singing group, and a life-drawing club. John joined the Ipswich Historical Commission and various church committees; Mary joined the garden club. They both attended town meetings about schools, sewage, and other civic matters. Some weeks there was a group activity nearly every night. And with their new friends they engaged in a whirl of cocktail soirées and clambakes, dinner parties and dancing, with some kind of get-together, planned or impromptu, almost every weekend.

But it was Sunday afternoon, perhaps even more than Saturday night, that bound the group together. The games began at about two o'clock, with some stragglers arriving late. They played for at most a couple of hours, after which they went off to one house or another, the venue chosen at the last minute, to drink a beer or a glass of wine or perhaps a gin and tonic. Sunday sports was a family occasion, though the wives played only if the game was volleyball or tennis. If the weather was particularly good, there would be a few spectators watching the game; often the numbers swelled toward evening when those who'd skipped the sports arrived for drinks. The children ran around in a pack, absentmindedly supervised, and the party broke up in time for their supper, tired families piling into station wagons and driving the short distance home. The Updikes attended faithfully. For John, it was a sequel to morning church. The sport itself was important to him; he played with enthusiasm and moderate skill, competition, as always, rousing him. Yet he also craved the human contact, the proximity of his new band of friends.

John and Mary had other friends in town, some of them of their parents' generation, and they had friends in Cambridge, Boston, and New York. They drove to Boston for concerts and to visit the museums. Their life, in other words, did not revolve exclusively around the Sunday sports crowd—but these new friends captured Updike's imagination, and soon enough they began popping up in his fiction.

WHO WERE THEY? The couples—his novel of that name makes it impossible to call them anything else—were white, mostly Protestant, college-educated,* and worldly in a way one wouldn't necessarily expect to find in a somewhat scruffy small town like Ipswich, with a sizable ethnic and blue-collar population (left over from the heyday of the hosiery mills). They were not natives (not "locals" or "townies"); they had moved to the area as a matter of choice—what a later generation would call a lifestyle choice. They had not, as a rule, come to Ipswich to take a job; the men were professionals, many of them commuting to Boston on the B&M line. There were two doctors, one of them a pediatrician; the owner of the town's newspaper; a pathologist; a lawyer who didn't practice law; a building contractor;

---

* Many of them had been to Harvard or Radcliffe, but with a few exceptions the friendships began only after college.

a minister; an administrator in the careers office at MIT and another at Harvard; a salesman for Wedgewood; and a couple of stockbrokers. All the women were pregnant, or recently pregnant, or about to be pregnant, and almost all were full-time housewives; some were active in community affairs, members of the League of Women Voters, and otherwise politically engaged, especially as the sixties wore on.* Several of the couples were wealthy; none were poor. For the first few years, the Updikes were the least financially secure of their friends.

Although there had been grand families in the vicinity since the nineteenth century—pockets of rich and refined summer residents who came up from Boston and Cambridge and built substantial houses along the North Shore's Gold Coast—Ipswich itself was less popular with the wealthy. The imposing houses on Argilla Road, which leads out to the beach, were mostly built in previous centuries as summer cottages, and in many cases the descendants of the original owners now lived in them year-round, and constituted the town's upper crust. One of the "genial grandees of Argilla Road" was Lovell Thompson, a distinguished publishing executive at Houghton Mifflin. Thompson would invite the Updikes for dinner with writers on the Houghton list; he also urged John and Mary to make use of his tennis court. Homer White, who wrote articles about Spain for *Harper's Magazine,* was another member of the "cultivated older generation," as Updike put it, "that had us frisky young folks in for drinks." Despite the presence of an established bourgeoisie, there was the perception that Ipswich had only recently been discovered as a desirable location just beyond the recognized commuter belt. The frisky young folks (known to the older generation as the "Junior Jet Set") were in a sense pioneers, establishing a new community, integrated with the town yet fractionally aloof. They were a privileged, affluent suburban crowd in an exurban setting.

And a remarkably cohesive group. That they remained so close for so long (about fifteen years) must be at least in part the result of a dynamic specific to the group—these particular individuals wanted

---

* For a few summers some of the women tutored African American children in Roxbury, a Boston neighborhood blighted by poverty.

to be together, perhaps even needed to be together, and found a way to make it work. It seems clear that the time and place were also ripe for an unbuttoned pursuit of happiness. Ipswich was congenial; idyllic, even—"a kind of playground for adults" is how Updike once described Tarbox, his name for Ipswich in his fiction. In the summer, there was the splendid beach; in the fall (football season) the intermittently picturesque downtown was beautified by turning leaves; in the winter the ponds and rivers froze obligingly for ice-skating, and on one or two nearby hills, rope tows dragged eager skiers to the top of gentle slopes (actual ski resorts were a few hours north, in New Hampshire); in the spring the municipal golf course beckoned and the warmer weather promised another round of seaside pleasures. The marquee of the downtown movie theater, the Strand, announced a new film every week.

History, too, played its part, pausing, so to speak, to let the couples take advantage of postwar prosperity and the post-McCarthy, post-Korea, pre-Vietnam political stability, epitomized by the reliably calm and moderate Dwight D. Eisenhower. If Ike's steady hand allowed them free and easy enjoyment of their leisure time, the election of his successor, John Kennedy, signaled a generational shift—young and glamorous, Kennedy blew in, a fresh breeze promising change. We can look back and with hindsight decide that Updike and his friends sensed in the air a new permissiveness, a loosening of the social fabric, and seized on it as a license to frolic. Also with hindsight, it's tempting to say that, like other members of their generation in other towns and other states, they went too far, frolicked too freely. But I suspect that, at the time, they merely thought they were making the most of happy circumstances.

The women seemed "gorgeous" to Updike, the men "knowledgeable and staunch," and he worked hard to gain their approval, mostly by making himself into a sparkling entertainer, a witty, clowning charmer. His Ipswich self, he once remarked, was a "delayed second edition" of his high school self. Bubbling over with enthusiasm, he all but begged to be acknowledged as the life of the party. And if he felt neglected, he was quick to do something about it; as one of his new friends told *Time* magazine, "If he's not being paid enough attention, he'll fall off the couch." He made fun of his eagerness to please in a poem composed in May 1959; he considered calling it "Post-Mortem" but settled on "Thoughts While Driving Home":

> Was I clever enough? Was I charming?
> Did I make at least one good pun?
> Was I disconcerting? Disarming?
> Was I wise? Was I wan? Was I fun?

The answer, inevitably, was yes—yes, he was fun, and quickly became a ringleader with the self-appointed task of organizing party games. He especially loved variants of Botticelli, in which whoever is "it" assumes a secret identity that the others must guess. Stepping back, we can see that by playing court jester to this group of affable but ordinary suburbanites, Updike was in a sense masking his identity as an artist, as someone whose true allegiance was not to his friends but to his writing. At work, during the hours he spent at his desk, he remained an outsider (a teenager with a special destiny; a hick among sophisticates; a poor boy among the rich; a churchgoer among the faithless). At play, he insinuated himself into the warm heart of things. Being a cherished member of the gang answered a deep need, and in that sense he was being true both to himself and to his friends. In his memoirs, he promotes them to the status of honorary siblings ("The sisters and brothers I had never had"); they certainly made an outsize impact on both his private life and his career. If his parents and grandparents gave him the bulk of his Olinger material, the couples gave him Tarbox. And if his mother's unwavering love and unconditional approbation fueled his early flight, the collective adoration of the couples sustained him as he soared higher still.

It was important to him that they knew him before he was famous, that the friendship was formed, as he said, "on the basis of what I did in person rather than what I did in print." The couples embraced him before his first novel was published. As far as they were concerned, the fact that he was a writer was incidental, at least in the first few years—unusual, somewhat intriguing, but otherwise insignificant. Books weren't of vital importance in this milieu—it was not a literary crowd—and that suited him, up to a point. Happy though he was to segregate his professional and social life, to leave literature behind when he left his desk, he could be fairly certain that his new pals would be aware of what he "did in print." Almost all of them had been *New Yorker* subscribers before he made their acquaintance, and almost all of them bought copies of *The Carpentered Hen* and *The Poorhouse Fair* as soon as they came out. As the years went by and his reputation grew, and scenes lifted from their lives began to crop up in his fiction, they of course read with sharpened interest. They were his audience, a representative sample of his readership right there on the other side of the volleyball net, demographically ideal. A new issue of *The New Yorker* would arrive in the mail every Friday morning, so that all of them had the opportunity to flip through in search of the latest Updike before the start of the weekend's entertainments. If he did have a piece in the magazine, however, it would usually go unmentioned; he wasn't quizzed or congratulated or scolded. There was never any explicit taboo forbidding discussion of his writing, or any incident that warned his friends to refrain from comment, but somehow the topic didn't come up, at least not in his presence, and reticence eventually became the norm, thereby preserving the illusion that his success as an author was irrelevant—not a factor in the group dynamic.

In the early days, actually, what he did during his solitary working hours—the mornings at the typewriter, the bookish afternoons—had little to do with the couples crowd and little to do with Ipswich. As a writer, up until early 1962, he was very much preoccupied with Berks County (Plowville, Shillington, Reading), both in his stories and in his novels; it's not too much of a stretch to say that he lived there most mornings. A particularly striking example of his immersion in that beloved Pennsylvania geography is "The Happiest I've Been," which is narrated by John Nordholm, the teenage protagonist of "Friends from Philadelphia" (not only the first story Updike sold to *The New Yorker* but also the first Olinger story and the first story in *The Same Door*, his debut collection).

Now a college sophomore, John has been home for Christmas at his parents' farm and is leaving again, heading to Chicago to see a girl he met in a fine arts course, hitching a ride from his friend Neil. But no sooner are the boys in the car, out of sight of the farm and presumably on their way, than Neil suggests a detour to a New Year's Eve party in Olinger. (The fictional John is surprised to learn about the party; the real-life John knew all about it—it was the "beautifully non-intellectual brawl" he'd been pining for up in Cambridge.) After the party, they take a further detour into Alton; only at dawn do they finally set off on their long westward journey. The farm, the town, the city—when an adult John Nordholm looks fondly back on the events of that night, Updike is taking us on a pilgrimage to all three of his holy sites.

He began writing "The Happiest I've Been" in late January 1958 and sent off a draft to Maxwell on February 7; *The New Yorker* published it eleven months later, in the first issue of 1959. (In those days the magazine had a fetish about running stories so that the fictional events coincided with the date on the calendar, and this one featured a New Year's Eve party.) A pivotal story in the evolution of his work, it marked both an ending and a beginning. Updike knew as soon as he finished it that it would round out the book of short stories he saw taking shape: placed at the end, it would provide a pleasing unity, with John Nordholm appearing first and last. (Hence the title: the reader goes in and out the same door.) To Elizabeth Lawrence he wrote that, in his mind, the story "clicked the collection shut."* He also claimed to have been tremendously excited by the possibilities it seemed to open up: "While writing it," he explained, "I had a sensation of breaking through, as if through a thin sheet of restraining glass, to material, to truth, previously locked up." A breakthrough is more dramatically satisfying than gradual improvement—he'd actually been working with similar material on and off for about five years—but because "The Happiest I've Been" is indeed markedly more successful and substantial

---

* He originally thought of calling the book *One of Us*, but changed his mind; Knopf published it as *The Same Door* in August 1959.

than the previous Olinger stories ("Friends from Philadelphia" and
"The Alligators"), Updike's account rings true. He had found, in
John Nordholm's tender reminiscence, in his muted, clear-eyed celebration of the mundane, an approach to his subject that was fresh
and compelling. "I believed," he later wrote, "that there was a body
of my fellow Americans to whom these modest doings in Pennsylvania would be news."

The modest doings are imagined with magical intensity. Here's
the moment at the farm when John is saying good-bye:

> I embraced my mother and over her shoulder with the cam-
> era of my head tried to take a snapshot I could keep of the
> house, the woods behind it and the sunset behind them, the
> bench beneath the walnut tree where my grandfather cut ap-
> ples into skinless bits and fed them to himself, and the ruts
> the bakery truck had made in the soft lawn that morning.

The detail grows more specific as the sentence progresses (as though
the camera were zooming in), and more telling, so that we begin
with the generic (house, woods, sunset), steal a glimpse of a meticulous and somewhat selfish old man, and finish with the fresh
ruts in the lawn, the objective correlative for the imprint that this
"snapshot" has made on John's memory. The valedictory tone of the
passage is sustained throughout the story, even in the midst of hectic
comings and goings at the Olinger party. "The party was the party I
had been going to all my life," John tells us—and focuses his mental
camera on his fellow revelers, his old high school crowd, his gang.
He's distressed by any hint that they have changed or are changing.
They are representative of his childhood; as he puts it, they had
"attended my life's party." He is at once eager to leave his childhood
behind (to fly, as most Updike mothers promised), and to preserve
the past intact, to protect and cherish it. The tension between these
two impulses supplies the emotional power here, as it does in many
of the Olinger stories.

In his 1985 speech on the creative imagination, Updike quoted
at length a passage from "The Happiest I've Been" about a game of

Ping-Pong played in the basement by John, another boy, and two girls, while the party carries on upstairs. Updike drew attention to two fragments of descriptive detail, a glimpse of a girl's shaved armpit "like a bit of chicken skin" and, on the basement floor near a lawn mower, "empty bronze motor-oil cans twice punctured by triangles"—insignificant, almost microscopic details that provide, in Updike's Jamesian phrase, an "abrupt purchase on lived life": in their insignificance and irrefutable authenticity, they acquire, he claimed, "the intensity of proclamation." But they resonate in other ways as well. While John is playing Ping-Pong, he spies the white cups of the girls' bras as they lunge forward in their semiformal dresses; after the game, one of the girls leans on John while she slips her heels back on. As Updike later noted, there's an undercurrent of "blurred sexuality" to this basement scene. Some of John's friends at the party are still involved in the maudlin romantic crises of late adolescence; a few wear engagement rings; and one awkward couple is already wed. John himself is itching to make his getaway to Chicago, the sooner to see the girl waiting for him ("a girl . . . who, if I asked, would marry me"). In this context, on the threshold of adulthood, a shaved armpit gleaming like chicken skin and triangular puncture holes in empty oil cans seem somewhat less random; they suggest, among other things, innocence lost and time draining away.

This is a story about leaving home, leaving friends behind, leaving childhood behind. Even as a college sophomore, the young man is already jealously hoarding memories; as he contemplates his classmates, he feels "a warm keen dishevelment." Looking back after the passage of an unspecified number of years, he wallows in sentiment, straining to recapture the unique sensation of an experience consigned to memory. Updike's task is to convey both the remembered sensation and the emotion (nostalgia's bittersweet tang) evoked by its passing. At the very end, the mood shifts: driving west across Pennsylvania in the early morning light while Neil snores beside him on the front seat, John is engulfed by a wave of happiness that lifts the story and gives it a quietly triumphant feel.

"The Happiest I've Been" tells us nothing about John Nordholm's adult life; we don't know why he feels so deeply nostalgic, though the title (nostalgia distilled) invites us to suppose that he's never been as purely, powerfully happy as he suddenly was that morning driving west. That doesn't mean, however, that he's currently *un*happy or regretful. In fact, the exultant note struck at the end of the story is entirely consonant with John Updike's own enviable situation at the time of writing: the college sophomore who drove with a friend from Plowville to Chicago, who married the fine arts major, who worked hard to become a successful freelance writer, had just bought a house of his own in Ipswich, Massachusetts, and surrounded himself with a brand-new circle of friends, a grown-up gang throwing grown-up parties. Acknowledging the autobiographical basis of the story in his speech on creativity, he told his audience,

> In 1958 I was at just the right distance from the night in Shillington, Pennsylvania, when 1952 became 1953; I still remembered and cared, yet was enough distant to get a handle on the memories, to manipulate them into fiction.

What he's measuring with the phrase "enough distant" is the gap between Ipswich and Shillington, between adulthood and adolescence, between the couples crowd and his old high school gang. Though he spent many a lonely morning getting a handle on Berks County memories, weekends he was living happily in New England, in a perfectly agreeable and abundantly sociable present tense. Any nostalgia of his own, he cultivated for literary purposes only.

His ability to parcel himself out between locations, to live as it were simultaneously in Ipswich and Olinger, is symptomatic of a talent for compartmentalization that he perfected as he grew older. Already, by the time he moved into the Polly Dole House, he had taken up two new pastimes, poker and golf, activities he established as realms separate from both his domestic and his professional life. Other compartments, church and adultery among them, leaked in awkward ways, but poker and golf were reliably watertight.

Because it fitted with a fantasy of what college life might be like, Updike had listed poker (along with chess and cartooning) as one of his "special interests" in the 1950 Harvard *Registrar*; in fact his only high school memory of the game was "a shy try at strip poker in someone's parents' attic." A Harvard classmate, Austin Briggs, first met Updike during a freshman year penny-ante game in Hollis. "He was an utterly striking figure with his lean almost emaciated frame and bird-beak nose," Briggs recalled. "He was playing big-time gambler more than poker, a cigarette dangling from his mouth and in costume with a green eyeshade and sleeve garters on his shirt."* He might have been tempted to dress up in a similar style when he was invited, on a chilly afternoon in December 1957—nine months after he'd arrived in town—to the first poker night organized by the owner of an Ipswich auto parts store and the local pediatrician. It was an all-male contingent, more socially diverse than the couples crowd. (The town cobbler first took a seat at the table in the late sixties and was still playing forty-odd years later.) They convened every other Wednesday, for low stakes: nickels and dimes until they made the minimum bet a quarter in 1960. Poker night was a raucous event in the early days, drenched in beer and wreathed in smoke. The camaraderie, and the sense of belonging, was for Updike the principal attraction; he confessed, in fact, to being only a mediocre player: "I am careless, neglecting to count cards, preferring to sit there in a pleasant haze of bewilderment and anticipation." In 2004 he noted that he'd been playing with more or less the same men for nearly half a century, and that in the meantime he'd "changed houses, church denominations, and wives. My publisher has been sold and resold. Only my children command a longer loyalty than this poker group." Perhaps the most remarkable thing about this durable attachment is that he was far *less* passionate about poker than he was about golf.

His first swing of a golf club came just a few months after the move to Ipswich. A relative of Mary's—she was actually her mother's cousin, but Mary called her aunt—lived in Wellesley, Massachusetts; she was a keen golfer, and in her shady backyard showed Updike how

---

* The green eyeshade, probably a memento from his stint at the *Reading Eagle*, was actually part of his regular freshman year outfit—he put it on for concentrated bouts of studying. The sleeve garters could be dismissed as a trick of Briggs's memory if they didn't seem like a touch of pure Updike ebullience.

to grip a driver, then told him he had a "wonderful natural swing." She took him to her local club to get him started. "The average golfer," he later wrote, "is hooked when he hits his first good shot." In his case, the addiction was immediate and enduring. In the fall of that year, he wrote his first golf story, "Intercession," in which Paul, a young man who resembles Updike—he writes the plot for a syndicated cartoon strip—has recently been "initiated" into the game by his wife's uncle. Out on a golf course on his own for the first time, on a drought-stricken summer's day, he feels guilty—guilty about leaving his wife alone in the house with their little girl, "about not working all day long like other men, about having grown up at all and married and left his parents alone together in Ohio, about being all by himself in this great kingdom of withered turf" (all sentiments Updike might have shared). The day goes badly; the story ends with a curse ("Damned game"), and it's entirely possible that Paul's first outing will be his last. For Updike, things went very differently: he shrugged off any twinges of guilt and continued to play golf, to think about it, to dream about it, to write about it, for the rest of his life— "the hours adding up," he admitted, "to years of *temps perdu*." The easiest explanation for his long love affair with this "narcotic pastime" is that the game gave him huge amounts of pleasure: "I am curiously, disproportionately, undeservedly happy on a golf course." Rounds of golf, he wrote, were "islands of bliss."

Bliss and frustration—with his "modest" eighteen handicap, he described himself as a "poor golfer, who came to the game late, with frazzled eye-hand connections." He practiced and practiced, dutifully studying the reams of advice aimed at his fellow duffers— advice he gently mocked in a succession of satiric essays. Golf is a cruel and exasperating sport for anyone with a perfectionist streak as pronounced as Updike's; it dangles hope—the tantalizing prospect of self-improvement—then yanks that hope out of sight with the next errant shot. He described, in a burst of colorful prose, the torments of this humbling cycle:

> The fluctuations of golfing success were charted on a graph craggier than those of other endeavors, with peaks of pure

poetry leaping up from abysses of sheer humiliation—the fat shot that sputters forward under the shadow of its divot, the thin shot that skims across the green like a maimed bird, the smothered hook which finds the raspberry patch, the soaring slice that crosses the highway, the chunked chip, the shanked approach, the water ball, the swamp ball, the deeper-into-the-woods ricochet, the trap-to-trap blast, the total whiff on the first tee, the double-hit putt from two feet out.

It's a sign of his sturdy self-confidence that he was able to endure these trials on a weekly or twice-weekly basis. One wonders whether the game didn't satisfy some masochistic need on his part for mild chastening punishment, whether the pain wasn't part of the pleasure.

Like every golfer, he had to endure the famous insults the game attracts, and parry oft-repeated accusations about its being the chosen pastime of wealthy philistines—"the idle and idiot well-to-do," in Osbert Sitwell's acid phrase. In his Pennsylvania youth, Updike remembered, "golf was a rumored something, like champagne breakfasts and divorce, that the rich did." But in Ipswich, once hooked, he conveniently discovered that it was a pleasure "democratically exploited"—by working-class golfers, say, flocking to the municipal course at the end of a long shift. (Wishful thinking contradicted by the sinister line from his poem "Golfers," in which those who play the game "take an open stance on the backs of the poor.")

It's true that he played with all kinds of people in all kinds of settings. "Golf," he wrote, "is a great social bridge." For many years, he was joined in a foursome by a local druggist, the same pediatrician who played in the poker group, and the owner of an automatic car wash; they played weekly from April to October on public courses in Ipswich and neighboring towns such as Essex, Topsfield, Wenham, and Newburyport. Although Updike was content with humble layouts, he gladly accepted invitations to enjoy the "spongy turf of private fairways." Eventually, in his early fifties, when the sport's expanding popularity meant that his favorite public courses were more and more crowded, he joined the exclusive and expensive

Myopia Hunt Club in Hamilton, Massachusetts, which boasts a famously beautiful course designed in the late nineteenth century by Herbert Corey Leeds.

A round of golf, for Updike, was no more an occasion for literary chatter than a poker game; what he "did in print" was not a topic his regular foursome would be apt to broach. Although in later years he played frequently with a psychiatrist turned writer who claimed that he and Updike would ritually discuss, when they reached the eighth fairway, what they were reading and writing, this brief bout of book banter was an exception. The novelist Tim O'Brien had a very different experience playing with Updike; he said he found himself consciously suppressing literary questions: "I sensed that for John, at least in part, golf was a way of getting away from artistic and professional pressures." Updike repeatedly remarked that he cherished the game's "relative hush," the "worshipful silence" on the green; "Golf," he explained, "is a constant struggle with one's self, productive of a few grunts and expletives but no extended discourse." As if in warning to garrulous companions, he wrote, "Basically, I want to be alone with my golf." Too polite to play a round in silence, he was also too fond of verbal display. O'Brien remembered having conversations about "ludicrously insignificant stuff"; even then, "John spoke very much as he wrote, with grace and precision and irony and impish humor and striking miracles of expression. I was never unaware that I was strolling down the fairway with John Updike."

He worked at his golf, struggled with it, the way a less naturally talented writer might struggle with a tricky passage, revising, honing, maybe tearing it up in frustration; his emphasis on the mental effort the sport demanded, the intense concentration, the need for each player to act as his own coach, invites the comparison. But of course Updike's good days at the typewriter, days when polished prose poured out of him, were more frequent than his good days on the links, where he was nagged by the sense that the basics of golf had to be relearned every week. "He seemed delighted when he won a hole or when he scored well," said O'Brien, "and he concentrated fiercely over his shots, but for the most part he struck me as wistfully (sometimes wryly) resigned to the inconsistencies and imperfections of his swing." When he did hit a sweet shot, however, his sense of exultation was dramatic. He wrote, "In those instants of whizz, ascent, hover, and fall, an ideal self seems mirrored." The urge to recapture that golden moment contributed to the power and persistence of his obsession.

He reveled also in the range of competition the game affords. Thanks to handicap strokes, players of widely different ability can compete on terms of equality; this was the "inexhaustible competitive charm" that turned a struggle with oneself into the excitement of a contest with others. The presence of partners and opponents meant that when he wasn't engrossed in his own shot, he had his eye on his companions, absorbing every last detail, registering not just the outline of a golf persona but the inner life as well. "Golf," he explained, "is . . . a great tunnel into the essences of others, for people are naked when they swing—their patience or impatience, their optimism or pessimism, their grace or awkwardness, their life's motifs are all bared." What he saw of their essence seems not to have dismayed him; on the contrary, he felt joined to his regular foursomes by a powerful bond: "My golfing companions . . . are more dear to me than I can unembarrassedly say."

When I interviewed him in 2003, more than forty-five years after his first swing, he humorously suggested that his continued devotion to the game (by now he was playing twice weekly) was perhaps hampering his career: "If I thought as hard about writing as I do about golf," he told me, "I might be a better writer—maybe win the Nobel prize." In fact, his obsession brought him good material right from the start; as he acknowledged, "Golf converts oddly well into words." "Intercession" and "Drinking from a Cup Made Cinchy (After Reading Too Many Books on How to Play Golf)," a parody he wrote for *The New Yorker* in 1959 lampooning the inexhaustible genre of golf instruction, were the earliest fruits of his passion. Late in life he wrote "Elegy for a Real Golfer," a lament in verse on the bizarre and tragic airplane accident that killed Payne Stewart in 1999. In between came several poems and short stories; notable golfing interludes in three of the *Rabbit* novels and in *A Month of Sundays* (which features a foursome composed exclusively of disgraced clergymen); and "The First Lunar Invitational"—a *jeu d'esprit* inspired by astronaut Alan Shepard's famous antics with an improvised six iron—about a tournament on the moon under the joint sponsorship of NASA, ALCOA, MIT, and Bob Hope.

As Adlai Stevenson noted in a 1952 campaign speech poking fun at President Eisenhower's famous enthusiasm for golf, "Some of us worship in churches, some in synagogues, some on golf courses." Updike spread his bets, worshipping in church and also casting his golfing experience in theological terms. A secular pastime commonly associated with material well-being, golf, oddly, gave Updike a spiritual thrill; from the very beginning, he was acutely sensitive to what he called "the eerie religious latency" of the game; when he wrote about it, he invariably invoked the supernatural. "Intercession" set the pattern, ending with a curse and turning on a seeming miracle. On his second time around, long after his progress across the course has become "a jumbled rout," Paul yearns for divine intervention:

> All he wanted was that his drive be perfect; it was very little to ask. If miracles, in this age of faint faith, could enter anywhere, it would be here, where the causal fabric was thinnest, in the quick collisions and abrupt deflections of a game. Paul drove high but crookedly over the treetops. It dismayed him to realize that the angle of a metal surface striking a rubber sphere counted for more with God than the keenest human hope.

On Paul's next drive, however, it seems that his halfhearted prayer is answered, that God does intervene: "The ball bounced once in the open and, as if a glass arm from heaven had reached down and grabbed it, vanished." Quitting in disgust, walking off the drought-parched course, he imagines that the one green he's missed seeing is "paradisiacal—broad-leaved trees, long-tailed birds, the cry of water."

For Updike, golf was like a cycle of mystery plays covering the entire Christian calendar from Creation to Judgment Day. An unplayed course is a Garden of Eden, from which the duffer is expelled with his first wayward shot ("We lack the mustard-seed of faith that keeps the swing smooth"); during a bad round one suffers torments of the damned; yet "miracles . . . abound"—not least the "ritual interment and resurrection of the ball at each green"; and next week's game holds out the promise of paradise regained. He found it hard to resist the urge to draw moral lessons: "Our bad golf testifies, we cannot help feeling, to our being bad people—bad to the core." Original sin may be inescapable, but any concerted effort to improve one's game resembles a righteous struggle for salvation.

Two years after "Intercession," teeing off on the page for only the second time, Updike pitted Harry ("Rabbit") Angstrom against an Episcopalian minister, the Reverend Jack Eccles, and used their first round together as a pivotal moment in *Rabbit, Run*. The novel is usually associated with basketball, the sport that briefly turned Rabbit into a local teenage celebrity, but it's on the golf course that Updike supplies his hero with tardy justification for the impulsive act that sets the narrative in motion.

Feeling trapped by drab domesticity, Rabbit has run away from his pregnant wife, Janice, and young son, zigzagging into the arms of a blowsy part-time prostitute. Eccles, by inviting him to play golf, thinks he's doing his pastoral duty, coaxing home a parishioner's wayward husband. In the car on the way over to the Chestnut Grove Golf Course, the minister chats about the theological wrangles between his father and grandfather (who was, he explains, the bishop of Providence); the talk is of family worship and belief in hell, of atheists dwelling in "outer darkness," the rest of us in "inner darkness"—all of which sets the scene for a round of golf freighted with religious significance.

Updike once described Harry Angstrom as a "representative Kierkegaardian man":

> Man in a state of fear and trembling, separated from God,
> haunted by dread, twisted by the conflicting demands of his

animal biology and human intelligence, of the social contract and the inner imperatives.

"Twisted," indeed. Rabbit feels "dragged down, lame"; at the first
tee, his drive "sputters away to one side, crippled by a perverse top-
spin." Although Eccles encourages him, praising his "beautiful natural swing" (Updike's "natural" swing was similarly admired), his
play deteriorates: "Ineptitude seems to coat him like a scabrous disease." His vision warped by guilt, he looks down the fairway and
sees Eccles in the distance; the clergyman's shirt resembles "a white
flag of forgiveness, crying encouragement, fluttering from the green
to guide him home." Rabbit's nightmare round resembles Paul's
"jumbled rout"—until he reaches the fifth tee, where he produces
a superb shot, a drive that climbs and climbs "along a line straight
as a ruler-edge." He exults: "That's *it*!" His miracle drive washes
away the nightmare and utterly defeats Eccles—not in the game,
but in their simmering wrangle over Rabbit's unorthodox religious
beliefs and his reasons for leaving home. The "it" in Rabbit's jubilant
"That's *it*!" is at once the supernatural "something" he identifies
as his faith in God ("I do feel that somewhere behind all this . . .
there's something that wants me to find it"); the element missing
from his marriage ("There was this thing that wasn't there"); and
the essential kernel of his self, his soul ("Hell, it's not much. . . . It's
just that, well, it's all there is"). This multipurpose "it" offers Rabbit
absolution of a kind that makes the prospect of Eccles's forgiveness
irrelevant. With one miraculous swing of a golf club, he has legiti-
mized, in his own mind, his defection from married life; "it" shows
him that he was right to abandon his pregnant wife and toddler son,
and no mere argument will persuade him otherwise.

For Rabbit, this is a moment of redemption celebrated with "a
grin of aggrandizement." For the reader, it's equivocal, thrilling yet
deeply worrisome, in that it harks back to Rabbit's high school glory
days. His sense of himself as a "first-rate" athlete, the idea that he's
a natural and should follow his "inner imperatives," is at the root
of the sudden restless impulse that sent him scampering from his
marriage. Whatever "it" is, it does nothing to reconcile him to his

responsibilities as a social being, a husband, and a father; on the contrary, it hardens his resolve, and two months later he's still AWOL, still in the arms of Ruth Leonard, the other woman. He returns home only when Janice goes into labor. Eccles, in the meantime, perseveres with his unique approach to pastoral care: "Playing golf with someone is a good way to get to know him," he tells Harry's aggrieved mother-in-law, assuring her that he's learned, thanks to their games, that Harry is "a good man." He believes that Harry is "worth saving and could be saved," but their weekly games mostly pander to Rabbit's flattering conception of himself as a hero on a quest and as a star athlete in tune with the "harmless ecstasy" of sporting excellence. Eccles notes that on the golf course, Harry is both better and worse than he, an apt judgment in all respects: Harry is as good as his game—wonderful at times, at times appalling.

As Updike regularly told interviewers, Harry Angstrom is a portrait of the author in straitened circumstances—without a Harvard degree or a marketable talent, as though Uppie had lingered in Shillington after high school, married young, and skidded into a dead-end job: "Although Harry hasn't studied the things I did or taken up my line of work, he still is fairly alert." Rabbit was a product of the author's imagination and intelligence working with intimately familiar material, superimposing elements of his own character on memories of stories his father used to tell about the top athletes at Shillington High and their fate, postgraduation. ("Shillington was littered . . . with the wrecks of former basketball stars.") Into the mix, too, went the Sunday basketball Updike was playing with the Ipswich crowd; the golf he was playing (often with the Episcopalian minister in Ipswich, Goldthwaite Sherrill, whose father was the bishop of Massachusetts); and the "clutter and tensions of young married life" (Mary was five months pregnant with their third child, Michael, when Updike started the novel). Like "The Happiest I've Been," *Rabbit, Run* grew out of the tension between Shillington and Ipswich, between his past and his present.

He began writing in January 1959, and finished in less than nine months. Three and a half decades later he still vividly recalled the rush of excitement with which he worked, sequestered in a small corner room on the second floor of the house, looking out over a busy intersection from one window and at the spreading branches of a huge elm tree from the other. He wrote hurriedly, in soft pencil. Under the old-fashioned upright desk with its fold-down writing surface, his kicking feet wore bare spots in the varnished pine floorboards. The momentum of the accumulating sentences thrilled him. Writing in the present tense, an unconventional choice at the time, had a liberating effect on him; it felt "exhilaratingly speedy and free." At first he thought he was working on a novella, and imagined that the headlong pace of the prose was cinematic; he even considered giving the book the subtitle "A Movie," to capture the sense of continuous forward motion.

He was excited, too, by the sex. As he later acknowledged, a "heavy, intoxicating dose of fantasy and wish-fulfillment went into *Rabbit, Run.* . . . Rabbit ran while I sat at my desk, scribbling"—and kicking his feet with excitement.

Having left Janice, Rabbit moves in with Ruth, who on their first night together allows him to make love to her "as he would to his wife." Thanks to Rabbit's tender ministrations, Ruth achieves the sensual equivalent of the breakthrough Harry later experiences on the fifth tee. Here, too, Updike introduces a numinous "it":

> "I'd forgotten," she says.
> "Forgot what?"
> "That I could have it too."
> "What's it like?"
> "Oh. It's like falling through."
> "Where do you fall to?"
> "Nowhere. I can't talk about it."

The word *orgasm* never appears in the book; *climax* figures once (as does *orgasmatic climax*, in a snippet of scabrous dialogue). My guess is that Updike avoids more clinical terms not for propriety's sake, or even for aesthetic reasons, but because a vague "it" does more to suggest transcendence. In general, he substitutes impressionistic descriptions for exact anatomical labeling. When, for example, Rabbit insists that Ruth be entirely naked before they make love, Updike concentrates on the effect of Ruth's bare skin on Rabbit's aroused sensibility without naming any more of the exposed body parts than strictly necessary.

Later in the book, Rabbit demands that Ruth perform oral sex, though in fact he's "too fastidious to mouth the words." Updike again chooses to suggest the act rather than describe it; he arranges a tableau:

> He takes his [clothes] off quickly and neatly and stands by the dull wall in his brilliant body. He leans awkwardly and brings one hand up and hangs it on his shoulder not knowing what to do with it. His whole shy pose has these wings of tension, like he's an angel waiting for a word.

Ruth undresses, kneels at his feet. As far as today's reader is concerned, the idea that under these circumstance Rabbit could be in any way angelic is possibly the only disturbing aspect of the truncated scene that follows. At the time, however, even to hint at fellatio was to court censorship. Particularly objectionable to readers in 1960 was Ruth's reaction after the deed is done, after Rabbit has bolted: "When the door closes the taste of seawater in her mouth is swallowed by the thick grief that mounts in her throat so fully she has to sit up to breathe." The sudden access of visceral accuracy (and the congregation in one sentence of the words *taste, seawater, mouth, swallowed,* and *throat*) was at the limit of what contemporary sensibilities could bear. Unable to bring himself to describe the offending sentence in English, Victor Gollancz resorted to Latin: "*gustum in ore feminae post fellationem consummatam.*"

Updike's publishers recognized at once the literary value of the novel, and also foresaw the legal difficulty in publishing a book likely to be judged obscene by the powers that be. Gollancz, not a man who'd led a sheltered life, nonetheless circulated an internal memo in which he declared, "I have . . . never read a novel which approaches this one for absolute sexual frankness." To Updike he telegraphed: RABBIT RUN A SUPERB NOVEL BY AN ALREADY MAJOR

AND POTENTIALLY VERY GREAT NOVELIST. The reaction from Alfred Knopf was muted by comparison ("we all admire it greatly") and accompanied by an understated caveat: "There are one or two little matters to discuss." Gollancz's telegram and Knopf's letter reached Updike on the Caribbean island of Anguilla, where he had taken his family on an extended winter vacation (the first of many trips to the West Indies in search of a sun cure for his psoriasis), so a month went by before Updike presented himself at his publisher's Madison Avenue offices. He was ushered into the presence of Knopf himself, who announced to his author, milking the moment for drama, that his lawyers had warned that publishing *Rabbit, Run* would land them both in jail. Faced with this opening gambit, Updike rapidly calculated the odds of finding a reputable publisher who would print the uncensored manuscript—and consented to cuts. As he put it, "I agreed to go along with the legal experts, and trim the obscenity to the point where the book might slide past the notice of hypothetical backwoods sheriffs vigilant against smut."

It's possible that the cuts were unnecessary, that no legal challenge would have been forthcoming. Vladimir Nabokov's *Lolita* had been published by G. P. Putnam's Sons in 1958, attracting considerable controversy but no prosecutions; by January 1959, *Lolita* had reached the top spot on the *New York Times* bestseller list. In July 1959, the U.S. Post Office ban on the unexpurgated Grove Press edition of *Lady Chatterley's Lover* was overturned in federal court, and Lawrence's novel also climbed the bestseller list. But two years later, when Grove published an American edition of Henry Miller's previously banned *Tropic of Cancer*, dozens of booksellers were arrested and obscenity cases filed coast to coast. In a bizarre twist, as if to fulfill Knopf's dark prophecy, charges of conspiracy were filed in a Brooklyn court against both the publisher, Barney Rosset, and Henry Miller himself; when Miller declined to appear before the grand jury, a bench warrant was issued for his arrest. Neither man went to jail, and in any case *Tropic of Cancer* is a much bawdier book; it's deliberately, even gleefully salacious in a way *Rabbit, Run* isn't. ("The novels of Henry Miller," Updike once quipped, "are not novels, they are acts of intercourse strung alternately with segments of personal harangue.") Yet Updike, in this uncertain climate, was perhaps wise to conclude that self-censorship was preferable to state censorship. No scenes were removed from his novel, only a few "dirty" words; as he later acknowledged, "none of the excisions really hurt." The sex was still there. Updike felt that in agreeing to the changes, he had sold out, but he wasn't, in fact, being asked to compromise his artistic integrity. If, as he told an interviewer in 1990, his aim was "to write about sex on the same level, as explicitly and carefully and lovingly as one wrote about anything else," the bowdlerized version did the job as thoroughly as the original.*

But even with the obscenity trimmed, the book presented an insuperable problem for Gollancz, who anguished and dithered and pleaded for additional changes—and finally concluded that despite his fervent admiration, he couldn't publish it. The British rights were immediately snapped up by André Deutsch Ltd., a small but highly regarded house, run on a shoestring and named for the Hungarian-born publisher who founded it in 1952. Having weathered an injunction against the British publication of Norman Mailer's *The Naked and the Dead* (although Mailer had substituted *fug* for *fuck*, the F-word was still omnipresent and unmistakable), Deutsch had acquired a reputation for fearlessness, which he embraced with characteristic verve. He hardly blinked at *Rabbit, Run*. Impetuous and irascible, but also charming and charismatic—"effervescent," Updike called him—the diminutive Deutsch made yearly trips to New York, and occasionally ventured north to Ipswich to visit Lovell Thompson. Deutsch quickly became a friend, as did his colleague Diana Athill, Updike's editor. André Deutsch Ltd. continued to publish Updike's books until the early 1990s, well after Deutsch himself had retired.

Updike was naturally keyed up about venturing into the risky, uncharted territory of sexual realism, and yet that was only part of the adventure he'd embarked on. The novel was conceived as a character

---

* Moreover, he restored the excised material as soon as he had the chance, in a British paperback edition of 1964.

study of a moral type: "the creature of impulse," jittery, uncomfortable Rabbit Angstrom, with his animal urge to untangle himself from a web of obligations. This was the first time Updike had plunged so deeply and at such length into the consciousness of a single character. The present tense carried him along as he chased after his restless Rabbit, the author's reach extending as the pages piled up.

The most harrowing scene, the accidental drowning of Janice's newborn baby, testifies to a dramatic expansion of his capacity for empathy. In *The Poorhouse Fair* he relied on his familiarity with his beloved grandparents to create elderly characters who were not only plausible but engaging; in *Rabbit, Run* he managed to channel, sympathetically, the thoughts of an inebriated housewife, not a class of citizen he was well acquainted with. The bumbling of the drunken Janice is terrifyingly convincing, leading with a dreadful inevitability to the moment when the baby "sinks down like a gray stone" into the overfilled bathtub:

> With a sob of protest she grapples for the child but the water pushes up at her hands, her bathrobe tends to float, and the slippery thing squirms in the sudden opacity. She has a hold, feels a heartbeat on her thumb, and then loses it, and the skin of the water leaps with pale refracted oblongs that she can't seize the solid of; it is only a moment, but a moment dragged out in a thicker time. Then she has Becky squeezed in her hands and it is all right.

Of course it's not all right; baby Becky, dead, is now just "the space between her arms," a space that can be filled only by sorrow. The whole catastrophic scene (seventeen manuscript pages) poured out of Updike in one sitting during a week in mid-August that he and the family spent with Mary's parents in their Vermont farmhouse. At the end of his very long day, he came downstairs and announced, "Well, I just drowned the baby."

Michael Updike was three months old at the time, and his father later acknowledged that he'd dreaded writing the scene: "Obviously, there was no real baby involved; only a few sentences and adjectives on some pieces of paper. But I had babies of my own at the time, and I found the prospect of writing about infanticide unsettling." He steeled himself and got it done. Tempering his ruthlessness, he managed, in the midst of horror, to keep alive a spark of tenderness for Janice. We pity her, knowing that what she tells herself is true, that "the worst thing that has ever happened to any woman in the world has happened to her."

It's happened to Harry, too; his baby daughter's death resonates not just in *Rabbit, Run* but also in the other volumes of the tetralogy. Janice evolves, recovering, growing in stature and importance (without ever losing her taste for tipple); their son, Nelson, eventually plays an important role as his father's antagonist; and the pregnant Ruth, though she threatens to have an abortion, gives birth to a baby girl (note the symmetry) who decades later will become the object of Rabbit's fitful attention—but *Rabbit Angstrom*, as Updike called the completed work, is nonetheless all about Harry. It gives us the measure of the man in all dimensions over the course of three decades. When Updike defined his "aesthetic and moral aim" as a "non-judgmental immersion," he meant immersion in the particulars of Harry's existence. That's especially true of the first volume. Critics have praised the style of *Rabbit, Run*, and scholars have tracked with great ingenuity complex patterns of imagery, but the novel ultimately succeeds or fails as a portrait of its central character. From the beginning there were readers who found Rabbit reprehensible and rejected the novel along with its protagonist; others, including the influential Granville Hicks, managed to admire it in spite of their distaste for the "irresponsible and troubled young man" whose agitated movements it tracks. But Updike, it seems clear to me, wanted us to root for Rabbit even at his most abysmally selfish, to sympathize when he tells Eccles, "I once did something right. I played first-rate basketball, I really did. And after you're first-rate at something, it kind of takes the kick out of being second rate." We're meant to respect his ideal of excellence, to treasure the signs of goodness in this manifestly fallible individual.

In a sense, and only in partnership with Updike, Rabbit does do something right, something first-rate. Never a great success in the workplace, and a serial failure as a family man, he became an excellent conduit, an obliging medium channeling the spirit of the times, the spirit of the nation. Harry Angstrom was a "ticket," Updike wrote, "to the America all around me. What I saw through Rabbit's eyes was more worth telling than what I saw through my own." There's just enough in *Rabbit, Run* of Harry scoping out his surroundings—listening to the car radio and observing the lay of the land—to set a precedent; it's a role he grew into, seeing more and more over time with an ever-keener eye, so that *Rabbit Redux* becomes a nightmare reflection of late-sixties social turmoil, and *Rabbit Is Rich* and *Rabbit at Rest* bring us a running commentary on the headline news of subsequent decades. Updike's nonjudgmental immersion began with Harry and his local orbit and moved on to America as a whole.

There is no such thing as static happiness. Happiness is a mixed thing, a thing compounded of sacrifices, and losses, and betrayals.
—Updike to a *Time* reporter in March 1968

V.

The Two Iseults

Had he run as far as Ipswich, Rabbit would have seen some familiar sights, among them a loosening of the social weave. An impulse not entirely unlike the one that led him to walk out on Janice and move in with another woman was taking root in the town Updike had learned to call home. It's obvious that if Updike himself wasn't yet having extramarital affairs, he was feeling the urge and thinking hard about it. Rabbit's dash for freedom and his dalliance with Ruth are in some measure an expression of displaced desire, a symptom of restlessness and anxiety in a twenty-seven-year-old freelance author tied down by his responsibility for a young family—hence Updike's remark about the "heavy, intoxicating dose of fantasy and wish-fulfillment" that went into the writing of *Rabbit, Run*. By the time the novel reached bookstore shelves in early November, the fantasy was, by his own account, becoming a reality: he was "falling in love, away from marriage." The woman in question was living in Boston, on Beacon Hill. She was not at home when Updike knocked hopefully on her door on the afternoon of Wednesday, September 28, 1960—so he went instead to Fenway Park and watched his great hero Ted Williams hit a home run in his last ever at-bat. Updike tells us next to nothing about this woman he was falling in love with, just a teasing hint slipped into a preface to a special reprinting of "Hub Fans Bid Kid Adieu," his celebrated essay about the historic baseball game he saw that afternoon. We learn that on the woman's door a bright brown mail basket was hanging—and that's about it. We don't know how he met her or when or whether the affair or fling was ever consummated, though at the end of the preface, he refers to "love forestalled," which may imply a romance that came to nothing. In any case, if Updike hadn't volunteered the information, we would know nothing at all of this anonymous woman's existence. (It's also possible that he invented the whole episode to add spice to the story of how he came to be at the ball game, or that he adjusted the time and venue of the assignation-that-wasn't to preserve dramatic unities.)

The preface is dated August 1, 1977, about a year and a half after he and Mary petitioned for divorce, and just two months before he married his second wife, Martha Ruggles Bernhard. I believe that the deliberate, unprompted mention of a failed tryst was a formal gesture of farewell to a chapter in his life that began or nearly began on the day of Williams's last at-bat, a chapter that would be coming to a close with his new marriage. He was saying good-bye to years of philandering, retiring as a womanizer, and choosing to mark the occasion in a preface to an essay about his hero's swan song.

Updike wasn't the first in his Ipswich crowd to commit adultery, and it's possible that he wasn't even the first in his marriage. Mary had blossomed as a young matron; surrounded by four lively and demanding children, she remained serene and graceful. With her wide, encouraging smile and calm, appraising eyes, she reminded many of her friends and neighbors of a kind of earth mother. She had a quiet, shy, passive side—and also a propensity to flirt at parties. It would be hard to be married to John without enjoying the back-and-forth of teasing banter. In the early sixties she took a lover; asked whether her affair, which lasted several years, began before or after John's first fling, she said she didn't know. Although she couldn't be sure when his infidelity began, or with whom, she thought it might have been more or less simultaneous with hers. This lack of certainty isn't surprising; she had children to look after, and her own secrets to hide, and couldn't keep track of his comings and goings.

For one thing, he was no longer around the house in the mornings. Immediately after the family's monthlong vacation in Anguilla, in late March 1960, Updike rented a one-room office in a "scabby tenement" in the center of Ipswich. This was another step in the process of becoming a professional author; it chimed with his childhood conception of an artist as someone "who, equipped with pencils and paper, practiced his solitary trade as methodically as a dentist practiced his." And Updike's trade was going well. His target, when he left Manhattan to become a freelancer, was to sell six stories a year to *The New Yorker*. In 1959 he managed seven; in 1960, four; in 1961, seven. He was right on target, selling eighteen stories in three years—as methodical as a dentist, but with the satisfactions of public recognition: two months after setting up the office he received the Rosenthal Award for *The Poorhouse Fair*. His first significant literary prize, it was bestowed at a ceremony at the National Institute of Arts and Letters on the Upper West Side of Manhattan.

His office was in the center of town, just four blocks from the house: a dingy second-floor room looking out over the Ipswich River, minimally furnished with a large dull green metal army desk bought for thirty dollars, a chair, a leather sofa, a bureau in which to store his manuscripts and working drafts ("everything artistic is kept down here," he told Maxwell), a crowded bookcase, and yellowing newspaper photographs of Proust and Joyce. The initial rent was eight dollars per week. For the next fourteen years, this is where he wrote, between a lawyer's office and a beautician, upstairs from the Dolphin Restaurant, where he often went for lunch when his writing day was done. To Victor Gollancz he explained, facetiously, "I've rented a little room . . . so that I can devote more time to my literary troubles and less to my children." He might have added that leaving the house every day would give him more opportunity to have an affair.

He didn't have to look far to find a lover. Several of the couples had already had affairs before moving to Ipswich, and once they were all settled and best friends, romantic intrigue was very much in the air. It's safe to say that the group's unusual closeness (and a large part of the pain that followed) had something to do with the collective willingness to indulge in extramarital sex. This "weave of promiscuous friendship" wasn't a purely local phenomenon. "Welcome to the post-pill paradise" is perhaps the most famous line from *Couples*, which Updike set in 1963, three years after he claimed to have first fallen "in love, away from marriage"—and three years after the first birth-control pill was approved for use in the United States. Did the advent of oral contraception unleash a frenzy of adulterous coupling in suburban communities all over the country? That theory seems a little pat, yet there's a measure of truth to it. There's no doubt that by the time of JFK's assassination, the junior jet set of Ipswich were already hopping in and out of one another's beds with impressive frequency. Whatever moral qualms Updike might have had were long since banished, and any lingering shyness had dissipated. He threw himself with reckless enthusiasm into the tangle of Ipswich infidelities. It's worth stressing, however, that it wasn't his idea; he wasn't the instigator. He made suburban sex famous, but he didn't invent it.

For the first few years, the proliferating affairs caused little trouble; any upset was kept tactfully out of sight. They were a promiscuous group but not blatant. The adultery was clandestine, discreet if not invisible. With one or two exceptions, there was no actual wife-swapping; there were never any key parties or orgies. And in the beginning, at least, no homes were wrecked; appearances were preserved, separation and divorce avoided. The taboo against casual or semi-casual sex may have been breached, but the integrity of the family (for the sake of the children) was still considered of paramount importance. The possibility that serial adultery would gradually undermine most marriages and put the welfare of the progeny at risk seems to have been overlooked—until it was too late and the town was dotted with broken homes.*

---

* In Updike's crowd there were two couples who joined in all the fun, the sports, the parties, the community projects, but *not* the extramarital sex. Those two couples were still together decades after the rest had split up.

Updike slept around in Ipswich, "a stag of sorts," as he wrote in his memoirs, "in our herd of housewife-does." And when his success as an author meant that he began to travel around the country and abroad, he permitted himself sexual adventures away from home. Without explicitly admitting that for most of the Ipswich years he enjoyed an active and varied extramarital sex life, he made clear in *Self-Consciousness* his disdain for this promiscuous period of his life, describing his behavior with a chain of derogatory adjectives: "malicious, greedy . . . obnoxious . . . rapacious and sneaky . . . remorseless." The fact of his promiscuity is important; a hyperactive libido is a component of his character that can't be ignored. And it explains in part the sheer volume of verbiage he devoted to sex over the next half century: he was writing about what he knew. But however infatuated he may have been with some of the women he hooked up with—and however useful, from a writer's perspective, his observation of their most intimate gestures—these casual arrangements are of interest only in a cumulative sense. Where the incidents are fleeting, the individuals will remain, for our purposes, nameless, as anonymous as the mystery woman who wasn't home on the day of Ted Williams's last at-bat.*

There are only two extramarital affairs of real significance in Updike's life. The first was with Joyce Harrington; she and her husband, Herbert, were core members of the couples crowd. The second was with Martha Bernhard; she and her husband, Alex, were late additions. The first affair came within a whisker of ending the Updikes' marriage in the fall of 1962; the second did end the marriage: John separated from Mary in 1974, and they were divorced two years later. John and Martha married soon afterward. And then, as if to demonstrate what a snarled web it was, Alex Bernhard, Martha's ex-husband, married Joyce Harrington, John's ex-mistress.

Even if we can't name the day when Updike fell in love with Joyce Harrington, we do know that by the spring of 1961 he was al-

---

* To protect their privacy, and to encourage those I met to tell me about their encounters with Updike, I agreed not to name any of the women with whom he conducted casual affairs.

ready writing about a husband whose unconsummated but entirely reciprocated lust for "a woman not [his] wife" leaves him literally panting: in "Packed Dirt, Churchgoing, a Dying Cat, a Traded Car," David Kern's highly charged flirtation with another woman sparks a religious crisis not dissimilar to the one he suffered the first time he appeared as Updike's alter ego, as a teenager in "Pigeon Feathers." In the summer of the following year, Updike began drafting stories about a passionate extramarital affair, stories so transparently autobiographical that he couldn't publish them—to do so would have been to broadcast the parlous state of his marriage and the naked fact of his adultery to the entire readership of *The New Yorker*, including his parents, his wife's parents, and every one of his Ipswich pals.

Ever since *Rabbit, Run*, the sexual element in his writing—principally the ache of a male's physical desire—had become more and more pronounced. "Wife-Wooing," an intimate portrait of the Updike marriage completed soon after he'd sent off the manuscript of the novel, is brimming with carnal energy, the narrator lusting after his wife in a kind of hymn to domestic eroticism.* Written like *Rabbit, Run* in the present tense, "Wife-Wooing" is elaborately, self-consciously literary; James Joyce, invoked in the first paragraph, supplies a coinage, "smackwarm," which is playfully appropriated, so that we get in the second paragraph this comic pastiche: "your thigh's inner side is lazily laid bare, and the eternally elastic garter snaps smackwarm against my hidden heart." The wife, understandably distracted and fatigued by three young children, rebuffs the husband's semisurreptitious attempts to seduce her, then surprises him the next night by making her own gratefully accepted advances. But before that happy ending, while the disappointment of sexual rejection still rankles, the hymn of praise turns into something more like a curse, one of the cruelest paragraphs in Updike's oeuvre:

---

* The characters are unnamed, but Updike eventually included "Wife-Wooing" among *The Maples Stories*, a chronicle of his twenty-two-year marriage parceled out in eighteen stories written over the course of thirty-eight years.

In the morning, to my relief, you are ugly. Monday's wan breakfast light bleaches you blotchily, drains the goodness from your thickness, makes the bathrobe a limp stained tube flapping disconsolately, exposing sallow décolletage. The skin between your breasts a sad yellow. I feast with the coffee on your drabness, every wrinkle and sickly tint a relief and a revenge. The children yammer. The toaster sticks. Seven years have worn this woman.

The sudden vindictive bitterness comes as a shock—but it works, effectively dramatizing the intensity of the husband's unsatisfied connubial lust.

Updike was surprised when Maxwell let him know that *The New Yorker* had accepted "Wife-Wooing." However lifelike the detail, however deep the current of feeling, it still has the feel of an experiment, a finger-exercise monologue that grew into a narrative. The much-anthologized "A&P," written six months later, also first person, also present tense, achieves much greater dramatic power and has the feel of a completed action. The lust, here, is comparatively lighthearted. The three girls who walk into the A&P in their bathing suits, especially Queenie, the one with the gloriously naked shoulders, trigger a visceral response in nineteen-year-old Sammy ("it made my stomach rub the inside of my apron"); when the store manager lectures the girls, Sammy quits in protest, a quixotic, self-defeating gesture that nonetheless wins the reader's admiration. Sammy's voice may indeed, as Mary Updike complained, sound too much like J. D. Salinger, but his tributes to Queenie's sex appeal have the ring of genuine adolescent yearning. "Lifeguard," written a month after "A&P," is another present-tense monologue, this one delivered by a divinity student who spends the summer months working as a lifeguard. "Lust stuns me like the sun," he says, and zeroes in on its source: "the arabesque of the spine. The curve by which the back modulates into the buttocks." He adds, "It is here that Grace sits and rides a woman's body."

Updike had sex on his mind—and death, too. In "The Blessed Man of Boston, My Grandmother's Thimble, and Fanning Island," a remarkable story he finished on September 27, 1960 (the day before Ted Williams's last at-bat, the day before Updike's failed tryst with the mystery woman of Boston), he pauses to reflect on an old Chinese man he once glimpsed in the stands of a baseball stadium; tells the story of his grandfather's death; attempts the resurrection of his dead grandmother; and imagines the inexorable, serial extinction of a band of castaways, all male, on an uninhabited but inhabitable Polynesian island. As that summary and the story's comically long-winded title suggest, Updike is stitching together disparate elements, a collage construction he thought of as an innovation. He told *Time* magazine that the "conversation" between the different parts of the story creates "a new kind of fictional space." He may have been exaggerating the novelty of the technique—it's not very different from the effect achieved, say, by the inter-chapters in Hemingway's *In Our Time*—but it's true that the story adds up to more than the sum of its parts.

The unnamed narrator could be David Kern, but he could just as easily be John Updike. Identifying himself as a writer, he claims authorship of one of Updike's published poems, "Shipbored," and tells us that he composed it sitting by the bedside of his ailing grandmother in his parents' kerosene-lit house. Though he reminds us of the digestive process whereby "would-be novelists" such as he condense and transform experience ("We walk through volumes of the unexpressed and like snails leave behind a faint thread excreted out of ourselves"), and though he does fictionalize certain minor details (his father-in-law is a surgeon rather than a Unitarian minister), it's more than usually tempting to treat the personal elements of this story as undiluted autobiography.

Much as *The Poorhouse Fair* had been a tribute to his maternal grandfather, John Hoyer, "Blessed Man" is a tribute to Updike's tenacious maternal grandmother, Katherine Hoyer, who died in 1955. Inspired by an heirloom, a silver thimble engraved with her initials, a keepsake Katherine gave to John and Mary as a wedding present (their *best* present, he told his mother), the story is an explicit attempt to bring her back to life ("O Lord, bless these poor paragraphs, that would do in their vile ignorance Your work of resurrection"), and a meditation on the extent to which it's possible to recapture experience and preserve it through writing. The death of his grandparents diminished his family by two fifths and deprived him of a treasured part of his past, the sheltered years of his youth and childhood. Could he make his grandmother live again on the page? It's certainly one of his finest prose portraits, tender, clear-eyed, wonderfully vivid. At one point the narrator remembers how, as a high-spirited teenager, he would scoop up his tiny grandmother, "lift her like a child, crooking one arm under her knees and cupping the other behind her back. Exultant in my height, my strength, I would lift that frail brittle body weighing perhaps a hundred pounds and twirl with it in my arms while the rest of the family watched with startled smiles of alarm." When he adds, "I was giving my past a dance," we hear the voice of John Updike exulting in his strength.

Katherine takes center stage only after an account of the dramatic day of her husband's death. John Hoyer died a few months after John and Mary were married, on the day both the newlyweds and Mary's parents were due to arrive in Plowville. From this unfortunate coincidence, the Updike family managed to spin a pair of short stories.

Six months before he wrote "Blessed Man," Updike's mother had her first story accepted by *The New Yorker*. For years her son had been doing his filial best to help get her work published—with no success. In college he sent out the manuscript of her novel about Ponce de León to the major Boston publishers, and when he landed at *The New Yorker* he made sure her stories were read by editors instead of languishing in the slush pile. These efforts finally bore fruit when an editor at the magazine named Rachel MacKenzie championed "Translation," a portentous family saga featuring Linda's version of her father's demise. Maxwell assured Updike that his colleagues all thought his mother "immensely gifted"; if that sounds like tactful exaggeration, Maxwell's idea that he could detect "the same quality of mind running through" mother and son is curious to say the least.

Published in *The New Yorker* on March 11, 1961, "Translation" was signed Linda Grace Hoyer and narrated by a character named

Linda—but it wasn't likely to be mistaken for a memoir. The story is overstuffed with biblical allusion, psychodrama, and magical thinking, most of it Linda's. She believes that her ninety-year-old father plans to be translated directly to heaven, ascending like Elijah in a whirlwind, with chariots of fire, and to pass his mantle to a new generation, again like Elijah. It's not clear whether this grand design is his obsession, as she claims, or hers. As it happens, the whirlwind is only a tussle with his wife that lands the old folks on the floor beside the bed. Linda finds them there and says, "Of all things. . . . What are you two doing?" Her father answers, his voice "matter-of-fact and conversational": "We are sitting on the floor." Having spoken these words, he dies. Linda's son Eric (a writer, of course) arrives on the scene almost immediately. When she tells him, "Grampy *died*," he replies, "I know, Mother, I know. It happened as we turned off the turnpike. I felt him going." Eric climbs the stairs to view the body and announces on his return, "He died *well*."* Linda laughs at the oddity of the remark. "Perhaps," she tells us, "I had expected Eric to see the chariot of fire and feel the whirlwind and show me the mantle." For her, the important thing is that Eric felt her father "going"—proof that he has inherited the "prophetic spirit," that the mantle has been passed.

Updike never commented on the fanciful mythology his mother elaborated in her fiction (the idea that she married only to conceive a son, and that her son's writing career was somehow related to her father's "prophetic spirit"—in other words that she was a crucial link in a generational chain of spiritual and creative greatness), but *his* version of the story she embroidered so lavishly in "Translation" is utterly free of supernatural agency—nobody feels anybody "going." Updike's approach suggests that when he chose to revisit his grandfather's deathbed scene, essentially rewriting the passage from Linda's story, his aim was to debunk; he wanted both to set the factual

---

* This is a direct quote from a letter John sent Linda from Harvard a few weeks after her father's death: "I miss Grandpa, even at this distance. . . . But he died well . . . and I am glad that his final utterance was such a level-headed and snappy one."

record straight and to remind Maxwell (and anyone else in a position to compare) that he possessed a "quality of mind" quite *un*like his mother's.

Updike's version begins with a delusional episode. The old man becomes convinced that his bed is on fire, bellows, and tries to spring from it. His wife struggles to restrain him, and they fall together to the floor, which is where their only daughter, bursting into the room, finds them. She asks what they're doing, and her father ("with level sarcasm") answers, "Why, we're on the floor." Whereupon he dies—"his heart stopped." When the grandchild (the unnamed narrator) arrives with his wife and in-laws, his father greets them with the news: "Jesus . . . you've come at a funny time; we think Pop's died." At the crucial moment, when the old couple are on the floor by the bed, Linda has the dying man addressing her in a "matter-of-fact and conversational" tone; Updike substitutes "level sarcasm"—that sarcasm, I suspect, was intended to deflate his mother's grandiose mythic notions about the "prophetic spirit." The only remaining trace of biblical allusion in Updike's version is the burning bed—a figment of a ninety-year-old's delirious imagination, part of a pattern of imagery rather than a supernatural occurrence. As if to underline his distaste for mystical mumbo-jumbo, the narrator mentions that the grandfather's funeral was made "ridiculous" by the "occult presumption" of his fellow Masons.

It would be misleading to say that Updike's story is devoid of religious sentiment. If "Blessed Man" registers his response to the death of beloved grandparents (his first intimate exposure to death of any kind), the lesson he seems to have learned is that ceremonies are of limited use, but that faith may be helpful. With trembling knees, the narrator comes downstairs from the room where his grandfather's body lies and is "shocked to discover . . . that we have no gestures adequate to answer the imperious gestures of nature." As the family waits for the undertaker, they carry on with their impromptu wake; the narrator is "amazed" by the poverty of their social gestures. In addition to the death of the grandparents, elsewhere in the story Updike presents us with the inexorable dwindling of a company of Polynesian men cast ashore on a remote island

("No women were among them, so their numbers could only diminish"), a story, he says, "of life stripped of the progenitive illusion." He quotes this famous, disheartening passage from Pascal's *Pensées*:

> Let us imagine a number of men in chains, and all condemned to death, where some are killed each day in the sight of the others, and those who remain see their own fate in that of their fellows, and wait their turn, looking at each other sorrowfully and without hope.

Pascal tells us that this is an image of man's condition—it's also Updike's worst nightmare. Condemned to death, we devise social rituals that are ineffectual, offering scant comfort, let alone hope. There *is* hope, however, for the efficacy of faith—or at least that's what the balance of the story seems to suggest. Faith bridges the gap between our good intentions (the desire, say, to resurrect a grandparent with words alone) and what we actually achieve: a dozen pages of prose fiction. The story is impressive and profoundly moving, but it can't mitigate the crushing certainty of our doom or the possibility (very real to the narrator) of imminent collective extinction ("I feel the world is ending"). This is how Updike leaves it: "I thought that this story, fully told, would become without my willing it a happy story, a story full of joy; had my powers been greater, we would know. As it is, you, like me, must take it on faith."

Seven months after "Blessed Man," he wrote a sequel of sorts, also in stitched-together, "fugal" form. It's hard to read "Packed Dirt, Churchgoing, a Dying Cat, a Traded Car," which he sent off to Maxwell in early May 1961, and not think that we're once again reading raw autobiography. Here's another death-haunted young writer, this time consumed by adulterous passion and horrified by the idea of actually cheating on his wife: "The universe that so easily permitted me to commit adultery became, by logical steps each one of which went more steeply down than the one above it, a universe that would easily permit me to die." And yet these are the words of a character, David Kern, subject to fears and scruples not necessarily shared by the author. Updike was surely quite aware that he could break a vow spoken at the altar without being struck dead or ejecting God from the heavens—without, indeed, disturbing the universe in any way. There's no doubt that he's working here with intimate autobiographical material, dogmatically inserting at every opportunity incidental detail plucked from real life, such as the name of the street where he lived in Oxford and the exact day and hour of his daughter's birth—and that he's counting on the sense of authenticity those details convey. In the letter he sent to Maxwell along with the manuscript, he reported that the events "shadowed" in the story continued to unfold in his own life, making him wonder where to end the tale.

There are backward glances in "Packed Dirt," but there's nothing like the sustained nostalgia of "Blessed Man." David Kern's narrative—or, rather, his string of juxtaposed narratives—is rooted in the present, and certain scenes buzz with an astonishingly urgent immediacy. The kernel of the story is again an actual event. On March 18, 1961, his twenty-ninth birthday, Updike learned that his father had been taken to the Reading hospital with heart trouble. Wesley had been experiencing chest pains and shortness of breath, and when Linda finally convinced him to see the doctor, an electrocardiogram revealed the seriousness of his condition: he had suffered a mild heart attack. Like David Kern, Updike made the eight-hour drive down to Pennsylvania. He spent the night at his parents' farm, and in the morning he drove with his mother to sit by his father's hospital bed. Then he drove home again, straight back to Massachusetts. All in all, a 750-mile round-trip.

In the story, on the night before David's birthday (which falls on a Saturday, just as Updike's did in 1961), he and his wife attend a party. He dances with another woman, a "friend"; as they dance, they touch, and between dances touch some more, ratcheting up the erotic tension:

> Her back seemed mysteriously taut and hard. . . . In a sheltered corner of the room we stopped dancing altogether and talked, and what I distinctly remember is how her hands, beneath the steady and opaque appraisal of her eyes, in agita-

tion blindly sought mine and seized and softly gripped, with infantile instinct, my thumbs. Just my thumbs she held, and as we talked she moved them this way and that as if she were steering me. When I closed my eyes, the red darkness inside my lids was vibrant, and when I rejoined my wife, and held her to dance, she asked, "Why are you panting?"

The specificity of the gestures is a powerful, almost hypnotic moment for the reader—as it is for David. Later, home in bed, he and his wife make love: "Irritated by whatever illicit stimulations, we took it out on each other." Then, unable to sleep, he replays the events of the party ("That feathery anxious embrace of my erect thumbs tormented me in twenty postures. My stomach turned in love of that woman") and plunges into a spiritual black hole, terrified by the unavoidable certainty of death and the nonexistence of God. The crisis is fueled by his Sunday school conviction that "to lust after a woman in thought is the same as committing adultery." For comfort he turns to his wife ("Wake up, Elaine. I'm so frightened"); the irony goes unmentioned. The next day, his birthday, the crisis continues, at least until his mother's phone call; when she delivers the bad news about his father's illness, David perks right up: "All day death had been advancing under cover and now it had declared its position. My father had engaged the enemy and it would be defeated."

From the moment his mother telephones about his father, there's no further mention of Friday night's events, of "illicit stimulations" or his "love of that woman." On the contrary, David becomes a cheerleader for marriage, telling a hitchhiking soldier he picks up on the way to Pennsylvania that the young man should "absolutely" marry his girlfriend: "I told him I had married at the age of twenty-one and had never been sorry." At his parents' farm he sleeps badly: "I missed my wife's body, that weight of memory, beside me. I was enough of a father to feel lost out of my nest of little rustling souls." The irony again goes unmentioned. The proximate cause of this astonishing transformation from would-be adulterer to model family man is the thought of his ailing father—whose role as his son's protector assumes a vast importance now that he's unwell. When David is cold during the night after his long drive ("My mother had mistaken me for a stoic like my father and had not put enough blankets on the bed"), he drapes an old overcoat over his blankets to keep him warm; the overcoat belongs to his father, of course. The next morning, when mother and son set off for the hospital, David insists that they drive his car. He doesn't want to get behind the wheel of the family's '53 Dodge—not just because it's an old secondhand heap but also because he doesn't want to assume the role of the patriarch: "My father's place was between me and heaven; I was afraid of being placed adjacent to that far sky." Fear of his own death, love of his father, fear of his father's death—a potent blend of emotion reinforces David's conservative streak. Having driven so far to perform a time-honored ritual, the bedside visit to a relative in the hospital, he discovers what he believes to be the moral of his story: "We in America need ceremonies, is I suppose . . . the point of what I have written."

Though hesitant (hedged by that tentative "I suppose"), David's formulation is straightforward, a prescription for troubled times: when in crisis or assailed by doubt, cleave to well-established social rituals, follow the rules. David's mother tells him that his father, a stalwart of the local Lutheran church, has lost his faith; she adds that he "never was much one for faith. . . . He was strictly a works man." When David affirms that we need ceremonies, he's aligning himself with his father; but Updike allows room for a more equivocal reading of the cautionary advice that caps the story. So abrupt is David's metamorphosis from incipient adulterer to straitlaced champion of family values that one wonders whether his flight from temptation will do any good. Is it really ceremonies we need? Perhaps, as the narrator of "Blessed Man" would say, we should take it on faith. Or perhaps it's faith itself we in America need. That we need *something* can't be denied; the need is woven into the fabric of this story and its predecessor, both written, as Updike acknowledged, "under a great pressure of sadness."

Wesley Updike's medical emergency—in the story, he's given an apt and poetically suggestive diagnosis: an enlarged heart—was a shock to his son. The ripple of alarm that prompted Updike to make his marathon road trip inspired not only the central incident in "Packed Dirt" but also the novel begun just weeks later. Though he claimed to have conceived of *Rabbit, Run* and *The Centaur* at the same time (as "a biune study of complementary moral types: the rabbit and the horse, the zigzagging creature of impulse and the plodding beast of stoic duty"), the profoundly affecting portrait of George Caldwell in the new novel was clearly informed by more recent concerns. "The main motive force behind *The Centaur*," he told an interviewer, was "some wish to make a record of my father"— Wesley's hospitalization and the real possibility of his death made the need for such a record seem suddenly urgent.

In *The Centaur*, George Caldwell has convinced himself that he's dying of cancer ("I'm carrying death in my bowels"), a worry that infects his wife and son (and figures, in the mythical dimension, as Chiron's intention to sacrifice himself for Prometheus's sake). His hypochondria has its humorous aspect, but alongside the comedy—Updike thought of the novel as his "gayest" book—there's an elegiac strain. The gloomiest passage comes in chapter 5, which is simply Caldwell's obituary as it might have appeared in the local newspaper. In fact George's Olinger doctor pronounces him cancer-free, good news that does nothing to relieve his comically lugubrious sense of encroaching doom. At the very end, he embraces his fate. In mythic terms, this means giving up his immortality: "Chiron accepted death." The centaur's sacrifice earns him a place in the firmament as the constellation Sagittarius. In everyday terms, it means that George Caldwell's martyrdom continues; the plodding beast will carry on with his duty, teaching school so his clever son, Peter, can make an escape.

Updike was worried about his father's health and also about his own. A routine medical examination undertaken to secure a life insurance policy revealed that his lungs were "slightly emphysematous," a condition he regarded as fatal; "young as I was," he wrote prophetically, "I had death in my lungs." He renewed his efforts to quit smoking and consulted his own doctor, who pooh-poohed the idea that emphysema might kill him—but did note that he had the spread rib cage of a chronic asthmatic. Updike took to heart this distant glimpse of the grave; echoing *The Centaur*, he wrote, "I was mortal. I carried within me fatal wounds."

In *Self-Consciousness*, Updike describes this period—during which he produced some of his finest fiction—as a time of "desperation"; he felt smothered by "an oppressive blanket of funk," a "grayness" he associated with death and decay. In these "gray moments," he reported, his "spirit could scarcely breathe"; he was in the grip of a chronic low-level spiritual crisis. Seeking a cure, or at least temporary relief, he self-medicated; his idea of how to treat his complaint was nothing like David Kern's—in fact, it was pretty much the opposite. "[T]o give myself brightness and air," he wrote, "I read Karl Barth and fell in love with other men's wives." He battled death with God and romance.

Barth was possibly the less efficacious of the two remedies. A bracingly stringent Calvinist, he did supply Updike with one of the enduring tenets of his personal creed (the idea that God is "Wholly Other": "We cannot reach Him, only He can reach us"), and he did become, in the sixties, Updike's favorite theologian ("Ipswich belonged to Barth")—but as Barth himself insisted, theology cannot protect faith from doubt. For Updike, it was one buttress in a system of reinforcements necessary to sustain belief. Like his father, he found comfort in the sense of *belonging* to a particular congregation. After several unpromising trips to a nearby Lutheran church, Updike joined the First Congregational Church in Ipswich, became an usher, and served conscientiously on church committees. Every week, he shepherded his children to Sunday school, where Mary, though she rarely if ever attended services, accompanied hymns on the battered piano; at night in their bedrooms, he recited prayers with the children. His peace of mind depended on conventional religious observance, regular doses of theology administered by those authors who helped him believe (especially Barth and Kierkegaard), and a dose also of his own, internally generated faith. This last, wavering item required periodic renewal. It began with an act of will; as an adolescent in Plowville, he had made a conscious effort to preserve his faith, a commodity he reluctantly recognized as rare and getting rarer. Surrounded by disbelief more or less politely concealed, he refused to play along—"I decided . . . I *would* believe." Though he disapproved of pragmatic faith, he was well aware of the utility of his own special brand of piety: "Religion enables us to ignore nothingness," he wrote, "and get on with the jobs of life." He explained the tenacity of his faith by pointing to the part played by fear: "The choice seemed to come down to: believe or be frightened and depressed all the time." On a good day, faith in God gave him confirmation that he *mattered*—"that one's sense of oneself as being of infinite value is somewhere in the universe answered, that indeed one is of infinite value." Religion eased his existential terror, allowing him to do his work, and to engage in the various kinds of play that best amused him—among them the hazardous sport of falling for his friends' wives. He was caught in a vicious circle: he fell in love, and his adulterous passion made him feel alive, but also sparked a religious crisis that renewed his fear of death—so he fell in love some more and read some more theology. Not surprisingly, his wife found that she couldn't tell, when he exhibited signs of angst, whether he was suffering from religious doubt or romantic torment.

David Kern's terror strikes at night; he lies next to his sleeping wife, breathing the dust of his grave. Updike's own version of the crisis could come at any time. Once, while he was in the basement building a dollhouse for Liz, he suddenly felt "that I was hanging on with my fingernails to the side of a cliff." A gray moment might descend on him during Sunday sports, with the entire couples crowd on hand: "[A]s I waited, on a raw rainy fall day, for the opposing touch-football team to kick off, there would come sailing through the air instead the sullen realization that in a few decades we would all be dead." If there's a frenetic, compulsive edge to his engagement with the Ipswich scene—what he himself called his "incessant

---

* Updike recycled this episode, and indeed the entire vicious circle of thanatophobia and adultery, in *Toward the End of Time* (1997). The narrator's first affair brings with it a "colorful weave of carnal revelation and intoxicating risk and craven guilt [which] eclipsed the devouring gray sensation of time."

sociability"—it's partly because his instinct was to drown out doubts and fears with the clamor of a party. He writes in *Self-Consciousness*,

> Egoistic dread faded within the shared life. We celebrated each other's birthdays and break-ups in a boozy, jaunty muddle of mutually invaded privacies. . . . The weekend get-togethers supplied courage to last the week.

Boozy weekend get-togethers also supplied the chance to clown, to dance, to flirt—to attract attention, amorous and otherwise.

Another way to mask terror was to keep constantly busy. When a friend bought the *Ipswich Chronicle* in early 1961, Updike volunteered "as a favor and a lark" to write reviews of the summer concert series held at Castle Hill, a grand nineteenth-century mansion near Crane Beach. John and Mary had been going to the concerts since their first year in Ipswich; these days, they went with their crowd, the women in their summer dresses, the men in seersucker jackets. Before the music there was a picnic washed down with white wine; during the concert, Updike kept his plastic glass upright between his feet and scribbled notes on his program. He liked the sense that he was surrounded by his friends, and yet in "an elevated position," the critic poised to pass judgment. His reviews, signed H.H. (his middle initial doubled), were banged out on the typewriter on the Monday morning after the weekend concert and handed in at lunchtime; the *Chronicle* offices were just up the street from his office. He wrote twenty-two of them over the course of five summers. Breezy and brash, they were written, in essence, for his pals—an attenuated form of flirtation.

More time-consuming than the Castle Hill distraction, and more perplexing, was his two-month stint in the classroom. On July 3, 1962, shortly after he sent off the typed manuscript of *The Centaur*, he found himself teaching a creative writing course at the Harvard Summer School. His father had announced his retirement in April, on doctor's orders, after nearly thirty years at Shillington High. There is of course a big difference between slaving away for decades at a public school and taking charge for eight weeks of an advanced composition class at an Ivy League college, but the irony is nonetheless remarkable: Updike had agreed to the Harvard job nine months earlier, while he was still at work on a novel about the travails of a teacher (the spitting image of his father) who refers to the classroom as the "slaughterhouse" and the "hate-factory," who thinks teaching is killing him. Money can't have been a motive. (At this point Updike would have earned more by selling a single story to *The New Yorker* than by teaching a term of summer school.) Perhaps he felt compelled to try his hand at the profession his mother had failed at, the profession his father had both thrived and suffered in—the profession, as *The Centaur* elaborately demonstrates, that allowed the teacher's son to make his famous escape. He knew it was the kind of invitation he should refuse, but somehow he couldn't say no to Harvard.

Admission to his class was restricted; he chose his students on the basis of writing samples submitted in advance. Once accepted, they were required to produce, each week, at least a dozen pages of writing, which he marked with conspicuous care. Guided by the example of his father's dedication, he treated his class with kindness and respect, a conscientious approach that earned the students' gratitude but demanded a great deal of time and effort. Though he was a rising star in literary circles—just two weeks after the end of the course, *Life* magazine named him one of its "Red Hot Hundred," leaders of a new generation—and though on the first day he had to turn away a small crowd of eager students who hadn't been admitted to the class but hoped to be allowed to sit quietly in the back and listen, he declined to act the part of a virtuoso condescending to a roomful of impressionable novices. He was friendly but serious, with flashes of charm and humor; he stuttered, but only a bit. He read his students' work promptly and handed it back with a typed comment (generally half a page, single-spaced) and scrawled notes in the margins. He remained tactful, even when faced with inferior work. Next to a notably lame passage in one student's story, he wrote in gentle rebuke, "Your literary energy has failed you here."

Two of his students, Nicholas Delbanco and Jonathan Penner, went on to have successful literary careers; both became university professors and taught creative writing for decades. Delbanco applied for Updike's class on a whim; he'd barely heard of the young author. It was the summer between his junior and senior years at Harvard, he was nineteen years old, and he'd wanted to stay in Cambridge only to be near his girlfriend—but Updike, he said, turned him into a novelist: "The first word I wrote for him was the first word of my first novel." Updike praised his first chapter ("For a beginner, you seem remarkably knowing in the trade of the novelist"), and Delbanco, having finished a second chapter, realized he was hooked. By the time he was twenty, he had a contract with a publisher—the book was the novel he started writing for Updike. Delbanco sat next to Updike in class and watched him doodle while his students read from their work. He remembered with pleasure Updike's high, braying laugh. "What was unforgettable," Delbanco said, "was how smart he was."

Penner recalled the day Updike came in and read with mock gravity a letter from the Tootsie Roll company sent to him because he had mentioned the candy in *Rabbit, Run*. The company thanked him for choosing its product as a representative symbol of American life and begged him to accept as a token of gratitude a six-gross box of Tootsie Rolls. Updike put the letter down and addressed the class: "Such are the benefits of the literary life."

Toward mid-August, with four classes left to go, Updike admitted to Maxwell that agreeing to the teaching job had been "sort of foolish"; he complained that "after ten short stories I could have Chekhov in my class and give him a B plus." At the very end of term he told one student that this would be the last class he taught. Dismayed, she asked him why. "I can't make friends with twelve people all at once again," he answered. If the letter to Maxwell is falsely modest, and the remark to the student a sweet bit of flattery, the prosaic explanation Updike gave to an interviewer in 1981 sums up his main objection to the profession: "Teaching takes a lot of energy. It uses somehow the very brain cells that you should be writing with." No arrangement that interfered with his writing was ever going to last.

HIS LOVE AFFAIR with Joyce Harrington disrupted his writing life in the short term, because he found himself compelled to write about their relationship even though he knew that what he wrote couldn't for now be published. But the affair also cracked open the seemingly inexhaustible topic of suburban adultery. It heated up dangerously during the spring, and at the beginning of summer, just before he began teaching, he confessed to Mary, who had begun to suspect that something serious was going on. She in turn confessed to her own affair and asked him to wait before taking any drastic steps, to do nothing and keep everything secret until summer's end. So the affair carried on—with a deadline for decision looming and both marriages in jeopardy—during the eight summer weeks when Updike was driving to Harvard Square on Tuesday and Thursday afternoons. Once again, his remarkable ability to compartmentalize guaranteed a smoothly functioning professional life.

Joyce Harrington turned thirty in the summer of 1962. She was the mother of three, two boys and a baby girl. Not classically beautiful but striking and sexy, with a long narrow face, a brilliant toothy smile, and lots of auburn hair, she stood out in the couples crowd, a bright, compelling presence. A description of one of Updike's fictional lovers captures the essence of her look: "Her eyes were the only glamorous feature of a freckled, bony, tomboyish face, remarkable chiefly for its sharp willingness to express pleasure." (The freckles are his concession to fiction.) He had met her soon after moving to Ipswich, while he was living at Little Violet. The Harringtons and the Updikes were as yet barely more than acquaintances when Herbert and Joyce asked if John and Mary would be willing to babysit for their infant son, Gus, who was the same age as David. The Updikes were surprised to be asked, but the plan went ahead all the same; the Harringtons dropped Gus off at Little Violet, drove to Boston for the evening, stayed out late, and picked him up on the way home. The ice was broken.

Herbert Harrington was a Harvard graduate, a building contractor and property developer who had inherited money from his father. The couple lived well, with flashes of extravagance. Joyce had a flair for clothes and furniture; glamorous, she dressed stylishly, for show, and the interior of her house was sleek and modern. They were very sociable, conspicuously outgoing even by the standards of this gregarious group. They had a motorboat and arranged trips to Plum Island and picnics on the beach. Mary thought their sophistication superficial, and was annoyed by Herbert's habit of dispensing glib psychoanalytic insights into the behavior of others. He had a diabolical streak, a way of manipulating people into uncomfortable situations so that he could then observe the consequences. John's early impression, at one of the Harringtons' dinner parties, was that Herbert had "the manner of the local undertaker, and indeed does somehow embalm his guests."

When Herbert found out about the affair (thanks to a close examination of the household telephone bill), he forced a dramatic showdown. Late one evening in early October, he called up and demanded that the Updikes come right away to the Harringtons' house, on Argilla Road, so that the four of them could thrash it out. Mary arranged for last-minute babysitting, and she and John dutifully drove over. Herbert sat them down with Joyce in the living room, served them all wine, and insisted that they resolve the situation there and then. His forceful attitude goaded John into taking precisely the step he knew he couldn't take, which was to declare his intention to leave Mary for Joyce. The next day, Herbert persuaded Mary to consult a lawyer—she and John would have to divorce so that John could marry Joyce. When Mary did drive down to Boston to see a lawyer (Herbert's own lawyer, in fact), she was sitting in the office, about to set the legal process in motion, when the telephone rang; it was John, asking to speak with his wife. "I took the phone," Mary remembered, "and John was saying that he'd changed his mind, that he wasn't going to leave me, that he didn't want a divorce—so I went home."

Herbert's reaction to John's change of heart was typically peremptory; first he threatened to sue John for alienation of affections, already an antiquated concept in 1962; then he decreed that the Updikes would have to leave Ipswich for a while—a banishment they accepted. John and Mary threw themselves a farewell cocktail party, packed up the family, and on the eighth of November boarded an Italian ocean liner and set sail for Europe. Traveling the "sunny southern route," the SS *Leonardo da Vinci* steered close to the Azores (hence the charming poem "Azores," about a "rural landscape / set adrift" in the mid-Atlantic) and through the Strait of Gibraltar en route to Naples, where John joined some other passengers for a disappointing tour of Pompeii. The family eventually disembarked at Cannes, and spent several days at the Hotel Savoy before finding a villa to rent in the hills just above Antibes. The house, called La Bastide, was modern, of modest size, and not particularly charming, but the terrace was warm in the sun, with a view of the Mediterranean, the orange roofs of Antibes, and to the east the snow-covered peaks of the Maritime Alps. A brief exile on the Riviera a few miles from where Gerald and Sara Murphy had played host to the leading lights of the Lost Generation doesn't sound especially grim, but Updike was indifferent to the glamour (except when he spotted Marlene Dietrich at the Nice airport). "He was pretty darn miserable," according to Mary. "He needed a lot of cheering up."

This sudden crescendo of momentous decisions and equally momentous reversals was the predictable result of Updike's affair. He'd known for months that he would have to choose between Mary and Joyce. In late September he'd taken the extraordinary step of writing to Alfred Knopf and asking him to remove from the biographical note to *The Centaur*, which was then in production, the line stating that he lived with his wife and four children in Ipswich; by the time of the book's publication, he confided, his circumstances might have changed. It was a likelihood, not a certainty. In fact he knew—though he needed to be pushed to the brink before admitting it—that his conscience would compel him to choose Mary. The predicament is mapped out in "Solitaire," an anguished story written in early August, two months before Herbert issued his ultimatum. The first words ("The children were asleep . . .") alert us to the crux of the dilemma confronting a husband who must decide between wife and mistress:

> How could he balance their claims and rights? The list was entirely one-sided. Prudence, decency, pity—not light things—all belonged to the guardian of his children and home; and these he would lose. . . . And he would as well lose

his own conception of himself, for to abandon his children and a woman who with scarcely a complaint or a quarrel had given him her youth was simply not what he would do.

Updike's own children now numbered four. Elizabeth, the eldest, was seven; the two boys, David and Michael, were five and three; Miranda was a toddler not yet two. Abandoning them would indeed dent the self-esteem of a father with any claim to prudence, decency, and pity. The narrator of "Solitaire," we're told, "was the son of parents who had stayed together for his sake." Updike felt that this was true of his parents as well; it's a theme that recurs regularly in his fiction.

And what of the other woman? In "Solitaire," the rights and claims of the mistress are dismissed as "nothing, or next to nothing." Her desire for him, her sense of him "existing purely as a man," is gratifying. The two women are roughly sketched, certain qualities vaguely suggested ("His wife had the more delicate mind, but his mistress, having suffered more, knew more that he didn't know"), yet the larger questions (Why does he desire his mistress? Why doesn't he desire his wife?) are left hazy—possibly to imply that this unhappy man is himself in the dark. With duty ranged against desire, he's stuck: "Back and forth, back and forth, like a sore fist his heart oscillated between them."

"Solitaire" was Updike's attempt to imagine how he might actually bring himself to make a decision overshadowed by the stubborn fact of his four young children. From the day Liz was born and he made a tiny, darling sketch of her to send to Plowville, he was a delighted and meticulous observer of his progeny. As the first baby grew and the others were born, he continued to watch with unflagging intensity. To his mother he sent detailed reports on the children's progress, weekly bulletins that were clearly as much for his benefit as hers. As so often with Updike, looking, seeing, and noting on paper were acts of worship: description expresses love.

"My Children at the Dump," a poem he sent to *The New Yorker* in the midst of the Harrington fiasco, hints at how the children weighed on his mind. It is, we learn in the first line, "The day before divorce." Shedding "remnants" of "a life / no longer shared," a father takes his three children on an excursion to the dump.* (Updike thought of the Ipswich dump as "one of the most peaceful and scenic places in the town.") Innocently oblivious of the looming trauma, the kids are "enchanted" by the "wonderland of discard"; the girl wants to take home "a naked armless doll," the boys covet bent toy tractors. The father's guilty imagination transforms them into "stunted starvelings cruelly set free / at a heaped banquet of food too rich to eat." Their poignant willingness to make do with damaged goods puts to shame the wasteful profligacy of the father who, one gathers, has thrown away his marriage, tossed it "among tummocks of junk"—"These things," he says by way of self-justification, "were considered, and dismissed / for a reason." Updike twists the knife at the very end of the poem; the father tells his daughter that she cannot keep the broken doll she's scavenged: "Love it now," he tells her. "Love it now, but we can't take it home." Home, the last word of the poem, resonates along with the repeated exhortation to love, sending us back to the root cause of this dismal situation. Father and children will no longer live together; the family home, having suffered like the amputated doll an irreparable loss, is now broken—ready for the scrap heap, which is where his children find themselves, wandering in a "universe of loss."

The New Yorker rejected "My Children at the Dump." Howard Moss, the poetry editor who did so much to encourage Updike, gave an uncharacteristically dopey account of the reasoning behind the decision. "The general feeling," Moss wrote, "was that a personal situation is its central point and the poem tends to avoid that point, though, at the same time, having been brought up, it's inescapable to the reader." Why not praise instead the poet's calculated (and evidently effective) indirection? I suspect that the editors felt squeamish about the "personal situation" in this intensely sad poem (originally entitled, as if to ram home the personal element, "My Children at the Dump at Ipswich"); they were uncomfortably aware that Updike was, as Maxwell put it, "a conspicuously autobiograph-

---

* Two-year-old Miranda was apparently left behind—too young for the dump.

ical writer" and weren't quite ready to hear about "the day before divorce."

But the "personal situation" remained Updike's obsessive concern for the next few years, causing difficulties for Maxwell as it did for Moss. "Solitaire" was accepted by *The New Yorker*, but Updike knew it couldn't be published just yet. In early October, as the storm was breaking, he submitted another story about a love affair in tatters, "Leaves." He asked that it not be put "on the bank"—that is, with the other stories ready to be printed in an upcoming issue. Dutiful and discreet, asking no awkward questions, Maxwell agreed to put it to one side until circumstances (the state of the marriage, the state of the affair) allowed its publication. Eventually Updike had more than half a dozen stories about unhappy adulterers parked on what he called "the shadow-bank," some for longer than two years. Among them were "Solitaire," "Leaves," "The Stare," "Museums and Women," "Avec la Bébé-Sitter," "Four Sides of One Story," and "The Morning"; about the last of these he wrote, "though the vessel of circumstantial facts is all invented, libel-proof, etc. the liquid contained may, if spilled soon, scald somebody." He was well aware that heaping the magazine with stories it couldn't run was an imposition, but as he admitted, stories of the "non-troublesome" variety didn't seem to engage his interest. Even after he'd renounced the dream of marrying Joyce, he was still thinking about her, still writing about her—or, rather, about the misery of renouncing her. The stories that did engage his interest were dense, bitter meditations on loss and longing, all short, all notably artful, not to say baroque.

In "Leaves," grief comes crashing down: "It does not stop coming. The pain does not stop coming." The narrator has given up his lover ("My heart shied back"), and is now in despair. Updike inserts an accurate thumbnail version of Mary's trip to the lawyer and the phone call that granted his marriage a last-minute stay of execution. The wife drives off to Boston "to get her divorce," dressed in a black sheath dress (as Mary often was); while she's conferring with the lawyer, the husband changes his mind: "By telephone I plucked my wife back; I clasped the black of her dress to me and braced for the pain." In "The Stare," another piece of the drama is played out. The adulterous husband faces the fury of his lover when she realizes that he won't be leaving his wife. "Don't you love me?" she asks. "Not enough," he replies. He states his answer "simply, as a fact, as something that had already been made plain." Updike emphasizes the shameful weakness of a character whose courage has failed him: "Two households were in turmoil and the rich instinct that had driven him to her had been transformed to a thin need to hide and beg." In "Museums and Women," after a half-dozen gorgeous pages based on reminiscence (memories of his mother taking him to the Reading Museum as a child, memories of meeting Mary outside the Fogg Museum as an undergraduate), Updike once again presents us with the forsaken lover. The woman, still distraught though the breakup occurred some time ago, asks what went wrong; the Updike alter ego shrugs: "Cowardice," he tells her. "A sense of duty." The story ends with a melancholy reflection on the steady diet of disenchantment that awaits him.

Compounded misery is the keynote of these stories; for the first time in his career, Updike's writing was unrelentingly dour, drastically short on hope and humor. Instead of celebrating the mundane, he brooded; introspection usurped the place of lively observation—"abstract-personal" was the label he affixed to this mode of writing. Though this somber mood cast its pall for a couple of years, the most intense phase (mid-August to mid-December 1962) was relatively brief. It was characterized by a kind of self-inflicted punishment. The protagonist of "The Stare" is dismayed to find the pain of his breakup receding: "[H]e discovered himself so healed that his wound ached to be reopened." Reopening the wound is what Updike did in story after story, a masochistic aggravation of the initial trauma. He felt guilty and ashamed and bereft. Still, however unhappy, he was essentially undamaged. He carried on churning out his daily pages, correcting proofs, keeping up his end of a voluminous, chatty, cheerful correspondence. His writing was as fluent as ever; "The Leaves," a virtuoso display of exquisitely controlled prose, was written "swiftly, unerringly." He boasted, "No memory of any revision mars my backwards impression of it." In other words, his

torments weren't such that he ceased to function professionally—
and his awareness of that fact triggered further remorse. At the same
time, knowing that he had emerged from the ordeal more or less
unscathed—and raring to write about it—could only bolster his already sturdy confidence in his career prospects. Decades later, when
he wrote in his memoirs about the "distress and emotional violence"
of this failed attempt to break out of his marriage, he claimed to feel
proud of his bravery: "I had at last ventured into harm's way. I had
not only been daring but had inspired daring in another." And yet
his daring deserted him: "A door had opened, and shut. My timidity
and conscience had slammed it shut." There are many contradictions at work in this passage, not least the jarring juxtaposition of
bravado and cowardice, infidelity and conscience. It's a sad muddle,
a classic case of mixed feelings.

Though he had made a mess of things, he was an inherently
disciplined and tidy writer. He didn't bleed onto the page; there
was no wailing, no gnashing of teeth. He bottled up his pain, labeled it with scrupulous accuracy, then spooned it out in neatly measured doses. Moreover, he was cheerful by nature. In time, therefore, as he organized domestic disarray into the ornate designs of his
"abstract-personal" meditations —"taut and symmetrical" is how he
described "Leaves"—he recovered his sense of humor. He also began
to examine his circumstances with detached, dispassionate curiosity.
Thwarted love, doomed love, love for the unattainable woman became for him a subject of intellectual and artistic inquiry.

Updike had been in Antibes for about a month when he wrote
"Avec la Bébé-Sitter," his first lighthearted look at the "personal situation." It begins with a swift scene-setting declaration: "Everybody,
from their friends in Boston to the stewards on the boat, wondered
why Mr. and Mrs. Kenneth Harris should suddenly uproot their
family of three young children and take them to the South of France
in the middle of November." The answer, of course, is that the trip
is the alternative to divorce. But instead of replaying the upheaval
of the affair and its sequel in Kenneth's consciousness as he mopes
around his rented villa with its "postcard view" of Antibes, Updike
makes comic use of a distancing device: the language barrier be-

tween the American couple and their middle-aged French "*bébé-sitter*," Marie. (The Updikes' own *bébé-sitter* was named Rosette.) While his wife is visiting the museum in the center of Antibes, Kenneth suggests that Marie give him and the children a French lesson; after some cute exchanges that amuse the kids and establish a degree of complicity between the adults, the children are sent out to play in the garden. The babysitter then asks why the Harris family has come to France. Kenneth's startling answer, which in English would have been woefully melodramatic, in French seems matter-of-fact, even when accompanied by a sentimental gesture:

> He said what he next said in part, no doubt, because it was the truth, but mainly, probably, because he happened to know the words. He put his hand over his heart and told the baby-sitter, "*J'aime une autre femme.*"

His impromptu, hand-on-heart confession soothes him ("He felt the relief, the loss of constriction, of a man who has let in air"), and when Marie asks whether he doesn't love his wife, he replies, ungrammatically but again truthfully, "*Un petit peu pas.*" To the accidental accuracy of this second confession (he loves his wife a little bit not) he adds an explanation universally understood and accepted: "*Pour les enfants.*" Thanks to this bizarre tête-à-tête, the story ends on a light, cheery note. Though Kenneth still suffers from a "preoccupied heart," the household now runs smoothly, harmoniously: "They had become a *ménage.*"

Because of the abundance of sensitive and accurate autobiographical detail, "Avec la Bébé-Sitter" had to be consigned to the shadow-bank along with the abstract-personal meditations that preceded it, but it's clearly a different kind of story, an entertainment with a comic lilt designed to charm the reader. Though there was room in Updike's own preoccupied heart for only one topic, he could now at last step back, take a breath, and laugh a little at the absurdity of his predicament.

In the new year, Updike's parents visited Antibes. Though Linda may have guessed at the reason for the family's sudden transatlantic relocation, the topic wasn't discussed. When John offered to pay for them to fly over, they were excited and worried in equal measure ("we could turn what should be a happy adventure for you into a grisly business"), but eventually agreed to come. John picked them up at the Nice airport in the little rented Renault the family used to explore the Côte d'Azur. Neither Linda nor Wesley spoke any French, and yet they bravely agreed to stay at La Bastide with the children while John and Mary flew to Rome for few days—a circumstance the Plowville couple also accepted without question. They were rewarded with a stopover in Paris on their homeward journey—a few days of sightseeing and a hotel on the Champs-Elysées, all paid for by their son.

The Roman interlude was mined for a story as soon as Updike was back in Ipswich. "Twin Beds in Rome" is again about the agony of marital collapse, but the tone is wry and teasing, exposing misery to gentle ridicule. His characters, Richard and Joan Maple, were by now familiar figures, with a shared history and established traits, which helped him to maintain a modicum of ironic distance. As Updike put it in the foreword to a collection of Maples stories, "people are incorrigibly themselves"; Richard Maple had developed an identity subtly separate from Updike's—Richard is a touch coarser, his failings minutely amplified—and the author could contemplate his character's quandary with a healthy degree of detachment. He later claimed, "Richard and Joan Maple had become so much characters that I lost track of where they were made up."

After their first appearance in "Snowing in Greenwich Village," the Maples faded from view, reappearing six years later, when Updike wrote "Giving Blood" in March 1962. Having moved to a small town north of Boston, and having acquired four children of the same age and gender as the Updike children, the Maples find their marriage now visibly under threat, partly because of Richard's infatuation with another woman and partly because his "strategy" is to encourage Joan to find a love interest of her own. Quarreling bitterly all the way (the squabble provoked by Richard's complaints about how hard he works to support the family), they drive to Boston to give blood—a relative of Joan's is scheduled for an operation for which multiple transfusions will be required. (As usual, this is based on a real-life incident, though in fact the blood was intended for an elderly Ipswich friend, not a relative.) Squeamish Richard has never given blood before, and he nervously seeks comfort from the helplessly maternal Joan. Their shared sacrifice begins to reknit the frayed marital bond. Richard imagines his blood merging with Joan's; as they leave the hospital, he whispers to her, "Hey, I love you. Love, love *love* you." Over lunch at a pancake house on Route 128, Richard promises "never never to do the Twist, the cha-cha or the schottische with Marlene Brossman," the married object of his infatuation. Joan replies, "Don't be silly. I don't care." The deliciously clever ending reverts to the initial quarrel. Richard offers with mock gallantry to pay for lunch; opening his wallet, he discovers that he has only a dollar on him and begins to rant again about "working like a bastard all week for you and those insatiable brats." Joan says, with a prophet's vatic calm, "We'll both pay."

With "Twin Beds in Rome," things have gotten much worse: "Bleeding, mangled, reverently laid in its tomb a dozen times, their marriage could not die." Conjugal habit and mutual dependency keep them together despite their "burning" desire to split up. All this unhappiness might have made for a miserable visit to the Eternal City, but except for John's psychosomatic complaints (his feet hurt, his stomach hurt), the Updikes enjoyed themselves. In the story, Richard's sufferings are comically exaggerated, first the foot torture ("In the soft, damp air of Roman winter, his shoes seemed to have developed hot inward convexities that gnashed his flesh at every stride"), then the abdominal ache ("The pain, having expanded into every corner of the chamber beneath his ribs, had armed itself with a knife and now began to slash the walls in hope of escape"). The shoes that pinch, the pain that seeks to "escape"—the symptoms suit a man who feels trapped; he frankly admits that the stomach ailment is a "nervous" condition. Why is he so neurotically eager to get out? There's no mention of another woman. The focus is entirely on the Maples themselves, on Richard's deep-seated ambivalence (his desire to leave his wife and concomitant reluctance to do so) and Joan's mysterious self-shielding emotional remove. They have come to Rome to "kill or cure"; the story teeters back and forth with the marriage—will it last or not?

The extraordinary thing is that Updike, when he wrote it, had no idea. He sent the story to Maxwell a week or so after his return from Antibes. The plan had been to stay in France until the spring, but the weather was damp and chilly, and there was no social life at all. Two-year-old Miranda wasn't well, and her parents were having difficulty communicating with the French doctors, so they seized on this excuse to cut short their stay. When they flew home in late January, John was still mired in gloom. He was not yet "over" Joyce, according to Mary, but "lost interest over the next six months, gradually." Herbert Harrington registered no objection to the premature curtailment of the Updike exile. When the two couples met in the months after the Updikes' return, it was usually in a crowd of friends. Though the greetings were polite all around, John apparently found these accidental reunions painful; he circled back in his fiction again and again to the scene where ex-lovers meet at a party and endure fresh agony. Eventually the Harringtons moved out of Ipswich, to nearby Manchester. They spent a year in Greece. Not quite out of sight, they were only intermittently out of mind.

The afterimage of the unattainable beloved lingered on, as desirable as ever in her absence. Two weeks after finishing "Twin Beds in Rome," Updike sent Maxwell "Four Sides of One Story," in which he poured the tragic tale of John and Mary and Herbert and Joyce into the ready-made vessel of the Tristan and Iseult legend. Following in the footsteps of many a twelfth-century troubadour, he took bold liberties with the Tristan material. He cast himself as a mock-heroic Tristan aboard a luxurious Italian steamship "heading Heaven knows where," self-banished from his impossible love; Joyce as an Iseult the Fair "distracted" by grief over her lover's departure; Mary as a long-suffering Iseult of the White Hands, the wronged wife; and Herbert as a bullying King Mark taking practical measures to keep hold of his adulterous queen, measures that include sending her to a psychoanalyst, mobilizing his lawyer, and scaring off Tristan by insisting that if he loves Iseult, he must marry her. Though there are passing references to the magic potion that bewitched the lovers, to the dragon of Whitehaven slain by Tristan, to King Mark's drafty castle, this epistolary version of the courtly romance is in spirit absolutely up-to-date, a medieval tale told in letters postmarked 1963.

Channeling Tristan and Iseult, archetypes of illicit passion, was another one of Updike's distancing devices. Tristan, writing to his beloved from the comfort of a well-appointed ocean liner, issues a long, torturous lament. Desperate and histrionic ("I am bleeding to death"), he's also blatantly, comically self-absorbed, intent on his own pain and aware of the pain of others only when he makes a conscious effort to consider it. Knowing this ("I had never, in my heart," he tells his lover, "taken your suffering as seriously as my own"), he twists himself into logical knots to justify his egotism. Cerebral in the midst of passion, he acknowledges the possibility that what he wishes to "possess forever" is not Iseult's presence but her "good opinion." He explains that marriage is the enemy of love: "We are in love," he tells Iseult. "The only way out of it is marriage, or some sufficiently pungent piece of overexposure equivalent to marriage"— cohabitation, in his view, would extinguish their passion. His love thrives on separation: the greater the distance from his beloved, the better. Self-imposed banishment is an expression of his purest devotion. (Skeptics might argue that he's simply a coward putting a fancy spin on a bad case of cold feet. As Mark puts it, "Confronted with the actuality of marriage, the young man bolted.")

Despite tantalizing autobiographical echoes, "Four Sides of One Story" isn't particularly compelling. The courtly love conceit is ingenious but limiting, the characters diminished rather than enhanced by their role in a medieval tragedy reconfigured as contemporary farce. The story is burdened, moreover, with a surplus of incompletely digested theory about romantic love—theory gleaned from Swiss philosopher Denis de Rougemont's wildly ambitious *Love in the Western World*, a book famous at midcentury (and now nearly forgotten) that exerted a strong and enduring influence on Updike.

In the early summer of 1963, Updike wrote a review for *The New Yorker* of *Love Declared*, a collection of essays in which de Rougemont expanded on the "mythanalysis of culture" begun in *Love in the Western World*. The review, as Updike later remarked, was mostly an excuse to write an essay about romantic love, the topic monopolizing his preoccupied heart. He couldn't have chosen a more apt book for the occasion. Cutting across disciplines with manic swagger to provide "an etymology of the passions," *Love in the Western World* is certainly thought provoking; it seeks to explain everything about our culture from the "inescapable conflict" between passionate love and marriage to the rise of nationalism and the barbarity of twentieth-century warfare. For Updike the appeal lay mostly in de Rougemont's exhaustive analysis of the legend of Tristan and Iseult, the representative myth of romantic love—an analysis Updike quibbled with yet couldn't resist.

"Tristan and Iseult do not love one another," de Rougemont declared. "*What they love is love and being in love.*" They are in the grip of passion, which he describes in *Love Declared* as a "form of love which refuses the immediate, avoids dealing with what is near, and if necessary invents distance in order to realize and exalt itself more completely." His remarks on the twelfth-century prototype could as easily be applied to the modern lovers in "Four Sides of One Story":

> Tristan loves the awareness that he is loving far more than he loves Iseult the Fair. And Iseult does nothing to hold Tristan. All she needs is her passionate dream. . . . What they need is not one another's presence, but one another's absence.

Passion feeds on denial, on obstacles such as the famous "sword of chastity" placed between the lovers. Pushing his analysis in a darkly Freudian direction, de Rougemont insists that this kind of unappeasable passion "disguises a twin narcissism," and that the suffering it entails betrays a "longing for what sears us and annihilates us"—a longing for death itself. (Poor Tristan! Poor Iseult! As *Time* magazine quipped when the book first appeared, de Rougemont "hangs on their necks more weight than Freud ever hung on Oedipus.")

Updike balks at the charge of narcissism, arguing that in all forms of love the "selfish and altruistic threads" are inseparable. He also points out that a symbol such as the "sword of chastity," which de Rougemont interprets as a telltale sign of our obsession with obstructed love, should be thought of as a narrative device—a troubadour's nifty trick for dragging out his tale. Yet Updike is nevertheless persuaded that de Rougemont is "dreadfully right" to assert that "love in the Western world has by some means acquired a force far out of proportion to its presumed procreative aim." Updike illustrates the power of "Tristanism" with a rhetorical question that can only be described as heartfelt: "But what of that thunderous congestion in the chest, that suffusion of emotion as harsh as a blow, which Tristan endures at the sight of the Unattainable Lady, or even the mention of her name?" One could be forgiven for reading the end of Updike's essay as a series of covert confessions. "Only in being loved," he writes, "do we find external corroboration of the supremely high valuation each ego secretly assigns itself." And again: "The heart *prefers* to move against the grain of circumstance; perversity is the soul's very life. Therefore the enforced and approved bonds of marriage, restricting freedom, weaken love." De Rougemont served up a high-flying theoretical explanation for adulterous longing, and Updike devoured it.

For at least half a year, at home and in Europe, the marriage verged on collapse—and yet proved sturdier than either John or Mary would have guessed. They had been together nearly ten years and would remain together for another twelve. In 2003, when he published *The Early Stories*, Updike grouped most of the stories written at the time of his affair with Joyce Harrington (including all those in the abstract-personal mode) in a section called "The Two Iseults." He was obviously thinking of Iseult the Fair and Iseult of the White Hands, and of the choice he had to make between Joyce and Mary ("[H]anging between us," says Iseult of the White Hands, "he won't let go with either hand"). But I suspect that with four decades' worth of hindsight, he had come around to the idea that Mary, too, was an Unattainable

Lady. There are hints of it in the Maples stories, even those written in 1963. In "Giving Blood," Joan twice presents Richard with a face that is a "porcelain shell of uncanny composure," effectively removing herself from all emotional engagement; and in "Twin Beds in Rome" Richard recognizes that Joan is a "secret woman he could never reach and had at last wearied of trying to reach." My guess is that Updike's self-diagnosed case of "Tristanism" extended, paradoxically, to conjugal love, and that Mary's knack of keeping her husband at a distance, her studiously unruffled passivity—leavened by dry humor, bolstered by tenacious dignity, and sealed with maturing beauty—helped to hold the marriage together. Like many of his damaged fictional couples, they "hunkered down in embattled, recriminatory renewal of their vows, mixed with spells of humorous weariness."

In his essay on de Rougemont, Updike maintains that a man in love "ceases to fear death"; Updike, having forced himself to renounce his love, saw death everywhere. After Antibes, still mooning over Joyce, still writing his way all around the topic of romantic love, he endured an "angst-besmogged period" in which his panic manifested itself as breathlessness. Maxwell, listening over the telephone to his author's labored wheezing, urged him to come to New York to see a doctor (Maxwell's own), who diagnosed the problem as bronchial asthma and prescribed a Medihaler to treat the symptoms. As for Updike, he wondered whether his breathlessness wasn't "an ingenious psychosomatic mechanism to make my wife feel guilty about being still married to me."

After all the tumult of the affair, the workings of his unconscious were open to new angles of interpretation. Denis de Rougemont held up one mirror, Freud another. "When we got back from Antibes," said Mary, "it was pretty clear that we both needed to go see shrinks, which we hadn't done before. We both started going twice a week." Updike never discussed in public his brush with psychotherapy, which Mary remembered lasting a year or two ("he may have dropped it and then picked it up again"), and there's no mention of it in his memoirs. He told a journalist in 1966 that therapy ("which in Boston means sitting up, as opposed to analysis, which means lying down") had made him "more relaxed"—but then stipulated that his remarks remain off the record.

He believed therapy did more for Mary, who was by nature more reserved, than it did for him, but he admitted to learning that he was "wrapped up in the idea of families," that he made a habit of trying to turn the people closest to him into a family—which he accomplished in Ipswich as in Shillington. He also learned that he was at once "invulnerably detached" and "quite vulnerable to the facts of separation and death."

In mid-July 1963, he sent Maxwell a story that begins with a woman walking into a man's office, ends with her walking out, and in between records the lopsided conversation of their "session." The word *session* hints at the nature of the transaction, but the word *analysis* never appears in "My Lover Has Dirty Fingernails," nor *patient*, nor *doctor*. And yet the ritual performed in the office—the flow of the woman's words interrupted by heavy pauses, the man's terse questions and prodding comments—is instantly recognizable. Updike is playing on our familiarity with the therapeutic techniques of Freudian analysis, which by the early sixties had become the stuff of cliché. The woman has picked up the jargon and shows it off self-consciously; she says twice that she's "suppressing" something, offers at one point to "free-associate," and at the end concedes, "I *am* neurotic." The climax of the story is a complaint based on her expectation of how analysis should proceed: "I'd got the idea from somewhere that by this time something would have happened between us, that I in some sort of way, perfectly controlled and safe, would have . . . fallen in love with you." She's expecting to experience transference, and hasn't. She tells her analyst that she thinks the opposite has happened, that he has fallen in love with her. Her "outburst," however, is taken by the doctor (and the reader) as a sign that he's "winning," that transference is indeed occurring. Whether that's a good thing is another question. At the heart of the story is the contrast between the passion of the lovers and the "perfectly controlled and safe" emotion fostered by analysis, which is intended to restore her to the tame safety of marital contentment.

"My Lover Has Dirty Fingernails" takes to an extreme the narrow focus of many of the stories from this period; it's as though Updike could think of nothing except his sorry predicament. Inside the doctor's bland, air-conditioned office, with its venetian blinds and "black slab sofa," the sole topic is the love affair recently ended. Everything the patient says, every detail she supplies, relates back to her lover, including the remark that gives the story its title: "I'd sometimes notice—is this too terrible, shall I stop?—I'd notice that his fingernails were dirty." The frame of the story, the psychoanalytic session, necessarily constricts the action, and yet in a sense it suggests a whole wide world in which marriages are foundering, and anxious wives and husbands look to psychiatry for answers. ("I need help," says the woman. "I'm ridiculously unhappy, and I want to know why.") Updike chooses not to label the scene, not to identify the man as a doctor and the woman as a patient, because he wants to underscore how immediately familiar it all seems, and how unsurprising it is for a bourgeois housewife from the suburbs (impeccably dressed in a gray linen suit with white shoes and a white pocketbook) to drive to the city on a weekly basis to consult a Freudian analyst about her affair with a married man. Any *New Yorker* reader would have recognized her in a flash.

As would Updike's Ipswich gang. Mary and John were neither the first nor the last among their friends to see a shrink. It became an accepted next step, after adultery. Alfred Schweigen, the narrator of "The Music School," sees a psychiatrist, as does his wife ("She visits a psychiatrist because I am unfaithful to her. I do not understand the connection but there seems to be one"). A remarkable story written at the end of 1963 and sent off to Maxwell under the title "Take, Eat," it includes a sad, helpless overview of suburban marital woes:

> My friends are like me. We are all pilgrims, faltering towards divorce. Some get no further than mutual confession, which becomes an addiction and exhausts them. Some move on, into violent quarrels and physical blows; and succumb to sexual excitement. A few make it to psychiatrists. A very few get as far as the lawyers.

This is an atypical passage; a difficult story, intricately, rhythmi-
cally patterned, "The Music School" is unmistakably in the abstract-
personal mode, as its daring first line foretells: "My name is Alfred
Schweigen and I exist in time." Schweigen's remarks about his
friends, a burst of sociology in the midst of an introspective meditation on religion, adultery, and death, are a radical distillation of a
very different kind of story written a few months earlier, "Couples."

And "Couples" is itself the germ of *Couples*; or, rather, the novel
is a vast extension of the territory sketched out in the story, which
Updike finished on May 16, 1963, and sent to Maxwell—who
promptly turned it down, probably because it was too nakedly autobiographical and too "crowded," as Updike himself put it. "Couples"
was finally published thirteen years later, when Updike was no
longer living in Ipswich, and then only in a limited edition of 250
numbered copies produced by a small Cambridge press; it has not
been reprinted, which is a pity, because it's the original Tarbox tale,
Updike's first attempt to think about what had happened to him in
terms of the community where it happened—his first attempt to
paint a panoramic portrait of the seaside town in which suburban
adultery thrived.*

"Couples" is indeed crowded, packed with people and their frenetic interaction—which is part of what makes it so engaging. David, the narrator, looks back on six years of married life in the thick
of an exceptionally tight-knit group of friends, all of them residents
of Tarbox. Now separated from his wife, David intends to marry his
lover, who was part of his gang of friends; he's in a kind of limbo
between marriages, and hence temporarily excluded from the world
of couples. Updike is imagining what might have been had he gone
a step further with Joyce—but if it's wish fulfillment, it's wish fulfillment of a dark and unhappy kind: "The leap that had wrenched
every joint in my skeleton had landed me in the same place, only
torn from my home and robbed of my children." From the vantage
point of no-man's-land ("I am a parenthesis—a boat adrift between

---

* The name Tarbox was actually coined a year earlier, in "The Indian," a story
devoid of adultery (and of narrative incident, for that matter).

two continents"), David has realized that his future will be very much like his past—except that by swapping wives, he has destroyed his family.

David and his wife, Ann (their last name isn't given, but it might well be Kern), came to Tarbox from New York City six years ago. They made the acquaintance of other young couples in town, and this at first seemed a wholly good thing; their new pals "looked like safeguards, echoes, reinforcements of our happiness." Six of the couples, including David and Ann, quickly formed a cozy bond—"We were folded in." For three years they enjoyed enviable harmony:

> In memory it seems we were playing at being adults, at being fathers and mothers and homeowners. We had all, it chanced, come to it new together, this incredible America where we managed, and controlled, and mattered; we paid taxes and mowed lawns and poured ourselves a deserved drink in the evenings.

Suburban bliss, circa 1960. Several scenes evoke with appealing tenderness the "simple party pleasures of the youngly married." But a subtle shift occurs, the core friendships reconfigure, other couples join in. Somewhere along the line, David falls in love with Peggy Williams. The Williamses, Peggy and Morton, arrived in Tarbox at the same time as Ann and David. A tall woman with "the brittle figure of a tomboy" (until she fills out over the years with "womanly weight"), Peggy is a snappy dresser: "Her clothes were the essence of my love. She had a way of wearing anything so that the cloth seemed glad and independently animated." She also has a "tireless touch with furnishings." Her husband, though pretentious, has "moments of great charm." Early on, before their friendship was fully formed, the Williamses asked (as the Harringtons had done) if they could leave their infant with David and Ann while they went to Boston for the evening. At the time, David's impression of Peggy was of someone "shrill" and "silly"; he thought she had "the demeanor of a secretary." And yet he falls in love, almost without

realizing it. He and Peggy don't even kiss until a full year after he
has at last admitted to himself that he's in love; six months after
that, they make love for the first time. Several months after the affair has finally blossomed, he confesses to Ann—who stuns him by
confessing in turn that for two years she has been sleeping "now and
then" with another one of their married friends (*not* Peggy's husband, Morton, for whom she has "no use whatsoever"). David asks
Ann for a divorce, but she convinces him to "hold off everything
until the end of summer."

Meanwhile, the scales have fallen from his eyes. David believes
that he was, "among the six couples, the last innocent" (which accounts for the glacial pace of the early stages of his affair with Peggy)
and that when his innocence was corrupted, "all our furtive woes
and suppressed miseries were free to swarm across the social field."
He now sees signs of adultery and marital dysfunction everywhere.
What he had assumed were untroubled friendships were plagued, he
belatedly understands, by "frantic . . . emotional storms." He had
thought, for example, that the previous winter his wife had been
suffering from a "mysteriously prolonged bout of intestinal flu"; in
fact it was a "violent mental crisis" triggered when she broke off her
own affair. The closeness of the couples has turned toxic. One friend
has a loud and public nervous breakdown and becomes the first of
the group to enter psychoanalysis; Peggy and others soon follow. It
is all, as Ann says, "a fantastic mess."

But is it, as David claims, somehow *his* fault? "We need a sacrifice," he declares. "We're so full of infection we must bleed." Because
he blames himself, he forces a crisis; as he tells it, "dazed with fear
and numb with resolution, I went to Morton Williams and asked
him for his wife." This unconvincing moment of odd, greedy self-
sacrifice has the desired result: "Under Morton's guidance, the four
of us became . . . expertly coöperative at obtaining divorces." Which
brings us to the grim, solitary present: David adrift, living "without
illusions," fingering like worry beads memories of friendships that
have melted away.

There's more incident in these few pages than one would expect to find in a half-dozen Updike stories. He tried to cram all of

Tarbox into one tale, a project, he later realized, that required the scope of a novel. Though overstuffed, "Couples" is exhilaratingly engaged with the world; after the claustrophobia and solipsism of the abstract-personal mode, it feels like a window thrown open. The story ends, however, on a violently misanthropic note. Living alone, David comes to the conclusion that solitude is man's natural state. (Having never yet lived on his own, Updike had a somewhat theoretical concept of solitude.) He envisions a constant battle being waged against the existential threat of isolation; deploying an elaborate metaphor, he equates a community of married couples with a "bewitched armaments factory whose workers, in their frenzy to forge armor for themselves, hammer, burn, and lacerate one another." Updike noted, in a foreword to the limited edition, the "clangor" of the last two paragraphs, and let slip, pointedly, that they were first scrawled on the "blank insides of an eviscerated envelope from the Mental Health Association of the North Shore." It's always hard to think of Updike unhinged; his cool professionalism discourages it. The image of his ripping apart an envelope that reminded him of psychiatry and scribbling a furious screed against the self-inflicted wounds of coupledom owes more than a little to romantic stereotype; it seems barely plausible—yet that's clearly the image he was hoping to plant in the reader's mind. (The Mental Health Association of the North Shore actually did exist; it occasionally solicited funds to provide counseling for the families of psychiatric patients in state care.)

Its grim ending notwithstanding, "Couples," like the Olinger stories, celebrates a time and place. The "bucolic pleasures" of Tarbox are fondly recalled, as is the warmhearted camaraderie of friends in the first blush of their acquaintance. David's affair is also celebrated; as he explains in his foreword, Updike wanted to say "something good" for the "sad magic" of suburban adultery.

That same "sad magic" is the obsessive subject of *Marry Me*, a flawed novel that nevertheless seems to me Updike's most underrated. Begun in the spring of 1962 and completed two years later, it was not published until 1976, just after the Updikes were divorced, when the Harrington fiasco—which it chronicles in excruciating, barely fictionalized detail—was a fading memory. Updike wrote *Marry Me*, in other words, alongside the sequence of stories consigned to the limbo of the *New Yorker* shadow-bank; in the true chronology of his novels, it follows *The Centaur* and precedes *Of the Farm*; more significantly, he finished it two full years before he began work on *Couples*, the bestselling novel that planted in the public imagination the idea that the adulterous society was territory belonging to him by right of discovery. It's likely that if *Marry Me* and *Couples* had been published in the order in which they were written, the critical reception and popular appeal of each would have been quite different.

Updike's circumstances changed markedly during the time he spent writing *Marry Me*. When he began it, age thirty, with a pair of novels, three short story collections, and a slim book of light verse to his credit, he could contemplate his career with a justified sense of satisfaction—but as yet it was his promise rather than his accomplishment that drew the attention of others. He was someone whom older writers were keeping an eye on; he was on the cusp. Mary McCarthy told her *Paris Review* interviewer in the winter of 1961, without feeling the need to preface the remark or identify the subject, "I was talking to someone about John Updike . . ."; she went on to praise *The Poorhouse Fair* and say that *Rabbit, Run* was the most interesting American novel she'd read in quite a long time. *Pigeon Feathers* was published in March 1962 and was a finalist, along with Nabokov's *Pale Fire*, for the National Book Award. After *The Centaur* was published in February 1963 (a week after the Updikes came home from their exile in Antibes), accolades, prizes, honors, and riches piled up in rapid succession. The novel was widely reviewed, for the most part ecstatically. The usually ferocious Renata Adler, writing in *The New Yorker*, admired its "delicate symmetry and balance"; it seemed to her "a fragile and colorful mobile suspended in slow rotation." Even critics who expressed irritation at the pretentiousness of the mythological parallels, among them the daily reviewer at *The New York Times*, Orville Prescott, felt compelled to praise the author; "brilliantly talented and versatile" was Prescott's line. *Time* magazine, though similarly irritated, announced that

"Updike finds his way more accurately than almost anyone else now writing to the small touchstones of mind and memory." *The New York Times Book Review* judged him to be "the most significant young novelist in America." *The Centaur* went on to win the National Book Award. Just a year later, Updike was elected to the National Institute of Arts and Letters, and invited by the State Department to make a goodwill tour of the USSR and other Soviet Bloc countries, part of a cultural exchange program in which John Cheever also participated. In other words, when he finished *Marry Me*, the thirty-two-year-old Updike was all at once a leading American novelist, embraced by both the literary establishment and a significant portion of the reading public. This darling of the literati was also a commercial success; he earned more than fifty thousand dollars in 1963, and for the first time felt the need to hire a tax accountant.

Marry Me began as a short story, "Warm Wine," about a tryst in the dunes of a beach in the late spring, two lovers sharing an idyllic moment, their bliss shadowed by the havoc they know their affair will unleash. Updike was a private citizen at the time, writing about a part of his life only he and Joyce knew anything about. Because the affair was still secret, actually *publishing* "Warm Wine" was out of the question. But John was beginning to dream of escaping from his marriage, and the story was an expression of that dream, a silent hymn to an illicit love. By the time he finished *Marry Me* (feeling "wobbly," he told Maxwell—and convinced his book would never see print), he was a public figure, and the affair with Joyce, well known to his crowd of Ipswich friends, was last year's gossip. Cruelly tested, the bond between John and Mary had survived, but the terms of the relationship were inevitably altered. Neither one now expected the other to be faithful, yet both expected the marriage to last. John told Maxwell in September 1964 that his wife, unlike her fictional avatar, was "strongly on the scene." But even a flexible arrangement toughened by time and bitter blows can withstand only so much. Though she had been costarring in her husband's fiction since 1956, *Marry Me* would have been too brutal an invasion of Mary's privacy. John didn't even show her the manuscript; "I was not privy to *Marry Me*," she said. He claimed to have aesthetic reservations about the novel (he even put quotation marks around the word when discussing it: the "novel"), but prudence and pity must have played a large part in his decision to stow it away in a safe-deposit box at the First National Bank in Ipswich.

The book that spent twelve years under lock and key tells the by now familiar story. This time around, John and Mary figure as Jerry and Ruth Conant, Herbert and Joyce as Richard and Sally Mathias. Though Updike later confessed to "unease about the book's lack of . . . sociology," he did give them a specific time and place to inhabit: the seaside suburb of Greenwood, Connecticut, in 1962. The two couples are, alas, the only citizens of Greenwood, or at least the only ones Updike breathes any life into—their friends and neighbors, babysitters and housekeepers are all minimally sketched. The focus is exclusively, obsessively on the four principals, with their small children (three on each side) occasionally intruding. The plot is a seesaw psychodrama; like so many other Updike stand-ins, Jerry is hanging between wife and mistress, unwilling to let go with either hand, and the suspense, such as it is, consists of will-he, won't-he. One new twist is symmetry in the couples' adulterous liaisons: Ruth and Richard were also once lovers, a rare fictional component in a novel that otherwise hews closely to the facts.

Another new element is a serious effort to see the events from the wife's perspective. Updike had made earlier attempts to illustrate the workings of a female mind (most memorably when the drunken Janice accidentally drowns the baby in *Rabbit, Run*), but never before had he engaged as closely and at such length with a lucid, educated, intelligent woman; nearly half of *Marry Me* is told from Ruth's point of view, an intimate third-person narration that allows us to see her, and the others, as she herself does.

A credible, sympathetic character, Ruth shares Mary's background and family history (she's the elder daughter of a civic-minded Unitarian minister), but not necessarily her mind-set; indeed, when Mary finally read *Marry Me* in the mid-seventies, she was dismissive of Updike's female psychology. Possibly she noticed that Ruth spends a disproportionate amount of her time brooding about her errant husband. A failed cartoonist who now works as an animator making television commercials, Jerry is in many ways less interesting than Ruth (mostly because he's entirely preoccupied with his romantic longing), yet he dominates the book. His vacillations draw attention, whereas Ruth's passivity deflects it. The "other woman," Sally, is beautiful—or so we're repeatedly told; the words *greedy*, *silly*, and *shrill* stick to her as well. Updike never gives a convincing explanation (other than potent sexual attraction) for Jerry's infatuation with her. The fact that when we first meet her she's reading a novel by Alberto Moravia (highbrow Italian literature!) seems a transparent attempt to give her some depth. Her husband, Richard, is bullying, needy, pretentious—a wise guy with a blind eye (literally) and a vulgar streak; he's a grotesque rather than a fully rounded character. When Richard learns of Jerry and Sally's affair (by examining the phone bill, of course), Updike brings all four of his characters together for a dramatic showdown at the Mathiases' house—a replay of the events at the Harringtons' in October 1962. Relying heavily on dialogue, he presents an agonizing scene that's harrowing for the characters (and the reader), though leavened by flashes of panicky humor. Richard's histrionics are both maudlin and amusing, more amusing, even, than Jerry's frantic witticisms and weaselly evasions.

Complex religious motifs thread themselves through the novel. Jerry, naturally, is a Lutheran who dreads death and reads neo-orthodox theologians (Barth, Berdyaev); Ruth is a Unitarian, a "pale faith" Jerry despises; Sally is a lapsed Catholic, superstitious and susceptible to pangs of guilt; and Richard is an atheist, a devotee of Freud and Dr. Spock.* The first chapter, the tryst in the dunes, represents a kind of Edenic, prelapsarian moment, with foreshadowings of the Fall and a sacrament of sorts (the warm wine the lovers drink). The second chapter, "The Wait," takes place mostly in the limbo of an airport lounge, the modern traveler's Purgatory. The four-way

---

* In an early draft, Richard was a Jew; Mary wisely advised him to abandon that idea; when Judith Jones, his editor at Knopf, echoed Mary's advice, Updike turned him into an atheist.

confrontation at the Mathiases' house offers a glimpse of existential damnation ("Hell is other people"). And at the very end, Jerry discovers an island paradise, heaven on earth, proof that there was a "dimension" in which he could say to Sally, *Marry me*—another sacrament holding out hope of redemption.

Denis de Rougemont hovers over the action like a heavy, dark cloud, never more oppressively than when Jerry spouts theories about his "ideal love" for Sally, "ideal because it can't be realized." Jerry also waxes sociological about the state of contemporary marriage: "Maybe our trouble," he muses, "is that we live in the twilight of the old morality, and there's just enough to torment us, and not enough to hold us in." (One is tempted to respond with Ruth's observation about the economic underpinnings of this particular brand of immorality: "If we all had to sweat for our food we wouldn't have time for this—this folly. We're all so spoiled we stink.") But it's neither the big ideas nor the complex themes that make the novel worth hauling up from the bottom rungs of Updike's oeuvre. Its virtues are the familiar ones: keen observation, stylistic brilliance, and painful emotional honesty (in this case, about the turmoil of a disintegrating marriage).

And what if *Marry Me* had found its way into readers' hands in the mid-sixties instead of the mid-seventies? Had it appeared magically in bookstores on May 4, 1964 (the day he finished it), it would have been his first published account of suburban adultery*—in fact, it would have been his first extended treatment of romantic passion. It was only after he had locked the manuscript away—drawing a line, as it were, under the Harrington saga—that he allowed *The New Yorker* to begin printing some of the abstract-personal stories written two years earlier in the throes of his love for Joyce. In 1964 no one would have complained, as Maureen Howard did in *The New York Times Book Review* twelve years later, about Updike's "obsession with adultery," and it would never have occurred to Alfred Kazin to identify Updike's "one big situation" as "the marital tangle." *Marry*

---

* I exclude Rabbit's dalliance with Ruth on the basis that she was an unmarried part-time hooker; the whole episode is emphatically *anti*-suburban.

Me would have been seen as a fresh departure for Updike, a daring book with a risqué subject. After the Summer of Love, the trauma of Vietnam and the antiwar protests, and the long national nightmare of Watergate, Jerry's line about living in the twilight of the old morality could only sound like quaint, cooing nostalgia. In 1964 it would have seemed brave and enlightened for Updike to try to see out of Ruth's eyes; in 1976, on the far side of feminist consciousness-raising, it was more likely to have been held against him. The marital anguish of the Conants and Mathiases would have made sense to middle-class readers in 1964, before the sharp rise in divorce rates that began in the mid-sixties and continued through the seventies, before "no-fault" divorce made the prospect of ending a marriage less daunting, and stories about it decidedly more banal.

A great novel both illuminates its historical context and transcends it; this one, though brilliant in patches and certainly far more rewarding than its critics acknowledge, is not great. The morning after the big confrontation arranged by Richard, Jerry glances at the newspaper; all the headlines are about standoffs: between black and white (James Meredith's admission to the University of Mississippi and the deadly riots in Oxford); between China's Zhou Enlai and the USSR; between the Giants and the Dodgers, tied in a pennant race; and between Kennedy and Khrushchev, caught in a spiral of rising tension over Cuba. In a different kind of novel, Updike might have made telling use of this brief, sweeping glimpse of current events, but here he lets it drop without comment. The news flash fixes the date of the Mathias-Conant showdown (September 30, 1962), and connects it for a fleeting instant with national and global crises— but only to remind us that the drama of marital meltdown has cut off the two couples from the wider world. When Updike called the novel *Marry Me: A Romance*, his idea was to sequester it from history, and he was also thinking nostalgically of the glamour of the early days of the Kennedy administration: Camelot and the elegance of the young couple in the White House. The white-knuckle trauma of the Cuban Missile Crisis doesn't figure in *Marry Me*, nor does the simmering violence of the civil rights movement—nor the assassination of the president.

In fact . . . the literary scene is a kind of *Medusa*'s raft, small and sinking, and one's instinct when a newcomer tries to clamber aboard is to stamp on his fingers.

—Updike on Cheever (July 1990)

VI.

Couples

When shots were fired at the presidential motorcade in Dallas on the morning of Friday, November 22, 1963, Mary Updike was in Cambridge, in the office of her psychoanalyst. Her husband was at the dentist having new crowns fitted. There was a dance scheduled that night in Manchester, Massachusetts, a Democratic Party fund-raiser; but the president was dead, and the dance was promptly cancelled. The Updikes had also been invited by a couple in their set, owners of a big house on the edge of town, to a pre-dance dinner party. The hostess was at the hairdresser when she heard the horrible news; after the initial shock wore off, she started worrying about what to do with the ten pounds of fillet of sole she had in her refrigerator. She phoned around to the other couples, including the Updikes, to ask if they thought it would be appropriate to get together, a telephonic negotiation Updike later characterized as "much agonizing." A consensus emerged: they would go ahead with the dinner as planned. As Updike explained it, "We didn't know what gesture to make, so we made none."

On Sunday, they all played touch football, as on any other autumn weekend.

In *Couples*, Updike exaggerates these bare facts with broad satiric intent. The Tarbox gang barely hesitates before deciding to attend a black-tie party on the Friday night of the president's assassination. The food and liquor have been bought, the women have shopped for new dresses ("The fashion that fall was for deep décolletage"), the men have had their tuxedos cleaned—why stay at home and mourn? Updike devotes twenty-five pages to the party: the drinking, the dancing, the flirting, the gossip. The climax is a kind of black Mass: a baked ham is brought in ceremoniously; the host carves; laying the sliced meat on a plate, he intones, "Take, eat. . . . This is his body, given for thee." It's a shocking scene, even without the blasphemy, as damning as any in the novel. To cap it off, a man jumps from a bathroom window with his mouth full of his pregnant mistress's milk. Obviously the evening's corrupt revelry is intended to give the reader a jolt, to bring home the full meaning of this damning sentence: "the dancing couples were gliding on the polished top of Kennedy's casket."

It would be neat and tidy to say that the shock of the killing marked the beginning of an outward turn, that on the morning of November 23, Updike woke from his sybaritic suburban slumber, looked hard at the world around him, and resolved to broaden his perspective and re-create in his fiction a "dense reality" through thick description charged with cultural and political energy—daily data with a kick. He did write the "Comment" in the first *New Yorker* after the assassination, a curiously pallid piece that begins, "It was as if we slept from Friday to Monday and dreamed an oppressive, unsearchably significant dream," and ends, "We pray not to fall into such a sleep again." In fact, he slumbered on for another few years. It was the civil rights movement and the protests against the Vietnam War—along with his travels behind the Iron Curtain late in 1964—that did the most to open his eyes. When the president was assassinated, Updike and his fellow suburbanites were still complacently self-involved. "We had become detached from the national life," he remembered. "Our private lives had become the real concern. There was a monstrous inflation of the private life as against the merged life of the society." As in Tarbox, the party in Ipswich carried on regardless.

Updike, having pretty much exhausted Tristanism, embarked on Don Juanism, cutting a swath through the ranks of the town's young matrons. He embarked on a string of affairs with his friends' wives, some of which were merely flings, some more extended, though none of the women engaged his emotions as deeply as Joyce had done. He did get one of them pregnant (his paradise wasn't wholly post-pill); the woman in question, thanks to a timely case of German measles, was able to obtain a legal abortion. Updike was greatly relieved, and the affair ended—by mutual agreement.* More flings followed. A friend from the couples group who managed to resist his charms told me, "At a certain point I thought, 'Am I the only woman in our crowd who hasn't slept with John?'" She was not, in fact, unique—but nearly. Another friend told me, "It was a matter of a certain pride to be sleeping with John."

He was a lusty man, and after Joyce, he had no scruples about adultery, yet he needed to dress up garden-variety infidelity as the inescapable consequence of some grand passion. Like Tristan, he was in love with love—and at the same time, he made no attempt to disguise his eagerness to hop straight into bed. One of his lovers reported that he felt compelled to cast their affair in romantic terms; "he needed a woman to adore," she said. She was crazy about him, too—but she was also flattered: here was this brilliant and charming friend bombarding her with amorous attention, always desperate to get her clothes off. "I would've preferred," she added, "to talk and tease."

In his memoirs, celebrating the healing effects of sunshine on his psoriasis, he gives us this glimpse of himself as all-conquering Casanova:

> [W]hat concupiscent vanity it used to be, playing volleyball bare-chested, leaping high to spike the ball down into a pretty housewife's upturned face, and wearing tomato-red bicycle shorts that as if casually slid down to expose an inch or more of tanned, normal-appearing derrière, even to the sexy dent where the cleavage of the buttocks begins.

---

* There was a brief second act to this affair, in the early seventies.

This preening display puts the emphasis on his physique. Like many men who succeed thanks to their brains, he would have liked to be worshipped for his body. He wanted us to believe (and perhaps believed himself) that the pretty housewife playing beach volley-ball was enthralled by a bare-chested hunk. Many of his friends and acquaintances remarked that he grew handsomer, less gawky, as he aged, yet it seems obvious that his wit, his intelligence, and his grow-ing fame seduced more women than his buttocks. Charm is com-posed of curious elements, and in his case something undefinable went into the mix—it could have been the flirting twinkle in his eye, the hint of malice in his teasing, or perhaps his willingness to telegraph lust frankly and fearlessly to the women he desired.

Though brilliantly equipped for hands-on research into the adulterous society, and rapidly acquiring expertise in the field, he was not yet ready to present his preliminary findings to the gen-eral public. In April 1964, even before he'd quite finished *Marry Me*, he explained to Alfred Knopf that "complicating factors" might force him to sit on the book—but he offered to try to write another, shorter novel by the end of the year. In late summer Updike went to work on a novella provisionally titled *The Farm*; he finished a penciled draft in the autumn, just before his State Department jun-ket to the Soviet Union and beyond. The novella was a return to Berks County, to the epicenter of his past—but at the same time, as Updike once acknowledged, it "takes place in the future." He was imagining the farm in Plowville as it would be a decade hence, with his father dead (*The Centaur* after the centaur has died, as he put it) and his mother living alone, a recent widow with a rapa-cious hunger for her only son's attention and affection. And in an even bolder prophetic inspiration, he was imagining making a week-end visit to his mother after having divorced and remarried. (One wonders whether this wasn't a deliberate attempt to extinguish the last embers of his romantic longing for Joyce by imagining how she would cope with Linda as a mother-in-law.) Along with his bride comes her precocious son, an eager-to-please eleven-year-old, who rounds out the cast of characters: two mothers, two sons, together in the old sandstone farmhouse. Like *Marry Me*, *Of the Farm*—he added the preposition to the title six months prior to publication—is an intricately choreographed dance in which four characters engage and disengage, grappling in a slippery push-and-pull that sometimes gives comfort but more often does damage.

The outside world is rigorously excluded from *Of the Farm*; we're allowed *off* the farm only for a quick trip to a shopping mall and a Sunday morning church service. There are only four voices—a quartet.* The voices belong to Joey Robinson, a public relations consultant who once dreamed of being a poet; his garrulous mother, Mary; his second wife, Peggy, a long-legged redhead with a bony face; and her young son, Richard. The selective focus pays off; it's one of Updike's best books, a small, quiet triumph. It was the first time he used a first-person narrator in a novel, and the intimacy of Joey's voice telling his story ("a kind of chamber music" is how he described it to Alfred Knopf) adds to the sense of events and characters isolated from the hurly-burly of daily life—a quartet in a spotlight, performing flawlessly for our benefit.

"It's a book people mention to me," Updike said more than forty-five years after it was published, "and I feel kind of embarrassed about it, like I was somehow too naked when I wrote it." Inasmuch as he was exploring his unusually close bond with his mother in a cruelly honest, minimally fictionalized piece of writing, it's no surprise that he felt exposed and ill at ease when called upon to discuss it. He was certainly nervous about what his mother would think of what he told her was "a little flight among imaginary moments that I hope won't annoy anyone"; in the months before publication, he repeatedly advised her not to bother reading it. He may have found it painful, also, to see himself in Joey, a thirty-five-year-old mama's boy easily manipulated by his mother into agreeing that his second wife is vulgar and stupid, and that divorcing his first wife was a mistake. But what Joey's mother knows about Joey, Linda could not have known about Updike—for the simple reason that Updike had not yet left his wife and children, and wouldn't do so for nearly a

---

* That there are just four voices is only technically true, since in church the minister delivers a sermon, which Updike paraphrases.

decade. Updike was testing out in fiction his mother's reaction to what might have been had he followed through and left Mary for Joyce. He was reopening the old wound—this time to gauge the degree of his guilt and the price of expiation.

Updike once wrote that the novel's "underlying thematic transaction . . . was the mutual forgiveness of mother and son"—but that makes the novel seem kinder and gentler than it is. Before we get to forgiveness, blame must be apportioned—not, in this case, a pretty process. Joey's guilt and his mother's emerge from an emotional melee worthy of Edward Albee; the three adults hammer, burn, and lacerate one another, to borrow the startling phrase from "Couples." Mrs. Robinson's crime is the familiar one central to the Hoyer/Updike saga: she forced her husband and son out of their beloved Olinger and onto the farm. In this version, the move had fatal consequences: it hastened her husband's death. Joey's crime, his divorce, cost him four thousand dollars in lawyers' fees alone— the same amount, he realizes, that the farm had cost his mother.* By this strict accounting, Joey and his mother are even—both took what they wanted and paid for it. But the true price can't be counted in dollars and cents. To get the farm, Joey's mother sacrificed her husband; to get Peggy, Joey sacrificed his first wife and his children. Not exactly victimless crimes.

When all the mother-son skirmishes are done, when all the wounds are neatly bandaged by forgiveness and the visitors are ready to leave, Joey's mother engages in a bit of pointed banter about selling the farm after she's dead. She refers to it as "my farm," and before he replies, Joey reflects, "We were striking terms, and circumspection was needed. I must answer in our old language, our only language, allusive and teasing, that with conspiratorial tact declared nothing and left the past apparently unrevised." His answer ("'*Your* farm?' I said. 'I've always thought of it as our farm'") is meant to reassure her that their conspiracy is intact.

Critics have spotted the prophetic strain in *Of the Farm*. One goes so far as to cite Eliot's dictum that the test of a true poet is that

---

* The purchase price of the Plowville farm was $4,743.12.

he writes of experiences before they have happened to him. Updike's vision of his mother's widowhood (after Wesley died in 1972, Linda lived alone on the farm for seventeen years, until her own death in 1989) is indeed eerily clairvoyant. Equally eerie is the "transaction" in which one crime is forgiven in exchange for a kind of immunity from prosecution for another crime that hasn't yet been committed—or not quite. A few years after Linda's death, Updike described the book as an attempt "to show an aging mother and her adult son negotiating acceptance of what seems to each the sins of the other." I suspect that when he wrote *Of the Farm*, he was negotiating acceptance of his sins—sins of the past (Joyce) as well of the future—by confessing them in fiction, a language in which his mother was fluent.

And what of his father? John evidently had to remove Wesley from the picture before he could imagine himself divorcing and remarrying. My guess is that Wesley would have known without knowing that the message in *Of the Farm*—delivered with "conspiratorial tact"—was not for his ears. He was accustomed to the sotto voce murmurings of Linda conversing with John in their "old language," and besides, a man who could embrace *The Centaur* and declare George Caldwell a true likeness of himself was unlikely to object to being killed off in his son's next novel—or to being left out of the loop. Wesley wouldn't have wanted to hear about the near-miss of John's marital crisis (the infidelity, the romantic passion, the threat of divorce), and John wasn't prepared to confess to him, even in code—that much had been made clear several years earlier, in "Packed Dirt, Churchgoing, a Dying Cat, a Traded Car," when the mere mention of his father's illness cuts off David Kern's thoughts of adultery and turns him into a model husband, a champion of family life. Like David, John was unwilling to puncture the illusions of a bighearted man; one of Wesley's cherished beliefs was that John was a good son and a good father.

The first draft of *Of the Farm* was finished less than a month before Updike set off on his six-week trip to Russia and other Communist Bloc countries. The State Department invitation to act as an ambassador of the arts was flattering but also unsettling. Unnerved by the prospect of a journey behind the Iron Curtain, he wrote to Maxwell, declaring his intention to draw up his last will and testament—and to name Maxwell as his literary executor (proof, if any were needed, of the unshakeable trust he placed in his editor). Updike promised to do his best not to inconvenience anyone by actually dying. On the eve of his departure, clearly more nervous than his giddy tone implied, he reminded Maxwell that he'd named him executor and mused with mock horror on the "puniness" of his legacy: "Maybe in Russia," he wrote, "I'll learn to think big." He mentioned the two unpublished novels in safe-deposit boxes at the local bank (*Home* and *Marry Me*). They were, he declared, "unreadable"—he had no idea what could be done with them in the "unthinkable" event that something were to happen to him. He instructed Maxwell to release all the stories on the shadow-bank—but again, only if the unthinkable were to occur.

He flew down to Washington in mid-October to receive his marching orders from Foggy Bottom; by the end of the month he and Mary were in Moscow. (Mary eagerly accepted the invitation to accompany her husband, even though the Updikes had to pay for her plane ticket.) William Luers, second secretary at the American embassy, was waiting at the airport to greet them. Luers looked after Updike for most of the trip, offering a corrective counterweight to the omnipresent Soviet "interpreters" assigned to Western visitors. Having done the same for John Steinbeck and Edward Albee, Luers was struck by the conscientious effort Updike made to establish meaningful contact with his Communist hosts. "He was so good about it," said Luers, "so intent on giving what he thought at the moment was the answer to the question. He felt duty-bound to do the best job he could. He was a patriot, a believer in America and its role in the world." But his patriotism was only half of the equation; he also felt obliged "to be a good guest of the Soviet state."

An author on exhibit—"wearing abroad," as he put it, "my country's colors"—he met with writers and artists and students, gave speeches, and signed books. Whisked from here to there in black ZiL limousines, he toured literary monuments; attended readings and operas and ballets; endured formal, two-hour banquets; and consumed quantities of vodka. "There I was everything I'm not here," he told *Life* magazine, "a public figure toasting this and that." The role-playing left its mark. Overcoming an aversion (instilled by *The New Yorker*) to "the artistic indecency of writing about a writer," he conceived of a character who was a successful author, a paid-up member of the literary establishment—"a vehicle," as he put it, "for impressions that only a writer could have collected." He returned to Ipswich in the first week of December outwardly intact but harboring within this new identity—which he unburdened in a story, "The Bulgarian Poetess," about an American novelist touring Communist countries at the behest of the State Department. Thus was born Henry Bech. A Lutheran family man from Pennsylvania had given birth to a Jewish bachelor from New York—it proved in time a wonderfully fruitful reconfiguration of Updike's essential self. Bech is a comic character—sometimes merely a figure of fun, sometimes an excuse to make fun of others—but he also represents a crucial part of his creator's personality and experience. Harry Angstrom is Updike's middle American, his Everyman; Bech is a more rarefied, less wholesome creature, his natural habitat the literary world centered in Manhattan, a landscape utterly alien to Rabbit. Harry is a version of what Updike might have been had he never left Pennsylvania; Bech is a version of what Updike might have been had he started out in New York and stubbornly stood his ground.

The first Bech story catches up with our hero in Sofia, after a stint in Moscow and briefer visits to Prague, Bucharest, Kiev, and other more remote capitals. ("I am transported around here like a brittle curio," writes Bech in his Russian journal; "plug me into the nearest socket and I spout red, white, and blue.") Just days before his scheduled return to America, he meets and instantly falls in love with Vera Glavanakova, a blond Bulgarian poetess modeled on Blaga Dimitrova (1922–2003), whom Updike met in Sofia. Knowing it will be his last glimpse of Vera, Bech inscribes for her a copy of one of his novels: "It is a matter of earnest regret for me that you and I must live on opposite sides of the world." Updike inscribed a copy of *The Centaur* for Blaga: "It is a great sadness for me that you and I must live on opposite sides of the world. You have been lovely." He emended the last sentence to "You are lovely." Dimitrova was a strikingly good-looking woman, and Updike's expression of romantic yearning clearly heartfelt—Bech's, too. Updike and Dimitrova corresponded briefly; her tender, wistful letters suggest that his inscription struck a chord.*

"The Bulgarian Poetess" offers only a glimmer of Bech's comic potential. In fact, the exotic setting (as Updike noted, Bulgaria in 1964 was, for Americans, "almost the dark side of the moon") and the snippets of serious literary discussion are almost more conspicuous than the personality of the protagonist, "this fortyish young man, Henry Bech, with his thinning curly hair and his melancholy Jewish nose." Like Rabbit, Bech evolved; his versatility as an alter ego dawned on Updike only gradually.

In "The Bulgarian Poetess," Bech is a solitary ambassador of the arts passed from one embassy secretary to the next as he makes his way around Eastern Europe and Transcaucasia. As for Updike, he started out on his excursion with plenty of company: Mary was with him for the first two weeks, and for the first ten days the Updikes saw a good deal of John Cheever, who was also staying at Moscow's Hotel Ukraine. In Moscow and Leningrad the two authors appeared at official functions as a double bill. Cheever flew home in early November, and Mary followed several days later; Updike stayed on for another month, spending two weeks in Russia, then flying south for a whirlwind tour of Eastern Bloc countries: four days each in Romania, Bulgaria, and Czechoslovakia.

Updike and Cheever had met fleetingly at literary events, such as the National Book Award ceremony on March 10, 1964, at the Grand Ballroom of the New York Hilton, where Updike accepted the prize for *The Centaur*. Cheever served on the panel of judges, and boasted of having steered the award toward Updike's novel (at the expense of Thomas Pynchon's *V*). This was a larger, more glittery crowd than any Updike had ever faced. A lively record of the occasion survives in paragraphs penned by Tom Wolfe, then a young reporter for the *New York Herald Tribune*:

---

* Knowing how proud she was of the inscription, her husband included a photograph of it in her collected works, published the year she died.

No sensitive artist in America will ever have to duck the spotlight again. John Updike, the Ipswich, Mass., novelist, did it for them all last night, for all time. Up on the stage . . . to receive the most glamorous of the five National Book Awards, the one for fiction, came John Updike . . . in a pair of 19-month-old loafers. Halfway to the podium, the spotlight from the balcony hit him, and he could not have ducked better if there had been a man behind it with a rubber truncheon.

First he squinted at the light through his owl-eyed eyeglasses. Then he ducked his head and his great thatchy medieval haircut toward his right shoulder. Then he threw up his left shoulder and his left elbow. Then he bent forward at the waist. And then, before the shirred draperies of the Grand Ballroom and an audience of 1,000 culturati, he went into his Sherwin-Williams blush.

Peeping past Wolfe's trademark hyperbole, we catch a precious glimpse of a rumpled Updike—he'd taken the train down from Boston with Mary just that morning—on the cusp of celebrity, still most comfortable with his aw-shucks pose. His short, earnest acceptance speech offered a contrast in style: slick and mellifluous, he extolled in spit-shined sentences the virtue of accuracy; invoked Proust, Joyce, and Cézanne; and left no one in doubt as to the scale of his ambition.

Cheever had also nominated Updike for membership in the National Institute of Arts and Letters. These gestures of goodwill helped make their Moscow meeting, eight months after the ceremony in the Grand Ballroom, a jolly occasion. But the camaraderie masked ambivalence on Cheever's side, a hidden animosity that flared when Updike's back was turned. As his biographer noted, Cheever was of two minds about Updike even before meeting him. A Knopf executive had sent Cheever an advance copy of *The Poorhouse Fair*, hoping for a blurb; he refused to provide one, explaining that Updike was an "unusually gifted young man . . . but perhaps not a novelist. His eloquence seems to me to retard the movement of the book and to damage his control." Having sent off this reply, he felt compelled to write again, saying that though he hadn't changed his mind about the blurb, he wanted to stress that Updike was indeed "unusually brilliant." In his journal he wrote, "Sometimes I like the thought of [Updike] and just as often he seems to me an oversensitive changling [*sic*] who allows himself to be photographed in arty poses." Complicating matters was the fact that the pair of them were close friends with Bill Maxwell, who edited their stories and acted on occasion as mentor to both—there was in Cheever's attitude toward Updike a hint of sibling rivalry.

For his part, Updike felt toward Cheever, who was born in 1912, none of the competitive aggression that sometimes gripped him when he was confronted with promising youngsters. He was grateful to Cheever for having provided the "crystallizing spark" for "Friends from Philadelphia," and he and Mary read each new Cheever story with avid pleasure ("John Cheever was a golden name to me"). The twenty-year age gap meant that for Updike, the older man belonged to a different generation of writers; as he put it, "Aspiring, we assume that those already in possession of eminence will feel no squeeze as we rise." Cheever was possibly only dimly aware of the difference in their ages, and was in any case unsuited to an avuncular role, though for the purposes of their adventure, the diminutive Cheever was "Big John" and Updike, who was at least a head taller, "Little John."

Big John had arrived in Russia a few weeks before the Updikes, and so acted like a genial host, full of charm and contagious enthusiasm. The two Johns joked about being the last non-Jewish writers in America. Cheever invented stories about the glum Soviet literary officials they encountered, turning them, Updike remembered, into "a bright scuttle of somehow suburban characters"—that is, into Cheever characters. Fueled by vodka and brandy, champagne and caviar, the proceedings took on a giddy carnival air. Cheever was courtly to Mary, who was thrilled to be in such lively company; "during that excursion," Updike wrote, she was transformed into "a kind of Russian beauty, with a friendly dimple and a sturdy capacity for vodka."

The Updikes assumed that Cheever was enjoying himself as much as they were. Perhaps he was—but an unfortunate and somewhat bewildering antagonism toward Little John creeps into Big John's journal entries. After one of their events at the University of Leningrad, he groused about how Updike "hogged the lecture platform." A high school dropout, Cheever may have been intimidated by Updike's intellect, but that doesn't quite explain why he chose to remember their interaction as continual "back-biting." In a sequence of letters to Frederick Exley in June 1965, he launched into a rant about Updike—"I think his magnanimity specious and his work seems motivated by covetousness, exhibitionism and a stony heart"—then dramatized his complaints with a born storyteller's flair:

> Our troubles began at the Embassy in Moscow when he came on exclaiming:
> "What are you looking so great about? I thought you'd be dead." He then began distributing paper-back copies of the Centaur while I distributed hard-cover copies of The Brigadier. The score was eight to six, my favor. When we went to Spasso [*sic*] House [the U.S. ambassador's residence] the next day he forgot to bring any books and I dumped six. On the train up to Leningrad he tried to throw my books out of the window but his lovely wife Mary intervened. She not only saved the books; she read one. She had to hide it under her bedpillow and claim to be sick. She said he would kill her if he knew. At the University of Leningrad he tried to upstage me by reciting some of his nonsense verse but I set fire to the contents of an ashtray and upset the water carafe.

This fantasy, obviously concocted for Exley's amusement, came to light only in 1988 with the publication of Cheever's letters. Updike didn't deign to deny the story (though Mary did, strenuously); the malice behind it surprised and saddened him, and opened his eyes to the ubiquity of the competitive reflex in writers. "[T]he literary scene," he wrote by way of explanation, "is a kind of *Medusa*'s raft, small and sinking, and one's instinct when a newcomer tries to clamber aboard is to stamp on his fingers." Cheever died in 1982, six years before the correspondence was published. If Updike was tempted to retaliate by speaking ill of the dead, he showed no sign of it. He did tell the dismal story of Cheever's last bender, but with sympathy rather than rancor.

THE LITERARY SCENE, with its minute calibration of rising and falling reputations, was taking up more and more of Updike's time. His election to the National Institute of Arts and Letters (as secure a purchase on *Medusa*'s raft as one is likely to achieve) meant that he was mingling with such eminent American authors as John Dos Passos, Marianne Moore, Ogden Nash, and Thornton Wilder. His former English professor Harry Levin was a member, as was Archibald MacLeish. Cheever had been elected in 1957, Saul Bellow in 1958, and William Maxwell in 1963, and Bernard Malamud (one of the models for Henry Bech) came in with Updike in 1964. Of all these, Updike was by far the youngest—in fact, at the tender age of thirty-two, he was the youngest writer elected to the institute for nearly half a century. Newly inducted and called upon to speak at a dinner meeting in the library of the splendid Beaux Arts headquarters on West 155th Street, a grand landmark building designed by McKim, Mead and White, he prefaced his remarks with a charming acknowledgment of the yawning generation gap: "I feel in this company like hiding behind the dictum that children should be seen and not heard."

A year after his election, and nine months after his Foggy Bottom briefing, Updike was back in Washington for an occasion that testified to his rising stature: he had been invited to dine at Lyndon Johnson's White House and entertain National Honor Students with a reading. He and Mary flew down and checked into the Hay-Adams. In the hotel lobby he spied a fellow Pennsylvanian—and fellow member of the National Institute of Arts and Letters—John O'Hara. Famous for a considerable oeuvre stretching back three decades to his first novel, *Appointment in Samarra* (and notorious

for his social insecurities and his obsession with the Ivy League—
hence Hemingway's well-known quip about starting a fund to send
O'Hara to Yale), the sixty-year-old author was reaching the end of
his career, a millionaire celebrity with a prickly temper and a flag-
ging literary reputation, despite the popularity of the film versions
of two prewar triumphs, *Pal Joey* and *BUtterfield 8*. Updike, an avid
reader of the older man's *New Yorker* stories, approached him with
a deferential, "Mr. O'Hara?" After a "laconic and characteristic dialogue," it was established that they would both be attending the
same function. Because Updike was providing entertainment, the
White House was sending a limousine for him. He asked O'Hara if
he'd like a ride—which seemed a good idea until it became obvious
that the celebrated author would have to sit in the front with the
driver ("the Negro chauffeur"), while the Updikes "settled regally"
in the backseat, a social irony Updike found mortifying, conscious
as he was of O'Hara's "acute nerves." The anecdote, which Updike
served up in an essay a few years later, when he himself was basking
in the klieg-light publicity surrounding *Couples*, captures the moment when a writer on the way up bumps awkwardly into a writer
on the way down.

The weighing of reputations had become for Updike a new sideline. A month before his encounter with O'Hara he had published
Assorted Prose, the final section of which reprints seventeen book
reviews that originally appeared in *The New Republic*, *The New York
Times*, *The American Scholar*, and *The New Yorker*. Collecting them
was a statement of intent; he wanted to be known as a critic as well
as an artist. One of the earliest reviews is of J. D. Salinger's *Franny
and Zooey*—a brilliant example of how to gently pan a writer one
admires, neatly balancing praise and blame:

> As Hemingway sought the words for things in motion,
> Salinger seeks words for things transmuted into human sub-
> jectivity. His fiction, in its rather grim bravado, its humor,
> its privacy, its wry but persistent hopefulness, matches the
> shape and tint of present American life. It pays the price,
> however, of becoming dangerously convoluted and static.

Having placed Salinger on a pedestal as proud as Hemingway's, he topples him with a tender, regretful shove, accusing him of a grave writerly sin, a self-indulgent obsession with certain of his characters, namely the Glass family.

> Salinger loves the Glasses more than God loves them. He loves them too exclusively. . . . He loves them to the detriment of artistic moderation. "Zooey" is just too long; there are too many cigarettes, too many goddamns, too much verbal ado about not quite enough. The author never rests from circling his creations, patting them fondly, slyly applauding.

The review ran on the front page of *The New York Times Book Review*, and despite Updike's evident respect, it outraged some ardent Salinger fans. Damning but not malicious, it set a precedent that distinguished Updike among reviewers; even when he disparaged a book, he never adopted a hostile tone. His jabs were cushioned by kindness—or at the very least a show of forbearance.

On a few occasions he tumbled unresisting into parody, as in his review of Samuel Beckett's novel *How It Is*, which concludes, memorably, after a few pages of punctuationless meandering in the style of the text, "the end of review the END of meditating upon this mud and subprimate sadism NO MORE no more thinking upon it few books have I read I will not reread sooner SORRY but that is how it is." The attraction of unkind, ungentle reviewing is immediately apparent, but unlike many critics, Updike preferred to write about books he liked. *Assorted Prose*, for instance, contains valentines to Nabokov and Muriel Spark. Nabokov was one of Maxwell's writers, and he and Spark both wrote for *The New Yorker*, but there's no doubt that Updike's enthusiasm was genuine and disinterested.

He was also on the receiving end. Mixed reviews of his work were not uncommon, but outright attacks were rare, at least until the mid-sixties, when his fame made him a target (and *Assorted Prose* had established him as a critic, and therefore fair game, on the theory that if you dish it out, you have to learn to take it). On November 21, 1965, *Book Week*, the book section of the *New York*

Herald Tribune, ran an astonishingly spiteful review of *Of the Farm* by a University of Michigan professor, John Aldridge, who considered himself a specialist in American literature. (He was a stalwart champion of Norman Mailer's work.) The overt aim of Aldridge's essay was to demote Updike to "the second or just possibly the third rank of serious American novelists." He begins by acknowledging "Mr. Updike's charming but limited gifts" and later allows that he "does on occasion write well," but these gestures in the direction of civility are buried by an overload of ad hominem reproach. Even the compliment to Updike's writing turns into an insult: writing well is revealed as the author's "private vice," a phrase that captures the insidiously personal drift of Aldridge's argument. Consider this unrelenting barrage:

> He does not have an interesting mind. He does not possess remarkable narrative gifts or a distinguished style. He does not create dynamic or colorful or deeply meaningful characters. He does not confront the reader with dramatic situations that bear the mark of an original or unique manner of seeing and responding to experience. He does not challenge the imagination or stimulate, shock, or educate it.

There's no attempt to disguise the animus at work here—on the contrary, the repetition of the personal pronoun at the beginning of each sentence makes the intent refreshingly clear: he (Aldridge) wanted to inflict pain.

The assault had long-term repercussions. The final thrust of the blade was the revelation that "behind the rich, beautiful scenery of [Updike's] descriptive prose" lay a hidden secret: "Mr. Updike has nothing to say." That this was merely an echo of a Norman Podhoretz slur ("To me he seems a writer who has very little to say") did nothing to ease the pain. Aldridge's essay not only left a lasting scar on Updike's admittedly sturdy ego, but also formed the basis of many subsequent attacks. It lies behind Harold Bloom's oft-quoted quip about Updike being "a minor novelist with a major style"; Dorothy Rabinowitz's discovery of a "vacuity" at the heart of his stories; and Gore Vidal's conviction that Updike "describes to no purpose." No matter how many prizes he won, no matter how many reviewers confirmed his position at the forefront of the first rank, Aldridge's dissent continued to rankle; that short, scathing put-down—"nothing to say"—never lost its sting.*

I believe it hurried him along a path he had just begun to explore. He started to allow a wider spectrum of his immediate experience into his fiction. Little by little, he embraced the notion that the personal is political—a phrase coined later in the decade, after civil rights marches, antiwar protests, and the women's liberation movement had crowded into the consciousness of even the most solipsistic citizen, when the interpenetration of private life and public policy had become obvious, a truism. Updike had always assigned unusually high value to his personal experience; he seemed to cherish whatever happened to him. Now he was beginning to place that experience in a national and international context.

Mary was a catalyst in this regard. Like her father, she had a strong commitment to the civil rights movement. After attending lectures on the theory and practice of nonviolence with a view to participating in the voting rights protests in the South, she flew down to Montgomery, Alabama, with another woman, a close friend from Ipswich; spent the night; then joined the last two days of the third and largest march from Selma, a protest that eventually attracted some twenty-five thousand supporters. Mary and her friend flew back from Montgomery late at night, landing in Boston in the small hours of the morning, exhausted and exultant.

A month later she persuaded John to come along on a protest march from Roxbury to the Boston Common. The object of the march, led like the Birmingham marches by Martin Luther King Jr., was to denounce segregation in schools, jobs, and housing. The ex-

---

* Eight years later, out of the blue, Aldridge invited Updike to participate in a writers' conference. Updike declined with an impish display of wit: "I guess I've recovered from your review of Of the Farm, but it was nip and tuck for a while, with intravenous glucose and months of staying quiet in a dark room, and I'm still too weak to do anything like the conference . . . that you describe."

perience is described, with only a few fictional flourishes (and a capsule version of Mary's adventures in the South), in a Maples story, "Marching Through Boston." After a dozen years of feeding voraciously on private moments, Updike for the first time chose a public event—an event destined to become an item in the newspapers, part of the historical record—as the basis for a short story. Needless to say, this didn't mark the end of his investigations into domestic life, but from now on, headlines were to play an increasingly prominent role, especially in his novels.

A reluctant and comically self-involved protester, Richard Maple is more inclined to mockery than indignation. Feverish on the day of the march, he struggles to turn his attention outward. Though he registers with uncanny precision the effects of the timed-release medicine he's taken for his cold ("Within him, the fever had become a small glassy scratching on the walls of the pit hollowed by detonating pills"), he seems barely capable of focusing on the purpose of the protest. Chilly at first, then drenched as they listen on the Common to speeches by King and Ralph Abernathy, he starts parodying, on the drive home, the revival meeting oratory of the speakers, then slips into a minstrel show accent and an Uncle Tom persona: "Ah'ze all raht, missy, jes; a tetch o' double pneu*mon*ia, don't you fret none, we'll get the cotton in." Joan asks him to please stop, but he finds he can't. It's a peculiar, unsettling performance only partly redeemed by the fact that he really is ill, and that at some level he identifies with the people he's mocking: "He was almost crying; a weird tenderness had crept over him . . . as if he had indeed given birth, birth to this voice, a voice crying for attention from the depths of oppression." Richard is crying for attention, and he's also goading Joan, needling her because he's trapped (shackled) by his marriage. And yet any identification between Richard Maple and slaves and their descendants is grotesque. To call his behavior politically incorrect is of course an anachronism; it's nonetheless willfully contrarian and intentionally offensive. When Joan tells him he's embarrassing the children with his Uncle Tom act, she might as well be saying that he's embarrassing the reader. Even in 1965, an author who put into the mouth of a white character the words, "Ef Ah could jes' res' hyah foh a spell in de shade o' de watermelon patch, res' dese ol' bones . . ." could count on making a sizable portion of his audience (his enlightened *New Yorker* audience) cringe.

This is pretty much a transcription of Updike's own behavior. The sound of civil rights oratory triggered his urge to mimic and mock. He would launch into his blackface routine with the apparent aim of amusing the children (and himself) and irritating his wife. That doesn't make him a racist or an opponent of the civil rights movement—he and Mary were charter members of the Ipswich Fair Housing Committee—but it does remind us of his delight in malicious teasing, and his resistance to righteous protest, however noble the cause. "I distrusted orthodoxies," he wrote in his memoirs, "especially orthodoxies of dissent." Though the rumor that a black family had been prevented by subterfuge from buying an Ipswich property inspired him to join a local campaign to promote equal-opportunity housing, broader protests made him uneasy. As he would soon prove in *Rabbit Redux* and *The Coup*, he was perfectly capable of identifying imaginatively with individual black people, whether American or African, yet marching in a civil rights demonstration provoked in him, like a kind of allergic reaction, a perverse and self-defeating display of callow humor.

A similar pattern was repeated in his more famous refusal to oppose the war in Vietnam, a saga that began in the summer of 1966, when he obligingly replied to a request from a pair of British editors who were collecting statements by writers from around the world (among them Italo Calvino, W. H. Auden, Norman Mailer, Doris Lessing, and Harold Pinter) for a book entitled *Authors Take Sides on Vietnam*. Here is Updike's contribution in its entirety:

> Like most Americans I am uncomfortable about our military adventure in South Vietnam; but in honesty I wonder how much of the discomfort has to do with the high cost, in lives and money, and how much with its moral legitimacy. I do not believe that the Viet Cong and Ho Chi Minh have a moral edge over us, nor do I believe that great powers can always avoid using their power. I am for our intervention

if it does some good. Specifically, if it enables the people of South Vietnam to seek their own political future. It is absurd to suggest that a village in the grip of guerrillas has freely chosen, or that we owe it to history to bow before a wave of the future engineered by terrorists. The crying need is for genuine elections whereby the South Vietnamese can express their will. If their will is for Communism, we should pick up our chips and leave. Until such a will is expressed, and as long as no willingness to negotiate is shown by the other side, I do not see that we can abdicate our burdensome position in South Vietnam.

From today's perspective, it's hard to understand why this cautious, moderate, even-tempered statement should have caused so much fuss—and why *The New York Times*, when it reported on the book's publication in England, should have proclaimed that Updike was "unequivocally for" American intervention. And yet that's what happened. He then wrote a letter to the *Times* (a *long* letter, more than three times the length of the paragraph he'd sent off to England), clarifying his position and politely defending himself against the newspaper's misrepresentations. Publicly explaining his private political views was a novel situation for him (his occasional "Comment" pieces in *The New Yorker* had been unsigned); it was a role for which he had little appetite and less aptitude. The more he embroidered his original statement, hedging and qualifying, the more apparent it became that he wasn't in fact opposed to the war—which in those "quarrelsome times" meant that he supported it. If his aim was to stake out some reasonable middle ground, he failed. And the failure stung. More than two decades later, he still felt the need to explain himself, to justify his position, notably in an essay included in *Self-Consciousness*, "On Not Being a Dove." (The convoluted title is implicit acknowledgment of the awkwardness of his stance.)

His public pronouncements on Vietnam were mild and restrained—"apologetic" is how he describes his letter to the *Times*. But in private (especially after being outed, as it were, by the *Times*), he was gripped by what he called a "strange underdog rage about the whole sorry thing." His Ipswich friends were all antiwar, one or two of them passionately so. Confronted with what seemed to him a safe and smug consensus, he would argue. Like his obnoxious blackface routine, it was a kind of compulsion: "I wanted to keep quiet, but could not. Something about it all made me very sore. I spoke up, blushing and hating my disruption of a post-liberal socioeconomic-cultural harmony I was pleased to be a part of." His memory of these occasions is distressingly visceral: "My face would become hot, my voice high and tense and wildly stuttery; I could feel my heart race in a kind of panic whenever the subject came up, and my excitement threatened to suffocate me."

Mary had a theory about it: Lyndon Johnson, she pointed out, was a former schoolteacher, and John, she thought, identified him with his father, whose struggles with classroom discipline had been a "central trauma" in John's childhood, a source of "fear and pity." Defending the president against the misbehavior of the antiwar protesters was a way of defending his father—and, by extension, himself. John found this theory interesting enough to mention it in his memoirs. And in revenge, as it were, he set out a counter-theory:

> [T]he possibility exists that, along with my . . . delusional filial attachment to Lyndon Baines Johnson, my wife's reflexive liberalism helped form my unfortunate undovish views—that I assumed these views out of a certain hostility to her, and was protesting against our marriage.

Whatever the precise mix of motives, the result was a kind of feedback loop. The dovish consensus irritated him, and the visible signs of his own irritation embarrassed him, and fueled his "underdog rage"; he became obsessive about it: "I was, perhaps, the most Vietnam-minded person I knew." And this, in the end, is what angered him most: Vietnam "made it impossible to ignore politics, to cultivate serenely my garden of private life and printed artifact."

An encounter with Philip Roth on Martha's Vineyard shows the process at work. The two writers were dinner guests in the summer of 1967 at the tiny house in West Tisbury rented by Bernard Taper, a *New Yorker* colleague of John's. The conversation turned to Vietnam, with predictable results; Updike recalled the "puzzled expression" on the faces of the two men as he mounted a spirited defense of Johnson and the American military.

> In my mind I was beset, defending an underdog, my back to the wall in a world of rabid anti-establishment militants. At one point Roth, in the calm and courteous tone of one who had been through many psychiatric sessions, pointed out to me that I was the most aggressive person in the room. It gave me pause. On reflection, it seemed possibly true. Why *was* I so vehement and agitated an undove? I did not just have a few cool reservations about the antiwar movement; I felt hot. I was emotionally involved. "Defending Vietnam"—the vernacular opposite of being "antiwar"—I was defending myself.

The anecdote is especially revealing because it's so rare to see Updike losing control of his public persona; hot and bothered was never the image he wanted to project, especially in the company of other writers.

He had first met Roth in 1959, at the house of Jack Leggett, a Houghton Mifflin editor who lived near Ipswich. Roth's initial impression was favorable ("I found him lively, funny, and mischievous, a kind of engaging, elongated leprechaun"), and Updike, according to Mary, was fascinated. The argument at Bernie Taper's little summerhouse ("a good row," according to Roth, "gifted debaters on both sides") did no harm; Roth's high opinion of John was unchanged, and from the very first, he found Mary "utterly charming and a wonderful looking woman." Subsequent encounters were always "genial," according to Roth.

The two writers were very nearly the same age (Updike was a year and a day older) and equally precocious; both were conspicuously intelligent, intellectually adventurous, and brimming with literary ambition. Roth won the National Book Award for *Goodbye, Columbus* in 1960, at age twenty-seven, and *Portnoy's Complaint*

(1969) was a succès de scandale on the order of *Couples*. From that point on, Roth and Updike remained neck and neck in the American author sweepstakes, both repeatedly hailed by critics as the leading talent of their generation. Whatever rivalry they felt, they buried it under mounds of cleverness; for instance, Updike asked his publisher to send Roth a copy of his book of poems, *Midpoint*, retitled *Poor Goy's Complaint*. They met for lunch on occasion and, as Roth put it, they entertained each other with their "distinctive brands of irony, satire, burlesque, and smartest-boy-in-the-class cultural superiority." They sent each other teasing notes—Roth, for example, warning Updike to steer clear of New Jersey: "Have I not stayed away from the Amish in order not to tread on your toes?"—and also letters of genuine, wholehearted praise. Roth was especially flattering about the last two volumes of the Rabbit tetralogy, which he thought of as the "twin peaks" of Updike's achievement. All in all, over the years they met perhaps a dozen times, and managed to remain friendly up until the nineties.

Updike's review of Roth's *Operation Shylock*, which ran in *The New Yorker* in March 1993, wrecked any chance that the two of them would continue to cozy up in old age. The review itself wasn't exactly negative (though Updike did assert that Roth had become "an exhausting author to be with," mostly because of his "narrowing, magnifying fascination with himself"); it was gently mocking, which for Roth was probably worse. Three years later, Roth's ex-wife, the actress Claire Bloom, published a memoir, *Leaving a Doll's House* (1996), in which she claimed that their marriage came unstitched shortly after the publication of *Operation Shylock*, when Roth sank into depression. According to Bloom, when Roth checked himself into the Silver Hill psychiatric hospital in the summer of 1993, he explained to his doctors that he was distressed by Updike's "ungenerous" review of his latest novel. When Updike read the Bloom memoir ("skipping the boring parts"), he dashed off a playful postcard to his friend Michael Arlen:

> A good woman wronged, that was my impression. . . . Also that they were a pretty good couple while it lasted, at least

on quiet Connecticut evenings, with only the sound of the
whippoorwill and the pages of the classics turning. And to
think that my friendly little review broke it up. Well, you
never . . .

Updike was being funny, and remarkably unsympathetic, but at
least that was in private. Unfortunately for Roth, Updike then cited
Bloom's memoir in a *New York Review of Books* essay on literary biography. He classed her book as a "Judas biography" and recapped
the action for the reader's benefit:

> Claire Bloom, as the wronged ex-wife of Philip Roth, shows
> him to have been, as their marriage rapidly unraveled, neur-
> asthenic to the point of hospitalization, adulterous, callously
> selfish, and financially vindictive.

As Roth saw it, Updike was taking Bloom's characterization at face
value, which to Roth seemed "cruelly obtuse—and I knew he wasn't
obtuse." Roth categorically denied that Updike's review of *Operation
Shylock* had anything at all to do with his bout of depression. But
that was ancient history; after the essay on literary biography, which
appeared in early 1999, they never spoke again.

Another literary friendship, with Joyce Carol Oates, fared better
over the years. Oates wrote Updike a fan letter about *The Centaur*
in 1964, when she was a newly published twenty-six-year-old. They
didn't actually meet until 1968, at the National Institute of Arts
and Letters, when Oates received the Rosenthal Award (the same
prize Updike had won in 1960). When she and her first husband,
Raymond Smith, founded a literary journal, the *Ontario Review*,
they asked Updike to contribute. His first poem in the magazine,
"Leaving Church Early," was published toward the end of 1977;
forty years later, in the spring/summer issue of 2007, he published
five poems, his final contribution. In between, he and Oates kept up
a lively, gossipy literary correspondence as voluminous as you would
expect from a pair of authors who were at the same time producing
at least a book a year, decade after decade.

Roth, Oates, and Updike were all prolific, but compared with Updike, the other two were slow off the mark. In November 1966, when a long and loving profile of Updike appeared in *Life* magazine, he had fourteen books to his credit: four novels, four collections of short stories, two volumes of poetry, three children's books, and *Assorted Prose*, his first miscellany. At that point, Roth and Oates had published only a couple of books apiece. So when the editors of *Life* asked Updike's opinion of other writers, it wasn't necessarily a slight on his part that he failed to mention either of them. The living Americans he weighed up, each in a phrase or two, were John O'Hara, Thomas Pynchon, J. D. Salinger, Norman Mailer, Jack Kerouac, Bernard Malamud, Saul Bellow, and John Cheever. Pynchon he dismissed ("like reading a very long Popeye strip, without the spinach"); the rest he gave mixed reviews, praising and panning in the same breath—until he got to Cheever, for whom his praise was unequivocal: "I've never met anyone quicker on his feet, both fictional and real, than Cheever."

THE *Life* PROFILE catches Updike and his family in their Ipswich prime, basking in what he called "sixties domestic bliss." After eight years, the Polly Dole House had become an emblem of their identity; describing it was a reporter's easy shorthand: "a 17th century house with enough rooms for everybody to get lost, a remodeled kitchen, a piano, splashes of blue-and-green Design Research upholstery fabrics, good paintings, many plants, myriad books." The paintings were mostly Mary's own, semi-abstract canvases that looked good in the large living room with its wide floorboards and cavernous fireplace. The curtains were Marimekko, the furniture a mix of austere Danish modern and antiques bought at local auctions; there was a glass-and-chrome coffee table and a butterfly chair. Some of the bookshelves bearing the myriad books had been built by Updike, hammering away in the basement. The small, scruffy backyard with its ragged forsythia hedge and rope swing was well used by the children and their pack of friends. A small vegetable patch was planted with lettuce, radishes, lima beans, and kohlrabi. The family cars, a station wagon and a dove-gray convertible Corvair, both dented, were parked on the street under dying elms. He took, he admitted, "snobbish pride" in the frayed, faintly shabby look he and his family adopted. He himself dressed carelessly, with holes in his sweaters ("I wear them until they get quite big at the elbows and oblong at the necks"), rumpled khakis, worn-out canvas sneakers, a shaggy haircut.

Updike chose his own label for this brand of unbuttoned prosperity: "By my mid-thirties," he wrote in his memoirs, "I had arrived at a lifestyle we might call genteel bohemian." It was funded, he liked to say, by a "parasitic relationship with Steuben Glass" (a major advertiser in *The New Yorker*). But he was also earning steady money from Knopf. He didn't take advances, partly because his *New Yorker* income meant that he didn't need to, and partly because he wanted to avoid the pressure of being in his publisher's debt. To avoid sudden spikes in earnings (and the consequent tax burden), for each successive book he would ask for a per-annum cap on the money Knopf would pay out from royalties and the sale of foreign rights. But even with these caps in place, he was easily making more than he was spending. He estimated, for example, that in 1967 he earned $70,000; in January 1968, sale of the film rights to *Couples* brought in a windfall of $360,000. With all four children in public school, the cost of supporting the family—frequent Caribbean jaunts and the summer rentals on the Vineyard excepted—could hardly be called extravagant.

In 1966 the Updikes spent the whole of August on Martha's Vineyard, the first of many family vacations on the island. They rented a gray shingle house with a view of Menemsha Harbor and a little studio for John to write in. The family eased into a blissful, school's-out distillation of their Ipswich life, with more beach, more sun, and a new cast of characters. One nearly new face was that of Nicholas Delbanco, who had been a student in Updike's Harvard writing class four years earlier. Now twenty-three, Delbanco had just published *The Martlet's Tale*, the novel he'd begun under Updike's supervision. Having worked several summers at Poole's Fish Market in Menemsha, he knew the Vineyard well, and offered to show the Updikes around the island. On his days off he cavorted with the kids in the South Beach surf, or took them kayaking on Menemsha Pond.

In "Bech Takes Pot Luck," the third Bech story (and the first set in the United States), Updike borrowed the basics of his history with Delbanco to create a comic caricature of literary hero worship. Bech is on vacation with his mistress, Norma Latchett; her sister Bea (who's in the midst of a divorce); and Bea's three children. They've rented a cottage on an instantly recognizable Massachusetts island—

> whose coves and sandy lanes were crammed with other writers, television producers, museum directors, undersecretaries of State, old *New Masses* editors possessively squatting on seaside acreage bought for a song in the Depression, movie stars whose forties films were now enjoying a camp revival, and hordes of those handsome, entertaining, professionless prosperous who fill the chinks between celebrities.

Also on the island is Wendell Morrison, Bech's former writing student at Columbia, whose familiarity with the area and "easy intermingling with the children" make him a welcome addition to Bech's little entourage. Wendell's adoration of his erstwhile teacher is played for laughs. He asks Norma, "He's beautiful, isn't he, Ma'am?" Norma replies, "He'll do." The situation is complicated by Bech's mixed feelings—about being worshipped, about Norma, about the possibility that Norma is attracted to Wendell—and further complicated by the "gram of LSD" in Wendell's possession. Eager for new experience, Norma demands that Bech arrange for her to trip with Wendell; instead it's agreed that all four adults will try some of the young man's Mexican marijuana. A mild sexual farce plays out against the backdrop of Bech's adverse reaction to the pot (nausea, vomiting). In the end, it's Bech and Bea who wind up in bed together. As for Wendell, his undimmed veneration for his old teacher leads him to flush the LSD down the toilet—and to ask Bech to read his manuscript.

Updike cooked up this sex-and-drugs comedy with ingredients supplied by Delbanco, who told him about some LSD he'd owned and disposed of. Updike mixed that morsel with a judiciously scrambled account of an evening when two friends from Ipswich came to the Vineyard for a visit. The houseguests, both part of the couples crowd, were a divorced man and a woman, an ex-lover of John's who was going through a rough patch in her marriage. Delbanco came to dinner and, after the meal, when the children had been tucked up in bed, offered to share some marijuana with the assembled company. Delbanco remembered John's wooziness when he was high—and taking home with him the female friend from Ipswich.

Updike wrote "Bech Takes Pot Luck" a little more than a year after the event that inspired it, and the story wasn't published in *The New Yorker* until the following year, whereupon Updike wrote a note to Delbanco urging him not to read himself into the "little fantasy" featuring young Wendell Morrison—"other than in the undeniable way the two of you know your way around the drug culture, and eat up aging writers of fading vitality." In fact, Delbanco knew exactly how to read both Updike's fiction and his teasing, self-deprecating letters; he didn't take offense, and the two remained friends and correspondents for the next four decades.

A few weeks after the Updikes' return from that first summer on the Vineyard, *Life* magazine came calling—not just the reporter, a young woman named Jane Howard, but also a photographer who posed the family, scrubbed up for the occasion, in the spacious living room at 26 East Street, the brick of the great fireplace just visible behind their heads. In the photo, John and his two sons are wearing button-down shirts, Mary and her two daughters summery cotton dresses. Seven-year-old Michael, an exasperated twist to his lips, leans toward his mother; five-year-old Miranda, with bangs and freckles, gazes cheerfully at her father. The two eldest stand behind their seated parents, looking straight at the camera, nine-year-old David eager and excited, Liz wise beyond her eleven years, her mouth a wary slant. She shares with her father an amused, ironic detachment, a hint of distrust. About Mary's wide smile and bright eyes, set off by a late-summer tan, there's nothing remotely distrustful; the easy happiness she exudes sets the tone—the image makes you want to say, *What a sweet family!* As if to reinforce that impression, the headline reads, "Can a Nice Novelist Finish First?" The accompanying text describes John as "oddly good-looking, with an arresting hook nose and sea-captainish crinkled eyes."

It requires a flexible worldview to keep in mind simultaneously the wholesome domestic scene of the *Life* photo and the adulterous shenanigans detailed in Updike's memoirs. The most shocking instance is packed into one unforgettable sentence describing the return journey of a ski trip up north:

> I seem to remember, on one endless drive back home in the dark down Route 93, while my wife sat in the front seat and her hair was rhythmically irradiated with light from opposing headlights, patiently masturbating my back-seat neighbor through her ski pants, beneath our blanketing parkas, and taking a brotherly pride in her shudder of orgasm just as we hit the Ipswich turn-off.

That lurid anecdote should perhaps be balanced by a few words about "Your Lover Just Called," a Maples story written in the summer of 1966 and based, as usual, on an incident in the Updikes' marriage. Richard Maple, returning home through the backyard from a quick errand, spies through the kitchen window his wife kissing a friend of his. The friend, Mack, is the soon-to-be ex-husband of Eleanor, with whom Richard shared a torrid embrace in the previous Maples story, "The Taste of Metal." Joan and Mack protest their innocence ("A mere fraternal kiss. A brotherly hug"), but infidelity is by now a tacitly accepted feature of the Maples' marriage; they both have lovers they conceal with varying degrees of success. The kiss Updike actually saw through the kitchen window of the Polly Dole House *was* innocent (according to the man who was kissing her), but at the time, both John and Mary were embroiled in affairs and flirtations—which is the premise of yet another Maples story, "The Red Herring Theory." Joan explains,

> The properly equipped suburban man . . . has a wife, a mistress and a red herring. The red herring may have been his

mistress once, or she may become one in the future, but he's not sleeping with her now. You can tell, because in public they act as though they do.

This brief sociological treatise is delivered in the immediate aftermath of a typical party at their house; their friends had come and gone and, in between, had "shuffled themselves" or had "been re-shuffled." Joan complains, "What messy people . . . Grinding Fritos into a shag rug. They're so *sloppy*." A faint echo of this complaint can be heard in Updike's memoirs, where he looks back at the Ipswich parties of the late sixties: "At moments of suburban relaxation, in our circle of semi-bohemian homes, we smoked pot, wore dashikis and love beads, and frugged ourselves into a lather while the Beatles and Janis Joplin sang away on the hi-fi set." The frugging ground many a Frito into the shag rug, and Updike, never a heavy drinker and only an occasional smoker of marijuana and hashish, was always in the thick of the reshuffle.

In her *Life* profile, Jane Howard noted how "enmeshed" Updike was in the town, both his civic engagement (the church committees, the town Democratic committee) and the avid socializing with the Ipswich gang—the parties, the sports, the poker, the recorder group. (In another *Life* photo, Mary and John soberly play their instruments, alto and tenor, respectively.) Updike meant something similar when he remarked that in Ipswich he felt "enlisted in actual life."

Enlisted, enmeshed, entangled . . . and yet he claimed still to feel, in his "innermost self," like an outsider—which is consistent with his belief that a writer should remain to some degree estranged. The *Life* photographer caught him in the act, snug in his own living room, posing for a magazine portrait: the celebrated young author in the bosom of his family. Part of him is conspicuously detached, eyeing the photo shoot charade from a distance. Impersonating the author as wholesome family man, he couldn't stop *being* a writer, his "inner remove" apparent in the backward tilt of the head, the slight squint, the half-smile. He was relaxed in front of the lens, unfazed by the rapid click of the shutter, but he wasn't an actor; he couldn't control what the camera revealed.

He was hard at work on *Couples* at the time, putting his friends and neighbors under the microscope, scrutinizing them with merciless sociological precision. Hailed as an exposé of "the adulterous society," *Couples* is both a celebration and a satire, a hymn to the joy he experienced in the company of the Ipswich set—especially the women he slept with—and a denunciation of a faithless, sexually promiscuous community, derelict in its most essential duty (the care of its children), and willfully, culpably detached from the outside world. Updike liked to say that the dinner he and Mary attended on the night of the assassination of President Kennedy—a dinner neither the Updikes nor their friends had "the patriotic grace to cancel or not attend"—was the "core" of *Couples.* In the novel, the party on November 22 is one of the few scenes where the satire is so blatant as to be unmistakable, where the action is designed to elicit contempt ("the dancing couples were gliding on the polished top of Kennedy's casket"). In other words, Updike believed that the spark that gave *Couples* life was essentially satiric: an urge to cry foul and point the finger at "monstrous" self-absorption and disregard for the civic life of the nation. He knew, perhaps even in the midst of the party on that tragic night, that soon he would be exposing in his fiction the moral failings of his fellow guests—and his own, too.

In an elaborately patterned novel, the chain of significance that links sex, children, the Kennedys, adultery, divorce, and abortion is just one strand of meaning among many, but it's worth teasing it out to show the scale of Updike's ambition in *Couples* and to illustrate an important shift in his method.

In the novel's first scene, the Hanemas, Piet and Angela, are getting ready for bed after a party. In an attempt to seduce his wife, Piet does a handstand in the bedroom; Angela, who's seen this stunt before, tells him, "Shh. You'll wake the children." This rebuke only eggs him on; he toddles toward the bed on his knees, imitating their younger daughter: "Dadda, Dadda, wake up-up, Dadda. The Sunnay paper's here, guess what? Jackie Kenneny's having a *ba*by!"

---

* Though surely truthful, this claim had the added benefit of deflecting attention from the autobiographical basis of the numerous Tarbox infidelities.

His antics (which Angela calls "cruel") remind her of what one of their friends told her, that their children, the children of the Tarbox couples, are "suffering" as a result of the adults' hyperactive social life, which (as we are about to learn at great length and in gorgeous detail) is accompanied by hyperactive adulterous coupling. Here, in a nutshell, is all of *Couples*—the marital stress, the tight-knit circle of friends, and the individual and social cost of the new sexual freedom.

The reference to Jackie Kennedy's pregnancy turns out to be a memento mori; the baby boy she gave birth to prematurely on August 7, 1963 (the year in which the novel is set), lived only two days. Several months (and two hundred-odd pages) after the opening scene, the Hanemas' younger daughter bursts into their bedroom and echoes Piet's parody, with a grim twist: "Daddy, wake up! Jackie Kenneny's baby died because it was born too tiny." This pathetic announcement foreshadows the death of the baby's father just a few months later, and also the disturbing consequence of Piet's affair with Foxy Whitman. Foxy and her husband are the new couple in town. When we meet her, she's two months pregnant (by her husband). Not long after giving birth to a healthy baby boy, she gets pregnant again—by Piet this time—and decides to have an abortion (which was of course illegal in Massachusetts in 1963, and indeed in the rest of the nation). The abortion is arranged by Freddy Thorne, the sinister ringleader of the couples set, who is a dentist. It's while she's having a cavity filled in Freddy's chair that Foxy hears news of Kennedy's assassination (and thinks of the dead president, already notorious for his philandering, as "a young man almost of her generation, with whom she could have slept"), and it's at Freddy's house that same night that the couples assemble for their black-tie dinner. Just to make this unwholesome set of circumstances undeniably repulsive, Freddy insists that as payment for facilitating the abortion, he be allowed to sleep with Angela, just once—an arrangement Piet, Foxy, and Angela all agree to, however reluctantly. One last detail brings it all full circle: Piet's "Kenneny"-obsessed younger daughter is listening at the door of Freddy's office while he and Piet hammer out their shameful agreement: "Her lips were pursed around the stem of a lollypop, and her eyes, though she had no words, knew everything."

There is a price to pay for the couples' feckless carousing. "All these goings on would be purely lyrical, like nymphs and satyrs in a grove," Updike told *Time* magazine, "except for the group of distressed and neglected children." The damage caused by promiscuity and collective self-absorption was much on Updike's mind as the novel was going to press. The fourteen-year-old daughter of a couple at the heart of the set, suffering from anorexia, died of an overdose of sleeping pills in January 1968. Though the overdose was presumed to be accidental, her death shocked the group and prompted some short-lived talk of restraint—perhaps, it was said, there should be fewer parties. But the manic socializing carried on as before.

Angela calls Tarbox a "sexpot"—to which Piet replies, "A sexpot is a person, not a place." But Angela knows she's right: "This one's a place." *Couples* exaggerates only slightly the closeness of the Ipswich couples and the frequency and complexity of their extramarital entanglements. What Updike liberally exaggerates, in order to keep his readers amused, is the cleverness of the repartee and innuendo when the couples get together for their dinners, their tennis parties, their parlor games, or when two of them (any two, every two) are trysting. Some of their banter weaves in topical references, information gleaned from the television news or a cursory glance at the newspaper; these scraps serve to situate us, to fix the precise date of the action, and to help us get our bearings. The fluid morality of the couples, their daisy chain of betrayals, is dizzying for the reader. When a news event intrudes—the sinking of the nuclear-powered submarine *Thresher*, say, or the toppling of a government in Southeast Asia, or the assassination of the American president—we can gauge the Tarbox reaction against our own. Talking about the Kennedys to her mother who lives in Washington, Foxy asks if there's truth to the rumor that Jack's promiscuity might lead the First Couple to divorce; listening to her mother's answer ("Of course, with his back, he's *not* as active as apparently he was"), Foxy happens to glance at the headline of her husband's neatly folded newspaper: "Diem Overthrown." (The U.S.-sanctioned coup against

Ngo Dinh Diem occurred on November 1, 1963; the deposed Vietnamese president was assassinated the next day.) News of turmoil in a war-torn country where more than sixteen thousand American military personnel are already stationed means nothing to Foxy. She thinks to herself, "Diem. *Dies, diei, diei, diem.*" Declining the Latin noun for "day," as in *carpe diem* (seize the day), she does just that; she confesses to her mother that she's thinking of divorcing her husband. As with the Kennedys, the proximate cause is infidelity (Foxy's engrossing affair with Piet).

Strip away the layers of elaborate patterning, and *Couples* is reduced to a simple love triangle, Piet and Foxy and Angela, with Angela cast in the role of the wronged wife. Piet and Foxy's affair has a spiritual element—they are the only two regular churchgoers among the ten couples—but there's clearly something wrong with their romance; a moral boundary has been crossed. Foxy's abortion, linked in myriad ways to the successive Kennedy tragedies, alerts us to the gravity of the crime—that and the thunderbolt that strikes the steeple of the Tarbox Congregational Church. But I would argue that the apocalyptic thunderbolt ("God's own lightning") is primarily a literary joke, a spoof on divine judgment. The burning of the church is a "great event" in town, a spectacle—the crowd that gathers to watch the blaze is in a carnival mood, festive rather than contrite. And there's a postmodern twist; this implausible, heavy-handed literary symbol of God's wrath is based on an actual event: the Ipswich Congregational Church, struck by lightning on a June Sunday in 1965, burned to the ground.

If there's a judgment handed down, it's the Kennedy saga rather than the church fire—the assassin's bullet rather than the deity's thunderbolt—that tips off the reader. The real world is the yardstick against which we measure these fictional characters, and yet to them the real world is unreal. "Television brought them the outer world. The little screen's icy brilliance implied a universe of profound cold beyond the warm encirclement of Tarbox, friends, and family." We might hear in that last sentence a distant echo of the Cold War; the couples crowd would not—their focus is entirely and unwaveringly on the "warm encirclement" they offer one another. The rest, they reject: "Not since Korea had Piet cared about news. News happened to other people." The news belongs to "the meaningless world beyond the ring of couples." But the careful reader remembers that in the very first scene of the novel, in Piet and Angela's bedroom, Jackie Kennedy's doomed baby is mentioned; the real world, with all its potential for tragedy, was right there all along, smuggled into the heart of their home.

Curiously muffled, the satiric element in *Couples* lies buried under two layers: Updike's exuberant prose, which wraps in baroque splendor whatever it touches, and the mass of sociological detail provided about Tarbox and its inhabitants. The result is a cloud of ambivalence noted by several critics, among them Wilfred Sheed, who wrote in *The New York Times Book Review* of the "loving horror" with which the author describes the couples' fun and games: "The incidents of wife-swapping are a nice blend of Noel Coward and Krafft-Ebing." Other critics noted that there was simply too much of everything: *Couples* is too long, a perverse effect of Updike's determination to produce a "big book." He got carried away and overshot the mark. Reading it, one is conscious, sometimes uncomfortably so, of the delight Updike takes in his material. In a letter to Joyce Carol Oates, he confided, "I wrote the book in a spirit, mostly, of love and fun." The censure he intended can't compete with the ebullience.

Updike dedicated *Couples* to Mary, the first novel he dedicated to her—an ironic gesture, certainly, and possibly hostile. Of all the characters, the only easily recognizable ones are Angela and Piet, the long-suffering wife and the antic husband who sleeps around. Angela is a sympathetic character (more appealing, anyway, than Foxy or even Piet), but that was small consolation. Mary's tart reaction to the novel—she told John she felt "smothered in pubic hair"—gives some indication of how touched she was by the dedication. Everyone in their circle of friends was naturally intrigued and somewhat nervous as rumors about the book swirled; to their relief these friends found that the other characters were jumbled up, so that the game of playing who's who—by all accounts the principal pastime on the North Shore in the months after the novel's publication in April 1968—could continue without reaching any defamatory conclusion.

This was largely thanks to warnings voiced by Alfred Knopf and Judith Jones, a Knopf editor who began to work closely with Updike in the mid-sixties. He had met her in a Knopf corridor in the summer of 1959, shortly after the departure of Sandy Richardson. Jones was a slim, handsome woman, elegant and sophisticated, married, and about ten years older than Updike; he guessed at once that she would suit him as an editor. He said as much to Knopf, who promised to arrange a lunch meeting, but nonetheless continued to manage Updike's affairs himself. It wasn't until *Couples* that Jones became in effect his editor—though Knopf, until he retired in the early 1970s, demanded in his peremptory style to be kept abreast of developments. When Jones read the manuscript of the novel, she immediately assumed that it was based on the author's exploits among his friends and neighbors. In her reader's report, she noted that Tarbox was "blatantly recognizable as Ipswich"; she added, "I trust we will impress on Updike the need to cover his tracks carefully enough." When her boss read the report, he was quick to point out to Updike that he was courting legal trouble. Knopf mentioned lawsuits for "libel and invasion of privacy," asked if the identity of all the characters was carefully covered up, and advised his author to show the manuscript to a lawyer. Updike's reaction was in part defensive; he assured his publisher that the book looked more libelous than it was, that no Ipswich woman he knew of had had an affair while pregnant, and that no local dentist had arranged an abortion. He insisted on this point—"indeed I know of no abortions at all"—which was of course a lie. With his next breath he agreed that Mary should scour the book for identifying details, and that he would consult *The New Yorker*'s libel lawyer—which he did. And he immediately set about moving Tarbox from Boston's North Shore to the South Shore, and further scrambling the composite characters. Freddy Thorne, for instance, lost all his hair between the first draft and the first edition, and his dentist's office moved to a cottage by itself on Divinity Street. All mention of the couples' favorite Sunday sport, volleyball, was deleted from the book.

A libel-proof *Couples* was loosed upon the world in tandem with the *Time* cover story, with its "grim" portrait of a "fretful," squinting author posed in a green turtleneck against an expanse of Ipswich marsh. To the magazine's reporter, Updike protested halfheartedly that his "real life experience has been quite mild compared to that of Piet"; Tarbox, he declared in the article itself, "is purely fictional." A few months later, with *Couples* already a bestseller, he told *The Paris Review*, "I disavow any essential connection between my life and whatever I write." No one was fooled. Tarbox was Ipswich, and the couples were his circle of close friends. When a columnist said as much in the *Ipswich Chronicle*, Updike flatly denied the allegations in a letter to the editor:

> The Tarboxians are not real people but conglomerations of glimpses and guesses and thefts and slips of the pen into which I, in the author's usual desperate endeavor, have tried to breathe life. They seemed alive to me, and in that sense became my friends; but I never confused them with reality, and think no one else should.

Of course one can recognize the difference between characters in a novel and real people and yet still maintain that Updike was offering up to the reading public a group portrait of his Ipswich gang. But his friends were used to his habit of pilfering bits and pieces from their lives; if they were annoyed, they kept it to themselves. Other locals on the periphery of the crowd—casual friends and acquaintances who weren't part of the inner circle—complained that the novel made the town sound like the adultery capital of America, a latter-day Sodom and Gomorrah. Updike had known all along that it would stir up trouble—he mentioned to Maxwell the possibility that it would create a "furor"—and this adds a further twist to his dedication; he was throwing a bomb into the main street of Ipswich with Mary's name printed on it in bold letters.

Did anyone notice the irony when Updike wrote the pageant for Seventeenth-Century Day? The occasion was the town's celebration of its Puritan past. There he was—the celebrity author who had trained a spotlight on suburban sex—dressed up in antique garb, a Pilgrim father for a day. That was in early August, and the resentment stirred up by *Couples* was a fading memory obscured by the novel's handsome commercial success. But Updike's literary reputation had been permanently skewed. The luscious prurience of the sex scenes made the author's name a byword for "cerebral raunch," the tag applied to Updike's oeuvre by a *New York Times* critic more than fifty years later. The headline of Wirt Williams's review of *Couples* in the *Los Angeles Times*, "America's Most Explicitly Sexual Novel Ever," summed up the sentiment of countless scandalized critics. (Williams himself was actually delighted that the author was so candid in his erotic descriptions.) Diana Trilling, writing in *The Atlantic Monthly*, expressed her distaste with prim remarks about how "wearying" she found the "sexual redundancies" of his "fancied-up pornography." Updike dismissed her review as "a banshee cry of indignation," but his publishers found it useful to quote her on the jacket of the mass-market paperback: "I can think of no other novel, even in these years of our sexual freedom, as sexually explicit in its language . . . as direct in its sexual reporting, and abundant in its sexual activities."* Sex, as they say, sells; Updike later acknowledged that the book earned him a million dollars.

Couples made him rich and famous—and, in a sense, notorious. But his notoriety—the winking acknowledgment of his dizzy ride on the merry-go-round of Ipswich adultery—is misleading. The novel was made possible not because he made a habit of bedding down with the wives of his friends but rather because he remained detached, because his "inner remove" freed him from the moral and social constraints most adulterers surrender to. Updike professed to believe that "artistic creation is at best a sublimation of the sexual instinct," a Freudian formulation he fleshed out in the person of Henry Bech, about whom he once remarked, "Art is his pastime, but love is his work." If that makes Bech a representative writer (and human being), then Updike is an anomaly: what mattered most profoundly to him wasn't sex or even love; what mattered was writing.

---

* Missing from the blurb was Trilling's acid kicker: "But to what purpose?"

In the era of jet planes and electronic communication, a writer in
gathering truth should set foot on as much of the globe as he can.
—*Self-Selected Stories of John Updike* (1996)

VII.

Updike Abroad

In a rented house near Chilmark Pond on Martha's Vineyard, in
August 1968, just a month before he and his family embarked on
a year abroad in London, Updike finished the longest, most ambitious poem of his career. "Midpoint" is a searching look back over
his thirty-six years, a summing-up after a prolific decade as a professional author, and an excavation of his identity as a son, a lover,
a husband, a father. Capping this wide-ranging retrospective, and
reinforcing the blithely optimistic notion that after this "midpoint"
a second act would unfold, the poet makes a startling resolution:
"henceforth, if I can, / I must impersonate a serious man." The very
last line of a difficult, five-canto, forty-page poem replete with formal
tricks, far-flung allusion, incidental pornography, and typographical
high jinks, it's both a tease and a blunt declaration of intent. The
hint of paradox—would a serious man embrace impersonation?—
shouldn't deter us from taking him, well, seriously. He's proposing
that he become what his career has made him: a public figure—as
Yeats would say, a "smiling public man"—a literary celebrity. (He
considered capitalizing "Serious Man" to emphasize the theatrical
aspect, the role-playing.) That particular kind of impersonation was

much on his mind. One reason he hatched the plan to spend a year in England was to dodge the publicity *Couples* was sure to generate; he and Mary started thinking about leaving town immediately after he'd finished the novel. (The publicity, however, proved hard to avoid; he permitted himself to be fêted by literary London and, with the novel lodged comfortably atop British bestseller lists, freely granted interviews to Fleet Street hacks.) Also on his mind was the kind of impersonation he did on the page: the making of fictional characters in general, and Henry Bech in particular.

The idea of giving Bech his own book first occurred to him when he wrote the second of the stories, "Bech in Rumania," in April 1966; a couple of years later, as he was working on "Midpoint" and looking forward to the London adventure, he wrote Bech's Russian journal and dreamed up a full bibliography, both eventually published as appendixes to *Bech: A Book* (1970). On the way to England he savored his latest story in *The New Yorker* ("Bech Takes Pot Luck," in the September 7 issue), reporting back to Maxwell with alliterative satisfaction, "It was good to read about Bech on the boat." Going abroad and burrowing deeper into Bech are related activities. Leaving home and living in the skin of an invented character are ways of escaping from oneself, and in both cases the distance achieved is instructive; impersonation teaches us something about who we are—as does travel, which uncovers, as Updike wrote, a "deeper, less comfortable self."

Bech is sometimes self-consciously aware of being a character created by John Updike (and sometimes even by Henry Bech), and being away from home often gave Updike the impression that he was posing as himself. Over the years, this hypersensitive postmodern pair collaborated extensively, and the doubling conjured up a receding infinity of mirror images—the giddy fun of Bech interviewing Updike; or giving him his blessing, as he did in the foreword to *Bech: A Book*; or wondering, with comic resignation or mounting panic, whether he isn't boring his creator. There's no academic theory weighing on these lighthearted, Nabokov-inspired displays of cleverness; the metatextual stunts never interfere with the narrative or obscure the scene. Like Updike, Bech is a sharp-eyed observer of the world around him, especially abroad. It's perhaps not too much to say that by impersonating Bech, Updike learned how to travel; the character gave the displaced author a purpose and a point of view—gave him, you might say, a new sense of his identity.

Updike had a stay-at-home childhood; during his first eighteen years, he hardly ever left Berks County. As a young man he was a nervous traveler. He never boarded an airplane before he was twenty-four, when he flew anxiously with Mary and one-year-old Elizabeth to California to visit Mary's sister. But by the time Bech was conceived, during the six-week tour of the Soviet Bloc in late 1964, Updike was more comfortable with foreign travel. His first trip abroad, to take up his Knox Fellowship at the Ruskin School in Oxford, was also his longest, lasting a little more than ten months. In early 1960, just after he finished *Rabbit, Run*, he packed up the whole family and flew them to Anguilla, the cheapest Caribbean island they could find, for a five-week adventure, an extended holiday in an unknown place. Though it was excitingly exotic at first, they grew bored when the novelty wore off. Then there was the two-month banishment to the South of France at the end of 1962, with the side trip to Rome. And there were many short hops to various sunny spots in the West Indies, including a return visit, with Mary, to Anguilla. But it was only after the family arrived in London in mid-September 1968 that the trips abroad started coming fast and furious. Over the next nine months he visited seven different countries, including Egypt, Denmark, and Morocco, and in the decades that followed he circled the globe with great relish, and a lingering sense of his own incompetence as a traveler—going to Africa, Australia, South America, the Far East, the Indian subcontinent, the Mideast, Eastern Europe, and Scandinavia. The small-town boy became a citizen of the world.

When he sailed for England aboard the SS *Rotterdam* accompanied by his wife and four children, he was Henry Bech in disguise: a peripatetic, cosmopolitan author ready and willing to perform the "basic and ancient" function of bringing news from abroad home to armchair travelers. Half of the twenty Bech stories take place in foreign countries; of the first five, only "Bech Takes Pot Luck" is set in

America, and even that—about Bech's summer escapades on a small Massachusetts island (Martha's Vineyard)—has a travelogue feel to it. A native of the Upper West Side, Bech thinks anywhere outside Manhattan ("the imaginary territory beyond the Hudson") is a distant land. Driving up the Eastern seaboard in his beat-up Ford, then crossing to the Vineyard on the ferry, is for him a nervous-making journey, his destination less exotic than the USSR but still distinctly foreign.

England was both familiar and congenial. John and Mary knew it from their Oxford days, and English literature supplied a cast of characters and a panorama of backdrops to help them make sense of the national foibles. Wordsworth prepared them for the "nodding" daffodils, Eliot for "pigeons the color of exhaust fumes." In a day's sightseeing you could compile an anthology; "every shire," Updike wrote, "has been the site of a poem." Yet aspects of British life remained irreducibly strange; as he acknowledged, "there are recesses of England that exist only for the initiates." And in the thirteen years since their first stay, the nation had been transformed. Postwar austerity was a dreary memory; London was now the swinging capital of cool, alive with youth and affluence and bright creative energy. Chic shopping streets were full of "bustling bravura" and novel sights; the women, Updike noted, "parade in everything from yak hides to cellophane." The mod fashions and high-decibel popular culture did not entirely detract from the essentially civilized urban atmosphere, the parks and monuments, tokens of a great empire, the gracious civic life. The bobbies in their helmets were polite; even the poor were polite. "Here," Updike wrote, "things are . . . cheap, pretty, educational, clean, green." He declared, "An American in London . . . cannot but be impressed and charmed by the city."

Their lodgings were implausibly grand: 59 Cumberland Terrace—the house found for them by André Deutsch's vivacious colleague Diana Athill—is part of a vast neoclassical edifice, completed in 1828, that stretches along the eastern side of Regent's Park. An imposing sequence of colonnades and arches, topped in the center by a large sculptural pediment, it features fleetingly in "Bech Swings?" and is first glimpsed from a taxi at night: "They entered a region where the shaggy heads of trees seemed to be dreaming of fantastically long colonnades and of high white wedding-cake facades receding to infinity." Moving from an Ipswich saltbox to the Regency splendor of Cumberland Terrace was disorienting for the whole family, though only the youngest, Miranda, admitted to homesickness. The children were enrolled at the American School in London. Liz and David were old enough, at thirteen and eleven, to enjoy exploring the city by riding on the tops of the double-decker buses. Michael, age nine, was proud that he could take the bus to Hamleys and Carnaby Street all on his own. Miranda got into the habit of doing imitations, and Liz, according to her father, acquired "a somewhat womanly air of expectation." All of them, he decided, were "turning a touch cosmopolitan." Mary picked out a trendy khaki pantsuit at Harrods; John found a pair of shoes at Russell and Bromley and was fitted for a suit at stylish Mayfair tailor Cyril A. Castle; they bought a new family car, a huge green Citroën sedan they shipped back to Ipswich at the end of their stay.

Mary was confronted with the task of keeping house in a strange city. Shopping for six with just a basket under her arm was a challenge in a neighborhood composed almost exclusively of mansions; to fetch groceries, she walked up to Camden Town. A malfunctioning washing machine meant that she did the laundry in the bathtub. As John conceded in a letter to Maxwell, their elegant house was "full of unworkable antiques and devices." It was the sort of property that generally housed foreign diplomats and high-flying executives who employed servants to look after the housekeeping details. The rent, moreover, was "princely": £455 a month, which looks innocuous but translates, in today's money, to roughly $10,000, a staggering sum, considering that they stayed in London for ten months. The payments were made by André Deutsch Ltd. out of Updike's account, which, luckily, was well stocked with pounds sterling earned from the seven books he'd published in Great Britain since *Rabbit, Run*.

Paying that kind of exorbitant rent, and knowing he could comfortably afford it, stirred up his misgivings about prosperity and sophistication. He was at times suspicious of the satisfaction he derived from having fulfilled his ambitions. Writing to Maxwell from London, from the splendor of his Regency terrace, he brooded about the fact that he was now irrefutably "successful"—"the adjective I hear since *Couples*." Success, he declared, was not the proper aim of writing; he wondered whether it was promoting in him "a kind of rotundity not only in the mirror but in the spirit." These grumblings shouldn't necessarily be taken at face value—he hadn't actually gained any weight; there was no visible sign of the dread "rotundity," and besides, he was feeling feverish, a condition he blamed on some chestnuts in syrup he'd eaten at supper the night before. When he was feeling ill, or after a disappointment or a perceived slight—in short, when he was feeling sorry for himself—he would feign indifference to his accomplishments and offer to give up his career. On this particular occasion, perhaps feeling a touch homesick, he allowed his musings on success to segue into a familiar refrain: "It occurs to me the world would not be significantly poorer if I stopped writing altogether. Only a bottomless capacity for envy keeps me going. That and the pleasure of reading proofs and designing book jackets." To anyone who didn't know him, these dramatic renunciations and self-recriminations could be somewhat alarming. After a string of *New Yorker* rejections in early 1958—but in the same month that *The Carpentered Hen* was published—he announced to Howard Moss with apparent finality, "[A]s a light verse writer I am through." Moss didn't panic, partly because along with his letter Updike enclosed a poem. Two decades later, Roger Angell was semi-spooked by a humorous aside from the magazine's most prolific contributor: "I may have reached the age," wrote the forty-seven-year-old Updike, "when I should hang up my short-story shoes along with my light-verse Keds, and turn to the slippers of the multi-volume memoir." In time, self-deprecation became a kind of tic; his submissions, in the last decades, were more often than not accompanied by the suggestion that the well had run dry, inspiration had deserted him, his talent was worn out, only hard work was keeping him going, and surely this story or poem would be the end of his writing career. In the early seventies he complained of feeling "like each thing is produced on the verge of silence and like each thing is the last thing I can think of to say." His Beckett-like tone of resignation and disappointment was a tease; he was playing it for laughs and also, oddly, sympathy.

There was no sign, in the fall of 1968, that the well was running dry. He quickly reestablished his work routine, an anchor that helped him settle easily in strange surroundings. He bought a new typewriter and a stamp bearing the Cumberland Terrace address. (It's possible that he remains the only resident of a snazzy Regent's Park terrace ever to personalize his stationery with a rubber stamp.) The first story he wrote in London, "The Corner," is firmly rooted in Ipswich—literally in his backyard—a sign that he was missing it. A minor car accident supplies the story line, but really "The Corner," as the title suggests, is about a place; Updike explained to Maxwell that he wanted the neighborhood houses and automobiles to substitute for people. The final sentence offers a retreating perspective in the style of James Joyce or Thornton Wilder: "the corner is one among many on the map of the town, and the town is a dot on the map of the state, and the state a mere patch on the globe, and the globe invisible from any of the stars overhead." He was clearly very conscious of being three thousand miles from home. The second story he wrote, "Cemeteries," is also rooted in place—many places, actually. It skips here and there with a death-denying restlessness, visiting graveyards around the world, in Soviet Georgia, London, Cairo, the West Indies. This "necrotic meditation" ends close to home, first at the family burial plot in Plowville, in the company of his mother, who's halfheartedly trying to convince him that he should be buried alongside his parents and grandparents; then he's in Ipswich, giving his son a bicycle-riding lesson along the "ample smooth roadways of asphalt" at the top of the town cemetery. When he sent it to Maxwell, Updike was quite sure that "Cemeteries" was a short story, and he was surprised when it was rejected. Though *Transatlantic Review* eventually published it, he left it out of *The Early Stories*, having reclassified it as nonfiction.

In early November, he and Mary voted at the U.S. embassy in Grosvenor Square—the second successive presidential election in which he had cast his ballot abroad. In Moscow four years earlier he had voted for Lyndon Johnson; in London, he backed the losing candidate, Hubert Humphrey. The winner wasn't to Updike's taste; he deplored Richard Nixon's looks and his "vapid" campaign, but consoled himself with the thought that this was a president he wouldn't have to defend. Being away from home boosted his patriotism, and the anti–Vietnam War protests in London triggered his usual "underdog rage." (A week before the election, some twenty-five thousand demonstrators thronged Trafalgar Square; a large and belligerent splinter group marched on the American embassy.) When Anthony Lewis, bureau chief for *The New York Times*, invited the Updikes to a dinner party at his house in Islington, he was surprised to hear John speaking very patriotically about the United States, even venturing to support the war. "It had been years since we heard anybody talk that way," said Lewis, "and at first I thought he was teasing, because he spoke in an owlish, amusing way. He was droll, but he was being absolutely serious." As if to prove it, Updike wrote a gung ho poem about America, "Minority Report," dissenting from the bad reviews of his "beloved land":

> They say over here you are choking to death on your cities and
>   slaves,
> but they have never smelled dry turf,
> smoked Kools in a drugstore,
> or pronounced a flat "a," an honest "r."

However appealing, England reminded him that America was "the only land."

Still looking back across the Atlantic, he wrote "The Day of the Dying Rabbit," about a photographer, his wife, and their six children vacationing on an island immediately recognizable as Martha's Vineyard. A poignant, cannily observed domestic drama set in motion by the slow death of a rabbit half-killed by a neighbor's cat, it's a slice of Updike's summer vacation artfully repackaged for *The New Yorker*. Maxwell objected to the insistent references to photography—we're never allowed to forget that the narrator takes pictures for a living—but Updike held his ground, arguing for a thrifty approach to fictional resources: "having made him a

A cherished only child, Updike "soaked up strength and love."

With his mother, Linda, and his father, Wesley, circa 1940.

With his mother in Reading, Pennsylvania, circa 1947.

The sandstone farmhouse in Plowville: "The firmest house in my fiction."

With his Shillington High School classmate Joan George Zug on the night of their senior prom—they went as friends.

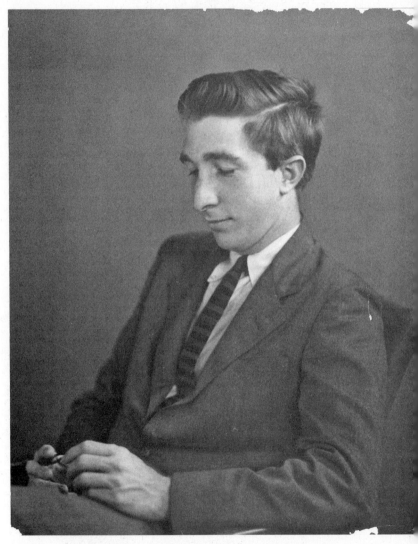
No longer a raw youth: Updike as a Harvard man.

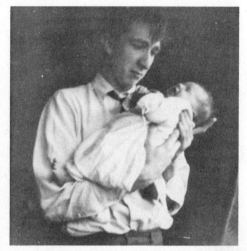

Elizabeth Updike,
born April 1, 1955.

On a visit to Plowville,
Liz on her father's
lap, David in his
grandmother's arms.

David Updike, born January 19,
1957, held precariously aloft by
his father.

Updike's Talk of the Town colleague Tony Bailey, with his wife, Margot, in 1957. Bailey and Updike met in 1955 and remained friends for life.

William Maxwell, the *New Yorker* editor who kept Updike in a state of "writerly bliss" for more than twenty years.

With Judith Jones, his Knopf editor for nearly fifty years,
at a reading in Manhattan in October 1989.

The young author at work, photographed by his brother-in-law, circa 1964.

The happy family in September 1966, posing for *Life* in the living room of the Polly Dole House.

A favorite party trick demonstrated for the *Life* photographer.

Sunday volleyball
with the Ipswich
gang, circa 1967.

Doubles with Mary in
the late sixties.

"That's *it*!" Practicing barefoot on Martha's Vineyard
in the early seventies.

With Mary in Addis Ababa in February 1973, at the end of the African lecture tour.

With Bill Luers in Caracas in January 1981.

Newly inducted into the Celebrity Walk of Fame in Fargo, North Dakota, on October 11, 1989. Though he didn't yet know it, his mother had died the day before.

With his younger son, Michael, and two grandchildren,
Trevor and Sawyer.

With Elizabeth's two sons, Anoff and Kwame Cobblah.

With Martha in December 1998.

With Ian McEwan, flanking Henry Thoreau's grave
in Sleepy Hollow Cemetery, Concord, Massachusetts,
in November 2006.

Michael Updike securing the headstone in Plow Cemetery. The poem carved on the back was written in Plowville when the author was a very young man.

Why the Telephone Wires Dip
and the Poles Are Cracked and Crooked

The old men say
young men in gray
hung this thread across our plains
acres and acres ago.

But we, the enlightened, know
in point of fact it's what remains
of the flight of a marvelous crow
no one saw—
each pole, a caw.

photographer, one has to do something with it." He next turned to material gathered abroad, from a two-week trip he made on his own to Egypt, first to Cairo to deliver a lecture at the university, then to Luxor for a Nile cruise north to Abydos and south to Aswan. The result, "I Am Dying, Egypt, Dying," is an oddly static portrait of an opaque character, Clem, an American tourist with the same itinerary as Updike's who deflects the sexual advances of various women aboard their "floating hotel," and of a man onshore, a tailor in Luxor fitting him with a caftan. Fleeting and inconclusive, this homosexual encounter troubles Clem and raises questions about his own apparently conflicted desires. The story was rejected by *The New Yorker*; shrugging off disappointment, Updike asked Maxwell to forward it directly to *Playboy*, which accepted it gratefully, happy to print anything by the author of *Couples*, the man credited with peeling back the covers and exposing the adulterous society.

Beginning in the new year, he spent many hours in the Reading Room of the British Library researching the life and times of James Buchanan, fifteenth president of the United States and the only one born in Pennsylvania, about whom he planned to write a novel. He conceived of it as a return to his native soil after the detour to Tarbox in *Couples*. Updike's obsession with Buchanan—an underrated president, in his opinion—had been brewing since the mid-sixties and would endure until the early nineties. But his habitual fluency failed him when he sat down to write historical fiction, and soon he was referring in exasperation to "the futile Buchanan project." He plugged away at it all the same; in London, especially, Buchanan was his personal link, via Pennsylvania, to America as a whole.

In February he wrote "The Deacon," about a man who can't resist involving himself in church affairs, and "Rich in Russia," his fourth Bech story and the most successful of the impersonations attempted at 59 Cumberland Terrace. Leavened perhaps by the frothy atmosphere of swinging London, Bech's report from the other side of the Iron Curtain is conspicuously devoid of Cold War angst ("There seemed no overweening reason why Russia and America, those loveable paranoid giants, could not happily share a globe so big and blue"); Bech is in an antic mood, even ready to descend into slapstick, as when he tosses his royalty rubles into the air. Newly rich Updike, writing about newly rich Bech, is having fun, supplying his stand-in with a stream of witticisms, among them this bon mot worthy of a seasoned expat: Russia, says Bech, "must be the only country in the world you can be homesick for while you're still in it." In early May, turning his attention back to Ipswich and suburban adultery, he finished "I Will Not Let Thee Go, Except Thou Bless Me," in which an unfaithful husband who's moving out of town (a Connecticut iteration of Tarbox) enacts a farewell scene with the woman who was once his mistress, the John and Joyce roles played out all over again with a kind of weary resignation.

Only when he had returned home did he write a story about London. "Bech Swings?" illustrates the usefulness of the lustful, ir-repressibly bookish Bech—and opens another window on Updike's expatriate experience. Bech allowed the carefully compartmental-ized Updike to integrate various inclinations: to unleash his libido (on the page, anyway) and to put his expanding erudition to playful use, all in the same story. Bech suffers the genteel condescension of his British publisher, J. J. Goldschmidt (André Deutsch with bits of Victor Gollancz mixed in), who says he wants to lionize him. ("I'd rather be lambified," Bech replies.) He fences with an egregious American journalist, parrying deftly but also speaking seriously about the aims of art, a good deed swiftly punished. He makes small talk with the chattering classes, appears on both BBC radio and tel-evision, gives a reading at the London School of Economics, submits to a cocktail party in his honor at the U.S. embassy—all this *à clef*, with Updike's own professional activities compressed and tweaked for dramatic effect. Updike had told Deutsch that he hated being on display, that he didn't want to become "a huckster for myself," that his book should sell itself or not at all, but he somehow ended up giving half a dozen full-dress interviews and making a succession of "appearances," live and on television. Bech's unease with his public role is a facsimile of his creator's:

It was his fault; he had wanted to be noticed, to be praised. He had wanted to be a man in the world, a "writer." For his punishment, they had made from the sticks and mud of his words a coarse large doll to question and torment, which would not have mattered except that he was trapped inside the doll, shared a name and bank account with it.

Luckily, there are perks to compensate for the "punishment" he endures as a celebrity, among them the adoration of pretty young things.

Precedent demanded that Bech have a love interest; in "Bech Swings?" Updike gives him Merissa, a diminutive twenty-seven-year-old gossip columnist who exudes an elfin femininity as treacherous as it is arousing. She takes him home from Goldschmidt's dinner party and serves up the kind of no-strings-attached sex that reeks of wish-fulfillment fantasy. Merissa is no figment of Bech's imagination; she's perfectly real: "her hand was as small as a child's, with close-cut fingernails and endearing shadows around the knuckles." And yet Bech searches reflexively for a literary source: "He felt he had seen the hand before. In a novel. *Lolita*? *Magic Mountain*?" When they make love, the sex is literally words on the page:

> He did all this in ten-point type, upon the warm white paper of her sliding skin. Poor child, under this old ogre . . . whose every experience was harassed by a fictional version of itself, whose waking life was a weary dream of echoes and erased pencil lines.

In bed, they're both ecstatically fictive.

Bech's flesh-and-blood creator enjoyed being wined and dined in London; he seized the opportunity to admire the "dreamy disdainful poise" of the local beauties, who in turn admired him—he declared them "masterful flirts." After attending a party crowded with young people, he wrote to Maxwell, "I see why they call English women birds; they chirp, and peck, and hop on one foot, leaving very precise tracks in the snow." (Bech, trying out the native lingo, calls Merissa a "bird.") Stimulated by novelty, Updike sparkled. Diana Athill found him to be "an extremely pleasant and intelligent man over the dinner-table"; she saw the Updikes "fairly often," as did André Deutsch. According to Mary, "Tony Lewis and his wife Linda sort of adopted us." The Lewises' daughter, Eliza, who was fourteen at the time, was struck by Updike's magnetism; she said, "There was this sense of tremendous intellectual energy and *fun*." The literary critic George Steiner invited Updike to a high table dinner at Churchill College, Cambridge; Steiner remembered the author being "delightful company" but felt he had to hide his inscribed copy of *Couples* from the curious eyes of his own young children.

John's parents flew over for a two-week visit in the spring, prompting a flurry of sightseeing: Canterbury Cathedral, Stonehenge, Hampton Court, Windsor Castle, the Keats House in Hampstead. The addition of Linda and Wesley meant that the Cumberland Terrace house was teeming with Updikes. Being away from Ipswich, away from their crowd of friends, made for a more concentrated family life, a domestic intensity reflected in a sequence of five short poems Updike wrote in London. "Living with a Wife" is narrowly personal; the reader feels thrust into an intimately private zone, not a place on the map, but rather an atmosphere, an evolving state of tension that binds the poet/husband to the wife he's contemplating. The poem's only punctuation is two question marks squeezed at the end of one stanza:

> You slip in and out of beauty
> and imply that nothing is wrong
> Who sent you?
> What is your assignment?

There is no answer; it's an honestly conflicted love poem, as the final stanza of the last section, "All the While," reveling in the casual intimacy of a shared life, suggests:

> Though years sneak by like children
> you stay as unaccountable
> as the underwear left to soak
> in the bowl where I brush my teeth

The tight focus on the gritty details of cohabitation reads like a confession, though the nature of the transgression is unclear. If she is "unaccountable," he is manifestly ambivalent, which may be the uncomfortable sum of what he's saying. Mary was certainly very much on John's mind. She's mentioned in most of the letters he wrote to Maxwell during the year abroad, sometimes in reference to her daily activities, but more often with regard to his work; he cites her opinion, or says he'll seek it out. She's plainly a trusted reader, an old friend, an ally in this foreign land; he may have been ambivalent about the marriage, but his faith in her literary judgment was unwavering.

The family flew back to America on June 14, 1969, all of them ready to come home. "I have felt like a balloon on too long a tether," Updike wrote, repeating (as he did only very rarely) a sentence lifted from a letter to Maxwell. It's no surprise that the whole adventure had seemed to him somehow unreal—in the nine months abroad he was almost constantly in motion. In Egypt he toured the mosques of Cairo and sailed the Nile. In Holland he saw six Vermeers that were new to him, including *View of Delft*. For Christmas, he took Mary and the children skiing in Austria. In Denmark they visited the haunts of John's hero Kierkegaard. In Milan, with André Deutsch, he celebrated the Italian publication of *Couples* (*Coppie*). A two-part Easter holiday began in Morocco, where they made an exhausting five-hundred-mile dash in a rented car from Tangier to Agadir; they then flew to Paris for two days, but were too weary of living out of suitcases to enjoy it much. They went up the Eiffel Tower and strolled in the Tuileries. Updike found that the strength of the French franc made the city painfully expensive; "a meal for six," he groused, "cost roughly the price of an English suit."

This traveling frenzy is a compact version of the next four decades. Not a year went by without several trips abroad, some of them purely vacations, many tied to work. Eight months after their return to Ipswich, the whole family flew to Tortola for some winter sun; four months later John took Liz with him to Japan and Korea to attend the PEN International Congress in Seoul, the first of a long series of conferences and symposia in distant lands. As he once remarked about the business of author appearances, media events, and other marketing ploys, "What frightens me really is not how much I dislike it but how much I kind of like it. It's kind of fun." The topic in Seoul was "Humor in Fiction." The next year, in addition to a holiday in Florence (with Mary and André Deutsch and Deutsch's girlfriend), he traveled to Venezuela to give a talk on Rómulo Gallegos's *Doña Bárbara* and the American Western. In early 1973, funded by a Fulbright grant and accompanied by Mary, he traversed central Africa from Ghana to Ethiopia, delivering at intervals along the way a lecture on the American writer's cultural situation. (The African lecture proved awkward; he found himself "shedding large chunks of it" as it dawned on him that the one thing audiences in sub-Saharan nations did not want to hear about was "parallelisms with the United States.") In March 1974 he flew alone to Australia for the weeklong Adelaide Festival of Arts and gave a speech entitled "Why Write?"

Bech followed in his footsteps.* Two stories, "Bech Third-Worlds It" and "Australia and Canada," track the movements across five continents of an author promoting his work (and his country) in a jet-lagged blur. Updike cuts back and forth between locations (and hemispheres), giving the stories the kaleidoscopic feel of scenery partially glimpsed in a haze of fatigue and disorientation. However tired, however far from home, Bech is always Bech. Embattled, sensitive to slights against his work and his nation, he fights back with displays of teasing wit, allowing on occasion a flare-up of the "ugly patriotism" he shares with his creator. He is charming—women love him; children, too. He marvels at the out-of-body sensation media attention provokes in him, and nevertheless performs flawlessly. He pays minute attention to any female (even when the female pays no attention to him). He bristles at any hint of male competition. He suffers sharp pangs of existential dread. Looking back at the end of

---

* Or was it the other way around? From Australia, Updike wrote a friendly postcard to Maxwell reporting that the weather was balmy and the skirts short; "Henry Bech is bleary," he added, "but in good voice."

his career, after being awarded a Nobel Prize nobody seems to believe he deserves, he thinks, "A few countries, a few women."

To Maxwell, Updike expressed the hope that each country he visited would yield a short story. Not quite, but nearly. Less immediately rewarding, but useful in the long run, was the authority that extensive travel bestowed on him. Thanks to a decade of cultural mission work and literary hobnobbing, by the mid-seventies he'd been practically everywhere; if he happened to go somewhere new, he could assimilate the novelty with dizzying speed and assurance. When he first saw Helsinki in 1987, for instance, he confidently compared it with Copenhagen, Stockholm, and Oslo, hatching opinions with the unhesitating conviction of a seasoned traveler. It was with the same easy confidence that he turned a slight acquaintance with a country or region into a novel, a feat he accomplished with both *The Coup* (1978) and *Brazil* (1994).

In January 1973, a month before journeying to Africa, he drew up a new will, just as he had done before setting out for Russia. (This time he named Judith Jones as his literary executor.) Despite the usual jitters—a sense of insecurity sharpened in Nairobi—the trip went smoothly, with Kenya providing both urban unease and the wildlife bonanza of a brief photo safari. Mary remembered that she and John weren't getting along well—certainly not as well as they had been on the Russia trip. On their return, Updike flew down to Washington, tanned and long-haired, to deliver a public debriefing at the State Department, where he explained that he was never happy with the lecture he'd planned to deliver in each of five countries visited, and that eventually he'd substituted remarks about himself—which seemed to be what his audience wanted. He looked back with some satisfaction on an experience that, he later said, "slightly enlarged my sense of human possibilities."

It also helped expand his literary range. He waited three years before mining his African expedition for material he could use in a novel; the four weeks spent traveling eastward across the continent were essential to the invention of Kush, the landlocked sub-Saharan nation, not unlike Chad or Ethiopia, at the heart of *The Coup*. Updike supplemented memories of his journey with copious research—

this is the first of his novels to include an acknowledgments page listing source materials. He also let his fancy roam more freely than ever before—*The Coup* is his first novel set abroad, but more important, it's his most radically experimental novel; the many critics who seemed incapable of resisting the urge to call it a "departure" weren't just pointing to the exotic setting. Updike was deliberately turning his back on the domestic realism readers and critics expected from him. For the first time in more than a decade, he produced a novel in which adultery played no significant part.

The Coup was liberating in all sorts of ways, opening up space and time, making room for a wild freedom of invention. A land of "delicate, delectable emptiness," Kush covers nearly half a million square miles and seems to be exempt from conventional chronology ("even memory thins in this land"), so that it's difficult, sometimes impossible, for the reader to track the passage of days and years (though the action, we're told, occurs sometime around "the last year of Richard Nixon's presidency, with flashbacks to the Eisenhower era"). On a map, Kush "suggests . . . an angular skull whose cranium is the empty desert"; it's less a geographical entity with an unfolding history than a fantasy played out in a jumbled, dreamlike sequence.

Whose head dreams the dream that is Kush? Our narrator is Colonel Hakim Félix Ellelloû, the country's deposed dictator, who is now writing his memoirs—sometimes in the first person, sometimes in the third—in a seaside café in Nice, "dreaming behind his sunglasses, among the clouds of Vespa exhaust, trying to remember, to relive." As Joyce Carol Oates noted in her review of the novel, *The Coup* is at heart Nabokovian; behind Ellelloû stands Charles Kinbote, the exiled ruler who scribbles in the margins of *Pale Fire*. Within the framework of Updike's novel, Colonel Ellelloû's opposite number, so to speak, is Colonel Sirin, the officer in charge of a secret Soviet missile installation buried in the Kush hinterland; Sirin was the nom de plume adopted by Nabokov in his twenties and thirties, while he was still writing in Russian. The outrageous pyrotechnics of Ellelloû's language ("mandarin explosions," Updike called them) bring to mind Nabokov's more florid moments. Consider, for example, this dazzling description of the Kush landscape as glimpsed from the air-conditioned comfort of Ellelloû's presidential Mercedes: "the low, somehow liquid horizon, its stony dun slumber scarcely disturbed by a distant cluster of thatched roofs encircled by euphorbia, or by the sudden looming of a roadside hovel, a rusted can on a stick advertising the poisonous and interdicted native beer." This is Updike on a tear, spooling out his prose, letting his sentences take whatever rococo shape strikes his fancy.

As the presence of Soviet missiles deep inside Kush suggests, domestic politics are inseparable from global politics, the push and pull of the superpowers waging their Cold War, what Ellelloû calls "the paramilitary foolery between the two superparanoids." A day after leaving the Soviet installation, he thinks he spies in the distance "two golden parabolas": the golden arches of McDonald's, inevitable symbol of American cultural hegemony. The Russians' missile silos are no match for the insidious encroachment of their enemy's crass commercialism. Ellelloû is rabidly anti-American, a prejudice that gave Updike license to satirize both anti-American rhetoric and those aspects of the national culture he himself deplored. When Ellelloû calls the United States a "fountainhead of obscenity and glut," we hear the echo of Updike's laughter and a little bit, too, of his scorn.

He wrote *The Coup* in part because he had things to say about Africa and about geopolitics, and in part for more personal, not to say selfish, reasons. He wanted to go back to Africa (which he eventually did, for two and a half weeks in the spring of 1984); inventing Kush was a way of taking a trip without leaving New England. And he also wanted to explore his own domestic experience, distanced by an exotic setting. One reason adultery is not an issue in the novel is that Ellelloû has four wives. When Updike began *The Coup*, he and Mary had already filed for divorce; by the time he finished, he was married to his second wife, Martha.

FOR MORE THAN three decades, Updike and Martha traveled indefatigably. Not a year went by without two or three foreign excursions—

and sometimes, when Updike was promoting a new book, several more. New scenery still thrilled him, and still stimulated his writing: "Out-of-the-way places," he noted in the mid-nineties, "seem to excite me to my best and brightest prose." And if a foreign publisher or the sponsors of a far-flung festival offered sufficient monetary inducement, avarice compelled him to say yes. Posing as a writer, he complained, often paid better than staying home and actually writing. But whether he was traveling for money or for pleasure, some part of him always wanted to be back at his desk, absorbed in his work.

Six months before his second marriage, while he was still writing *The Coup*, he escorted his widowed mother and the sixteen-year-old Miranda to Spain for eight days, mostly to satisfy Linda's craving for things Spanish and to facilitate her research for yet another unpublishable historical novel. Arriving in the capital, he suffered from insomnia, and took advantage of his sleeplessness to write a remarkable sequence of eight sonnets that mix impressions of Madrid, Toledo, Ávila, and Valladolid with yearning for Martha back at home. Howard Moss of *The New Yorker* thought "Spanish Sonnets" contained some of the best poetry Updike had ever written. Certainly there's a bracing freedom and a daring to some of the lines:

> The land is dry enough to make the rivers
> dramatic here. You say you love me;
> as the answer to your thirst, I splash,
> fall, and flow, a varied cool color.
> Here fountains celebrate intersections,
> and our little Fiats eddy and whirl
> on the way to siesta and back.
> They say don't drink tap water, but I do.

The imagery is jumbled like the cascading thoughts of the sleep-deprived.

After the trip to Spain, which figures in a late short story as a "fraught and sad . . . expedition," there were no more family excursions to foreign countries, no more holidays abroad with the Updike children (who by the eighties were grown up and beginning to have children of their own). He traveled either alone, alone with Martha, or with Martha on guided tours. He also went on a handful of rain-sodden golfing trips to Scotland and Ireland organized by the Myopia Hunt Club.*

In January 1981 he paid a second visit to Venezuela, this time with Martha. They were the guests of Bill Luers, the young diplomat who looked after Updike in Russia and was now the American ambassador in Caracas. Luers sent the tourists on an expedition, via helicopter, to see the remote and spectacular Angel Falls, but the helicopter crashed as it was landing atop Auyán-Tepui. In his memoirs, Updike gives a dramatic account of the accident:

> As it hoveringly descended, with its battering big rotor blades, toward the cross painted on a flat rock as a landing field, it swerved out of control and plopped down on a nearby set of rocks shaped like diagonally stacked loaves of bread. The amazed helicopter, its rotors still cumbersomely battering the air, came to rest at a sharp tilt, and the tipped interior of the plane was flooded with excited Spanish in which the word *puerta* distinctly sounded. I was next to the door, and deduced that the general wish was that I open it and jump out; this I did, running out from under the whirling blades. I assumed that my youthful wife would irresistibly follow, but evidently I should have stopped and let her jump onto me, for when another man, an officer of the American Embassy, saw her balk and attempted to help her down, both fell, and she sprained her ankle so severely I had to push her, a day or two later, in a wheelchair through the Caracas airport.

Updike was pleased by his "inner coolness" in the midst of this emergency, but the anecdote, as recited at dinner parties in years to

---

* A typically damp and blustery week in Scotland in October 1990 inspired one of his best golf stories, "Farrell's Caddie."

come, turned into a tale of Updike's cowardice. It was in any case not the only unfortunate story to emerge from this South American adventure. Four months after his return, *The New Yorker* ran a travel piece, "Venezuela for Visitors," in which Updike anatomized the country's class system with broad satiric strokes. He begins with this: "All Venezuela, except for the negligible middle class, is divided between the Indians (*los indios*) and the rich (*los ricos*)," and ends with this: "*Los indios* and *los ricos* rarely achieve contact. When they do, *mestizos* result, and the exploitation of natural resources. In such lies the future of Venezuela." In between, there's more of the same facetiousness. Needless to say, the Venezuelans who read it were unimpressed with the way he chose to repay their hospitality.

Five years later, Updike was again Luers's guest, in Prague this time, on his own and behaving with his accustomed good manners. Two notable events from this trip to Communist Czechoslovakia are recorded with only minimal adjustment in "Bech in Czech": a visit to Kafka's grave and a book signing at the U.S. embassy. On the day Updike arrived, Luers whisked him in the embassy limousine to the "newer" Jewish cemetery on the outskirts of the city, where Kafka is buried with his parents—but the gates were locked shut, the caretaker unmoved by the ambassador's flag-waving assertion of diplomatic privilege. Luers was about to give up when two young men in plaster-splattered overalls appeared with a key. Although Luers did his best to convince them that he and his guest must be allowed in, his appeals were met with blank indifference—until Updike's name was mentioned, whereupon the men exclaimed, "Updike! *Rabbit, Run*! We love his works!" The men were only too happy to unlock the cemetery gates for the distinguished author and escort him to Kafka's grave. Though gratifying, this unexpected display of literary ardor was less stirring than the long, patient line of Czechs of all ages, many of them young, spilling out of the embassy and onto the sidewalk, waiting for Updike to sign tattered volumes of his work. They waited in plain sight, despite the presence of policemen taking photographs. (The Communist authorities kept a keen eye on anyone eager for an American's autograph.)

Updike bestows all this adulation on Henry Bech, who feels flattered and flustered—and inadequate. He feels like an impostor—Updike's cue to supply him with this teasing reflection: "That was why, he supposed, you travelled to places like this: to encounter fictional selves, the refreshing false ideas of you that strangers hold in their mind." As if poor Bech didn't have enough to contend with, he has to cope with the baggage of his ethnic identity: "For a Jew, to move through post-war Europe is to move through hordes of ghosts, vast animated crowds that, since 1945, are not there, not there at all—up in smoke." Here of course, Updike is the impostor. He and Bech combine to produce a kind of comic postmodern duet:

> More fervently than he was a Jew, Bech was a writer, a literary man, and in this dimension, too, he felt a cause for unease. He was a creature of the third person, a character. A character suffers from the fear that he will become boring to the author, who will simply let him drop.

In bed on his last night at the ambassador's residence, a sumptuous palace built by a Jewish banker whose family was forced to flee Hitler's menace, Bech panics, his sense of imposture and of his own insignificance magnified by the extreme seriousness of literary endeavor in a country ruled by a "Kafkaesque" Communist state. He worries that he will "cease to exist," and Updike makes a tidy package of the whole by looping back to the phrase he uses as a synecdoche for the Holocaust: Bech worries that he, too, will go "up in smoke."

Just before his sixtieth birthday, in March 1992, Updike spent a week touring Brazil on his own, sampling a small section of a country the size of the continental United States. He visited São Paulo, the well-preserved colonial mining town of Ouro Prêto, Brasília, and Rio de Janeiro, where his Copacabana hotel room overlooked the beach, which he described to Joyce Carol Oates as "one of the globe's great animate spectacles." Simultaneously enchanted and repelled by the easy hedonism of the near-naked crowd, excited by the idea of a world of mixed skin colors, he used this glimpse of "teeming bodies" as the starting point of his new novel. His week of sightseeing was the impetus for *Brazil*, but not the principal ingredient; much of the book is set in parts of the country where Updike never set foot. He acknowledged his reliance on other books, principally *Rebellion in the Backlands*, by Euclides da Cunha, and *Tristes Tropiques*, by Claude Lévi-Strauss. He benefited from the liberating influence of that great South American literary export, magic realism, and from his hard-earned familiarity with the theme that obsessed him during the sixties: courtly love as exemplified by his favorite archetypes of illicit passion, Tristan and Iseult.

Tristão and Isabel, Updike's hero and heroine, meet on Copacabana Beach in the mid-sixties. Their love overcomes barriers of race and class—he is poor and black; she is rich and white—survives marriage and children, and endures for more than two decades, longevity that would have surprised Denis de Rougemont. It certainly strained the patience of many book reviewers, who felt that the narrative petered out toward the end, particularly after our hero and heroine, thanks to powerful sorcery, swap skin colors. It would be unfair to say that Updike was taking it easy—he was never less than hardworking—but he did think of *Brazil* as a lark, a "little" novel with enough open space to let his imagination roam free. Critics who approached it hoping to match their own high seriousness with a correspondingly lofty literary tome were baffled or dismayed; some were angered. It collected fewer friendly reviews than any other Updike novel.

Just after he finished *Brazil*, he and Martha went on a quasi-educational two-week cruise of the Mediterranean, complete with onboard lecturers—"ill-advised" was Updike's verdict. Nine months later, "Cruise," a slight, sour fantasy, appeared in *The New Yorker*. For three years running in the late nineties, they spent a couple of weeks traipsing around Italy on their own, peering at churches and picture galleries, indulging their shared passion for art. These Italian adventures resulted in a clutch of poems and a single short story, "Aperto, Chiuso"—two words that govern the tourist experience in Italy. A quarreling couple features in many of the stories Updike set abroad; in this case the sightseers bicker from beginning to end.

In April 2002, on a trip to southern Spain, Updike and Martha were mugged on the narrow streets of Seville, pushed over by purse snatchers. Updike smacked into the asphalt facedown, and his right eyebrow was cut open; at the hospital a doctor closed the wound with nine stitches. A month later, his eyebrow still occasionally hurt—but a short story followed in due course, "The Accelerating Expansion of the Universe," with a blow-by-blow description of the mugging. (The narrator regrets not having dragged the culprit "down to the dirty asphalt with him, and pulverized his . . . face with his fists.")

When their destination was more exotic, they signed up for expensive guided tours. In September 1998, they were in China for three weeks under the auspices of the Smithsonian Institution. The *New Yorker* essay he wrote promptly on his return is as much about the experience of being on a tour—lumped with 120 others and shepherded by three bilingual tour guides and a tour manager from the Smithsonian—as about the vast, crowded, "still imperfectly tourist-friendly" nation pivoting from communism to "superheated mercantilism."

They were back in Asia two years later, and again in 2006, when they spent two weeks temple hopping in India—more curated group travel. Updike confessed to a friend that he found the Indian expedition "existentially damaging"; it forced him to contemplate "how many people the world contains, and what weird and dank religions they hold to as shields against their hunger and struggle." Resilient as ever, he made efficient use of the experience in a short story called "The Apparition," about a museum-sponsored tour of the splendors of South India.

In his seventies, he was less and less eager to travel. Although he managed to glean new material from every destination, the law of diminishing returns was at work. After the trip to India, he complained, "It shatters my composure to leave my little shell . . . but my wife's lust for adventure and warmer weather drives me to it." He felt he'd seen the world; Martha wanted to see still more, so he accompanied her to Cambodia in 2007, and to Egypt and Jordan the year after that. The first third of his final novel, *The Widows of Eastwick* (2008), is essentially a sequence of travelogues. The narrative takes us to the Canadian Rockies, where the Updikes had toured for ten days in September 2006; then to Egypt; then to China—all to see the sights. The Updikes' last foreign excursion was a three-week tour of Russia and the Baltic republics in September 2008. It came too late to be transformed into fiction.

> In Ipswich my impersonation of a normal person became as good as
> I could make it.
>
> —*Self-Consciousness* (1989)

VIII.

Tarbox Redux

A thick, smoky summer beam, three hundred years old, held up the
ceiling of the Updikes' living room at 26 East Street. On the underside of the beam were an outsize nut and washer; this hardware—
also antique in appearance, though of more recent vintage—was
fastened to the end of a long bolt, an iron rod that ran all the way
up to a truss in the attic, a triangular configuration of timbers that
provided structural support. Updike used to tell his children that if
they loosened the nut the whole house would collapse: "If that nut
goes, everything goes." They never tried it—and eventually, after
a dozen years in the Polly Dole House, the family left East Street.
Later, unable to resist a dramatic flourish, Updike tacked an ending
onto his little fable: "Once we moved, things fell apart. The big nut
and bolt were holding us together as well."

John and Mary had been thinking about moving before they
left for their year in London. They looked at some new houses in
and around Ipswich, grand and spacious dwellings, and also at plots
of land on which they could build. Nothing was quite right, and
they put the plan on hold. Then, in the fall of 1969, several months
after their return from England, they were offered the chance to

buy a property they knew of and liked, a handsome white clapboard house, built in the late nineteenth century, with a broad, symmetrical facade. Standing on the site of an old farmhouse that had burned down, the house came with a barn, a cottage, and seven and a half acres of land with waterfront access to a tidal creek—all this not much more than a mile from the center of Ipswich. They bought it without hesitation.

The children, they felt, needed more space; their bedrooms in the Polly Dole House were tiny, as was the backyard, where there was scarcely room to kick a soccer ball. The noisy, busy corner was a hazard for the family dog, and for the younger children, too. But it was the first house the family had owned and the only home Michael and Miranda had ever known, so there were mixed feelings about the move, regrets about leaving the place that had sheltered them for so long. A pack of kids roamed the East Street neighborhood from yard to yard, the Updike children among them. From the new house at the end of Labor-in-Vain Road, it was a twenty-minute walk to the center of town; the children could bicycle, but their playmates were no longer on the doorstep. According to Mary, the idea behind the move was not to put distance between the young Updikes and downtown Ipswich, and yet at the back of John's mind may have been a protective impulse similar to the one that prompted Linda to lead her thirteen-year-old son out of Shillington and into his rural Plowville exile.

Liz was fifteen when the family moved out of East Street, David thirteen. Not exactly rebellious, the oldest Updike child held herself aloof from her siblings. "I sort of ignored them," Liz remembered. "I led a separate life, a little bit." During the last year in the Polly Dole House, she began to make life somewhat difficult for her parents, developing relationships that they may have thought of as inappropriate but couldn't bring themselves to criticize. They had always been very relaxed about discipline, allowing their children wonderful freedom to roam. Although Liz remained ignorant of her parents' extramarital affairs, she was dimly aware that they were "racy"; she noted, for instance, that they played Twister at their cocktail parties. "They had a friend's painting of a naked man on a beach hanging in the dining room—very muted colors, more suggestive than graphic—but I couldn't handle it; it was just so weird for me." When she was ten and her Girl Scout troop came to dinner, she asked her parents to take the painting down. This prudish streak was later offset by typical adolescent defiance: "I remember saying I wanted anarchy in the house. My father was angry—that ruffled his feathers." As for David, he was a sensitive child, bright and athletic, but he was prone to unexplained headaches and fits of bad temper. Distracted by work, by his gang of friends, by his many flings, Updike was only fitfully aware of his children's problems.

And yet the first story he wrote on his return to Ipswich suggests that he may have been a little worried about his children blending too seamlessly with the local kids, and newly ambivalent about the town itself. A Tarbox sketch in which the narrator speaks with a collective voice (imagine the town elders acting as a chorus), "The Hillies" offers an ironic assessment of the interaction between "the town" and a flock of young people ("the hillies") squatting on the slope between the main street and the hilltop green. As usual, Updike was writing about actual events. In the summer of 1969, two years after Haight-Ashbury's Summer of Love, bands of disaffected youths were making their presence felt in town centers all over the country; Ipswich was no exception. When some local kids were evicted from their hangout in the corner drugstore, they took up residence on the slope of the hill overlooking the downtown. The town fretted about this obtrusive local manifestation of the counterculture. Updike, who walked past them on the way to and from his office, saw this motley crowd up close every day—but took a wider view.

His sketch is political and literary; the antiwar protests and race riots of the late sixties hover in the background, as does the shade of Nathaniel Hawthorne, who would haunt Updike for the next three decades, supplying material for a trio of novels. The hillies, we're told, aren't exactly hippies or flower children; less exotically, they're the town's own offspring, some of them from prominent local families. A disturbance but not a danger, they "make no threat-

ening moves" and yet exude "the hostile strangeness of marauders."
Though they take drugs and drink alcohol and doubtless engage in
carnal activity ("it was supposed that their congregation was sexual
in motive," the narrator primly pronounces), what really rankles is
their refusal to embrace the American way: "The town discovers
itself scorned by . . . an implacable 'no' spoken here between its two
traditional centers"—that is, between the main street (commerce)
at the bottom of the hill and the church and meetinghouse (civic
society) at the top.

To Updike, Ipswich scorned was Shillington scorned. The hillies were saying no to the steadfast, beneficent world order young
Johnny had basked in as a boy; they were saying no to his patriotism,
no to the America he cherished. If his instinctive response to the
"vague mockery" of this ragtag gathering was to condemn it, his second thoughts complicated the issue. Most of the sketch is about the
different reactions the hillies provoke, and the range is wide enough
to undermine any consensus on the significance of their very visible
presence. Even our collective narrator's contribution is suspect: "We
need our self-respect," he announces. "That is what is eroding on the
hill—the foundations of our lives, the identities our industry and
acquisitiveness have heaped up behind the flag's blessing." Is identity
compounded of industry and acquisitiveness? Is the flag's blessing,
earlier identified as the pursuit of happiness, merely a license to earn
and consume? Are these the foundations of self-respect? The hillie
who declares that he was driven from his own home by "the stench
of ego" may have a point.

The somber final paragraph does nothing to answer the questions raised by the hillies' implicit rebuke. In the town, we're told,
"Fear reigns, and impatience." Updike makes fun of the panic of the
Tarbox bourgeoisie, many of them busy erecting fences and adding
locks to their doors and shutters to their windows. This defensive
reaction harks back to the first sentence of the sketch, which describes the town's origins (and by extension, the nation's): "Tarbox
was founded, in 1634, as an agricultural outpost of the Boston col-
ony, by men fearful of attack." The Pilgrim fathers' fear is with us
still; only the source is new: the threat now comes from within.

The hillies are also afraid, worried that the establishment will strike back: "They are getting ready for our attack."*

That's the last line of the story. The gloom of the ending, with its fresh threat of violence, comes as a surprise after the amusing vacillations of the earlier passages, the air of measured, historical exposition comically scrambled by the clamor of competing perspectives. Both the lighter and the darker strands smack of Hawthorne. But the tip-off, in case the reader missed it, is the hillies' "implacable 'no,'" which recalls the "grand truth" Melville famously pronounced about Hawthorne: "He says No! in thunder." (Hawthorne, whose "no" is that of a solitary individual refusing any compromise with conventional wisdom and the status quo, is emphatically *not* a proto-hillie; he mistrusted crowds of any kind.) The congregation of quasi-hippies gathered on the hill in Ipswich, in close proximity to sites associated with the town's Puritan heritage, set off a train of historical association that led back to the author of *The Scarlet Letter*—which Updike liked to call "the first American masterpiece." Like Hawthorne, he was measuring present-day America against a more robust past. Neither the hillies nor the town's bourgeoisie were made of the same stern stuff as the Pilgrim fathers.

When Updike made fun of the paranoia stirred up by the hillies, he was caricaturing his own discomfort; his description of the young people's pale faces smeared with dirt raises the suspicion that he felt viscerally offended by them. As he often remarked, he was alarmed and disturbed by the sixties rhetoric of social protest and revolt; he found the whole concept of civil disobedience "antithetical" to his fifties education. In one of the more startling passages from "The Hillies," the narrator reminds us that the young people causing all the ruckus "came from our own homes"; he then asks, "And in honesty do we want them back?" Whatever the answer— the question is layered with irony, the narrator's attitude dubious at best—it's safe to say that Updike would have been dismayed to see his own children mingling with the hillies.

---

* This isn't as paranoid as it sounds. "The Hillies" was finished at the end of August 1969, a little more than eight months before the Kent State shootings.

When they left East Street, the Updikes' "genteel bohemian" lifestyle didn't change much. And yet the move to Labor-in-Vain Road was a step up, a conspicuous sign of affluence. Updike was by now a millionaire, and was making as much money every year as any of the leading American writers, with the possible exception of Norman Mailer. Updike's wealth was in itself a reason for leaving the Polly Dole House and the busy small-town corner on which it stood. If he could easily afford a more substantial property, shouldn't he then buy one? Upward mobility is the cornerstone of the American dream; to opt out would be to echo the hillies' scorn.

The new house, for which he paid $85,000, was visible proof that, at least in worldly terms, the labors of John Updike were not in vain. One can tell at a glance that it is a splendidly situated property: the house is perched on a gentle rise above a tidal inlet known as Gould's Creek. At the back, a long, deep screened-in porch, L-shaped, looks out over a wide expanse of saltwater marsh, with no other house in sight. Owned in the thirties by a playwright named George Brewer Jr. (who cowrote *Dark Victory*, on which the Bette Davis film is based), it's the kind of house bound to appeal to an author. Though only a mile from town and in plain sight of Labor-in-Vain Road, it's secluded, calm, and peaceful, with marshes and the ebb and flow of the tidal creek providing ever-changing scenery. While still in the midst of moving in, Updike was already writing to Maxwell about the play of light on the water outside his windows; a couple of months later, he was boasting about the utter tranquillity of his surroundings, turning his delight into a complaint: "It is so quiet in my new house a cat mewing wakes me right up, just in time for the sun to blast through the window at 5:30."

Proud of the new property, he took on responsibility for up-keep of the house and outbuildings; for the mowing, pruning, and trimming; the putting up and taking down of storm windows and window screens. He liked to be useful around the house, a Mr. Fixit; practical carpentry skills mattered to him. "Enemies of a House," a poem written in the late eighties, demonstrates considerable expertise about the consequences of shoddy home maintenance. On Labor-in-Vain Road, he built a wooden pier to improve access to the creek. When a new stove was delivered for the kitchen, he con-structed the base for it and extended the existing counters. When Liz decided she wanted to keep chickens, he built the coop; when Miranda decided she wanted to keep sheep, he built the pen. (There were two sheep, Madeline and Medea.)

It's hard to believe that someone as prolific as Updike, who guided his writing through the editing and production process with such meticulous care and without the assistance of an agent; who read voraciously, as though cramming constantly for a final exam in universal knowledge; who carried on voluminous correspondence with a wide array of professional colleagues, played golf twice a week, volunteered for numerous civic duties, and enjoyed an agitated social and romantic life, also found time to wrestle the vines off the roof of the barn or to fit a new door in the living room, taking extra care to make sure the latch worked properly. Even so, there was work that he simply couldn't do, such as replacing leaky, antiquated pipes. For that he hired a plumber, who not only fixed the pipes but also supplied the impetus for "Plumbing," a story written a month after they moved into the new house. If "The Hillies" gives us a glimpse of public Ipswich, a scene played out in an open, communal space, "Plumbing" shows us what's happening indoors, out of sight, in the privacy of the family home.

About a decade after he'd written it, Updike decided, based on "internal evidence," that "Plumbing" was a Maples story, that the unnamed narrator's voice belongs to Richard Maple.* The old plumber doing work on the Maples' new house marvels at the work-manship of an "antique joint" and warns about the seam on a care-lessly mounted soil pipe: "Don't touch it. It'll start to bleed." This is no ordinary plumber: "He is a poet. Where I see only a flaw, a vexing imperfection that will cost me money, he gazes fondly, mus-ing upon the eternal presences of corrosion and flow." His fondness for "tender meditations" seems to be catching; soon Richard, too, is waxing philosophical: "We think we have bought living space and a

---

* Updike hadn't written a Maples story since "Eros Rampant," in 1966; his next would be "Sublimating," written a year after "Plumbing," in May 1971.

view when in truth we have bought a maze, a history, an archeology of pipes and cut-ins and traps and valves." When Updike revised the story in the late seventies, he added a parallel sentence to make explicit the connection between domestic plumbing and human anatomy: "We think we are what we think and see but in truth we are upright bags of tripe." Mortality and the transience of the material world are the overarching theme, but another concern is the state of Richard and Joan Maple's marriage, a joint less well crafted than the one that caught the plumber's eye; it's a pipe with a bleeding seam.

The Maples' old house is a mile away. Emptied of the family's belongings, it holds only the "ghosts" of their past selves; Richard imagines these ghosts arranged in a series of tableaux that together sum up the dozen years they lived there. First there's the husband and wife at two o'clock in the morning on Easter Sunday; drunk, still dressed for the formal dinner party they've evidently just left, they are hiding chocolate eggs in the backyard for the children's Easter egg hunt. Another scene shows the husband saying prayers with his children; a younger child prays with him, an older child refuses. In the next tableau the husband and wife quarrel bitterly in the large living room, weeping, exchanging blows, scaring the children and the family dog. Contemplating this distressing dumbshow, Richard asks, "What are they saying, what are these violent, frightened people discussing?" Knowing the Maples, we can be certain that the fight is about infidelity; we can imagine the back-and-forth of accusation and denial, confession and ultimatum. Richard, however, wants us to see the bigger picture, and tells us that the couple are in truth discussing the human condition: "change, natural process, the passage of time, death." He's suggesting that at the root of their unhappiness, of the violence and the fear, is transience, the appalling brevity of our existence.*

Trading one house for another (the moving van assisting in a practical demonstration of transience) stirred Updike's memories of

---

* In the concluding lines of "Enemies of a House," Updike neatly, chillingly extends the list of threats that menace one's home: "voracious ivy; frost heaves; splintering; / carpenter ants; adultery; drink; death."

the relocation to Plowville, especially as the family was leaving the center of town for a more rural spot; it triggered a wave of nostalgia for the house in Shillington. In "Plumbing," Richard compares his memories of the recent past, of the life he shared with Joan and the children ("feeble ghosts"), with mythic memories excavated from the sacred site where he spent his early years. Drawing an explicit contrast, he goes into rhapsodies over the "potent, powerful, numinous Easter eggs of my childhood." Potent, powerful, numinous—not just the eggs but the memories themselves; the distant past has a bonded grip on him, as though his connection with his childhood had been crafted with the same care as the plumber's "antique joint." The distant past has weight and dignity; the recent past is pale and trivial—"frivolous," like that partying couple in their finery tiptoeing drunk around the yard in the small hours of the morning with a stash of chocolate eggs wrapped in tinfoil.

Religious concerns, flagged by the heavy, repeated emphasis on Easter and prayer, were clearly weighing on Updike's mind. In the broadest terms, the story pits time against the eternal, death against resurrection. For Richard, nostalgia involves hankering after an uncomplicated childhood faith in the "impossible-to-plumb well of mystery where the stars swam, and old photographs predating my birth were snapped, and God listened"—an unplumbed well of mystery that's also, we're told, the source of those potent, powerful, numinous Easter eggs. Like his nine-year-old daughter, who dreads growing older and tells him she doesn't want a birthday, Richard is wishing not to age, not to die, not to be "outlasted."

Loaded, possibly overloaded, with metaphysical significance, "Plumbing" offers only hazy clues to the here and now—to the rate at which, for instance, the Maples' battered marriage is deteriorating. Joan appears as a "feeble ghost"; she's given no dialogue. In the quarrel tableau, Richard dramatizes his conception of himself as a prisoner (an old complaint) by sitting slumped, head bowed, ankles together, as if shackled. Contemplating a dozen years at the old house, he's strangely numb; mild regret is what he seems to feel about his marriage, and a twinge of guilt. The story also provides a glimpse of Richard with his offspring, an increasingly common thread in the Maples stories. Richard is a loving father—but worn out, distracted, self-involved, ashamed of his shortcomings as a parent. Despite his good intentions, he fears that he's failing his children. With remarkable economy, Updike packs nearly all this into a brief paragraph featuring Richard and two of his progeny:

> A man bends above a child's bed; his voice and a child's voice murmur prayers in unison. They have trouble with "trespass" versus "debts," having attended different Sunday schools. Weary, slightly asthmatic . . . anxious to return downstairs to a book and a drink, he passes into the next room. The child there, a bigger child, when he offers to bow his head with her, cries softly, "Daddy, no, don't!" The round white face, dim in the dusk of the evening, seems to glow with tension, embarrassment, appeal. Embarrassed himself, too easily embarrassed, he gives her a kiss, backs off, closes her bedroom door, leaves her to the darkness.

The phrase "trouble with 'trespass' versus 'debts'" refers to competing versions of the Lord's Prayer. It could also serve as a condensed description of a family being pulled apart by adultery, a home where fighting parents hit each other in front of bewildered children. The parents trespass; they default on debts owed to each other and to their sons and daughters; trouble brews. The older child's pleading refusal to join her father in prayer, most easily explained as the rebellion of a young girl who feels she's outgrown what she thinks of as a childish ritual, could also be seen—if, for example, you were a father with a guilty conscience—as the rebuke of a daughter who senses a hint of falsity in your rote display of piety. You might think that she's uneasy about saying her prayers with an enervated man anxious to be elsewhere, a man who has "trouble with 'trespass' versus 'debts.'"

As Updike would say, "internal evidence" identifies the "bigger child" as Judith, eldest of the Maple children. The others are Richard Jr. ("Dickie"), John, and Margaret (nicknamed "Bean" as a baby). First introduced as a foursome in the early sixties in "Giving Blood," they began to emerge as full-fledged characters several years later, beginning with "Eros Rampant"; from that point on, it was obvious that Updike had no compunction about using Liz, David, Michael, and Miranda as his models. Lightly fictionalized, the young Maples are as much like the young Updikes as Richard and Joan are like John and Mary—which is to say that in each case the outline is more or less accurate. There's no scrambling of identities: Friends and relatives recognized all the children immediately, and the children recognized themselves.

The prayer scene in "Plumbing" was probably played out in real life essentially as Updike wrote it; by the late sixties, an adolescent Liz had grown out of saying prayers with her father, but the other children continued with what had become a family ritual: John would go into each of their rooms separately, sit on the bed, and repeat with them the Lord's Prayer.

The children began to figure more prominently in the Maples stories, and elsewhere in Updike's fiction, in part because they were more involved in grown-up activities. During the Labor-in-Vain years, Liz began to play volleyball with the adults during Sunday sports. David took up golf and photography. Michael helped his father, more than the others, with carpentry projects around the house. Each of the four children was now a vocal, even articulate, presence. But another reason for their prominence in the fiction is the moral weight they carried. As in "Plumbing," children are a reminder of the parents' obligations, their duties and responsibilities. The actions of the parents vis-à-vis the children are an important gauge of decency, a gauge that exposes failure more often than success. Over and over again in Updike's fiction from the late sixties and early seventies, children see things they shouldn't; their presence, or even just the possibility of their presence, shames the parents—or *ought* to shame the parents—into behaving better. At times, John felt uncomfortably sandwiched between his children on the one hand and Wesley and Linda on the other. As he once remarked, he belonged to "a generation . . . that found itself somewhat pushed around by its parents, and now feels it's being pushed around by its children— we're a generation that never got on top." Wesley wasn't pushy (he left that to Linda), but he was an exemplar—however eccentric and irritating—a good man who showed what it meant to be a good son, a good husband, a good father. How heavily John's children weighed on him is harder to measure. When he was trying to leave Mary for Joyce Harrington, the thought of abandoning them was not in itself enough to tip the balance, not enough to make him stay. And yet he *did* stay (his father possibly the deciding factor)—and wrote movingly of the torment of a parent poised on the brink of breaking up his family.

Richard Maple occupies a clearly defined space in the constellation of Updike alter egos. He is the character into whom Updike poured, over a span of thirty-eight years, his feelings about being a husband and father. Outside that narrow segment of the domestic realm, Richard scarcely exists. We're told in "Snowing in Greenwich Village" that he works in advertising, but his professional life has no bearing at all in the later stories; he might as well be unemployed, or the beneficiary of a trust fund sufficient to maintain a middle-class existence in an Ipswich-like Boston suburb. He has parents and a hometown (in West Virginia), but what little pre-Joan past he's given is lifted straight from Updike's own background, with only minor cosmetic adjustments, such as substituting West Virginia for southeastern Pennsylvania. Neither Harry Angstrom (an indifferent husband and an epically bad father) nor Henry Bech (a bachelor at heart and not a father until his seventies) offered Updike much chance to explore the role of paterfamilias; Richard Maple was tailor-made for exactly that.

And in that role, he's an almost exact facsimile of Updike. More consistently than Bech or Rabbit, Richard presents an undistorted reflection of his creator's inner being. His wildly oscillating emotions about Joan; his yearning to leave her and his chronic love for her; the pangs of sexual desire he experiences in her presence, even when their marriage is in ruins; the bitter frustration; the revulsion—all this is very close to home. So, too, his hypochondria, his sadistic pleasure in harmful teasing, and his instant (but passing) remorse. And so, too, his misgivings about his parenting skills, his sense that he's somehow doing damage to the very beings he least wants to harm. Updike occasionally tried to distance himself from his doppelgänger—"there's more fiction to those stories than would meet the eye"—but the attempt was always halfhearted and transparently disingenuous. There is one crucial distinction between the character and his creator: unlike Richard, Updike hoarded his experience as a husband and father for use in his writing. He observed with intent, monitoring his teetering home life with a loving, greedy eye, precisely aware of its value as material. His undoubted affection was accompanied by an opportunistic urge to make use of what he was witnessing. Conscious of a sliver of inner detachment, a gap between thought and feeling that made surreptitious surveillance possible, he felt guilty about it, another layer of regret and remorse.

The converse of his detachment was his fierce concentration when he was at work. David remembered going with a couple of his siblings to visit their father in his downtown Ipswich office sometime in the sixties. As they climbed the stairs they could hear the busy noise of his typewriter, a continuous clickety-click that ceased the instant they knocked. The children piled into the office and delivered some message or made some trivial request. Their father was perfectly happy to see them and faultlessly attentive; he wasn't remotely grumpy about being disturbed. After a few minutes, their business settled, the kids trooped out again, shutting the door behind them—and before they reached the stairs, the clatter of the typewriter had resumed, rapid-fire, unbroken.

There were of course times when he was stymied, when his powers of concentration and magical fluency were unavailing. For example, he was unable to make progress on the novel about James Buchanan that he had begun researching and writing in London. Back home in Ipswich, he struggled, and finally gave up in the first weeks of the new decade. He later declared himself incapable of the "vigorous fakery" essential to historical fiction. Feeling he owed Knopf a novel, he turned to an "old friend" firmly rooted in realist detail: Harry Angstrom, last seen running through the streets of Brewer, fleeing complications and entanglements—"Ah: runs. Runs." For nearly a decade, people had been asking what happened next; where did Rabbit run to? Updike began cooking up an answer, and in the first week of February 1970, he started work on the novel that became *Rabbit Redux.*[*] As he later put it, "the perpetual *presentness* of my former hero beckoned as a relief"; or, more simply, "Rabbit to the rescue."

The courage to contemplate a sequel came in part from his success with serial installments of the Maples' marital woes and Bech's far-flung literary adventures. *Bech: A Book*, in the works for a year or so, appeared in June and, to Updike's surprise, was greeted with voluble pleasure by reviewers, many of whom proclaimed it his best book. To Judith Jones he complained, only half seriously, "I am beginning to wince at the way they praise this little jeu at the expense of all the other books. Somehow, as everybody treats Bech so courteously, I am beginning to wonder if there isn't indeed a Jewish Mafia." The miseries of the Maples, meanwhile, were the subject of nakedly prurient fascination. With two thriving alter egos close by and in regular contact, it's not particularly surprising that Harry, presenting himself as a character ripe for revival, should be invited to join them. Updike's dismay at "all the revolutions in the air"—the same disquiet about the counterculture voiced in "The Hillies"— needed a fresh outlet. As a middle American, representative of the socioeconomic class Updike had left behind, and as a member of Nixon's "silent majority"—the mass of ordinary, law-abiding citizens feeling overwhelmed by raucous jeers of dissent from a "vocal minority"—Harry became a "receptacle" for Updike's concerns. Patriotic resentments, Updike realized, would sit more becomingly on a paunchy thirty-six-year-old Linotype operator scraping payments on an apple-green ranch house and a quarter-acre of lawn than on a trim millionaire author, recent resident of a London terrace with a $10,000-a-month price tag.

Looking through Harry's eyes, Updike surveyed a nation in torment, riven by rioting and assassination, anguished protest and uncomprehending reaction. Not surprisingly, the novel, by Updike's

---

[*] He typed the first draft, an anomaly; the first drafts of the other three Rabbit books were all handwritten with a soft pencil.

own admission, is "violent and bizarre," the violence and bizarrity invading Harry's little world in the shape of Jill, an upper-class teenage runaway; and Skeeter, a black Vietnam veteran with a messianic streak, also on the run. Even before these two fugitives move into Harry's Penn Villas ranch house, his home has been turned upside down; Janice, who's been having an affair with Charlie Stavros, a savvy salesman at her father's Toyota franchise, moves in with her lover, leaving her husband in sole charge of twelve-year-old Nelson—an augmentation of parental responsibility for which Harry is ill-equipped. His own father is aging, his mother slowly dying of Parkinson's disease—"having the adventure now we're all going to have," his father says bleakly. Rabbit himself is sunk in apathy; he reacts but seems sadly incapable of asserting himself, his passivity in marked contrast to the tumult all around him.

It's the summer of 1969, and man is bound for the moon; Harry and his father watch reruns of the Cape Canaveral blast-off in the Phoenix Bar, down the street from Verity Press, where they've worked together for a decade. In York, Pennsylvania, just fifty miles away, a race riot is in full swing; snipers target firemen; policemen patrol the streets. In Vietnam, the body count escalates; it's one of the worst years of the war, with more than eleven thousand American casualties. On Martha's Vineyard, Senator Edward Kennedy drives off a bridge in the wee hours and a young woman from Pennsylvania drowns. "If the novel seems hectic, so were the times," Updike wrote decades later. "[T]he news had moved out of the television and into our laps, and there was no ignoring the war, the protest, the civil-rights movement, the moon shot, and the drugs and sexual promiscuity that were winning favor in the middle classes." With the moon shot as framing metaphor (Harry launched into the outer space of radically new experience), the novel blends national trauma and domestic disarray so smoothly that they merge; the political and the personal are indistinguishable on every level—plot, characterization, and imagery all contribute to a highly suggestive confusion of categories. In her review of *Couples*, Diana Trilling had scolded Updike for using the tragic public events of the Kennedy era as mere backdrop: "We recognize them," she wrote, "as the fashionable trappings of all contemporary fiction that pretends to big meanings." With *Rabbit Redux*, no one could complain that history serves "only a decorative function."

Rabbit and America, both drastically demoralized, need to be nursed back to health; "Pray for rebirth," Harry's ailing mother tells him.* Whether or not that happy result is actually achieved, there's certainly a concerted effort to reeducate our hero by anatomizing the flaws of the nation he loves, beginning with slavery and the ongoing saga of racial oppression and exploitation, then veering into the horrors of Vietnam. The venue is the living room of the ranch house, and the cast of characters consists of Harry, Nelson, Jill, and Skeeter—another of Updike's quartets. The waiflike Jill, a flower child who's fled a drug problem and the stifling family manse in Stonington, Connecticut (though she could easily have been a hillie from Tarbox), moves in first, and makes herself at home in various agreeable ways. She's Harry's lover and his daughter; she's a big sister for Nelson and the object of the boy's lust-tinged affection. Then Skeeter, a trickster figure who's jumped bail on a drug charge, crashes the party, promising to be gone in a few days; instead, casting a sinister spell, he stays on, even though Jill and Nelson both beg Harry to throw him out. Skeeter stays until disaster forces him to flee.

The living room teach-ins intended to raise Rabbit's consciousness quickly descend into something much more emotionally complex and volatile, Skeeter ranting and raging with terrifying rhetorical skill. Each character is in an altered state: Harry mesmerized; Skeeter unhinged; Jill drugged and increasingly spacey; Nelson frantic with worry about Jill—until Rabbit is roused to banish him upstairs. Unable to resist the messianic power of Skeeter's wild sermons, Harry fails to recognize Jill's peril. The reader, too, is under a spell, lulled by fearless, majestically assured writing:

---

* *Redux*, a word Updike claimed to have brought back into circulation, means "brought back"—back to health, back to life; it shares with *educate* the Latin verb stem *duc-*.

Physically, Skeeter fascinates Rabbit. The lustrous pallor of the tongue and palms and the soles of the feet, left out of the sun. Or a different kind of skin? White palms never tan either. The peculiar glinting lustre of his skin. The something so very finely turned and finished in the face, reflecting at a dozen polished points: in comparison white faces are blobs: putty still drying. The curious greased grace of his gestures, rapid and watchful as a lizard's motions, free of mammalian fat. Skeeter in his house feels like a finely made electric toy; Harry wants to touch him but is afraid he will get a shock.

As the weeks go by, the political theater played out in the living room degenerates into an orgiastic, drug-fueled romp, with Harry and Skeeter high on marijuana, and Jill on mescaline, then heroin. The drugs are sacraments administered by Skeeter, the self-styled "black Jesus" arranging a psychedelic black Mass. As Rabbit, stoned, weirdly acquiescent, reads aloud from *The Life and Times of Frederick Douglass*, Skeeter "rapes" Jill.* Alone with Harry, Skeeter masturbates—again to the tune of the ex-slave's narrative—and Harry has to smother a spark of homoerotic desire kindled by the naked man on his sofa: "His heart skips. He has escaped. Narrowly." Nelson glimpses enough of this mayhem to send him sobbing to his room. It's a brutal sequence, repellent and compelling in equal measure.

If *Rabbit Redux* is Updike's most powerful novel—and I would confidently argue the case—part of that power comes from high stakes: the soul of the nation and the soul of the hero teetering in the balance. The psychodrama played out in Rabbit's living room culminates in the shock of Jill's degradation; her death in a house fire deliberately set by Peeping Tom neighbors outraged by glimpses of a black man having sex with a white woman occurs offstage, a

---

* Skeeter certainly assaults her sexually, but the extent of the assault is unclear. In the first edition of the novel, Harry thinks that "she is liking it, being raped." In later editions, the reference to rape was deleted: Harry thinks that "she is liking it, this attack."

mercy to the reader.* Violence was rare in Updike's fiction up to this point; Jill's fiery death is a sure sign that we're all being pushed to extremes, the characters, the reader, the author; it's a high-wire act for all concerned.

To Updike, a "vehement and agitated . . . undove" who harbored a half-hidden conservative streak and couldn't kick the unfortunate habit of mocking civil rights rhetoric (as in "Marching Through Boston"), it must have felt as if his own soul were also in play. Harry's "angry old patriotism" (as Updike remarked, "the rage and destructiveness boiling out of the television set belong to him") is an echo of the "strange underdog rage" provoked in Updike by any mention of antiwar sentiment. The flag decal on the back window of Harry's car finds its equivalent in the large American flag given to Updike by his family—"in loving exasperation"—as a Christmas present just before he started *Rabbit Redux*. When Harry tells Stavros, "It's not all war I love . . . it's *this* war. Because nobody else does. Nobody else understands it," we're catching a glimpse of Updike launching into the "good row" he had with Philip Roth (and many others) over Vietnam. The teach-ins were part of Updike's own reeducation; he was putting his prejudices and political convictions to the test, subjecting them to the full force of a ferocious counterblast: Skeeter's insidiously persuasive attack on racist America as a big pig wallowing in a muck of greed. Updike loathed this kind of critique. As we know, he bristled at any form of organized social protest: sit-ins, marches, rallies. He sometimes claimed that this aversion was the result of his apolitical fifties education, but the "immutability" of his Shillington childhood was surely at the root of it. Growing up safe and happy in a town that was "abnormally still," in an unchanging family structure, taught him to associate happiness and well-being with stability. "To me," he wrote in his memoirs, "authority was the Shillington High School faculty"—his father and his father's colleagues. He was never

---

* Updike went out of his way to explain that Jill's death was inspired by "a piece of authentic social violence": Updike's parents had told him of a biracial couple's house in Berks County that had been burned to the ground in a racist arson attack. The black man who was living in the house had attended Shillington High School.

going to agitate for the overthrow of institutions, or even wholeheartedly endorse social idealism; he couldn't bring himself to believe that the status quo could be "lightly or easily altered." And yet he gave the firebrand Skeeter a starring role (like Satan in *Paradise Lost*) and allowed him to vent his spleen with hypnotic eloquence. When the novel appeared, Updike told an interviewer that "[r]evolt, rebellion, violence, disgust are themselves there for a reason . . . and must be considered respectfully." He gave equal billing to the radical and the reactionary, and equal weight to their grievances.

Neither patriotism nor protest gets the last word. The teach-ins end when Jill dies, victim of the flames engulfing the nation and Harry's home. When it's all over we're left to sift through the ashes. As Updike put it, "The cost of the disruption of the social fabric was paid, as in the earlier novel, by a girl." Or in Harry's pithy formulation, linking the fire with Janice fumbling for their infant daughter in too-deep bathwater, "Her trip drowns babies; his burns girls." Passive, hard-hearted, callously egocentric, Harry gives little sign of grief for his dead lover; the business of mourning Jill, of raging against her death, falls to Nelson, further complicating the bruised relations between father and son. If any good news can be said to come out the whole sorry mess, it's that Harry—who sees himself as "the man in the middle"—has *listened*; his curiosity and his native openness have led him to entertain ideas that would otherwise be anathema to him.

For Updike, as for Harry, Skeeter was a revelation. Taking a black man into his home, offering him even temporary asylum, is a huge step for Harry. You would think that for Updike, who noted that he had "hardly met a black person" until he arrived at Harvard, creating a credible black character to play a major, catalytic role in the novel would have been similarly daunting. And yet the finished product bears no trace of authorial jitters. On the contrary, there are three notable black characters, all presented with aplomb: Skeeter; Buchanan, who works at Verity Press with Harry and his father; and Buchanan's friend Babe, a singer-cum-hooker.

Invited by Buchanan, Rabbit ventures into Jimbo's Friendly Lounge, and discovers that he's the only white man in the bar:

Black to him is just a political word but these people really are, their faces shine of blackness turning as he enters, a large soft white man in a sticky gray suit. Fear travels up and down his skin, but the music of the great green-and-mauve-glowing jukebox called Moonmood slides on, and the liquid of laughter and tickled muttering resumes flowing; his entrance was merely a snag. Rabbit hangs like a balloon waiting for a dart; then his elbow is jostled and Buchanan is beside him.

"Come meet some soul," says Buchanan, and leads him to a booth where Babe and Skeeter sit, Babe smoking "a yellow cigarette that requires much sucking in and holding down and closing of the eyes and sighing." It's hard to resist quoting from the twenty-page scene; it's a virtuoso turn, magnificently conceived and executed. From a narrative point of view, the aim is to connect Harry and Jill and Skeeter, and to unload Jill, who's been staying with Babe, onto Harry. But the details of the encounter are so gorgeous, the interaction between the black characters so tense and intricate, that the reader never notices that the plot is being eased forward. Babe is old and wise and tragic, in touch with psychic powers (she reads Rabbit's hand, extolling the virtues of his thumb—"extremely plausible," she calls it); Skeeter is young and fierce, taunting the others with lacerating wit; and Buchanan is a conciliator, a patient negotiator working his angle. Updike was indulging in a bit of fun with Buchanan, namesake of the pragmatic president from Pennsylvania whose story had stymied him: "Having told a number of interviewers that I was writing a book about Buchanan," he later explained, "I painted him black and put him in, too." Like Rabbit's thumb, Buchanan is extremely plausible—and appealing, whereas Skeeter is plainly nasty and dangerous.

Daring to make a black man not just a villain but a would-be Antichrist; daring to stage the rape of a white girl by a black man; or simply daring to dip into a black man's point of view—in the morally strident sixties, in the heyday of the Black Power movement, Updike was taking a risk, as demonstrated by the fate of William

Styron's *The Confessions of Nat Turner*. Styron chose to write in the voice of Nat Turner, the messianic leader of a bloody slave rebellion, and though his novel was warmly received when it was first published in 1967 (it was awarded the Pulitzer Prize), a year or so later it was loudly and repeatedly condemned as racist, a tag that stuck for decades. Though defended by his friend James Baldwin, Styron was vilified in print by a group of black writers and intellectuals; he was pronounced "psychologically sick" and "morally senile"; he was accused of having "a vile racist imagination"—partly because he was a white southerner assuming the persona of a key figure in African American history, and partly because he invented a sexually charged relationship between a black man and a white teenage girl he eventually murders. Updike was well aware of this bitter, much-publicized controversy. He'd read the book when it came out and found it "laborious." When he was six months into the writing of *Rabbit Redux*, he told Maxwell about a long subway ride from the National Institute of Arts and Letters on the Upper West Side down to Fourteenth Street, during which he endured "a very eloquent and intelligent negro critic shouting in my ear, above the roar, about how bad Styron's book was and how much 'coercive self-righteousness' was in the air now." A load of coercive self-righteousness (what today we would call political correctness) could easily have landed on Updike had Skeeter, and the graphic descriptions of Skeeter having sex with Jill, been misconstrued.

Updike thought Rabbit's "reluctant crossing of the color line" was a sign of progress. And so it was, in more ways than one. Anatole Broyard, the daily reviewer for *The New York Times*, was unstinting in his praise of Updike's accomplishment:

> Skeeter is something new in black characters, including those in books by blacks. He goes beyond the familiar anger and rhetoric into the wild humor blacks no longer seem to allow themselves. He is an inspired preacher. . . . Skeeter is a compound of drug-induced delusions of grandeur, real indignation, homicidal rage and quirky genius. He has a talent for provoking, for getting to the absolute bottom, for trav-

eling through disillusion and coming out on the other side, where *everything* is exposed.*

Broyard's praise includes a hint of sympathy for Skeeter. His villainy has its reasons; his outrageousness makes sense. It fits; it chimes with the outrageousness of the era.

So much in the sixties was too big, too bright, too loud, especially when it came to flaunting newly won sexual freedom. Updike later conceded that there was in the novel a "possibly inordinate emphasis on sexual congress." There are fewer sex scenes than in *Couples*, but they're raunchier, more blatantly pornographic. Fellatio and miscegenation feature prominently. And a good deal of the sex takes place in Harry's head—for example, his masturbatory fantasy featuring a "hefty coarse Negress," and his incestuous compulsion to imagine the graphic details of his sister, Mim, copulating with Stavros, his wife's lover. Rabbit has come a long way. When we first met him, he was "too fastidious to mouth the words" to say that he wanted Ruth to perform oral sex. Now, when Mim asks him what he's learned, he tells her flatly, "I learned I'd rather fuck than be blown."

Like the decade, the novel is strong poison, and it will always have its detractors, among them Christopher Ricks, whose essay in *The New York Review of Books* bore the telltale title "Flopsy Bunny." But some of the reviews were among the most ecstatic Updike ever received. Broyard positively gushed: "*Rabbit Redux* is the complete Updike at last, an awesomely accomplished writer who is better, tougher, wiser and more radically human than anyone could have expected him to be."† A week after that panegyric, Richard Locke, an editor at *The New York Times Book Review*, declared *Rabbit Redux* "by far the most audacious and successful" of Updike's books.

---

* Though he concealed the fact, Broyard was himself African American, a light-skinned black man who passed as white. His judgment is complicated by that experience but not necessarily invalidated; few critics can have devoted more thought to what it means to be black in America.

† "I'm rather baffled," Updike told Jones, "by this book's progress . . . and wonder if it wasn't somebody else who wrote it. Skeeter Johnson, perhaps."

Locke's long front-page essay looked back over the breadth of his career; Locke noted that this was the first time Updike had dealt "in a large way with public subjects."

Concentrating on the new, and on the risks he took, shouldn't distract us from the carefully planned continuity between the second Rabbit novel and the first. They were designed as a set; the sequel, he wrote, was "meant to be symmetric" with the earlier novel. In *Rabbit Redux*, Janice leaves her husband and saves a life (that of her lover); Harry stays home, and a girl dies on his watch. In *Rabbit, Run*, Eccles, the milquetoast clergyman, tries to rescue Rabbit with rounds of golf;* in the next installment, the messianic Skeeter preaches apocalypse and passes the sacramental joint. The fun-house mirroring is pervasive—as Updike helpfully suggested, "Anybody who really cared could get some interesting formal things out of the two books together." Between them, Harry and Janice cancel out the events of the first novel and inch, at the end of the second, toward a tentative reconciliation. The tranquil, uncertain ending, which finds husband and wife in bed together at the Safe Haven Motel, invites a sequel: "He. She. Sleeps. O.K.?" According to Updike, "The question that ends the book is not meant to have an easy answer"—but it seems more hopeful than not, and a third installment of the Rabbit saga was already taking shape in the author's mind. In the mid-seventies, Updike told Joyce Carol Oates, "I feel at home in Harry's pelt and may not have spent my last term there."

The major incidents in *Rabbit Redux* were entirely made up. There was never a Jill in Updike's life, no nineteen-year-old flower-child lover moving into his house, strumming on the guitar and cooking him fillet of sole; and there was no Skeeter, no black Jesus prophesying revolution and promising to return in glory. Here, as in *The Poorhouse Fair* and *Rabbit, Run*, Updike uncoupled fiction from autobiography. He went right back to the well, of course, dip-

---

* Updike crafted a scene for Eccles in *Rabbit Redux*, but decided to leave it out. Harry sees his old golf partner on the bus in Brewer, and they talk briefly. Telling Janice about the encounter, Harry remarks, "The Sixties did a number on him, too." The scene was restored in the omnibus *Rabbit Angstrom*.

ping into his personal experience when it suited him, writing about himself and those around him without a second thought. But *Rabbit Redux*, which spilled out in a rush—looking back, he remembered that it "kind of wrote itself"—released him into a new and expansive freedom. It paved the way for *The Coup*, the most outlandish of his creations.

He took brave leaps of imagination with *Rabbit Redux*, and invited into the pages of his novel all the disorienting upheaval of what he identified as "the most dissentious American decade since the Civil War." He worked harder than ever to achieve his goal of "intuition into the mass consciousness and an identification with our national fortunes"—and yet the writing didn't take him far from home. His fundamental concern was domestic and quotidian; "the basic action remains familial," he noted; "marital fidelity and parental responsibility are still the issues."

He sported, in the months after the novel's publication, an increasingly thick and bohemian-looking beard. But though it looked like a statement of solidarity with the counterculture, it wasn't; he had broken his leg playing defensive end in a game of Sunday football, and being on crutches made it hard to shave. Hobbling, hirsute, he went back to work on James Buchanan.

The hundred pages of his abandoned historical novel seemed to him "stiff, unreal, and lacking in electricity." Unable to vivify those pages, he convinced himself that the material he'd laboriously accumulated over the last four years required a dramatic form—he decided to turn the novel into a play. It was a peculiar decision. He was not, as he candidly admitted, a theatergoer; in fact, he found most plays "pretty silly." He knew next to nothing about stagecraft. And the unattractive and fatally passive Buchanan was hardly ideal as the hero of live drama. Updike was aware, even as he was writing it, that the play would be unplayably long (seven hours, according to one estimate), not to mention static and pedantic. But he persevered, calculating that if he called it a "closet drama," spiced up the text with lively stage directions, and tacked on a historical afterword, it would be, as he wrote to André Deutsch, "bindable and thence forgettable." As it happened, *Buchanan Dying* was twice brought to the stage (in abbreviated form): first at Franklin and Marshall College, near Buchanan's home in Lancaster, Pennsylvania, in a fully staged production; and a year later in San Diego, as a dramatic reading. A delighted Updike escorted his mother to the Franklin and Marshall production. Linda wore a gray fox fur he had brought back from Russia; she looked, her son thought, "every inch a first-nighter." There was no opening night disaster, certainly nothing like the jeering that Henry James endured at the premiere of *Guy Domville*. Updike remained fond of his play (as he was of all his work), though he couldn't suppress the suspicion that his theatrical foray was a disappointment. He somehow still wasn't done with Buchanan, but it would be nearly two decades before he found a way to get the fifteenth president off his back for good.

A PATTERN, ALREADY emergent in the mid-sixties, solidified in the seventies: Updike zigzagged, from short story to short story, between the conspicuously experimental and the comfortably familiar. He later grouped the experimental stories under the rubric "Far Out," a tip of the hat to the spirit of the times. "During the Jurassic" and "Under the Microscope," written in 1965 and 1967, respectively, are early attempts to wrap the mundane in a radically unfamiliar package. Each takes an ordinary cocktail party and makes it strange. In "During the Jurassic," the guests are a taxonomy of dinosaurs, from *Hypsilophodon* to *Stegosaurus*; in "Under the Microscope," they're a sampling of pond life—water mites, rotifers, flatworms. In "The Baluchitherium," an enterprising journalist time-travels to an interview with the largest-ever land mammal, extinct since the Oligocene. Three historical fantasies offered an easy avenue of escape from the here and now: "The Invention of the Horse Collar," a tale of fratricide set in the "darkest Dark Ages"; "Jesus on Honshu," an alternative life of Christ; and "Augustine's Concubine," a fictional elaboration of the bare facts known about the mother of Augustine's child, the woman he renounced after thirteen years as her lover. "Commercial"—a different kind of experiment, classed by Updike as a Tarbox tale—first analyzes the script of a saccharine television advertisement replete with cozy images of family togetherness, and then, still casually spoofing advertising conventions, follows a man (Updike in thin disguise) preparing for bed and trying with difficulty to fall asleep next to his slumbering wife. The cleverness on display in this and other stories only partly conceals an underlying restlessness, an intermittently urgent need to rethink his methods, to tackle domestic issues without automatic recourse to the domestic realism he had long since thoroughly mastered—and would never abandon for long.*

In "Sublimating," a fresh episode of the Maples saga written a few months after he'd finished *Rabbit Redux*, marital fidelity and parental responsibility are again the central concerns. The story begins with the announcement that Joan and Richard, still hoping to salvage the marriage (though their respective involvement in serial adultery is now frankly acknowledged), have sworn off sex—"since sex was the only sore point in their marriage."† For once the Maples are in sync; abstinence affects them in much the same way, sharpening their senses, putting them on edge, fueling morbid daydreams. Emphasizing this common ground, Updike tells us that the Maples' eyes had "married and merged to three" and that the shared eye in the middle allows them, on occasion, to read each other's mind. This elaborate image was suggested by a drawing made for Mary and John by a "picturesque" Russian artist during their trip to the Soviet Union in 1964. The sketch was of two overlapping heads with a third eye shared between them. The artist insisted that it was a portrait of the Updikes as husband and wife. John saw his point; as he wrote in *Self-Consciousness*, "It was true, [Mary] and I saw many things the same way, and never had much trouble understanding

---

* The "Far Out" stories were also Updike's way of keeping up with the avant-garde—Donald Barthelme, whose strikingly original stories began appearing in *The New Yorker* in the early sixties, and also John Barth, John Hawkes, Thomas Pynchon, and William Gaddis.

† Pure fiction, according to Mary. She and John never pledged to give up sex—and besides, sex was hardly "the only sore point"; politics and religion also caused trouble.

each other." But what sounds like an asset turns out to be a liability: "We rarely needed . . . to talk, and under this quietness resentments and secret lives came to flourish. Had we had two eyes each, we might have made a better couple." This interpretation—arrived at more than a decade after they had ceased to be a couple—is clearly skewed by hindsight. In "Sublimating," the shared third eye makes it *more* difficult for the Maples to hide secrets from one another; it allows them to sense each other's thoughts and punctures self-deceit.

Abstinence, alas, fails to make the heart grow fonder, and by the end of "Sublimating," the Maples' marriage is as rickety as ever. The children, meanwhile, are omnipresent, each of them acting out a predictable Freudian role, as one would expect in a story with a psychoanalytic catchphrase as its title. Bean, the youngest, flirts with her father, yet retains a measure of infantile polymorphous perversity; she's fixated on any nearby "warmth-source." John, still in the latency stage, is building a guillotine in the cellar ("Jesus," Richard exclaims, underlining the point, "he better not lose a finger"). Newly adolescent Dickie is threatened by his older sister's maturing body; her "blind blooming" pains him. And it drives her father crazy: Judith flaunts her nubile charms, doing stretching exercises in front of the poor sex-starved man. The children are distinct, fully particularized characters (as in the earlier "Eros Rampant"), and yet they function as a unit, a mute chorus offering implicit comment on the behavior of their parents. The object of love and the source of love— and of guilt, regret, and frustration—they are foils, mirrors, prods to the conscience. They bind their mother and father and drive them apart, like every couple's children.

Like the Updike children. But the Updike children—*un*like most other children—were also fodder for a fictional record of their parents' failing marriage, a record published serially in *The New Yorker*, and read with relish by family friends and neighbors, and any number of the magazine's subscribers (of whom there were nearly half a million by the early seventies). Their father claimed to have no qualms about broadcasting intimate details of his family life in stories with titles such as "Your Lover Just Called" and "Eros Rampant"; he pointed out that his "nearest and dearest of that time didn't complain, I think because among other things there was some respect for what I was trying to do—something that transcended the personalities around me." Tell-all in print, he was utterly discreet in conversation. One of his friends told me, "I don't remember any boy-talk about our different romances. We never exchanged war stories." Another friend, the young Nicholas Delbanco, who for many years harbored a platonic, worshipful love for Mary, asked Updike during this period about the ubiquity of adulterous liaisons in his fiction, particularly the Maples stories. He found it hard to believe that anyone with such an attractive, engaging wife would be sleeping around. Updike assured him that it was merely a socially validated form of daydreaming—in other words, harmless fantasy. With Judith Jones, who was by now officially his editor at Knopf, he turned the topic of his fictional lovers into a salty joke; after writing the flap copy for *Museums and Women* (1972), a collection of twenty-nine stories, nearly half involving adultery, he suggested the following "cap-line": "Wonderful *contes* from a veteran *conte*-chaser."

Occasionally the Updike children appeared in sketches (barely fictional) anatomizing the filial bond. "Daughter, Last Glimpses Of" is essentially a snapshot of the Updike family at the moment when Liz left home at eighteen to live with a man in his thirties. (They spent a year in England together, broke up upon their return, and later married—a brief, unhappy union that ended when the husband died of alcoholism at age thirty-seven.) The tone of the story, written just weeks after she moved out, is mildly sad, nostalgic, haunted by the passage of time, and troubled by the problem of perspective. The father (who narrates) asks his wife why their eldest child, Joy, doesn't go out with boys; he wonders whether she's ugly. Shocked, his wife asks if he's serious, to which he replies, "I am. I can't tell. She's my daughter." The father's inability to gauge his daughter's looks—she's gorgeous, according to the mother—is a symptom of a larger problem; he's too close to his wife and children to appreciate them as he should. He takes the everyday blessing of family life for granted, a lesson made explicit in the final paragraph, which is about a rooster that is in a sense Joy's parting gift to her family. (Like Liz, she insisted on keeping chickens in the backyard.) At dawn, just outside the father's bedroom window, the rooster "gives a crow as if to hoist with his own pure lungs that sleepy fat sun to the zenith of the sky." This jubilant cock-a-doodle-doo supplies the moral of the story:

> He never moderates his joy, though I am gradually growing deafer to it. That must be the difference between soulless creatures and human beings: creatures find every dawn as remarkable as the ones previous, whereas the soul grows calluses.

Growing gradually deaf to the rooster's joy is analogous to being blind to Joy's good looks. For Updike as a writer, calluses on the soul would be nothing short of catastrophic; after all, his self-appointed mission was to "give the mundane its beautiful due." For Updike as a father and a husband, the deadening calluses were inescapable, a stubborn fact of family life; he became hardened not just to its joys but to its sorrows.

Like "Daughter, Last Glimpses Of," "Son" is less a story than a meditation. It begins with a portrait drawn from life, an exact likeness of the guitar- and soccer-playing David as a sensitive, precocious, emotionally volatile fifteen-year-old with an adolescent's impatient yearning for perfection. Updike then travels back in time to give us a quick look at himself as a son, of his father as a son, and even of his grandfather as a son. Of the many threads linking the generations, the most conspicuous are blocked or conflicted emotion ("I love touching him," Updike writes about David, "but don't often dare") and the sons' urge to escape, their disappointment, their rage. The absence of any kind of narrative seems entirely appropriate to the many-sided relations between a son and his parents; the confusing admixture of love, hate, yearning, and disdain is almost too clotted and messy for the stricture of organized plot.

And yet Updike tried to work three generations' worth of conflicted father-son feeling into "The Gun Shop," which was inspired by a trip John and David and Wesley took to have a Remington .22 repaired during the family's Thanksgiving visit to Plowville in 1971. Firing the gun, which Wesley had given to John the Christmas after they moved to the farm (the exact weapon wielded by David Kern in "Pigeon Feathers"), was one of the treats David and Michael associated with visits to their grandparents. On this occasion, the rifle refused to fire, David threw a tantrum, and Wesley suggested they take it to a nearby gunsmith, who fashioned a new firing pin on the spot. The arc of the story Updike constructed from this "adventure" runs from the tantrum the boy (Murray) throws in front of his father (Ben) after the gun refuses to fire to the father's relief and pride the next day when the repaired gun works and the boy hits the target. Simmering below the surface, and sometimes erupting into full view, is a fierce, almost deadly oedipal struggle declared in the first paragraph: Ben remembers Murray's fourteenth birthday party, when he had "tapped the child on the back of the head to settle him down, and his son had pointed the cake knife at his father's chest and said, 'Hit me again and I'll kill you.'" This note is sounded throughout: After Murray's "infantile" tantrum when the gun won't fire, Ben is in a "murderous" mood; in the gun shop, which "smelled of death," the talk is of combat, "blood and guts"; Ben's father, also called Murray, says wryly that his motto is "Kill or be killed"; and at the end of the story, when his son's shots, aimed with "murderous concentration," are hitting the target and his own are not, Ben tells the boy, "You're killing me."* The age-old pattern—the new generation pushing the old out of the way—was much on Updike's mind, not just because the adolescent David was crowding up from behind but because his father, now past seventy, was visibly unwell.

The elder Murray is the spitting image of Wesley; imagine George Caldwell from *The Centaur* after he has plodded on for another twenty-odd years. A retired schoolteacher who had trouble maintaining classroom discipline, he's a kindhearted, garrulous, irrepressibly enthusiastic man who nonetheless embarrasses and irritates his son. It's a vivid likeness:

---

* Updike revised "The Gun Shop" when it was collected in *Problems* (1979). The revisions accentuate oedipal aggression at the expense of other, more nuanced aspects of the father-son relationship.

Ben's father . . . had become an old man, but a wonderfully strange old man, with a long, yellow-white face, a blue nose, and the erect carriage of a child who is straining to see. His circulation was poor, he had been hospitalized, he lived from pill to pill, he had uncharacteristic quiet spells that Ben guessed were seizures of pain; yet his hopefulness still dominated any room he was in.

Wesley had been in poor health since his heart attack in 1961, and was hospitalized after suffering a mild stroke in late 1969. Updike was clearly anticipating his death when he wrote "The Gun Shop" in February 1972—and two months later, Wesley was rushed to the hospital, again with heart trouble. John and Mary were in Florence, on vacation with André Deutsch, when Linda telephoned to say that Wesley was gravely ill. They took the next flight to London, rushing to catch a connection to New York, but in London they learned that Wesley had died only a few hours after Linda's call. Updike's story, when it was published in *The New Yorker* in November, became a kind of memorial to his father, a clear-eyed and affectionate tribute, as honest and unsparing as *The Centaur*.

The old man in "The Gun Shop" is, as he himself would admit, "a pain in the old bazoo"—and at the same time unquestionably virtuous, a good man, like George Caldwell. When Ben tells his wife, "I'd like to be nice like my father, but he was so nice I can't be," it has the ring of autobiographical confession. Ben knows what a good father he's had; he knows that he's been "much less a father than his own had been"; he knows that he's "hard" on his son, teasing and troubling him, itching to correct his faults. Generally exasperated by his father's bumbling kindness, Ben is especially annoyed when the elder Murray's awkward and fulsome flattery is directed at his grandson; one Murray praising the other means that Ben has been bypassed. He resents being squeezed out by the generation on either side.

Read in the context of Updike's family life, "The Gun Shop" is a highly personal and revealing self-assessment. It underscores a sad paradox: although he could anatomize his own failings with perfect clarity, he seemed incapable of changing how he behaved. He wanted to be as kind to David as Wesley had been to him, but couldn't. Similarly, he wanted *not* to be embarrassed and irritated by his father, but couldn't. He was powerless to make up for his own shortcomings as a father and as a son—a fact he saw plainly as a writer.

His father's death brought with it regret, liberation, and a weight of responsibility. In another memorial, "The House Growing," a melancholy poem he wrote less than a week after the funeral, Updike imagines that each new death—first his grandparents', now his father's—is "adding rooms of silence" to the old sandstone farmhouse. The poem doesn't mention Linda, now its sole occupant, but she was never far from his thoughts. Wesley's absence gave John a new burden to shoulder: a sixty-seven-year-old widow living alone on an isolated farm 350 miles from her only child. She had become for him exactly the mother he'd invented in *Of the Farm*.

In June, John and Mary and the children took an American vacation: three weeks of driving around western states from motel to motel, starting in Albuquerque and ending up in San Francisco, at Mary's sister's house. (The bereaved Linda, writing from Plowville, waved them on cheerfully, advising them to "stay on the right side of the road.") Thrifty as ever with his experience, and fast as ever, Updike recycled his impressions in a short story—an expert distillation of the trip—and sold it to *The New Yorker*, which ran it in mid-August. "How to Love America and Leave It at the Same Time"—the title a sly twist on the ubiquitous sixties bumper sticker—is charmingly evocative of both the American West and happy family life, and salted with epigrams about the nation, such as "America conceals immense things" and "America is a vast conspiracy to make you happy" and "This is America, a hamburger kingdom, one cuisine, under God, indivisible, with pickles and potato chips for all" and "[W]hen we say 'American' it is not a fact, it is an act, of faith, a matter of lines on a map and words on paper, an outline it will take generations and centuries more to fill in." The children on this road trip aren't given names (nor is the wife, who develops a headache when the husband's sexual interest is aroused by her nakedness); they're a corporate entity that the parents must bargain with and satisfy by supplying them with food and distractions at scheduled intervals. The paterfamilias observes minutely (and narrates in the second person), registering a mellow, musing contentment. The constraints of a sightseeing vacation with four kids aged eleven to seventeen leave plenty of space for his stubborn patriotism, his undisguised love of the "natives" and the landscape they inhabit. His eye takes in the "tawny" valley and, beyond it, "a lesser range of mountains, gray, but gray multitudinously, with an infinity of shades—ash, graphite, cardboard, tomcat, lavender." He adds, "Such beauty wants to make us weep."

It's difficult to avoid the impression that the family portraits Updike executed in the early seventies were merely warm-up exercises, studies he made in preparation for a more ambitious and powerful work. He was feeling his way toward something bigger, and two years after his father's death he bumped up against it. "Separating" is the dramatic climax of the Maples saga. Richard, who now hopes to marry another woman, is intent on making his "escape," but before he goes, he must tell his children that he is leaving their mother, leaving home, leaving the family. More minutely accurate than its predecessors in the depiction of a real-life episode, and vastly more distressing, "Separating" was written in mid-July 1974, just a couple of weeks after the events it so faithfully describes.

This is a true story about telling the truth—and concealing it. The Maple parents, we're told early on, "stood as a thin barrier between the children and the truth"—the sad truth, that is, of the imminent breakup of the family. However, there are some aspects of that truth Richard and Joan are unwilling to reveal: the offstage presence, for instance, of Richard's lover. They also pretend the decision to split is one they arrived at together, though it's clear that Richard is the instigator. They delay the unveiling of this partial, repackaged truth, and try to stage-manage the announcement. Though surely convinced that their prevarications are in the children's best interest, the parents stand between the children and a full and accurate understanding of the circumstances; the "thin barrier" remains. At the last moment, Richard is granted an epiphany, and discovers another, equally sad truth—not one he would be inclined to share.

The lobster-and-champagne dinner he and Joan arrange for the family (ostensibly a homecoming for Judith, who has been away in England for a year, as Liz had been) is meant to set the stage for a serial breaking of the bad news, first to Judith, then John, then Margaret, who is thirteen now and no longer called Bean. Dickie is at a rock concert in Boston, and Richard is to tell him last, after picking him up at the train station. The plan misfires thanks to the copious flow of Richard's tears, a soggy display of grief that begins as soon as he sits down to dinner:

> They became, his tears, a shield for himself against these others—their faces, the fact of their assembly, a last time as innocents, at a table where he sat the last time as head. Tears dropped from his nose as he broke the lobster's back; salt flavored his champagne as he sipped it; the raw clench at the back of his throat was delicious. He could not help himself.

The tears were Updike's own, a glandular secretion rather than a literary device, and yet they take on the multivalent meaning of a cleverly chosen metaphor, a token of Richard's guilt, of his yearning for absolution, and of his stubborn separateness. The tears also demonstrate his ample gift for self-dramatization, self-pity, and the self-serving manipulation of others; they remind us of his fondness for irony, and that he's essentially incorrigible—he can't help himself.

Taking a step back from the fiction (in this case, bare fact artfully arranged), we see Updike's tears flowing at the same prodigious rate, with the same range of significance, and more: the added amazement that he could sit weeping through this traumatic meal and navigate its equally traumatic denouement, all the while gathering up and filing away the detailed impressions that would later give life to a short story. According to two of the three children present, when their father began to cry, their mother said to him, "Coward!" Mary herself had no recollection of saying it, though she thought her children were probably right; "I must at least have thought it," she said, "that John was using his tears to let the children know right then and there instead of telling them individually as I had wanted him to do." Whether or not she called him a coward, the tears were certainly his "shield" against the others, behind which the never-resting author was busy doing his work. And in a sense his fiction was a shield, too, a way for him to relive (and reorder) events and emotions at a slight remove from the intensity of the actual, real-time experience of announcing the end of family life as he knew it.

In the story, the tears that distance and protect also hasten the moment of reckoning. Asked why Daddy is crying, Joan is forced to supply the answer, thereby relieving Richard of the obligation to tell his children one by one, face-to-face—"You were having your way," Joan later points out, "making a general announcement." Now that the secret is out, Joan elaborates, "levelly, sensibly, reciting what they had prepared." The younger boy, John, slightly tipsy on champagne, becomes hysterical, and Richard leads him outside, past the clay tennis court the Maples—just like the Updikes—had recently built ("Years ago the Maples had observed how often . . . divorce followed a dramatic home improvement"). They sit together on a grassy rise in the last of the sun. As he comforts his son, he begins to take measure of his actions: "How selfish, how blind, Richard thought. His eyes felt scoured." The sore eyes are a taste of penance, but the moment of contrition is short-lived. In bed, Richard congratulates himself on having cleared a hurdle; he points out to Joan that the children "never questioned the reasons we gave." In other words, they never entertained the idea that "a third person" (Richard's lover) was involved. Joan's reply drips with irony: "That *was* touching." She reminds him, "You still have Dickie to do."

The thought of telling Dickie shatters Richard's "cozy" complacency and sets before him a "black mountain," a vast weight of guilt. "Of the four children," we're told, "his elder son was most nearly his conscience," an arrangement consonant with the character of a man who has trouble—to borrow the phrase from "Plumbing"—with trespass versus debts. The contours of his trespass are revealed almost as soon as he's made the announcement to Dickie, who's clearly stunned by the news. Richard lets him know that he's finding it difficult, too, that the hour he's spent waiting for the boy's train has been "about the worst" of his life. He says, "I hate this. *Hate* it. My father would have died before doing it to me." Richard's father has never figured in the Maples stories, so the remark, though striking, lacks resonance—it gestures vaguely at deterioration in moral standards from one generation to the next. Richard's son is "nearly his conscience," and so, it seems, is the memory of his father; as soon as Richard has mentioned his father, he feels "immensely lighter." He has passed on the burden of conscience—"dumped the mountain onto the boy."

For Updike, writing the sentence "My father would have died before doing it to me" must have felt like entering a guilty plea. It's a terrible admission—terrible and true: Wesley would indeed have died before breaking up John's childhood home.* And John would probably have found it exponentially more difficult to separate from Mary had his father still been alive. As Mary put it, "I think the fact that all of our parents had died—except Linda—gave John some sort of extra permission to start a new life, to do something different. Psychologically, that's part of what happened." Updike himself came close to giving an explanation during a filmed interview. Discussing the adulterous shenanigans of the *Couples* gang, he remarked, "One's continued need to be loved, to be glamorous, is basically very disruptive." He added, "In our attempt to be beautiful, we often break a lot of innocent bystanders' bones." Even as he cautiously maintained the illusion of authorial distance, he was admitting to the vanity and self-indulgence of the motive behind his affairs, and the painful cost of the consequence.

As for poor Richard Maple, he's not destined to have an easy night. Just before he goes out to pick up Dickie, he tells his wife, "Joan, if I could undo it all, I would." He's referring to the affair he's having, to the woman we know only as a "white face" he yearns to

---

* David told me that he had no specific memory of his father mentioning his grandfather that night, but that the account of their conversation was essentially accurate. The only element of fiction was the rock concert in Boston; in fact, David had been to a jazz club in Harvard Square.

"shield from tears." (Note the ironic asymmetry of that chivalrous sentiment.) Of course, before this latest affair there were the others; the idea that he could "undo it all" is preposterous. And it also hints at rich reserves of ambivalence. Joan's brilliant reply—"Where would you begin?"—is the first of two unanswerable questions that begin to expose the scale of his blunder:

The second question—"*Why?*"—is asked by a passionate and tearful Dickie, and instead of an answer, it's met with a heartbreaking passage that ends the story:

> *Why.* It was a whistle of wind in a crack, a knife thrust, a window thrown open on emptiness. The white face was gone, the darkness was featureless. Richard had forgotten why.

THINGS FELL APART. How did it happen? A couple of years earlier, Updike had made the following philosophical pronouncement to a visiting journalist: "There's something irredeemably perverse and self-destructive about us," he said. "The basic human condition of being a social animal is hard on the animal and hard on society." The phrasing pleased him, but blaming the human condition is a bit like blaming a nut and bolt fastened to a beam on the ceiling of your living room—in both cases, personal agency is removed from the equation. If the antique hardware on an old beam is what binds a family, and if a perversity common to us all is what unscrews the nut from the bolt, then nobody in particular is to blame when the house comes tumbling down.

Updike's whimsical fable about the big nut and bolt holding the family together has the unintended effect of redirecting our gaze toward the new owners of the Polly Dole House. The Updikes sold their home to Alexander and Martha Bernhard, a young couple who were moving to Ipswich from Wellesley with their three boys. Martha, a very pretty blond woman five years younger than John, had a captivating smile, intense blue eyes, and a tantalizing anecdote about one of his literary heroes, Nabokov, whose lecture course on

European literature she had taken at Cornell in the late fifties. Having moved into 26 East Street, Martha joined the Updikes' recorder group and made friends with them; soon the Bernhards were part of the gang, and several years later John and Martha launched into an affair that broke up both marriages.

If the Updikes' Ipswich friends were asked to identify fingerprints on the loosened nut, they would all point to Martha, who was, after all, living right there. A chorus of neighbors, some of them plausibly professing fondness for the alleged culprit, testified that Martha "went after" John with a single-minded resolve readily apparent to all. They told the same story in interview after interview: "It was all Martha. Martha set out to do it. It's just as simple as that. She had set her sights on John." Or: "Martha was as determined as any woman I've ever seen to have her way." Or: "She was very overt in her running after John—and he fell for it." Or: "Martha knew what she wanted and used everything in her charm bag to get it." The unanimity raises the suspicion that forty-year-old gossip has congealed into dogma. John's role in the breakup of his marriage barely gets a mention. That Mary might have had a hand in it seemed to occur to no one. It's as though John and Mary were both bystanders—part of the audience at Martha's one-woman show.

Her unswerving determination played its part in breaking up the marriage, but so did Mary's affairs and John's. Mary already had a lover when she found out about John and Martha—as far as she knew, her affair, which began early in 1973, predated his. John knew about her latest affair but didn't let on, and eventually cited it as a reason for wanting to separate. Marriages wear out, and in this case husband and wife had both been having affairs on and off for more than half of their twenty-one years together; the strain of those infidelities eventually weakened the bond. Given the complexity of the overlapping adulteries, and the affection that endured on both sides, it seems clear that if there's blame to be apportioned, it should be divided equally between the principals. After all, the Updikes sought and were granted a no-fault divorce (among the first in Massachusetts). Why should we waste our time pointing the finger when they reasonably chose not to? There were no villains, and in the end no victims, just an acutely painful family mess.

Had there been victims, had the Updike children, say, suffered any more than children inevitably suffer when their parents split, I would be tempted to describe the breakup by inverting Marx's formula: history repeats itself the first time as farce, the second time as tragedy. First came Joyce Harrington and the comic melodrama of John's abortive attempt to escape his marriage, the spectacular showdown at the Harringtons' house, the banishment to Antibes, the slow, pouty return to the status quo ante. A decade later, along came Martha Bernhard (Joyce redux), and we get an extended replay of John's indecision, hanging once again between Mary and another woman, unwilling to let go with either hand. When Mary found out about the affair, there were public scenes of jealous bad behavior and vicious private scraps before the heartbreaking endgame captured indelibly in "Separating"—which, though not a tragedy, is hard to read without a lump in the throat.

In June, Updike moved out of the house on Labor-in-Vain Road and rented a dingy apartment in a housing development in Ipswich. The family vacation (August on Martha's Vineyard) was split into shifts, Mary and John staggering their time on the island. He left town in September, and though he couldn't have known it because he was still wavering and nothing was settled, the Ipswich years were over.

What had been unthinkable under Eisenhower and racy under Kennedy had become, under Ford, almost compulsory.

—Memories of the Ford Administration (1992)

IX.

Marrying Martha

Updike was alone, living by himself for the first time in his life, without parents, roommates, a spouse, children. In September 1974 he moved into a small apartment on Beacon Street in Boston, a few blocks from the recently erected though still unoccupied John Hancock Tower, a mirrored slab famous for shedding panes of its reflective glass; he had a "gorgeous" view of this expensive fiasco, the tallest building in the city, and in several stories wrote hymns to its "huge blueness" and the disastrous blemish of its falling panes. In the wake of the separation from Mary, he felt like damaged goods, and the Hancock Tower became his secret sharer, a companion in his loneliness. In "Gesturing," the Maples story that follows "Separating," Richard rents a Boston apartment because it has a view of the tower; the building "spoke to him . . . of beauty and suffering." In "From the Journal of a Leper," the narrator associates his psoriasis with the vexed skyscraper ("the building had shed windows as I shed scales"), but the association is not unhappy; as the "leper" writes in his journal, "I reflect that all art, all beauty, is reflection." The mirrored immensity of the building reminded Updike, inevitably, of Stendhal's epigram "A novel is a mirror, taking a walk down a big road." At the time, alas, his own fiction reflected the wreckage of a marriage in its death throes.

Sunstruck and overheated, his apartment anchored him only loosely for the twenty months he rented it. His living "derangements," he wrote, entailed "a lot of driving from point to point in the scattered map of my emotional involvements." Like the protagonist of another story from this period, he "lived rather shapelessly," ricocheting from the isolation of his bachelor pad to his wife, to his mistress, to his children. (Liz was at Bennington College in Vermont; David in his last year of prep school at Phillips Academy, Andover; the younger two at home with their mother.) Also separated from her husband, Martha was still living in the Polly Dole House with her three boys, John, Jason, and Ted.* At first Updike zipped around in a lime-green convertible Mustang; after it was totaled by David's girlfriend, he bought a "rakish" Volkswagen Karmann Ghia, also convertible, handy for tight parking spaces in Back Bay but otherwise thoroughly impractical—a "guiltily self-destructive" purchase, he called it. The rattletrap Karmann Ghia shed nuts and bolts and even, once, a front wheel; he could watch the road fly by under his feet thanks to the rust holes in the floor; it felt, he wrote, like driving a bird's nest—another apt metaphor for the precarious limbo of his "furtive semi-bachelorhood."

"Domestic Life in America" is not a Maples story, but it might as well be; it bears, in any case, a similar proximity to the facts of Updike's domestic life during his self-imposed Boston exile. The names are new, but the family is the same (four children, recently separated parents), and the emotional currents crisscross in a familiar pattern. Fraser, the story's torn protagonist, bounces back and forth between wife and mistress, who live in the same town. As a result, we get a good look at both households. Greta, the other woman, is the mother of three young boys, the youngest of whom, Billy, is only five, and not adjusting well to his parents' separation. Nor, to be fair,

---

* Updike never wrote about a man visiting a mistress who lives in a house he used to own, a house where he once lived with his wife and children—too complicated a setup, perhaps, for fiction.

is Greta; "Because of me," she says with neurotic hyperbole, "Billy has no father." Billy does in fact have a father, and that father has a lawyer (as many wronged husbands do); the two of them are playing hardball—or, as Greta puts it, "the bastard and his lawyer are making me feed his own children cat food." Whether or not Martha recognized herself in the histrionic Greta, Alex Bernhard, the husband Martha left behind, had no trouble spotting his children when the story appeared in *The New Yorker*; a partner in a high-powered Boston law firm, Bernhard made it perfectly clear that he would sue Updike if he used them again in his fiction. Who knows? If he hadn't lodged that threat, we might have had a sequence of stories about Fraser's gradual adjustment to life with a trio of boys and their high-strung mother. As it is, the boys all but disappeared from Updike's oeuvre for the next several decades. (Second wives continued to feature prominently.)

Alone in Boston, he took German lessons and tried out a new cure for his psoriasis. Whether or not, as he suspected, his sense of guilt "triggered a metabolic riot," the condition of the skin on his face, shoulders, and neck deteriorated alarmingly. He flew down to St. Thomas hoping the Caribbean sun would once again work its wonders; he came home tanned but still scabby. Then Martha heard from her psychiatrist about an experimental program at Massachusetts General Hospital, just a few blocks from his apartment, where dermatologists were developing PUVA therapy, a treatment that combines ultraviolet light with a dose of psoralen. After only a few sessions in the "magic box," his complexion improved; within months he was "clear." For the first time since the age of six, he was no longer at war with his skin. Cured, like Updike, by the high-tech ministrations of an Australian dermatologist, the narrator of "From the Journal of a Leper" exults, "I am free, as other men. I am whole."

Yet Updike still had to contend, in the words of one of his divorcé narrators, with "clouds of grief and sleeplessness and moral confusion." Suspended between Mary and Martha, he wavered, and opted for the consolation of literature. Escaping into other writers' work, he accepted book review assignments from *The New Yorker* at a rate that would have been unsustainable if he hadn't been holed up on his own. Solitude gave him time for reading; as he admitted in a frightening aside, "I read slower than I write." He was also, during the first several months in Boston, collecting his reviews and other miscellaneous writings for a sequel to *Assorted Prose* called *Picked-Up Pieces*, a collection that revealed him as the best novelist-critic of his day. The introduction to *Picked-Up Pieces* makes it clear that Updike was giving the art of the book review serious thought. This is where he set out his "code of reviewing," guidelines that remain essential reading for critics starting out in the profession. The impetus for drawing up the code was, as he put it, "youthful traumas at the receiving end of critical opinion"—John Aldridge's review of *Of the Farm*, among others that stuck in his craw. Operating under the critical equivalent of the golden rule, and hoping to maintain "a chemical purity in the reaction between product and appraiser," he urged critics to stay honest by not accepting for review books they are "predisposed to dislike, or committed by friendship to like." Along with some pithy uplift ("Review the book, not the reputation" and "Better to praise and share than blame and ban"), he provided five concrete rules, all of which extend the benefit of the doubt to the book in question. His basic assumption was that criticism should be written not for its own sake but for the sake of the book under review, never forgetting the intelligent lay reader who might be encouraged to buy it, or avoid it. In short, he hoped to add to the joy of reading.

Although he feared that on occasion he failed to live up to his own high standards, he almost always practiced what he preached. The hallmarks of his criticism are catholic taste; a refreshingly friendly, casual, and pragmatic approach to the task; and of course sheer volume: he was not only the best novelist-critic of his day but also among the most prolific.* With a mixture of bravado and chagrin, he confessed the obvious: "Evidently I can read anything in English and muster up an opinion about it." Gathered together and grouped by subject, as they are in *Picked-Up Pieces*, his reviews re-

---

* Competition was provided by Gore Vidal and Joyce Carol Oates; Norman Mailer, another worthy contender, couldn't quite keep pace.

main stubbornly separate from each other, a collection of discrete entities. That may sound like a vice, but actually it's a virtue: he pushed no larger agenda, espoused no grand theory of literature. Nor was he concerned to have the last word on an author or a topic; he had no qualms about admitting ignorance, or even bewilderment. In these respects, he was very different from Edmund Wilson, *The New Yorker*'s regular reviewer from the mid-forties to the mid-sixties; and from George Steiner, who succeeded Wilson. A distinguished academic, Steiner was unabashedly erudite, a fearless champion of the highbrow. Wilson immersed himself unreservedly, sometimes pedantically, in topics that appealed to him; having mastered a topic, he surveyed it in toto, delivering with uncompromising high purpose a complete package pegged to an all-encompassing narrative. Updike was more modest than either of these critics, more versatile, and more practical; he approached his task with unheroic professionalism, with the tacit acknowledgment, hinted at in the title of *Picked-Up Pieces*, that this was piecework—well-remunerated piecework: as he later remarked, "the payment for a monthly review roughly balanced out the monthly alimony payment that was mine to make." His subjects were very often chosen for him, mostly by Shawn in consultation with the gruff, sharp-tongued Rogers Whitaker, a jack-of-all-trades *New Yorker* editor who joined the staff of the magazine the year it was founded, helped shape its famous fact-checking department, and eventually did much of his work in the books department (when he wasn't writing about trains as the pseudonymous E. M. Frimbo, or about college football as "J.W.L."). Whitaker edited Updike's reviews from the mid-sixties until his retirement in 1975; *Picked-Up Pieces* is dedicated to him, in gratitude.

A collection of reviews assigned by magazine editors will usually have a random feel to it, and this one is no exception. Certain preoccupations are nonetheless apparent, chief among them Updike's abiding interest in Nabokov. Updike had been reading him with avid pleasure ever since the Pnin stories began appearing in *The New Yorker* in the mid-fifties; a decade later he began writing about him. In the seventies, a pattern of influence began to emerge: the two novels written after *Rabbit Redux*—*A Month of Sundays* and

The Coup—are blessed or cursed, depending on your taste, with the trickiest, flashiest Updike prose, a sure sign that the author of *Pale Fire* was casting a long shadow.

Writing reviews of Nabokov's work, Updike often permitted himself to engage in reflexive one-upmanship. In his lengthy, ambivalent piece on *Ada*, for example, he gives a brilliant demonstration of how to review fairly, sensitively, and intelligently—all the while showing off to maximum effect his own writerly agility. Urbane and self-assured ("Rape is the sexual sin of the mob, adultery of the bourgeoisie, and incest of the aristocracy"), he declines to spend his time "unstitching the sequined embroidery of Nabokov's five-years' labor of love" but can't resist sewing a few sequins of his own: "[T]he last pages of *Ada* are the best, and rank with Nabokov's best, but to get to them we traverse too wide a waste of facetious, airy, side-slipped semi-reality." Would he have allowed himself that alliterative glut in a review of a less glittery writer? Perhaps, but something about Nabokov seems to call forth the characteristic foibles of his critics—that was certainly the case with Updike, as it was with Wilson and Steiner.

Updike's ideas about Nabokov spring from a root sympathy: shared delight in the aesthetic bliss of wordplay. Updike understood that they were both afflicted with "a writer's covetousness," a complaint he thought of as "akin to the fear of death"; the telltale symptom is a "constant state of anxiety compelling one to fix indelibly this or that evanescent trifle"—in other words, they suffered from a compulsive urge to translate into writing, into words printed on the page, as much of the universe as they could render. In his 1964 review of the English translation of *The Defense*, he declared with comical precision that "Vladimir Nabokov distinctly seems to be the best writer of English prose currently holding American citizenship." He never retreated from that opinion, though he made it clear from the start that there were limits to his enthusiasm, and that he would not be engaging in hero worship. For every bouquet ("His sentences are beautiful out of context and doubly beautiful in it. He writes prose the only way it should be written—that is, ecstatically"), there's a brickbat: mention of "aimless intricacies" and "mannered" devices, and more sinister failings, such as Nabokov's "cruelty" to his own characters and his peculiar "teasing of cripples." In 1977, when the great man died, Updike offered handsome tribute in *The New Yorker* to the "resplendent oeuvre" of a Russian novelist who had achieved the remarkable feat of "inventing himself anew, as an American writer." Yet while Nabokov was alive and working, Updike's aim was not to sum up and codify; he simply told us what we needed to know about each successive post-*Lolita* novel, scattering praise and itemizing sadly (or, in the case of *Transparent Things*, with cheery bafflement) any failings.

An American born in a small town at the nadir of the Depression is unlikely to identify too closely with an aristocrat born in czarist Russia in the last year of the nineteenth century, and yet Updike's descriptions of Nabokov sometimes sound like wish-fulfillment fantasies: "Rich, healthy, brilliant, physically successful, he lacks the neurasthenic infirmities that gave the modernism of Proust, Joyce, Kafka, and Mann its tender underside." Was Updike auditioning for a similar role, imagining a suave suburban iteration of the textual titan, playing beach volleyball on Sunday afternoon, and the next morning bending his attention to the masterpiece in his typewriter? And when he marvels at the mental energy of Nabokov (whose "brain was so excited" he could scarcely sleep), was it his own "cerebral self-delight" he was admiring? Whether or not he daydreamed his way into some half-conscious identification, he endorsed with enthusiasm Nabokov's artistic ambitions: "He asked . . . of his own art and the art of others a something extra—a flourish of mimetic magic or deceptive doubleness—that was supernatural and surreal in the root sense of these degraded words." Updike was by temperament wary of pure artifice; he needed to keep a foot on hard ground and an eye on humble, well-thumbed detail. Yet during the seventies, the glories of Nabokov's literary sleight of hand, his "deceptive doubleness," exerted a powerful pull. With his domestic life in disarray, Updike enveloped his novels in a protective carapace of stylistic and imaginative flamboyance. The wedge of distance provided by a Nabokovian dose of the supernatural and the surreal offered a break from the stubborn fact that he had left his wife and children.

Oddly enough, Martha Bernhard (née Ruggles), the woman at the epicenter of the disarray, bore the stamp of Nabokov's approval. Enrolled in the last course he taught at Cornell, she had fallen "deeply under his spell"—deeply and lastingly. She told Updike she never forgot the lessons learned from his lectures: "I felt he could teach me how to read. I believed he could give me something that would last all my life—and it has." Updike proudly repeated a neatly polished version of the anecdote about her only one-to-one encounter with her teacher:

> When our Miss Ruggles, a tender twenty, went up at the end of one class to retrieve her blue book from the mess of graded "prelims" strewn there, she could not find it, and at last had to approach the professor. Nabokov stood tall and apparently abstracted on the platform above her, fussing with his papers. She begged his pardon and said that her exam didn't seem to be here. He bent low, eyebrows raised. "And what is your name?" She told him, and with prestidigitational suddenness he produced her blue book from behind his back. It was marked 97. "I wanted to see," he told her, "what a genius looked like." And coolly he looked her up and down, while she blushed; that was the extent of their exchange.

Who could resist a mistress who'd been certified a genius by Vladimir Nabokov? Updike's evident delight in this incident suggests that falling under Martha's spell was yet another way of falling under Nabokov's spell.

Updike wrote a fictionalized account of the genesis of their affair, "A Constellation of Events," a little more than a year after the fact, in March 1975. In the story, Betty and Rafe—married, but to other people—first get together thanks to a book Rafe is reading by a professor of literature Betty had studied with at college: She sees it on the seat of his car; he offers to lend it to her, and drops by her house the next morning to deliver it. She offers him a coffee and they kiss, drawn to each other, as it were, by literary affinity. We witness the action through Betty's eyes as she realizes that she's falling in love with Rafe, a lean, loosely knit, hatchet-faced man with a "humiliated clown's air" and a wife who has a lover. Because Updike included in the story Betty's husband, Rob (a lightly disguised version of Alex Bernhard), he felt he had to delay publication of the story—even though he'd gone to the trouble of changing the venue of a key scene to mask its factual basis. *The New Yorker* was eager to publish the prudently revised version in early 1979 (a full five years after the wreck of the two marriages), but Updike told the magazine that the possibility of a "legal assault" from Alex Bernhard was still too real; he couldn't trust the efficacy of his attempts to make the story libel-proof. "A Constellation of Events" finally appeared in 1985, when the damage done was an even more distant memory.

The story gives the strong sense that the protagonists are helpless as they drift into adultery. "We're going to be a lot of trouble," Rafe says to Betty. "Yes," she replies, resigned to the breakup of two families. They're helpless and therefore somehow blameless. (There's also the mitigating factor of Rafe's wife's infidelity, which Betty knows about, but perhaps not Rafe.) Inconvenient and inevitable, their romance, Updike hints, is blessed by divine sanction:

> And, though there was much in the aftermath to regret, and a harm that would never cease, Betty remembered these days . . . as bright, as a single iridescent unit, not scattered like a constellation, but continuous, a rainbow, a U-turn.

That's the last sentence of the story. Although the U-turn ends two marriages and inflicts enduring harm, it also takes the shape of a rainbow, God's covenant promising no recurrence, no more wreckage. The flood passes, and Betty and Rafe survive the aftermath—it adds up to a happy enough ending. But life is messier than fiction, and the rainbow's iridescent curve, harbinger of a bright future with Martha, is inverted in the author's note to *Problems and Other Stories* (1979), where "A Constellation of Events" would have appeared if not for fear of legal assault. He begins facetiously ("Seven years since my last short-story collection? There must have been problems") and ends on a tender, melancholy note: "[T]he collection as a whole, with the curve of sad time it subtends, is dedicated lovingly to Elizabeth, David, Michael, and Miranda." That haunting phrase, "the curve of sad time it subtends," is Updike's elliptical way of saying sorry publicly for his part in a trauma he not only precipitated but also publicized.

Half the stories in *Problems* were written after he separated from Mary, and in all but one of those we read about the guilt and regret of a man whose first marriage has failed or is failing. His guilt is aggravated by the pain and confusion his "dereliction" has inflicted on various children. "Guilt Gems," the title of one of the stories, could easily serve as the title for all the others. Sometimes the poor man is torn between wife and mistress; sometimes he's adjusting uneasily to a rather brittle and demanding second wife, who's guilt-racked, too. Alone or with the other woman, he's almost always lashed by remorse. Updike in this period could be as single-minded as he had been in the months and years following the near-miss with Joyce Harrington. Divorce and its discontents had replaced adultery as his simplex theme. He worried about a glut in the market for suburban guilt.

To compound the sense of déjà vu, Denis de Rougemont and the legend of Tristan and Iseult make a return appearance. In the title story of *Problems*, charmingly configured as a six-part math test, Updike invokes Tristan's Law: "appealingness is inversely proportional to attainability." Here's the premise: "During the night, A, though sleeping with B, dreams of C." And here's the question: "Which has he more profoundly betrayed, B or C?" Translated out of fictional terms, this is the gist of Updike's own problem: as soon as separation made her seem unattainable, Mary grew more appealing to him—he dreamed of his wife, even though he was now free to sleep with his mistress. In the story, he appends a "helpful hint" in the guise of Midas's Law: "Possession diminishes perception of value, immediately." Anything but helpful in his actual situation, this second law twists the knife: he had left Mary for Martha, and now Martha's value was diminished—not hugely, but just enough to fog his emotional landscape and add to his "life-fright." He knew that he was making both women unhappy, straining their patience, betraying them both, but he couldn't help himself. In a late story he described the condition as "emotional bigamy." He began seeing a psychiatrist again, every other week. All this anguish and uncertainty provided rich material for fiction. As before, it made him miserable, but not too miserable to write.

Perhaps the oddest feature of his Boston limbo is that it loosely resembled the situation he had mapped out in *A Month of Sundays*, which is about a philandering husband banished in disgrace from his community as a direct result of his adulterous shenanigans. He wrote the novel in a rush, beginning in early November 1973 and finishing just sixteen weeks later—well before the breakup and more than half a year before he left Ipswich. The whiff of prophecy adds to the impression, already strong after *Of the Farm*, of a man who steeled himself for action or braced himself to endure an event by writing it out. Having somehow understood, consciously or not, that exile from Ipswich was inevitable, he devised a way to explore the experience on paper.

The novel consists of a journal kept by the Reverend Tom Marshfield, who has been relieved of his clerical duties for a month by his bishop. Shipped out to a desert retreat in an unnamed western state, he's required to add a new entry to the journal every morning of his stay, the daily stint at the typewriter being a form of therapy or penance. In the afternoon he plays golf with his fellow exiles, also clergymen in disgrace. Married and the father of two young sons, Marshfield had embarked on an affair with the church organist, his first infidelity, and then with several other "seducing" parishioners ("by way of being helpful"), before his indiscretions were exposed. The premise might lead you to expect a somber, regretful tone. But contrite he is not. His reaction to the scandal and his punishment is a kind of manic clowning. He indulges in an orgy of glib wordplay. His diary, complete with typos and footnotes (and even a transcribed comment said to have been scrawled in pencil, in a reader's hand), is a mixture of confession, reminiscence, clever disquisition, polemic, and sermon—with plenty of sex for spice. After his long struggle with the recalcitrant Buchanan material, Updike had reason to rejoice in a hyperfluent torrent of language; the tone of the novel is exuberant in part because of the author's relief at the ease with which he was writing.

Adultery is one of the many topics Marshfield playfully juggles (he drafts a sermon in praise of it); divorce is another. He asks, "When is it right for a man to leave his wife?"—and supplies an answer that gives a good idea of both his state of mind and the texture of his prose: "When the sum of his denied life overtops the calculated loss of the children, the grandparents if surviving, the dog, and the dogged *ux.*, known as Fido, residual in himself." The style might be described as excitable Humbert Humbert: a virtuoso performance, but somewhat off-putting in its razzle-dazzle and stiff-arm irony. A sentence from Updike's review of *Ada*—"His prose has never . . . menaced a cowering reader with more bristling erudition, garlicky puns, bearish parentheses, and ogreish winks"—applies perfectly well here. But Nabokov is not the novel's only godparent; *A Month of Sundays* tips its hat repeatedly to Hawthorne's *The Scarlet Letter*, the earliest and perhaps greatest American contribution to the literature of adultery. Thomas Marshfield, whose wife's maiden name is Chillingworth and who tries, while exiled, to seduce a Ms. Prynne, is a militantly unrepentant descendant of Hawthorne's wayward minister, Arthur Dimmesdale.*

Not surprisingly, Marshfield's verbal acrobatics get in the way of feeling. The scene in which the banished minister says good-bye to his two sons is notably bereft of emotion—compared with "Separating," it's as dry as an old stick. Updike told an interviewer that he "wanted to make the book kind of abrasive and offensive," and in the eyes of many reviewers, he succeeded. Anatole Broyard, who'd raved about *Rabbit Redux*, was particularly disappointed by the "virtuosity . . . too gleefully displayed." He went so far as to throw one of

---

* *A Month of Sundays* is only the first installment in a trilogy of novels linked to *The Scarlet Letter*; in the second, *Roger's Version* (1986), a modern-day Chillingworth, also an elderly cuckold, takes center stage; and the third, *S.* (1988), is a tribute to Hester Prynne herself. As even a cursory comparison of Marshfield and Dimmesdale would suggest, Updike's serial appropriation of Hawthorne's characters is part homage, part subversion—*askew* is the apt word Updike uses.

Updike's best put-downs back at him: "In a review of J. D. Salinger, Mr. Updike once remarked that sentimentality is a writer's loving his characters more than God loves them. Something similar might be said about his own love of language." Other critics objected to the sexual content, and to Marshfield's unabashed sexism, which they attributed to Updike. It's a mistake to casually conflate character and author, especially with respect to a book as sophisticated as *A Month of Sundays*, which plays clever games with narrative voice and the notion of the implied reader—and yet the critics' complaints are understandable, a predictable reaction to the grating tone of Marshfield's braggadocio.

By the time Knopf published the novel in February 1975, Updike may have found himself somewhat less amused by the defiantly impenitent posturing of his exiled philanderer.* After living away from his family for more than half a year, he was still unsure whether the break with Mary was the right idea; in any case, he was neither defiant nor impenitent. A semi-bachelor perched in his Boston pad, he was "living like a buzzard in a tree"; when he visited the house on Labor-in-Vain Road, as he did most Sundays, he was circling the cold periphery of a family life that had sustained him for two decades. One of his protagonists recalls "those embarrassing, disarrayed years when I scuttled without a shell, between houses and wives, a snake between skins, a monster of selfishness, my grotesque needs naked and pink." If Updike still saw anything funny about being a "divorcing bachelor," his laughter would have been wry, bitter, disgusted.

He could at least reflect that he was in better shape than John Cheever, who had come to town to teach two writing classes at Boston University and was doing his level best to drink himself to death. Early in the fall term, Updike bumped into him on Newbury Street, outside Brooks Brothers; they went in together, and Cheever bought two pairs of tasseled loafers. Then they had a drink at the Kon-

---

* Whatever his private sentiments, in public Updike never spoke ill of any of his books. Once or twice he claimed to have special affection for *A Month of Sundays*.

Tiki bar at the Park Plaza Hotel—or rather Updike had a drink and Cheever a succession of drinks, all doubles (the dosage urgently insisted upon by the older man). They parted on Commonwealth Avenue, Cheever toddling off unsteadily. "I felt badly," Updike remembered, "because it was as though a natural resource was being wasted." Although Cheever complained in the months that followed that Updike never made contact, they did get together several times, and on each occasion the plan went awry. Updike tried to take him to the Museum of Fine Arts to see the revival of a Greta Garbo film, but when they got there they found it was sold out, so they went instead to dinner at the Café Budapest in Copley Square. Cheever convinced Updike to participate in a two-hour question-and-answer session at BU; after less than an hour, peeved because he felt his tongue-tied students weren't taking full advantage of this special opportunity, Cheever suddenly cut the proceedings short. And then there was the night Updike dropped by to pick up Cheever and take him to Symphony Hall; when he arrived he found the celebrated sixty-two-year-old author drunk and stark naked on his fourth-floor landing, the door to his apartment swinging shut behind him. Luckily it didn't lock. Updike, absent a better idea, went about getting his friend ready for the concert: "I primly concentrated on wedging him into his clothes." In March, Cheever faced facts for long enough to resign from his teaching job; he persuaded Updike to stand in for the remaining six weeks of the term. Updike agreed because he thought Cheever was doomed, literally about to drop dead. But after one last epic Boston bender, the author of *The Wapshot Chronicle* woke up and found himself in Manhattan—at the Smithers Alcoholism Treatment and Training Center. Released after twenty-eight days, he remained sober. Drying out had saved his life. In midsummer, driving back from a visit to Plowville, Updike dropped in to see him at home in Ossining, New York, and thought he looked well but frail "with all the alcohol squeezed out of him."

MARY HAD STOPPED drinking, too—not because she was suffering from alcoholism, or was even in any danger of it, but because successive traumas (the death of both parents in the space of two years, the final collapse of her marriage) had pushed her to the edge of exhaustion. Her psychiatrist recommended a two-month spell on the wagon and as much peace and quiet as she could arrange. She spent most of July in Vermont, hoping that the remove from Ipswich and the tranquillity of the isolated farmhouse she and her sister had inherited would help her recover her sense of well-being. In her absence, Updike moved back into the house on Labor-in-Vain Road for three weeks, glad to spend time with the children. He was struck afresh by the loveliness of the house, and when Mary returned at the end of the month, he found it a shock to trade bucolic Ipswich for two rooms in muggy Back Bay. In early August he took Martha to East Hampton, New York, near the tip of Long Island, for a weeklong vacation at the Sea Spray Inn, a nineteenth-century hotel perched on a dune overlooking the ocean.

At this point—in fact, for the first fifteen months of the separation—his affair with Martha was still a secret. His mother and his children, who knew nothing about his mistress, had to make sense of the separation as best they could, swallowing euphemistic explanations such as the ones the Maples foisted on their children: "For some years now, we haven't been doing enough for each other, making each other as happy as we should be." Mary had known about Martha all along, and her resentment grew as he dithered and the affair began to look as though it might last. She managed to keep quiet until Christmas, then abruptly gave the game away—throwing, as John put it, "the shadow of my girlfriend over the holidays." Once Martha's role in the breakup had been revealed—once John's hand, in effect, had been forced—the paralysis ended. He sent a photograph of Martha (posed next to a tombstone) to his mother, he convinced Mary to agree that it was time for the "next step," and he began looking for a house he could share with his mistress and her children.

Before he could embark on a new life, he had to formally renounce the old one. On a sunny Monday morning in early May 1976, he and Mary drove to the courthouse in nearby Salem to petition for divorce. At the hearing—replayed with unerring accuracy in

"Here Come the Maples," written just eight weeks later—the judge asked them both in turn if they believed the marriage had suffered an "irretrievable breakdown" (the legal language of "no-fault"); each replied, "I do." When it was all over, John kissed Mary, remedying, as he remarked, "an old omission." He told his mother that the ceremony was very like a marriage, a poignant irony he also exploited in the story.

A week after the hearing in Salem, Updike took possession of a red clapboard house on West Main Street in Georgetown, Massachusetts. The town, which he described as "an unassuming population knot on the way to other places," was twenty minutes inland from Ipswich, in a flat, featureless part of the state. He'd noticed the house with its For Sale sign from the car as he was driving through; set perpendicular to a busy street, it was a long, narrow Colonial with a big yard out back—an oasis of relative calm. The low-ceilinged front rooms were noisy, with truck traffic rattling the windows, but Updike's large, drafty office was at the rear, so the rumble of the trucks didn't bother him. From his window he could see the lot where the town parked its fleet of yellow school buses. When Joyce Carol Oates and her husband, Ray Smith, dropped by in mid-July to take John and Martha out to lunch at a local restaurant, Oates was perplexed to find them living in a tiny town, in a house where the traffic noise threatened to drown out conversation. She wondered in her journal, "With all Updike's money, and his and Martha's good sense, how has it come about that they've bought a house in such a location?" The answer is that Updike's habitual thrift—his lingering fear of the poorhouse, exacerbated by the fact that he'd signed over to Mary the house on Labor-in-Vain Road and agreed to pay her a comfortable alimony—made him hungry for a bargain. And just as important, the shape of the Georgetown house, the outline he glimpsed from the car window, reminded him of the white brick house he grew up in, the haven of his Shillington boyhood. The town, too, reminded him of Shillington—"I was at home in America, all right."

Oates's visit was the first chance for the two writers to spend time together; it cemented their friendship and set the tone for four decades of animated correspondence. Lunch was a leisurely affair, two hours of "lightweight, amusing gossip," according to Oates, "nothing malicious, nothing extreme." Roth, Bellow, and Kurt Vonnegut were mentioned, along with Erica Jong, whose *Fear of Flying* Updike had reviewed glowingly three years earlier. Updike mocked a facial tic the critic Alfred Kazin had developed: "I couldn't help but admire," he said, "how Kazin's mouth seemed to disappear under his ear." Oates thought the tone of this last observation was "amiable." (From this distance it sounds suspiciously like Nabokov teasing cripples.) She enjoyed Updike's self-deprecation and listed his other likable qualities: he was gentle, sly, clever, witty, charming. She detected an element of impersonation in his character, and caught hints that his modesty was exaggerated. "[H]e's a hillbilly from rural Pennsylvania," she wrote, "somehow masquerading as a world-famous writer, and the role makes him uneasy and ironic." She also spotted an undercurrent of competition with the other writers whose names came up, a tendency she recognized in herself, even in relation to her new friend. Over the years, the gossip carried on, but the spark of competition between them, which so nearly flickered to life over lunch, never ignited; perhaps it was smothered by the many professions of mutual admiration. To Oates, John was "immensely attractive," and Martha "his equal in every way"; she could see at once why they'd fallen in love. Having read "Separating," she spared a thought for "the various agonies they experienced, and caused, in coming together." John had introduced Martha as an "old and ardent Oates reader," and this surely helped make the lunch go smoothly, promoting friendly feelings all around. The two couples remained on good terms, seeing each other once or twice a year over the next decade or so. Martha occasionally added cheerful, affectionate handwritten notes at the bottom of John's letters; to judge from the brisk confidence of those postscripts, she, too, thought she was John's equal in every way.

Updike's letters to Oates are not unlike his letters to Maxwell: warm and unbuttoned, full of little jokes, odd digressions, and literary insight. A treasury of snappy judgments about members of the National Institute of Arts and Letters, and about the stream of writers nominated for one prize or another, the correspondence is a brilliant record of the affectionate shoptalk of two authors at the top of their profession. As a friend, and as his publisher at the *Ontario Review*, Oates was in cahoots with him, and he liked that—they were a gang of two. Her letters to him were not entirely unlike his mother's—his mother having been in cahoots with him since infancy. Part of what encouraged him to write so brilliantly to Oates was his faith in the brilliance of her replies. He had the same faith in Maxwell, and in his mother. "Nobody can read like a writer," he told Oates; he might have added that nobody can write letters like a writer.

"I'd go mad in such a small town myself," Oates confided to her journal after her necessarily brief tour of Georgetown and lunch in the empty Chanticleer restaurant in neighboring Rowley—but she added that Updike appeared to be thriving in his near seclusion. At first he didn't sleep well in the new house, but that was before Martha moved in with her children and her furniture. The cellar was "foul," and a scavenging rat in the kitchen caused some consternation, disrupted Martha's cooking, and inspired a poem about the "rotten places" in a house. When Updike counted up his Georgetown friends, he stalled at four: the mailman, the milkman, the newspaper boy, and the electrician. But for the most part he was pleased with the house and delighted to be out of the city—no more waiting in line at the bank, no need to navigate an urban obstacle course just to buy a loaf of bread. Georgetown "made negligible communal demands," he wrote; compared with Ipswich, where he had been a generous, hardworking volunteer, piling up civic obligations, it represented a blissful simplification of his life, a chance for him, he liked to say, to rededicate himself to his writing.

You can't expect to lead a simple life when you have four children aged sixteen to twenty-one. After the summer holiday, Michael announced that he would like to live in Georgetown with his father for his senior year in high school. Mary was dismayed, and John perplexed and a little worried about preserving the serenity of his new household, but Martha was willing, and the seventeen-year-old moved into a little room at the back of the house. His siblings figured that Michael was trying to forge a closer bond with his father.

He stayed only a few months before moving back to Labor-in-Vain Road. Meanwhile, Liz, who had left Bennington to study nursing, announced that she was going to marry the much older man she had spent a year with in England, a match Updike deplored but felt powerless to prevent; he thought of his future son-in-law—whose alcohol dependency was perceptible to those willing to acknowledge it—as "a patch of human quicksand down which Liz's nursing career and a lot of my hard-earned money will be thrown." David, who started at Harvard in the fall of 1975, had long outgrown his headaches and his temper tantrums and was proving himself, in his father's estimation, to be competent and confident. He was trying to break into the varsity soccer team, and would soon develop an interest in creative writing. Miranda, home alone with Mary, was troubled by math tests, her fluctuating weight, and the health of Helen, the family's aging golden retriever. Almost all these details filtered into Updike's fiction and poetry.

A poem set in his new Georgetown surroundings, "An Oddly Lovely Day Alone," luxuriates in the domestic peace of an empty house: "The kids went off to school, / the wife to the hairdresser." He reads a book, receives a visit from the man from "Pest Control" (the rat problem again)—"Time went by silently." The spare language matches the emptiness of the day and the house. A metaphor adds depth and breadth: "Each hour seemed a rubber band / the preoccupied fingers of God / were stretching at His desk," a daring glimpse of a bored creator. And then, in the midst of postprandial torpor, distraction arrives: "More time passed, darkening. / All suddenly unbeknownst, / the afternoon had begun to snow." The moral that wraps up this charming lyric—"If people don't entertain you, / Nature will"—is a deft reminder of Updike's talent for making something out of what most people would think of as nothing.

Much as he liked being home alone, and though he told himself that public speaking was "a whorish thing to do," when asked to give a talk, he more often than not said yes; time and again, the promise of an adoring audience, solicitous journalists, and a long line of readers waiting to have their books signed proved irresistible. Six months after moving to Georgetown, he flew to Washington to deliver a lecture, "The Written Word," at the Smithsonian Institution. He agreed to do some publicity while he was in town to help promote the newly published *Marry Me*. Sally Quinn of *The Washington Post* interviewed him over lunch at a restaurant the day after the lecture and produced the kind of lunchtime interview-cum-profile often found in magazines and the arts pages of newspapers: questions and answers are lobbed back and forth between mouthfuls, and the choice of entrée, the table manners, the crumbs scattered on the placemat are all scrutinized as though the mechanics of the meal supplied clues to the author's character and the mystery of literary inspiration. Over the next several decades, Updike submitted to dozens and dozens of these live-action interviews. The Quinn Q&A is notable only because it's one of the few times Updike tried and failed to charm a journalist.

He was by this time well practiced in the art of handling interviews. After *Couples* made him famous, after the critical acclaim that greeted *Rabbit Redux*, journalists expected to meet someone puffed up with self-importance, or anyway aware of himself as a literary celebrity. Instead they came face-to-face with an appealingly awkward character with an almost imperceptible stutter. "Gracious, self-deprecating, and casually attentive" is how a young Michiko Kakutani found him. As his *Lampoon* friend Michael Arlen said in the early seventies, "John is one of the few people I know who's been literally made larger and more attractive by success." The British novelist Ian McEwan interviewed him in London in the early nineties and was impressed by how obliging he was. Updike flew in from New York in the morning and spent most of the afternoon in the television studio filming the interview. When it was over, the producer asked him to read a long passage from his new novel for the camera, and then asked him to do it over—twice. As far as McEwan could tell, "Updike read faultlessly each time"; and yet, jet lag or no jet lag, he didn't grumble when asked to start again. He was always careful to avoid prima donna posturing and any whiff of literary pretension. Faced with media scrutiny, he aimed to be smart and engaging, to be nice.

Sally Quinn was unwilling to settle for nice; she had her heart set on naughty.

The headline read, "Updike on Women, Marriage and Adultery." Barely nodding in the direction of his books, she asked first about his marital status. He explained about the recent divorce hearing. His laugh, she noted, was uncomfortable, "the kind of laugh 13-year-old boys have when they are being teased." She threw back at him lines from the lecture he'd delivered the night before:

> Now I live with yet another family group . . . and the lady of the household is indeed a reader. She has told me she cannot let a day pass without its hours of reading, which makes her an ideal counterpart for me, whose chemistry must daily secrete a written page or two. Speaking economically, she consumes what I produce.

Updike undoubtedly intended the playfully risqué double entendre in the last sentence. And yet, confronted with it over lunch (and realizing at once that Quinn would milk it, so to speak), he blushed. Quinn then extracted Martha's first name, and pressed him on the difference between being married and living together. "There's a delicate but kind of fragrant difference," he said. "There's just a touch of the voluntary that lingers, that would be a pity to lose. The lady I live with is very scared of changing it. She was married for 17 years. She felt very captive then." According to Quinn, Updike began to relax. Or perhaps he knew he couldn't win and was adjusting to the inevitability of mild public humiliation. In any case, he continued to spout semiconfessional musings: "The older I get I'd say I'm more monogamous. After all I'm conserving energy enabling me to get on with my life's work. Monogamy is very energy-conserving. To be unmonogamous is a great energy consumer." In the article, Quinn capped this ill-considered quote with a description guaranteed to make her subject cringe: "He takes a prideful puff from his cigarillo and laughs at his own philosophy." He got up from the table—having consumed mushroom soup, a chicken salad sandwich, and potato chips—knowing that Quinn's profile would portray him in an unflattering light, and loathing her for it already. With his help, she had maneuvered him into exactly the pose feminist critics expected of him in the wake of *Couples* and *A Month of Sundays*: priapic narcissism.

Many women (and some men, too) were now reading Updike with a skeptical squint. A full-blown feminist critique, Mary Allen's "John Updike's Love of 'Dull Bovine Beauty,'" had recently been published. Like many of the complaints lodged against him in the decades to come, Allen's polemic suffers from a slippery tendency to conflate the author's attitudes with those of his characters (especially Rabbit), and swerves dangerously close to ad hominem attack. Yet her essay piles up so many instances of casual male chauvinism (Rabbit again, but also Tom Marshfield) that it threatens to tip the scales and make even an otherwise favorably disposed reader wonder whether Updike might indeed be a chauvinist. Why, in the fiction of the sixties and early seventies, are so many of the girlfriends and wives of his characters described as dumb or stupid? Is the profusion of lovingly described sexual activity, and the Updikean man-child's avid focus on female anatomy, indicative of an obsession that blinkers his attitude toward women? Are these symptoms of misogyny?

Updike was sufficiently troubled by this kind of question to issue a protest: "I can't think of any male American writer who takes women more seriously or has attempted more earnestly to show them as heroines." But just to be safe, he also issued a blanket apology— "Whatever I don't know about women I apologize for"—and reaffirmed his writerly intention to encompass as much of humanity as he could. Faced with direct questions about sexism, he mostly avoided combative or defensive answers; he mentioned the influence of his mother, who first stimulated his interest in writing, and the crucial role that women editors, Katharine White and Judith Jones chief among them, had played in his career. And on the page he pushed deeper into the minds of his female characters, gave them better jobs and greater psychic independence. (Janice Angstrom would soon become a prime beneficiary of these efforts.)

In January 1978, a month after the Quinn debacle, as if submitting to classroom penance, he signed his name more than twenty-five thousand times for a Franklin Library "Signature Edition" of *Rabbit, Run*. He did the deed over a two-week stay at the Pineapple

Beach Resort on St. Thomas, a mind-numbing junket exactly like the one he inflicted on Henry Bech in "Three Illuminations in the Life of an American Author"—except that Bech was paid a little more than forty thousand dollars, Updike nearly sixty thousand. This was the most lucrative venture in what might be termed Updike's shadow publishing career, a range of activity that included allowing fine presses to print broadsides, pamphlets, and chapbooks; selling his own manuscripts; and signing proofs and galleys and other collectible items that are part of the publishing process. The audience for this shadow career was not the reading public but collectors, assorted bibliophiles, and friends of the author; the impulse behind it was his love of the printed page (especially when the page was adorned with words he'd written), his sympathy with the collecting instinct, a very Updikean mix of avarice and generosity, and his usual reluctance to say no.

Art and money intersect repeatedly in "Three Illuminations." In the first vignette, Bech visits his most ardent collector, a sour fellow named Marvin Federbusch who acquires (and asks Bech to sign) every edition of his work, every scrap of "Bechiana"—"What Federbusch didn't collect deserved oblivion." But when the collector shows the proud collectee the stacked volumes prudently stored in a closet, Bech spies ("oh, treachery!") equally exhaustive collections of Roth, Mailer, Barth, and Capote. Mercenary calculation, not literary passion, motivates Federbusch. In the third vignette, Bech takes his mistress to the resort island of San Poco to sign 28,500 tip-in sheets for a special edition of his novel *Brother Pig* (bound, naturally, in genuine pigskin). There's an added metatextual twist to the humor here: a year after the story appeared in *The New Yorker*, Updike authorized Targ Editions to print a 350-copy edition of it, the numbered volumes priced at forty dollars each—and signed, of course.

Mixed reviews greeted *A Month of Sundays* and *Marry Me*, but otherwise, Updike's more conventional professional life was largely untroubled. At Knopf, Judith Jones proved a calm, steady presence; *A Month of Sundays* is dedicated to her. William Maxwell retired from *The New Yorker* in 1976 and passed Updike into the care of Roger Angell, Katharine White's son. It was a smooth segue, though

Updike complained that with Maxwell gone, another stitch had been dropped in his "once-close-woven relationship" with the magazine. He had been impatient, in Boston, to start something totally fresh and different—"a novel about penguins, perhaps, or Hottentots"—and when he was well and truly settled in the new house, that project took shape as *The Coup*. His study strewn with guidebooks to Africa, copies of *National Geographic*, and dictionaries of sub-Saharan languages, he conjured up the distant landlocked nation of Kush, overcoming his own early misgivings (after the first chapter, he stopped and thought seriously of not continuing) and every author's hunger for mindless distraction (he undertook, while writing the novel, to paint the entire exterior of the house—in a shade of red he feared might be too bright). In July 1977, when he was about halfway through the book (but done with the paint job), Vladimir Nabokov died. Updike flew down to New York for the memorial service on a stiflingly hot summer day—the hottest in forty years. He spoke briefly to the crowd in the baking auditorium about an author whom he revered but had never met in person, then read selected passages from the great man's work. He finished *The Coup*, his most Nabokovian novel, nine months later—a year and a half after he'd begun.

In the meantime, he had married Martha.*

THE CEREMONY TOOK place on a sunny Friday morning, the last day of September 1977, at Clifton Lutheran Church in Marblehead, Massachusetts. The youngest of John's children, Miranda, declined to attend. "It was a protest," she said; "I wanted my absence felt." She telephoned her father and told him that she wouldn't be there, that she was worried about her mother, and that she didn't want him to get remarried yet. "He was surprised and hurt," Miranda remembered. Michael was absent, too (and "glad not to be there"); he

---

* He was well aware of the comic effect of marrying in succession a Mary and a Martha. To Delbanco he wrote, "If I marry a third time, it'll have to be Lazarus."

was in his first year at Lawrence University in Appleton, Wisconsin. David and Liz were at the ceremony, as were Martha's sons. There were practically no guests. John's best man, an Ipswich friend from the couples crowd, liked to say, "I was the best man; I was the only man." There was no fanfare, no wedding reception; after lunch at a restaurant, Updike went back to work. He typed a letter to Howard Moss about changes to the galleys of his "Spanish Sonnets"; almost as an afterthought, he announced that Martha had that morning become Mrs. Updike.

They were married sixteen months after he and Mary petitioned for divorce—which was as soon as the divorce became final. In his interview with the hated Sally Quinn, he had let it be known that neither Martha nor he was keen to wed a second time; and yet they had seized the earliest opportunity to do so. Of the several reasons for him to be in a hurry, the urge to complete a gesture was foremost. As with Richard Maple, his aim was to "amalgamate and align all his betrayals." Fifteen years earlier he had tried and failed to leave Mary so he could marry Joyce Harrington. This time, having managed actually to leave, he completed his escape by marrying his mistress. Two families had been broken apart; now he and Martha formally established a third.

His new wife was intelligent, literary, and attractive, a fresh-faced, young-looking blond with a bright smile. He often went out of his way to emphasize their compatibility as a couple—in an intimate, physical sense. In a late story, Updike's protagonist quotes Emerson's famous line "We boil at different degrees" and explains his second marriage in those terms: "a woman came along who had my same boiling point." So it was with Martha.* She also played an active part in his professional life in a way Mary never had. Of course Mary had read all his early work and made helpful suggestions, but she stood back, her tact shading into reticence; he felt that over time they became "artistically estranged." (*Couples* can't have helped in that regard.)

---

* A story about a man and his mistress written while Updike was still a semi-bachelor begins bluntly, "She was good in bed."

Mary met John when he was a sophomore in college. Although she recognized his talent from the beginning, she knew him too well to be awestruck when that talent propelled him to literary stardom. Two decades of domestic life—diapers and dishes and dirty ashtrays—are the perfect antidote to hero worship. Martha met John when he was already a world-famous author; she looked at him and saw a great man, admiration welling up like tears in her startling blue eyes.

Never inclined to stand back, Martha marched straight into the role of gatekeeper and protector. When her husband wanted room to write, she held the world at bay, gradually assuming the management of his time, doing her best to make sure that nothing and no one encroached on the hours devoted to his work. And in their early years together she gave him unconditional support, rivaling his mother in her enthusiasm for every scrap of prose and poetry. He showed Martha whatever he wrote; as he put it, "I was very confiding and she was very interested." All this was motive and more for making her his wife. Nobody would have said, as Joyce Carol Oates said of Martha, that Mary was John's "equal in every way"—they were so very different, their respective spheres of competence so distinct. Compared with Martha, Mary was shy, passive, serene. The tough and fearless Martha was conspicuously purposeful, unhesitatingly vocal, and perfectly willing to bully John for his own good.

A month after they married, Updike took his new spouse down to Plowville—this was her first sight of her husband in his native habitat. (On their next visit, Martha brought along her youngest son, an eerie reenactment of the visit Joey Robinson makes to his widowed mother's farmhouse with second wife and stepson in tow.) In the five years since Wesley's death, Linda had mellowed somewhat, but her energy, determination, and ambition were unflagging. At first she was wary of Martha, noting in a diary signs of her new daughter-in-law's snobbery. Martha, in turn, flattered her, and tried to ingratiate herself.

As always, Linda's fiction is the best gauge of her temperament. After Wesley's death, she had invented for herself a new alter ego: Belle Minuit was replaced by the widowed Ada Gibson, who lives alone on an isolated farm with a profusion of cats. Ada's son is Christopher, a world-famous illustrator (who draws covers for *The New Yorker*); she and her son have been carrying on a form of teasing banter since he was a child. Now middle-aged, Christopher is married to Joan and has four lively children of his own, two boys and two girls. In a story about Ada's seventieth birthday, Christopher announces that he's leaving Joan and taking an apartment in Boston. Ada asks him why he's "abandoning" his children; he answers, "It's not easy to say. I'd rather not talk about it." Ada's displeasure at her son's evasiveness doesn't need to be spelled out; unspoken, it emanates in waves, like one of Linda's famous "atmospheres." This was the fourth of five Ada Gibson stories to appear in *The New Yorker*; it was published a little less than two years after John and Martha were married—perhaps Linda thought of it as a delayed wedding present.

Updike was used to seeing himself refracted in his mother's fiction, but suddenly, in the late seventies, his image came back to him from another source. His son David had a girlfriend with literary aspirations who suggested that he try to write; having shown no previous inclination to pick up a pen, David made an attempt in the summer after his junior year. Back at Harvard, he enrolled in a fiction writing course offered by Ann Beattie, whose first novel, *Chilly Scenes of Winter*, John had reviewed glowingly in *The New Yorker* a couple of years earlier. David got an A in the class, which encouraged him to show his work to his father.

Like his father and his grandmother, David was an autobiographical writer. He wrote about his family, the facts disguised only lightly, if at all—the siblings and the separated parents all easily recognizable. Updike read what his son showed him with a complicated mix of emotions, among them pleasure, pride, and protectiveness—"they were," he told Maxwell, "very *tender* stories." He was curious to see how his son saw him, deeply moved by the mere fact that David would want to write, and frankly threatened by this new encroachment on his established literary territory. With Linda writing about Plowville and David writing about Ipswich (native turf in each case), Updike felt hemmed in—an absurd reaction, given his eminence and their obscurity, but as usual he couldn't help himself, especially after David had a story accepted by *The New Yorker*. John's competitive instinct kicked in at once: David had cracked the magazine only a year after first trying his hand at writing, with the first story he submitted—and at a younger age than his father.

David, however, was not prolific; he never even matched his grandmother's *New Yorker* tally. He published seven short stories in the magazine in his father's lifetime, along with several Talk pieces, all from the late seventies to the mid-eighties. But he could rightly claim to be a *New Yorker* writer, just like his father and his father's mother. John had founded a dynasty of sorts: three generations published in the magazine, a unique accomplishment. Although sincerely pleased for them—the acceptance of David's first story was "a soul-stirring event"—he couldn't always suppress the irrational idea that he was being squeezed. His anxious pangs surfaced as humor; he joked to André Deutsch, who was publishing a British edition of Linda's first book, that he might as well bring out a collection of David's stories and "box it with his grandmother's."

Feeling crowded was an unwelcome, jarring sensation in the tranquil seclusion of Georgetown, where his domestic life was tailored to give him plenty of space to write. On the whole, the town suited him nicely. He and Martha made little or no effort to find new friends. A manically crammed social calendar had once seemed to him essential; now he preferred it blank. Though he occasionally drove over to see his children when they gathered at Labor-in-Vain Road, his contact with his gang of Ipswich friends was virtually nil. Sunday sports were a thing of the past; so, too, the weekly parties—all that frantic commingling had ground to a halt when he left Mary. His intimate association with the crowd he'd been so close to for so long was abruptly severed. He saw one or two of the men on the golf course, and every other week for poker night, but otherwise he disappeared from view, as if abducted. The couples (nearly all by now divorced, many still living in Ipswich) blamed Martha for his sudden absence. How else to explain the fact that he was living nearby and yet remained entirely out of touch? A few acknowledged that Updike must have acquiesced in the decision to cut off contact, but most heaped the blame squarely on the shoulders of his new wife.

His old friends, many of them also his old lovers, decided that she'd snatched him away in a fit of jealousy and possessiveness.

As if to compensate for the loss of the Ipswich gang and the busy Ipswich community life, he turned to New York City, to the less ardent but still satisfying embrace of the literary establishment. Having been elected in 1964 to the National Institute of Arts and Letters, he was "elevated" in 1976 to the Academy of Arts and Letters, a club within the club, so to speak. There were 250 members of the Institute, only 50 in the Academy, each with his or her own carved Italian walnut chair and a special boutonniere.* Soon after marrying Martha, he told a journalist that the writing of the Bech stories, and the kindly welcome they received, had made him more comfortable with the New York literary scene. Election to the Academy had a similar effect. Being honored in this way was of course agreeable, but having accepted the honor, he could have kept his distance. Some members of the Academy rarely set foot in the grand mansion on West 155th Street. Updike, however, plunged into the fray. He signed up, along with Joyce Carol Oates, to serve on one of the numerous prize committees, a duty that entailed heaps of compulsory reading and long meetings not always briskly chaired. In the spring of 1978 he gave a talk at a conference of Soviet and American writers held at the Academy-Institute; a year later he delivered an address on "Hawthorne's Religious Language." He became a regular on prize committees and began to chair them himself. He served as secretary of the Academy from 1979 to 1982, and as chancellor from 1987 to 1990—he joked that he ascended to the latter position because he was the only member who could make it to the podium without a walking frame. In the centennial year, 1998, he edited a hefty historical tome called *A Century of Arts & Letters*, to which he contributed a foreword and a chapter. Though he liked to complain about the absurdities of the place and the burdens of his committee work—he

---

* The hierarchical distinction within the Academy-Institute was abolished in 1992 when the fifty members of the Academy invited all the members of the Institute to join them. At the same time, the entire organization adopted the name American Academy of Arts and Letters.

and Oates exchanged many an exasperated missive on this topic—
the Academy gave him a sense of community and a social life of
sorts: members' dinners and lunches, where tributes to the recently
deceased were read out. He and Martha regularly attended the May
"Ceremonial," where in a marquee crowded with three hundred–odd
guests they might see friends such as Oates and Kurt Vonnegut and
his second wife, the photographer Jill Krementz, and rub shoulders
with other luminaries: Aaron Copland, Saul Steinberg, Ralph Elli-
son, Eudora Welty, Allen Ginsberg, Stephen Sondheim. Although
it also provided material, notably "Bech Enters Heaven" (about his
election to the Institute) and "Bech Presides" (about the vicissitudes
of running an honorary organization composed of cranky, eccentric,
and comically competitive geriatrics), Updike's commitment was at
heart disinterested. He believed sincerely, if not quite passionately,
in the overarching aim of the Academy, which is to honor artistic
achievement.

The gentle, affectionate satire and *à clef* playfulness of the later
Bech stories were as much fiction as Updike could wring from the
highbrow doings of his fellow academicians. "One of the problems
of being a fiction writer," he remarked nine months into his second
marriage, "is that of gathering experience. The need for seclusion,
and the respectability that goes with some success, both are very
sheltering—they cut you off from painful experience. We all want
to avoid painful experience, and yet painful experience is your chief
resource as a writer." In Georgetown, as at the Academy, he was
settled and safe—out of harm's way—and free from the time- and
energy-consuming entanglements of the riotously unmonogamous
Ipswich lifestyle. But he worried that he was putting too much distance between himself and the sources of his inspiration.

The household he shared with Martha inspired him in many
ways, but it wasn't the best spot to trawl for material, and not just
because of the danger of legal assault from Alex Bernhard. Unlike
Mary, Martha resisted the idea that successive portraits of her should
appear in his work. Several of Updike's friends reported that she
chided him publicly for revealing intimate autobiographical details.
Philip Roth, for one, remembered a dinner at the Updikes' when the

conversation somehow came around to that notorious moment in *Self-Consciousness*: the return journey of a ski trip up north, Mary sitting in the front seat of the car, Updike sitting in the back, patiently masturbating his neighbor through her ski pants. According to Roth, "Martha was very upset that John had included the scene in the book. John was boyishly silent while she spoke." Roth did his best to smooth the waters by quoting Poe: John, he suggested, was indulging "the imp of the perverse"—both in the car and in the memoir. Martha was possibly not mollified.

There was of course no chance that she would succeed in weaning Updike from the habit of lifting situations and characters from his daily life. He made use of her, but with caution; in many of his later novels she appears as the brisk, busy, slightly younger, sometimes impatient and peevish wife number two. There are glimpses of her in Bech's wife, Bea, especially when the couple are traveling abroad, as in "The Holy Land" and "Macbech," both written during the Georgetown years. But for the first twenty-odd years of their marriage, anyway, Martha's fictional disguise, the weave of invented particulars that offered her a measure of privacy, was never as flimsy as Mary's. The second wife wasn't exposed the way the first wife was.

Having left Ipswich, he could still revisit it in the manner he so often revisited Plowville and Shillington: with a backward glance. The difference is that he looked back at Ipswich with a more frankly ambivalent brand of nostalgia. Even before he left town, he was lamenting the good old days in ironic fictions that mixed celebration of the past with ominous hints of moral peril. The narrator of "When Everyone Was Pregnant," written while Updike was still at Labor-in-Vain Road, puts his past on a pedestal; the fifties, he proclaims, were "not only kind but beautiful years." He's fascinated with the memory of the swollen bellies of young matrons; a "curl of pubic hair" on the thigh of a woman whose maternity skirt is flipped up by the breeze fills him with a "sickening sensation of love." The erotic component casts his nostalgia in an unsettling light, so that when he bemoans the passing of a golden era "when everyone was pregnant guiltlessly," we suspect guilt willy-nilly. Even as he extols the innocence and glamour of bygone days, the reader scans for signs of a darker side—memories, for instance, of the gang's summer parties, the children "wandering in and out with complaints their mothers brushed away like cigarette smoke." Or this fondly remembered infidelity: while his wife was in the hospital with varicose veins, he slept in their bed with his lover, who got up in the night to comfort a crying baby, the youngest of his four children. He doesn't directly acknowledge that there's anything wrong with this episode, but his jotted notes hint at an uneasy conscience: "Too much love. Too many babies, breathing all over the dark house like searchlights that might switch on." And what would we see if those searchlights did switch on? Not guiltlessness. Despite the foreshadowing, the punch line of the story comes as a shock: "Our babies accuse us."

A similarly ambivalent tone complicates post-Ipswich tales such as "The Lovely Troubled Daughters of Our Old Crowd" and "Getting into the Set." The first of these is narrated by another self-deluded worshipper of "the best of times"—the days of parties when the young parents' young children ran around in a flock, "creating their own world underfoot as the liquor and the sunlight soaked in and the sky filled with love." He wonders why their daughters—girls who observed the tangle of extramarital affairs spawned by well-lubricated carousing, who suffered through the eventual epidemic of divorce—haven't themselves married, now that they're in their twenties. They're hanging around town, conspicuously unattached; just the thought of them dredges up memories of old times. A rueful smile on the face of an ex-lover's grown daughter sends our narrator spinning into the past: "Lou's exact same smile on little Annie, and it was like being in love again, when all the world is a hunt and the sight of the woman's car parked at a gas station or in the Stop & Shop lot makes your Saturday, makes your blood race and your palms go numb, the heart touching base." The blend of banal suburban detail with bodice-ripper cliché is exactly what you'd expect from someone who would look at these stubbornly single girls and ask, "What are they hanging back for? What are they afraid of?" He's blind to the irony, his senses overwhelmed by nostalgia for his own adulterous exploits.

"Getting into the Set" features an amped-up version of the impromptu cocktail parties that ritually followed Sunday sports. To an outsider, the clique in town seems exciting and alluring; the lucky few who've gained admittance to the in-crowd exude a "ramshackle and reckless yet well-heeled air." But Updike exposes the ugly reality: the betrayals, the petty violence, the carelessness.

In all these stories, his longing for lost time, for the coziness of a happy circle of intimate friends ("spokes of a wheel"), for the vivifying fervor of illicit lust, is neatly balanced against dismay at the inevitable result: broken homes, neglected children.

Though the Maples saga had come to an end, he continued to track the comings and goings of a collection of young people—children of divorce who bore an unsurprising resemblance to his own progeny.* In "Still of Some Use," a middle-aged divorced man's familiar guilt is accompanied by a tardy urge to protect his broad-shouldered but "sensitive" teenage son. The boy, modeled on Michael, is upset at having to help clear out the attic of his childhood home after his parents have split up; the unwanted games and toys are to be discarded, consigned to the "universe of loss" explored a decade and a half earlier in "My Children at the Dump." An identical teenager reappears—or at least his artwork does—in "Learn a Trade," about a highly successful sculptor, Fegley, who has grown rich selling his art, yet finds the idea of "artsy-crafty stuff" depressing; "He was like a man who, having miraculously survived a shipwreck, wants to warn all others back at the edge of the sea." He had hoped his four children would become scientists, or anyway do something useful, but every one of them, including his younger son, his only "practical, down-to-earth child," has drifted into the "limbo of artistic endeavor." Working with copper wire, pliers, and snippers, the boy has filled the basement with "unsold, unrequested" mobiles, a leafy forest stretching into dark corners.

---

* Although the divorce hearing in "Here Come the Maples" brought down the curtain, Updike summoned Richard and Joan for an encore a decade later in "Grandparenting," when their eldest daughter gave birth to their first grandchild.

Fegley blames his ex-wife, herself a painter. He tells her, "You've brought these kids up to live in never-never land." She gently reminds him that he, too, was indulged in the years before his commercial success, that she never urged him to do the practical thing, to abandon sculpture and resign himself to secure, white-collar work; she'd left him free to follow his muse. (One hears an echo of Mary mildly noting that she made no objection when Updike quit his safe, steady job as a Talk writer.) Unwilling to argue the point, Fegley merely says that he was driven in a way their children are not. He was, he reminds her, "desperate" to escape his provincial upbringing; "Our children aren't desperate," he says; "they're just kidding around."

By the time Michael began making mobiles in the basement at Labor-in-Vain Road, Updike was well aware that all four of his children might easily end up in the "limbo of artistic endeavor." Liz, after a year at the Byam Shaw School of Art in London and a couple of years at Bennington, had enrolled in the Mass General School of Nursing and become a student nurse at Spaulding Rehabilitation Hospital—but couldn't commit to the profession and dropped out after six months. There seemed, after this, little chance that any of the young Updikes would "learn a trade." None—not even David, despite his precocious *New Yorker* success—seemed in a hurry to make a mark; they gave no sign of having inherited their father's urgent need to outstrip the competition. Compared with the eager young man who rocketed out of Shillington High School with a single aim—a job at the magazine of his dreams—Updike's children seemed directionless, happy to drift. If they harbored any professional ambition, they disguised it brilliantly. He could be forgiven for thinking that they, too, were "just kidding around."

However disappointed or frustrated, he never scolded, never nagged, never tried to hurry them along a particular career path. As he observed to his mother, his children seemed to have "all the gifts but the one of making their way in the world." He was inclined to see their laid-back attitude as generational, a sign of the times. "The work ethic is crumbling," he told a journalist in the early seventies. By the end of the decade, as his two younger children were leaving their teenage years behind, the topic of work—how his fellow citizens earn a living, why they strive or fail to strive—had become something of an obsession. His worries about leading a sheltered life went hand in hand with a recurring worry about losing touch with ordinary, middling, nine-to-five Americans. "You grow up of course with these people who become car salesmen," he told a journalist, "but the older you get the less you see of them." He explained that "your average American writer is far too innocent of the actual workings of the capitalist consumerist society he's a member of."

Even as he was articulating the problem, he had in his sights a solution. Once again, Rabbit rode to the rescue: Harry Angstrom would become a car salesman.

THOUGH IN MOST ways utterly unlike *The Coup*, *Rabbit Is Rich* benefits from the lessons Updike learned when he decided, three and a half years after a four-week trip to Africa, to invent a drought-stricken sub-Saharan nation. This time around, he invented a working life. Harry's personality and social milieu, the push and pull of his desires, his fears, his loyalties—Updike knew these inside out; ditto the hometown geography. But what did he know about his hero's new job? What did he know about the business of running a Toyota dealership? As he did for *The Coup*, he rolled up his sleeves and hit the books. And he also enlisted outside help, hiring a researcher to untangle the arcane protocols of automobile finance and the corporate structure of a dealership—how salesmen are compensated, how many support staff work in the back office, what the salaries are for the various employees, what paperwork is involved in importing foreign cars, and so on. Updike visited showrooms in the Boston area, hunting for tips from salesmen and collecting brochures. He aimed for, and achieved, a degree of detail so convincing that the publisher felt obliged to append to the legal boilerplate on the copyright page a specific disclaimer: "No actual Toyota agency in southeastern Pennsylvania is known to the author or in any way depicted herein."*

---

* In fact, Updike very likely had in mind a Reading dealership on Lancaster Avenue, which in the seventies was lined with car showrooms.

The first scene of the novel presents us with Rabbit in his new element, the showroom of Springer Motors, one of two Toyota dealerships in the Brewer area. Updike plants us next to Harry as he surveys the dispiriting scene on the other side of the dusty plate-glass window with its paper banner bearing the latest Toyota slogan, "YOU ASKED FOR IT, WE GOT IT." The traffic on Route 111 is "thin and scared"; the energy crisis, manifest in long and fractious lines at gas stations, has spread disquiet; Jimmy Carter will soon deliver his famous "malaise" speech. The country is running out of gas, Harry thinks; "the great American ride is ending." But his gloom is skin deep. Fuel-efficient Toyotas are selling well, money is rolling in. "Life is sweet," he tells himself, savoring his personal prosperity in the midst of a national anxiety bordering on panic. "Bourgeois bliss" is how Updike described Rabbit's state of mind.

Janice's father died five years ago, and now Harry "co-owns a half-interest" in Springer Motors. He's "king of the lot," his place validated by the cheery patter of his salesman's pitch, which he tries out on a couple of country kids who drive up in a rundown station wagon, the girl "milky-pale and bare-legged," with a snub nose and pale blue eyes. His reaction to the girl is typically sexual, but also fatherly; by the time he takes them for a test drive, chatting smoothly about base models, extras, trade-in value—"paternal talkativeness keeps bubbling up in Harry"—he's already wondering whether the girl is his daughter, the child he believes, he hopes, he fathered with Ruth Leonard some two decades earlier. Hints pile up, and Rabbit eagerly convinces himself that she is indeed his child, her white skin a mirror, her pale blues eyes conclusive evidence of a genetic link.

It's worth pausing to admire the efficiency of the setup. Despite the apparently leisurely pace, Updike has already established his essential themes: the parlous state of the union, money, sex, fatherhood ("this matter of men descending from men"). When the workday is done, Harry leaves the showroom, stepping out into a golden early summer afternoon. In the seconds it takes him to walk across the lot to his car, Updike makes time for an extraordinary aria: Harry reflects that sales peak in June, and from there launches into a calculation of the monthly profits of Springer Motors, a single-sentence stream of consciousness that extends for more than a page and touches on topics as various as pneumatic tools ("*rrrrrrt*"), OPEC ("the fucking Arabs are killing us"), Medicaid, and "his poor dead dad." Perched on Harry's shoulder, we hear the echo of his scattered thoughts. The technique is remarkably flexible, opening up interior space, the inner dimensions of a sentient being, and at the same time allowing us to see Harry from above, as it were: We know what he knows and also what he doesn't know. We sympathize with him and his failings, at once superior to him and keenly aware of a shared humanity. Immersed in Harry, we're immersed in ourselves.

The free indirect style is only one strand of Updike's virtuosity. In his ambition to leave behind a faithful record of the second half of the twentieth century—an ambition that dates back to his Harvard years but that began to take a concrete shape only after *Rabbit Redux*—he paid minute attention to the delicate art of weaving popular culture, politics, and economics into the fabric of his narrative. Harry drives home through rusting Brewer, snug in his "Luxury Edition" 1978 Toyota Corona, "the four corners of the car dinging out disco music as from the four corners of the mind's ballroom." Donna Summer sings "Hot Stuff," and Harry imagines the backup singers "standing around on some steamy city corner chewing gum and who knows what else." The music blends with the scenery in a magically tight weave.* Elsewhere he charts the fate of Johnny Frye's Chophouse, an old-fashioned Brewer establishment that once fed pork chops and sauerkraut to an old-fashioned clientele. The Chophouse became Café Barcelona (paella and gazpacho), then morphed into the Crêpe House, serving "glorified pancakes wrapped around minced whatever." This latest incarnation is a hit with the "lean new race of downtown office workers," and that elicits a wry reflection: "The world keeps ending but new people too dumb to know it keep showing up as if the fun just started"; the relaxed syntax and colloquial diction paper over the profundity of the observation and tie it securely to Harry. At home, our hero reads *Consumer Reports*; the parade of goods in the magazine forms a running commen-

---

* MTV was launched just a few months before the novel was published.

tary on the way we lived then. A stack of *Playboy* and *Penthouse* magazines from earlier in the decade gives him a lesson in evolving pornographic fashion; he flips to each centerfold and discovers that the modesty of the models recedes inexorably: "An invisible force month after month through each year's seasons forces gently wider their flawless thighs until somewhere around the bicentennial issues the Constitutional triumph of open beaver is attained." (Note the exquisite mingling of patriotic celebration, First Amendment rhetoric, and crass schoolboy slang.) Inflation is nibbling at Rabbit's savings account—how to dramatize this dreary topic? Updike turns it into an erotic romp: Harry and Janice making love on a bedspread scattered with the thirty Krugerrands bought at Fiscal Alternatives in downtown Brewer, Rabbit's first speculative foray. The scene is a comic gem, and suggestive as well of the metaphoric link between sex and speculation. The coins come in tightly packed cylinders; hidden away in Harry's coat, they feel "like a bull's balls tugging at his pockets." The rising price of gold and the Angstroms' newly buoyant sex life seem to go together naturally, like disco and urban decay.

Pleased with his newly flush and frisky wife, Rabbit works, Rabbit plays, Rabbit runs—his jogging is an affirmation of health and vitality, and inevitably a reminder of the opposite. His new blue-and-gold running shoes skim "above the earth, above the dead." The novel is punctuated with memorials to the dead, Harry naming them again and again: Mom and Pop; Skeeter, gunned down by policemen; Jill; and the baby, Becky. Harry tells himself he will never die. In fact, nobody dies in *Rabbit Is Rich*, and this makes it unique in the tetralogy; instead of a funeral, we get the wedding of Nelson Angstrom and the five-months-pregnant Teresa ("Pru") Lubell, a twenty-five-page set piece almost exactly in the middle of the book. The ceremony at the Episcopalian church makes sentimental Harry weep as the couple stand at the altar:

> And the burning in his tear ducts and the rawness scraping at the back of his throat have become irresistible, all the forsaken poor ailing paltry witnesses to this marriage at Harry's

back roll forward in hoops of terrible knowing, an impalpable suddenly sensed mass of human sadness concentrated burningly on the nape of Nelson's neck.

Even in the midst of this timeless ritual, current events impinge. The father of the groom marvels at the effect of inflation on the cost of the wedding ("one hundred and eighty-five American dollars for a cake, a *cake*") and feels the pain of OPEC's squeeze: "What a great waste of gas it seems as they drive in procession . . . through the slanted streets of the town." He flicks on the car radio and listens to the news: Russian tanks in Kabul, a natural gas pact with Mexico, the pope's visit to nearby Philadelphia.

Step back from the parade of detail, and the larger pattern begins to look familiar: from the hope and despair of the American scene, Updike has fashioned a tapestry that looks a lot like history unfurling. It unfurls to the tune of the extraordinary speech Jimmy Carter delivered in midsummer, a televised address in which he told his fellow citizens that there was something wrong with America. Threatened by "paralysis and stagnation and drift," the country was suffering from a "crisis of confidence." His diagnosis of the problem sounds as if it might have been hatched in Brewer, after an extended sociological study of our own Harry Angstrom. Said Carter:

> In a nation that was proud of hard work, strong families, close-knit communities, and our faith in God, too many of us now tend to worship self-indulgence and consumption. Human identity is no longer defined by what one does, but by what one owns. But we've discovered that owning things and consuming things does not satisfy our longing for meaning.

Rabbit reflects several times on the transformation that has devalued hard work in favor of "a whole new ethic." Men under thirty "just will not work without comfort and all the perks"—whereas his father ("poor dead dad") slaved away and "never got out from under" and "didn't live to see money get unreal." Money is now "unreal" because it's divorced from honest toil. As for self-indulgence and consumption, at the end of the novel, having returned from a frolicsome, sex-filled holiday in the Caribbean, Harry allocates to himself a Celica Supra, the "ultimate Toyota," a model "priced in five digits"—this after spending the afternoon furniture shopping for the new house he and Janice have bought but not yet moved into. All in all, an orgy of owning and consuming. The one-word refrain in the last pages of the novel is the possessive pronoun "his." And yet ownership isn't enough somehow; he still feels compelled to drive out toward Galilee, to the farm where Ruth lives, to ask about the girl he believes is their daughter. President Carter would say that Rabbit's riches have not satisfied his "longing for meaning."

Oddly enough, the president's speech was shaped in part by a critique elaborated by Updike's Harvard roommate Kit Lasch in *The Culture of Narcissism*, published seven months earlier. A surprise bestseller, Lasch's book was widely discussed in the wake of prominent reviews and a profile of the author in *People* magazine. He warned of America's ebbing confidence, the erosion of the work ethic, weakened family bonds, and a creeping permissiveness—ideas that struck a nerve with Carter, who was interested in their political implications. Lasch was astonished to receive an invitation to dinner at the White House.

Updike was only very sporadically in contact with his old roommate, and didn't write to him about the success of *The Culture of Narcissism* or make explicit use of it in the novel (though Harry's narcissism is in full bloom).* In fact, he never publicly discussed Lasch's ideas or his career as a cultural critic, a sign that his memories of his erstwhile friend and rival were not exclusively fond. But Updike did acknowledge the centrality of Carter's pronouncements, which Lasch had influenced; to a British journalist he explained that in the "malaise" speech, Carter "was trying to put his finger on what he thought, as a good Christian, was somehow wrong"—and that he, in his novel, was "mucking about the same area."

---

* In "Rabbit Remembered," Nelson gives his diagnosis: His father was "narcissistically impaired. . . . Intuitive but not very empathic. He never grew up."

Despite the clear echoes of a president's sermonizing address and the mass of cleverly embedded sociological detail, *Rabbit Is Rich* is less political than *Rabbit Redux*—there's no Vietnam to rile Harry—and just as focused on domestic and quotidian concerns; family is once again the big event. Family is also where Harry diverges from the norm, where our American Everyman, the self-proclaimed "man in the middle," begins to look more like an oddball on the fringe. There's nothing run-of-the-mill about his relations either with the son he'd like to get rid of or with the daughter he'd like to acquire.

At the end of *Rabbit, Run*, when the young Harry tries to dissolve the responsibilities weighing on him, his son, not yet three years old, is the stubborn fact that cannot be wished away: "Nelson remains: here is a hardness he must carry with him." The hardness endures; you might say it hardens. An oedipal struggle unleashed in *Rabbit Redux* escalates in the last two novels. In *Rabbit Is Rich*, Harry resents Nelson crowding up behind him; the king of the lot feels his place is being usurped, both at work and at home. He's not entirely wrong: Nelson, feeling stifled, wonders, "Why doesn't Dad just die?" Of course oedipal conflict is not unusual, but its naked expression—"Harry wanted out of fatherhood"—is nonetheless startling. Actually, Harry only wants out of being father to a *male* child; the thought of Nelson's genitals is what disturbs him most. The idea of having a daughter thrills him—and sends him out into the country to stalk the girl he met at the lot, whose name, he eventually learns, is Annabelle Byer. Only when Nelson has skipped town, following the family tradition by running out on his wife and child, is Rabbit satisfied: "The kid was no threat to him for now. Harry was king of the castle." Updike had no firsthand experience of hopelessly bitter father-son relations, but it's not too hard to imagine that he was prodding a sore point, that the travails of Nelson and Rabbit are a nightmare extension of his anxieties about his feckless children, a product of the guilty sense that he himself was holding them back—that his single-minded and monolithic success was at the root of their aimlessness.

Harry's obsession with Annabelle is usually explained as a symptom of his unacknowledged (in fact, loudly denied) guilt over

Becky's death. Ruth's pregnancy begins, so to speak, when Janice lets her baby girl sink into the bathwater—the symmetry is essential to the internal logic of the novel. And Rabbit's refusal to believe that a pregnant Ruth would go through with a threatened abortion gives birth, metaphorically, to a phantom daughter. Until Rabbit catches sight of Annabelle at the beginning of *Rabbit Is Rich,* he has to make do with surrogates: enter the doomed Jill, whose fiery death still haunts him. But could the obsession with a fantasy daughter also be the product of the author's own long-term guilt—could Updike have been thinking back to his lover's abortion fifteen years earlier? Did Updike, like Harry, moon over might-have-beens, plotting the hypothetical future of a child who was never born? I very much doubt it. Rabbit's baby daughter died on paper on a summer afternoon in 1959, at the Penningtons' farmhouse in Vermont. Once the work-weary young author came downstairs and announced to his family that he had "drowned the baby," his hero's obsessive yearning for a daughter was inevitable. It's a literary conceit, not some kind of slip an amateur shrink might decode.

Annabelle threads through the tetralogy, in utero in the first volume and nearly a spinster in the last. As long as she's only possibly, wishfully, Rabbit's daughter, she's pure potential. She's his most reliable source of hope and wonder. Conservative, nostalgic, occasionally morbid, acutely sensitive to signs of national decline, Harry is nonetheless eager to look on the bright side, to detect glimmers of renewal. This complex attitude, the mix of elegy and longing, is on display in his late-night meditation on the unexpected, awkward beauty of Pru, Nelson's pregnant wife-to-be, a flight of poetic prose that shows again how far Updike can push Harry's point of view:

> She breathed that air he'd forgotten, of high-school loveliness, come uninvited to bloom in the shadow of railroad overpasses, alongside telephone poles, within earshot of highways with battered aluminum center strips, out of mothers gone to lard and fathers ground down by gray days of work and more work, in an America littered with bottlecaps and pull-tabs and pieces of broken muffler.

Pru's pale loveliness shines out against this grim backdrop, a harbinger of good things to come; at the novel's end she will place in Harry's lap what he's been waiting for without knowing it: not a daughter but a granddaughter.

Updike thought *Rabbit Is Rich* the "happiest" novel of the tetralogy, despite "shadows" such as Harry's elegiac brooding on dying and the dead. He gallantly gave credit for the upbeat mood to his new marriage; "an invigorating change of mates," he explained, cleared his head and sharpened his talent. Martha, he also suggested, was the inspiration for "Janice's lusty rejuvenation"; Rabbit's sex life improved with his creator's. And once he was truly settled in Georgetown, the shock of divorce and alimony receding, he allowed himself to feel rich like Rabbit. Both were content, and the result was happy endings all around, the author's exuberance spilling over.

Updike's happiness, his own bourgeois bliss, swelled with the tremendous reception of the novel, which was published in late September 1981. Most reviewers loved it. Mark Feeney, writing in *The Boston Globe*, pronounced it "unquestionably" Updike's finest novel; loyal champion Anatole Broyard judged it "the best book I've ever read about an ordinary man." Even skeptics came around. In *The New York Times Book Review*, a grudging Roger Sale listed a series of caveats before concluding that "*Rabbit Is Rich* is the first book in which Updike has fulfilled the fabulous promise he offered with *Rabbit, Run* and *The Centaur* twenty years ago." As if to ratify the critics' verdict, the book scooped up all three major prizes: the National Book Critics Circle Award, the American Book Award, and the Pulitzer. This comprehensive triumph naturally stirred up some ill will. Jonathan Yardley of *The Washington Post*, a rare dissenter among reviewers, was dismayed to see so many prizes lavished on a "thoroughly bad novel"; he argued that it put on display "all of Updike's worst characteristics" and that the author was sneering at the common man rather than celebrating him. "What comes through most vividly," Yardley wrote, "are Updike's condescension and contempt."

It was easy to ignore Yardley, especially when the eminent British critic V. S. Pritchett, writing in *The New Yorker*, declared Updike "both a poet and a historian" and the three Rabbit books a "monumental portrayal of provincial and domestic manners." The sense of a cumulative achievement was especially gratifying to Updike, whose book-a-year rate of production sometimes made his fiction seem like units rolling off the assembly line; any praise that suggested a substantial, enduring accomplishment was particularly pleasing.

On January 28, 1982, when he should have been at the New York Public Library in Manhattan receiving the first of his three prizes, the National Book Critics Circle Award, Updike was in Los Angeles being sued for libel. This was the farcical climax of a slow and tortuous litigation that began six years earlier with a seemingly innocuous *New Yorker* review of Doris Day's "as-told-to" autobiography. What got Updike into trouble was a passing reference to "a swindler named Rosenthal," whose schemes had swallowed up buckets and buckets of the star's money. Jerome B. Rosenthal had been Day's lawyer, and his swindle was well documented: Day sued Rosenthal for legal malpractice and fraud, and won a $26 million judgment, at the time the largest civil judgment in the state of California. In addition to being a swindler, Rosenthal was almost pathologically litigious; he went after Updike despite the blatant futility of his suit. His legal shenanigans were the factual basis of "Bech Pleads Guilty," in which Bech is sued in L.A. for calling a disgraced Hollywood agent an "arch-gouger." But it's worth noting that Updike waited fifteen years before repackaging the courtroom drama of *Rosenthal v. The New Yorker Magazine, Inc.* as a short story, a rare show of restraint. The whole episode was a nightmare enactment of the "legal assault" he had feared from Alex Bernhard.

When the case came to trial before L.A. Superior Court in early January, Updike and Martha flew out to California. They stayed in a wedge-shaped room in the Hotel Bonaventure, and spent the first week sightseeing, Martha enjoying the warm, sunny weather and the La Brea Tar Pits; John, the Forest Lawn Cemetery. Updike was disappointed that the only living movie star he spotted was Goldie Hawn. Two more weeks were spent observing the operatic comedy of the plaintiff's lawyer's bumbling bombast. Martha eventually flew home to take care of eleven-year-old Ted, whom she'd left behind in wintry New England, but Updike stayed on to testify in his own defense. This in spite of bad news from Plowville: his mother had been sent to the hospital with severe chest pains. After formally asserting his innocence in the witness box—loudly and carefully, with no trace of a stammer—he caught the red-eye to Philadelphia, arriving at dawn and making his way to the farmhouse to feed the horse, the dog, and the herd of semiferal cats before visiting his mother on the ward. More happy endings were brewing: Liz rushed down to take over the feeding of the animals and to bring a rapidly recovering Linda home from the hospital; and back in California the jury found unanimously for the defense.

Between the trial in L.A. and the medical emergency in Plowville, Updike had been away from his desk for an entire month.

At the National Book Critics Circle Awards ceremony, Judith Jones read out to the assembled guests a letter from Updike apologizing for his absence and expressing his gratitude to his editor and to Knopf in general. The letter also thanked Martha, "not only for her many reassurances and suggestions . . . but for standing foremost in that band of intimates who surround with forbearance the homely and sometimes hopeless-seeming labor of concocting fiction." Last, he thanked his characters "for coming to life as best they could and for enduring in resilient style the indignities I had planned for them." This eccentric courtesy was not the only sign that, for him, Harry, Janice, Nelson, et al. lived and breathed. At the end of *Rabbit Is Rich*, Rabbit moved into a new house; Updike, shortly after finishing the novel, announced to his mother that he and Martha were doing the same. They were negotiating the purchase of a property in the Gold Coast town of Beverly Farms—no truck route outside the front door this time, he promised; the rumble of traffic would no longer disturb a visiting parent. The new house, he told her, was "a largish white edifice with a distant look at the sea."

> An adult human consists of sedimentary layers. We shed more skins than we can count, and are born each day to a merciful forgetfulness. We forget most of our past but embody all of it.
>
> —Introduction to *Rabbit Angstrom* (1995)

X.

Haven Hill

Updike spotted a pattern in his comings and goings, and drew attention to it in the foreword to his third collection of essays and reviews, the mammoth *Hugging the Shore* (1983). When his first marriage broke up, he noted, "I had left a big white house with a view of saltwater"; now, after "an inland interim of reconsolidation"—a snappy euphemism for twenty months of Boston semi-bachelorhood followed by six years with Martha in unassuming Georgetown—he was back where he started: "I live again in a big white house with a view of saltwater."* This was a false symmetry; the new property, Haven Hill, was in fact a mansion, much grander and more imposing than the handsome yet utterly unpretentious house on the edge of the salt marshes where he'd lived with Mary. Built as a summer "cottage" at the turn of the century by a Boston banker, Franklin Haven, the aptly named Haven Hill was hidden away on a craggy

---

* He also thought of the Shillington house, where as a child he "soaked up love and strength," as a "big white house," though it was big only in comparison with the cramped Plowville farmhouse and the modesty of his family's means.

wooded hilltop; except for its "distant look at the sea," it was sheltered from the world, a private place for private comforts. To the few
who saw it, gleaming and magnificent, it signaled wealth, status,
and the safety of secure privilege. When Updike thought of it during
the long months before the papers were signed and the property was
his, the image in his mind was of "a pale white castle in a fairy tale."

On a rainy Saturday morning in early June 1982, carrying on an
old tradition, he formally marked the beginning of his residence by
erecting a mailbox at the foot of the steep, curving driveway, within
sight of a small pond. Still thrifty in his plush new surroundings, he
invested in yet another rubber stamp to personalize his stationery;
henceforth his correspondence would bear in blue ink an address
that gave little away: 675 Hale Street, Beverly Farms, MA 01915.

Joyce Carol Oates, who'd also been an early visitor to the house
in Georgetown, stopped by about four months after the planting
of the mailbox. She and her husband arrived by car from Boston, a
journey of a little less than an hour. At the top of the drive, they were
confronted with a sight so extravagant that only a reference to an
American masterpiece could do it justice. "As we drove up the lane,"
Oates wrote in a letter to Updike, "I found myself thinking not of
poor Gatsby's house but of Tom and Daisy's—the splendid white
mansion overlooking the bay—at which Gatsby stared."* If Oates
was teasing him, he took it well, writing back to say that there was
indeed a green light at the end of Marblehead Neck, visible across
Salem Sound, there to remind them of ineffable glory and things
unobtainable.

Haven Hill made a similarly strong impression on other friends.
An irreverent golfing buddy liked to call it The Palazzo. The mere
mention of upscale Beverly Farms was enough for Michael Arlen to
tease him: "Now that I think of it[,] wasn't 675 Hale the house once
occupied by General Patton . . . ?" Austin Briggs, Updike's Harvard
classmate, was reminded of Xanadu in *Citizen Kane*. Briggs and his
wife were served dinner in the gigantic dining room. "We ate at a

---

* The Buchanans' house was actually a red-and-white Georgian Colonial
mansion, presumably built of brick. Haven Hill was all white and clapboard.

table that was much too large for only four people," he remembered. "As the daylight faded, we were left with only two or three candles, and I could scarcely see the walls of the room, or even, almost, the faces of the others." Briggs marveled at the formality and grandeur of his surroundings, and at the distance Updike had traveled from Shillington. Like the others, Briggs associated Haven Hill with unreal privilege, a fantastical remove from ordinary life. Sheer size (the Plowville farmhouse could have fitted comfortably inside, several times over) had something to do with it, and so did the unusual access: the only way to get to the Updikes' ten-acre property was to cross the railroad tracks that run between Boston and Cape Ann. On one side of the tracks was the hilly strip of coastal land where Haven Hill, from its lofty perch, looked out to the southeast over Misery Island, Salem Sound, and the Atlantic; on the other side of the tracks—the wrong side of the tracks—was the rest of America. Although the railroad cut him off, it kept him in touch, too, as he remarked in an essay about the Boston commuter line:

> My own house, up a wooded hill, trembles when the train passes, and the effect is of a caress, a gentle reminder, like the sight of airplane lights circling in over Massachusetts Bay toward Logan Airport, that an urban congeries lurks over the arboreal horizon.

The trains also provided "a rumor of motion, a suggestion of potential escape"—not that one would want to escape from a house blessed with an "arboreal horizon."

Why was the man who liked middles, the self-proclaimed bard of "middling, hidden, troubled America," living in a part of the North Shore known as the Gold Coast, "a bucolic enclave" of elegant summer places built by "quiet Boston money"? Updike disliked reckless expenditure and admired things practical and convenient; why would he move into a huge house that was awkward to maintain and hard to heat—especially if only three, then two, people were going to live there? (Martha's older sons were already away at boarding school; Teddy lived with his mother and stepfather until the mid-eighties, before he, too, went off to school.) The Ipswich crowd and some of his own children believed that Updike had been largely content in the Georgetown house, truck route or no truck route, that it suited him, that he didn't want to move at all, let alone to a mansion. They said that Haven Hill was the kind of property Martha wanted to own, and it's true that she threw herself into decorating and tending the extensive gardens with a gusto that suggested a full measure of pride. But even if buying a grandiose house was his wife's idea, even if he bowed only reluctantly to her wishes, it was still a joint decision, and the money that paid for it was his. And as it turned out, Beverly Farms suited him just as well as Georgetown had.

On the second floor of the new house, over the kitchen, were the old servant quarters, a corridor with a pair of small rooms on each side; he parceled out his professional life between them. In the largest he built a bookcase to house all his own books, including two sets of the collected Knopf first editions, one with the dust jacket, the other without; on a small rolling table with folding wings sat his typewriter. In another room was a word processor acquired a year after he moved in, for the typing of second drafts. There was a reading room crammed with books written by other people. And finally there was a room with the large green metal army desk that had been the centerpiece of his office in downtown Ipswich. To the left of the desk, a window looked out over treetops (the arboreal horizon) to the Atlantic Ocean. Having grasped the beauty of the setup in this last room—perfect for the longhand composition of first drafts—Oates wrote, "I envy John the metaphorical resources of Infinity at his left hand."

The literary production line housed in the suite of offices ran full tilt. The hiccups of the early seventies, the false starts and dead ends and emotional turmoil, were now a fading memory. Even before leaving Georgetown, he'd already settled back into his book-a-year rhythm. In the eighties and nineties, in his warren of little rooms, his output peaked and never again faltered: in twenty-seven years at Haven Hill, he wrote thirteen novels; his memoirs; nearly a hundred short stories; more than 250 poems; some three hundred reviews; and countless odds and ends, the essays and miscellaneous scraps of commissioned prose all scrupulously collected in the hefty omnium-gatherum volumes produced like clockwork every eight years.

This unstoppable flow of writing was the result of the rededication he promised himself when he set up housekeeping with Martha. With her help, he constructed a well-defended life*—a life designed for devotion to the written word (and to golf). The transformation was gradual, the six years in Georgetown a time of transition. Oates, when she visited him in the house on West Main Street, thought he resembled a character in an Updike story. She was right. The Georgetown house was a quirky, attractive old place—noisy, unspectacular, but convenient and friendly, the sort of place where one could imagine the Maples living. The rumble of the trucks was like an admission of guilt, an explanation, so to speak, for the incompletely obscured traces of wreckage, of harm done. The rumble also warned of more trouble to come—a danger that couldn't be ruled out, given this particular character's track record. His flaws were on display, flagged by the presence of family number two (three boys living apart from their father) and the periodic intrusion of the children from a defunct first marriage.

By the end of the Georgetown years, the flaws were harder to spot. His reputation boosted by the triumphant success of *Rabbit Is Rich*, Updike had perfected a convincing, engaging impersonation of an eminent man of letters. Here was a mask he could present to the world—and the world, its expectations met, would signal its approval by keeping its distance. He gave a bravura performance playing John Updike in a BBC documentary, *What Makes Rabbit Run?* Filmed in New York, Pennsylvania, and Massachusetts during the fall of 1981 (while he was still negotiating the purchase of Haven Hill), the documentary was aired on public television in the United States nearly two years later. Relaxed, self-assured, reasonable, and painstakingly modest, Updike floats through his scenes dispensing low-key bonhomie, equally at home wherever the camera finds him:

---

* Updike once observed, writing about Harry Angstrom, that Rabbit's life was less "defended" than his own.

in the Knopf offices in midtown Manhattan with Judith Jones (slim, elegant, evidently attuned to her author's charms); in an auditorium, reading his work to rapturous applause; undaunted on the set of *The Dick Cavett Show*; stuttering innocuously in a bookstore as he signs a fan's copy of *Rabbit Is Rich*; in Plowville with Linda, who is looking handsome but somewhat glazed, as though the camera lights are too bright for her; munching on parsley in the garden of the Georgetown house, and inspecting with Martha the last of the kohlrabi crop. Reviewing *What Makes Rabbit Run?* and taking note of its hero's blandly affable demeanor, *New York Times* critic John Corry concluded that the "television Updike" was a "respectable, uncomplicated fellow":

> What is clearest in the documentary is that Mr. Updike is blessed with easy charm and possessed by quiet conviction. . . . If Mr. Updike has demons he does not show them; if he has Angst he keeps it to himself. In a culture where self-exposure knows no bounds, he places his psyche under wraps.

It was perfectly obvious to Corry, as it was to any Updike reader watching the film, that the casual, seemingly reflexive modesty ("I feel in most respects that I am a pretty average person") was undisguised self-fashioning. The lack of guile was in itself appealing; it was as though he were saying, with a wink, *As long as they're filming me, I might as well put my best foot forward.* Offered a chance to present himself to posterity in a flattering light, he cheerfully grabbed it, bequeathing to us the dutiful son, the genial colleague, the bashful public speaker, the loyal, frolicsome husband.

This polished new persona pushed back into the dim reaches of the past all previous incarnations, so that earlier selves, even relatively recent ones, became the stuff of legend. The humble origins of the hick from rural Pennsylvania were now ancient history; traces could still be unearthed—he could be spotted putting the storm windows up on his mother's isolated farmhouse—but there was something comical in thinking that this distinguished gent once actually lived there, back in the days when the house lacked indoor plumbing. Gone were the ragged sweaters and shaggy haircuts of the bohemian interlude in Ipswich. Updike did his best to quash rumors of bad behavior: *Couples* was reinvented as a novel about "friendship" rather than adultery; the autobiographical basis of the Maples stories was called into question—he claimed he had lost track of what was real and what was invented, and that there was more fiction in the stories than met the eye. As for the guilty disarray of the Boston days— the vulnerability of the emotional bigamist dithering between wife and mistress—those ugly cracks had been papered over. The psyche may have been under wraps, decorously out of sight, but the "sedimentary layers" remained accessible; he could still excavate them for fictional purposes, a process he referred to as "personal archeology."

Also out of sight were his children, who felt less than entirely welcome at the grand mansion on the hill. Back in Georgetown, they had dropped in when they liked; Beverly Farms was another matter. According to Michael, "That was when you really got the impression that a casual stop-by was not something that could happen. You needed to announce your intention to come by." It was their father's house, but it certainly was not their family home.

There's no question that Updike loved his children. Over the years, his letters to his mother were punctuated with acutely observed reports of their comings and goings. He watched them with a full heart. And they never doubted his affection, even though they recognized that in the Martha era, the hours he spent with them were strictly rationed. As Michael put it, "It felt like we're his mistress and he's sneaking away from Martha to see us." But he was also sneaking away from his work, the realm Martha fiercely guarded. She took responsibility for limiting intrusions and was blamed by friends and family for cutting off access. Filter out the children's resentment of a stepmother and the old friends' resentment of a second wife, and all that's left of this complaint is the bedrock fact of the last three decades of Updike's life: his professional activities— not just the writing but the single-handed management of a vast, ever-expanding backlist of work published all over the globe—took up a huge amount of time. Merely keeping up with his business correspondence would have been a full-time job for anyone less fluent and less focused. And he needed time not only to write but also to let his imaginings percolate, time to spend on routine, relatively mindless chores such as spreading mulch, mowing the lawn, raking leaves, shoveling snow. A certain ruthlessness was required to divest the day of unwanted distractions, to keep business matters and family matters and the daily press of niggling demands at bay. Martha wanted to teach him to say no. Failing that, she was happy to say no for him. Her unyielding rigor in this respect could hardly escape notice, but it was her husband's will to work that invited her to take up the role of gatekeeper—the ruthlessness was as much his as hers.[*] It was during his very brief appearance in *What Makes Rabbit Run?* that David, looking pained, stated the case with unhappy precision: his father decided early on that his writing would "take precedence over his relations with real people."

The first novel Updike wrote in Beverly Farms, *The Witches of Eastwick*, begins with a mysterious bachelor arriving in the seaside town of Eastwick. Darryl Van Horne, our devilish hero, buys a house with a "chasteningly grand" silhouette; his property is cut off from the mainland whenever high tides flood the causeway connecting it with the town beach. Van Horne's mansion may resemble Haven Hill, but Darryl is not Updike, nor even a satanic alter ego—and yet a dose of fantasy and wish fulfillment spices up the *Witches* brew. It's useless to try to pick out real-life models for the novel's three weird sisters; Alexandra Spofford, Sukie Rougemont, and Jane Smart are composite characters, jumbled like the circle of friends in *Couples.* But when Van Horne seduces all three simultaneously after soaking with them in his scalding hot tub, Updike is compressing into one orgiastic Halloween night the highlights of his erotic history: Mary, Joyce Harrington, and Martha, the three most important romantic attachments of his life, were undoubtedly on his mind.

---

[*] This kind of complicity crops up regularly in the stories from this period. In "The Journey to the Dead," the recently divorced protagonist is involved with a woman who's "possessive of his time," who "kept watch on it." He reflects, "His life seemed destined never to be wholly his own. By his choice, of course."

"Replete but airy" is the phrase Updike used to describe *The Coup*, *Rabbit Is Rich*, and *Bech at Bay*—all products of the Georgetown years; it suits *Witches* just as well. Charmingly wicked, mischievous like the Bech books, it's pointed and provocative, balancing playful cleverness with a sustained meditation on women, power, nature, and evil. Harold Bloom described the novel as "engagingly half-mad with a storyteller's exuberance." And it does seem that Updike was enjoying himself; his sheer delight in the comic spectacle of suburban witches casting spells in a ranch house kitchen is plain to see. Although the witchcraft turns deadly, with violent death and fatal disease crashing into the narrative, the comedy never palls—a testament to his nimble artistry. He again did extensive research, poring over volumes on demonology and sorcery, but didn't allow the scrupulous authenticity of the coven's grotesque spells to spoil the fun. To his scholarly investigations he added distant memories of Berks County "witch doctors" and more recent experience closer to home. The novel is set in Rhode Island, but "semi-depressed and semi-fashionable" Eastwick is quite clearly another of his many portraits of Ipswich.* In fact, the novel contains some of his best writing about place; he tracks the New England seasons with his unerring eye and instinct for metaphor: "Bald November reigned outside. Lawn chairs had been taken in, the lawns were as dead and flat as floors, the outdoors was bare as a house after the movers had come."

But it's the three women who make the novel, especially Alexandra, the eldest and earthiest, whose impressively complex inner life is opened up for the reader. Our experience of her private thoughts and feelings is tender and intimate, as well as raw, strange, and scary. Depressed, she mopes in the bedroom of her untidy mid-nineteenth-century farmhouse:

---

* He wrote, "I once moved to a venerable secluded town, not far from Salem, where there had been a scandal"—an allusion to rumors of witchcraft that haunted Ipswich long before the Updikes arrived in town. Also, in March 1960 a double suicide by cyanide poisoning marked the grisly end of an "unorthodox" Ipswich romantic triangle; this was the germ of the novel's equally grisly murder-suicide: Sukie's lover batters his wife to death, then hangs himself.

[T]he world poured through her, wasted, down the drain. A woman is a hole, Alexandra had once read in the memoirs of a prostitute. In truth it felt less like being a hole than a sponge, a heavy squishy thing on this bed soaking out of the air all the futility and misery there is: wars nobody wins, diseases conquered so we can all die of cancer.

By the end, we know her inside out; her sensations are vivid and precise: "[S]unlight pressed on Alexandra's face and she could feel the hair of her single thick braid heat up like an electric coil." The novelist Diane Johnson, reviewing the book, cited this description as evidence that Updike "had a very good spy in the female camp to tell him things." Bloom, similarly impressed by the imaginative sympathy on display, declared that Updike "loves Alexandra better even than Rabbit Angstrom."

Updike made a deliberate decision to put the women at the center of the novel. He freely acknowledged that he did so in answer to accusations of sexism and misogyny leveled at his earlier work: "I've been criticized for making the women in my books subsidiary to the men," he told *The New York Times*, and conceded that there could be some truth in the charge. "Perhaps my female characters have been too domestic, too adorable and too much what men wished them to be." The witches' powers come to them in the absence of men, and although they eventually leave Eastwick and take refuge in marriage, what matters to them (and to us) is the interval when they are scandalously single, "gorgeous and doing evil." Updike was paying tribute to the power of women, acknowledging the inferiority of magical powers in the face of entrenched patriarchal power, and amusing himself by conflating "sinister old myths" with the "modern female experiences of liberation and raised consciousness." Unable, as always, to join any chorus chanting liberal pieties, he made fun of feminism even as he embraced it—naturally incensing his more dogmatic critics.

His book was twice transmogrified, first by Hollywood, into a jazzy battle-of-the-sexes horror-comedy hybrid starring Jack Nicholson as Van Horne, and Cher, Susan Sarandon, and Michelle Pfeiffer as Alexandra, Jane, and Sukie; and then by the impresario Cameron Mackintosh into a musical comedy on the London stage. John and Martha saw the film, sneaking into an afternoon showing at a local mall. She loathed it; he was less bothered, especially as the screenplay veered away from the book and the whiz-bang special effects took over, leaving him free to enjoy the three witches, each lovable in her own way. In the book he had been careful to keep Van Horne from stealing the show, as the devil tends to do, but Nicholson, who had no such scruple, gave an outrageously exuberant performance; Updike was pleased that the filmmakers had nonetheless managed to convey that the story was about women.

The novel was praised by many women writers, among them Johnson and Margaret Atwood, but others came to it with minds closed to the possibility that Updike could ever convincingly explore feminine awareness; to them he was "a male author notoriously unsympathetic to women," incapable of seeing females as anything but sex objects. Academic critics blinkered by ideology denied themselves the pleasure of reading *Witches* as a kind of self-mocking feminist manifesto, the mischief omnidirectional; or as a Rabbit novel subverted, the domestic realism of a male-centered world bewitched by the sorcery of the Eastwick coven. (They would have made short work of poor Harry, those three.) Magic realism, the literary fashion imported from South America a decade or so earlier, is here repurposed as a release from, and a challenge to, the inherent repressive tendency of the status quo. Two games of tennis illustrate the difference. At the Springers' cabin in the Poconos, Harry and Janice play with another couple from the lakeside community. Harry doesn't like tennis, mostly because Janice, who's had lessons, is better at it than he is: "The decade past has taught her more than it has taught him." Janice has internalized conventional advice: "Harry, don't try to *steer* it . . . Keep your knees bent. Point your hip toward the net." She's dutifully parroting the tennis pro at the Flying Eagle Tee and Racquet Club, abiding by rules and regulations the three witches riotously flout. At Van Horne's estate in Eastwick, they play doubles with their host—and their spells turn the court into a mad circus, the ball morphing into a bat or a toad, the painted baseline snaking over a sneaker. The battle of the sexes is joined in both these games, but in *Witches* a shot of surrealism has reinvigorated Updike's favorite topic, "the sexual *seethe* that underlies many a small town."

HALF A YEAR after the publication of *Witches*, on a punishingly cold evening in January 1985, Updike found himself in the waiting room of the Hartford Hospital in Hartford, Connecticut. It was the day of Ronald Reagan's second inauguration, and because it fell on a Sunday, the oath of office was administered in a private White House ceremony; the outdoor events scheduled for the next day's public inauguration were cancelled because of the record-setting cold forecast up and down the East Coast. On the West Coast, where Super Bowl XIX was being played between the Miami Dolphins and the San Francisco 49ers, the afternoon was mild, with clouds and fog; President Reagan, freshly sworn in for his second term, appeared at the game (via satellite) and tossed the coin. Updike followed the football on television in the hospital waiting room. He was awaiting the birth of his first grandchild.

A baby boy, John Anoff Cobblah, was born to Liz and her new husband, Tete Cobblah, an artist and art teacher from Ghana. Liz had met Tete in 1983 while studying at the Rhode Island School of Design, three years after the death of her first husband. It was to Anoff and his younger brother, Kwame, that Updike addressed "A Letter to My Grandsons," the genealogical disquisition in *Self-Consciousness*. The circumstances of Anoff's birth—the cold evening in Hartford, the football game, and the news that the baby had been given his paternal grandfather's name—are recorded in "Grandparenting," the very last Maples story, an epilogue of sorts, with Richard and Joan both remarried. The new spouses are half the fun. Once Richard's mistress, now his wife, Ruth has "a crisp way of seeing things; it was like living in a pop-up book, with no dimension of ambiguity." She is "decisive and clear-headed"—so much so that Richard "rarely had to think." No one would have any trouble recognizing Martha from that description. As for Joan's new husband, Andy Vanderhaven, he's a gently comic portrait of the man Mary married in 1982, Bob Weatherall—with a few details scrambled. Foppish and fussy, peering over gold half-glasses, Andy resembles a "skeptical schoolmaster." Still obscurely tied to his ex-wife, Richard can't help speculating about her sex life:

> Richard wondered if Andy was this fastidious in bed. Perhaps that was what Joan had needed—a man to draw her out, to make her feel relatively liberated. "No matter where I go," she had once complained to Richard, not only of their sex, "you're there ahead of me."

As in so many Maples stories, Joan gets the best lines. Inspired by watching her daughter in the delivery room (while her husband and ex-husband were watching the Super Bowl), she gushes about the "apparatus" that sustains an unborn child: "You think of the womb as a place for transients, but it's a whole other life in there. It's a lot to give up." Later that night, shivering in the cold of his motel room bed, feeling like "a homunculus burning at the far end of God's indifferently held telescope," Richard typically links Joan's remark—"It's a lot to give up"—to his own mortality: "He was a newly hatched grandfather, and the universe wanted to crush him, to make room for newcomers."

Character and author came to the same conclusion: a couple of weeks before he hatched as a grandfather, the coming generation weighing on his mind, Updike wrote his will. He had written wills before, in 1964 and 1973, only to find that altered circumstances forced him to start over. But the only change he ever made to the will dated January 8, 1985, was a scribbled amendment bequeathing to his children Plowville acreage inherited from his mother. Such was the settled nature of his life in Beverly Farms: aside from his mother's death, nothing in the last twenty-four years of his life caused him to him rethink the disposition of his estate.

No grandchildren were named in the will, one reason it never had to be rewritten.* Instead, he divided his estate between Mar-

---

* Anoff was the first of seven grandchildren. Liz, Michael, and Miranda had two children each; David, one.

tha and his four children. Through the instrument of the John H. Updike Revocable Literary Trust, the children and their stepmother inherited the rights to his literary property, so that after his death the income from all his books and the ancillary rights would be shared five ways between them. (After Martha's death, the surviving children would be sole beneficiaries.) The children would also receive $500,000 split four ways. The rest—the house and its contents, his savings and investments—would all go to Martha. There were also smaller cash bequests: $35,000 for his mother and $15,000 each for Martha's three boys. And there were personal items for his own children: his two-volume edition of Samuel Johnson's dictionary for Liz; for David, a small gateleg table known in the family as "the Updike table"; for Michael, a cartoon Saul Steinberg had inscribed to a teenage John in 1945; and a Thurber drawing for Miranda.

Although the bulk of his estate would go to his new wife, he also mentioned his ex: to Mary, he left a seventeenth-century veneered bench, a two-seater with armrests and a decorative back that they had bought together from an antique dealer in Ipswich in the mid-sixties.

Stable but hardly static, life in Beverly Farms was interrupted by frequent trips to New York (to the Academy of Arts and Letters, to the offices of Knopf and *The New Yorker*), author appearances in scattered locations across the continent and overseas (for readings, talks, and book festivals; to give and receive awards; and to accept honorary degrees, which he found he could never turn down), and vacations abroad with Martha at least twice a year. Starting in the mid-eighties, he had another reason for traveling to Manhattan: reviewing museum exhibitions as an occasional art critic for *The New Republic*. He had written a number of short essays about specific artworks for the American edition of a French magazine, *Réalités*, the modest beginnings of a new sideline that turned to practical use a passion stretching back through art classes in Oxford and at Harvard to the hours spent as a child lying on the floor tracing cartoons and magazine illustrations. Writing about the visual arts suited him so well that it's a wonder he hadn't turned his hand to it earlier—for example, when he was living in Manhattan and could stroll, as he often did, from his office to MoMA (or the Modern, as it was known then) to admire the Cézannes and the Matisses or mingle in the Sculpture Garden with a bevy of bronze nudes.

His reviews of museum exhibitions displayed all the virtues of his book reviews: unpretentious, open-minded, and acutely perceptive, they are sensitive to artistic intent and immune to theoretical dogma. His great talent, as Arthur Danto argued in a review of Updike's first collection of essays on art, *Just Looking* (1989), was for "ruminative ekphrasis"—poetic description of an artwork combined with a tentative movement toward aesthetic judgment. Reviewing the Renoir show at the Boston Museum of Fine Art in 1985, he wrote, "The peaceable Renoir moment is a kind of naptime; his dancing couples drowse in one another's arms, and his outdoor cafés exist without clatter or the possibility of conflict"—the kind of inspired observation that led by soft steps to a verdict, in this case that "Renoir does not quite rank with . . . his friends Monet and Cézanne." But even with all the hours spent in art classes, even with his modest ability as an amateur painter, Updike knew far less about art than he did about literature, and the difference ultimately showed. The accounts he gave of his museum visits were invariably compelling, sometimes dazzling, and he did his homework so he could dish out historical context and tidbits from an artist's life story, yet he lacked the kind of expert knowledge that comes with dedicated scholarship or lifelong immersion. It was an extracurricular activity, a hobby of sorts (an enthusiasm he shared with Martha). Still, he turned out the art reviews with his usual cool professionalism—a writer doing his job.

He certainly wasn't doing it for the money: *The New Republic* paid very poorly. After receiving a paltry eight cents per word for a literary piece in 1975, he complained. The editors came back to him with an offer of $250 per review, not nearly enough to keep him on board. But writing about art was a different matter. He was happy to review the Renoir show for a tiny fraction of what *The New Yorker* would have paid for a book review of similar length. Starting in 1990 he switched his allegiance to *The New York Review of Books* (despite several sharply negative reviews of his work that had appeared in its pages), where the pay was better and the circulation wider.

On trips to Manhattan, the Updikes sometimes stayed with Michael Arlen, who lived with his wife, Alice, in a sumptuous apartment on Fifth Avenue, a dozen blocks north of the Metropolitan Museum of Art. But the luxurious accommodation at "the Arlen Arms" couldn't quite make up for what Updike saw as the city's sad decline. He wrote in 1987, "I feel confident in saying that disadvantages of New York life which led me to leave have intensified rather than abated, and that the city which Le Corbusier described as a magnificent disaster is less and less magnificent." If the tone of this pronouncement seems peevish, it chimes with a number of grievances nurtured during the decade, grumbles about conglomerate ownership of publishing houses, the shrinking pool of American readers, and hostile feminist critics.

It echoes, too, the caustic tone of the novel he began even before the publication of *Witches. Roger's Version* (originally titled *Majesty*) is narrated by a latter-day incarnation of Hester Prynne's cuckolded husband, the sinister Roger Chillingworth. The modern-day Roger, called Lambert and also a cuckold (at least in his imagination), is a depressive divinity school professor with a "sullen temper" and a mordant wit who debates theological points great and small with a young computer scientist intent on discovering scientific proof of the existence of God. Once again, Updike is playing with the love triangle from *The Scarlet Letter*: Roger imagines in pornographic detail an affair between the computer programmer, Dale Kohler (the Dimmesdale figure), and his wife, Esther (as in Hester). The novel stretches in directions Hawthorne could not have conceived, and required extensive research into the workings of a computer lab, theories about the origin of both organic and inorganic matter, and heresies of the Early Church.

To achieve the "informational abundance" of this ambitious, formidably intelligent novel, Updike turned to experts amused by the prospect of assisting a famous writer. He consulted no less an authority than Michael Dertouzos, director of MIT's Laboratory for Computer Science, who took a keen interest in the idea of a computer whiz trying to catch a glimpse of God courtesy of binary code and graphic interface. Dertouzos advised him on technical details as well as larger scientific issues and vetted portions of the manuscript. He told Updike about physicists in his lab who were trying to explain all physical phenomena with computational theories, young men who liked to "play God" at their terminals—real-life counterparts of Dale Kohler. Updike studied articles on cosmology in *Scientific American* and *Sky & Telescope*. He exchanged letters with a college classmate, Jacob Neusner, director of the Program in Judaic Studies at Brown University, concerning Genesis Rabbah and the writings of Tertullian, subject of Roger's scholarly investigations.

Roger's Version reshapes *The Scarlet Letter*'s romantic triangle into a quadrangle—a configuration more appropriate to a novel profoundly invested in binary systems and computation, and more congenial to an author already deeply invested in foursomes. Character number four is Verna, daughter of Roger's half sister; nineteen and a single mother of a biracial child, she's paired with her uncle, whom she calls Nunc, in binary opposition to Dale and Esther. Verna lives in a housing project in a dilapidated precinct of a northeastern city so obviously based on greater Boston that it seems oddly coy of Updike to leave it unnamed. As part of his research for the novel, he wandered through unsavory Cambridge neighborhoods, notepad in hand, scribbling observations about the clothes and hairstyles of the citizens he passed on the sidewalk. He took snapshots, gritty black-and-white vistas of urban decay. He pored over government documents on food stamp eligibility. Having decided after *Witches* to "attempt a city novel"—this was in fact his first novel set in a major metropolis—he paid meticulous attention to the cityscape, taking his notepad with him to the top of the Prudential Tower and scrawling notes labeled according to the points of the compass. Making good use of fresh data, he sent Roger and Verna to eat lunch in a "crassly swank" rotating restaurant atop a skyscraper; their dialogue is punctuated by detailed topographical descriptions of the 360-degree panorama.

The novel skips back and forth across the socioeconomic divides of Reagan's America. Roger lives in a leafy academic enclave near the university; his neighbors do aerobics on their redwood deck to an upbeat Bach fugue. In a grim neighborhood on the other side of town, Verna and eighteen-month-old Paula live on welfare in a yellow-brick building that smells of "urine and damp cement and rubber-based paint, paint repeatedly applied and repeatedly defaced." Lusting after his nubile niece, inching his way to incest, Roger pays several visits to their dismal one-room apartment. Before the flirtation is consummated, Verna announces that she's pregnant again, and Roger convinces her to have an abortion. Now thoroughly entangled, he agrees to take her to the clinic. On the appointed day, he chauffeurs her "beyond the project, deeper into that section of the city where [he] never used to go." In the dingy anteroom, surveying the other "prospective mothers," he spots a black girl with wet cheeks and an otherwise impassive face, "an African mask, her lips and jaw majestically protruding." Later, seeing that her tears have dried, he marvels at this "princess of a race that travels from cradle to grave at the expense of the state, like the aristocrats of old." It's typically mischievous of Updike to insert a flagrantly provocative sentence about race and welfare into a scene that puts liberal thinking on abortion (which he endorsed) into action: Roger believes that Verna should terminate her pregnancy on the grounds that the abortionist would be "killing an unborn child to try to save a born one." When Verna's habit of smacking Paula lands the child in the emergency room with a broken leg, the wisdom of preventing any increase in a small dysfunctional family currently subsisting "at the expense the state" seems unimpeachable. (Small comfort to Updike's liberal readers.)

Despite the sociology and the scientific bells and whistles, despite the long, abstruse passages devoted to Dale's doomed experiment on the computer lab's VAX 8600, *Roger's Version* is a book about theology; "an essay about kinds of belief," Updike labeled it. While little Paula is staying overnight in the hospital "under observation," Verna tempts Roger onto her musty futon, where he's graced with an epiphany:

> When I was spent and my niece released, we lay together on
> a hard floor of the spirit, partners in incest, adultery, and

child abuse. We wanted to be rid of each other, yet perversely clung, lovers, miles below the ceiling, our comfort being that we had no further to fall. Lying there with Verna, gazing upward, I saw how much majesty resides in our continuing to love and honor God even as He inflicts blows upon us—as much as resides in the silence He maintains so that we may enjoy and explore our human freedom. This was *my* proof of His existence, I saw—the distance to the impalpable ceiling, the immense distance measuring our abasement.

Verna's abortion doesn't figure in Roger's tally of the couple's sins—sins that reveal, paradoxically, the majesty of faith. This is a faith that thrives on the absence, or at least the silence and distance, of the divinity. The theological motto Roger lives by is distilled from his favorite theologian, Karl Barth: the god who stood at the end of some human way would not be God. Dale's technology-driven attempt to flush out our creator by digitally replicating creation is trumped by a truth perceived in abasement and founded on faith alone. That, anyway, is the gospel according to Roger.

Reviews of the novel were respectful and for the most part favorable, with much praise for Updike's prodigious capacity for assimilating scientific knowledge. But one critic, Frederick Crews, a professor of English at Berkeley and the author of an influential Freudian exegesis of Hawthorne's work, took the opportunity to write a scathing essay in *The New York Review of Books* lamenting what he saw as the wrong turn Updike took sometime in the sixties, a swerve that eventually transformed him, on the evidence of *Roger's Version*, into a crank and a militant snob. Crews accused Roger (and Updike) of "class-based misanthropy." Leaving poor Roger out of it, he also complained of the author's "belligerent, almost hysterical callousness" and his "outbursts of misogyny"; he called Updike "morally obtuse" as well as "morbid and curmudgeonly"; he hinted darkly that he was a closet nihilist. Updike, in sum, bore the brunt of Crews's displeasure; Roger got off lightly.

What turned Updike into such a miserable, twisted soul? According to Crews, the damage came from Updike's having "radically divorced his notion of Christian theology from Christian ethics." He also divorced his wife "after twenty-one years together," a fact Crews seems to have gleaned from the "many stories and novels that dwell upon that trauma." It's not entirely clear how fiction alone could have formed Crews's opinions about the author's private life, yet he confidently asserts that Updike quashed the voice of his conscience, while at the same time clinging to a "me-first Salvationism." In his conclusion, Crews locates "a certain bleakness at the center" of Updike's mind, which is perhaps less gratuitously insulting than John Aldridge's claim that "Mr. Updike has nothing to say." Bleakness may be preferable to blankness, but both essays reek of personal animus and willfully punitive misreading.

Attempts at character assassination by reputable critics are alarming but rarely fatal. Updike survived Aldridge when he was young and relatively unknown. By the time Crews published his mean-spirited polemic, Updike's work had been reviewed in newspapers and magazines more than two thousand times, with the raves easily outnumbering the rest. An author of his stature could afford to shrug off even the ugliest assault. When Joyce Carol Oates commiserated over Crews, Updike calmly replied that being called a racist curmudgeon made him feel quite detached from himself. And yet there *was* a hint of gloom in Updike's remarks at the time of the novel's publication, a murmur of discontent. Perhaps Crews had seen the *New York Times* interview in which the novelist volunteered that his fiction contained his "sense of futility and of doom and of darkness . . . of death being behind everything in life, a sort of black backdrop." Bleak indeed.* Was he unhappy at age fifty-three, at the peak of his success, living with his new wife in his splendid white mansion with its distant look at the sea?

A broken-down F. Scott Fitzgerald, having decided to give up trying to be a person ("It was strange to have no self") and become "a writer only," declared that "the natural state of the sentient adult is a qualified unhappiness." Updike's own view was considerably sun-

---

* Bleaker, in fact, than *Roger's Version*, which is prickly rather than gloomy, and much funnier than Frederick Crews would have you believe.

nier. His memoirs, begun while he was writing *Roger's Version*, end with an essay, entitled "Being a Self Forever," that includes testimony to his "good-tempered" disposition. He presents himself as someone whose natural state is a qualified happiness, his good temper balanced against a recurring sense of being "smothered and confined, misunderstood and put-upon." He was not without complaints. Two of the first four chapters of *Self-Consciousness* are devoted to physical afflictions: his psoriasis, his stammer, and his asthma. One chapter is devoted to the awkward business of "not being a dove" during the Vietnam War (and to his bad teeth). But all these troubles were overcome, the various ailments treated or brought under control, and the ideological tension diffused by the fact that the war eventually ended. In other words, despite his cheery disposition, he was quite often annoyed by circumstances that he recognized and understood—but that made him grumpy all the same.

"Happiness," he writes in *Self-Consciousness*, "is best seen out of the corner of the eye." Yet he goes on to take a forensic look at one blissful moment, a walk back up the drive from his mailbox to his house on a sunny Sunday morning. He lists the components of his happiness: postcoital satisfaction ("My wife and I had just made love, successfully all around, which at my age"—his mid-fifties—"occasions some self-congratulation"); pleasure in his property ("a cobalt-blue sky precisely fitted against the dormered roof-line of my house"); a keen interest in his professional activities ("preparing the final draft of this long-savored and -contemplated book"); eager anticipation of an afternoon visit from Liz, Tete, and his two grandsons (the second, Kwame, still an infant); and the prospect of his "invariable" breakfast, granola and orange juice. "Can happiness," he asks, "be simply a matter of orange juice?"

He notes that his sense of well-being is complicated by his "inner remove," the writer's habit of stepping back and squinting at everything, including his own bourgeois contentment. If America, as he once memorably put it, "is a vast conspiracy to make you happy," his job was to unravel the conspiracy and skeptically examine its constituent parts. He felt disdain for his well-protected life, his careful management of his worldly affairs, his self-pampering concern for tranquillity and material comfort. Adding a theological dimension to his disdain, he quotes from the Gospel: "He that gains his life shall lose it."

Although Crews suggested that Updike's religious beliefs were turning him into an insufferable grouch, and although Updike himself conceded that when he wrote about organized religion in his novels, the tone was sometimes "kind of acid," his personal faith had in fact been less troublesome to him since his late thirties, and was now the source of some security, a mostly reliable reassurance. Never robust, his faith at least began to have the virtue of longevity. He held fast to the idea that God was the "guarantor" of his existence, "a protector and a reference point." He held fast to crisis theology, his views unaltered since the days when he countered paralyzing dread by immersing himself in Barth and Kierkegaard. Visiting Florence with Martha in the fall of 1999, he woke up in the night feeling "fearful and adrift"; he prayed for sleep. A sudden, furious thunderstorm came up and comforted him with the sense of "exterior activity"; he felt that "the burden of being was shared." The storm, he decided, was "an answered prayer." These episodes of late-night panic grew less and less frequent over the decades. In his early seventies he reported nothing more distressing than the odd anxious moment at four in the morning. Perhaps the mere endurance of his beliefs and his faithful attendance at church helped cure him. Perhaps, as he aged, his dread of dying and being dead gradually lost its cruel edge, the fear, blunted by passing years, too familiar at last to frighten.

On that Sunday morning when he experienced a sudden access of happiness strolling up the driveway from the mailbox, he was wearing, he tells us, his "churchgoing clothes." He and Martha had joined St. John's Episcopalian Church in Beverly Farms. A replica of an English country church set back from the road behind a low stone wall, it was just a brisk ten-minute walk from the house. John almost always went on his own, and favored a pew on the baptistery side. A frequent lector at services, he occasionally supplied introductions to the lessons he read. But though he helped out with St. John's annual book fair, he was no longer an active churchman as he had been at the Congregational church in Ipswich. He dodged the committee work—"I have stayed out," as he put it, "of the business end of St. John's."

Golf, another reassuring constant in his Beverly Farms life, provided equally essential uplift. Sometimes, choosing the fairway over the pew at St. John's, he arranged his second round of the week for a Sunday morning. Having joined the venerable Myopia Hunt Club, he now mostly played on its gorgeous, undulating, tree-lined links. His foursome might have a sandwich in the clubhouse looking out over the eighteenth hole, before their round or after. The dining room, with its understated old-school club décor, became a favorite spot for family dinners—on John's birthday, or if Linda was visiting from Plowville, special occasions his children remember as relaxed and jolly.

"Relaxed and jolly" is what his next novel, *S.*, should have been, to judge from the premise. The concluding installment of his Scarlet Letter trilogy, it's a chance for Hester—reinvented as Sarah Worth, a rich, snobby housewife from the North Shore of Boston who leaves her philandering husband for the spiritual adventure of life at an Arizona ashram—finally to have her say. *S.* is funny in places and sharply satiric, but for the most part it's thin and stretched and uncomfortably manic, as though Updike were straining for an effect beyond his reach, or trying to reconcile incompatible aims. He had hoped to pay fitting tribute to Hester Prynne, whom he thought of as the only flesh-and-blood female in American fiction before Henry James's heroines.

Updike gave an unfortunate interview just as the novel landed in bookstores, in early March 1988. Meeting a *New York Times* journalist in the Knopf offices, he announced that *S.* was another attempt to "make things right" with his "feminist detractors":

> I saw this as being a woman's novel by a man. And indeed, the binding of the book is pink. It's really sort of rose, I'd like to think, but it looks pretty pink to me—a feminine, hopeful, fresh pink.

To signal to the reader that Updike was being facetious, teasing in his wicked, unsettling way, the journalist (male, and apparently sympathetic) drew repeated attention to the "permanent twinkle" in the author's eyes. Much of the interview was tongue-in-cheek, in the manner of Updike's self-mocking exchanges with Henry Bech. Updike went on to declare that *The Witches of Eastwick* was "a very determined effort to write about women who did have careers of a sort—they were professional witches," a preposterous remark that might have endeared him to ironists but could only exasperate the feminist critics he claimed to want to mollify. *S.*, he said, was "a sincere attempt to write about a woman on the move"—sure, except that her move is to an ashram presided over by a fraud who not only exploits her but enlists her help in exploiting others, hardly liberation as the women's movement conceived it. Updike was keenly aware that his readership was mostly female (as any readership generally is), but his misguided attempt to kowtow ("a feminine hopeful, fresh pink") careened in the direction of satiric, self-defeating mischief. Reviews of the novel were sour, and sales, despite Knopf's high hopes, underwhelming. A decade later, when he came across a well-thumbed copy of *S.* in a small public library in the Hudson Valley, he remembered how he had put his "heart and soul" into the heroine and concluded that the novel had at last been "recognized": "A sort of blessing seemed to arise from the anonymous public; I had been, mutely, understood." Forsaking irony, he embraced a retrospective sincerity that smacks of wishful thinking.

Infinitely more complicated than *S.*, and far more rewarding, *Self-Consciousness* was published a year later, on his fifty-seventh birthday. Its genesis, Updike acknowledged, was defensive: having heard that someone might be eager to write his biography, and repulsed by the mere thought of anyone appropriating his life story ("this massive datum that happens to be mine"), he resolved to write his memoirs—a tactical maneuver, purely preemptive. And indeed, the best way to make sense of these six linked autobiographical essays is to think of them as a kind of damage control: here was his chance to put a factual frame around the poetry and prose into which he'd poured so much of his experience. That frame would naturally draw attention to the aspects of his life he considered most important, just as it would obscure whatever he preferred not to publicize. Though indiscreet, a peepshow revealing flashes of cruelty, promiscuity, narcissism, and petty vindictiveness, the essays are only *selectively* indiscreet. His fits of avarice, for example, and his tendency to meet emotional crises with a vacillating indecision that amounted to what he elsewhere called emotional bigamy—those faults are not on show. In a draft ending eventually dropped from the manuscript, he conceded that he was peddling a kind of "cagey candor" and proposed that the title of the book should be *Self-Serving* or *Self-Promotion*. Like the author of every memoir ever published, he was engaged in a calculated attempt to shape his reputation. "These memoirs feel shabby," he wrote. It made him uncomfortable to be burnishing his personal rather than his literary reputation, his self rather than his books.

As a record of his life as experienced from within, the memoirs are wonderfully, distressingly intimate. "A writer's self-consciousness," he tells us, "is really a mode of interestedness." In these pages, he offers a demonstration of how that intense interestedness turned both inward and outward; one minute he was picking psoriatic scabs (figuratively and literally) and the next looking out the window of the house in Shillington and noting exactly how the mailman walks, "leaning doggedly away from the pull of his leather pouch." We get as rich an account of his boyhood as anyone would wish—and in the fifth essay, a genealogical digression that's more than most readers can bear; as Martin Amis quipped, "here we see Updike nude, without a stitch of irony or art." As an objective record of his life, especially his adult life, a record of the facts an acquaintance or a loyal reader might find useful, it's sketchy at best. Neither of his wives is named, and Martha ("my second wife") barely figures. Of his children, only David is named (in passing); they, too, barely figure. Whereas family life in Shillington and Plowville is lovingly evoked, there's precious little sense of how he lived after leaving home. If the details of his first marriage are hazy, the second is utterly opaque. There's no career narrative. He provides very few glimpses of himself as a friend or a colleague. Reading *Self-Consciousness*, you would probably not suspect that up until his self-inflicted banishment from Ipswich, Updike was a clown, a manic entertainer, an aficionado of the pratfall and the silly gag. You might not even grasp that he was funny, that an enduring part of his charm was an eagerness to make others laugh. Instead of humor, he offers up a veteran hypochondriac's litany of complaint, his bodily ills aggravated by social insecurities and political quarrels—"a parading," as he put it, "of my wounds."

A lifelong habit of self-deprecation made the opposite unthinkable: he would never parade his triumphs—prizes, riches, accolades. When self-satisfaction spills out onto the page, he adopts a self-mocking tone: "I have preened, I have lived." Although he knew it was laughable for a "good-tempered," supremely successful author to insist on telling sob stories about the trouble he'd seen ("Suffering and I," he admitted, "have had a basically glancing, flirtatious acquaintanceship"), he nonetheless felt compelled to dwell on infirmities and obstacles, disagreements and imminent decline, circling back in every essay except "A Letter to My Grandsons" to some physical or emotional hurt, as though his wounds were his essence.

And in a curious way they were. Relentlessly metaphorical, *Self-Consciousness* is the trace of a mind speeding back and forth like a weaver's shuttle between idea and thing, knitting together abstract and concrete, word and flesh. In the first essay, a nostalgic stroll through rainy Shillington blurs the boundary between his physical being and the enchanted precincts of his childhood: "I had propelled my body through the tenderest parts of a town that was also somewhat my body." In the second, musing on his "troubled epidermis," he asks, "What was my creativity, my relentless need to produce, but a parody of my skin's embarrassing overproduction?" In the third, he describes the "obdurate barrier" in his throat that trips up his speech, then tells us that the "paralysis of stuttering stems from the dead center of one's being, a deep doubt there"; he explains the "ingenious psychosomatic mechanism" of his asthma: "I tried to break out of my marriage on behalf of another, and failed, and began to have trouble breathing." In the fourth, he pivots from "not being a dove" to his epic, lifelong ordeal in the dentist's chair—and ends facetiously, "I gave my teeth to the war effort."* In the last essay, written when he was fifty-five, he complains of being old, repeating the word as though he were banging on a funeral drum. Everywhere, he sees symptoms of his deterioration: "As I age, I feel my head to be full of holes where once there was electricity and matter." Similar laments sound throughout the book; he was actually only fifty-three when he composed the maudlin final paragraph of "At War with My Skin":

> Between now and the grave lies a long slide of forestallment, a slew of dutiful, dutifully paid-for maintenance routines in which dermatological makeshift joins periodontal work and prostate examinations on the crowded appointment calendar of dwindling days.

Even in the genealogical essay, the body, the skin we live in, gets the last word. He wraps up "A Letter to My Grandsons" with a saying attributed to his maternal grandfather, John Hoyer: *"You carry your own hide to market."*

His body was his self, and vice versa, so he wrote his memoirs as though he were tattooing the words on every inch of his hide—inscribing his story on the body, inside and out. "Truth," he writes, "is anecdotes, narrative, the snug, opaque quotidian." An anecdote is a body in motion, animated clay. Truth, for Updike, reveals itself in the interaction between the corporeal (skin, teeth, throat, lungs) and the spirit. Is it any surprise that he was prone to psychosomatic illness? Or that sex meant so much to him? This is how he conceived of human meaning: memory, emotion, conscience, all the precious intangibles of our consciousness, affixing themselves to living tissue, to flesh and bone.

He was still at work on the last two essays in November 1987 when he spent a couple of nights in Plowville. He visited his mother frequently during these years, usually by himself and in conjunction with a journey to New York or farther afield. This particular

---

* He's referring here to World War II, not the Vietnam War, but the acrobatics are impressive all the same.

visit was sandwiched between a trip to Missouri to pick up a literary award at Saint Louis University and a research expedition to Trenton, New Jersey, to hunt for traces of his paternal grandfather, Hartley.* He slept badly in the cold, damp guest room, brooding about his mother. During the summer, she had taken a bad fall in the kitchen. Bruised on her back and abdomen, she retreated to her bed—and stayed there for weeks, getting up only to feed the dog, the many cats, and sometimes herself. She had lost her appetite for food, and for reading and writing, and even for her favorite television game shows. She was eighty-three, and though she was livelier now that she was back on her feet, her health remained fragile. He worried with every visit that this would be his last.

A year and a half later, in April 1989, she was hospitalized with cardiogenic pulmonary edema, an accumulation of fluid in the air sacs of the lungs—she could barely breathe. He spent much of the month traveling back and forth from Plowville, visiting her in the hospital, and looking after the farmhouse. The underlying cause of her condition was a weak heart. The cardiologist recommended open-heart surgery and a coronary bypass. To her son's unspoken relief, she refused, saying she wanted to go home and "take what comes." That summer, breathing more easily and regaining some of her feistiness, she worked with John on the proofs of her second book, which was scheduled for October publication. Pencil in hand, he went over her stories, making changes; he was amused to note that when she looked back over what he'd done, she erased a few of his emendations. She insisted on riding the lawn mower and put him to work digging stones from the lawn. She announced that she wanted to put an end to the visits of the nurses monitoring her condition. But she couldn't summon the indomitable spirit of her younger years. She was frail, fragile; her son wondered how soon he would be making decisions for her.

---

* In 1984, when it was first offered to him, Updike turned down the Saint Louis Literary Award, pleading a crowded schedule. In the interim it had been accepted by Walker Percy (1985) and Saul Bellow (1986); the luster of those names apparently made up for the modest prize money, a mere $1,500.

Early on the morning of Tuesday, October 10, she suffered a fatal heart attack standing by her kitchen sink with her coat and hat on. (Although she'd been forbidden to drive by her doctor, she was planning that morning to take her car to the garage in nearby New Holland.) Falling, she broke her glasses and cut her eye. Updike was told by the coroner—and believed—that she died instantly. Her body was discovered only the next day, when the neighboring farmer, alarmed by her repeated failure to answer the door or the telephone, finally broke into the house and summoned the undertaker and the local minister.

On the Tuesday she died, her son was giving a reading at Minnesota State University Moorhead. On Wednesday, before flying back to Boston, he allowed himself to be persuaded to visit Moorhead's twin city, Fargo, North Dakota. He was ferried across the Red River in a swollen stretch limo adorned inside with a tiny chandelier. Outside a downtown print shop, he was inducted into Fargo's newly established Celebrity Walk of Fame. He gamely pressed feet and hands into wet concrete, and signed his name—and all the while, as he wrote to Oates, his mother's body was cooling on the kitchen floor, between the sink and the stove. When he reached Haven Hill, he found on the front door a neighbor's note announcing her death.

His immediate reaction was guilt. He wrote a poem nine days later, "The Fall," describing the moment he arrived at the empty farmhouse and discovered on the kitchen floor the broken glasses and bloodstained hat:

> "O Mama," I said aloud, though I never called
> her "Mama," "I didn't take very good care of you."

Feeling guilty and inadequate, he summoned his children for the funeral. Afterward came the dismal work of sorting through the vast jumble of her possessions, emptying the house and cleaning it. From countless shelves and drawers and trunks emerged mementos of her life and his, so that as he worked he relived his childhood in random, haunting flashes. Michael had stayed behind after his siblings left and helped his father load furniture into a rented van, which they drove together back up to Massachusetts. In early November, Updike drove back down to Plowville to finish the job, a sad, lonely visit. After sleeping in the farmhouse for the last time, he locked up and drove north, the car loaded with maternal souvenirs destined for storage in the barn at Haven Hill. He stopped at a service area on the New Jersey Turnpike for a coffee and a cinnamon doughnut. Sitting there, gazing out at the exit ramps, he was visited by an emotion remembered from adolescence, a feeling that came to him when he was stranded after school for a long stretch in Stephen's Luncheon-ette, waiting for his father so that they could drive the eleven miles home from Shillington: "I was an orphan, full of the triumphant, arid bliss of being on my own."

After seventeen years of worrying about a widowed mother living alone on an isolated farm, and seven years of worrying about her declining health, his sorrow was tinged with relief. He missed her Saturday phone calls, a recap of her week salted with her distinctive wit and self-deprecating irony. He pored over the treasure of knickknacks and snapshots salvaged from Plowville, and in the new year began a long story, "A Sandstone Farmhouse," a sequel to *Of the Farm*, in which his mother is resurrected with unsentimental candor and evident affection. Feeling that he now possessed her life made him at once sad and exultant. He filled the story with incidents snatched directly from her last six months, quoting her verbatim and giving the precise circumstances of her demise.* It was both a memorial—an attempt to immortalize the most important person in his life—and a kind of therapy.

Joey Robinson, narrator of *Of the Farm*, is here a third-person protagonist suddenly orphaned by the death of his widowed mother. At the funeral, he's treated gingerly by relatives and neighbors: "He knew he and his mother were regarded as having been unusually, perhaps unnaturally close." But Joey harbors an old grudge against her for having turned him, at age thirteen, into a yokel by mov-

---

* There were of course fictional elements, but almost all of them had to do with her son: Joey is given three ex-wives, a lucrative career in advertising, and a more urban pre-farmhouse boyhood than Updike himself had enjoyed.

ing the family out of town, out into the countryside, back to the farm where she was born, her paradise regained. Although he feels that "she betrayed him with the farm and its sandstone house," he makes a conscious effort to channel his resentment: "He couldn't blame his mother, he still needed her too much, so he blamed the place." Updike did something similar in writing the story, working through memories of the embarrassment, boredom, and discomfort of his rural exile, and his galling sense that his mother loved the farm as much as or more than she loved him, that he and her eighty acres were rivals. When Joey cleans out the house, he does it "ruthlessly, vengefully," gradually erasing all trace of her life there and his. Updike, in a "frenzy of efficiency," did the same in the late fall of 1989, calling in an auctioneer for the unwanted furniture and sifting through a "stifling" amount of stuff worthless to anyone but a nostalgic relative. Like Joey, he asked his ex-wife to take the dog, and the county humane society to trap and gas the cats. He quickly sold the house and thirty acres to a second cousin (keeping fifty acres that were rented out to Mennonite farmers). But unlike Joey, he could transfer all this onto the page, thereby turning a ruthless and vengeful activity into a form of unblinking tribute. The reader recognizes the essential beauty of the place, and also the semi-squalid condition in which his mother left it. The place is an extension of the person. One admires the monstrous force of her will, her vitality, her youthful aspirations, even while cringing at the revelation of her obscure sexual incompatibility with Joey's father. The story won the O. Henry Prize and was included in *The Best American Short Stories 1991*.

To Maxwell, Updike confided that Linda had never been well suited to the role either of mother or of writer, but that she made "gallant stabs in both directions." His ambivalence about her talent as a mother is less pronounced than his ambivalence about her writing talent, which is summed up by the peculiar inconsistency of the hardcover edition of *Self-Consciousness*: On the dust jacket's flap copy, his mother is described as "a writer"; between the covers, in the Note About the Author, she's merely "an aspiring writer"—even though her second book was about to be published. It's unlikely, given the care with which Updike checked and rechecked galley proofs, that the discrepancy was accidental.

"A SANDSTONE FARMHOUSE" was by no means his final farewell to Plowville—or to his mother. Ten days before she died, he finished the longhand draft of *Rabbit at Rest*. Her "unignorable" decline during the year he spent writing it contributed to what he called the "mortal mood" of this final volume of the tetralogy; her stints in the Reading hospital under the care of cardiologists provided medical details he "shamelessly" fed into his terrifyingly vivid descriptions of Harry Angstrom's cardiovascular traumas. (Anyone wondering how it feels to have an angioplasty under local anesthetic will find out midway through the novel.) Rabbit's second heart attack kills him in the city of Deleon, Florida, so named in honor of Juan Ponce de León, hero of Linda's oft-revised and perennially rejected novel. Saying good-bye to Rabbit, Updike was also saying good-bye to his mother, and to Berks County, a part of the world that he knew he would be visiting only very rarely from now on. All this leave-taking affected him viscerally. He suffered chest pains like Rabbit ("that singeing sensation he gets as if a child inside him is playing with lighted matches"), a kind of empathetic heartache. "Deciding to wind up the series," he remarked, "was a kind of death for me."

Making light of his genuine grief, he exaggerated for comic effect: "You might say it's a depressed book about a depressed man, written by a depressed man." In fact, *Rabbit at Rest* resembles in tone and texture *Rabbit Is Rich*, the volume Updike thought of as the happiest, most buoyant of the tetralogy. Although the ever-present drama of Harry's deteriorating health hangs threateningly over the action, in other respects the final installment is no less cheerful than its predecessor (which begins with Harry's downbeat verdict: "The fucking world is running out of gas"). The new book was hugely successful, again winning three prizes: a second Pulitzer, a third National Book Critics Circle Award, and the William Dean Howells Medal, bestowed by the Academy of Arts and Letters for the most distinguished work of American fiction published in the previous five years. The critical acclaim was louder than ever, in part because it was cumulative. Reviewers were shouting hurray for all four novels at once; some, including Michiko Kakutani of *The New York Times*, hardly Updike's most sympathetic critic, decided to spread the praise even more widely. Kakutani declared that Updike was "working at the full height of his powers, reorchestrating the themes that have animated not only his earlier Rabbit novels but his entire oeuvre." *Rabbit at Rest* became the measure of his achievement as a novelist. Jonathan Raban, a British writer whose rave ran in *The Washington Post*, boosted Updike into exalted company, insisting that he had produced "one of the very few modern novels in English . . . that one can set beside the work of Dickens, Thackeray, George Eliot, Joyce and not feel the draft."

Much of the critics' praise was heaped on Harry Angstrom, his irreducible individuality and his emblematic ordinariness. Reviewers marveled at Updike's ability to funnel so much of American life through his hero's sensibility. In a ten-page account of the Mt. Judge Fourth of July parade, Rabbit, dressed up as Uncle Sam to please his granddaughter, achieves his apotheosis as the American Everyman. Here Updike was reporting on his own experience: as a celebrated former resident, he'd been invited to march, though not in costume, in that summer's Georgetown parade. He grafted onto Harry the eerie experience of walking alone on the yellow double line of a main street rimmed with citizens celebrating Independence Day as they do every year, a friendly, unbuttoned congregation, a "human melt."

Once again, Updike was pledging allegiance "to the mild, middling truth of average American life." That particular phrase comes from a lecture he delivered at Harvard in May 1987, a 150th-birthday tribute to William Dean Howells in which he'd praised the novelist's realism. He described Howells's agenda in terms that made it sound very much like his own, quoting with approval from a letter in which Howells reaffirmed that he was "always . . . trying to fashion a piece of literature out of the life next at hand." Rabbit's parade, which is refreshingly free of drama and extreme effects, was made from the "common, crude material" that Howells considered "the right American stuff." Harry worries about his goatee coming unstuck, and the reader worries, as always, about Harry's heart as he trudges in the summer heat up and down the streets of his hometown, but nothing actually happens except for the step-by-step unfurling of everyday life, witnessed by Harry in the top hat and striped trousers of our national symbol. As Updike remarked in his Howells lecture, "It is, after all, the triumph of American life that so much of it should be middling."

There's no drama to the Fourth of July parade, but there's a punch line, a venting of our hero's gung ho patriotism, the twist that turns a set piece into "a piece of literature":

> Harry's eyes burn and the impression giddily—as if he has been lifted up to survey all human history—grows upon him, making his heart thump worse and worse, that all in all this is the happiest fucking country the world has ever seen.

Coming from a corpulent ex-athlete who still hears ringing in his ears the cheering of fans jammed into the high school gym, Harry's expression of patriotic pride doubles as an ironic comment on the inalienable rights enshrined in the Declaration of Independence. Rabbit recognizes that he's living in a consumer paradise; his ravenous pursuit of happiness has clogged his "typical" American heart, which is now "tired and stiff and full of crud." As he would say, "Enough."

If Updike was sad to say good-bye, he was also relieved to get Rabbit off his desk. He enjoyed the sense of tidying up, the neatness of "a squared-off tetralogy, a boxed life." After *Rabbit Redux*, he realized he was headed not just for a tetralogy but for a fifteen-hundred-page "mega-novel," and it was the mega-novel he had in mind when he designed the last installment so that it echoed the first in structure and imagery. In the final volume (Updike's longest novel), Rabbit's younger incarnations jostle on the page with our middle-aged hero, echoes and allusions piled on top of the steadily accreting wealth of new images and information, a superabundance Updike ruefully acknowledged: "So many themes convene in *Rabbit at Rest* that the hero could be said to sink under the burden of the accumulated past." Rabbit running away to Florida in *Rabbit at Rest*, as he tried unsuccessfully to do in *Rabbit, Run*, is only the most obvious of the structural parallels Updike engineered to anchor the end to the beginning. Our very first glimpse of Harry comes when he's a twenty-six-year-old watching a handful of Brewer kids playing basketball: "Legs, shouts." The same two-word sentence recurs at the end of *Rabbit at Rest*, along with other echoed phrases, when Harry again finds himself watching kids shoot baskets, this time black kids in Deleon. The youthful Harry thought, "[T]he kids keep coming, they keep crowding you up." Three decades later, on the brink of oblivion, he's charmingly relaxed about the youngsters pushing up from behind. These black kids have "that unhurried look he likes to see." Harry has found an apt stage for his swan song—"the world isn't yet too crowded to have a few of these underused pockets left." When he collapses after his last layup, there's pathos and even a hint of grandeur in the isolation of his stricken body, "as alone on the court as the sun in the sky, in its arena of clouds."

Many readers noted that Harry was old before his time. Updike inclined the same way: he seemed to be practicing for old age while still a young man. In his late twenties he began to complain about his hair being grizzled with gray. When he was thirty-six and writing "Midpoint," this is what he saw in the mirror:

Ten thousand soggy mornings have warped my lids
and minced a crafty pulp of this my mouth . . .

At forty-five he was "over the hill." By the time he was in his mid-fifties, his hair had turned almost entirely white—but what he said and wrote did more to shape impressions than his hair color or the crow's-feet around his eyes. As *Self-Consciousness* amply demonstrated, he felt the need to tell everyone within earshot that he was already old and sprinting toward the grave. He was not yet sixty when he wrote with an insider's authority a poem called "Elderly Sex." And he was not yet sixty when *Rabbit at Rest* was named the winner of the 1991 Pulitzer Prize—yet he told *The New York Times* that he'd decided to make it the final volume because he wasn't sure he'd be around to write another in a decade's time. He wasn't particularly concerned about the early onset of dementia when he wrote, "I wanted to cap my series and make it a tetralogy while I still had most of my wits about me," but referring to his age had become a habit he couldn't shake. All the time he spent reliving the past in his fiction made him acutely conscious of his otherwise irretrievable youth. And after decades of observing himself intently and minutely, he couldn't help registering every new wrinkle, every stiff joint, every trivial memory lapse.

One of his aims in *Rabbit at Rest* was to offer a plausible portrait of "a specimen American male's evolution into grandpaternity." A poor dad, Harry tries to be a better grandpa; his nine-year-old granddaughter in particular brings out his willingness to empathize, his openness to experience. Contemplating Judy, "Harry tries to imagine the world seen through her clear green eyes, every little thing vivid and sharp and new, packed full of itself like a satin valentine." This sweet moment of identification, necessarily brief given Rabbit's attention span, is typical of the tugs of hope that pull against the tide of his encroaching doom. His appalling relations with his coke-addled son hit bottom when Nelson learns that Harry has welcomed Pru, his daughter-in-law, into his bed; that semi-incestuous encounter seals off the possibility of any meaningful father-son reconciliation. As Harry lies in extremis in the Deleon intensive coronary care unit, Nelson cries in anguish, "Don't *die*, Dad, *don't!*"—but it was always too late for them. If Harry ever wanted to think of himself as a patriarch, head of the Angstrom clan, the grandchildren were his best bet. When his slapstick heroism keeps Judy safe after their Sunfish capsizes, the "it" he sought on the golf course with Eccles thirty years earlier returns in predatory mode, in the shape of his first heart attack: "Whatever it is, *it* has found *him*, and is working him over." Delivering Judy unharmed to the safety of the beach while racked with pain is perhaps his finest moment as a family man.

Updike's son David married a Kenyan woman, Wambui Githiora, in the summer of 1989. Their son, Wesley, born that same year, was Updike's third African American grandson. Michael and

Miranda had two sons each during the 1990s, bringing the total of Updike's grandchildren to seven, without a single granddaughter among them. Martha's sons narrowed the gender gap by producing six girls and one boy. But the Updike and Bernhard grandchildren rarely mixed. Martha preferred not to blend the two families, and so at Christmas, for example, the youngsters were entertained in two batches.* For the most part, John went to see his grandsons at their parents' houses, dropping by for tea every month or so; or he took them to Disney movies. He dutifully marked their birthdays, sometimes a little late, with hand-drawn cards, asked what they might want for Christmas, and made an effort to spend some time with each of them. But he found it difficult to get past the polite, awkward stage, to make himself seem less remote. "I think he was emotionally shy with us, and with his grandchildren, too," said David. "He was always looking for something to do with them but not sure it was the right thing." Michael was less charitable, saying his father "just didn't have room for grandchildren." John's attempt to forge a bond was more successful with the older boys. In later years, a round of golf with Grandpa was his most popular offer.

If a pack of small children invaded Haven Hill, it was much more likely to be the Bernhard grandchildren visiting during school holidays. For the rest of the year, the house was often empty except for the writer working quietly in his suite of rooms over the kitchen, interrupted only by the Federal Express truck's daily visit and the faint rumble of passing commuter trains. Martha was not often at home. When her youngest, Teddy, followed his brothers to boarding school, she enrolled in a master's program in social work at Simmons College in Boston; she earned her degree in 1988 and took a job at Massachusetts General Hospital as a psychiatric social worker. The commute made for a long day; in the winter months she set off in the early morning dark, returning home with grisly tales of broken lives

---

* The grandchildren and stepgrandchildren did mix between the covers of Updike's books: *Bech at Bay* (1998) is dedicated to three of Martha's and two of his, "the youngest people I know"; and the posthumous *My Father's Tears* (2009), to all fourteen of them, his and hers listed on separate lines. *Trust Me* (1978) is dedicated to his three stepsons, "trusting and trustworthy."

and domestic violence. When she wasn't working, there were bridge parties, church committees, and the North Shore Garden Club.

During the daylight hours it seemed to Updike, alone in the big house, that he spent much of the time tying up loose ends. With the Scarlet Letter trilogy completed, his memoirs assembled and published, and Rabbit laid to rest, he put together a fourth collection of essays and reviews, *Odd Jobs* (1991), as huge as *Hugging the Shore*, and even more eclectic. Despite all his efforts to give the book a shape, to establish categories and subcategories, to slot each scrap of prose into its assigned place, there was no disguising a great big grab bag—hence the title. He cheerfully admitted in the preface that he had a problem turning down editors' requests, and blamed his word processor for exacerbating the condition: "With his wonderful new tool of ease how can a writer say No?" He said yes to a bewildering array of editorial invitations, including an essay for *Popular Mechanics* on the engineering feats that produced our national monuments; for *Sport* magazine a meandering Ted Williams retrospective; for the *Harvard Gazette* a breezy reminiscence on the occasion of his thirtieth reunion; and for *W*, a paragraph about beauty: some two hundred words handsomely arranged.

In her capacity as self-appointed gatekeeper, Martha did her best to screen out some of the importuning editors. I'm not alone in having telephoned Updike to beg for some literary doodle (as I did, for example, in the late nineties to ask for his top five books about loving), only to hear the author's wife, in the background, urging him to reject the idea—telling him to hang up. John would be affable and charming, seemingly amused; Martha would be audibly unamused, reminding him of other, more pressing obligations and of his repeated promises not to take on ephemeral and unremunerative assignments. She wanted him to concentrate on serious work, and it's hard to look at *Odd Jobs* and the three collections that followed—*More Matter* (1999), *Due Considerations* (2007), and the posthumous *Higher Gossip* (2011)—and not agree with her. Behind the question of whether he should have bothered to preserve miscellaneous trifles such as the squib on beauty for *W* or "Five Great Novels About Loving" (which he included in *Due Considerations*) lies the deeper question of whether he should have written them in the first place. But as he would say, he couldn't help himself.

Martha kept a vigilant eye on his incoming mail. This was gatekeeping of an essential kind, made necessary by his fame. In addition to the editors soliciting work, and the academics from all over the world who wrote inviting him to read or lecture or participate in workshops and seminars, there were eager characters with more complicated agendas: literary groupies and other overzealous fans; avid and avaricious collectors; unscrupulous journalists hungry for a revealing interview; and dogged scholars with intrusive biographical queries. Martha occasionally made notes on letters of this kind, highlighting particularly egregious requests with a yellow marker and scrawling ferocious comments and directives in the margins. The gist was always that the supplicant was hoping to take advantage of Updike, invade his privacy, or profit in some nefarious way—and that Updike must protect himself with a categorical *no*. She warned again and again against agreeing to projects that would allow the curious and the greedy to eat up his time and encroach upon his private life or his copyright.

On the morning of Wednesday, March 18, 1992, he found his mailbox flooded, but with more welcome missives. Elizabeth had come up with the idea of contacting all his friends, along with a variety of celebrities, and asking them to send sixtieth-birthday greetings; hundreds complied. Saul Steinberg sent a drawing; Susan Lucci of the soap opera *All My Children* sent a signed photo; Norman Mailer sent a friendly note. Martha and John drove to Boston that morning, to the Gardner Museum, where they saw the empty frames marking the places where paintings had once hung, paintings stolen on his birthday two years earlier.* (This was the notorious heist in which thirteen works of art were snatched, including three paintings by Rembrandt and one by Updike's favorite, Vermeer.) In the after-

---

* More than a decade later, Updike made use of the missing paintings in a valedictory poem to William Maxwell, who died in 2000, age ninety-one. The last lines of the poem read, "When wise / and kindly men die, who will restore / disappeared excellence to its throne."

noon there was a small birthday party back at the house, with a cake. Later there was yet another cake: it was poker night, and his cronies had decided that they, too, would celebrate his big birthday.

The novel he wrote in his sixtieth year was another project that tied up loose ends. In *Memories of the Ford Administration*, he recycled his Buchanan material and paired it in a kind of prose diptych with an imaginative reworking of the many months of "sexual disarray" he spent in Boston, vacillating between Mary and Martha, a period more or less coterminous with Gerald Ford's presidency. "I've been carrying Buchanan around with me for years," he explained to Dick Cavett, "and I had to get rid of him." Updike succeeded at last in writing historical fiction, but with a postmodern twist: he invented a historian, Alf Clayton, who's also been carrying Buchanan around for years, and presented fragments of Alf's incomplete opus, a kind of speculative biographical history padded out with fiction. Alf's writings about a president criticized for vacillating between North and South ("There is a civilized heroism to indecision," says Alf defensively) fitted snugly with Updike's framing narrative, which is all about his own domestic dithering, circa 1975: Alf has left his wife but can't fully commit to his mistress. Updike was doubling back to the fork in the road that led to his life at Haven Hill. But there's another twist: he guides the wavering Alf along the road he himself did not take. At the end of the Ford administration, Alf does not marry his mistress or even divorce the mother of his children; dropped by his mistress, he returns to the family home, where he and his wife resume their marriage and are, for the next fifteen years and counting, "fairly content." Alf tells us, "Real life is in essence anti-climactic." Dizzying depths of irony are contained in that simple sentence, which reminds us, among other things, of the real-life climax of the story Alf and Updike tried so hard to write: the slaughter of the Civil War that began six weeks after the end of Buchanan's presidency.

Framing the Buchanan material, the memoir of Alf's domestic secession reads like a counterfactual history of Updike's own adventures: the story of the time he almost married Martha but ended up back with Mary instead. Alf's wife, Norma ("the Queen of Disorder": artistic, vague, maternal), and his mistress, Genevieve ("the Perfect Wife": peremptory, efficient, snobbish), bear only an incidental physical resemblance to Mary and Martha, but the psychic tug-of-war played out between them is a replay of what actually happened—except, of course, for the eventual outcome. Would John and Mary have been "fairly content" had they stayed together? Was John any more than "fairly content" with Martha? As Alf would say, real life is anticlimactic. On the back cover of *Memories of the Ford Administration*, a grinning Updike plays peekaboo, hands in front of his face; on his ring finger one can just make out a glint of gold, the wedding band he wore after his marriage to Martha.*

In keeping with the playful, mirroring mood of the novel, Updike (at *Vogue*'s behest) summoned Henry Bech to interview him about it. Bech calls the new book a mishmash, and Updike, playing the huffy author, calls it "my *Tempest*, my valedictory visit to all my themes," and, less grandly, a sequel of sorts to *A Month of Sundays*. Although both novels are narrated by promiscuous men separated from their wives, and both are saturated with sex and liberally footnoted, the earlier novel, full of frantic and abrasive wordplay, feels more like an anguished release; *Memories of the Ford Administration* is a more mellow and contemplative affair, a spinning out of might-have-beens, and a fond, lingering look at old memories. One senses the pleasure Updike took in make-believe. He even made room for a cameo appearance by his mother (in the guise of Alf's mother), a canny, widowed octogenarian who adores her only son, disapproves of his defection from his marriage, and revels in the kind of portentous family mythology that had been Linda's stock-in-trade. Meanwhile, Alf tells us that James Buchanan's mother—"like many a mother in the biography of a successful man"—was "sensitive, spiritual, fond of poetry," and fond, too, of bantering with her son: "What woman henceforth will entertain, ridicule, inspire, empathize as this one did?" That rhetorical question is followed by another: "Is it not the biological cruelty of mothers to leave, so to speak, too big a hole?"

---

* Updike never wore a wedding ring when he was married to Mary. She didn't expect him to—her father didn't wear one, and neither did Wesley Updike.

THREE WEEKS AFTER the publication of *Memories of the Ford Administration*, William Shawn died. (Like Linda, he died of a heart attack, also at the age of eighty-five.) He'd been ushered out of *The New Yorker* five years earlier by its new owner, S. I. Newhouse Jr.—a momentous event in literary circles, cataclysmic in the eyes of many of the magazine's editors and contributors aghast at the perceived mistreatment of "Mr. Shawn." When Newhouse announced that Robert Gottlieb would be the new editor, the staff promptly drafted a letter urging him not to take the job. There were 153 signatories, including a galaxy of illustrious contributors. (A few of these disaffected souls subsequently quit to register their protest more emphatically.) Updike declined to sign the letter. The precipitous retirement, however awkward, of the man who played such a huge role in his career ("What would have happened to me if William Shawn had not liked my work?") seemed to him in fact overdue. Although he remembered clearly a time when his fundamental sense of himself was mixed up with Shawn's approval, he believed that the great man's saintly devotion to the magazine had, in the twilight of his tenure, degenerated into a somewhat sinister megalomania. As he clung to power, his resistance to change became a fetish, and the magazine suffered. Once celebrated for its wit and bounce, it was now too often dull and didactic.

Unlike his agitated colleagues, Updike had no reason to be apprehensive about the new editor. Gottlieb came to *The New Yorker* from Knopf, where he'd been in charge for nineteen years. Just eleven months older than Updike, he was already a legendary figure in book publishing, with a reputation as a brilliant, prodigiously hardworking editor. He had no experience with magazines, but among the hundreds of books he'd edited were Joseph Heller's *Catch-22*, Michael Crichton's *The Andromeda Strain*, Robert Caro's *The Power Broker*, John Le Carré's *A Perfect Spy*, and Toni Morrison's *Beloved*— so there was little doubt about his versatility or his will to succeed. Like Shawn, he was thought of as an eccentric (in part because of his collection of more than five hundred vintage plastic handbags), and he, too, involved himself intimately in every aspect of the editorial process. But the similarities ended there: he was neither shy nor secretive nor devious nor crushingly polite. No reverent hush was likely to surround a character who bounded along the corridors in tennis shoes, who chatted easily and cheerfully with his colleagues and expected them to call him Bob.

Updike found it briefly disconcerting to have a spirited contemporary at the helm of the magazine he always thought of as his literary home. Gottlieb made it clear straightaway that he was not interested in cultivating the kind of "shamanistic mystique" associated with the cult of Mr. Shawn, but he was also obviously not interested in sweeping aside his predecessor's legacy. As a devoted, lifelong reader of the magazine, he saw himself as a conservator, the guardian of a noble tradition. What changes he made were subtle and sympathetic. There was never any chance that he would put in jeopardy the mutually beneficial alliance between Updike and the magazine.

But Gottlieb's reign was short-lived; five years after his tumultuous accession, Newhouse asked him to step down. Although *The New Yorker*'s finances had improved under his stewardship, it was still losing several million dollars a year. But money wasn't the main issue for Newhouse (who'd paid $170 million for the magazine); he was impatient with Gottlieb's policy of incremental change. To shake things up he brought in Tina Brown, a young British editor newly famous for breathing life into the relaunched *Vanity Fair*, another title in Newhouse's Condé Nast portfolio. Whereas Gottlieb was in many ways an obvious choice to run the magazine, Brown was not, and longtime contributors such as Updike needed to be reassured that this thirty-eight-year-old Brit wouldn't lay waste to cherished *New Yorker* values. Unsurprisingly, she invited Updike to lunch less than a month after the appearance of her first issue.

He liked her. She was attractive, calmly self-confident, and utterly undaunted at the prospect of reshaping an institution notorious for clinging to its traditions. But he did not like what she was doing to the magazine. He considered her taste coarse, her redesign a kind of vandalism. The sober, dignified pages he was used to were suddenly "sharply angled," splashed with crassly provocative layouts, and freighted with sensational content. Brown brought photography into the magazine, gave the writers bylines instead of taglines, inserted a contributors page, and printed letters to the editor—all unheard of under the old regime. Worse, Updike worried that she was printing the work of writers who wouldn't have made the grade in Shawn's day. Along with a host of disgruntled subscribers, he deplored Brown's reliance on shock tactics, her seemingly uncritical fascination with celebrity culture, and her mania for novelty and timeliness. He longed for the days before "Tina's barbarians" sacked and pillaged the elegant magazine he'd fallen in love with.

Her tenure lasted only a little longer than Gottlieb's. She became the first editor of *The New Yorker* to leave the job voluntarily, and was succeeded in 1998 by David Remnick, a Pulitzer Prize–winning journalist who joined the magazine as a staff writer in the final year of the Gottlieb era. Remnick was even younger than Brown, but although he had no experience as an editor, he was a fast learner, a hard worker like Gottlieb, and still in charge when Updike reached a rare milestone: by midsummer 2004, he'd been a *New Yorker* contributor for fifty years.

Tina Brown was a nine-month-old baby when "Duet, with Muffled Brake Drums" earned Updike a check for fifty-five dollars, the first of more than 150 of his poems published by the magazine in his lifetime. When he collected his verse in 1993, he included 128 poems that had first seen print in *The New Yorker*, an impressive haul for a full-time poet, let alone a writer busy in so many other genres. Working on *Collected Poems, 1953–1993*, he experienced the by now familiar pleasure of sorting, arranging, and polishing: "There is a bliss in making sets of things, and in bringing something imperfect closer to perfection." He was extending the scope of his housekeeping.* "My poems are my oeuvre's beloved waifs," he wrote in the preface, "and I feared that if I did not perform the elementary bibliographic decencies for

---

* There was a melancholy aspect to his tidiness. A few years later, when he was assembling *Bech at Bay* (1998), he wrote to Oates, "I have a little Bech book in the works—I seem to be wrapping up, one character and theme after another."

them no one would." That remark may smack of reflexive modesty, but it was also true enough; his poetry was often overlooked by both his critics and his fans. At this point in his career, any Updike novel or book of short stories was bound to be reviewed in newspapers from coast to coast, and in dozens of magazines and quarterlies. A book of his poetry was likely to attract fewer than twenty reviews all told, most of them in out-of-the-way places.

Updike was consciously evoking funeral rites when he talked of performing "the elementary bibliographic decencies" for his poems. Publishing *Collected Poems*, he said, was "packing my bag a little bit" and preparing for posterity's judgment: "Well," he asked, "why would you collect your poems unless you were getting ready to go on a journey?" Linda's death haunted him, just as the prospect of his own death had haunted him since adolescence, and yet his po-ems (which he chose to segregate from his light verse) had always been and continued to be predominately cheerful, characterized by a jaunty, chin-up defiance. "Perfection Wasted," for example, was written just a few months after he buried his mother.

> And another regrettable thing about death
> is the ceasing of your own brand of magic,
> which took a whole life to develop and market—
> the quips, the witticisms, the slant
> adjusted to a few, those loved ones nearest
> the lip of the stage, their soft faces blanched
> in the footlight glow, their laughter close to tears,
> their tears confused with their diamond earrings,
> their warm pooled breath in and out with your heartbeat,
> their response and your performance twinned.
> The jokes over the phone. The memories packed
> in the rapid-access file. The whole act.
> Who will do it again? That's it: no one;
> imitators and descendants aren't the same.

The in-medias-res opening line, the verve, the rapid flow, the cheeky cynicism of the complaint—even the deflated last line—all remind us that despite his worries about death (and however much he might miss Linda's "brand of magic"), the poet himself was very much alive. And thanks to the performance captured in "Perfection Wasted," he lives to this day, at least in the sense that his magic is preserved in the fourteen lines of the sonnet.

But the old Shakespearean ploy of cheating death by grafting the perishable self onto "eternal lines" of poetry works only if the sonnet continues to be read. *Collected Poems* was largely ignored by reviewers. In *The New Criterion*, X. J. Kennedy, defying received opinion, declared that "John Updike is a far better poet than the sort now growing up." Although he decided that "Updike isn't bitter enough to be our American Larkin," Kennedy listed a handful of poems he thought worthy of the beloved British poet Philip Larkin, stretching from "Shillington," written in 1958, to "Enemies of a House," composed three decades later. Thomas Disch's review in *Poetry* magazine appeared almost a year after the publication of *Collected Poems*; he noted that the "entertainment quotient" in Updike's verse "offends the poetry establishment and provokes its resolute inattention to his works"—perhaps a roundabout way of apologizing for the delay. Echoing Kennedy, Disch said that Updike was one of the best poets writing today and could be America's Larkin—if only there were an American audience for poetry. As if in fulfillment of a prophecy, Updike's next book of poems, *Americana* (2001), was greeted with near-total silence. Dismayed, he announced to Joyce Carol Oates that he had stopped writing poetry. (He hadn't, but his output slowed noticeably. He was unwilling to deprive himself entirely of his "secret bliss.")

In the spring of 1994 he was asked by the literary quarterly *Antaeus* to write a version of Borges's famous "Borges and I," a tiny, teasing conundrum of an essay in which the writer's private self ("I") struggles to stake out an identity distinct from the public persona of the author ("Borges"). The last sentence, "I do not know which of us has written this page," invites the reader to wander in an epistemological maze. Rather than get lost in it, we might as well skip straight to the issue of mortality and the posthumous fame of the author. The private self, says Borges (or "Borges"), is "destined to perish, definitively"; if some sliver is to survive, it will be in the work of the author. At times Updike embraced this hope; at times he mocked it, as in the comically escalating panic in the final paragraph of his preface to *More Matter*:

> [A]ny illusion of "permanent form" struggles against the realizations, come upon me late in life, that paper decays, that readership dwindles, that a book is a kind of newspaper, that the most polished composition loses edge to the flow of language and cultural context, that no masterpiece will outlast the human race, that the race is but an incident in the fauna of our planet, that our planet is doomed to die in a hiccup of the sun, that the sun will eventually implode and explode, and that the universe itself is a transitory scribble on the surface, so oddly breached fifteen billion years ago, of nothingness. Wow! Zap!

Brushing aside this excursion into cosmic pessimism, he reverted in a blink to human scale: "Nevertheless, the living must live, a writer must write." But his anxieties about posterity were actually closely related to precisely the question of how much living and how much writing he should be doing. Curating his reputation entailed not just producing new work but also tending to his "ponderously growing oeuvre"—forty books and counting, dragging behind him "like an ever-heavier tail." Squeezed between those two engrossing activities, he found that living his life had begun to seem a neglected hobby.

"Updike and I," his version of "Borges and I," presents what looks at first like a clear-cut division between two entities: "Updike," an awkward, golemlike creature fashioned from the sticks and mud of a Pennsylvania boyhood, is purely a writer; he "works only in the medium of the written word."* His counterpart, "I"—we'll call him

---

* In "Bech Swings?" Bech despises the creature publicity has turned him into: "For his punishment, they had made from the sticks and mud of his words a coarse large doll to question and torment, which would not have mattered except that he was trapped inside the doll, shared a name and bank account with it."

John—is a slick character who thinks fast on his feet, skimming over the "qualificatory complexities" that preoccupy Updike. John boasts that he moves "swiftly and rather blindly through life, spending the money" Updike earns. Yet instead of being grateful, John is irritated:

> That he takes up so much of my time, answering his cloying mail and reading his incessant proofs, I resent. I feel that the fractional time of the day he spends away from being Updike is what feeds and inspires him, and yet, perversely, he spends more and more time being Updike, that monster of whom my boyhood dreamed.

Every morning, John reluctantly goes upstairs to "face the rooms that Updike has filled with his books, his papers, his trophies, his projects." Sitting at the desk, in front of the "blank-faced word processor," John wonders, "Suppose, some day, he fails to show up? I would attempt to do his work, but no one would be fooled." The Borges conundrum returns the moment we start asking ourselves which one of these two wrote "Updike and I."

The answer is that there can be no meaningful distinction between the selves we've designated as John and Updike. The slick white-haired gent with the teasing manner and wolfish grin, the avid golfer and mediocre poker player who went to church on the Sabbath, mostly, and did his best to remember his grandsons' birthdays, is always also the sedentary writer, awkward and stuttery, who hogged a disproportionate number of the daylight hours.

"A Rescue," composed in early summer of 1999, addresses the issue by weighing the writer's accomplishment and his wavering faith in print-based immortality against a poignant, fleeting encounter with a trapped bird:

> Today I wrote some words that will see print.
> Maybe they will last "forever," in that
> someone will read them, their ink making
> a light scratch on his mind, or hers.

I think back with greater satisfaction
upon a yellow bird—a goldfinch?—
that had flown into the garden shed
and could not get out,
battering its wings on the deceptive light
of the dusty, warped-shut window.

Without much reflection, for once, I stepped
to where its panicked heart
was making commotion, the flared wings drumming,
and with clumsy soft hands
pinned it against a pane,
held loosely cupped
this agitated essence of the air,
and through the open door released it,
like a self-flung ball,
to all that lovely perishing outdoors.

There's little enthusiasm here for the tenuous "forever" of the artist's immortality; the action in the garden shed is far more compelling— wonderfully vivid and immediate. But as he explains in "Updike and I," "hours of time can be devoted to a moment's effect." We mustn't forget that Updike had to retreat upstairs to his office, sit alone, undistracted, and take the time to fix in perpetuity that evanescent moment, a process he thought of as the "packaging of flux." Releasing the yellow bird, that "agitated essence of the air," is a matter of instinct, done without thinking. Finding the words to convey, for instance, the sensation of the bird leaving his hand— the weirdly apt "self-flung ball"—is another matter. The title of "A Rescue" refers of course to the freeing of the trapped bird, but it applies equally to the rescue, through art, of this particular moment's effect, which would otherwise have been consigned to the oblivion of the unexpressed. Both bird and poem now have a small stake in a literary "forever."

One lesson here is about the value not of living but of reliving. An obvious solution for an author who finds himself short of time to gather fresh experience (who spends most of the day "being Updike") is to indulge liberally in nostalgia, to replay the past, frame by frame, and wring every last drop out of reminiscence—a technique Updike had mastered as early as 1958, in "The Happiest I've Been." But though a great deal of the material he worked with in the years at Haven Hill was dredged up from distant memory, and some of the writing he produced was clogged with full-fat nostalgia, Updike needed to feel that in the process of refining that raw material, he opened up new directions. "You have to be in some way excited," he said, "and in a way frightened." He acknowledged that the struggle to avoid repeating himself grew more urgent and more arduous with the passing years—"you reach an age when every sentence you write bumps into one you wrote thirty years ago"—and consoled himself with the thought that the wisdom of experience could be substituted for the innocent enthusiasm of youth. But young or old, the writer had to add one final ingredient: "You have to give it magic."

THERE WAS PLENTY of magic in *Brazil* (1994), but not the right sort, at least according to the critics. Two years later came *In the Beauty of the Lilies*, which was much more favorably reviewed. Of the novels he wrote in the nineties, it's easily the most ambitious, and in some ways just as adventurous and daring as his rash excursion into South American fantasy. His second-longest and most expansive novel, *Lilies* tracks four generations of the Wilmot family across the twentieth century and across the continent, from New Jersey to Hollywood to Colorado, where a climactic conflagration closes out the narrative. The story begins in 1910 with a nugget of Updike family history, a reimagined version of a seminal crisis: his grandfather Hartley's loss of faith. This was material Updike had first begun to research for the genealogical chapter of *Self-Consciousness*, but here he succeeds where elsewhere he had repeatedly failed: at last he managed to write straight historical fiction that satisfied him intellectually and aesthetically. Relocating the Updike saga from Trenton to Paterson, he juxtaposed a Presbyterian minister's apostasy with the making of a motion picture (D. W. Griffith's *The Call to Arms*, starring Mack

Sennett and Mary Pickford) and the doomed 1913 Paterson silk strike—a dose of theology, film, and history that establishes the thematic parameters of the novel.

The granddaughter of the lapsed clergyman becomes a world-famous movie star. Although she achieves her apotheosis in Hollywood as Alma DeMott, she was raised as Essie Wilmot in a "sweet small town" very much like Shillington, her childhood an idealized recapitulation of Updike's own. Essie is the twin sister he never had, another stutterer, cherished and self-cherishing, reveling in the joy of being herself, protected by an innocently solipsistic religious faith, and most ecstatic in the dark at the Roxie, the town's movie house. Her parents, unlike his, are as loving with each other as they are with their daughter, and that added comfort, which makes her doubly secure in "her power, her irresistible fire," does nothing to blunt her urge to escape, to make the successive leaps from young beauty pageant contestant to starlet to celluloid goddess. She becomes a celebrity in a way that no writer ever does, but her ambition and the fulfillment of that ambition are analogous to what Updike experienced in his flight from Shillington to Harvard and beyond. This was the first time he had poured so much of himself into a woman's body, and the result, especially as Essie is growing up, is a thoroughly convincing portrait of a sympathetic character with humanizing flaws. Her narcissism hardens in adulthood, starkly exposed by her failings as a mother and her radically self-serving theology. On her climb to the pinnacle of fame, Alma plays opposite Bing Crosby in a musical comedy, and recognizes in her costar an "inhuman efficiency": "She observed in him what she already sensed in herself, the danger of becoming a performer purely, of coming alive in proportion to the size of the audience, and being absent-minded and remote when the audience was small"—a trait Updike, too, would have recognized.

Alma's only child, the sorely neglected Clark (after Gable), drifts until he falls under the spell of a charismatic preacher, the self-appointed messiah of a Colorado religious commune. After several years at the Temple of True and Actual Faith, Clark earns the fifteen minutes of fame he never sought. Escalating friction with the local authorities leads to a Waco-style debacle, complete with helicopters, armored vehicles, swarming FBI and ATF agents, tear gas canisters, and the imminent threat of collective immolation—all avidly filmed by the television networks for the evening news. On impulse, perhaps assisted by divine revelation, perhaps conditioned by Hollywood cliché, Clark plays the hero.

The extreme violence at the end of *Lilies* is unlike anything in Updike's fiction. The shooting goes on for eight pages, the only sustained scene of mayhem he ever attempted, and, except for the murder-suicide in *Witches*, the only fatal violence of any kind that isn't distanced by an exotic setting (as in *The Coup* and *Brazil*, both of them, like *Witches*, rife with extravagant make-believe). The realist novels and stories Updike set in America are almost entirely devoid of even the threat of violence, but here, in the context of a military-style assault, we're caught in the cross fire of a protracted gunfight with multiple victims and the kind of gore usually associated with splatter porn. We see a woman shot from close range, her head "spouting blood . . . the hole spurting like a water bubbler, pulse after pulse until it quickly dribbled down to an ebbing red nub."

Published only eighteen months after *Lilies*, his next novel was fittingly postapocalyptic: *Toward the End of Time* is set in the year 2020, after a nuclear war with China has devastated large tracts of a now-defunct United States of America. Industrial pollution has given rise to "metallobioforms," a plague of deadly inorganic pests proliferating on the "blasted, depopulated planet." In the skies, new objects have appeared, including an abandoned space station and a mysterious "halo of iridescence," a vast torus that floats beyond the clouds. And the narrative itself forks at times, making "quantum leaps of plot and personality," taking us to places far away and long ago, parallel universes briefly illuminated. But these sci-fi embellishments are peripheral to the central drama, which is recorded in a year's worth of journal entries kept by a retired investment adviser named Ben Turnbull. That drama is nothing more exotic than Ben's panicky fear of growing old and dying. Oates, reviewing the novel in *The New Yorker*, described Ben as "morbidly narcissistic," and indeed, in the midst of planetary disaster, he recites with raging egotism complaints about his deteriorating health and the impotence, literal and figurative, of the elderly. (At sixty-six he seems far older.)

In the Beauty of the Lilies was in many respects a thoroughly conventional novel, but writing it pushed Updike into new territory. Conversely, the wildly unconventional *Toward the End of Time* hardly required him to step out the door. The social chaos implied by the postapocalyptic, "post-law-and-order" environment is little more than a rumor for Ben; he and his neighbors in Haskells Crossing, an affluent seaside community north of Boston, find their privileged lives largely undisturbed: "I am safe," he says, "in my nest of local conditions, on my hilltop in sight of the still-unevaporated ocean." Ben's lofty white mansion with its majestic saltwater view is a portrait of Haven Hill, faithful to the last detail. The best passages in the book lavish attention on the flora and fauna of the eleven acres of grounds around the house: the garden beds, the driveway winding down through the woods to the mailbox, the pond.

Updike was uncharacteristically nervous about the similarities between his life in Beverly Farms and Ben's in Haskells Crossing. For the first time since the publication of *Couples*, he went out of his way to distance himself from his fiction. Declaring forcefully that autobiography is "one of the dullest genres," he stressed the "considerable trouble of invention" that went into the making of his narrator. He stooped to listing comically trivial differences between Ben and himself: "He comes from the Massachusetts Berkshires and not from Pennsylvania's Berks County. He has more children and grandchildren than I." (Ben's five children from his first marriage have given him eleven grandchildren, two of whom have a Togolese father.) Updike's odd and oddly ineffective attempt to disavow the obvious autobiographical basis of the novel has in all probability nothing to do with the fact that Ben is distinctly unappealing, mostly because of his sexual rapacity. If you've already foisted on your readers characters as abrasive as Tom Marshfield and Roger Lambert, presenting them with the nasty, lecherous, and self-pitying Ben Turnbull scarcely seems an occasion for awkward disclaimers.

Updike was more likely worried about the portrait of Ben's second wife, the crisp and forbidding Gloria, a fanatic gardener and fearsome nag, five years younger than he and exasperated with his doddery behavior. She is, if possible, less appealing than her husband. According to Ben, "Symmetry, fine white teeth, and monomaniacal insistence on her own concept of world order mark her impress on the world." The novel begins with her crusade against the doe that eats her tulip shoots and euonymus hedge. She wants the deer killed—and Ben narcissistically translates this as a murderous impulse aimed at him: "In her guilt at secretly wishing me dead, she took an overactive interest in my health, from vitamin pills laid out beside my morning orange juice to a constant nagging about what I put in my mouth." With her ice-blue eyes, perfect smile, and crown of ash-blond hair, Gloria, in his estimation, is a "soigné vulture" eagerly awaiting his demise and her rich widow's reward: "well-heeled freedom."

Martha's comments on the manuscript suggest that if she recognized herself in this caricature of a shrewish, controlling wife, she wasn't going to let on.* Most of her notes dealt with horticultural issues (correcting details such as the proper time of year to prune clematis), but she did permit herself to question the passage where Ben crows about having had sex with three different women in one day—this when he was married to his first wife (the suggestively named Perdita) and immersed in "suburban polygamy." Martha wrote:

> Well, it's your call, but you already told us, the Readers, in a previous novel, about the time you fucked 3 women in 1 day. It's boasting too much, perhaps?

Updike let the passage stand.

Martha bravely proclaimed the book a delight to read, a verdict even its most generous supporters would have hesitated to endorse. *Toward the End of Time* summoned more bile from critics than any previous Updike novel, and it was the last, with the possible excep-

---

* The account of her relentless campaign against marauding deer was no caricature.

tion of the 9/11-inspired *Terrorist* (2006), to spark much controversy. Decidedly mixed reviews greeted the remaining four novels: *Gertrude and Claudius* (2000), a nimbly entertaining prequel to *Hamlet*; *Seek My Face* (2002), a guided tour of the New York art scene courtesy of the leading female abstract expressionist, now seventy-eight and raging, like Ben Turnbull, against the indignities of old age; *Villages* (2004), a doggedly autobiographical retelling of Updike's progress from Shillington (renamed Willow, in honor of the novel he attempted sophomore year at Harvard) to Beverly Farms (Haskells Crossing again), complete with the two wives, both scantily disguised; and *The Widows of Eastwick* (2008), a downbeat, valedictory sequel. Only *Gertrude and Claudius*, clever and engaging (yet slight), stirred any real enthusiasm. On the whole, the novels of Updike's last decade were more likely to be met with polite indifference than hostility. He was by now a landmark on the literary landscape so familiar and venerated that even a spiteful reviewer felt obliged either to salute his cumulative achievement or to regret that after a lifetime of acclaim he no longer measured up. His oeuvre could be a liability; as he pointed out, "Among the rivals besetting an aging writer is his younger, nimbler self, when he was the cocky new thing."

XI.

The Lonely Fort

In the fall of 1997, Updike's literary reputation was buffeted in rapid succession by Michiko Kakutani, the most prominent reviewer in America, and by a relative youngster, David Foster Wallace, who exploded onto the scene a year earlier with his gargantuan second novel, *Infinite Jest*. Kakutani dismissed *Toward the End of Time* as "particularly sour, ugly and haphazardly constructed"; she wondered how such a gifted writer could produce such a "lousy" novel. Wallace was even more scathing: "It is, of the total 25 Updike books I've read, far and away the worst, a novel so mind-bendingly clunky and self-indulgent that it's hard to believe the author let it be published in this kind of shape." Updike was spared immediate pain from this one-two combination. He'd learned to shrug off the "irrepressible Michiko"; he told a friend that since he had seen her "blow her top" so often, it was hard to take her seriously. The *Times*, as if to compensate for Kakutani, ran in its Sunday books section a breezy, enthusiastic endorsement from Margaret Atwood: "As memento mori and its obverse, carpe diem, *Toward the End of Time* could scarcely be bettered." As for Wallace's review, he didn't read it until years later.

The thirty-five-year-old Wallace presented himself as the spokesman for a new generation. "The fact is," he confided, "that I am probably classifiable as one of very few actual sub-40 Updike fans." He claimed to have discovered, among (female) friends of his age, a range of unflattering opinions on Updike, including "Just a penis with a thesaurus" and "Has the son of a bitch ever had one unpublished thought?" and the familiar accusation of misogyny. Worse, he announced with calm conviction that Updike, Roth, and Mailer, "the three Great Male Narcissists who've dominated American postwar fiction," were now in their "senescence"—a verdict so perfectly tailored to Updike's insecurities that it seemed sadistic. Wallace complained that Updike's prose, his "great strength for almost forty years," had deteriorated to the point where it seemed "less like John Updike than like somebody doing a mean parody of John Updike." (Writing about Renoir, Updike had observed, "Old artists are entitled to caricature themselves.")

A dismaying echo of Wallace's criticisms came wafting across the Atlantic in early 1998—dismaying because it issued from the pen of James Wood, a thirty-two-year-old Englishman regarded by many as the best literary critic of his generation. In his review of *Toward the End of Time*, Wood judged the novel to be "idly constructed . . . and astonishingly misogynistic." He added, "Of course it is 'beautifully written' if by that one means a harmless puffy lyricism." Zeroing in on the novel's "puerile misogyny," he dismissed, in this case, the argument that the author "is not identical with his misogynistic characters." Wood saw little daylight between Updike and Ben, but stopped short of declaring that Updike actually hated women. Instead, he added his voice to the chorus of critics who objected to the sexual content of Updike's fiction; "a lifelong distraction," he called it. In an essay about a later collection of stories, *Licks of Love* (2000), Wood argued that sexual obsessions "have recurred and overlapped thickly enough in his work to constitute, now, the equivalent of an artist's palette: this is how Updike chooses to paint the world." There's certainly plenty of evidence to support this claim: Tom Marshfield, Roger Lambert, and Ben Turnbull are all guilty of thinking of women as sex objects, worthy of atten-

tion only insofar as they are instruments of male sexual gratifica-
tion; Rabbit rarely thinks any other way. A list of Updike's priapic
characters, men whose fascination with women amounts to sexual
obsession, would be very long indeed. But Wood chose to ground
his criticism in aesthetics rather than the politics of feminism, to
keep his focus on the "artist's palette." He called the world Updike
painted "distasteful and limited" and suggested that it needn't be:
"Misogyny can animate, and very powerfully and interestingly, as in
Philip Roth's work." But by bringing in Roth, whose novel *Sabbath's
Theater* (1995) had provoked shrieks of outrage as well as hosannas,
Wood drains his argument of any force. He finds Roth's misogyny
compelling and Updike's distasteful—it's only a matter of which
palette suits the critic's palate.

The worry for Updike was a gradually forming consensus; again
and again, reviewers handed down a three- or four-part indictment
that began with misogyny, then accused him of being too prolific,
too fond of his own gorgeous prose, and too nostalgic (read: out of
date). He'd been typecast. Wood could write, "It seems to be easier for John Updike to stifle a yawn than to refrain from writing a
book," and be sure to elicit a knowing chuckle. His warnings about
the perils of too fancy a style were themselves pretty swank: "The
sentences have an essayistic saunter; the language lifts itself up on
pretty hydraulics, and hovers slightly above its subjects, generally a
little too accomplished and a little too abstract." Ten years earlier,
praising *Rabbit at Rest*, he had remarked that Updike's "plush attention to detail" amounted to "a nostalgia for the present"; now he
lamented a different, more common brand of nostalgia: "If Updike's
earlier work was consumed with wife-swapping, his late work is consumed by nostalgia for it." All this carping pointed in only one direction, Wood's blunt verdict: "Updike is not, I think, a great writer."*

With the new millennium looming and the critical tide running
against him, Updike called Henry Bech into action. In "Bech Noir,"

---

* "Woods [*sic*] is a great annoyance," Updike wrote, "in part because he is so
intelligent, in a needling, fussy kind of way." In 2007, Wood joined *The New
Yorker* as a staff writer and book critic—a bitter pill for Updike to swallow.

written as the reviews of *Toward the End of Time* began to appear, he sent his alter ego on a killing spree. Hitting back after "a lifetime of provocation," adopting as his motto the biblical phrase "Vengeance is mine," Bech slays his harshest critics one by one, rubbing them out ruthlessly, just as they had ruthlessly panned his work. Spiteful to the end, one of them says with his dying breath, "Bech . . . believe me . . . your stuff . . . won't last." Indulging himself with a less far-fetched fantasy in "Bech and the Bounty of Sweden," the author shipped his hero off to Stockholm to receive the Nobel Prize for Literature—a gesture of ramifying irony. Updike's motives were so mixed that only fragments showed, among them the impish urge to make mischief: if his moment had passed, if, age sixty-five, he was unlikely ever to wear the laurels, why not take himself definitively out of the running with a piece of calculated effrontery? Bech, we learn, receives the Swedish prize not on merit but because certain committee members were casting protest votes. In "Bech Presides," he'd already taken a swipe at prize committees. A fellow writer asks Bech if he ever wanted to be a literary judge:

"No," Bech admitted. "I always duck it."
"Me, too. So who accepts? Midgets. So who do they choose for the prize? Another midget."

Bech detects sour grapes behind this show of bravado. Updike, too: himself the recipient of countless awards, he was careful not to belittle the beneficiaries of Sweden's bounty, nor to let any hint of envy creep into his public remarks on new laureates. (The Italian Dario Fo won in 1997; the following year it was the turn of Portuguese novelist José Saramago, whose *Baltasar and Blimunda* Updike had reviewed without much enthusiasm, but politely, for *The New Yorker*.)

Accepting the National Book Foundation Medal for Distinguished Contribution to American Letters in November 1998, Updike spoke to a crowd of over eight hundred at the Marriott Marquis hotel in midtown Manhattan. (Martha was in the audience with two of her sons and a "glamorous" daughter-in-law; none of the Updike children was invited.) In the speech, delivered with his habitual teasing charm, he noted that medals for lifetime achievement are engraved on the reverse side with a subliminal message: "the time has come to retire." A new award piled onto his towering stack of honors only reminded him of that other, magnificent prize he hadn't won. The Nobel was the uncontested peak of his profession, and every October he fell short. Though he bottled up his disappointment, he found it hard to disagree with the pundits who wondered whether the antic Dario Fo was truly more deserving than he. As William Maxwell put it forty years earlier, if Updike didn't get the prize, it would be "the Swedes' fault, not his."

Crowning Bech with laurels, killing off Bech's critics, having one of them tell Bech that his work was destined for the dustbin—these gags cut in various directions, but all are related to Updike's anxiety about his own fame, present and posthumous. He whined to an interviewer that his books were no longer stocked in airport bookstores: "There's no Updike at all. I'm a vanished man, a nonentity as far as mass readership goes." Another symptom of his anxiety: he revived a long-simmering literary feud. Several weeks before the ceremony at the Marriott Marquis, nagged by the thought of prizes unbestowed and readers who got away, he dashed off a review for *The New Yorker* of Tom Wolfe's *A Man in Full* (1998).* This was Wolfe's second novel, his long-awaited follow-up to the huge commercial success of *The Bonfire of the Vanities* (1987)—which Updike claimed he couldn't read: "The blatancy of the icy-hearted satire repelled me." His resentment of the new novel was apparent from the first paragraph: "The book weighs in as a 742-page bruiser. . . . A book to muscle aside all the others on the 'New Releases' table. A book that defies you not to buy it." This chipper tone gives way to more sober assessment; despite Wolfe's vigor and his laudable ambition, "*A Man in Full* still amounts to entertainment, not literature, even literature in a modest, aspirant form." The rub was

---

* Although he warned his editor that the review was "a very hasty job and would admit of much improvement," the lethal finished product shows no sign of haste.

Wolfe's failure to be "exquisite"; "Such failure would not seem to be major," Updike writes, "but in the long run it is." A vulgar book— "cheesy," Updike called it in private—is an ephemeral book, and what mattered to Updike was the long run. He was confident that Wolfe's mass audience would eventually dwindle to nothing, but this conviction wasn't enough to neutralize his envy. His exasperation boiled over in a letter to Oates: "Wolfe not only demands to make his millions but wants <u>respect</u>, too."

Norman Mailer barreled in, lamenting at length Wolfe's "final inability to be great." *A Man in Full*, he judged, was merely a "Mega-bestseller": "At the highest level, it's a failure." With Updike, he argued that no matter how popular, Wolfe's novels were not literature.* Wolfe hit back, calling Updike and Mailer "two old piles of bones." Whereupon John Irving joined the fray: on any page of a Wolfe novel, Irving claimed, he could find a sentence that would make him "gag." Wolfe's rejoinder made it clear to anyone still in doubt that these high-profile literary figures were embroiled in a playground scuffle: "Larry, Curly, and Moe," he said. "Updike, Mailer, and Irving. My three stooges."

In the midst of the name-calling, Wolfe was elected to the American Academy of Arts and Letters—despite Updike's staunch opposition. Although he was in New York on the day of the May ceremonial when Wolfe was "apotheosized," Updike decided it was a spectacle he could miss.† Yet he did nothing to extend the quarrel. He felt queasy about scrapping with a writer who worked so hard at his fiction; he knew that jealousy and ill will had played a part in his review of *A Man in Full*.

The antagonism between Wolfe and Updike was decades old; it had taken root in 1965, when Wolfe was a young reporter and

---

* He also indulged in a classic Mailerism: "At certain points, reading the work can even be said to resemble the act of making love to a three-hundred-pound woman. Once she gets on top, it's over."

† Harold Bloom, who'd proclaimed Updike "a minor novelist with a major style," was inducted on the same day—another good reason to steer clear of West 155th Street.

published his notorious two-part parody (or "counter-parody") profile of William Shawn and *The New Yorker*, "Tiny Mummies!" Making cruel fun of the man who ran the magazine Updike thought of as his home was bad enough; worse were the swipes at *New Yorker* short stories in general ("the laughingstock of the New York literary community for years") and Updike's in particular: "more and more tabescent." Wolfe brandished the same adjective nearly twenty-five years later in his manifesto "Stalking the Billion-Footed Beast": "At this weak, pale, tabescent moment in the history of American literature." Designed as a cure for tabescence, the manifesto was meant to galvanize literary novelists and get them writing robust social realism. Wolfe urged them to "do what journalists do, or are supposed to do, which is to wrestle the beast and bring it to terms"—the beast being "this wild, bizarre, unpredictable, Hog-stomping Baroque country of ours."

Wolfe's "Stalking the Billion-Footed Beast" and Updike's "The Importance of Fiction," an essay he wrote for *Esquire* in 1985, contain between them the meat of the quarrel (as opposed to the playground insults), which is essentially a disagreement about the aim of literature. Updike argued for the importance of individual sensibility: "Fiction is nothing less than the subtlest instrument for self-examination and self-display that Mankind has ever invented." He specifically denied that fiction should be read for information of the kind a journalist uncovers. "Unlike journalism . . . fiction does not give us facts snug in their accredited truth," he wrote. The meaning of fiction emerges from a collaborative process—"we *make* fiction true, as we read it"—and the collaboration occurs between two solitary souls, one "sitting in a quiet room coding make-believe," the other elsewhere at a later date, trying to decipher it. A pair of rhetorical questions rounds out the essay and leaves no doubt as to the author's allegiance:

What is important, if not the human individual? And where can individuality be better confronted, appraised, and enjoyed than in fiction's shapely lies?

For Wolfe, conversely, the aim is to expose the "status structure of society." Not quite an afterthought, the individual matters only because of his "intimate and inextricable relation to the society around him." The inner life of a creature who stands on just two feet hardly figures in Wolfe's scheme; it's the billion-footed specimen he's after.

What's odd about this difference of opinion is that Updike, from *Couples* onward, and especially in the last three Rabbit novels, proved more than willing to "wrestle the beast." The novelist credited with uncovering the "adulterous society," who turned himself into an expert on the workings of a Toyota dealership, should have been Wolfe's hero, not his nemesis.

FOR DIVERGENT REASONS, both Wolfe and Updike cited a remark Philip Roth made back in the comparatively sedate year of 1961 about American reality "outdoing" the novelist's imagination. As if to prove him right, America in September 2001 turned frightening and bizarre in ways fiction, no matter how hog-stompingly baroque, could never match. On the morning of September 11, Updike and his wife woke up in Brooklyn Heights, where they were staying in the tenth-floor apartment of Martha's son Jason. Martha's four-year-old granddaughter and the babysitter called from the library and pointed across the East River to Lower Manhattan, less than a mile away, where one of the Twin Towers was unaccountably on fire: "smoke speckled with bits of paper curled into the cloudless sky, and strange inky rivulets ran down the giant structure's vertically corrugated surface." A building blocked the view of the second plane's screaming approach, so they were further mystified when the other tower burst into flames; the gorgeous day, the flames, the smoke—it all seemed unreal, a high-tech TV drama.

John and Martha went up to the roof of the apartment building and there witnessed the collapse of the first tower. He preserved his impressions in a Talk piece for the September 24 issue of *The New Yorker*:

[I]t fell straight down like an elevator, with a tinkling shiver
and a groan of concussion distinct across the mile of air.
We knew we had just witnessed thousands of deaths; we
clung to each other as if we ourselves were falling. Amid
the glittering impassivity of the many buildings across the
East River, an empty spot had appeared, as if by electronic
command, beneath the sky that, but for the sulfurous cloud
streaming south toward the ocean, was pure blue, rendered
uncannily pristine by the absence of jet trails. A swiftly expanding burst of smoke and dust hid the rest of lower Manhattan; we saw the collapse of the second tower only on
television, where the footage of hell-bent airplane, exploding
jet fuel, and imploding tower was played and replayed, much
rehearsed moments from a nightmare ballet.

The accuracy of the observation would have pleased the reporter in
Wolfe, less so Updike's deliberate insistence on his own sensibility,
on the act of perception rather than the phenomena perceived. The
piece begins: "Suddenly summoned to witness something great and
horrendous, we keep fighting not to reduce it to our own smallness."
His eyewitness account delivers both an indelible portrait of what he
saw and also a lesson in how to resist the smallness of reflexive solipsism. He ends with an implicit promise: resiliency and optimism
will secure a bright future for a larger entity—the city.

The next morning, I went back to the open vantage from
which we had watched the tower so dreadfully slip from
sight. The fresh sun shone on the eastward facades, a few
boats tentatively moved in the river, the ruins were still sending out smoke, but New York looked glorious.

A gesture of solidarity in the face of bewildering violence and loss,
the piece should be read with the opening sentence in mind. Updike
is urging us to keep looking, to keep fighting.

The combination of terrorists and airplanes had been vivid to
him for at least a decade, when he used the Lockerbie bombing as a

leitmotif in *Rabbit at Rest*. A little more than a year before 9/11 he added Islam to the mix in a poem called "Icarus":

> O.K., you are sitting in an airplane and
> the person in the seat next to you is a sweaty, swarthy
> gentleman of Middle Eastern origin
> whose carry-on luggage consists of a bulky black brief-
> case he stashes in compliance with airline regulations,
> underneath the seat ahead.
> He keeps looking at his watch and closing his eyes in
> prayer . . .

Playing with prejudice, and what we would today call racial profiling, Updike makes us complicit in his fear and his guilt. Our "praying neighbor" is of course revealed as a harmless passenger, and we are released from small-minded suspicion. As a parting gift, Updike bestows on us a gorgeous image of a plane aloft: "this scrape against the numbed sky."

In "Varieties of Religious Experience," a short story he wrote about a year after the events of September 2001, and *Terrorist*, the novel he began two years later, he reversed the strategy of "Icarus": instead of racial profiling, we get an intimate and, in the case of *Terrorist*, sympathetic portrait of a would-be suicide bomber, an honest attempt to understand sincere hatred for American life in the twenty-first century. In the story, Updike gives us a chilling moment with Mohamed Atta in a roadside strip joint in Florida, lets us feel the pressure of the deed just days from execution: "Within him his great secret felt an eggshell thickness from bursting forth." The germ of the novel was the mental image of a tunnel exploding and water crashing in—Updike scaring himself with a claustrophobe's hell. The Lincoln Tunnel during rush hour became the bomber's target. The bomber, at first, was going to be a young Christian, a seminarian convinced that he was surrounded by devils trying to rob him of his faith. Updike eventually settled on a similarly embattled protagonist, but one who had converted to Islam: a New Jersey high school student, half Egyptian, half Irish American, under the sway of a sinister Yemeni imam. Eighteen-year-old Ahmad is a distant cousin of another Updike extremist, Ellelloû, the rabid anti-American narrator of *The Coup*. Both characters offered Updike the opportunity to cast a jaundiced eye on American materialism, to give Muslim rage a voice.

Ahmad's hometown, New Prospect, is based on Paterson, the setting for the first part of *Lilies*. Updike hired a chauffeured car and toured storefront mosques in the scruffier neighborhoods. For forty dollars an hour, he employed a Harvard graduate student to help him with transliteration of the Koran and details such as the traditional attire of Islamic clerics. He sent away for a home-study course for a New Jersey commercial driver's license. He consulted army manuals on explosives, and did Web research on detonators. He tapped into his generous store of Shillington High School memories. And for the first and last time in his career, he tried to bring a thrillerlike plot to a suspenseful conclusion.

Although *Terrorist* made the bestseller list—and clung on for several weeks—the reviews were mixed at best; some, such as Christopher Hitchens's blast in *The Atlantic* (where, ironically, "Varieties of Religious Experience" had recently been published), were openly insulting: "Updike has produced one of the worst pieces of writing from any grown-up source since the events he has so unwisely tried to draw upon"—that is, since 9/11. Opinion was divided about whether Ahmad was a credible character: some reviewers praised Updike for having stretched himself; others blamed him for over-reaching.

Being told that he had no business imagining the interior life of a Muslim teenager was particularly galling after the relentless criticism he endured for revisiting old haunts in *Villages*: the word *familiar* had appeared in the headline of review after review. Even friendly critics felt that *Villages* suffered in comparison with earlier explorations of the same territory. The hero, Owen Mackenzie, emerges from an idyllic small-town boyhood that is essentially indistinguishable from Updike's. Owen escapes his beloved Willow with a scholarship to MIT rather than Harvard; works at IBM rather than *The New Yorker*; and makes a modest fortune, after going freelance, writing software rather than literature. All this is revealed in retrospect. In the opening pages of the novel we find Owen comfortably retired in Haskells Crossing, married to his second wife, Julia, who might as well be Ben Turnbull's nagging Gloria; husband and wife are rattling around in what might as well be Ben Turnbull's big white house. The sense of déjà vu is also overwhelming in the account of Owen's years with his first wife in Middle Falls, the second of the three villages that define his life, and the setting for his ecstatic participation in round after round of suburban adultery. The hanky-panky begins when the youngest of Owen's four children is still an infant, and ends, abruptly, when Owen leaves wife number one for wife number two. It was the numbing recurrence of this old dance that annoyed so many reviewers.

He couldn't help himself. The compulsion to circle back to any place where he felt some essence of his being was stored grew stronger as he grew older, and extended even to fictional locales—Eastwick, for instance, which he revisited in a sequel that again found little favor with the critics. One notable exception was Alison Lurie, writing in *The New York Review of Books*, who praised the return of Alexandra, Jane, and Sukie, thirty years after their misadventures with Darryl, in terms that offered sweet vindication: "It is to Updike's great credit, and a proof of his long-standing and ardent interest in women, that he is also interested in and deeply sympathetic to their experience of age." In its loving, sharp-eyed look at the elderly, *The Widows of Eastwick*, his final novel, doubled back to his first, *The Poorhouse Fair*.

Most of the accolades that came his way during these last years, if not focused on Harry Angstrom, featured his short stories rather than his novels. When he published *The Early Stories* toward the end of 2003, he was showered with the kind of reverential critical attention he hadn't met with since *Rabbit at Rest* a dozen years earlier. Gathering and arranging 103 of the stories written between 1954 and 1975 was a bittersweet experience; it was the kind of rigorous spring-cleaning he enjoyed and performed more and more frequently—Everyman's Library, a Knopf imprint, published *The Complete Henry Bech* in 2001 and *The Maples Stories* in 2009—but it also made him feel as though he were closing up shop. Cynthia Ozick's review can't have helped; her acclaim, distinctly funereal, began with a tombstone:

> John Updike: the name is graven. It stands, by now, along-side Cather, Faulkner, Fitzgerald, those older masters who lay claim to territory previously untrafficked, and who make of it common American ground. So enduringly stamped and ineradicably renowned is Updike that it was more tribute than gaucherie when, only the other day, someone (a de-mographer, as it happens, with wider views of the shiftings of lives) asked, "Is he still alive?"

As if worried that he might take offense, she offered to bury him alongside a crowd of illustrious figures:

> As for the plenitude of stories and novels: think of Balzac, Dickens, George Sand, Trollope, Chekhov and all the 19th-century rest. It scarcely seemed likely that the distracted and impatient 20th could throw up such prodigious abundance.

To be ranked with indisputably great writers was of course music to his ears, as close to the exact melody as the pitch-perfect Ozick could manage. Equally pleasing was Jay Cantor's more concise trib-ute: "These stories, I feel sure, will weather all times and tides." Lor-rie Moore came tantalizingly close to eclipsing the others, but her verdict had a sting in its tail: "It is quite possible that by dint of both quality and quantity," she wrote, Updike "is American literature's greatest short-story writer." So far so good—but then she wondered aloud whether he wasn't also "our greatest writer without a single great novel."

After twenty years of seeing it given to other distinguished writ-ers, Updike won the prestigious Rea Award for the Short Story in 2006. He told Oates, who'd been on the judges' panel along with Richard Ford and Ann Beattie, how very dear his stories had been to him, both because they earned him his living and because they recorded, "in an oblique way," his life. He added, "[I]t doesn't do to think overmuch about prizes, does it? Being a writer at all is the prize."

That remark, tossed off casually at the end of one of the thousands of print-crowded three-by-five postcards he mailed out over a lifetime, was another way of saying something he said again and again: how grateful he was just to write. More than fifty years after his first *New Yorker* check, he was still happily amazed that he could make a living this way, that his boyhood plan to ride "a thin pencil line out of Shillington, out of time altogether, into an infinity of unseen and even unborn hearts" had succeeded quite so brilliantly. And yet it seemed to him, as it did to many others, that his profession was in trouble, the industry ("Ink, Inc.") in decline, his pencil line in danger of being rubbed out:

> For who, in that unthinkable future
> when I am dead, will read? The printed page
> was just a half-millennium's brief wonder.

In the digital future suddenly upon us, the screen looked certain to displace the page. Hanging over literary enterprise for decades had been the threat of a dwindling readership as the book competed with various forms of electronic entertainment: first television, then computers. More recently, with the emergence of the Internet and the spread of handheld digital devices, a new villain was exposed in the ongoing plot to snuff out literature.

Fascinated and troubled since the early eighties by the speed and power of computing, Updike had been writing about it since *Roger's Version*. Dale Kohler's vain attempt to model reality on a mainframe computer and thereby furnish scientific evidence of God's existence was never likely to undermine the printed page or the livelihood of professional authors; it merely ruffled Roger Lambert's theological feathers—and Updike's. Owen Mackenzie's invention in *Villages* is potentially more worrisome. In his retirement Owen finds himself dizzied and disgusted by the "chip-power" of a desktop PC and the "Library of Babel" on the Internet, but in his heyday he created a software package called DigitEyes, "a method of drawing with a light pen on a computer screen"—an innovation that injects technology into the heart of the creative process. The logical next step is to do without the artist's hand entirely—to "DigitEyes" the creative act. Finding God through computation and graphic interface rather than faith and prayer, producing an illustration without putting pen to paper—in each case the electronic age was making a raid on an aspect of the culture Updike felt the urgent need to protect. As with *Terrorist*, he was examining his own fears.

Another excursion into the brave new world of technology points in a happier direction. Robin Teagarden, Bech's young girlfriend in the last two stories in *Bech at Bay*, has a job in a computer store; when Bech visits her, he's anxiously aware of the industry's "lightning-swift undertow of obsolescence," which makes the latest model outdated within months—and which, typically, Bech associates with his own "dispensability." He's seventy-two, his "sidekick" twenty-six; they represent past and future. She helps him navigate the new IBM his publisher talks him into buying, one thing leads to another, and together they make a baby; a successful "interface," Robin might say. Their infant daughter in turn helps Bech deliver his Nobel Prize acceptance speech, a collaboration that raises the possibility of some accommodation between technological advancement and old-fashioned literary values.

Despite the research he did for *Roger's Version* and *Villages*, in practical terms Updike remained something of a Luddite. He could grasp the science driving the digital revolution—and pepper a paragraph with daunting high-tech terminology—but the day-to-day applications didn't suit him. His computer competence evolved only slowly. He replaced his original Wang word processor, acquired in 1983, with a succession of more sophisticated models; then, in the early nineties, he made the jump to his first PC (an IBM with a Windows operating system)—a machine, he told Oates, that only his stepsons could help him with. He never felt completely at ease with the blank gaze of the computer screen, and even after using the buttons of a computer keyboard to type out a dozen books, he still preferred the feel of typewriter keys. The Internet made him nervous; he was fearful of viruses that might corrupt his files and wipe out his work. If he wanted to do research on the Web, he went down to the public library in Beverly Farms. Martha told him that if he had access to e-mail he would spend every waking hour responding to messages, so he steered clear, relying on the postal service and FedEx. He never owned a cell phone.

As for the e-book, he could conceive of it only as a threat to the paper book, his favorite object since childhood: "Smaller than a breadbox, bigger than a TV remote, the average book fits into the human hand with a seductive nestling, a kiss of texture, whether of cover cloth, glazed jacket, or flexible paperback." If books became obsolete, he reasoned, so would he: "Without books, we might melt into the airwaves, and become another set of blips." Even more distressing was the prospect, revealed by Google's plan to scan the contents of major research libraries, of a vast digital databank containing the sum of the world's knowledge. Sent by Knopf to promote *Terrorist* at a national booksellers' convention in Washington in May 2006, he mounted a vigorous defense of the "printed, bound and paid-for book." The title of his talk, "The End of Authorship," reflects the apocalyptic view he took of the anarchic future promised by Internet gurus. The idea of a universal library, accessible to all through the Web—what boosters envisioned as a paradise of free-flowing text—Updike saw as ruin for writers dependent on royalties. Defending not only the economic model that had sustained him but also his fundamental conception of literature, which he understood to be a private, silent communication between two individuals, author and reader, he was arguing for "accountability and intimacy." Because the paid-for book had made him rich years ago, his own prosperity was not at risk; his call for accountability wasn't motivated by petty self-interest. His concern was for an entire industry: writers, publishers, booksellers. A threat to that industry felt like a threat to his sense of self, which was always inextricably entwined with printed volumes, his own and others'. His identity was forged in solitary communion with an open book. The teenage boy who escaped the crowded Plowville farmhouse by immersing himself in a P. G. Wodehouse farce or an Agatha Christie murder mystery became in time the white-haired literary grandee on the podium warning that readers and writers of books were "approaching the condition of holdouts, surly hermits who refuse to come out and play in the electric sunshine of the post-Gutenberg village."

When he told that auditorium full of booksellers, "Defend your lonely forts," Updike had for a couple of years been the proud owner of not one but two lonely forts: his grand Beverly Farms mansion and also a small "casita" in a gated development in the foothills above Tucson, Arizona—a house he bought in 2004 as an escape from the harsh New England weather (which Martha found more and more painful) and to extend his golf season. For five years running, they went west for a month, leaving in early March, hoping to miss the late winter storms and the early spring mud. On March 18 they would go out for a celebratory meal.

> Our annual birthday do: dinner at
> the Arizona Inn for only two.
> White tablecloth, much cutlery, décor
> in somber dark-beamed territorial style.

That description comes from a series of birthday poems written out west, elegiac verses grappling with advancing age. Laced with worry that his powers are dimming, they are proof to the contrary—for instance this neat twinning of his two enduring preoccupations:

> How not to think of death? Its ghastly blank
> lies underneath your dreams, that once gave rise
> to horn-hard, conscienceless erections.
> Just so, your waking brain no longer stiffens
> with careless inspirations—urgent news
> spilled in clenched spasms on the virgin sheets.

The Arizona poems, along with a short essay, "A Desert Encounter," offer a glimpse of the author in a ruminative mood brought on by another milestone passed and uncommon amounts of free time: he had little to do in the desert but golf, garden under Martha's close supervision, and write poetry about the inexorable passage of time. It was as close as someone so tirelessly industrious could ever come to retirement.

Lonely forts: often on his own, sometimes on his own with Martha ("dinner . . . for only two")—that's the tenor of these years in both the Southwest and New England. A birthday poem composed in Beverly Farms when he turned seventy in 2002 strikes the characteristic note: "Wife absent a day or two, I wake alone, and older." He had his golf and poker buddies and his literary pen pals such as Oates, but few close friends, none of them intimate. He and Martha kept his children at arm's length, and none of her children lived nearby. The big house echoed with solitude, with the absence of his mother, his father, his grandparents, the constellation of loved ones who'd brightened his childhood.

ON VERY RARE occasions, John and Martha had houseguests to stay. In November 2006, Ian McEwan and his wife, Annalena McAfee, a newspaper editor, came to Beverly Farms for a long weekend, an uneventful, harmonious visit that lowers the drawbridge on Updike's lonely fort and allows us to take a farewell peek at his well-defended life.

He and McEwan were not close friends; in fact, they met only three or four times over the course of many years, and exchanged no more than a handful of letters. But McEwan was an Updike enthusiast. They first met in 1993, when Updike was in London promoting *Memories of the Ford Administration* and McEwan interviewed him for a BBC television program. At the time, McEwan was a promising novelist with half a dozen books to his name. He remembered being "awestruck" by Updike: "The fact that he seemed to enjoy talking to me was deeply flattering. When I was young I was always looking for intellectual father figures. That desire completely left me in my mid-twenties, but I found it reanimated in meeting Updike." A decade later, Updike wrote a rave review in *The New Yorker* of McEwan's *Atonement*, a widely acclaimed bestseller that ensured his place among leading British novelists. When they met for a second time, in London in early summer 2004, they taped an hour-long program for Channel 4: two authors on equal footing "in conversation" in front of the cameras. Because of the sixteen-year age gap, the ocean between them, and McEwan's unwavering admiration, there was never any hint of competition.

Updike was the star attraction that year at the Hay Festival of Literature and the Arts in Hay-on-Wye, a tiny market town in Wales, 180 miles west of London. At the time, the Hay Festival was sponsored by *The Guardian*, where McEwan's wife worked as the founding editor of the paper's literary supplement, *The Guardian Review*. It was McAfee's responsibility to give a short speech at a festival dinner and hand Updike a check for thirty thousand dollars—the carrot that had lured him across the Atlantic. Just two years earlier he had turned down twenty thousand dollars to spend a week at the University of Michigan, where he would have had to teach a writing seminar as well as give a reading and a "public lecture." His duties at Hay were lighter: a reading and an onstage interview with a BBC journalist.

Martha and McEwan sat next to each other in the audience watching the live interview, which was marred by the interviewer's spotty knowledge of Updike's work and an uncomfortable emphasis on the author's attitude toward the Vietnam War. As questions piled up about his nonparticipation in the antiwar protests of the late sixties, the audience grew restive, and Martha began to fume. Finally she leaned over and hissed in McEwan's ear, "*Who is this man?*" She was livid. This was McEwan's first glimpse of her protective instinct—"tigerish, strong, and loving," was how he described it.

The McEwans arrived at Haven Hill bearing a gift. Having read in *Self-Consciousness* about Updike's Dutch heritage, McEwan acquired (through his Dutch publisher) an eighteenth-century print of Elburg, the town in Holland on the edge of the Zuiderzee where the Opdyck family had lived before sailing for the New World. This tribute gratefully received, the Updikes took their guests out to dinner at Myopia Hunt Club, where they were joined by two other writers, James Carroll and his wife, Alexandra Marshall. The conversation turned to reviewing, and Updike said that sitting in his study still unread after five months was the Hitchens review of *Terrorist*, which he knew to be toxic. Martha stepped in, saying, "Oh, you don't need to read it; *I'll* read it." Her husband responded tetchily, or so it seemed to McEwan: "I can take it," he said.

The next day, Saturday, was Veterans Day, and the Updikes marked the occasion by ferrying the McEwans to Concord, Massachusetts, a forty-five-minute drive from Beverly Farms. Updike enjoyed the role of tour guide, eager to show off the precise spot near the North Bridge where the militiamen made their stand in the first skirmish of the Revolutionary War, the "shot heard 'round the world." The battlefields were crowded with tourists, and McEwan remarked on the large number of Muslim families. He said to Updike that it would be inconceivable in England—or France, or Germany—to find so many Muslims parading around historic sites on Remembrance Day, paying tribute to the fallen of past wars; whatever else one might say about America, it still had this powerful pull, making people want to be part of it, to be included. Updike agreed, saying that there was something about America that was still a success, though it was no longer fashionable to boast about it: it didn't fit the liberal frame of the Democrats or the xenophobic frame of the Republicans.

From the Minute Man National Historic Park, the two couples drove to Walden Pond, where they signed their names in the guest book inside the replica of Thoreau's hut, and thence to Sleepy Hollow Cemetery, where Thoreau and Emerson are buried. All in all, it was a long day of patriotic and literary tourism, and they were on their feet for quite a lot of the time, yet it seemed to McEwan that Updike, who walked a little stiffly, was in good physical shape.

Saturday night they stayed home. Martha didn't cook—she bought dinner from the local deli. Before they sat down to eat, John and Martha told a story in the classic contrapuntal style of a married couple, the one finishing the sentences of the other. They had decided to clear out their barn and cellar and so hired someone to cart away a load of unwanted junk; soon thereafter an article appeared in *The Boston Globe* about Updike selling off his honorary degrees: a bookseller in nearby Marblehead had a stack of them, priced at around $750 each. The Updikes explained that it was an accident, that the degrees had ended up in the wrong pile. The upshot of this unfortunate incident—and the climax of the couples' story—was a sudden onslaught of journalists arriving unannounced at Haven Hill looking for comment, maybe even a photo of the man who had so many honors stashed in his cellar that he could afford to put them out with the trash. Updike particularly enjoyed telling his guests how an incensed Martha shooed a pair of pesky paparazzi off the lawn and pursued them halfway down the driveway.

Having guests in the house did not mean that Updike altered his work schedule; he shut himself away as usual for his daily three hours. McEwan was again impressed by Martha's protectiveness. "She made a very good writing environment for him," he said, "and he clearly valued that. She made a lot of space around him, which meant keeping people away. She organized everything and left John to imagine." It was Martha who decided what restaurant they would go to on Sunday evening, Martha who made the reservation, Martha who set the time for leaving the house, Martha who made sure no one was late. "She was determined to make our stay a success," said McEwan, "and it was. She was fantastically hospitable and friendly and lively."

The house was spotless, though there was no suggestion that Updike had any hand in keeping it tidy. He did help out in the garden—and the guests joined in: for an hour or two they were all four busy on the lawn, raking and bagging leaves. One of the rakes was plastic, and McEwan made the connection with Ben Turnbull's hymn to the "silkily serviceable" excellence of his orange plastic snow shovel on the first page of *Toward the End of Time*—which detail Updike claimed to have forgotten. Doing yard work made Updike look like an Updike character (late Updike), and McEwan asked about the mailbox down at the bottom of the drive. Was it the same mailbox Ben Turnbull used to walk to? Was it the mailbox that yielded that memorable rush of Sunday morning bliss in *Self-Consciousness*? Updike gave a noncommittal answer.

Which McEwan understood entirely: "I felt my question," he said, "was a little vulgar."

Be with me, words, a little longer.

—"Spirit of '76"

XII.

Endpoint

Updike spent the last twenty-six hours of his life at the Hospice of the North Shore in Danvers, Massachusetts, about a quarter of an hour's drive from Haven Hill. His room was in a private suite in a low-slung, gray clapboard building called the Kaplan House, a mildly pretentious, tastefully landscaped example of suburban-sprawl architecture, a place he would have skewered in exact and loving detail in the Rabbit tetralogy. He would have noted, too, an unswerving devotion to euphemism; the promotional brochure available at reception never mentions the word Rabbit fingered like a rosary, *death*.

When Updike returned in late September 2008 from his last trip abroad (to Russia and the Baltic states), he was nursing "a cold," as he put it, "that wouldn't let go." *The Widows of Eastwick* was published in October, and he dragged himself through publicity duties in New York and Washington. Back home and still coughing, he went for his annual checkup at Mass General and was told by the doctor that he had pneumonia; X-rays revealed a cloud on his lungs. The news scared him, yet he resolved to go ahead with a weeklong four-city publicity tour on the West Coast. One event, in Seattle, was already sold out, and he couldn't conceive of disappointing his audience. He never did back out of a speaking engagement and never would, though he did cancel one other commitment: home again, he told *The New York Review of Books* that he was too feeble and wheezy to fly down and review the Joan Miró exhibition at MoMA.

Martha moved him into a "sickroom"—one of her sons' old bedrooms, a cozy spot for what he hoped would be a quick convalescence. Housebound, and bedridden for much of the day, far too ill to help with yard work, he watched from the windows as autumn leaves blanketed the lawn. He found the election of Barack Obama hugely consoling. As he wrote to a Harvard classmate, "What a great country we have here when it decides to be." And he distracted himself with work, reading and writing in bed. He was reviewing a "mammoth" biography of John Cheever, and feeling weighed down by the too-generous share of embarrassment and unhappiness his old friend had suffered.*

He knew he was sick, he knew that pneumonia could be a danger for someone his age, but he was utterly unprepared for the diagnosis that came at the end of the month, after a further visit to Mass General: stage-four metastatic lung cancer. The oncologist prescribed radiotherapy, and a round of chemotherapy in mid-December, but Updike decided to give up the treatment when it became clear, just before Christmas, how widespread and aggressive the cancer was.

He wrote a handful of poems, in his last months at Haven Hill, recording his ordeal with unflinching honesty and a complete absence of sentimentality. Fear, sorrow, pain, anger—all acknowledged—were pushed aside in the interest of clear-sighted observation. "Is this an end?" he asks. "I hang, half-healthy, here, and wait to see." He stopped living "as if / within forever"; he abandoned the idea that his endpoint "would end a chapter in / a book beyond imagining." He watched with resigned intensity to see what dying would do to him, to his cherished self, to the life he defended so conscientiously.

He surrendered to a world of medical technology, of invasive procedures made bearable by painkilling drugs. In these grim circumstances he remained an avid collector of jargon; he savored the

---

* The book was Blake Bailey's *Cheever*, and the review, Updike's last, appeared in *The New Yorker* posthumously, on March 9, 2009.

phrase "CAT-scan needle biopsy" even though it brought news of metastasis: cancer cells in one of the adrenal glands.

For the sake of others he was brave, masking grief and bitterness, but in the poems he hid nothing:

> My visitors, my kin. I fall into
> the conversational mode, matching it
> to each old child, as if we share a joke
> (of course we do, the dizzy depths of years)
> and each grandchild, politely quizzing them
> on their events and prospects, all the while
> suppressing, like an acid reflux, the lack
> of prospect black and bilious for me.
>
> Must I do this, uphold the social lie
> that binds us all together in blind faith
> that nothing ends, not youth nor age nor strength,
> as in a motion picture which, once seen,
> can be rebought on DVD? My tongue
> says yes; within I lamely drown.

A lifetime of writing about himself is here rewarded in a way he couldn't possibly be happy about. Lying in the hospital with the news of his death sentence echoing in his head, he could still manage gratitude and compassion—and note how those feelings fight for room against the selfish, viscerally powerful longing for comfort:

> My wife of thirty years is on the phone.
> I get a busy signal, and I know
> she's in her grief and needs to organize
> consulting friends. But me, I need her voice;
> her body is the only locus where
> my desolation bumps against its end.

His children asked their children to write to their grandfather; he answered the letters, and when they visited him just before he was moved to the hospice, when he could barely breathe and his mind was fuzzy from painkillers, he did his best, eager to please even on his deathbed, to ask them about their lives, to carry on with the "social lie." A golfing pal came to spend a few hours with him while Martha was in Boston, and found him dozy, eager to look through old photograph albums, angry rather than sad. The anger came from being at long last unable to write.

Writing, like poring over old snapshots, took him back to Shillington. Just as he so often did in his late stories, in his late poems he revisited his boyhood, his family, his playground friends. The kaleidoscope of memories, simple facts about his hometown ("their meaning has no bottom in my mind")—to put them down again on paper brought him a precious rush of happiness. He assured us one last time that Shillington "draped in plain glory the passing days." Distilled over the decades, his nostalgia was now as pure as sunlight in the dead of winter: "Perhaps / we meet our heaven at the start and not / the end of life."

Three days before Christmas, in his final poem, "Fine Point," he played with a combination of words that touched the core of his religious conviction, his lifelong inability to make what he called "the leap of unfaith." He took as his text the last lines of Psalm 23, the psalm that invites us to "walk through the valley of the shadow of death." In the first stanza, he questions the value of religious ritual practiced without faith: "Why go to Sunday school, though surlily, / and not believe a bit of what was taught?" The answer comes in the second stanza:

> The timbrel creed of praise
> gives spirit to the daily; blood tinges lips.
> The tongue reposes in papyrus pleas,
> saying, *Surely*—magnificent, that "surely"—
> goodness and mercy shall follow me all
> *the days of my life*, my life, forever.

A well-worn prayer, its rhythm as comfortably regular as the beat of a tambourine, elevates the everyday, gives it spirit; as he memorably remarked about his hopes for his fiction, the idea is "to give the mundane its beautiful due." But "blood tinges lips"—those three words neatly wrap up Christ's sacrifice and the ritual of the Eucharist, and cast a somber shadow. It's the unmistakable Updike touch, to ground the metaphysical mystery of transubstantiation in such an intimately physical phrase. Sticking with the corporeal, he observes the effect of the tongue uttering "papyrus pleas" (the psalm, in this case). He caresses the word *surely*—which sends us back to that curious *surlily* in the first line. The ritual or ceremony of religious observance, whether enacted surlily or cheerily, remained for him the best path to goodness and mercy, and to faith in the hereafter. Shaky or solid, his faith was essential to him; he could never do without it—especially not now.

When his eldest child visited, he asked if she was happy with her life. Elizabeth told him that she was—assuring him, in other words, that he had done well as a parent. Later, at the hospice, she and David and their father linked hands with the Episcopalian minister and recited the Lord's Prayer.

He was still at home when Mary telephoned Martha and said she'd like to come see her ex-husband. Martha suggested that she bring her daughter Miranda, which Mary readily agreed to. Martha met them at the door, and the two wives exchanged a tense hug. After sterilizing their hands, they went up to the sickroom. Miranda sat on one side of the bed, Mary stood at the foot; Martha was opposite Miranda. Updike tried to look cheerful, buried under the covers, trying to keep warm, but the effect, as far as Mary was concerned, was miserable. "I felt I shouldn't touch him," she remembered, "except for his feet, so I was massaging his feet, and that seemed to be all right." They talked about the children, very briefly, and about how he was feeling, also very briefly. Mary was struck in particular by a remark out of the blue: "He said to me, 'Now remember Aunt Polly'—my great-aunt, whom he knew, who lived to be ninety-something or other. He was telling me, I thought, that I should remember that and try to live as long as she had." After twenty minutes, Martha said it was time to go. On the way downstairs, Mary said she'd like to come again and was told that it would not be possible.

To the consternation of the Updike children, Martha continued to restrict access to her husband even after he'd been moved to the hospice, even after the point when prolonging his life was no longer the primary object of the nurses charged with his care.

He died eight weeks after the cancer was diagnosed, on Tuesday morning, January 27, 2009, less than two months shy of his seventy-seventh birthday.

There was a crowded funeral service at St. John's in Beverly Farms, austerely Episcopalian, with no eulogy, but several readings from his work woven into the service; Updike had chosen the hymns himself.

There were two memorial events. The first, hosted by Knopf and *The New Yorker*, was held in the New York Public Library. Judith Jones, Roger Angell, and David Remnick spoke, along with several other editors and two writers, Lorrie Moore and ZZ Packer, neither of whom knew Updike particularly well. David Updike also spoke, a late addition to the program. Although someone, possibly Martha, was opposed to the idea, David persuaded the organizers to let a member of the family say a few words. After a brief, poignant speech, he read passages from his father's last *New Yorker* story, "The Full Glass." The second memorial event was held a few months later, at the Kennedy Library in Boston. Elizabeth Updike spoke, as did Nicholson Baker, Updike scholar William Pritchard, and several others. Martha did not attend.

Some of Updike's ashes are buried four miles from Haven Hill, in a memorial garden behind the Emmanuel Chapel in Manchester-by-the-Sea, the spot marked only by his name on a bronze plaque, second on a list. The Emmanuel Chapel was Martha's summer church. (Services are held there from Memorial Day through Labor Day.) The rest of the ashes are buried next to his parents, in Plow Cemetery, downhill from Robeson Evangelical Lutheran Church in Plowville, in the plot his mother bought for him. Michael Updike carved a black slate headstone with a winged portrait of his father on the front, above a collection of the names he went by, all the signatures in faithful imitation of his hand: Johnny, John, John Updike, JHU, Dad, and Grandpa. On the back of the gravestone, Michael carved a crow in flight and, in its entirety, his father's best early poem, "Why the Telephone Wires Dip and the Poles Are Cracked and Crooked":

The old men say
young men in gray
hung this thread across our plains
acres and acres ago.

But we, the enlightened, know
in point of fact it's what remains
of the flight of a marvellous crow
no one saw:
each pole a caw.

The great stack of books Updike left behind is the monument that matters most. Several posthumous volumes have been added to the pile: a collection of stories, *My Father's Tears*; a final miscellany, *Higher Gossip*; and *Always Looking*, more essays on art. But as far as he was concerned, his final book, also posthumous, was *Endpoint*, a slim collection of poems he put together when he knew without a doubt he was dying; it includes the birthday poems from his last six years and the poems he wrote about his illness.* In a late essay, he expressed the "irrational hope" that his last book might be his best. It came mighty close.

In the late fall of 2005, he complained uncharacteristically to Joyce Carol Oates, "I find producing anything fraught with diffi-culty these days, and tinged with a certain word-disgust, for which there must be an excellent German term." Even as he was formulat-ing this complaint, enthusiasm was bubbling up for a hypothetical German locution, some formidable compound word that might cap-ture his meaning with Teutonic precision. In truth, he never tired of writing, never tired of "creation's giddy bliss." Up until the last

---

* The dedication of *Endpoint* reads, "For Martha, who asked for one more book: here it is, with all my love."

weeks of his life, when he was too sick to write, he was always that little boy on the floor of the Shillington dining room, bending his attention to the paper, riding that thin pencil line into a glorious future, fulfilling the towering ambition of his grandest dreams. "I've remained," he once said, "all too true to my youthful self."

Acknowledgments

For the five years that I've been working on this book, I've been piling up debts, both professional and personal.

Mary Weatherall, who was married to Updike from 1953 to 1976, has been an inspiration to me from the day of our first interview. She made me want to write a book she would recognize as a faithful portrait of Updike's life and work. The four children she and John raised together, Elizabeth Cobblah, David Updike, Michael Updike, and Miranda Updike, have been generous with their help, often in awkward circumstances.

Among Updike's Shillington friends, Joan Venne Youngerman, Jackie Hirneisen Kendall, Harlan Boyer, and David Silcox kindly granted interviews. Updike's Harvard friends, many of them Lampoon members, shared their anecdotes and insights. I want to thank James E. Barrett Jr., Austin Briggs, William M. Calder, David Chandler, William Drake, David Ferry, Charles Bracelen Flood, Edward Stone Gleason, Reginald Hannaford, Edward Hoagland, John Hubbard, Peter Judd, Ann Karnovsky, Benjamin La Farge, Samuel Stewart, Bayard Storey, and Eric Wentworth. Many of Updike's *New Yorker* colleagues took time to answer my questions and ferret out correspondence. I'm very grateful to Roger Angell, Anthony Bailey, Henry Finder, Ann Goldstein, Fran Kiernan, Susan Morrison, David Remnick, and Alec Wilkinson. Several members of Updike's Ipswich crowd offered friendly assistance. I'd like to thank Vera Cobb, Toni Crosby, Helen Danforth, Judy Fouser, David and Mary Louise Scudder, Dan Thompson, William Wasserman Jr., and Bob Weatherall. Two of the children of the Ipswich crowd, Gus Harrington and Hatsy Thompson, were kind enough to grant me interviews, as were Updike's golfing buddy Richard Purinton and his poker pal Charlie Tsoutsouras. Three of Updike's students, Nicholas Delbanco, Jonathan Penner, and Mary Webb, generously shared memories of his Harvard summer school writing class.

During the course of my research the following people were helpful in ways large and small: Stephen Aris, Diana Athill, James Atlas, Margaret Atwood, Blake Bailey, Nicholson Baker, Ben Batchelder, Sandy Batchelder, Katharine Bava, Ann Beattie, Timothy Beeken, Anne Bernays, Philip and Maya Bobbitt, Isabel Buchanan, Benjamin Cheever, Susan Cheever, Ron Chernow, Joel Conarroe, Jeffrey Cunard, Virginia Dajani, William Ecenbarger, Scott Eyman, Mark Feeney, Molly and Sarah Fisk, Arthur Fournier, Janet Groth, Judith and Victor Gurewich, Donald Hall, Eric Homberger, Glenn Horowitz, Michael Janeway, Ward Just, James Kaplan, Justin Kaplan, William Kennedy, Deborah Miller Lizasoain, William and Wendy Luers, Janet Malcolm, Nancy Malloy, Ian McEwan, John McTavish, David Michaelis, Leon Neyfakh, Joyce Carol Oates, Tim O'Brien, Jed Perl, Lucie Prinz, Francine Prose, Mary Rhinelander, Andrew Rosenheim, Philip Roth, Stacy Schiff, Robert Silvers, Peter Spiro and Merin Wexler, George Steiner, Sam Tanenhaus, Benjamin Taylor, David Thomson, David Ulin, David Wallace-Wells, Ted Widmer, Leon Wieseltier, John T. Williams, Brenda Wineapple, Barbara Woodfin, and Ben Yagoda.

Various Updike aficionados have been helpful along the way. I want to thank Ward Briggs, James Plath, William Pritchard, and James Schiff for their assistance and kind encouragement. Without the herculean efforts of Jack De Bellis, a tireless collector of Updike facts and Updike treasures, all Updike scholars would have to work twice as hard as they do.

A small army of librarians guided me through various archives: Leslie Morris and the helpful staff of Harvard's Houghton Library; Charlie Jamison and his colleagues at the Myrin Library, Ursinus College; the kind and patient folk in the Manuscripts and Archives Division, New York Public Library; the staff of the Harry Ransom Center, University of Texas in Austin; Sean Quimby of the Special Collections Research Center, Syracuse University Library;

Dennis Sears of the Rare Book and Manuscript Library, University of Illinois; Mary Huth of the Rare Books and Special Collections Department, University of Rochester Library; Alison Greenlee at the McFarlin Library, University of Tulsa; the staff of the Ipswich Public Library; and Sharon Neal of the Dr. Frank A. Franco Library Learning Center, Alvernia University.

My agent, Georges Borchardt, does exactly what an agent should do: lower the stress levels. My editor, Tim Duggan, came up with the idea that I should write about Updike—for which I am deeply grateful, as I am for his encouragement and his sharp critical eye. His colleagues at HarperCollins, Emily Cunningham, Jenna Dolan, and Martin Wilson, have been friendly, helpful, and efficient.

Two old friends, André Bernard and Michael Arlen, read the manuscript and gave me very useful advice. Bob Gottlieb read successive drafts and managed to make me laugh even as he was recommending that I cut great chunks of my precious prose.

The late Peter Kaplan, my boss, my friend, pushed me to write this book. I wish he could have read it.

My thanks to my mother, Sally Begley; my siblings, Peter Begley and Amey Larmore; my stepmother, Anka Begley; and my exceedingly generous father, Louis Begley, who has been an unfailing source of moral, intellectual, and financial support.

Speaking of financial support: I was very fortunate to receive fellowships from the John Simon Guggenheim Memorial Foundation and the Leon Levy Center for Biography.

Finally, I want to thank my wonderful wife, Anne Cotton; and my stepchildren, Tristan and Chloë Ashby. They have put up with me for more than a decade now—and for almost half that time have shared me graciously with John Updike.

Notes

The following abbreviations appear in the endnotes:

A	*The Afterlife and Other Stories.* New York: Alfred A. Knopf, 1994.
AAK	Alfred A. Knopf
AD	André Deutsch.
Am	*Americana and Other Poems.* New York: Alfred A. Knopf, 2001.
AP	*Assorted Prose.* Greenwich, CT: Fawcett Premier, 1969.
BL	*In the Beauty of the Lilies.* New York: Alfred A. Knopf, 1996.
BookTV	"In Depth with John Updike." *BookTV.* C-SPAN2, December 4, 2005.
C	*The Centaur.* New York: Alfred A. Knopf, 1963.
CB	*The Complete Henry Bech.* New York: Everyman's Library, 2001.
CC	Cass Canfield
CJU	James Plath, ed. *Conversations with John Updike.* Jackson: University of Mississippi Press, 1994.
Coup	*The Coup.* New York: Alfred A. Knopf, 1978.
Couples	*Couples.* New York: Random House Trade Paperback, 2012.
CP	*Collected Poems, 1953–1993.* New York: Alfred A. Knopf, 1993.
DC	*Due Considerations: Essays and Criticism.* New York: Alfred A. Knopf, 2007.
EL	Elizabeth Lawrence
EP	*Endpoint and Other Poems.* New York: Alfred A. Knopf, 2009.
ES	*The Early Stories: 1953–1975.* New York: Alfred A. Knopf, 2003.
GD	*Golf Dreams: Writings on Golf.* New York: Alfred A. Knopf, 1996.
Harper	Updike correspondence in the Harper and Brothers archive.
HG	*Higher Gossip: Essays and Criticism.* New York: Alfred A. Knopf, 2011.
Hiller	Cathy Hiller. "Updike at Forty." Unpublished profile of JU written in April 1972.
HM	Howard Moss
Houghton	John Updike Archive, Houghton Library, Harvard University.
HS	*Hugging the Shore: Essays and Criticism.* New York: Alfred A. Knopf, 1983.
Illinois	William Maxwell papers, University of Illinois Rare Book and Manuscript Library.
JCO	Joyce Carol Oates
JJ	Judith Jones
JL	*Just Looking: Essays on Art.* New York: Alfred A. Knopf, 1989.

JU	John Updike
KL	Robert Christopher ("Kit") Lasch
KSW	Katharine Sergeant White
Lasch	Kit Lasch's letters to his parents, Christopher Lasch Papers, River Campus Libraries, University of Rochester.
LGH	Linda Grace Hoyer Updike
LL	*Licks of Love: Short Stories and a Sequel, "Rabbit Remembered."* New York: Alfred A. Knopf, 2000.
LP	Letters to Plowville, JU to LGH and WU, John Updike Archive, Houghton Library, Harvard University.
MA	Michael Arlen
MEUU	Mary Ella Updike
MFA	*Memories of the Ford Administration.* New York: Alfred A. Knopf, 1992.
Michigan	Delbanco Papers, Special Collections Library, University of Michigan.
MM	*More Matter: Essays and Criticism.* New York: Alfred A. Knopf, 1999.
MS	*A Month of Sundays.* New York: Alfred A. Knopf, 1975.
MT	*My Father's Tears and Other Stories.* New York: Alfred A. Knopf, 2009.
MW	Mary Weatherall
ND	Nicholas Delbanco
NYPL	*New Yorker* records. New York Public Library.
OF	*Of the Farm.* New York: Alfred A. Knopf, 1965.
OJ	*Odd Jobs: Essays and Criticism.* New York: Alfred A. Knopf, 1991.
Orion	Updike correspondence in the archives of Victor Gollancz Ltd. Gollancz is now owned by the Orion Publishing Group.
OS	*Olinger Stories.* New York: Vintage Books, 1964.
P	*Problems and Other Stories.* New York: Alfred A. Knopf, 1979.
PF	*The Poorhouse Fair.* New York: Alfred A. Knopf, 1959.
PF77	*The Poorhouse Fair.* New York: Alfred A. Knopf, 1977.
PP	*Picked-Up Pieces.* Greenwich, CT: Fawcett Crest, 1976.
RA	Roger Angell
Ransom	Knopf Archive, Harry Ransom Humanities Research Center, University of Texas.
Rochester	Christopher Lasch Papers, River Campus Libraries, University of Rochester.
RRedux	*Rabbit Redux.* New York: Alfred A. Knopf, 1971.
RRest	*Rabbit at Rest.* New York: Alfred A. Knopf, 1990.
RRich	*Rabbit Is Rich.* New York: Alfred A. Knopf, 1981.
RRun	*Rabbit, Run.* New York: Alfred A. Knopf, 1960.
RV	*Roger's Version.* New York: Alfred A. Knopf, 1986.
SC	*Self-Consciousness.* New York: Alfred A. Knopf, 1989.
SR	Stewart ("Sandy") Richardson
Syracuse	Joyce Carol Oates Papers, Syracuse University Library.

TB   Anthony Bailey

TET   *Toward the End of Time*. New York: Alfred A. Knopf, 1997.

*T*d   *Time* magazine dispatches related to the April 26, 1968, Updike cover story. Houghton Library, Harvard University.

TM   *Trust Me and Other Stories*. New York: Alfred A. Knopf, 1987.

Tulsa   André Deutsch Collection, McFarlin Library, University of Tulsa.

Ursinus   Linda Grace Hoyer Papers, Myrin Library, Ursinus College.

VG   Victor Gollancz

WE   *The Witches of Eastwick*. New York: Fawcett Crest, 1985.

WM   William Maxwell

WMRR   *What Makes Rabbit Run?* David Cheshire, producer. BBC TV, January 26, 1982.

WU   Wesley Updike

Introduction

ix   "public, marketable self": *SC*, 238.

x   "he had a bona fide twinkle in his eye": Jane Smiley, from a tribute posted on Granta.com, January 31, 2009.

x   "I read and talked into the microphone": *SC*, 237.

xi   "[A]s Norman Mailer pointed out": *MM*, 824.

xii   "John could be funny": Author interview, MA, April 1, 2009.

xii   he "somehow withdrew a little": Roger Angell, "The Fadeaway," *The New Yorker*, February 9, 2009, 38.

xii   "a pretty average person": *WMRR*.

xii   declared "unreservedly" that Updike was a genius: Nicholson Baker, *U and I: A True Story* (New York: Random House, 1991), 126.

xii   "He was not a genius": Lionel Trilling, *The Moral Obligation to Be Intelligent* (New York: Farrar, Straus and Giroux, 2000), 262–63.

xii   "Here lies a small-town boy": *WMRR*.

xiii   he dreamed of becoming a "universal artist": LP, February 16, 1953.

xiii   "the refuse of my profession": *MM*, 852.

I. A Tour of Berks County

1   "*my* home turf": JU interviewed by Jeffrey Goldberg at the New York Public Library, June 15, 2006.

2   "I really think being interviewed": *CJU*, xi.

2   "I know all about him": E-mail, William Ecenbarger to author, April 5, 2009.

2   "He told me when he left for Harvard": William Ecenbarger, "Updike Is Home," *Philadelphia Inquirer Magazine*, June 12, 1983, 19.

3   "Chonny will be here tomorrow": E-mail, Ecenbarger to author, April 5, 2009.

3   "He often gets that way": Ecenbarger, "Updike Is Home," 19.

3   "Let's go," he said: Ibid.

3   "I'll drive so you can take notes": Ibid.

5   he helpfully spelled out the word: Author interview, William Ecenbarger, May 29, 2009.

5   "where we used to neck": Ibid.

5   "my only girlfriend": *SC*, 37.

5   "pilgrim's progress": *CJU*, 26.

6   "I become exhilarated in Shillington": *SC*, 220.

6   "We walk through volumes": *ES*, 92.

6   "Freud somewhere claims": *OJ*, 134.

7   Fiction is a "dirty business": *SC*, 231.

7   "a deliberate indulgence": Ibid., 40.

7   "scraps" that have been "used": Ibid.

7   "Nimble and bald": *AP*, 129.

7   "Artie for a joke": *SC*, 19.

7   "a town that was also" . . . "scribbling for my life": Ibid., 40 and 54.

7   "simultaneous sense of loss": *OJ*, 134.

8   "for providing a / sufficiency of human types": *EP*, 26.

8   "the drab normalities": *HS*, 855.

8   "Most of the best fiction": *SC*, 252.

8   "realize . . . the shape": JU, application for the 1959 Guggenheim Fellowship competition, mailed to the John Simon Guggenheim Memorial Foundation on November 10, 1958.

8   "We must write where we stand": *PP*, 48.

8   "relentless domestic realism": *SC*, 150.

8   "normal intra-familial courtesy": Ibid.

8   "[T]he nearer and dearer they are": Ibid., 231.

9   "decided at an early age": *WMRR*.

9   "My duty as a writer": Ibid.

9   "as 10-point Janson" *EP*, 10.

9   "teasing little connections": *CJU*, 27.

9   "I disavow any essential connection": Ibid.

9   "Creative excitement": *OJ*, 135.

9   "I don't really feel it's me": *WMRR*.

10   "Imitation is praise," he wrote: *SC*, 231.

11   "A wake-up call?": *EP*, 21.

11   "We read fiction": David Streitfeld, "Updike at Bay," *The Washington Post*, December 16, 1998.

11   "only the imagery we have personally gathered": *MM*, 293.

12   "I was never allowed": Ibid., 37.

12   "heart-tearing" cough: *SC*, 174.

13   "It was courtesy of Nora": Ibid, 174.

13   "hoping she would accidentally": Ibid., 39.

14   "I did not let Nora's satiny skin": Ibid., 38.

14   "This is the way it was, is": *CJU*, 28.

14   "Composition, in crystallizing memory": *OS*, vi.

15   "Once I've coined a [character's] name": *CJU*, 27.

15   "imitate reality with increasing closeness": JU, Guggenheim application.

16   "an ideally permissive writer's mother": *CJU*, 26.

16   "only truth is useful": *SC*, 231.

16   "He portrayed me as he saw me": Ecenbarger, "Updike Is Home," 20.

16   "I don't think I'm as witty": Steve Neal, *Rolling on the River: The Best of Steve Neal* (Carbondale: Southern Illinois University Press, 1999), 194–95.

16   "She paused and said": Author interview, Ron Chernow, August 19, 2009.

17   "would-be writer": *CJU*, 83.

17   "I had only a little gift": Ecenbarger, "Updike Is Home," 20.

17   "It probably wouldn't have occurred to me": *T*d.

18   "straight fiction": MEUU to LGH, March 21, 1931, Ursinus.

18   "one of the disadvantages": Remarks made at Ursinus College, November 1991.

18   "frequently revised and never published": *OJ*, 871.

18   "There was a novel": Ibid., 834.

19   "I had not hitherto realized": *SC*, 105.

19   "plodding out to the mailbox": *MM*, 763.

19   "I never see a blue mailbox": *OJ*, 120.

19   "the slave shack of the unpublished": *MM*, 765.

19   "My mother knew non-publication's shame": *EP*, 12.

20   "I took off from her failure": Ibid., 11.

20   "I always did think he could fly": *T*d.

20   "I was made to feel that I could do things": Neal, *Rolling on the River*, 194.

20   "the great leap of imagination": *OJ*, 68.

20   "trying to reach beyond" . . . "hiding from the town": Ibid., 834; *SC*, 27.

21   "synonymous" with his being: *SC*, 30.

21   "I began my life": Linda Grace Hoyer, *Enchantment* (Boston: Houghton Mifflin Company, 1971), 6. (Hereafter cited as LGH, *Enchantment*.)

22   a "revelation" that left her with "no choice": Ibid., 61–62.

22   "I had this foresight": Quoted in Hiller.

22   According to her son: JU to JCO, May 17, 1996, Syracuse.

22   "Possibly the household that nurtured me": *SC*, 256.

22   "pretensions to quality": Ibid., 221.

23   "a belle of sorts": Ibid., 27.

23   She found herself unable: *T*d.

23   "running scared financially": *BookTV*.

23   Updike was struck: *AP*, 130.

23   "I grew up": *CJU*, 167.

24   "locked into a star": *AP*, 121.

24   "The fifth point of a star": *CP*, 70.

24   a "lovely talker": *CJU*, 167.

24   "I was raised among quite witty people": "John Updike Comments on His Work and the Role of the Novelist Today" (New York: National Education Television, September 1966), produced by Jack Sommers for his "USA Writers" series.

25   "always serving, serving others": *OJ*, 64.

25   "My mother is pushing the mower": *AP*, 119.

25   "dear Chonny" . . . "However pinched": *SC*, 151 and 29.

25   "soaked up strength and love": Ibid., 25.

26   "squeamish": Ibid., 151.

26   he "strained for glimpses": Ibid., 172.

26   nervous tension that made his stomach ache: Ibid., 151.

26   the "cosmic party" going on without him: Ibid., 217.

26   "The paralysis of stuttering": Ibid., 87.

26   "red spots, ripening into silvery scabs": Ibid., 42.

27   "fits of anger": Ibid., 151.

27   "smoldering remarks": *CP*, 69.

27   "As I remember the Shillington house": *SC*, 84.

27   Her "stinging discipline": *MM*, 799.

27   "I still carry intact within me": *SC*, 104.

27   "The tribe of Bum-Bums": "View from the Catacombs," *Time*, April 26, 1968, 73. (Hereafter cited as "View from the Catacombs.")

27   "Have I ever loved a human being": *SC*, 256.

27   "What I really wanted to be": *MM*, 642.

28   "one of my favorite places": Ibid., 672.

28   "chunky little volumes": Ibid., 673.

28   Even at the age of five: Hiller.

28   the creative imagination "wants to please": *OJ*, 233.

28   "Even as a very small child": *A*, 131.

28   "Only in Pennsylvania": *PP*, 73.

28   "My geography went like this": *AP*, 128.

29   "Cars traveling through see nothing here": *OS*, viii.

29   "transcribe middleness with all its grits": *AP*, 146.

29   "I was a small-town child": Ibid., 125.

29   "hopelessly mired in farmerishness": *SC*, 166.

29   "consumer culture, Forties style": *MM*, 804.

30   "a flapper's boyish": *SC*, 169.

30   "stirring, puzzling" first glimpse: *JL*, 7.

30 "the best of possible magazines": *CJU*, 24.

30 "I loved that magazine so much": *PP*, 52–53.

30 "[P]eople assume": JU to SR, April 14, 1958, Ransom.

31 "The mystery that . . . puzzled me": *AP*, 143.

31 his "beloved" hometown: *SC*, 110.

31 "Time . . . spent anywhere in Shillington": Ibid., 8.

31 "My deepest sense of self has to do with Shillington": Ibid., 220.

31 "If there was a meaning to existence": Ibid., 30.

31 "Shillington was my *here*": Ibid., 6.

31 "The Playground's dust": *CP*, 100.

31 "I don't know why you always spite me": *A*, 265.

32 "We have one home, the first": *CP*, 15.

32 "the crucial detachment of my life": *OS*, ix.

32 "saw his entire life": *A*, 146.

32 "In Shillington we had never had a car": *AP*, 147.

32 "Somewhat self-consciously and cruelly": Ibid.

32 "dislocation to the country," which "unsettled": *DC*, 34.

33 "a rural creature": *PP*, 421.

33 "pretty much an outsider": *T*d.

33 "If I had known then": LP, October 31, 1950.

33 "man of the streets": *PP*, 74.

33 "I was returning to the Garden of Eden": *WMRR*.

33 "where she wore her hair up in a bandana": *MM*, 802.

33 a total of $4,743.12: LGH diary entry dated January 23, 1948, Ursinus.

33 "After reading White's essays": *PP*, 421.

34 "we should live as close to nature": *OJ*, 69.

34 "eighty rundown acres": *PP*, 421.

34 "Shillington in my mother's vision": *SC*, 37.

34 "She was of Shillington": *T*d.

34 "authority-worshipping Germanness": *SC*, 134.

34 "The firmest house in my fiction": *OJ*, 48.

34 "My reaction to this state of deprivation": *BookTV*.

35 "In this day and age": *ES*, 21.

35 "My love for the town": *SC*, 38.

35 "Take what you want": Ibid., 209.

35 She began going to church: *DC*, 35.

35 "You don't get something for nothing": *SC*, 77.

35 "a retreat from life itself": LGH, *Enchantment*, 6.

35 "felt like not quite my idea": *SC*, 41.

36 "extra amounts of solitude": *HS*, 840.

36 "A real reader": *OJ*, 837.

36   "a temple of books": *MM*, 855.

36   "A kind of heaven opened up for me there": *OJ*, 838.

36   "a place you felt safe inside": *MT*, 194.

36   *The Bride of Lammermoor*: BookTV.

36   "its opacity pleasingly crisp": *DC*, 659.

36   he finally finished *Ulysses*: LP, December 21, 1966.

37   he tried to write a mystery novel: *DC*, 666.

37   One of the poems in the anthology: JU to KSW, October 4, 1954, NYPL.

37   At age sixteen he had his first poem accepted: *MM*, 812–13.

37   "a kind of cartooning with words": *CP*, xxiii.

37   "O, is it true": Quoted in "View from the Catacombs," 73.

38   "I knew what this scene was": *C*, 293.

38   "developed out of sheer boredom": *CJU*, 167.

38   "[I]t is as if one were suddenly flayed": *DC*, 40.

39   He was impressed by the idea: *OJ*, 239.

39   "painful theological doubts": *SC*, 223.

39   "1. If God does not exist": Ibid., 230.

39   "Having accepted that old Shillington blessing": Ibid., 231.

40   In the summer of 1946: *DC*, 667.

41   "Towers of ambition rose": *ES*, 134.

41   "the saga of my mother and father": *OJ*, 835.

41   "[O]nce, returning to Plowville": *CJU*, 26.

41   Updike thought of *The Centaur*: Ibid., 106.

41   "make a record" of his father: Ibid., 49.

41   "It had been my mother's idea": *C*, 52.

41   "The poor kid. . . .": Ibid., 81.

42   As Updike pointed out: *PP*, 33.

42   "an ambivalence that seemed to make him": *CJU*, 51.

43   "[T]he stain of unsuccess": *SC*, 183.

43   "caught in some awful undercurrent": Ibid., 173.

43   "inveterate, infuriating, ever-hopeful": Ibid., 177.

43   "stoic yet quixotic, despairing yet protective": *P*, 233.

43   never quite "clued in": *CJU*, 51.

43   "Life," Updike concluded: *SC*, 33.

43   "really did communicate to me": *WMRR*.

43   Wesley's paltry salary: *Td*.

44   "the agony of the working teacher": *CJU*, 214.

44   "slights and abasements": *SC*, 33.

44   "admiration, exasperation, and pity": *A*, 235.

44   "the kids goaded him": *C*, 100.

44   "I hate nature": Ibid., 291.

44   She exerts a "magnetic pull": Ibid., 211.

44   "little intricate world": Ibid., 289.

44   "that sad silly man": Ibid., 63.

44   the "romance" of mother and son: Ibid.

44   "I thought guiltily of my mother": Ibid., 138.

45   "Why is it that nothing that happens": *PP*, 74.

46   "gaudy and momentous" gesture: *C*, 117.

46   "performed exquisitely": Ibid., 122.

46   the girl will nevertheless "sacrifice" for him: Ibid., 51.

46   "small and not unusual": Ibid., 117.

46   his "poor little dumb girl": Ibid., 118.

46   "delicate irresolution of feature": Ibid., 117.

46   he is, after all, an "atrocious ego": Ibid., 201.

46   "other people as an arena for self-assertion": Ibid., 241.

46   his own "obnoxious" teenage self: *SC*, 221.

46   Updike could never resist leapfrogging: Ecenbarger, "Updike Is Home," 24.

47   "Himself a jangle of wit and nerves": Draft of "Homage to Paul Klee," Houghton.

47   "I did not, at heart": *SC*, 80.

47   "In Shillington, to win attention": Ibid., 153.

47   "some pretty hairy rides": Ecenbarger, "Updike Is Home," 24.

47   "smoked and posed and daydreamed": *SC*, 7.

47   "high-school sexiness": Ibid., 10.

47   "how to inhale, to double-inhale": Ibid., 225.

47   "the original flower child": Ecenbarger, "Updike Is Home," 24.

47   "cigarette smoke and adolescent intrigue": *SC*, 7.

47   the pinball's "rockety-*ding*": *HS*, 842.

48   "I developed the technique": "View from the Catacombs," 73.

48   "clamorous and hormone-laden haze": *EP*, 35.

48   "an Olinger know-nothing": *OF*, 29–30.

48   "central image of flight or escape": *CJU*, 28.

49   "hothouse world / Of complicating": *CP*, 122.

49   "under some terrible pressure": *SC*, 103.

49   "The trauma or message": *CJU*, 28.

49   "If there's anything *I* hate": *C*, 69.

49   "I suppose there probably are": James Kaplan, "Requiem for Rabbit," *Vanity Fair*, October 1990, 116.

49   "The old place was alive": *OJ*, 838.

50   "a method of riding a thin pencil line": *AP*, 146.

50   "gnawing panic to excel": *CP*, 85.

50   "What did I wish to transcend?": *SC*, 110.

50   "Some falsity of impersonation": Ibid., 82–83.

50   "my dastardly plot": *CP*, 13.

50   "Leaving Pennsylvania": *SC*, 33.

II. The Harvard Years

53   "What is the past, after all, but a vast sheet of darkness": *ES*, 660.

54   "ready for posterity": LP, December 1, 1950.

55   "Goodnight—Is it Mamma?": LGH to JU, September 21, 1950, Ursinus.

55   "Harvard took me": *CJU*, 204–5.

55   "To take me in, raw as I was": *CP*, 121.

55   he felt "little gratitude": Ibid., 122.

55   "in some obscure way ashamed": *T*d.

55   "obscurely hoodwinked" and "pacified": *CJU*, 23.

55   "I felt toward those years": Ibid.

56   a "palace of print": *SC*, 225.

56   "the shock of Harvard": *ES*, 168.

56   "freshman melancholy": *CP*, 122.

58   "prickly," as Updike put it: *Am*, 38.

58   "rubbing two tomcats together": LP, September 25, 1950.

58   the "compression bends" of freshman year: *CJU*, 23.

58   "My roommate has stood the test of time": Lasch, September 26, 1950, Rochester.

59   the "unexpressible friction" between them: *Am*, 38.

60   a "haven from Latin and Calculus": *HG*, 377.

60   "It is too bad; he just seemed to be getting loose": Lasch, January 11, 1951.

60   "Harvard has enough panegyrists without me": *CJU*, 23.

63   "feigned haughtiness": *T*d.

64   "soft-spoken aristocrats": LP, September 26, 1950.

64   "an outcropping . . . of that awful seismic force": *PP*, 94.

65   "saved from mere sociable fatuity": Ibid., 94.

65   "It was a rainy night": Author interview, MA, April 1, 2009.

66   *wonky* is the term Updike preferred: *SC*, 223.

66   "John seemed a cut above": Author interview, MA, April 1, 2009.

66   More than half a century later: E-mail, Charles Bracelen Flood to author, September 15, 2009.

66   despite the "snobbish opposition": E-mail, John Hubbard to author, November 19, 2009.

66   "An undergraduate magazine": *PP*, 95.

67   "he was much fonder of his cartoons": Author interview, MA, April 1, 2009.

67   "The main problem with the gag sessions": Douglas Fairbairn, *Down and Out in Cambridge* (New York: Coward, McCann and Geoghegan, 1982), 134.

67   "romantic weakness for gags": *CJU*, 23.

67   orchestrated "social frivolity": *OJ*, 842.

67   his "one successful impersonation": *HS*, 844.

68   "At the end": E-mail, Charles Bracelen Flood to author, September 15, 2009.

68   According to Ted Gleason: E-mail, Ted Gleason to author, September 15, 2009.

70   "[T]he drawings now give me pleasure": *OJ*, 842.

70   "the happiness of creation": *MM*, 796.

70   "the budding cartoonist in me": Ibid., 795.

71   "Stravinsky looks upon the mountain": *CP*, 257.

71   "the mythogenetic truth": Ibid., xxiv.

71   "the flight of a marvelous crow": Ibid., 3.

72   "the smell of wet old magazines": *CJU*, 23.

72   He also remembered the lonely bliss: *MM*, 795.

72   "about the Peruvian": CC to JU, April 22, 1954, Harper.

72   Updike replied with a long letter: JU to CC, April 26, 1954, Harper.

73   Canfield made vague, encouraging noises: CC to JU, May 10, 1954, Harper.

73   Updike eventually promised: JU to CC, March 17, 1955, Harper.

73   As she wrote in the letter: KSW to JU, July 17, 1954, NYPL.

73   He didn't want to give any more interviews: JU to Eric Rayman, June 30, 2008. The letter is in Rayman's possession.

75   "John was always a striver": Author interview, MA, April 1, 2009.

75   "one of the most exclusive": LGH to JU, February 15, 1951, Ursinus.

76   he claimed to have "peaked" as a scholar: *OJ*, 841.

76   "As I settled into the first lecture": *SC*, 254.

76   "delivered with a slightly tremulous elegance": *OJ*, 840.

76   "That a literary work could have a double life": Ibid., 843.

77   "staid, tweedy" poet: *MM*, 764.

77   "the least tweedy of writing instructors": Ibid.

77   "the very model of a cigarette-addicted Gallic intellectual": *ES*, ix.

78   "None of his courses": Lasch, October 9, 1951, Rochester.

78   "Updike keeps plowing ahead": Lasch, October 14, 1951, Rochester.

78   "a kind of younger *Couples*": *Td*.

78   "eighty-five percent bent upon becoming a writer": *MM*, 789.

78   "the trouble was": Edward Hoagland, "A Novelist's Novelist," *The New York Times*, October 17, 1982.

79   "art was a job you did on your own": *DC*, 627.

79   "losing sight of his initial purpose": Lasch, February 2, 1952, Rochester.

79   when Kit finally met the "lady love": Lasch, February 24, 1952, Rochester.

79   "She sounds alright to me"; LGH to JU, February 2, 1952, Ursinus.

80   "I am no longer amused by her flutterings": LGH to JU, December 1, 1950, Ursinus.

80   "an air of slight unrest": Lasch, April 8, 1952, Rochester.

80   unpublished version of "Homage to Paul Klee": Houghton.

81   "I courted her essentially by falling down": "View from the Catacombs," 73.

82   "We need a writer": LP, November 3, 1951, Houghton.

82   "I feel I am on the lip": LP, March 10, 1953, Houghton.

84   One of his Lampoon colleagues: E-mail, John Hubbard to author, September 28, 2009.

84   "If only he would write": Lasch, September 22, 1952, Rochester.

84   "The financial aspect": Lasch, February 22, 1953, Rochester.

85   "Updike was elected": Lasch, April 12, 1953, Rochester.

87   He arrived in Cambridge a "cultural bumpkin": *SC*, 110.

87   "first and . . . most vivid glimpse": *HS*, 196.

87   "a yen to read great literature": LP, May 28, 1951, Houghton.

87   "worshipped, and gossiped about, Eliot and Pound": *OJ*, 840.

87   "like an encompassing gray cloud": *PP*, 256.

87   "The only thing that has sustained me": JU to Joan George Zug, quoted in *T*d.

88   literature "was revered as it would not be again": *MM*, 27.

88   " 'You know,' he told his old friend": *DC*, 538.

89   "Joe McCarthy (against)": *OJ*, 840.

89   "Not one class I took": Ibid., 839.

89   The sun burned his nose: LP, June 30, 1953, Houghton.

90   "About the job—": WM to JU, March 18, 1954, Houghton,

91   "I managed a froggy backstroke": *DC*, 83.

91   "a babbling display of ignorance": *OJ*, 841.

91   Asked by a classmate: E-mail, Benjamin La Farge to author, January 30, 2010.

91   When Updike saw it: LP, February 16, 1953, Houghton.

92   "If I were reasonable": LP, May 17, 1955, Houghton.

92   "That long face with the nose accentuated": E-mail, Peter Judd to author, March 24, 2010.

92   "He never liked intellectuals": *T*d.

92   "I was kind of a loner": Ibid.

93   John suggested they stay: Lasch, November 22, 1953, Rochester.

94   "sounds a programmatic note": Ward W. Briggs Jr., "One Writer's Classics: John Updike's Harvard," *Amphora* (Fall 2002): 14.

97   "to give the mundane its beautiful due": *ES*, xv.

97   the magazine was "delighted": WM to JU, August 5, 1954, NYPL.

97   "I felt, standing and reading": *MM*, 763.

97   "the ecstatic breakthrough of my literary life": *CJU*, 25.

98   "The point, to me, is plain": *OS*, vii.

99   "Cheever's story involved drunkenness": *MM*, 764.

99   "one of my greatest enemies"; LP, January 31, 1954, Houghton.

99   "owes something" to the dead Easter chick: *ES*, x.

99   In a letter to his editor: JU to WM, October 4, 1954, NYPL.

99   "everything outside Olinger": *OS*, vii.

100   "I had given myself five years": Ibid.

101   " . . . Perhaps / we meet our heaven": *EP*, 27.

101   "Four years was enough Harvard": *OJ*, 841.

102   "Just a note to tell you": Quoted in Ben Yagoda, *About Town: The* New Yorker *and the World It Made* (New York: Scribner, 2000), 18. (Hereafter cited as Yagoda, *About Town*.)

102   "The first time I took him to lunch": Hiller.

102   "passive-aggressive aw-shucks pose": Letter, MA to author, May 8, 2010.

102   "the object," as Updike put it: *MM*, 780.

III. The Talk of the Town

105   "Nothing like a sneering nude": JU to KL, November 10, 1954, Rochester.

105   "the sooty, leonine sprawl of the Ashmolean": *ES*, 193.

106   "I've never done anything harder": *CJU*, 105.

106   "Mary, in need of a bathroom": JU to WM, February 2, 1962, Illinois.

107   "The color of March": *CP*, 7.

107   "I think John really disapproved": Author interview, MW, April 7, 2011.

107   Updike confessed in *Self-Consciousness*: *SC*, 132.

108   "The English climate": JU to KL, September 23, 1954, Rochester.

108   "Englishmen are astoundingly ignorant": JU to KL, November 10, 1954, Rochester.

109   "He typed automatically": Author interview, MW, April 7, 2011.

109   A letter from Katharine White: KSW to JU, September 15, 1954, NYPL.

110   "We price every manuscript separately": Ibid.

110   "In many ways," he bravely claimed: JU to KSW, November 26, 1954, NYPL.

111   "More than any other editor": William Shawn, "Katharine Sergeant White," *The New Yorker*, August 1, 1977, 72.

111   "aristocratic sureness of taste": *OJ*, 771–75.

112   "A colon is compact, firm, and balanced": JU to KSW, November 26, 1954, NYPL.

112   "try to feel more kindly toward the dash": KSW to JU, December 1, 1954, NYPL.

112   in March, she suggested: KSW to JU, March 21, 1955, NYPL.

113   White suggested that he should avoid: KSW to JU, February 14, 1955, NYPL.

114   "the domestic scene": KSW to JU, March 23, 1957, NYPL.

114   "an entirely different locale": KSW to JU, February 14, 1955, NYPL.

114   "We think it is the best written prose": KSW to JU, April 5, 1955, NYPL.

114   Updike read his first Nabokov: *PP*, 220.

115   "[T]hey play flitting, cooing chorus": *HS*, 326.

115   "He is a saint of the mundane": Ibid., 312.

115   the "intensity of witnessing": Ibid., 311.

115   Green's "limpid realism": Ibid., 328.

115   Green's "formal ambitiousness": Ibid.

116   "Both quite bowled me over": *DC*, 660.

116   "full of a tender excitement": *PP*, 21.

116   Updike "rose to no bait": E-mail, Judd to author, March 24, 2010.

118   Updike remembered driving: *DC*, 102.

118   "[He] would make *this* trip alone": LGH, *Enchantment*, 114.

118   "meet the man who was going to be": Ibid., 112.

118   "seemed saddened, as if she had laid an egg": *SC*, 48.

119   "It was all pretty monastic": Author interview, TB, September 13, 2009.

119   "He struck *The New Yorker*": WMRR.

120   "John was the star": Author interview, TB, September 13, 2009.

120   "If ever a writer, a magazine": Yagoda, *About Town*, 302.

120   Updike praised Yagoda's book: *DC*, 102.

120   "ever since you accepted": JU to WM, May 19, 1995, Illinois.

120   "It is a slightly different": WM to JU, May 7, 1958, NYPL.

120   "continuously insolent and alive": Quoted in Yagoda, *About Town*, 214.

121   "the bull's-eye of our city": *PP*, 78.

121   "The city," E. B. White rhapsodized: E. B. White, *Here Is New York* (New York: The Little Bookroom, 1999), 29.

121   "pampered and urban": *OJ*, 135.

122   "the delicious immensity of the excluded": *PP*, 94.

122   "at least all of the following": Quoted in Mary F. Corey, *The World Through a Monocle:* The New Yorker *at Midcentury* (Cambridge, MA: Harvard University Press, 1999), 10.

122   "I loved that magazine so much": *PP*, 52–53.

125   "two hours of fanciful typing": *HS*, 847.

125   "It was perfectly obvious": Quoted in Yagoda, *About Town*, 306.

125   "a kind of contemptuous harried virtuosity": *HS*, 849.

126   Updike once defined "*New Yorker*-ese": JU interviewed by David Remnick, *New Yorker* Festival, 2005.

126   "It seemed unlikely that I would ever get better": *HS*, 849.

126   "innocent longing for sophistication": *PP*, 421.

128   "I began to read Proust": Ibid., 165.

130   On his second visit, he was invited to dinner: KL to Paula Budlong, October 19, 1955, Rochester.

130   "They invite you to dinner": KL to Paula Budlong, October 23, 1955, Rochester.

133   anxious theological investigations: *OJ*, 844.

135   "there was this really intense nonspeaking atmosphere": Author interview, TB, September 13, 2009.

135   Updike's fondness for gags: JU to TB, May 25, 1989, Houghton.

136   "He was participating in the life of the city": Author interview, MW, April 7, 2011.

137   "substantially" his own: JU to WM, April 16, 1957, NYPL.

138   "not only the best general magazine in America": *DC*, 100–101.

139   "from the real (the given, the substantial) world": *CP*, xxiii.

141   "sole ambition": *CJU*, 12.

141   "If there is anything to be": WM to JU, August 3, 1955, NYPL.

141   "the only gregarious man on the premises": *MM*, 785.

141   "everything," Updike remembered: Remnick interview, 2005.

142   Napoleon and St. Francis of Assisi: William Maxwell, "The Art of Fiction No. 71," *The Paris Review* 85 (Fall 1982). (Hereafter cited as Maxwell, "The Art of Fiction No. 71.")

142   "pinkly crouched behind his proof-piled desk": *MM*, 780.

142   "unfailing courtesy and rather determined conversational blandness": Ibid., 779.

142   "without moving a muscle": Ibid., 780.

142   "His sense of honor": *DC*, 103.

143   his "gratitude and admiration": William Shawn to JU, October 18, 1960, NYPL.

143   an "ineffable eminence": *DC*, 102.

143   "the message was commonly expressed": *MM*, 783.

144   "He was, in effect, the caretaker of my livelihood": Ibid., 783.

144   he "conveyed a murmurous, restrained nervous energy": Ibid., 780.

145   "If he doesn't get the Nobel Prize": WM, "Confidential Report on Candidate," 1959 Guggenheim Fellowship competition, received by the Guggenheim Foundation on December 18, 1958.

145   Maxwell said, "That's a short story": *MM*, 781.

145   Maxwell thought the finished product: JU to WM, January 21, 1958, NYPL.

145   "The relationship," as Updike acknowledged: *MM*, 783.

145   "meddlesome perfectionism" of *New Yorker* editors: *OJ*, 116.

145   "a good verbal tussle": JU to WM, January 12, 1961, NYPL.

145   "part of a machine": *MM*, 783.

146   "Could there have been an easier": WM to JU, undated [1975?], NYPL.

146   Updike waxed ecstatic: JU to WM, January 23, 1992, Illinois.

147   Updike wrote to Bailey: JU to TB, April 15, 2005, Anthony Bailey Papers, Houghton Library, Harvard University.

147   "a large, semi-ruinous mock-Tudor mansion": Brendan Gill, *Here at the New Yorker* (New York: Da Capo, 1997), 226.

148   He felt "crowded, physically and spiritually": *MM*, 806.

148   the city's "ghastly plentitude": *OJ*, 56.

148   "whatever you might do or achieve in New York": Letter, MA to author, November 29, 2010.

148   "Not quite right for me, as the rejection slips say": LP, May 21, 1956, Houghton.

149   Gill "came to *The New Yorker* young": MM, 786.

149   He wanted to be an artist, not an "elegant hack": LP, June 26, 1960, Houghton.

149   "easily the finest writing talent": Brendan Gill to VG, October 20, 1956, Orion.

149   "gallant, wise, and willing to lose money": JU to VG, January 31, 1957, Orion.

150   "While our baby cooed": *PP*, 165.

150   "It was a revelation to me": Ibid., 167.

150   "Those two woke me up": Remnick interview, 2005.

151   In some later accounts of his "defection": *DC*, 103.

151   "too trafficked, too well cherished by others": *SC*, 253.

151   "immense as the city is": Remnick interview, 2005.

151   "a vast conspiracy of bother": LP, January 27, 1957, Houghton.

151   "When New York ceased to support my fantasies": *AP*, vii.

151   "sweet as a mint paddy": LP, February 18, 1957, Houghton.

151   volunteered to find him a larger, more suitable apartment: *DC*, 103.

151   "The crucial flight of my life": *ES*, x.

152   "the crucial detachment of my life": *OS*, ix.

152   In 1968 he told *Time* magazine: *T*d.

152   "My money comes out of here": *WMRR*.

152   "There's a certain moment of jubilant mortality": *T*d.

152   "being in New York takes so much energy": *OJ*, 56.

152   The reviewer referred in the very first sentence: Maxwell Geismar, "The End of the Line," *The New York Times*, March 24, 1957.

153   "very shallow sophistication": Maxwell Geismar, "Fitzgerald: Bard of the Jazz Age," *Saturday Review of Literature*, April 26, 1958, 17.

153   William Maxwell felt obliged to send his "depressed" author: WM to JU, May 7, 1958, NYPL.

154   "We must write where we stand": *PP*, 48.

154   "Irwin Shaw when he was a young man": Maxwell, "The Art of Fiction No. 71."

155   Updike himself complained of a certain "prudery": *DC*, 101.

155   "anachronistic nice-nellyism": *OJ*, 116.

155   Dismissing what he called "Westport comedy": Alfred Kazin, "Broadway: The New Philistines," *Time*, June 6, 1960.

156   "I notice in *Time* a reference to 'the artist for *The New Yorker*'": JU to Alfred Kazin, June 13, 1960, The Henry W. and Albert A. Berg Collection of English and American Literature, New York Public Library.

157   "Harold Bloom's torturous dramatization": *HS*, 592.

IV. Welcome to Tarbox

158   "[M]y conception of an artist . . .": *AP*, 145.

158   "If Shillington gave me life": *SC*, 49.

159   "Children are what welds a family to a town": Ibid., 53.

159   "It felt," he wrote, "like a town with space": JU, "The Dilemma of Ipswich," *Ford Times*, September 1972, 10.

159   Updike once claimed that he'd moved: *SC*, 57.

159   "A small-town boy," he wrote: *ES*, x.

159   "the whole mass of middling, hidden, troubled": *SC*, 103.

160   "mini-city perkiness": JU, "The Dilemma of Ipswich," 10.

160   "a maverick kind of place": *SC*, 52.

160   "Ipswich is traditionally careless of itself": JU, "The Dilemma of Ipswich," 12.

161   "We are all looking forward greatly": CC to JU, April 3, 1957, Harper.

162   "It gathers power as it goes": EL to JU, May 10, 1957, Harper.

162   "[N]one of us feels that the book": CC to JU, June 13, 1957, Harper.

162   "It had been a good exercise to write it": *CJU*, 47.

162   "chalk it up to practice": Ibid., 3.

163   "every incident with any pith": LP, January 13, 1964, Houghton.

163   "wretched genre," he exclaimed: *CJU*, 3.

165   "a self-preserving detachment": *LL*, 89.

166   "one wife, one editor is all a man should have": WM to JU, September 24, 1957, Houghton.

166   "pricelessly sensitive reader": *CJU*, 29.

166   she advanced her shrewd opinions: Julieta Ojeda Alba, "A Relaxed Conversation with John Updike," *Atlantis* (June–December 1996): 499. (Hereafter cited as Alba, "A Relaxed Conversation with John Updike.")

166   "He was good with the first baby": Author interview, MW, November 1, 2011.

167   "I came up here to get into a novel-writing groove": JU to KSW, July 9, 1957, NYPL.

169   "The poetry book is a lovely job": JU to EL, March 1, 1958, Harper.

169   "Is the young man joking?": Found on JU letter to EL, April 14, 1958, Harper.

169   "troubled about the impact of the story": EL to JU, December 31, 1957, Harper.

170   "too good to lose": VG to Simon Michael Bessie, March 27, 1958, Orion.

170   "a mistake to publish [the novel] as it stands": EL to JU, January 17, 1958, Harper.

170   "I think we knew already": Found on JU letter to EL, January 20, 1958, Harper.

170   "not carried to a satisfactory or satisfying conclusion": EL to JU, January 27, 1958, Harper.

170   the novel's fate in the marketplace "could be dismal": JU to EL, January 20, 1958, Harper.

170   "I doubt whether we shall sell": VG to Simon Michael Bessie, March 27, 1958, Orion.

171   "You went to the heart": JU to EL, February 17, 1958, Harper.

171   "the doors at Harper's are wide open": EL to JU, February 20, 1958, Harper.

171   She replied with a long, exceptionally frank letter: KSW to CC, February 18, 1958, Harper.

172   "I am now deeply in debt and quite panicked": JU to WM, January 25, 1958, NYPL.

172   "ready to disgorge the whole mass": JU to WM, January 21, 1958, NYPL.

173   "I was full of a Pennsylvania thing I wanted to say": *CJU*, 25.

173   "a long account of the good old days in Shillington": LP, October 14, 1958, Houghton.

173   suggested that Updike send a carbon copy of the manuscript: JU to TB, March 23, 1967, Anthony Bailey Papers, Houghton Library.

173   a "wildly enthusiastic" Richardson: SR to JU, March 16, 1958, Ransom.

174   the "inner aspect of the book": JU to SR, March 13, 1958, Ransom.

174   "Do I sense here a universal man?": SR to JU, March 17, 1958, Ransom.

174   Updike described him as a cross: *MM*, 856.

175   "I wrote *The Poorhouse Fair* as an anti-novel": *CJU*, 45.

175   "a deliberate anti–*Nineteen Eighty-Four*": *PF77*, x.

175   a "queer shape," he called it: JU to EL, February 17, 1958, Harper.

175   "what will become of us": Ibid.

176   "Out of the hole where it had been": *PF77*, viii.

176   Updike "had no fear": *CJU*, 3.

176   "in his way a distinguished man": Ibid., 167.

176   "He loved me, and I loved him": *DC*, 11.

177   an "oblique monument": *CJU*, 3.

177   "The time is ap-proaching": *PF*, 117.

177   The inventory of items Updike borrowed: *PF77*, xiii.

177   "offhand-and-backwards-feeling": *PP*, 51.

177   "absolute empathy": *HS*, 320.

177   a "classic, if not flawless": Whitney Balliett, "Writer's Writer," *The New Yorker*, February 7, 1959, 138.

178   less a novel than a "poetic vision": Ibid.

178   a "poet's care and sensitivity": Ibid., 140.

178   a lack of "emotional content": Ibid.

178   "curiously, one never thinks of *liking* or *disliking* it": Ibid.

178   "Even more than black death": *PF*, 24.

179   Updike recalled "the thrill of power": *OJ*, 48.

180   "My father was always afraid": *CJU*, 12.

180   "My first novel . . . showed the rebellion": *MM*, 10.

180   "I love the magazine like a parent": JU to SR, May 5, 1958, Ransom.

180   a steady source of "whale-sized checks": JU to WM, February 25, 1958, NYPL.

181   "My wife and I found ourselves in a kind of 'swim'": *SC*, 51–52.

183   One of the "genial grandees of Argilla Road": Ibid., 52.

183   the "cultivated older generation": Ibid.

183   the "Junior Jet Set": "View from the Catacombs," 75.

184   The women seemed "gorgeous" to Updike: *SC*, 51.

184   a "delayed second edition" of his high school self: Ibid., 221.

184   "If he's not being paid enough attention": *Td*.

185   "The sisters and brothers I had never had": *SC*, 52.

185   "on the basis of what I did in person": *CJU*, 25.

187   "clicked the collection shut": JU to EL, March 1, 1958, Harper.

187   "While writing it," he explained: *OJ*, 134–35.

188   "I believed," he later wrote: Ibid., 135.

189   "abrupt purchase on lived life": Ibid.

190   "In 1958 I was at just the right distance": *OJ*, 134.

191   "a shy try at strip poker": *DC*, 84.

191   "He was an utterly striking figure": E-mail, Austin Briggs to author, March 6, 2011.

191   "I am careless, neglecting to count cards": *DC*, 84.

191   he'd "changed houses, church denominations, and wives": *DC*, 85.

192   a "wonderful natural swing": *GD*, 147.

192   "The average golfer," he later wrote: *MM*, 124.

192   "the hours adding up," he admitted: *GD*, xiv.

192   this "narcotic pastime": Ibid.

192   "I am curiously, disproportionately": Ibid., 169.

192   Rounds of golf, he wrote: Ibid., 189.

192   with his "modest" eighteen handicap: Ibid., xii.

192   a "poor golfer, who came to the game late": Ibid., 25.

192   "The fluctuations of golfing success": Ibid., 188–89.

193   "golf was a rumored something": Ibid., 24.

193   "Golf," he wrote, "is a great social bridge": *MM*, 126.

193   the "spongy turf of private fairways": *GD*, 111.

194   "I sensed that for John": E-mail, Tim O'Brien to author, February 17, 2012.

194   "Golf," he explained, "is a constant struggle": *MM*, 125.

194   "Basically, I want to be alone with my golf": *GD*, 40.

194   O'Brien remembered having conversations: E-mail, Tim O'Brien to author, February 17, 2012.

194   "He seemed delighted when he won a hole": E-mail, Tim O'Brien to author, February 18, 2012.

195   "In those instants of whizz, ascent, hover, and fall": *GD*, 149.

195   the "inexhaustible competitive charm": Ibid., 127.

195   "Golf," he explained, "is . . . a great tunnel": *MM*, 126.

195   "My golfing companions . . . are more dear to me": *GD*, 189.

195   "If I thought as hard about writing": Adam Begley, "A Jolly Geezer, Updike Is Back," *The New York Observer*, October 27, 2003.

195   "Golf converts oddly well into words": *GD*, 15.

196   "Some of us worship in churches": Adlai E. Stevenson, *The Major Campaign Speeches of Adlai E. Stevenson, 1952* (New York: Random House, 1953), 282.

196   "the eerie religious latency": *GD*, 51.

197   "We lack the mustard-seed of faith": Ibid., 46.

197   yet "miracles . . . abound": Ibid., 51.

197   "ritual interment and resurrection": Ibid., 152.

197   "Our bad golf testifies, we cannot help feeling": Ibid., 45.

197   "Man in a state of fear and trembling": *MM*, 852.

198   "sputters away to one side": *RRun*, 129.

198   "beautiful natural swing": Ibid., 130.

198   "Ineptitude seems to coat him": Ibid., 129.

198   "a white flag of forgiveness": Ibid., 131.

198   "along a line straight as a ruler-edge": Ibid., 134.

198   "I do feel that somewhere behind all this": Ibid., 127.

198   "There was this thing that wasn't there": Ibid., 132.

198   "Hell, it's not much. . . .": Ibid., 124.

198   a "first-rate" athlete: Ibid., 105.

199   "Playing golf with someone": Ibid., 151.

199   Harry is "worth saving and could be saved": Ibid., 167.

199   the "harmless ecstasy" of sporting excellence: Ibid., 168.

199   "Although Harry hasn't studied": *WMRR*.

199   "Shillington was littered . . .": *HG*, 450.

199   "clutter and tensions of young married life": *MM*, 817.

200   it felt "exhilaratingly speedy and free": *HG*, 451.

200   a "heavy, intoxicating dose of fantasy": *MM*, 817.

200   "as he would to his wife": *RRun*, 82.

200   "'I'd forgotten,' she says": Ibid., 85.

201   he's "too fastidious to mouth the words": Ibid., 186.

201   "He takes his [clothes] off quickly": Ibid., 187.

201   "When the door closes": Ibid., 192.

201   Victor Gollancz resorted to Latin: VG to Daniel George, September 11, 1961, Orion.

201   "I have . . . never read a novel": Undated memorandum, VG, Orion.

201   "RABBIT RUN A SUPERB NOVEL": VG to JU, February 10, 1960, Orion.

202   "There are one or two little matters to discuss": *OJ*, 845.

202   "I agreed to go along with the legal experts": Ibid., 846.

202   "The novels of Henry Miller," Updike once quipped: *PP*, 38.

203   "none of the excisions really hurt": *OJ*, 846.

203   his aim was "to write about sex": *CJU*, 223.

204   "the creature of impulse": *HG*, 449.

204   "With a sob of protest she grapples for the child": *RRun*, 264.

204   "Well, I just drowned the baby": Author interview, MW, November 1, 2011.

204   "Obviously, there was no real baby involved": *CJU*, 132.

205   his "aesthetic and moral aim": *HG*, 451.

205   "I once did something right": *RRun*, 105.

206   Harry Angstrom was a "ticket," Updike wrote: *HG*, 448.

V. The Two Iseults

207   "There is no such thing as static happiness": *Td*.

207   he was "falling in love, away from marriage": JU, *Hub Fans Bid Kid Adieu* (Northridge, CA: John Lord Press, 1977), xi.

209   a "scabby tenement" in the center of Ipswich: LP, March 27, 1960, Houghton.

209   someone "who, equipped with pencils and paper": *AP*, 145.

209   "everything artistic is kept down here": JU to WM, April 19, 1960, NYPL.

209   "I've rented a little room": JU to VG, March 23, 1960, Orion.

210   This "weave of promiscuous friendship": *LL*, 96.

211   "a stag of sorts," as he wrote in his memoirs: *SC*, 222.

211   "malicious, greedy . . . obnoxious . . .": Ibid.

214   "a new kind of fictional space": *Td*.

215   Maxwell assured Updike: WM to JU, May 5, 1960, NYPL.

216   "I miss Grandpa, even at this distance": LP, September 15, 1953, Houghton.

218   stitched-together, "fugal" form: *MM*, 768.

221   "under a great pressure of sadness": JU to Edward Hoagland, January 12, 1962, Houghton.

222   "a biune study of complementary moral types": *HG*, 449.

222   "The main motive force behind *The Centaur*": *CJU*, 49.

222   "I'm carrying death in my bowels": *C*, 54.

222   his "gayest" book: *CJU*, 35.

222   "I had death in my lungs": *SC*, 96.

223   "I carried within me fatal wounds": Ibid., 97.

223   a time of "desperation": Ibid.

223   "[T]o give myself brightness and air": Ibid., 98.

223   "We cannot reach Him, only He can reach us": *AP*, 212.

223   "Ipswich belonged to Barth": *SC*, 98.

224   "I decided . . . I *would* believe": Ibid., 230.

224   "Religion enables us to ignore nothingness": Ibid., 228.

224   "The choice seemed to come down to": *BookTV*.

224   "that one's sense of oneself": *WMRR*.

224   Once, while he was in the basement: Michiko Kakutani, "Turning Sex and Guilt into an American Epic," *Saturday Review*, October 1981, 21.

224   "[A]s I waited, on a raw rainy fall day": *SC*, 97.

224   what he himself called his "incessant sociability": Ibid., 54.

225   "Egoistic dread faded within the shared life": Ibid., 55.

225   Updike volunteered "as a favor and a lark": *MM*, 807.

225   he was surrounded by his friends, and yet in "an elevated position": Ibid., 809.

226   "Your literary energy has failed you here": Author interview, Mary Webb, November 16, 2009.

227   "The first word I wrote for him": Author interview, ND, July 28, 2011.

227   "For a beginner, you seem remarkably knowing": JU, "Two Communications to Nicholas Delbanco," in Frederick Busch, ed., *Letters to a Fiction Writer* (New York: W. W. Norton, 2000), 232.

227   "What was unforgettable," Delbanco said: Author interview, ND, July 28, 2011.

227   Updike put the letter down: E-mail, Jonathan Penner to author, August 2, 2011.

227   agreeing to the teaching job had been "sort of foolish": JU to WM, August 11, 1962, NYPL.

227   "I can't make friends with twelve people": Author interview, Mary Webb, November 16, 2009.

227   "Teaching takes a lot of energy": *CJU*, 157.

228   "Her eyes were the only glamorous feature": *ES*, 515.

229   Herbert had "the manner of the local undertaker": LP, May 18, 1958, Houghton.

229   "I took the phone," Mary remembered: Author interview, MW, July 14, 2012.

230   "He was pretty darn miserable": Author interview, MW, July 15, 2012.

231   description expresses love: *SC*, 231.

232   "one of the most peaceful and scenic places": LP, September 14, 1959, Houghton.

232   "a conspicuously autobiographical writer": WM to JU, June 25, 1965, NYPL.

233   He asked that it not be put "on the bank": JU to WM, June 15, 1963, Illinois.

233   "though the vessel of circumstantial facts is all invented": JU to WM, July 19, 1963, NYPL.

233   stories of the "non-troublesome" variety: JU to WM, June 15, 1963, Illinois.

234   characterized by a kind of self-inflicted punishment: See William H. Pritchard, *John Updike: America's Man of Letters* (South Royalton, VT: Steerforth Press, 2000), 122. (Hereafter cited as Pritchard, *Updike*.)

234   "No memory of any revision": *HS*, 853.

235   "A door had opened, and shut": *SC*, 98.

237   "we could turn what should be a happy adventure": LGH to JU, October 25, 1962, Ursinus.

237   "people are incorrigibly themselves": JU, *The Maples Stories* (New York: Everyman's Pocket Classics, 2009), 11. (Hereafter cited as *JU, The Maples Stories*.)

237   "Richard and Joan Maple had become": *WMRR*.

241   "mythanalysis of culture": Denis de Rougemont, *Love Declared* (New York: Pantheon Press, 1963), 34.

241   The review, as Updike later remarked: *CJU*, 29.

241   "an etymology of the passions": Denis de Rougemont, *Love in the Western World* (Princeton, NJ: Princeton University Press, 1983), 18.

241   "form of love which refuses the immediate": De Rougemont, *Love Declared*, 41

241   "Tristan loves the awareness": De Rougemont, *Love in the Western World*, 41–42.

241   "disguises a twin narcissism": Ibid., 52.

241   a "longing for what sears us": Ibid., 50.

241   de Rougemont "hangs on their necks": "Books: Liebestod," *Time*, September 2, 1940.

242   "selfish and altruistic threads": *AP*, 225.

242   de Rougemont is "dreadfully right": Ibid., 232.

242   "Only in being loved," he writes: Ibid., 233.

243   they "hunkered down": *LL*, 93.

243   a man in love "ceases to fear death": *AP*, 222–23.

243   an "angst-besmogged period": *SC*, 99.

243   "an ingenious psychosomatic mechanism": Ibid.

244   "invulnerably detached" and "quite vulnerable": LP, October 1, 1963, Houghton.

246   too "crowded," as Updike himself put it: *HS*, 854.

249   the "clangor" of the last two paragraphs: Ibid., 855.

249   say "something good" for the "sad magic": Ibid.

250   "I was talking to someone about John Updike": Mary McCarthy, "The Art of Fiction No. 27," *The Paris Review* (Winter–Spring 1962).

250   "delicate symmetry and balance": Renata Adler, "Arcadia, Pa.," *The New Yorker*, April 13, 1963, 185.

250   "brilliantly talented and versatile": Orville Prescott, "Books of the Times," *The New York Times*, February 4, 1963, 7.

251   "Updike finds his way more accurately": "Prometheus Unsound," *Time*, February 8, 1963, 86.

251   "the most significant young novelist in America": Peter Buitenhuis, "Pennsylvania Pantheon," *The New York Times Book Review*, April 7, 1963, 4.

251   feeling "wobbly," he told Maxwell: JU to WM, May 4, 1964, Illinois.

251   his wife, unlike her fictional avatar, was "strongly on the scene": JU to WM, September 1, 1964, Illinois.

251   "I was not privy to *Marry Me*," she said: Author interview, WM, November 2, 2011.

252   "unease about the book's lack of . . . sociology": *CJU*, 134.

254   Updike's "obsession with adultery": Maureen Howard, "Jerry and Sally and Richard and Ruth," *The New York Times Book Review*, October 31, 1976, 2.

254   Updike's "one big situation": Alfred Kazin, "Alfred Kazin on Fiction," *The New Republic*, November 27, 1976, 23.

VI. Couples

256   "In fact . . . the literary scene is a kind of *Medusa*'s raft": *OJ*, 117.

256   Her husband was at the dentist: *DC*, 114.

256   "We didn't know what gesture to make": *CJU*, 161.

257   "The fashion that fall was for deep décolletage": *Couples*, 357.

257   "Take, eat. . . . This is his body, given for thee": Ibid., 386.

257   "the dancing couples were gliding": Ibid., 375.

257   "dense reality" through thick description: *CJU*, 146.

257   "It was as if we slept from Friday to Monday": *AP*, 96.

257   "Our private lives had become the real concern": *CJU*, 161.

258   "[W]hat concupiscent vanity it used to be": *SC*, 78.

259   "complicating factors" might force him: JU to AAK, April 8, 1964, Ransom.

259   it "takes place in the future": *CJU*, 37.

259   *The Centaur* after the centaur has died: Ibid., 27.

260   "a kind of chamber music": JU to AAK, May 6, 1965, Ransom.

260   "It's a book people mention to me": *CJU*, 239.

260   "a little flight among imaginary moments": LP, July 3, 1965, Houghton.

261   "underlying thematic transaction": *PP*, 92–93.

261   "We were striking terms, and circumspection was needed": *OF*, 174.

261   One goes so far as to cite Eliot's dictum: Pritchard, *Updike*, 104.

262   an attempt "to show an aging mother": *MM*, 11.

263   "Maybe in Russia," he wrote, "I'll learn to think big": JU to WM, October 20, 1964, NYPL.

263   "He was so good about it," said Luers: Author interview, William Luers, November 5, 2011.

263   felt obliged "to be a good guest of the Soviet state": *SC*, 139.

263   "wearing abroad," as he put it, "my country's colors": Ibid., 137.

263   "There I was everything I'm not here": *CJU*, 15.

264   "the artistic indecency of writing about a writer": *CB*, 5.

264   "a vehicle," as he put it, "for impressions": *PP*, 486.

264   "I am transported around here like a brittle curio": *CB*, 147.

264   "It is a matter of earnest regret for me": Ibid., 55.

264   "It is a great sadness for me": Блага Димитрова, *Събрани творби*, Том 2, *Лирика и Поеми*, Тих-Ивел, София [Blaga Dimitrova, *Collected Works*, Vol. 2, *Lyrical Poems and Poems* (Sofia: Tih-Ivel, 2003), 209].

265   "almost the dark side of the moon": *MM*, 768.

265   "this fortyish young man, Henry Bech": *CB*, 40.

266   "No sensitive artist in America": *MM*, 853.

266   Updike was an "unusually gifted young man": Blake Bailey, *Cheever: A Life* (New York: Alfred A. Knopf, 2009), 261–62. (Hereafter cited as Bailey, *Cheever*.)

267   "Sometimes I like the thought of [Updike]": Ibid., 347.

267   "John Cheever was a golden name to me": *OJ*, 115–16.

267   "Aspiring, we assume that those already in possession": Ibid., 117.

267   the diminutive Cheever was "Big John": Bailey, *Cheever*, 348.

267   "a bright scuttle of somehow suburban characters": *PP*, 23.

267   "a kind of Russian beauty": *OJ*, 116.

268   "hogged the lecture platform": Bailey, *Cheever*, 349.

268   continual "back-biting": Benjamin Cheever, ed., *The Letters of John Cheever* (London: Vintage, 1992), 246.

268   "I think his magnanimity specious": Ibid., 245.

268   "Our troubles began at the Embassy": Ibid., 248.

268   "[T]he literary scene," he wrote by way of explanation: *OJ*, 117.

269   "I feel in this company": JU, ed., *A Century of Arts and Letters* (New York: Columbia University Press, 1998), 183.

270   The anecdote, which Updike served up in an essay: *PP*, 24.

270   "As Hemingway sought the words for things in motion": *AP*, 182.

271   "Salinger loves the Glasses more than God loves them": Ibid., 183.

271   "the end of review the END of meditating": Ibid., 248.

272   "He does not have an interesting mind": John Aldridge, "Cultivating Corn Out of Season," *Book Week*, November 21, 1965, 5.

272   "To me he seems a writer who has very little to say": Norman Podhoretz, "A Dissent on Updike," *Show*, April 1963.

272   "a minor novelist with a major style": Harold Bloom, ed., *John Updike* (New York: Chelsea House, 1987), 7. (Hereafter cited as Bloom, *John Updike*.)

272   a "vacuity" at the heart of his stories: Dorothy Rabinowitz, "Current Books in Short Compass," *World*, October 24, 1972, 52.

273   Updike "describes to no purpose": Gore Vidal, "Rabbit's Own Burrow," *Times Literary Supplement*, April 26, 1996, 5.

273   "I guess I've recovered from your review": JU to John Aldridge, September 18, 1973, John W. Aldridge Papers, Bentley Historical Library, University of Michigan.

275   "I distrusted orthodoxies," he wrote in his memoirs: *SC*, 142.

275   "Like most Americans I am uncomfortable": Ibid., 112–13.

276   "apologetic" is how he describes his letter: Ibid., 116.

276   a "strange underdog rage about the whole sorry thing": Ibid., 148.

277   "I wanted to keep quiet, but could not": Ibid., 126.

277   "My face would become hot, my voice high and tense": Ibid., 124.

277   a "central trauma" in John's childhood: Ibid., 127.

277   "[T]he possibility exists": Ibid., 134.

277   "I was, perhaps, the most Vietnam-minded person": Ibid., 124.

277   Vietnam "made it impossible to ignore politics": Ibid., 129.

278   "In my mind I was beset, defending an underdog": Ibid., 126–27.

278   "I found him lively, funny, and mischievous": Fax, Philip Roth to author, December 1, 2011.

279   "distinctive brands of irony": Ibid.

279   "Have I not stayed away from the Amish": Roth to JU, August 24, 1978, Houghton.

279   the "twin peaks" of Updike's achievement: Fax, Philip Roth to author, December 1, 2011.

279   Roth had become "an exhausting author to be with": *MM*, 298.

279   "A good woman wronged": JU to MA, November 10, 1996.

280   "Claire Bloom, as the wronged ex-wife": *MM*, 9.

280   "cruelly obtuse—and I knew he wasn't obtuse": Fax, Roth to author, December 1, 2011.

280   Roth categorically denied: Fax, Roth to author, December 2, 2011.

280   they never spoke again: Fax, Roth to author, December 1, 2011.

281   The living Americans he weighed up: *CJU*, 17.

281   "a 17th century house with enough rooms": Ibid., 12.

282   He took, he admitted, "snobbish pride": *PP*, 31.

282   "I wear them until they get quite big": LP, December 6, 1959, Houghton.

282   "By my mid-thirties," he wrote in his memoirs: *SC*, 122.

282   "parasitic relationship with Steuben Glass": *CJU*, 12.

282   He estimated, for example, that in 1967: *Td*.

284   the "little fantasy" featuring young Wendell Morrison: JU to ND, October 4, 1968, Michigan.

285   "oddly good-looking, with an arresting hook nose": *CJU*, 12.

285   "I seem to remember, on one endless drive": *SC*, 123.

286   "At moments of suburban relaxation": Ibid., 123–24.

286   Jane Howard noted how "enmeshed" Updike was: *CJU*, 13.

286   in Ipswich he felt "enlisted in actual life": *SC*, 253.

286   he claimed still to feel, in his "innermost self": *MM*, 806.

286   "inner remove" apparent in the backward tilt of the head: *SC*, 256.

287   "the patriotic grace to cancel": JU to JCO, January 22, 1985.

287   "the dancing couples were gliding": *Couples*, 375.

287   "monstrous" self-absorption: *CJU*, 161.

287   "Shh. You'll wake the children": *Couples*, 9.

288   "Daddy, wake up! Jackie Kenneny's baby died": Ibid., 256.

288   "a young man almost of her generation": Ibid., 356.

288   "Her lips were pursed around the stem of a lollypop": Ibid., 435.

289   "All these goings on would be purely lyrical": "View from the Catacombs," 67.

290   "God's own lightning": *Couples*, 536.

290   The burning of the church is a "great event": Ibid., 535.

290   "Television brought them the outer world": Ibid., 259.

291   "Not since Korea had Piet cared about news": Ibid.

291   "the meaningless world beyond the ring of couples": Ibid., 282.

291   "a nice blend of Noel Coward and Krafft-Ebing": Wilfred Sheed, "Play in Tarbox," *The New York Times Book Review*, April 7, 1968, 33.

291   "I wrote the book in a spirit, mostly, of love and fun": JU to JCO, January 12, 1976, Syracuse.

291   "smothered in pubic hair": "View from the Catacombs," 75.

292   Tarbox was "blatantly recognizable as Ipswich": JJ, August 7, 1967, Ransom.

292   "libel and invasion of privacy": AAK to JU, August 10, 1967, Ransom.

292   "indeed I know of no abortions at all": JU to AAK, August 12, 1967, Ransom.

292   its "grim" portrait of a "fretful," squinting author: *CP*, 70.

293   "I disavow any essential connection": *CJU*, 27.

293   "The Tarboxians are not real people": JU, "Letter to the Editor," *Ipswich Chronicle*, April 25, 1968.

293   the possibility that it would create a "furor": JU to WM, October 7, 1967, Illinois.

294   "cerebral raunch," the tag applied to Updike's oeuvre: Dwight Garner, "Sex, Drugs and E Chords While Seeking Remission," *The New York Times*, December 22, 2011, C1.

294   how "wearying" she found the "sexual redundancies": Diana Trilling, "Updike's Yankee Traders," *The Atlantic Monthly*, April 1968, 131. (Hereafter cited as Trilling, "Updike's Yankee Traders.")

294   dismissed her review as "a banshee cry of indignation": *CJU*, 25.

294   "I can think of no other novel, even in these years of our sexual freedom": Trilling, "Updike's Yankee Traders," 130.

294   Trilling's acid kicker: "But to what purpose?": Ibid.

294   "artistic creation is at best a sublimation": *HG*, 469.

294   "Art is his pastime, but love is his work": Ibid.

VII. Updike Abroad

295   "In the era of jet planes and electronic communication": *MM*, 769.

296   "It was good to read about Bech on the boat": JU to WM, September 27, 1968, Illinois.

296   a "deeper, less comfortable self": *OJ*, 4.

297   the "basic and ancient" function of bringing news: *MM*, 768.

298   "the imaginary territory beyond the Hudson": *CB*, 308.

298   Wordsworth prepared them for the "nodding" daffodils: JU to WM, April 14, 1969, Illinois.

298   "pigeons the color of exhaust fumes": *CB*, 103.

298   "every shire," Updike wrote, "has been the site of a poem": *PP*, 62.

298   "there are recesses of England that exist only for the initiates": Ibid., 59.

298   "parade in everything from yak hides to cellophane": Ibid., 57.

298   "Here," Updike wrote, "things are . . . cheap": Ibid., 55.

298   "They entered a region where the shaggy heads": *CB*, 111.

299   "turning a touch cosmopolitan": LP, February 25, 1969, Houghton.

299   "full of unworkable antiques and devices": JU to WM, September 27, 1968, Illinois.

299   The rent, moreover, was "princely": *CP*, 364.

300   he brooded about the fact that he was now irrefutably "successful": JU to WM, March 6 and 7, 1969, Illinois.

300   "[A]s a light verse writer I am through": JU to HM, March 5, 1958, NYPL.

300   "I may have reached the age": JU to RA, January 30, 1979, NYPL.

300   feeling "like each thing is produced on the verge of silence": Hiller.

301   he left it out of *The Early Stories*: *PP*, 16.

302   Richard Nixon's looks and his "vapid" campaign: JU to WM, November 8, 1968, Illinois.

302   "It had been years since we heard anybody": Author interview, Anthony Lewis, January 17, 2012.

302   "having made him a photographer": JU to WM, December 2, 1968, Illinois.

303   "the futile Buchanan project": JU to JJ, December 18, 1969, Houghton.

304   he didn't want to become "a huckster for myself": JU to AD, April 8, 1968, Tulsa.

305   he declared them "masterful flirts": *PP*, 61.

305   "I see why they call English women birds": JU to WM, October 24, 1968, Illinois.

305   "an extremely pleasant and intelligent man": E-mail, Diana Athill to author, October 3, 2011.

306   "Tony Lewis and his wife Linda sort of adopted us": Author interview, MW, July 14, 2012.

306   "tremendous intellectual energy and *fun*": Author interview, Eliza Lewis, January 19, 2012.

306   Steiner remembered the author being "delightful company": Letter, George Steiner to author, January 14, 2012.

307   "I have felt like a balloon on too long a tether": *PP*, 63.

307   a sentence lifted from a letter to Maxwell: JU to WM, June 4, 1969, NYPL.

307   "a meal for six," he groused: JU to WM, April 14, 1969, Illinois.

308   "What frightens me really is not how much I dislike it": *WMRR*.

308   The African lecture proved awkward: *PP*, 16.

308   "Henry Bech is bleary," he added, "but in good voice": JU to WM, undated, Illinois.

309   "slightly enlarged my sense of human possibilities": *CJU*, 68.

310   A land of "delicate, delectable emptiness": *Coup*, 4–6.

310   Kush "suggests . . . an angular skull": Ibid., 6.

310   "dreaming behind his sunglasses": Ibid., 298.

310   "mandarin explosions," Updike called them: *HG*, 473.

311   "the low, somehow liquid horizon": *Coup*, 21.

311   "the paramilitary foolery between the two superparanoids": Ibid., 57.

311   "fountainhead of obscenity and glut": Ibid., 3.

312   "Out-of-the-way places," he noted: *MM*, 768.

312   a "fraught and sad . . . expedition": *MT*, 115.

313   "As it hoveringly descended": *SC*, 152.

314   "All Venezuela, except for the negligible middle class": *HS*, 31.

314   "*Los indios* and *los ricos* rarely achieve contact": Ibid., 34.

314   "Updike! *Rabbit, Run*! We love his works!": Author interview, Luers, November 5, 2011.

315   "That was why, he supposed, you travelled": *CB*, 308.

315   "For a Jew, to move through post-war Europe": Ibid., 303.

315   "More fervently than he was a Jew, Bech was a writer": Ibid., 326.

315   He worries that he will "cease to exist": Ibid., 329.

315   "one of the globe's great animate spectacles": JU to JCO, March 18, 1992, Syracuse.

316   "ill-advised" was Updike's verdict: JU to JCO, July 3, 1993, Syracuse.

317   "still imperfectly tourist-friendly": *DC*, 17.

317   from communism to "superheated mercantilism": Ibid., 20.

317   he found the Indian expedition "existentially damaging": JU to Werner Berthoff, January 26, 2006, Houghton.

317   "It shatters my composure": Ibid.

VIII. Tarbox Redux

319   "In Ipswich my impersonation of a normal person": *SC,* 54.

319   "If that nut goes, everything goes": LP, February 9, 1958, Houghton.

319   "Once we moved, things fell apart": *OJ,* 59.

320   "I sort of ignored them," Liz remembered: Author interview, Elizabeth Cobblah, April 11, 2011.

323   "the first American masterpiece": *CJU,* 129.

323   civil disobedience "antithetical" to his fifties education: *HG,* 452.

324   "It is so quiet in my new house": JU to MW, June 3, 1970, Illinois.

325   based on "internal evidence": JU, *Too Far to Go* (New York: Fawcett Crest, 1979), 10.

329   "a generation . . . that found itself somewhat pushed around": *WMRR.*

331   "there's more fiction to those stories": Ibid.

331   the "vigorous fakery" essential to historical fiction: *HG,* 453.

331   he turned to an "old friend": *PP,* 491.

332   "the perpetual *presentness* of my former hero": *HG,* 453.

332   "Rabbit to the rescue": *HS,* 858.

332   "I am beginning to wince": JU to JJ, June 16, 1970, Ransom.

332   Updike's dismay at "all the revolutions in the air": *HG,* 453.

332   Harry became a "receptacle" for Updike's concerns: Ibid.

332   the novel, by Updike's own admission, is "violent and bizarre": *HG,* 454.

333   "having the adventure now we're all going to have": *RRedux,* 238.

333   "[T]he news had moved out of the television": *MM,* 818.

333   "We recognize them," she wrote: Trilling, "Updike's Yankee Traders," 129.

334   "Pray for rebirth," Harry's ailing mother tells him: *RRedux,* 198.

335   "Physically, Skeeter fascinates Rabbit": Ibid., 250–51.

335   "she is liking it, being raped": Ibid., 280.

335   "His heart skips. He has escaped. Narrowly": Ibid., 283.

336   inspired by "a piece of authentic social violence": *CJU,* 90.

336   "the rage and destructiveness": *HG,* 455.

336   given to Updike by his family—"in loving exasperation": *SC,* 129.

336   "It's not all war I love . . . it's *this* war": *RRedux,* 357.

336   a town that was "abnormally still": *CJU,* 167.

336   "authority was the Shillington High School faculty": *SC,* 128.

337   the status quo could be "lightly or easily altered": *CJU,* 60.

337   "[r]evolt, rebellion, violence, disgust": Ibid., 62.

337   "The cost of the disruption of the social fabric": *HS,* 858–59.

337   "Her trip drowns babies; his burns girls": *RRedux,* 395.

337   sees himself as "the man in the middle": Ibid., 330.

337   he had "hardly met a black person": *SC,* 196.

338   "Black to him is just a political word": *RRedux,* 114.

338   "Come meet some soul," says Buchanan: Ibid., 115.

338   "a yellow cigarette that requires much sucking in": Ibid.

338   "extremely plausible," she calls it: Ibid., 117.

338   "Having told a number of interviewers": *HS*, 858.

339   he was pronounced "psychologically sick": William Styron, *The Confessions of Nat Turner* (New York: Vintage International, 1992), 448.

339   He'd read the book when it came out and found it "laborious": JU to ND, November 29, 1967, Michigan.

339   "a very eloquent and intelligent negro critic": JU to WM, May 30, 1970, NYPL.

339   Rabbit's "reluctant crossing of the color line": *HG*, 454.

339   "Skeeter is something new in black characters": Anatole Broyard, "Updike Goes All Out at Last," *The New York Times*, November 5, 1971, 40.

340   "possibly inordinate emphasis on sexual congress": *HG*, 454.

340   a "hefty coarse Negress": *RRedux*, 378.

340   "I learned I'd rather fuck than be blown": Ibid., 358.

340   "*Rabbit Redux* is the complete Updike at last": Broyard, "Updike Goes All Out at Last," 40.

340   "I'm rather baffled," Updike told Jones: JU to JJ, November 8, 1971, Ransom.

340   "by far the most audacious and successful": Richard Locke, "Rabbit Returns: Updike Was Always There—It's Time We Noticed," *The New York Times Book Review*, November 14, 1971.

341   the sequel, he wrote, was "meant to be symmetric": *HG*, 454.

341   "The Sixties did a number on him, too": JU, *Rabbit Angstrom* (New York: Everyman's Library, 1995), 611.

341   "Anybody who really cared": *CJU*, 62.

341   "The question that ends the book": *HS*, 859.

341   "I feel at home in Harry's pelt": JU to JCO, January 12, 1976, Syracuse.

342   he remembered that it "kind of wrote itself": Unpublished outtakes from James Atlas's taped interview with JU for "John Updike Breaks Out of Suburbia," *The New York Times Sunday Magazine*, December 10, 1978.

342   "the most dissentious American decade": *HS*, 858.

342   "intuition into the mass consciousness": *SC*, 124.

342   "marital fidelity and parental responsibility": *MM*, 818.

342   "stiff, unreal, and lacking in electricity": Quoted in Josh Rubins, "The Industrious Drifter in Room 2," *Harvard Magazine*, May 1974, 45.

342   he found most plays "pretty silly": Ibid., 51.

342   "bindable and thence forgettable": JU to AD, December 29, 1973, Tulsa.

343   "every inch a first-nighter": JU, *Buchanan Dying* (Mechanicsburg, PA: Stackpole Books, 2000), vii.

344   sex was hardly "the only sore point": Author interview, MW, July 14, 2012.

344   "It was true, [Mary] and I saw many things the same way": *SC*, 102.

345   "nearest and dearest of that time didn't complain": *WMRR*.

346   "Wonderful *contes* from a veteran *conte*-chaser": JU to JJ, March 20, 1972, Ransom.

350   "stay on the right side of the road": LGH to JU, June 8, 1972, Ursinus.

352   their mother said to him, "Coward!": E-mail, MW to author, July 7, 2012.

354   David told me that he had no specific memory: Author interview, David Updike, April 12, 2011.

354   "I think the fact that all of our parents had died": Author interview, MW, April 7, 2011.

354   "In our attempt to be beautiful": *WMRR*.

355   "The basic human condition of being a social animal": Hiller.

IX. Marrying Martha

358   "What had been unthinkable under Eisenhower": *MFA*, 6.

358   he had a "gorgeous" view: LP, June 3, 1975, Houghton.

359   His living "derangements," he wrote: JU to William Koshland, November 14, 1974, Ransom.

359   he "lived rather shapelessly": *ES*, 823.

359   a "rakish" Volkswagen Karmann Ghia: *DC*, 89.

359   his "furtive semi-bachelorhood": *EP*, 24–25.

360   his sense of guilt "triggered a metabolic riot": *SC*, 73.

360   After only a few sessions in the "magic box": Ibid., 74.

360   "clouds of grief and sleeplessness and moral confusion": *TM*, 83.

361   he admitted in a frightening aside, "I read slower than I write": *PP*, 15.

361   "youthful traumas at the receiving end of critical opinion": Ibid., 14.

361   "Review the book, not the reputation": Ibid., 15.

361   "Evidently I can read anything in English": Ibid., 14.

362   "the payment for a monthly review": *HS*, xx.

363   "Rape is the sexual sin of the mob": *PP*, 206.

363   "unstitching the sequined embroidery": Ibid., 201.

363   "[T]he last pages of *Ada* are the best": Ibid., 203.

363   they were both afflicted with "a writer's covetousness": Ibid., 199.

363   "Vladimir Nabokov distinctly seems to be the best writer": *AP*, 248.

363   "His sentences are beautiful out of context": Ibid., 249.

363   "aimless intricacies" and "mannered" devices: Ibid., 255.

364   Nabokov's "cruelty" to his own characters: *HS*, 243.

364   Updike offered handsome tribute in *The New Yorker*: Ibid., 246.

364   "Rich, healthy, brilliant, physically successful": *PP*, 204.

364   whose "brain was so excited" he could scarcely sleep: *HS*, 242.

364   "cerebral self-delight": Ibid., 243.

364   "He asked . . . of his own art and the art of others": Ibid.

365   "When our Miss Ruggles, a tender twenty": Ibid., 232.

366   the possibility of a "legal assault" from Alex Bernhard: JU to RA, December 11, 1978, NYPL.

367   the pain and confusion his "dereliction" has inflicted: *P*, 246.

367   just enough to fog his emotional landscape and add to his "life-fright": LP, March 29, 1975, Houghton.

368   he described the condition as "emotional bigamy": *MT*, 21.

368   "seducing" parishioners ("by way of being helpful"): *MS*, 136.

369   "When is it right for a man to leave his wife?": Ibid., 192.

369   "His prose has never . . . menaced a cowering reader": *PP*, 199.

369   *askew* is the apt word Updike uses: *OJ*, 858.

369   he "wanted to make the book kind of abrasive": *CJU*, 75.

369   "virtuosity . . . too gleefully displayed": Anatole Broyard, "Some Unoriginal Sins," *The New York Times*, February 19, 1975, 33.

370   he was "living like a buzzard in a tree": LP, June 3, 1975, Houghton.

370   "those embarrassing, disarrayed years": *TM*, 89.

370   being a "divorcing bachelor": Michiko Kakutani, "Turning Sex and Guilt into an American Epic," *Saturday Review*, October, 1981, 22.

371   "I felt badly," Updike remembered: Bailey, *Cheever*, 499.

371   "I primly concentrated on wedging him into his clothes": *OJ*, 118.

371   "with all the alcohol squeezed out of him": LP, June 27, 1975, Houghton.

372   throwing, as John put it, "the shadow of my girlfriend over the holidays": LP, December 26, 1975, Houghton.

373   "an unassuming population knot on the way to other places": *HG*, 456.

373   "With all Updike's money, and his and Martha's good sense": Joyce Carol Oates, *The Journal of Joyce Carol Oates, 1973–1982* (New York: Ecco Press, 2007), 125. (Hereafter cited as Oates, *Journal*.)

373   "I was at home in America, all right": JU, "Why Rabbit Had to Go," *The New York Times*, August 5, 1990, 23. (Hereafter cited as JU, "Why Rabbit Had to Go.")

374   two hours of "lightweight, amusing gossip": Oates, *Journal*, 126.

374   "[H]e's a hillbilly from rural Pennsylvania": Ibid., 127.

374   "the various agonies they experienced": Ibid., 125.

374   John had introduced Martha as an "old and ardent Oates reader": JU to JCO, June 26, 1976, Syracuse.

375   "Nobody can read like a writer," he told Oates: JU to JCO, December 14, 1978, Syracuse.

375   "I'd go mad in such a small town myself": Oates, *Journal*, 125.

375   The cellar was "foul": LP, November 9, 1976, Houghton.

375   the "rotten places" in a house: *CP*, 144.

375   Georgetown "made negligible communal demands": *HG*, 457.

376   "a patch of human quicksand": LP, November 20, 1976.

376   public speaking was "a whorish thing to do": Hiller.

377   "Gracious, self-deprecating, and casually attentive": Kakutani, "Turning Sex and Guilt into an American Epic," 14.

377   "John is one of the few people I know": Quoted in Hiller.

377   "Updike read faultlessly each time": Author interview, Ian McEwan, December 5, 2012.

378   "Now I live with yet another family group": Sally Quinn, "Updike on Women, Marriage and Adultery," *The Washington Post*, December 9, 1976, C1.

379   A full-blown feminist critique: Mary Allen, "John Updike's Love of 'Dull Bovine Beauty,'" in *The Necessary Blankness: Women in Major American Fiction of the Nineteen Sixties* (Urbana: University of Illinois Press, 1976), 97–132.

379   "I can't think of any male American writer": *CJU*, 78.

381   his "once-close-woven relationship" with the magazine: LP, January 12, 1976, Houghton.

381   "a novel about penguins, perhaps, or Hottentots": Ibid.

381   "If I marry a third time, it'll have to be Lazarus": JU to ND, October 4, 1977, Michigan.

381   "It was a protest," she said, "I wanted my absence felt": E-mail, Miranda Updike to author, October 12, 2012.

381   Michael was absent, too (and "glad not to be there"): E-mail, Michael Updike to author, September 25, 2012.

382   "amalgamate and align all his betrayals": JU, *The Maples Stories*, 215.

382   Emerson's famous line "We boil at different degrees": *MT*, 206.

382   "She was good in bed": *ES*, 829.

382   he felt that over time they became "artistically estranged": Alba, "A Relaxed Conversation with John Updike," 499.

383   "I was very confiding and she was very interested": Ibid.

384   Ada asks him why he's "abandoning" his children: Linda Grace Hoyer, *The Predator* (New York: Ticknor and Fields, 1990), 37.

384   "they were," he told Maxwell, "very *tender* stories": JU to WM, February 6, 1978, Illinois.

385   the acceptance of David's first story was "a soul-stirring event": JU to WM, May 29, 1978, Illinois.

385   "box it with his grandmother's": JU to AD, March 5, 1981, Tulsa.

387   "One of the problems of being a fiction writer": Unpublished *Atlas* interview, December 10, 1978.

388   "Martha was very upset that John had included the scene": Fax, Roth to author, December 1, 2011.

390   "spokes of a wheel": *ES*, 447.

391   "all the gifts but the one of making their way in the world": LP, August 30, 1981, Houghton.

391   "The work ethic is crumbling," he told a journalist in the early seventies: Hiller.

392   "You grow up of course with these people": Unpublished *Atlas* interview, December 10, 1978.

393   "YOU ASKED FOR IT, WE GOT IT": *RRich*, 13.

393   The traffic on Route 111 is "thin and scared": Ibid., 3.

393   Harry thinks; "the great American ride is ending": Ibid.

393   "Life is sweet," he tells himself: Ibid., 6.

393   "Bourgeois bliss" is how Updike described Rabbit's state of mind: *HG*, 456.

393   He's "king of the lot": *RRich*, 5.

393   "paternal talkativeness keeps bubbling up in Harry": Ibid., 16–17.

393   "this matter of men descending from men": Ibid., 212.

394   a single-sentence stream of consciousness: Ibid., 28–29.

394   snug in his "Luxury Edition" 1978 Toyota Corona: Ibid., 30.

394   "standing around on some steamy city corner": Ibid., 36.

394   "glorified pancakes wrapped around minced whatever": Ibid., 87.

394   the "lean new race of downtown office workers": Ibid.

394   "The world keeps ending": Ibid., 88.

395   "An invisible force month after month": Ibid., 458.

395   they feel "like a bull's balls tugging at his pockets": Ibid., 211.

395   running shoes skim "above the earth, above the dead": Ibid., 141.

395   "And the burning in his tear ducts": Ibid., 244.

396   "one hundred and eighty-five American dollars": Ibid., 235.

396   "What a great waste of gas it seems": Ibid., 245.

396   "a whole new ethic": Ibid., 226.

396   his father ("poor dead dad"): Ibid., 29.

396   "never got out from under": Ibid., 69.

396   "didn't live to see money get unreal": Ibid., 402.

397   the "ultimate Toyota," a model "priced in five digits": Ibid., 434–35.

397   His father was "narcissistically impaired": *LL*, 248.

397   he, in his novel, was "mucking about the same area": *CJU*, 226.

398   "Nelson remains: here is a hardness he must carry": *RRun*, 305.

398   "Why doesn't Dad just die?": *RRich*, 323.

398   "The kid was no threat to him for now": Ibid., 456.

399   "She breathed that air he'd forgotten": Ibid., 189.

400   Updike thought *Rabbit Is Rich* the "happiest" novel: *HG*, 455.

400   "an invigorating change of mates": Ibid., 457.

400   the inspiration for "Janice's lusty rejuvenation": Ibid., 456.

400   "unquestionably" Updike's finest novel: Mark Feeney, "Rabbit Running Down: Intimations of Immortality in Updike's Finest," *The Boston Globe*, September 27, 1981, 1.

400   "the best book I've ever read about an ordinary man": Anatole Broyard, "Ordinary People," *The New York Times Book Review*, December 13, 1981, 43.

400   "*Rabbit Is Rich* is the first book": Roger Sale, "Rabbit Returns," *The New York Times Book Review*, September 27, 1981, 32.

400   "What comes through most vividly," Yardley wrote: Jonathan Yardley, "Rabbit Isn't Rich," *The Washington Post*, April 26, 1982.

400   declared Updike "both a poet and a historian": V. S. Pritchett, "Updike," *The New Yorker*, November 9, 1981, 206.

401   "a swindler named Rosenthal": JU, "Suzie Creamcheese Speaks," *The New Yorker*, February 23, 1967, 110.

402   a letter from Updike apologizing for his absence: *HS*, 875–76.

402   "a largish white edifice with a distant look at the sea": LP, May 25, 1981, Houghton.

X. Haven Hill

403   "An adult human consists of sedimentary layers": *HG*, 460.

403   "I had left a big white house with a view of saltwater": *HS*, xx.

403   He also thought of the Shillington house, where as a child he "soaked up love and strength," as a "big white house": *SC*, 25, 27.

404   "a pale white castle in a fairy tale": LP, September 10, 1981, Houghton.

404   "As we drove up the lane," Oates wrote: JCO to JU, October 9, 1982, Syracuse.

404   "Now that I think of it[,] wasn't 675 Hale the house": MA to JU, August 10, 1982, Houghton.

404   "We ate at a table that was much too large": E-mail, Austin Briggs to author, March 6, 2011.

405   "My own house, up a wooded hill": *OJ*, 61.

405   "middling, hidden, troubled America": *SC*, 103.

405   the Gold Coast, "a bucolic enclave": *HG*, 457.

405   summer places built by "quiet Boston money": *OJ*, 50.

406   "I envy John the metaphorical resources of Infinity at his left hand": JCO to JU, October 9, 1982, Syracuse.

407   Rabbit's life was less "defended" than his own: *HG*, 448.

408   "What is clearest in the documentary": John Corry, "A Documentary of John Updike," *The New York Times*, July 13, 1983.

408   "I feel in most respects that I am a pretty average person": *WMRR*.

409   "That was when you really got the impression": Author interview, Michael Updike, August 18, 2012.

409   "It felt like we're his mistress": Ibid.

410   "His life seemed destined never to be wholly his own": *A*, 64.

410   a "chasteningly grand" silhouette: *WE*, 10.

411   "engagingly half-mad with a storyteller's exuberance": Bloom, *John Updike*, 2.

411   "semi-depressed and semi-fashionable": *WE*, 2.

411   "I once moved to a venerable secluded town": *OJ*, 855.

411   "Bald November reigned outside": *WE*, 156.

412   "[T]he world poured through her": Ibid., 78.

412   "[S]unlight pressed on Alexandra's face": Ibid., 291.

412   Updike "had a very good spy in the female camp": Diane Johnson, "War-lock," *The New York Review of Books*, June 14, 1984, 3.

412   "loves Alexandra better even than Rabbit": Bloom, *John Updike*, 2.

412   "I've been criticized for making the women": Quoted in Margaret At-wood, "Wondering What It's Like to Be a Woman," *The New York Times Book Review*, May 13, 1984, 1.

412   "gorgeous and doing evil": *WE*, 343.

412   conflating "sinister old myths" with the "modern female experiences": *OJ*, 855.

413   "a male author notoriously unsympathetic to women": Nina Byam, "Re-view of *The Witches of Eastwick* and *Sex and Destiny*, by Germaine Greer," *The Iowa Review* (Fall 1984): 165.

413   "The decade past has taught her more than it has taught him": *RRich*, 138.

414   "the sexual *seethe* that underlies many a small town": *CJU*, 267.

417   "ruminative ekphrasis"—poetic description of an artwork: Arthur Danto, "What MOMA Done Tole Him," *The New York Times Book Review*, Oc-tober 15, 1989, 12.

418   "I feel confident in saying that the disadvantages of New York life": *OJ*, 53.

418   a depressive divinity school professor with a "sullen temper": *RV*, 9.

418   To achieve the "informational abundance": *OJ*, 869.

419   Having decided after *Witches* to "attempt a city novel": Ibid., 856.

419   a "crassly swank" rotating restaurant atop a skyscraper: *RV*, 309.

420   "urine and damp cement and rubber-based paint": Ibid., 59.

420   "beyond the project, deeper into that section of the city": Ibid., 221.

420   "an African mask, her lips and jaw majestically protruding": Ibid., 223.

420   "princess of a race that travels from cradle to grave": Ibid., 226.

420   "killing an unborn child to try to save a born one": Ibid., 221.

420   "an essay about kinds of belief," Updike labeled it: *CJU*, 254.

420   staying overnight in the hospital "under observation": *RV*, 269.

420   "When I was spent and my niece released": Ibid., 280–81.

421   Crews accused Roger (and Updike) of "class-based misanthropy": Freder-ick Crews, "Mr. Updike's Planet," *The New York Review of Books*, Decem-ber 4, 1986, 12.

422   Crews locates "a certain bleakness at the center" of Updike's mind: Ibid., 14.

422   his "sense of futility and of doom and of darkness": Mervyn Rothstein, "The Origin of the Universe, Time and John Updike," *The New York Times*, November 21, 1985.

422   "the natural state of the sentient adult": F. Scott Fitzgerald, *The Crack-Up* (New York: New Directions, 1993), 84.

423   his good temper balanced against a recurring sense of being "smothered and confined, misunderstood and put-upon": *SC*, 256.

423   "Happiness," he writes in *Self-Consciousness*, "is best seen out of the corner of the eye": Ibid., 254.

423   "Can happiness," he asks, "be simply a matter of orange juice?": Ibid., 255.

423   his sense of well-being is complicated by his "inner remove": Ibid., 256.

423   "is a vast conspiracy to make you happy": *ES*, 413.

424   "He that gains his life shall lose it": *SC*, 257.

424   the tone was sometimes "kind of acid": *CJU*, 188.

424   God was the "guarantor" of his existence, "a protector and a reference point": *WMRR*.

424   he woke up in the night feeling "fearful and adrift": *MM*, 40–41.

424   he was wearing, he tells us, his "churchgoing clothes": *SC*, 254.

425   "I have stayed out," as he put it, "of the business end of St. John's": *CJU*, 255.

425   "I saw this as being a woman's novel by a man": Mervyn Rothstein, "In 'S.,' Updike Tries the Woman's Viewpoint," *The New York Times*, March 2, 1988.

426   "A sort of blessing seemed to arise from the anonymous public": *OJ*, 761.

426   "this massive datum that happens to be mine": *SC*, xi.

427   he conceded that he was peddling a kind of "cagey candor": *HG*, 472.

427   "These memoirs feel shabby," he wrote: *SC*, 231.

427   "A writer's self-consciousness," he tells us, "is really a mode of interestedness": Ibid., 24.

427   "leaning doggedly away from the pull of his leather pouch": Ibid., 37.

427   "here we see Updike nude, without a stitch of irony or art": Martin Amis, *The War Against Cliché* (New York: Talk Miramax Book, 2001), 376.

428   "a parading," as he put it, "of my wounds": *DC*, 11.

428   he adopts a self-mocking tone: "I have preened, I have lived": *SC*, 78.

428   "a basically glancing, flirtatious acquaintanceship": Ibid., 154.

428   "I had propelled my body through the tenderest parts": Ibid., 40.

428   musing on his "troubled epidermis": Ibid., 72.

428   "What was my creativity, my relentless need to produce": Ibid., 75.

428   he describes the "obdurate barrier" in his throat: Ibid., 79.

428   the "paralysis of stuttering stems from the dead center": Ibid., 87.

428   the "ingenious psychosomatic mechanism": Ibid., 99.

428   "I tried to break out of my marriage": Ibid., 98.

429   "I gave my teeth to the war effort": Ibid., 163.

429   "holes where once there was electricity and matter": Ibid., 248.

429   "Between now and the grave lies a long slide": Ibid., 78.

429   *"You carry your own hide to market"*: Ibid., 211.

429   "Truth," he writes, "is anecdotes, narrative": Ibid., 234.

430   she wanted to go home and "take what comes": JU to WM, November 8, 1989, Illinois.

432   "I was an orphan, full of the triumphant, arid bliss of being on my own": *OJ*, 869.

433   Updike, in a "frenzy of efficiency," did the same in the late fall of 1989: Ibid., 867.

433   she made "gallant stabs in both directions": JU to WM, November 8, 1989, Illinois.

434   Her "unignorable" decline during the year he spent writing it: *OJ*, 872.

434   medical details he "shamelessly" fed into his terrifyingly vivid descriptions: *HG*, 458.

434   "that singeing sensation he gets": *RRest*, 91.

434   "Deciding to wind up the series": JU, "Why Rabbit Had to Go."

434   "You might say it's a depressed book": Ibid.

435   "working at the full height of his powers": Michiko Kakutani, "Just 30 Years Later, Updike Has a Quartet," *The New York Times*, September 25, 1990, C13.

435   "one of the very few modern novels in English": Jonathan Raban, "Rabbit's Last Run," *The Washington Post*, September 30, 1990.

435   a friendly, unbuttoned congregation, a "human melt": *RRest*, 371.

435   "to the mild, middling truth of average American life": *OJ*, 183.

435   "always . . . trying to fashion a piece of literature": Ibid., 189.

436   "It is, after all, the triumph of American life": Ibid.

436   "Harry's eyes burn": *RRest*, 371.

436   "tired and stiff and full of crud": Ibid., 166.

436   As he would say, "Enough": Ibid., 512.

436   the neatness of "a squared-off tetralogy, a boxed life": *HG*, 457.

436   "So many themes convene in *Rabbit at Rest*": Ibid., 459.

437   Brewer kids playing basketball: "Legs, shouts": *RRun*, 3.

437   These black kids have "that unhurried look": *RRest*, 487.

437   "as alone on the court as the sun in the sky": Ibid., 506–7.

437   At forty-five he was "over the hill": *CP*, 147.

438   "I wanted to cap my series and make it a tetralogy": *OJ*, 872.

438   "a specimen American male's evolution into grandpaternity": Ibid.

438   "Harry tries to imagine the world seen through her clear green eyes": *RRest*, 55.

438   Nelson cries in anguish, "Don't *die*, Dad, *don't*!": Ibid., 512.

438   "Whatever it is, *it* has found *him*, and is working him over": Ibid., 136.

439   "I think he was emotionally shy with us": Author interview, David Updike, January 18, 2013.

439   his father "just didn't have room for grandchildren": Author interview, Michael Updike, August 18, 2012.

440   "With his wonderful new tool of ease how can a writer say No?": *OJ*, xviii.

442   the many months of "sexual disarray": *MM*, 822.

442   "I've been carrying Buchanan around with me for years": *CJU*, 230.

442   "There is a civilized heroism to indecision": *MFA*, 13.

442   for the next fifteen years and counting, "fairly content": Ibid., 365.

442   Alf tells us, "Real life is in essence anti-climactic": Ibid., 357.

442   "the Queen of Disorder": artistic, vague, maternal: Ibid., 10.

443   "the Perfect Wife": peremptory, efficient, snobbish: Ibid., 24.

443   "my *Tempest*, my valedictory visit to all my themes": *MM*, 822.

443   "like many a mother in the biography of a successful man": *MFA*, 26.

443   "Is it not the biological cruelty of mothers": Ibid., 29.

444   "What would have happened to me if William Shawn": *HG*, 466.

445   "shamanistic mystique" associated with the cult of Mr. Shawn: *MM*, ix.

445   The sober, dignified pages he was used to were suddenly "sharply angled": Ibid., xxi.

446   the days before "Tina's barbarians" sacked and pillaged: JU to MA, March 5, 1994.

446   "There is a bliss in making sets of things": *MM*, xxiii.

446   "I have a little Bech book in the works": JU to JCO, December 30, 1997, Syracuse.

446   "My poems are my oeuvre's beloved waifs": *CP*, xxiv.

447   "Well," he asked, "why would you collect your poems": Televised interview with Charlie Rose, October 6, 1997.

448   "John Updike is a far better poet": X. J. Kennedy, "John Updike *Collected Poems*," *The New Criterion* (April 1993): 62.

448   "entertainment quotient" in Updike's verse: Thomas M. Disch, "Having an Oeuvre," *Poetry* (February 1994): 288.

448   He was unwilling to deprive himself entirely of his "secret bliss": JU to JCO, March 3, 1994, Syracuse.

449   "Nevertheless, the living must live, a writer must write": *MM*, xxiii.

449   dragging behind him "like an ever-heavier tail": *SC*, 86.

450   "That he takes up so much of my time": *MM*, 757.

451   a process he thought of as the "packaging of flux": *CP*, xxiii.

452   "you reach an age when every sentence you write": *DC*, 651.

452   "You have to give it magic": Rothstein, "The Origin of the Universe, Time and John Updike."

453   she was raised as Essie Wilmot in a "sweet small town": *BL*, 333.

453   secure in "her power, her irresistible fire": Ibid., 286.

453   recognizes in her costar an "inhuman efficiency": Ibid., 353.

454   "spouting blood . . . the hole spurting like a water bubbler": Ibid., 483.

454   "metallobioforms," a plague of deadly inorganic pests: *TET*, 110–11.

454   a mysterious "halo of iridescence": Ibid., 151.

454   "quantum leaps of plot and personality": *MM*, 833.

454   Oates, reviewing the novel in *The New Yorker*, described Ben as "morbidly narcissistic": Joyce Carol Oates, "Future Tense," *The New Yorker*, December 8, 1997, 117.

455   the postapocalyptic, "post-law-and-order" environment: *TET*, 271.

455   "I am safe," he says, "in my nest of local conditions": Ibid., 329.

455   autobiography is "one of the dullest genres": *MM*, 834.

456   "Symmetry, fine white teeth, and monomaniacal insistence": *TET*, 8.

456   "In her guilt at secretly wishing me dead": Ibid., 240.

456   Gloria, in his estimation, is a "soigné vulture": Ibid., 271.

456   her rich widow's reward: "well-heeled freedom": Ibid., 142.

456   immersed in "suburban polygamy": Ibid., 136.

456   "Well, it's your call, but you already told us, the Readers": Notes found on *TET* manuscript, Houghton.

457   "Among the rivals besetting an aging writer": *HG*, 5.

XI. The Lonely Fort

458   "particularly sour, ugly and haphazardly constructed": Michiko Kakutani, "On Sex, Death and the Self: An Old Man's Sour Grapes," *The New York Times*, September 30, 1997, E1.

458   "It is, of the total 25 Updike books I've read, far and away the worst": David Foster Wallace, "John Updike, Champion Literary Phallocrat, Drops One; Is This Finally the End for Magnificent Narcissists?" *The New York Observer*, October 13, 1997.

458   He'd learned to shrug off the "irrepressible Michiko": JU to MA, November 16, 2004.

458   since he had seen her "blow her top" so often, it was hard to take her seriously: JU to ND, November 21, 2002, Michigan.

458   "As memento mori and its obverse, carpe diem": Margaret Atwood, "Memento Mori—But First, Carpe Diem," *The New York Times Book Review*, October 12, 1997.

459   "Old artists are entitled to caricature themselves": *JL*, 82.

459   "idly constructed . . . and astonishingly misogynistic": James Wood, "A Prick in Time," *The Guardian*, January 29, 1998.

459   sexual obsessions "have recurred and overlapped thickly enough": James Wood, "Gossip in Gilt," *London Review of Books*, April 19, 2001.

460   "It seems to be easier for John Updike to stifle a yawn": Ibid.

460   "plush attention to detail" amounted to "a nostalgia for the present": James Wood, "The Beast in the American Ice Cream Parlour," *The Guardian*, October 25, 1990.

460   "If Updike's earlier work was consumed with wife-swapping": Wood, "Gossip in Gilt."

460   "Updike is not, I think, a great writer": James Wood, *The Broken Estate: Essays on Belief and Literature* (New York: Random House, 1999), 193.

460   "Woods [*sic*] is a great annoyance," Updike wrote: JU to John McTavish, June 13, 2008.

462   a subliminal message: "the time has come to retire": *MM*, 856.

462   if Updike didn't get the prize, it would be "the Swedes' fault, not his": WM, "Confidential Report on Candidate," 1959 Guggenheim Fellowship competition.

462   "There's no Updike at all. I'm a vanished man, a nonentity": David Streit-feld, "Updike at Bay," *The Washington Post*, December 16, 1998.

462   "a very hasty job": JU to Ann Goldstein, October 22, 1998.

462   "The blatancy of the icy-hearted satire repelled me": *MM*, 323.

462   "The book weighs in as a 742-page bruiser": Ibid., 320.

462   "*A Man in Full* still amounts to entertainment": Ibid., 324.

463   "cheesy," Updike called it in private: JU to JCO, December 15, 1998, Syracuse.

463   "Wolfe not only demands to make his millions but wants <u>respect</u>, too": Ibid.

463   Wolfe's "final inability to be great": Norman Mailer, "A Man Half Full," *The New York Review of Books*, December 17, 1998.

463   Wolfe hit back, calling Updike and Mailer "two old piles of bones": Tom Wolfe, *Hooking Up* (New York: Farrar, Straus and Giroux, 2000), 152–53.

463   when Wolfe was "apotheosized": JU to JCO, May 31, 1999, Syracuse.

463   "a minor novelist with a major style": Bloom, *John Updike*, 7.

464   two-part parody (or "counter-parody"): Wolfe, *Hooking Up*, 252.

464   "the laughingstock of the New York literary community": Ibid., 279.

464   Updike's in particular: "more and more tabescent": Ibid., 278.

464   "At this weak, pale, tabescent moment": Tom Wolfe, "Stalking the Billion-Footed Beast: A Literary Manifesto for the New Social Novel," *Harper's Magazine*, November 1989, 55.

464   Wolfe urged them to "do what journalists do": Ibid.

464   "Fiction is nothing less than the subtlest instrument": *OJ*, 86.

464   "Unlike journalism . . . fiction does not give us facts": Ibid., 87.

465   the aim is to expose the "status structure of society": Wolfe, "Stalking the Billion-Footed Beast," 52.

465   "intimate and inextricable relation to the society": Ibid., 50.

465   American reality "outdoing" the novelist's imagination: Philip Roth, "Writing American Fiction," *Commentary* (March 1961): 224.

466   "[I]t fell straight down like an elevator, with a tinkling shiver": JU, "The Talk of the Town," *The New Yorker*, September 24, 2001, 28.

466   "The next morning, I went back to the open vantage": Ibid., 29.

467   "O.K., you are sitting in an airplane": JU, *Am*.

467   "Within him his great secret felt an eggshell thickness from bursting forth": *MT*, 94.

468   "Updike has produced one of the worst pieces of writing": Christopher Hitchens, "No Way," *The Atlantic*, June 2006, 117.

469   "It is to Updike's great credit, and a proof of his long-standing and ardent interest in women": Alison Lurie, "Widcraft," *The New York Review of Books*, January 15, 2009.

470   "John Updike: the name is graven": Cynthia Ozick, "God Is in the De-tails," *The New York Times Book Review*, November 30, 2003, 8.

470   "These stories, I feel sure, will weather all times and tides": Jay Cantor, "Suburban on the Rocks," *Bookforum* (Winter 2003).

470   "It is quite possible that by dint of both quality and quantity": Lorrie Moore, "Home Truths," *The New York Review of Books*, November 20, 2003, 16.

471   "[I]t doesn't do to think overmuch about prizes, does it?": JU to JCO, September 12, 2006, Syracuse.

471   "For who, in that unthinkable future": *EP*, 8.

471   disgusted by the "chip-power" of a desktop PC: JU, *Villages* (New York: Ballantine Books, 2005), 45.

472   "a method of drawing with a light pen on a computer screen": Ibid., 132.

473   "Smaller than a breadbox, bigger than a TV remote": *DC*, 68.

473   "Without books, we might melt into the airwaves": Ibid., 70.

473   he was arguing for "accountability and intimacy": *HG*, 421.

474   readers and writers of books were "approaching the condition of hold-outs": Ibid., 422.

474   "Defend your lonely forts": Ibid.

474   "Our annual birthday do": *EP*, 19–20.

474   "How not to think of death?": Ibid., 19.

475   "Wife absent a day or two, I wake alone, and older": Ibid., 3.

475   "The fact that he seemed to enjoy talking to me": Author interview, Ian McEwan, December 5, 2012.

XII. Endpoint

479   "Be with me, words, a little longer": *EP*, 19.

479   he was nursing "a cold," as he put it, "that wouldn't let go": Ibid., 21.

480   "What a great country we have here": JU to Walter Kaiser, November 18, 2008, Houghton.

480   "Is this an end?" he asks. "I hang, half-healthy": *EP*, 21.

480   he savored the phrase "CAT-scan needle biopsy": Ibid., 27.

481   "My visitors, my kin": Ibid., 23.

481   "My wife of thirty years is on the phone": Ibid., 24.

482   "Perhaps / we meet our heaven at the start": Ibid., 27.

482   what he called "the leap of unfaith": JU, interview with the Associated Press, 2006.

482   "Why go to Sunday school, though surlily": *EP*, 29.

483   the idea is "to give the mundane its beautiful due": *ES*, xv.

483   "I felt I shouldn't touch him": Author interview, MW, July 15, 2012.

485   the "irrational hope" that his last book might be his best: *HG*, 7.

485   "I find producing anything fraught with difficulty these days": JU to JCO, November 23, 2005, Syracuse.

485   never tired of "creation's giddy bliss": *HG*, 7.

486   "I've remained," he once said, "all too true to my youthful self": *WMRR*.

Credits

Grateful acknowledgment is made for permission to reproduce the following:

Updike sitting on the gravel path: Unknown Photographer. John Updike Papers, Houghton Library, Harvard University.
With his parents: Unknown Photographer. John Updike Papers, Houghton Library, Harvard University.
With his mother in Reading: Unknown Photographer. John Updike Papers, Houghton Library, Harvard University.
The sandstone farmhouse: Photograph by Mary Weatherall. John Updike Papers, Houghton Library, Harvard University.
With his Shillington High School classmate: Unknown Photographer. John Updike Papers, Houghton Library, Harvard University.
Updike as a Harvard man: Photograph by W. Earl Snyder. John Updike Papers, Houghton Library, Harvard University.
Elizabeth Updike: Photograph by Mary Weatherall. John Updike Papers, Houghton Library, Harvard University.
Liz on her father's lap, David in his grandmother's arms: Photograph by Mary Weatherall. John Updike Papers, Houghton Library, Harvard University.
David Updike held precariously aloft by his father: Photograph by Mary Weatherall. John Updike Papers, Houghton Library, Harvard University.
Tony Bailey and his wife, Margot: Photograph by Greg Doherty. Courtesy of Anthony Bailey.
William Maxwell: Photograph by Walter Daran. Getty Images.
Judith Jones: Photograph by Dorothy Alexander. John Updike Papers, Houghton Library, Harvard University.
Updike at his typewriter: Photograph by Irving L. Fisk. Courtesy of the estate of Irving L. Fisk.
Family portrait: Photograph by Truman Moore. Getty Images.
Juggling: Photograph by Truman Moore. Getty Images.
Playing volleyball: Photograph by Antonia McManaway. John Updike Papers, Houghton Library, Harvard University.
Playing tennis with Mary: Photograph by André Deutsch. John Updike Papers, Houghton Library, Harvard University.
Playing golf barefoot: Photograph by David Updike. Courtesy of David Updike.
With Mary in Addis Ababa: Courtesy of the U.S. Department of State. John Updike Papers, Houghton Library, Harvard University.
With Bill Luers: Photograph by Wendy Luers. John Updike Papers, Houghton Library, Harvard University.
The Celebrity Walk of Fame: Photograph by Jeff Wheeler, *Star Tribune*. John Updike Papers, Houghton Library, Harvard University.

With Michael and two grandchildren: Photograph by Janice Updike. Courtesy of Michael Updike.

With Elizabeth's two sons: Photograph by Tete Cobblah. Courtesy of Elizabeth Cobblah.

With Martha: Photograph by Timothy Greenfield-Sanders. John Updike Papers, Houghton Library, Harvard University.

With Ian McEwan: Photograph by Annalena McAfee. Courtesy of Ian McEwan.

Securing the headstone: Photograph by David Silcox. Courtesy of David Silcox.

The back of the headstone: Photograph by David Silcox. Courtesy of David Silcox.

Index